Copyright © History of Wrestling 2014. All Rights Reserved.

Published by lulu.com

All rights reserved. This book may not be reproduced, in whole or in any part, in any form, without written permission from the publisher or author.

This book is set in Rockwell Extra Bold, Impact and Arial.

10 9 8 7 6 5 4 3 2 1

This book was printed and bound in the United Kingdom.

ISBN 978-1-291-81693-8

THE COMPLETE WWF VIDEO GUIDE VOLUME #5

James Dixon
Arnold Furious
Lee Maughan
Bob Dahlstrom
Rick Ashley

THE COMPLETE WWF VIDEO GUIDE VOLUME #5

MEET THE TEAM

All of the contributors in this book have been wrestling fans for a long time, probably longer than we would care to admit. Some of our favourite memories of our early wrestling fandom involved renting video tapes and watching them repeatedly. However, there had never been one truly all encompassing guide to those tapes, and what turns up on them. Yes, there are some great sites on the internet here and there, but nothing ever published. No guide book. Here at *History of Wrestling*, we decided that *we* would write that book, and we did! With a century of combined viewing between us, we have lived through all of this many times over. We decided to bring that knowledge and love of wrestling, to you. While the opinions you will read are often controversial, off-the-wall or just plain moronic, they are from likeminded people who put wrestling before almost anything else. Disagree with them if you wish, certainly the office has seen its fair share of furniture thrown and occasional bloodshed (there was an unpleasant incident with a stapler that was later resolved with a pint). This is the fifth in our series of books profiling WWF video tape releases.

THE TEAM AT WWW.HISTORYOFWRESTLING.INFO:

ARNOLD FURIOUS
Arnold Furious likes… Mitsuharu Misawa, Jushin Liger, Eddie Guerrero, Bret Hart, Raven, Toshiaki Kawada, Vader, Samoa Joe, Bryan Danielson, Kenta Kobashi, Star Wars, Martin Scorsese, Arnold Schwarzenegger, Bill Hicks, Wall-E, Akira Kurosawa, Johnny Cash, Scott Pilgrim, Tintin, The Wire, Firefly, The Simpsons, Jackie Chan, AC/DC, Rocky, Simon Furman, Danny Wallace, Aerosmith, The British Red Cross, Garth Ennis, Batman, Kiss, Asterix, Alan Moore's Top Ten, Astro City, Christopher Walken, Juliette and the Licks, Quentin Tarantino, Goodfellas, Kurt Busiek, Watchmen (the book, not the film), White Out (the book, not the film), Super Troopers, Swingers, Death's Head, Iron Maiden, Will Ferrell, Clint Eastwood, Trish Stratus, Everton FC, Tom Hanks, The Blues Brothers, Simon Pegg, Clerks, Terry Pratchett, Richard Pryor, Viz, Mutemath, Joe Bonamassa, How to Train Your Dragon, Stevie Ray Vaughan, Dexter, Jimi Hendrix, Alien, Aliens, Predator, Frankie Boyle, Secret Wars, Woody Allen, True Romance, Lethal Weapon, Takashi Miike, Graham Linehan, Big Bang Theory, Darren Aronofsky, John Woo, Charlie Chaplin, films with ridiculous shoot-out sequences in them, Douglas Adams, Chow Yun Fat, 12 Angry Men, Wilson Pickett, Studio Ghibli, Pixar, The Avengers, Fable II, history, Bill Bailey, Skyrim, Stephen Fry, Top Gear, kung fu movies, Alan Wake, Meet the Feebles, Die Hard, Sin City (the books and the film), zombies, Red Dwarf, Peter Sellers, Peter Cook, Michael Caine, Planet of the Apes, conspiracies, steak, The Princess Bride, Grimlock, Mel Brooks, top fives, 30 Rock, Preacher, Pringles, Pirates of the Caribbean, Back to the Future, Klaus Kinski, The Sopranos, boxing, Casablanca, Stephen King, Hunter S. Thompson, Mike Leigh's Naked, Captain America, Hawkeye, Spaced, Flight of the Conchords, Monty Python, Pearl Jam, Carol Danvers, 100 Bullets, Indiana Jones, The Goon, Thorntons, Jack Nicholson, Jim Beam, real ale, cartoons, novelty underwear, the Joker, Frank Miller, Robert Brockway, The Breakfast Club, Far Cry 3, Freddy Krueger, Alec Baldwin's speech in Glengarry Glen Ross, John Carpenter, Bill & Ted, MMA, John Wayne, Terrence Howard, The Terminator, Guy Forsyth, nudity, coffee, crazy Japanese films that make no sense, crazy Japanese wrestling that makes no sense, crazy Japanese people that make no sense, Greg Benson, Tony Cottam, Bernard Rage, Redje Harris, Ezet Samalca…and forever Maria.

JAMES DIXON
James Dixon has been watching wrestling for over 20 years. Inspired by the likes of Davey Boy Smith, Bret Hart and The Undertaker, Dixon was drawn to the business like any other fan, for reasons that are difficult to explain. A hobby quickly became an obsession, and Dixon was determined to get involved in wrestling by utilising the one thing he could do: write about it. In previous books James wrote alongside his "writing partner" Evil Ste. The truth is, the Evil Ste character was merely an extension of Dixon's own personality, his way of sharing his Jekyll and Hyde opinions on things. The writing choice worked fairly well at first, but the team all feel it has perhaps become more gimmicky that was hoped, so Dixon has reverted to just writing as himself. Well, we say himself. In reality James is a former British professional wrestler, but he has adopted the pseudonym to retain relative anonymity and to distance himself from his past career in the industry. However, that past experience does give him a unique and more inside perspective on things than the others, though he is still a "mark" at heart. James has limited patience for anything in wrestling post-2002, and much prefers 80s and 90s grappling. Curious really, because as you will see in these pages, he spends a lot of time complaining about it. James currently lives in the North of England, where it rains the majority if the time.

LEE MAUGHAN
Lee Maughan has been a fan of the professional wrestling industry for as long has he can remember, dating back to an embryonic memory of sitting on his grandparent's living room floor, his eyes transfixed to British household names Big Daddy and Giant Haystacks belly-busting their way through ITV's *World of Sport*. Somehow this wasn't enough to deter him, and young Lee was rewarded with having the incredibly good fortune to be within the WWF's target demographic just in time its early 90s UK boom period. He was hooked, his bedroom quickly becoming a wall-to-wall palace of video tapes, action figures, magazines, posters and any piece of tat all stamped with the WWF insignia. His thirst for the quasi-sport was ravenous but unfortunately, his family were too cheap to subscribe to Sky television, home of the WWF. His quencher? WCW *International Pro*, broadcast well past his bedtime on regional terrestrial station Tyne-Tees. Those WWF magazines soon found themselves piled up alongside copies of *Pro Wrestling Illustrated* and *Superstars of Wrestling*, making Lee possibly the most clued-up eight year old wrestling superfan in the entire TS14 postcode. It's possible, nay probable thanks to a further 20 years of research, that Lee is still the most clued-up wrestling superfan in the entire TS14 postcode. A trader of tapes, a distributor of DVDs and a purveyor of pixels, Lee keeps up with everything from New Japan to CHIKARA whilst continuing to catch up with the classics of pro wrestling's territorial days. Away from the grapple game, Lee likes to watch sitcoms, rock out in punk bands, and play video games with a strong preference for old school platformers and kart racers. Despite this, he even found the time to graduate from the University of Teesside in 2005 with a degree in media production, and after much soul searching and stints making Christmas cards for a living and working as a producer and on-air talent for a community radio station, is now taking the tentative first steps into the world of film video editing. He also tweets with a reverently dry sense of humour @atomicbombs, but reserves the right to ignore you entirely unless you want to pay him to write about wrestling, guitar bands or 80s pop culture for your book, website or magazine.

BOB DAHLSTROM
Bob Dahlstrom is many things. A son, a brother, an uncle; but also is a dude who likes to draw. And more importantly than that, a lifelong wrestling fan. It all started back at WrestleMania III, which hooked young Bob. He would then go onto rent every wrestling tape from every video rental place around, and watch them over and over. He's never looked back. All the artwork in this book has been loving crafted exclusively by Bob, specially for this publication. He lives in Illinois with his girlfriend and pet guinea pig. His wrestling artwork and autobiographical webcomic *Egomaniac* can be found at www.robertpfd.com.

TWITTER
@HOWwrestling

FACEBOOK
Facebook.com/historyofwrestling.info

THE SCORING SYSTEM

We have used the popular star system in order to rate the matches that appear in this book. For those who are unaware of it, here is the key:

*****	Perfect
****½	Very close to perfect
****	Superb
***½	Very good
***	Good
**½	Decent
**	Average
*½	Nothing to it
*	Bad
½*	Terrible
DUD	Utterly worthless
SQUASH	Not rated (too short)
N/R	Not rated (for various reasons)
Negatives	Any match that goes into negative stars is one of the worst you will ever see

Sometimes things will be so bad, that we go into negative stars. These are matches that will make you want to stop watching wrestling and find a new hobby. We also dabble frequently in quarter stars, just when we cannot quite decide which of the above criteria a match falls under, and decide that it is somewhere in between.

It is important to remember that all star ratings are entirely subjective to the person awarding them. One man's **** bout could be another man's **. There is no set judging system for these things, this is not gymnastics or synchronised diving. That is the uniqueness of wrestling; everyone likes it for different reasons. There are a few times in this book that the writers will review the same matches due to their appearance on more than one tape, and give different ratings. This is not a typographical mistake, rather just an example of how different people perceive things. Rather than corroborate all of the ratings so they align, we have chosen to keep them this way, as to give a true reflection of the bout from different angles. So if your favourite match is not rated as highly as you might have hoped, don't worry, it shouldn't change your enjoyment of it. In fact, many a good natured argument has occurred in our offices about whether a match is "*****" or "****¾", that is just the nature of the business and one of the things that makes it so unique and fun to watch.

Some may also be wondering how we reached the scores that each tape receives at the end of each review. Rest assured, it is not just a figure plucked out of the sky, like in some video games magazines. Rather, we have created a complex algorithm that takes into account various factors and data. These include; length of the show, the ratings of the matches (and segments) broken down into weighted points that are awarded to the tape, the number of matches, historical relevance, and many other factors. Unfortunately this is top secret, and we cannot go into a full explanation here. However, we can guarantee that many hours have been spent on this in order to make it the fairest and most consistent overall review scoring system you will ever find. Of course, you can still get the opinion of the writers about whether it is worth buying, regardless of the score, in the verdict section of the book.

The score it produces is not so much an overall rating for the tape, but rather a "watchability" rating. Basically, how easy the tape is to sit through in one sitting and enjoy. Some shows have genuine, all-time classic matches, on long cards full of dull wrestling otherwise. While that match will improve the score of the show, it alone is not enough to make the whole show watchable on its own. The match yes, the show no.

Some tapes inevitably end up with very high scores, and can even surpass the 100 point limit that we set. Our cap is 100, so that is the highest score a tape can get. Similarly, a tape can drop below zero if it is so bad, but we cap the minimum at zero so it cannot. If a tape receives a full 100 score, it does not necessarily mean that all of the content is perfect. Rather, as a whole, it is generally so good and consistent and in places outstanding, that it is entirely watchable and the time flies by when viewing it. These scores crop up now and again, but not too frequently. The score is the overall equivalent of a 5* match. In our eyes at least, anyway.

A complete list of the tapes in order of score is available at the back of the book.

We have used a combination of US and UK releases when compiling this book. Because of that, there may be the odd discrepancy when it comes to content, though every effort has been made to avoid this. VHS covers are a combination also. We didn't want to display all of the different versions, so we just picked the ones we preferred.

The catalogue numbering system for WWF tapes is a bit of a mess, with some numbers missed out, different series (some with the same name, but different catalogue numbers) and vast discrepancies between US and UK releases. We have gone with the US catalogue numbers to order these tapes and in the listings, but depending on your location, these could differ.

CONTENTS

CONTENTS

11	WWF Home Video	(WWF230 - WWF288)
12	WWF230	No Mercy 1999
16	WWF232	Capital Carnage
22	WWF233	Steve Austin - Hell Yeah
24	WWF234	The Rock - Know Your Role
26	WWF235	Come Get Some - The Women of the WWF
28	WWF236	Best of RAW Vol. 1
32	WWF237	No Mercy (UK)
36	WWF238	Andre the Giant - Larger Than Life
40	WWF239	It's Our Time
44	WWF240	Austin vs. McMahon
46	WWF241	Rebellion 1999
50	WWF242	Survivor Series 1999
56	WWF243	Armageddon 1999
62	WWF244	Royal Rumble 2000
68	WWF245	No Way Out 2000
72	WWF246	WrestleMania 2000
78	WWF247	Backlash 2000
82	WWF248	Judgment Day 2000
88	WWF249	King of the Ring 2000
92	WWF250	Fully Loaded 2000
96	WWF251	SummerSlam 2000
100	WWF252	Unforgiven 2000
104	WWF253	No Mercy 2000
108	WWF254	The Rock - The People's Champ
112	WWF255	Mick Foley - Madman Unmasked
114	WWF256	Eve of Destruction
116	WWF257	Chyna Fitness
118	WWF258	Insurrextion 2000
122	WWF259	TLC - Tables Ladders Chairs
126	WWF260	Stone Cold Steve Austin - Lord of the Ring
128	WWF261	Divas - Postcard From the Caribbean
130	WWF262	Chris Jericho - Break Down the Walls
132	WWF263	Kurt Angle - It's True It's True
134	WWF264	Rebellion 2000
138	WWF265	Survivor Series 2000
144	WWF266	Armageddon 2000
148	WWF267	Royal Rumble 2001
152	WWF268	No Way Out 2001
158	WWF269	WrestleMania X-Seven
166	WWF270	Backlash 2001
172	WWF271	Judgment Day 2001
176	WWF272	King of the Ring 2001
182	WWF273	Invasion
186	WWF274	SummerSlam 2001
190	WWF277	Mick Foley - Hard Knocks and Cheap Pops
194	WWF278	Hardcore
198	WWF279	Lita - It Just Feels Right
202	WWF280	Best of RAW Vol. 2
206	WWF281	Divas in Hedonism
208	WWF282	Insurrextion 2001
212	WWF283	Triple H - That Damn Good
216	WWF286	Best of RAW Vol. 3
220	WWF287	Action!
224	WWF288	The Undertaker - This is my Yard

228   WWF/WWE Home Video

230	WWF54101	Unforgiven 2001
236	WWF54103	No Mercy 2001
242	WWF54105	Hardy Boyz - Leap of Faith
246	WWF54107	Before they were WWF Superstars
250	WWF54109	Survivor Series 2001
256	WWF54111	The Rock - Just Bring It!
260	WWF54113	Vengeance 2001
266	WWF54115	Rebellion 2001
270	WWF54117	Royal Rumble 2002
274	WWF54121	No Way Out 2002
278	WWF54125	WrestleMania X8
284	WWF54127	Divas - Tropical Pleasure
288	WWF54129	Stone Cold Steve Austin - What?
292	WWF59313	Backlash 2002
296	WWF59327	Funniest Moments
300	WWF59331	nWo - Back in Black
304	WWE59333	Insurrextion 2002

308   WWF "800" SERIES

310	WWF808	Hulk Hogan's Rock N Wrestling Volume 4
312	WWF809	Hulk Hogan's Rock N Wrestling Volume 5
314	WWF810	Hulk Hogan's Rock N Wrestling Volume 4
316	WWF825	Most Memorable Matches 1999
320	WWF826	Most Memorable Matches 2000
324	WWF827	Taking it 2 Xtremes
326	WWF843	Hits and Disses

328   MISC OTHER RELEASES

330	867863	Behind WWF Tough Enough
334	874463	Tough Enough - The First Season Boxset
344	NW001(UK)	Wild in the UK
346	WF298(UK)	Best of the WWF 2001 Viewers' Choice
350	WWF9998	Castrol Presents Best of SummerSlam
354	N/A	Stone Cold Demolition

356	Coliseum Classics - What the World was Watching
361	Hall of Shame
363	The 41st Annual Volume #5 Awards
366	Tape Rank Index

(L) = Date of live show, not VHS release.

KEY		
AF	-	Arnold Furious
LM	-	Lee Maughan
JD	-	James Dixon
Furious About	-	Arnold Furious
Evil Eye	-	James Dixon

WWF HOME VIDEO

WWF230

To

WWF288

NO MERCY 1999

CAT NO: WWF230
RUN TIME: 163 minutes (approx)

Arnold Furious: This is a show I begged off James Dixon as I wanted to see the famous ladder match again. I could just watch it by itself, but I never seem to get time for such leisurely activity when we have tapes to review. This came from a time when I was meticulous about recording details of shows, and inside the tape case is a complete match listing of the show, complete with the star ratings I gave out at the time. If only I'd been so meticulous when it came to cataloguing my Japanese tape collections, which appear to have been dumped in large cardboard boxes with no labelling whatsoever. I probably have 40 unmarked VHS tapes in my collection that are completely unidentifiable without sitting down and watching the tape. With all the Japanese matches that have found their way onto YouTube since I acquired all these tapes it makes such a job both excruciatingly dull and utterly pointless. But I'll hang on them anyway in case I one day need a load of random Japanese matches from the 1990s to keep me amused.

We're in Cleveland, Ohio. Hosts are Jim Ross and Jerry Lawler. *No Mercy* has some of the most unfortunately awful theme music of all time. It's a rubbish techno soundtrack with about three notes repeated over and over again. Garbage.

The Godfather vs. Mideon
The Godfather gets a hearty pop, because he brings a collection of fine looking ladies with him, but this is not an ideal PPV opener. This is before the WWF decided to pair up actual talent with Godfather to leech his pop. Mideon is still in his Ministry garb and he was supposed to have a Soothsayer gimmick, but that never amounted to anything so he was just a jobber who sucked in the ring. Godfather is limited but at least he's over. Viscera uses his ample size to help out Mideon as the crowd sit on their hands waiting for something interesting to happen. It probably won't be in this match, Cleveland. The Hos are all terrible actresses and can't quite fathom that they're supposed to be scared of Vis. They just stand near him cheering Godfather. If the idea of this match wasn't bad enough, they give it over 7-minutes. Ample time for them to kill the crowd, stink the joint up and make me wish the PPV started in a few matches time. It's one of the shortest matches on the card, but it could stand to be shorter. About 7-minutes shorter. Mideon runs into a load of bumps when Vis isn't cheating on his behalf, which makes him look like an incompetent clown. The crowd is so dead after the first few minutes that it's like watching a match from a Japanese undercard. The crowd finally wake up for the Ho Train and Mideon isn't even worthy of a Pimp Drop and loses to a friggin' roll up. As we all know, histrionics are more important than an actual finisher. Match sucked the meat missile and loved it, just like the Hos.
Final Rating: DUD

Backstage: Ivory belittles the Fabulous Moolah for being really, really, really, really, really, really, really, really, really old. Normally that's a bad play for a heel as when you lose you look a chump. But Moolah *was* really old so it's hard to avoid.

WWF Women's Championship
Ivory (c) vs. The Fabulous Moolah
Moolah is 72 and has been a pro for 50 years (first winning the WWWF Women's title in 1956!!). So when you complain about guys hanging around in the spotlight for too long, just remember none of them can compete with Moolah for hanging on. What makes matters worse is Ivory isn't one of these useless Divas (like Terri or Miss Kitty) but an actual wrestler. I could stand a useless worker going down to Moolah here, but a competent wrestler? It's a crime. Moolah hurts her knee early and decides to ignore Ivory's offence after that. It's a goddamn embarrassment. Ivory gets her jollies dropkicking Mae Young off the apron, which is good for a laugh. Moolah was fucking horrible in the 80s and another 20 years has turned her into your gran. Moolah wins the title with the worst roll up in wrestling history, just in case you didn't realise the division was an absolute joke. Ivory would have been better off wrestling herself. It amazes me how much shit she had to eat in this women's division, trying to drag it out of the gutter only to be forced into jobs like this. At least her third reign was ended by Chyna. The only plus for me here is that even though she's ancient, Moolah is still a wrestler, which puts her above the likes of Miss Kitty who would be Women's Champion a few months later.
Final Rating: -**

The New Age Outlaws vs. The Hollys

A strange situation here where the Outlaws aren't the tag team champions, having lost them to the Rock N' Sock Connection on *SmackDown!* The Hollys interfered in that match, hence this one. The winners will be number one contenders on *RAW* tomorrow. It's an odd situation as the Rock has no interest in being tag champs whereas both these teams are desperate to get the straps. The tag titles switched hands every other week during 1999, until the Outlaws locked them up in November as part of the heel DX group. They're still babyfaces here so Road Dogg eats a load of heat, even from the smaller Crash. It's not particularly thrilling and isn't helped by the poor opening two matches having killed the crowd, but at least Bob gets in his swank dropkick. After running the tag team formula business, Mr. Ass gets a hot tag and hits something you could loosely call a Jackhammer on Hardcore. Bob slides a chair in, Billy catches Crash with a Fameasser on the chair and the ref DQs the Outlaws giving us a shocking result. The Outlaws still get their music played and stand around celebrating a loss. I'm still not sure why the Hollys went over here, or the following night when they won the tag titles.
Final Rating: **

Good Housekeeping Match
WWF Intercontinental Championship
Jeff Jarrett (c) vs. Chyna

This match is worthy of three music videos to shill it. Jeff had gotten ludicrously over, more so than at any point in his WWF career, by belittling and beating women. Naturally Chyna stood up for womankind and the two feuded over the IC Title. Jarrett started to abuse Chyna with household objects, because that's where women belong. His words, not mine. They've been trading women too with Miss Kitty replacing Debra as Jeff's valet after Debra left him in support of womenfolk everywhere. This match is also responsible for a complete change in WWF contract policy. Jarrett's contract expired the day before this PPV, with the WWF not having the common sense to notice, and Vince McMahon was forced to pay Jarrett some $200,000 for one night's work and one job. Otherwise he could have walked off to WCW with the IC Title and dumped it in the trash, a fate the WWF Women's Title never recovered from. If you're a misogynist you could argue that the IC Title never recovered from Chyna winning it anyway, so it was always a lose/lose situation. I wouldn't agree, as Chyna would eventually job the belt to Chris Jericho in a decent series of matches. The whole Jarrett scheme was rumoured to be the brainchild of one Vince Russo, who'd recently jumped ship to WCW while the WWF were on tour in the UK. The internet predicted that Russo's departure would leave the WWF in chaos as he'd booked all the successful storylines over the preceding two years. Instead of his jump reviving WCW, it actually killed WCW and the WWF sauntered to the top based on the superior booking of Chris Kreski.

Anyway, the match is billed as Good Housekeeping, which means only household objects can be used in this hardcore environment. So we get a unique garbage match with both using assorted household crap like toilet seats, whipped cream, salami, pots and pans. Chyna has to earn her IC Title courtesy of various garbage shots, including a piece of fish. JR and Lawler bring a rich strain of misogyny to the commentary desk with Ross suggesting Chyna wasn't too familiar with an ironing board before tonight. Miss Kitty is eliminated from the match by getting a cake mix dumped on her head. Jarrett, covered in flour, gets a figure four as he switches from goofy to serious in a heartbeat. Chyna uses the ropes to escape and then uses salad tongs on Jarrett's spuds. The kitchen sink, an actual one, gets a near fall. Chyna goes for a Pedigree on a cake, as if that makes it worse somehow, but a counter knocks the ref over. Jarrett knocks Chyna out with the IC belt and retains, thus taking the title with him to WCW and dumping it on the trash live on *Nitro* the following... wait... that's not right. Teddy Long points out that Jeff can't win the title by using the title because it's not a household item. To be fair, it IS in Jeff's house! Jarrett responds by slapping the figure four on Teddy, so Chyna waffles him with a guitar for the belt. Silly booking aside this was a fun garbage match and well within Chyna's abilities. Too bad Jarrett had to jump to WCW when he actually had heat in the WWF.
Final Rating: **¾

The Rock vs. The British Bulldog

Davey returned to the WWF the previous month and they immediately thrust him into the big leagues by having him screw with the Rock and stop the 'Brahma Bull' from winning the WWF Title. Bulldog had been in WCW after Montreal but landed badly on a trapdoor during his time there and was hospitalised for 6 months. WCW, always classy, fired him via FedEx. The WWF re-hired him to get the Harts onside after Owen's accidental death, but as an in-ring talent Davey was a shadow of his former self. He'd be retired a year later and dead two years after that. A tragic end for a great performer and another horrible downside to Montreal. If Davey had never left with Bret, he wouldn't have gotten injured in WCW and probably would have wrestled for another decade. He certainly would have been in much better condition here. The WWF billed this as a top contendership match based on Bulldog's aspiration to win the one title he'd never won; the WWF Title. If Bulldog's condition wasn't bad enough, the WWF made him wrestle in jeans, which made him look like a non-wrestler. Davey manages to take his corner bump, at half pace, but he doesn't land on his head. He is just a quarter step behind and is slow rotating on a neckbreaker and slow ducking under a clothesline and slow kicking Rock in the gut, making him look stupid. It's like watching a youngster who's been working for a couple of years and hasn't quite got his timing down. Or like Rock three years earlier. Watching Bulldog launch himself into a backdrop before Rock is even in position for it is just sad.

FURIOUS ABOUT: JACQUELINE

Jacqui debuted way back in 1989 and before her WWF run began, in 1998, she'd already worked for the USWA in Memphis and WCW, as Kevin Sullivan's valet. Her original role in the WWE was as a valet for Marc Mero, a replacement for Sable. In this role she won the women's title, which had been vacant since Alundra Blayze quit the WWF in 1995. After the Mero-Sable storyline ran its course Jacqui teamed up with Terri as PMS, managing D'Lo Brown and later Meat (Shawn Stasiak). She resumed an in-ring career after that, winning the title again, from Harvey Wippleman. When Trish Stratus became the star of the women's division it was Jacqueline who put her over in Trish's first title defences. As she began to wind down her in-ring career Jacqui became a referee but continued to compete in the women's division. She left the WWE in 2004.

FURIOUS ABOUT: MICHAEL COLE

We've spent most of our Michael Cole coverage complaining about what an odious, clueless little shit he is. Cole began his career in journalism, covering political campaigns, the Waco siege and, famously, the Yugoslavian civil war. Believe it or not he was hired on the advice of Todd Pettengill, as if I didn't already hate Todd enough. Todd pointed out that Cole "knew a hell of a lot more than I did". That's not saying much. Cole's early WWE days were mainly doing voice overs, hosting unimportant TV shows and doing interviews. It wasn't until 1999 that he stepped into a big role, replacing Jim Ross as RAW announcer as JR had Bell's Palsy. Cole was rewarded for his passable performances by becoming the lead announcer on *SmackDown!* later in the year. His grinding persistence at remaining the WWE's lead announcer have turned him into the "Voice of the WWE".

You can see he's done, or at the very least rusty. Davey hits the running powerslam, then realises he's done it wrong and pushes Rock toward the ropes before pinning. It's just sad. Davey stumbles like a drunk man into the Rock Bottom, and the People's Elbow finishes.
Final Rating: *½

Tangent: Davey's career went completely downhill from here. He was addicted to prescription painkillers and when that didn't sort his back out he got hooked on morphine. He really shouldn't have been wrestling and got released from his WWF contract in mid-2000 and died of a drug related heart attack in 2002. Another in a long list of wrestling tragedies.

Terri Invitational Tournament Final
Ladder Match
Edge & Christian vs. The Hardy Boyz
The winner gets $100,000 and Terri's services. The Hardys were working as the New Brood and have Gangrel in their corner, which brings up the question of why Gangrel would want them to win as he'd have to share management duties with Terri, and was actually replaced by her. The Hardys went through a load of managers before the WWF finally teamed them up with Lita and found a winning combination. This is the first tag team ladder match and an absolute game-changer. Not only for the individuals involved, who all benefitted enormously from this exposure, but also for tag team wrestling, which leapt to importance in 2000, and the hardcore style, which gained massively in popularity in 2000 too. It's amazing looking back to see Cleveland's total lack of interest in the match to begin with. The lack of tags benefits the Hardys as they have more team moves. Timmy White gets sick of Gangrel in a hurry and sends him to the back. The early ladder spots seem quite tame compared to later ladder matches, but it works because they build to bigger things and it's organic. Christian and Jeff fighting over a ladder leads to Jeff getting jammed in the corner, allowing Christian to run up the ladder and dropkick him. As the danger increases during the match the pops get bigger. Christian does an inverted DDT off the middle of the ladder and that's a "WOW" moment for 1999. Matt goes up and Edge powerbombs him off and that gets a meaty pop too. But they're just getting going. Edge climbs and Jeff missile dropkicks him off the ladder. The spots get progressively more brutal and dangerous. At this point Christian was the biggest talent of the four, and his timing is impeccable. But it's Jeff who's the showiest and he slingshots over a ladder to hit a big legdrop. I love the planning in this match, which compared to the TLC matches is a lot better, albeit with less carnage. The spots make sense. As the match escalates they start into the trademarks off the ladders with Edge hitting the Downward Spiral on Jeff, a move he stopped doing not long after. Because they build to big spots the selling compares favourably so they can throw in the fatigue stuff, and they start climbing slower to allow spots to be set up. It's smart work. What's really important is how they got the crowd, slowly but surely, and eventually they're hanging on every spot. The seesaw spot where Christian and Matt battle over a set up ladder and Jeff dives onto the other end is inspired and gets a standing ovation. They can milk the hell out of that and just lie around afterwards as everyone gets hurt. They move up to duelling ladder spots with all four guys involved and everyone falls off apart from Jeff who grabs the cash. The finish is underwhelming but the stuff that proceeded it was smartly worked, escalated nicely and got over four guys in one fell swoop. The WWF very rarely went out of their way to get four new guys over in one night, but they did here. All of them moved on to greatness and only Matt never won a World Title. Without this match to showcase their skills it could have taken them years longer to get to the top of the mountain. One of the best matches of 1999 and MOTY for most people. Follow on TLC matches would get crazier and have tremendous spots, but this was a smarter work all round.
Final Rating: ****½

Video Control takes us to Heat where Mick Foley makes fun of Crash Holly before interacting with the Rock and getting his ass kicked by Val Venis.

Promo Time: The Rock
Seeing as his match sucked the Rock decides to come out and entertain the fans with a promo. He's here to issue a challenge to the winner of tonight's main event, whether it be Steve Austin or Triple H. He runs through catchphrases and claims he'll win the title soon, but as he leaves Triple H comes down and works him over with a sledgehammer. It's a gimmicked hammer, which allows him to swing for the fences rather than jab while covering the end. EMT's take Rock out of here, including the future BB who I preferred as a sexy EMT rather than as a performer, which she was a bit useless at.

Val Venis vs. Mankind
This was at a point where Mick was run down and relying heavily on comedy and tag matches to cover his injuries. He did have a bit of a sidebar plan to make a few replacement stars for when he left, one of which was Val, well thought of by the WWF but horribly booked and limited by his porn star gimmick. I think Mick's initial plan was to put over a few guys on his way out to make them look good, but the only jobs anyone ever remembers are to Triple H in their two matches in early 2000. Also the Radicalz showed up early in 2000 to take over the mantle of midcard workrate freaks. Val was further handicapped by being an inferior worker to all the new arrivals, not that he bad or anything, but just inferior to the top level WCW guys that came in. Here Mick uses his insanity and love of ridiculous bumps to get the match over and takes a back bump on a set up chair as well hitting the ring post with the back of his head before taking a Russian legsweep on a chair. I can't think of a good reason for working the back of the head,

other than aiming to kill someone, but that's the target of Val's aggression. It makes the match uncomfortable to watch. Even when a lot of the shots are pulled, there are enough that connect to make it unsettling. The psychology behind it makes sense but it's not much fun. I appreciate attempts to make wrestling more realistic, but not at the expense of my entertainment. That arrives with Mandible Claw vs. Testicular Claw, which causes Mankind to collapse and Val falls on top for the surprise win. The finish is stupid as all the nut shots in the world won't keep your shoulders down. I guess he passed out from pain, but this is Mick Foley so the finish deflates the work.
Final Rating: **¼

Kane vs. X-Pac vs. Bradshaw vs. Faarooq
This is under elimination rules. Kane and X-Pac's team was a cute big brother routine, like Kenta Kobashi and Tsuyoshi Kikuchi, but with the switch of X-Pac being mentally stronger. The Acolytes are a better team, with absolutely no teases of dissention and they don't seem to care about beating each other up. The Acolytes put a beating on Kane until he tags Faarooq with an enzuigiri, and X-Pac tags in blind. Pac decides he wants to fight Kane, because he's a little twat, so Kane takes his head off with a clothesline. The difference is that X-Pac wants to fight his partner. The Acolytes do fight each other when they're both tagged in, but rather than be personal it's just a solid match. Clothesline from Hell should finish X-Pac off but Kane steps in to break it up, perhaps thinking he'll get double teamed if the APA are left alone with him, or perhaps anxious to help his little buddy. The Acolytes get their jollies by teaming and beating the crap out of X-Pac. This gives JR plenty of opportunities to talk about X-Pac's courage and Lawler to make fun of his "big heart". Kane has seen enough and tags himself in, with X-Pac trying to carry on fighting. Chokeslam sees off Bradshaw.

As Kane stands up X-Pac catches him with a spinning heel kick off the top. A shock pin, for sure, but it makes X-Pac look like a total ingrate. Kane literally saved him and he repays his benefactor by spin kicking him off the top rope.

X-Pac vs. Faarooq then, in a contest no one was expecting to take place as the semi-main event. Faarooq even gets cheered a bit as X-Pac's actions have been those of a punk. Spinebuster cuts off the Broncobuster but Faarooq manages to dive straight into the X-Factor. X-Pac goes over. The crowd were a lot happier when X-Pac was getting his ass kicked. I know I prefer when wrestling is not about size and all about talent, but the fans were not happy with the booking here, although seeing as X-Pac would turn heel shortly afterwards I guess this is okay.
Final Rating: **½

Backstage: The Rock gets treated for his busted ribs. He's refused to go to the infamous medical facility and is getting taped up instead.

No Holds Barred
WWF Championship
Triple H (c) vs. Steve Austin
This goes back to Triple H causing Austin to lose the title at *SummerSlam* and promptly taking possession of the championship. Hunter then spent two months pissing off Austin and the feeling was that a reckoning was coming here, and that Austin would reclaim his title. But this is the first piece of booking where Triple H was made to look like something other than a heel de jour. He was a main eventer and here to stay as such (unlike Kane, whose main event flirtation lasted all of 24 hours). Austin's subsequent injury lay off left Hunter as "the man" for most of 2000, with Rock replacing Austin as the top babyface. This match exists as a way to transition from the Austin main event era, which was repetitive brawling, into the Hunter era where they reverted to a mixture of Main Event Style and smarter in ring work. When Austin is in charge it remains an Austin era aimless brawl all over the building. Austin switches up the brawling for a creative use of a boom camera. It's my second favourite weird use of a camera, after Rock-Austin at *Backlash '99*. The brawl eventually gets to the ring, after the ref has been knocked out, and Hunter eats a Stunner. Another Stunner is countered and the ref takes another awesome bump, off the apron to the rail, before the Pedigree. Earl Hebner runs down to replace the injured Mike Chioda and Hunter immediately gets into a shoving contest with the new ref. Hunter used to sell a shit load for Hebner. They're both part of the Montreal Club. Screw Bret Hart? You're in! They go back to brawling with Hunter getting opened up on the announce table and Austin taking a suplex on the Spanish table. As they settle into an actual match Hunter works over the knee, which is a cerebral move as Austin has two bad legs. They work in a nice counter where Austin goes for a spinebuster and Hunter counters right into the facebuster. All in one move. Seeing as it's no DQ a chair comes into play. They start shooting for epic as Austin gets a long two count off a superplex. Austin goes to town on Hunter, getting receipts for *SummerSlam*, and kills his knees with a chair as a receipt for this match. The Rock comes down with a sledgehammer but accidentally hits Austin. Hunter lays him out with a Pedigree and just pins the winded Austin to retain. I remember liking this a lot more at the time, but the lengthy crowd brawl is a waste and by the time they actually get into the meat of the match half of it is gone. You could argue that's similar to Bret Hart's matches only with brawling replacing the technical stuff, but the second half wasn't hot enough to compensate.
Final Rating: ***½

VERDICT

Obviously the big match here is the Hardys vs. Edge & Christian as it made both teams and all four individuals into stars overnight. You can't ask for more from one match and every now and again the WWF creates a scenario with the sole intention of getting the participants over. Prior to this none of them were particularly over, maybe Edge, but afterwards the WWF had four new superstars. Job done. The rest of the card is less than enthralling, although Austin vs. Hunter is much better than the standard fare of Austin vs. "anyone but Mick Foley" run of 1998-99. It also has the historic Good Housekeeping match where Vince got held up for serious cash by the departing Jeff Jarrett, with Jeff putting in one final decent shift before signing for WCW and never coming back. The opening two matches are absolutely dreadful but if you can hold on past those, the PPV is pretty good after that. If you can't catch the whole show at least see the ladder match. That's essential viewing.

54

CAPITAL CARNAGE

CAT NO: WWF232
RUN TIME: 165 minutes (approx)

www.jrsbbq.com:

"Mother's Day brings back a cascade of memories for me as I was in London, as I recall, when word came from the States from my wife that my Mama had suddenly died of a heart attack at the age of 64. This info was received a few hours prior to a WWE produced UK PPV which, by the way, will naturally spawn the obligatory and worn out question: "Is WWE going to promote another UK PPV?" of which I have no idea. The McMahon family offered to fly me home immediately so I could attend to my mom's funeral arrangements with having no siblings and with my Dad passing away just a few years prior. Knowing my mother's work ethic and love of the genre, I opted to stay in the UK, do my job and then come home the next day to deal with the funeral arrangements. The only thing that I wasn't expecting was to come down with my second bout of Bells palsy while I was actually on the air live during that particular show. It wasn't the greatest weekend on record for me personally, but I did have the greatest Mom one could ever ask for as she loved me unconditionally, supported my passions, almost to a fault, and gave me a unrelenting work ethic and a no BS approach to many aspects of my life."

Kudos to Ross for remaining so professional throughout the show in the face of such adversity.

Lee Maughan: You may be wondering why a show from December 1998 appears in a book that picks up in October 1999, but you can thank the WWF for releasing the VHS of this show so long after it actually took place, resulting in a later catalogue number, the method we've chosen to simplify the ordering of the mammoth task we've elected to undertake in covering all and sundry on the promotion's home video market. This show marks the WWF's long-awaited return to UK-only pay-per-view after 1997's inaugural *One Night Only* event, with *Mayhem in Manchester* earlier in the year having been scheduled for the Sky Box Office treatment, only for a disagreement over the revenue split between the WWF and Sky resulting in a blackout of sorts that saw the card wind up as a non-televised house show, later seeing a half-hearted "highlights" release on VHS as a way for the WWF to try and recoup at least some of the overblown advertising that they put into the event.

Hosts are Jerry Lawler and Jim Ross, who unfortunately suffered his second attack of Bell's palsy during the broadcast after learning of his mother's death. In Jim's own words, from

Gangrel vs. Al Snow
Gangrel may have had the coolest entrance theme out of anybody during the entire Attitude era. Dude Love of course had the catchiest. Gangrel gets the obligatory "first guy on the main card out" pop (Droz had already beaten Mosh in a dark match), but the reaction to Snow (and Head in particular) dwarfs it. I don't think the WWF ever truly understood the rave party aspect of the Styrofoam head entrance, even though a lot of the audience in London has cottoned onto it despite ECW tapes having not (legally) reached the country yet. Not that the promotion would ever have spring for the rights to 'Breathe' by the Prodigy, but there you go.

Despite a tasty wheelbarrow German suplex from Snow, the two only manage to cobble together a decidedly average match, let down by a plethora of botches. First, Snow doesn't get enough height on a leapfrog (or Gangrel doesn't duck down low enough), resulting in Snow taking a headbutt to the balls, which he doesn't even stop to sell. That's followed by an awkward crossbody and Snow "missing" a moonsault, his knees actually hitting Gangrel who doesn't move out of the way in time. Finally, following a sloppy tornado DDT, the Brood arrive at ringside with Christian distracting the referee long enough to render Snow's Head shot to Gangrel null, as Edge comes off the top with a missile dropkick to give Gangrel the duke. A pretty bad opener from two guys who should really have done much better, but who actually managed to take a jacked up crowd and completely deflate them in less than five minutes. Well done, lads.
Final Rating: *½

The Headbangers vs. The Legion of Doom
As noted, Droz had already beaten Mosh in a dark match prior to the pay-per-view going live, so this looks to be something of a revenge match for the 'Bangers. For the rest of the viewing

audience however, it's an excuse to replay the God-awful angle from three weeks prior where Hawk "tried to commit suicide" (or, more blatantly, was pushed off the top of the Titantron by Droz, his implied enabler.) As a consequence, the fans boo Droz a lot, since everybody hated the angle so much and what the once-mighty LOD had been reduced to, but they still like Animal, so he gets cheered. The Headbangers also get cheered, but it's really weird as they get the heat on Droz. You know, the heel. Have I ever told you how much I hated Vince Russo's continually confused booking philosophies?

Animal gets the hot tag and runs wild as it all breaks down, so Droz shoves him out of the ring while the referee isn't looking, leading to his getting rolled-up from behind and pinned in just three minutes. Yes, they made their hot new heel look like a total moron, and sacrificed him to a team that was very much on the downswing by this point. Post-match, Droz and Animal finally comes to blows, signalling the end of their union, which is about the only thing of any importance on this entire show. I say "importance", all it inevitably led to was Droz being turfed from the LOD and the LOD being turfed from the WWF before they could get any revenge as the angle limped to its unfulfilled conclusion in early 1999. What a thorough waste of time for all concerned.
Final Rating: *

Val Venis vs. Goldust
What happens when you take two midcard babyfaces but give them both heel characteristics then ask the audience to pick a side between the one douchebag and the other douchebag? Why, you have a match where nobody really gets over of course! Yes, once again Vince Russo attempts to rewrite the wrestling playbook by giving everyone an edge, killing all their heat in the process and ensuring neither will ever mean anything again as long as he remains in charge. Brilliant. The angle here is some convoluted horseshit in which Goldust callously dumped his wife Terri Runnels in late 1997, remerged as the sexually deviant Artist Formerly Known as Goldust, then repented his sins as a Born Again Christian desperate for forgiveness. Terri meanwhile did what any woman in her emotionally unstable condition would do and made a sex tape with a porn star, which she broadcast to the world. For some reason, she then decided to announce that she was pregnant with Val Venis' child, so Venis dumped her, revealing that he had previously undergone a vasectomy and thus couldn't be the baby daddy. What third-rate soap opera garbage this is, only emphasised further by poor old JR having to recount it in a serious tone rather than call any wrestling holds.

Of course, the believed-to-be-lying Terri then attempted to reconcile with Goldust, his Bible-thumping Dustin Runnels character having gone over about as well as the idea of Judas Iscariot showing up for a kissing contest and the whole thing managed to not only come full-circle, but kill any superstar aura Goldust had left. Her advances rebuffed, Terri instead formed a pact with the also recently scorned Jacqueline, who in turn proceeded to kick Goldust and Marc Mero in the balls for a cheap pop. How the hell anybody was supposed to be able to determine who the babyface was in all this is anybody's best guess, and crowd here are completely confused by it all, cheering Venis initially as he cuts a babyface promo, before turning on him completely after he cheats to avoid getting a kick in the goolies of his own. And why were these two even playing second-fiddle to a union of two valets anyway? How was that supposed to help anyone? Terri and Jacqueline weren't going to be teaming up for a series of four star matches with Goldust and Venis, so all it really accomplished was to emasculate the two guys who were actually working the matches. Again, have I ever told you how much I hated Vince Russo's continually confused booking philosophies?

To top it all off, Terri isn't even here, so all that's left is yet another short, average match in a parade of them tonight. JR soon begins questioning whether Terri is really pregnant or not, which only serves to remind me that she would soon fake a miscarriage in yet another deeply unpleasant angle from the creative shitstorm that is Vince Russo's brain. The match itself somewhat resembles a 90's All Japan match, albeit a largely heatless undercard one that you'd see eating up a few minutes of TV time underneath one of those classic 30-minute six-man tags. Venis breaks out a nice fisherman suplex and they work in some penile spots and a head-on collision leading to Goldust inadvertently headbutting Val squarely in the plums. Goldust goes for Shattered Dreams (penalty kick to the bollocks) but Val pulls the referee in the way to avoid that, then uses the distraction to roll Goldust up for the pin with a handful of tights, our second roll-up finish of the night. Goldust isn't best pleased with that, and boots Val in the nuts anyway.
Final Rating: **

- Earlier in the weekend, Vince McMahon gave a lecture at Oxford University, something I wish would have been broadcast instead of this undercard.

- Speak of the devil, Mr. McMahon arrives in the arena, along with Shane McMahon, Pat Patterson and Gerald Brisco, because we're deep into the era of lengthy promos that accomplish little of note being more important than short matches (the longest we've seen thus far was the previous match at an endurance sapping 5:33) that also accomplish nothing of note. Patterson announces that the previously advertised Rock vs. Triple H title match has been cancelled and replaced with Rock defending the strap against X-Pac instead, and Triple H now going up against Jeff Jarrett, for reasons which are never adequately explained. And wasn't it nice of him to let you know you weren't getting what you'd previously been promised *after* you'd already paid your £15 to see the show?

Shane follows up by referencing George Michael's interview on *Parkinson* the previous evening, in which Michael publicly addressed his arrest for attempting to cottage with an undercover police officer in Beverly Hills the previous April. He notes that Michael had brought up the subject of his boyfriend without ever revealing a name, leading Shane to conclude it must be Vinnie Jones, suggesting that's where his reputation as a "hard man" came from. Because even in the progressive 90s, freakish beings like homosexuals are to be derided, spat at, looked down up and generally made fun of for the sake of generating heel heat. Vince finishes by declaring "tea time" as "a load of pious crap" and claiming that every single Brit in the audience wishes they were American.

Tiger Ali Singh vs. Edge
What's the absolute best way possible to follow up a pointless, rambling, xenophobic anti-British heel promo on a UK-only PPV you ask? Why, by rolling out Tiger Ali Singh for another one! And wasn't it just dandy of them to confirm earlier in the night that, yes, the Brood are definitely heels, only to then send out Edge as a happy, clappy babyface three matches later? The match winds up the shortest of the night (clocking in a paltry 2:52) on account of how bad Singh is. He'd actually debuted with the WWF to much fanfare in 1997 as an attempt to cash-in on the Asian market, but had been so rotten that

JACQUELINE

essentially beating themselves, and if you count the slam reversal as a variant, third roll-up finish in a row. It's like they're scared to let anybody actually win a match on their own merit in case they get accused of "lacking creativity" or it damages the loser, but it does nothing to enhance the winner either, and who cares about "protecting" midcarders on a show with such a limited broadcast outreach anyway? Say, have I ever told you about how much I hated Vince Russo's continually confused booking philosophies?
Final Rating: *

- Former Wimbledon "Crazy Gang" footballer and *Lock, Stock and Two Smoking Barrels* star Vinnie Jones comes out and promises that tonight is "gonna be emotional!" Steady on, Vinnie, this is hardly Davey Boy Smith going for the Intercontinental Title against his brother-in-law at Wembley Stadium!

Sable & Christian vs. Jacqueline & Marc Mero
This is essentially a rematch from *SummerSlam*, only with Christian taking Edge's place. Again, you've got a Brood member having worked as a heel in the opener now as a de facto babyface for lack of anything better to do, whilst the Jacqueline/Mero union has the odd dynamic of the pair having already split up. As the pre-match video package reminds us, Jacqueline tripped Mero from the outside during a recent episode of *Sunday Night Heat*, costing him a match with fellow heel the Big Bossman. Incensed, Mero ended their relationship, leading to already-mentioned angle in which he and Goldust got kicked in the nads by Jacqueline and Terri Runnels, the newly-dubbed Pretty Mean Sisters. On a losing streak, Mero then announced on *RAW* that if he couldn't knock off Dwayne Gill, he'd leave the WWF, which went badly for 'Marvelous' when the Blue Meanie ran-in and cost him the match. Here, he's simply "fulfilling his final contractual obligation" before riding off into the sunset.

Mero actually works almost the entire match for his team, getting into a shoving contest with Jacqueline before things even get going, then working some basic spots with Christian before challenging Sable to go one-on-one with him. Pulling his shorts up to his nipples and raising his shoulders as broadly as they'll go, Mero opens himself up for some wacky comedy with Christian jumping in from behind and pantsing him. At least he

he'd been sent out to the minor leagues for seasoning before receiving a call-up for the *One Night Only* show, where he entered such a crappy performance that he was farmed back out for further tutoring. Back again here and he's still completely rotten, yet he actually goes over which tells you a lot about how much of an eye the WWF had for actual talent back then.

Singh wins after catching Edge coming off the top with a crossbody, and slams him for a pin with his feet on the ropes. Edge carried it as best he could, but he was still pretty young and somewhat inexperienced at this level himself at this point. May I also point out that's now the fourth finish in a row with either interference, someone looking stupid, or someone

didn't get pinned from the resultant roll-up. He does however manage to crotch himself on the top rope, get hoofed in the love spuds (what is this promotion's obsession with women kicking men in their wedding tackle around this time? Was Vince Russo just a simple fetishist on top of everything else?) and eat a Sablebomb before deciding enough's enough and scarpering. Sable finally brings Jacqueline into the match for some piss-weak punches and she quickly ends it with Mero's own TKO. Post-match, Jacqueline takes out her frustrations on the referee, so Sable sneaks up from behind and rips her top clean off, revealing her enormous amplified breasts for all to see, something the WWF had been trying to get onto pay-per-view for months only to face strict restrictions from US PPV carriers. The UK was much more lenient in that department, and the incident even remains intact on the home video release. A perfectly fine comedy match, with a clean finish to boot. And hey! Boobies! If you're into that sort of thing.
Final Rating: **½

WWF Intercontinental Championship
Ken Shamrock (c) vs. Steve Blackman
JR promises a "dandy" here but it's decidedly dull stuff, the crowd instead having to amuse themselves with chants of "Shamrock sucks!" and "You fat bastard!" aimed at the Big Bossman. Shamrock takes over very early and while his fundamentals are sound, they're not particularly invigorating. It doesn't help that neither guy has much in the way of personality to speak of, and that Blackman offers absolutely no resistance, no fire, or really any signs of life as Shamrock methodically works him over, until he suddenly makes his big comeback with an Irish whip. He follows with a leap over the top, giving Shamrock a neck snap in the process, before finally waking up the crowd after levelling the Bossman with a baseball slide, Bossman having not even interfered in the match. Bossman retaliates by striking Blackman in the ankle with his ASP baton, setting up Shamrock's match-winning ankle lock in 6:50. Another short match (not that I was screaming out for it to go any longer, mind you), and another fuck finish where the guy losing looks like a total twerp. Bossman beats Blackman down some more after the match, audibly shouting "Fuck you, man!" at Earl Hebner for trying to call it off.
Final Rating: *½

- Meanwhile, the Rock is hanging out in the back, eating fruit and being cool as Hulk Hogan might say. On being asked about his upcoming match with X-Pac, Rock references a previous meeting between the pair on *RAW*, where "The Rock almost put that bony jabroni in a coma when he gave him the Corporate Elbow!" He tops it off with an amusing bit where he runs through Hogan's, Steve Austin's, Ric Flair's and Bret Hart's catchphrases, a gag he would later recycle on *RAW*.

Triple H vs. Jeff Jarrett
At least three-and-a-half years too early, it's the ultimate showdown for supremacy in the grand wrestling war that is WWE vs. TNA. As noted earlier, Triple H was supposed to face the Rock for the WWF Title on this show, so we can presume that Jarrett was originally going to face X-Pac here. Given that Rock and Triple H had been feuding throughout the last few months, and given that Jarrett and X-Pac had been feuding throughout the last few months, I can only assume that made far too much sense in Vince Russo's mind, hence the switch. Still, I appreciate the fresher match-ups.

This is actually Triple H's first televised singles match back after his knee surgery in September (and subsequent flirtation with WCW). He hits a spinebuster early which, devastating a move as it's supposed to be, Jarrett no-sells. That's why, unless it's part of the story you're trying to tell, you don't hit moves like that three minutes into a match. Then again, there's only about three more minutes left, and there's still shenanigans to pack in! Debra tries to distract Triple H be threatening to whip her baps out, which I'm sure a great many members of the audience figured might actually happen after the Jacqueline incident earlier. It backfires however, as Jarrett brings a steel chair into the ring only for Chyna to grab it, allowing Triple H to land the Pedigree for the pin.
Final Rating: **¼

- Michael Cole interviews Steve Austin backstage in yet another nondescript promo tonight, uttering the words "Friday night on *RAW*, you and Kane were working together like a hand in a glove." I didn't know wearing a glove was something you had to work at?

WWF Tag Team Championship
The New Age Outlaws (c) vs. D'Lo Brown & Mark Henry
None of this actually ties directly into the match, but just to bring you up to speed on where everyone was, character-wise in this match: D'Lo Brown has been on a tour of Buckingham Palace and the River Thames (pronounced with a soft 't'), deludedly believing himself to be of British origin after having recently held the European Title (which is kind of a babyface move on this card for someone who's supposed to be a heel); Mark Henry has recently been on a romantic date with Chyna, standing up for her honour when a bunch of douchebags began harassing her at a bar (which is kind of a babyface move for someone who's supposed to be a heel); and the New Age Outlaws have been considering a standing offer to join Mr. McMahon's evil Corporation (which is kind of a heel move for a couple of guys who are supposed to be babyfaces).

The Outlaws are still hugely over here and work some typical back-and-forth with D'Lo before Henry comes in for an always electrifying bearhug. Billy escapes that and the Outlaws hit a nice double dropkick to put him down, and that's when the match falls apart. Henry gives Road Dogg a legdrop square across the head and a massive splash, and that's the last of Road Dogg. Billy has to actually get in and drag him clean across the ring just so he can make his own hot tag (which actually comes across as both smart and comical, drawing a big pop), and Gunn works the rest of the match at a 2-on-1 disadvantage. Despite having never been much of a ring wizard, him being the senior guy in the ring means he's left to improvise a new finish after Road Dogg confirms that he's done, and after a Fameasser (not yet named), a double down and a small package, he calls a piledriver (loudly) out of nowhere, adding a "Stay here! This is it! This is it!" just to make sure the people watching at home could tell it was all fake. Hell, I think the folks back in the US probably heard him yelling out his instructions there, and what a sloppy piledriver too. Match was perfectly fine until it all fell apart at the end, and Road Dogg leaves still holding his head and clutching his chest.
Final Rating: **

WWF Championship
The Rock (c) vs. X-Pac
X-Pac is also European Champion here, so the earlier reshuffling of the card means there's no European Title match on this card, the belt that was introduced for just such an occasion. Not only that, but these two have already done this match on *RAW* a couple of weeks ago, ending when Shawn Michaels swerve turned with a steel chair shot to the head of X-

Pac, joining the Corporation as WWF commissioner. And speaking of RAW matches, that's exactly what this is like, something which wouldn't feel out of place on free TV, but doesn't quite reach the level you may hope of a pay-per-view outing.

They start out how with X-Pac landing a series of spinning wheel kicks and armdrag takeovers, with Rock attempting to bail only to have Triple H and Chyna block his exit. From there what follows is one of those matches where, when the guys are actually doing stuff it's pretty good, and when they're not it isn't. And unfortunately, the Rock has disappointing tendency to keep going back to a tedious chinlock in between all of his highspots. Has he been studying his IRS tapes? And then, just because the booking hasn't been backwards enough already tonight, Triple H distracts the referee, allowing Chyna to jump into the ring and low blow Rocky during a Rock Bottom attempt (again with the testicular offence) to give X-Pac a near fall. He gets another one after the referee takes an accidental bump and Triple H decks Rocky with the European Title. The whole story of this match is presented as X-Pac being a monumental underdog, but the only close counts he's getting are off his buddies interfering freely!

Rock finally decides enough is enough and goes after Chyna, so Triple H decks him (from behind mind you) to draw the super lame disqualification at 12:36. After the match, DX put the boots to Rocky like the babyfaces they are until Ken Shamrock runs out to make the save, and gets his head kicked in too. Because everyone knows if you're the Intercontinental Champion, you're supposed to look like a total dork. Perhaps this was all acceptable in its time since Shawn had turned on X-Pac a couple of weeks prior, but viewed in isolation this was completely ass backwards psychology-wise and just served to put sympathy on the Rock. X-Pac seemed to be working harder than just about anybody else on the show however.
Final Rating: **¾

In a bit lifted from *Over the Edge* earlier in the year, the Corporation are out to stack the deck against Austin with "Academy Award winner" Shane McMahon as the special guest ring announcer, Mr. McMahon as the special guest commentator, Pat Patterson as the special guest timekeeper, Gerald Brisco as special guest referee (replacing the Big Bossman for no given reason), and the Bossman as "special guest enforcer", a role that was supposed to go to Vinnie Jones. Jones comes out to take umbrage with that and shoves Bossman through the ropes, earning him a red card from Brisco! He follows that with such classic crooked referee spots as faking a knee injury, declaring a clearly down shoulder to be up, and getting dust in his eyes, all reasons for him not to count any of Austin's pinfall attempts.

As you might expect, the bulk of the match is a gigantic brawl, but Mankind peppers that steak with a hearty side-helping of comedy, trying to form an alliance with former partner Austin that earns him a Stone Cold Stunner. Annoyed by this, he then attempts to form a union with the currently feuding Undertaker and Kane, two guys he also has much history with, which earns him a double chokeslam. Austin then drops Kane with a Stunner, but Brisco is busy checking Patterson's watch for the time limit, so Austin finally just decks him and hits another Stunner on Kane, counted this time by replacement referee Earl Hebner. Brisco doesn't take kindly to that and goes after Hebner, so Austin drops him with another Stunner before Vinnie Jones returns to block Bossman's path to Austin. Hebner then goes absolutely bonkers and kicks the stuffing out of Bossman, flipping the bird and yelling like a maniac the whole time. The show goes off the air with a beer bash, although despite his heroics, Hebner comes across like a total hanger-on as Austin gets his celebrity rub from Jones. A good match to finish, but not quite the anarchic fun that some of the Austin-Dude Love matches earlier in the year were.
Final Rating: ***¼

Steve Austin vs. Kane vs. Mankind vs. The Undertaker

VERDICT

At the time, this card was heavily slated by British wrestling magazine *Power Slam*, as well as by many fans who felt that being asked to pay good money for a show full of sloppy, lethargic performances while weekly episodes of *RAW* offered much more excitement was an insult. While the show does dress itself up as being someway important thanks to continual references to recent TV angles, the fact that none of the happenings travel back to America (as news of Shawn Michaels beating Davey Boy Smith for the European Title did after *One Night Only*) render the whole card nothing more than a glorified house show.

In fairness to the WWF, it would have been difficult to book anything with lasting consequences even if they'd wanted to, as the next edition of *RAW* (due to air the next evening in the US and the following Friday in the UK) had already been taped six days earlier, and everything was already in place for the promotion's next supercard, incidentally another pay-per-view, *Rock Bottom*, back on home soil the very next week. The fact that *Rock Bottom* featured a WWF Title change (albeit overturned), plus Steve Austin earning a berth in 1999's *Royal Rumble* by virtue of his victory over the Undertaker in a Buried Alive match, just added further frustration for *Capital Carnage* viewers, as that show, like all other "regular" pay-per-view events of the day, aired essentially for free in the UK (albeit on Sky Sports, a subscription-only package that offered the rest of the WWF's televisual output in the country). No, being asked to pay for a show on which nothing mattered just seven days before the *real* big show aired at no extra cost did *not* go over well. Sadly, it was a trend that was to continue for several years to come.

Viewed strictly *as* a glorified house show, *Capital Carnage* really isn't all that bad, but there's nothing to really recommend about it either, especially as you can probably Google an animated .gif of the topless Jacqueline in mere seconds to satisfy any curiosities you may have about that. I also just want to note that the version of the show I reviewed for this book was Silver Vision's Tagged Classics DVD dub of the original VHS mastertape, which includes a very grainy picture and lots of little tracking lines flickering over the screen. For a show filmed in 1998, the fact the master could wind up in such poor condition so quickly is very disappointing, and in fact, my own home-recorded VHS from the original Sky Box Office showing is actually in better nick. Poor show, Silver Vision.

37

PAT PATTERSON & GERALD BRISCO

STEVE AUSTIN - HELL YEAH

CAT NO: WWF233
RUN TIME: 60 minutes (approx)

Arnold Furious: This may seem strange to any DVD era readers but there was a time when we shelled out hard earned cash for VHS tapes that barely tipped the playing scales at 60 minutes. Such was the popularity of the WWF in the late 90's wrestling boom that they could get away with releasing tapes, usually dedicated to one of their big draws, and seriously skimp on the content. As the company's number one star and biggest draw, Steve Austin was a natural choice for several VHS releases. Austin tapes came out at a rate only previously associated with Hulk Hogan tapes. The difference being that in Attitude actual wrestling wasn't as important. At least those Hogan tapes had a series of matches, usually fairly complete, on them. Attitude profile tapes generally were total clipfests.

Host is Michael Cole and he announces they'll be following Steve Austin around for three days and that will form the content of this tape. Steve starts by saying he's an original and 'Stone Cold' is just him with the volume turned up. He points out that all the really successful guys are just playing themselves. He talks about the WWF Title belt and how much it means to anyone in the business. "That means you're at the fucking top". The behind-the-scenes look at Austin is terrific as he is able to shoot the shit and play up to the cameras, ever so slightly out of character. Which means him bullshitting backstage and claiming his roll of wrist tape was given to him by Wayne Gretzky before chuckling. He's a lot of fun to be around.

King of the Ring 1998
We get clips of Austin-Kane and their First Blood match. It's far closer to a music video than actual highlights. Every time I see the match I am reminded that Mick Foley came running down after his Hell in a Cell double bump. I always forget! Undertaker causes Austin to bleed by missing Foley with a chair shot and Kane gets the title. Austin cuts a less shooty promo into the travel camera although he gets to litter it with profanity, swearing at drivers he's passing. We clip right ahead to Austin vs. Kane on *RAW* the following night. Austin escapes a Tombstone and hits the Stunner to regain his title just 24-hours after Kane won it. Undertaker runs in so Austin gives him a Stunner too for causing Kane's 24-hour title reign.

Video Control gives us Austin's vehicular rampages with Austin claiming he can drive anything with four wheels. The interview continues as Austin drives somewhere and god damnit he's drinking a beer. Why did the WWF think *that* was a good idea? Austin gives us a good inside look at the vehicles he's driven. He points out the monster limo that he drove over eight cars either would have worked or he'd have broken the front axle "and had to walk into the damn building". This was a fun little segment but I really could have lived without the drinking and driving business. Maybe I'm wrong and it was a non-alcoholic beer or something, but it doesn't exactly send out the right message.

SummerSlam 1998
Austin points out he got knocked silly after kicking Taker in the guts and Undertaker stood up and hit his head on Austin's jaw. When he came around the ref asked him if he was alright. "Where am I?" "You're in the Garden". "Oh, really?" Clips from the match follow and a Stunner finishes. Again, the clips are more like a music video and the constant stream of loud heavy metal music is giving me a headache by this point. And I like rock music as much as the next man, but combined with a deluge of violent imagery it's akin to the torture scene in *A Clockwork Orange*.

We thankfully slow things down while Austin talks about the Smoking Skulls belt, which he calls a "fuck you to Vince McMahon". Austin thinks it's the best looking championship belt he's ever seen. This leads into Austin's acts of rebellion against Vince, which is a bit strange as they've now gone backwards chronologically.

Over the Edge 1998
So we've gone from June to August to May for some bizarre reason. Clips of Austin-Foley follow with loud rock music playing over the top of it, naturally. Austin hits Dude with the Stunner and counts him down with Vince's unconscious hand. This is the shortest segment on the tape, which is a shame considering how good the match is.

Breakdown
Then it's back into the original chronological order of things as we flash ahead to September and Austin losing to both Kane and the Undertaker for the WWF Title. "You don't have it anymore, it's mine" yells Vince. Video Control takes us to a series of Austin's assaults on the chairman of the board including pouring cement into his Corvette. Cole finally adds something of worth by pointing out the 'Vette is on display at Titan Towers.

Judgement Day 1998
This is the tedious Taker-Kane title match where Austin was the referee. He knocks both guys out and counts them both down. Vince fires him. Luckily this is brisk and we don't get extended highlights of a terrible match. We segue right into *RAW* the next night where Austin turned up with a gun, which is another angle I wasn't overly keen on. It might have ended with BANG 3:16 but the set up with the guns and the crossbow had a bad vibe about it. Totally irresponsible.

Video Control then takes us to the nonsensical Shane McMahon rehiring Austin, then turning heel on him angle. You got rid of him, why would you want him back? We go from there to the Undertaker trying to embalm Austin, which is another ridiculous and stupid angle. Most of the Undertaker's crap has no business in wrestling, but this was yet another irresponsible angle. Interesting to note that Taker crucified Austin, considering Kurt Angle once refused to sign for ECW because Raven crucified Sandman, and Scott Levy even had to apologise for it. Seeing as Angle was in the WWF system at the time, it seems a bit weird.

Rock Bottom
This is the Buried Alive match between Taker and Austin, which Austin had to win just to qualify for the Rumble. Naturally he does. Because there's nothing else to say, that's the entire segment.

Royal Rumble 1999
This is stripped right down to the Austin-McMahon battle that takes place at the end of the match. This is another one of those moments where Austin being a total ass cost him a big match. If he'd just thrown Vince out he'd have won. Austin, in a less-shooty comment, calls it a "rookie mistake". We move on to *RAW* the next night with Vince waving his title shot so Shawn Michaels, drunk in Texas, gives Austin the shot instead thus negating the booking at the Rumble. Sometimes I swear they booked PPVs to deliberately swerve people and screw with predictions and office pools.

St Valentine's Day Massacre
The February PPV only existed so Austin could put a beating on Vince and extend the bit at the end of the Rumble by another month. The highlights show Vince taking a hiding for the entire match, which is exactly what happened. Vince blades and the Stunner should finish, but Paul Wight shows up fresh from WCW to interfere. This backfires as Wight throws Austin into the cage and the side gives way. Austin goes to 'Mania. It makes you wonder how much of the beating was Vince's plan. If he planned for Wight to save his ass at the end of the match, why didn't he just arrive earlier and save Vince a shoeing?

Video Control gives us another chat with Austin. He really goes all over the place with his musical interests saying 85% is country music. Urgh. He recovers by saying Stevie Ray Vaughn is one of his favourite musicians of all time. He moves on to his entrance music, saying he asked for something that sounded like Rage Against the Machine song *'Bulls on Parade'* and Jim Johnston did the rest. See, this is interesting material. I have no idea why they didn't insert more of this. Presumably Michael Cole couldn't come up with any meaningful questions to get Steve to open up.

WrestleMania XV
During this tape the Hardys' music crops up quite often as Jim Johnston wrote it before the Hardys were pushed, so it's just filler music. It must have been played four times by this point. The Rock-Austin match looks pretty good in highlights, but I think it was a bit overbooked and I much prefer their *Backlash* match the following month. This is the longest highlights package on the tape, as it's the culmination of another Road to *WrestleMania* for Austin. As the match reaches a conclusion Vince runs down followed by Mankind, amusingly to the Hardys' music, as it finishes and kicks in again. Stunner finishes.

Video Control goes back to Austin and him talking about his fame, saying if he missed those opportunities he'd have missed the boat. Austin talks about "crossover audience" and while it burned him out a bit doing *Nash Bridges* on his day off, it was important for his staying power. To hear Austin talking about business is really weird, but he's a smart guy. Just because he's a profane redneck doesn't mean he's not clever. In closing Austin says he's proud to be a part of the one of the hottest runs in the history of wrestling, and that it drives him to show up every day and bust his ass.

Backlash 1999
The Rock takes things into overdrive by throwing Austin into a river and holding a funeral service for him. The match highlights follow again, this time with different generic rock music and Shane McMahon as referee. The bit with Rock filming himself getting a Stunner makes the cut. A wonderful piece of Gonzo filmmaking from the WWF. Vince stops Shane's evil ways and Austin wins with a belt shot, with this being part of Vince's maniacal plan to screw Austin as the Higher Power. But first he has to earn his trust, for whatever reason.

Video Control gives us another chat with Austin, who gets philosophical about his injuries and thinks everything happens for a reason. He figures he wouldn't be where he is if he'd not walked the path he did. "I love my fucking job". We see screaming fans and Austin says it's what the business is all about.

VERDICT

This started so promisingly with Austin BS'ing with people backstage and offering insight into his actions. The bits with vehicles and Austin recalling how much fun he had doing various stuff was good, but the tape rapidly goes downhill as it becomes a clip-fest of bad matches. It's as if they forgot their original intention to make a different style tape and instead just let Video Control cobble together a highlights package for each PPV and the relevant storyline stuff around that. Like many superstar tapes from the Attitude Era it's not worth getting.

40

THE ROCK - KNOW YOUR ROLE

CAT NO: WWF234
RUN TIME: 60 minutes (approx)

Arnold Furious: It's amazing to think that the late 90s were still as kayfabed as they were. What with Vince Russo and his million worked shoots in WCW, you'd think even the dimmest mark would have cottoned on to the internet and got themselves smartened up. But, if memory serves correctly, I've personally had to explain how wrestling works to people older and supposedly wiser than me (including one deluded fellow who claimed Kane wore his mask everywhere and really was scarred from a fire. I bet he felt pretty stupid when Kane unmasked). Not to mention a hoard of idiots I've encountered over the years on the internet and at live shows who seemed to have no clue as to what was occurring in front of them (being resident guru of SmashWrestling was an eye opener). So maybe it's not so shocking that a trip down memory lane like this one reveals the WWF still desperately churning out kayfabe products. This being at the same time as Mick Foley was writing books detailing how wrestling works. I guess this DVD was aimed more at the non-literate market. If you smell what I'm cooking.

Tangent: During the course of these books I've remembered both a sentimental love of VHS as a format (tape trading was an absurdly fun time) and an incredible loathing. The latter normally stemming from how horribly deteriorated the tapes have become when WWF Home Video decided to use cheap quality tape. Like Lee, I've noticed stuff I taped off TV is in far better condition than official WWF releases. It's frustrating and I'm glad DVD arrived when it did, thus preserving wrestling in a better format.

We're in South Beach, Florida. The tape is hosted by The Rock, as if anyone else could do it. In a remarkable piece of business he runs through his opponents including "that half queer" Triple H, "a big piece of monkey crap" Mankind and "the biggest piece of trash walking God's green Earth" Steve Austin. We start off by watching Rock shooting a commercial, which seems to involve him driving around with his shirt open. He has three women hanging off his arm during the shoot but refers to them as "jabronis" and the Nation of Domination too. "Faarooq. Faarwho?"

On *RAW*, Rock presents the Nation with solid gold Rolexes to win their favour. Kama, D'Lo and Mark Henry get $15,000 gifts but Faarooq gets a framed photo of the Rock. In a kayfabe interview The Rock talks about lying and then lying about lying and backstabbing because that's what he was about, but that sometimes he'd just hit you in the face with a chair. That leads to footage of Rock hitting Ken Shamrock square in the face with a chair, which is one of the most brutal unprotected chair shots, ever. "Are you ribbing the Rock?" says Rocky when Shamrock beckons him to use the chair. The Rock next addresses the rivalry with Faarooq and suggests there was no rivalry as the Rock just laid the smack down on his candy ass. This leads into footage of the Nation turfing Faarooq out, mainly because Rock had given them all expensive gifts. I like how Rock just totally skims over this whole segment as if the Nation meant nothing to him compared to the actual talent he's about to work with.

We head straight into Rock making fun of Chyna for wanting the Rock in a sexual manner. "Chyna, you just need to get some". The rest of the Nation put her "down on her knees where she belongs". The Rock eventually refuses to kiss her because she's a big piece of trash. The IC Title feud with Triple H leads into the Nation battling DX and after Rock uses a ladder on Hunter, they have a ladder match at *SummerSlam '98*. When quizzed as to if he'll accept the match the Rock says "you bet your pretty ass". Rock goes on to shoot on Hunter again calling him "part queer". Do you think they didn't get along? Extended highlights of the *SummerSlam '98* ladder match follow. I happen to think it's one of the most overrated ladder matches of all time, but any time the WWF give two stars a ladder match on PPV it means they're serious about pushing them. Even the highlights are lame as both guys slowly, slowly, slowly walk after the ladder and get cut off. You know how we make fun of slow ladder climbing? You'd be surprised at how little of it exists in the really great ladder matches whereas this one has laughable ladder climbing. At least there's a bit of psychology regarding Hunter's slow climbing as Rock works his leg over. The knee stuff is easily the best part of the match. Another interesting point from this match is how careless Rock can be and he shows no attempt to protect Hunter when he shoves a ladder over. Watching these highlights does remind me of some of the better psychology the match has and of Rock's brutal facial injury from getting a ladder dropkicked into his nose. Chyna gets in a low blow to allow Hunter the win. I have the match at around ***½, and I could live with four if someone wanted to rate it that, but for me it's not MOTY or anything.

I love a little offshoot from the Rock where he says how anyone can just come out and say "this Friday I'm gonna kick your ass". After saying no one can cut a promo like the Rock, we get a collection of them. He's tremendously entertaining. "Here's a guy who looks like Tarzan and he wrestles like Jane" – of Triple H, during a match against him. "You put his brain in a parakeet, ZING, flies backwards" – of Kane.

Rock had a brief flirtation with being a babyface, where he was getting monster reactions. This leads into *Survivor Series* where Rock beat Bossman and Shamrock, both Corporate members, in dubious circumstances. Kane, also in the Corporation, then cost Undertaker his match with the Rock. Eventually Vince McMahon screws Mankind and the booking of the tournament makes perfect sense as Rock advanced thanks to the Corporation, all the way. One of Vince Russo's better evenings of booking, albeit at the expense of actual wrestling. Rock denies being a Corporate puppet as it was his plan to use the Corporation like he used the Nation; to become the man. Rock still makes me chuckle when desperately trying to stay heel. "This ain't sing-a-long with the champ. The Rock says it by himself". His facial reactions to the fans finishing his catchphrases are wonderful. They even finish his "this is not sing-a-long with..." I love his nursery rhyme stuff too. "Piss on the lamb, piss on Mary and piss on you". By late 1999 the fans were eating up every single word that came out of his mouth. Austin's injury was actually well timed for the People's Champ. Back to the interview and Rock mentions the fans are loud for him regardless of whether he's a face or a heel, which is the first "insider" terminology on display.

The Corporate piece leads into footage from the Rock-Mankind "I Quit" match at *Royal Rumble '99*. This includes Rock's entire pre-match promo, his entire entrance and then clips of the match, most of which involve Rock hitting Mankind with inanimate objects and refusing to quit in humorous fashion. The match is a mixture of brutality, comedy and high spots. It's a decent match. Rock was certainly improving as an in-ring talent during early 1999 and getting the hang of being a main event star. The finale comes with Mankind taking a big bump onto an "electrical" thing, which causes the lights to go out before Rock handcuffs Mankind and waffles him repeatedly with sickening chair shots. Rock ignores the blatant pumped in "I Quit" words and claims he dominated that match. This leads into the Empty Arena match from Superbowl *Halftime Heat*. I had totally forgotten that Vince McMahon commentated on the match, in somewhat biased fashion. The cinematic nature of the photography is a letdown as it takes away from the competitive nature of the bout although I'm sure they wanted to do something stylish to appeal to potential Superbowl viewers. It's not a traditional wrestling match as there's no wrestling in it and they garbage brawl all over an arena before Mankind wins with a forklift truck. The final shot of Rock being pinned with a camera in his face is stupid. We also get footage of their final match; the ladder match on *RAW*. I guess there wasn't room on the tape for their Last Man Standing match at *St. Valentine's Day Massacre*. Putting it close to the HHH match from *SummerSlam* the previous year means we can see the similarity of Rock's ladder spots in this match. Eventually Big Show comes down to chokeslam Mankind off the ladder and Rock reclaims the WWF Title. They covered an important run in Rock's career here and did it reasonable justice, considering the tape's run time.

They quickly bring in the historical importance of Rock-Austin by covering the IC Title feud they had. Rock's semi-shoot into camera promo gets hysterical at this point as he builds up the feud while, in total sincerity, claims he made the IC Title famous. We skip ahead to *WrestleMania XV*, having suitably set the table, and the WWF Title match. Seeing as the match is hugely important, we get extended highlights again. Austin might have won this match but Rock headlined *WrestleMania* and once you've been there and delivered, you're set. Austin's bump on the entranceway lighting rig shows up here and it makes me wonder how deliberate the spot was considering how bad it must have been for his knee to take it. Austin manages to kick out of the Rock Bottom, rolling his shoulder when Rock drags him too far up with the legs. You need to get an even weight distribution across the shoulders. They have a few good counters, especially around the finishing moves. Austin just barely kicks out of a chair shot and a Samoan drop, keeping the fans on the edge of their seats. Rock then kicks out of a Stunner, thus putting him over big time. The booking kicks in as Rock hits a Rock Bottom and sets for the People's Elbow but Austin dodges it. Another Rock Bottom is countered into the Stunner and despite an enormous oversell Rock stays down for three. Rock points out it took two Stunners to beat him before mentioning the record business they did. The feud continued because Rock throws Austin off a bridge and his title belt follows. We get a few clips from the funeral for Austin and move on to *Backlash* as talking head Rock claims Rock vs. Austin is the best sportz entertainment there is. In order to prove that, we get the Gonzo camerawork from the Rock leading to the Stunner. I love that spot. Rock does another enormous oversell on the Stunner before Austin wins with a follow up belt shot. Rock compares Austin to a loaf of Wonderbread, stating he'll go stale eventually but that will never happen to the Rock whose book has "infinite chapters" because he doesn't slap hands or kiss babies. This segment summed up exactly why the Rock became a massive star.

Rock points out he used the Corporation and won three world titles but then got sick of carrying them and left. Rock closes out by saying it's only just begun as he's the People's Champion and lives to entertain his millions of fans.

VERDICT

This is much better than expected as the whole tape flows from one major event to the next and even the link pieces feel correctly positioned. Each segment is strong and Rock's charisma is all over this tape. Considering he was a heel for most of it, that makes this tape all the more extraordinary. The WWF could actually put out a profile of a guy who was a heel, behaves like a heel and doesn't give a crap about anyone but himself and make it not only a good tape but a much better tape than say, *Steve Austin: Hell Yeah*. The Rock's tape is more entertaining, is more coherent and is a far better showcase of his talent.

76

COME GET SOME - THE WOMEN OF THE WWF

CAT NO: WWF235
RUN TIME: 49 minutes (approx)

James Dixon: We start with a brief video package set to music that sees the women featured doing amongst other things running to the ring, staring at a fire, dicking around on a beach and hitting bad wrestling moves. Oh boy.

We get a couple of talking heads discussing the role of women in the WWF, with Road Dogg pulling no punches when he states: "As far as wrestling goes, I don't think they have a place". Jerry Lawler has a much different opinion, as you would probably expect, and attributes the WWF's monster ratings and crowds of 1999 to the women. He is senile. Jim Cornette speaks half in character and half shooting, expressing that he believes women shouldn't be involved in a contact sport and that no woman can beat a man. A mix of opinions then. Michael Cole hosts the main presentation, which is just swell. "Like it or not they are here, and they're here to stay" says Cole. Pardon me while I go and jump for joy.

Sable
Sable doesn't consider herself to be a sex symbol. Yeah, right. Explain the Playboy shoots then... We then get more music, as footage of Sable walking with her horse, washing her hair in the shower and staring into a fire accompanies. Next, she walks down some steps. What a fantastic use of video tape. Sable says she had some issues to resolve in her life, but they were solved by posing for Playboy. That's sound advice girls; if you have any problems, just whip your kit off and take some pictures so you can regain your battered self esteem by having horny teenagers jerk off over you. Oh man... that voice! That shrill, unbearable, awful, screeching voice. And that's just Michael Cole! I can't listen to Sable either of course, she sounds so disingenuous with everything she says. I would rather have a root canal without Novocaine than listen to her speak for thirty seconds. More music, more Sable doing a great deal of nothing, because she is not actually a wrestler at all and has no place in the business. She is a big titted blonde who got a mega push because of her looks, and nothing else. We finally see some footage of Sable in "action", starting and ending with her horrible match against Tori at *WrestleMania XV*. The most notable thing about the match is Tori's bizarre outfit, which looks like it has been painted on. What Road Dogg said earlier is rather vindicated by this match, and the botched powerbomb reversal towards the end is particularly gruelling on the eye. The match ends when the manliest woman alive, Nicole Bass, interferes and beats up Tori. Sable's only match in her bio piece, and she needs help to win it.

Jacqueline
The tape gives us an exclusive interview with Jacqueline, who says she enjoys wrestling guys more than girls. Jim Cornette and Road Dogg won't be happy. Jacqueline is actually among the better workers of the women around at the time, but she is a terrible interviewee. Her story of how she got into the WWF? "I was in WCW. Then Jim Ross called and asked me if I wanted to be in the WWF. I said yes. So I signed a contract and now I am here". What insight! We see footage of Jacqueline's debut when she is introduced by Marc Mero, which extends to her walking to the ring. Jacqueline then says that in WCW, Eric Bischoff didn't like that she was being pushed because he didn't believe women had a place in wrestling. But, if she was being pushed then Eric, as the head honcho, would have been the one pushing her! "I showed him, now I am here, and I am happy". It's about as interesting as listening to a monotone child read out a phonebook. Jacqueline gets a match too, against Sable from *RAW* in September 1998, and it is clipped to hell. That's probably for the best. The bout in question is for the reinstated WWF Women's Championship, and Jacqueline wins thanks to an assist from Marc Mero. Shane McMahon on commentary, gets far, far too excited. "They're really nice here, they treat you really well here" she says, which contradicts everything anyone who was there has ever said about the company during the Attitude era. Jackie's feature finishes off with footage of her running on a beach in slow motion as Michael Cole waxes lyrical about her beauty and unique talent. The little letch.

Chyna

"Here's an exclusive look at Chyna" says Cole. No, an exclusive look at Chyna was her sex video with X-Pac, which gave us *far* too much of a look at Chyna and her bits. Let's just say that out of the two, X-Pac was by far the more feminine in that eyesore. Chyna doesn't do running on beaches, instead she lifts weights. Lots and lots of weights. The Big Bossman chimes in that he thinks Chyna is tough for competing against men of his size, while Road Dogg says he is friends with Chyna and accepts her as a wrestler. What, did he forget about her in the opening rant? "Now I don't look like a man" says Chyna, neglecting to mention that it is because of extensive plastic surgery. More boring gym stuff follows. Going to the gym to workout is boring enough, but watching someone else do it is paint drying territory. The music that accompanies close-up shots of Chyna's muscles flexing makes this like the softest of soft-core porn. Ironic, given her later career choices. Finally we get something involving a wrestling ring, just, as Mark Henry asks Chyna out on a date and reads a poem. Chyna accepts begrudgingly, then acts like a complete dick to him when they go out. "Let's just get this over with, Mark!" she says when he greets her. Well, why accept the thing in the first place then!? Ungrateful cow. Triple H quite rightly gets some talking head time, and goes over some of the issues Chyna faced when she first joined the company. He doesn't say it directly, but implies what is actually the truth: that guys didn't want to sell for her, put her over or have her involved in their matches. As Ahmed Johnson once succinctly put it: "Ain't gonna let no bitch hit me!" Back in the gym, some apparently notable large muscled folk who I have never heard of, offer their support. At one point Chyna is surrounded by four guys and asks them to "take it off" before inviting them to "check this out". I don't mean to keep bringing up her future porn career but... The Chyna story ends as she tells some whoppers about why she looks so different now than when she first arrived in 1997, claiming that she broke her jaw on a house show and lost 30lbs because she couldn't eat, and she liked the way she looked so decided to stay that way. Never in my life have I heard of someone losing that much weight, and the majority of it coming off the jaw. Nice try, Chyna, nice try.

Debra

Now the dumb as dishwater Debra, who I always think looks about ten years older than she actually is. Jeff Jarrett puts her over, which is amusing considering his shoot comments about her when he returned to the WWF on *RAW* in 1997, where he described her as "the definition of the term "dumb blonde"". Debra likes working with the WWF because they have people who do your hair. Yeah, so do salons. We go to the build-up for the Goldust-Jeff Jarrett match at *Rock Bottom*, where the stipulation stated that if Jarrett won then Goldust would have to strip naked, but if Goldust won then Debra had to show her "tasty cakes". Jarrett wins thanks to a guitar shot, but commissioner Shawn Michaels comes out and reverses the decision and calls it DQ, so Debra has to strip. The WWF hams it up with stripper music while Shawn Michaels fumbles excitedly in his wallet for some singles. Yes folks, encouraging a randy crowd to whoop and holler as she takes her clothes off is the highlight of her WWF run at this point. Of course the WWF always promised big fake baps and very rarely delivered, and that is the case here too because the Blue Blazer and Jeff Jarrett come out to prevent her fun bags from getting out. Debra says "the real Debra" would never do that, then describes her tomboy childhood. Yeah, sorry, I tuned out. I have no clue what relevance that has to any of this.

Terri Runnels

Probably my least favourite of all the non-wrestling pieces of eye candy is the equine Terri Runnels. I can't stand Sable, but at least she was hot. Terri is not, and she is even worse a performer than Mrs. Lesnar. After seeing Terri at a wine tasting, we battle potential epilepsy with a psychedelic music video, before Terri discusses "the characters I've portrayed". Goodbye, kayfabe. Terri shares her views on parenthood and then tells potential suitors that she doesn't like overly macho men. Well, she was with Goldust, so I think we knew that. "We look forward to seeing more of her" says the little pervert Cole, as we wrap up Terri's feature, which frankly offered absolutely nothing. Why? Because she has done nothing of note. At all. Ever.

Ivory and Tori

These two get lumped together because they are relatively new to the company, but they are both better than most of the other girls featured. Both are fairly verbose and easy to listen to, especially Tori, but there is hardly any footage on offer because they haven't been around for long enough. Instead they both talk in an empty arena about their hobbies. Tori likes yoga, Ivory likes working out and movies. Riveting. Ivory talks about her scarf, which she used to carry to the ring for every match, and she says she will never go to the ring without it. She lied.

We wrap up with a "warm weather look" at the women from the tape, which means lots of teasing shots of posing on beaches with tits out but covered up, seductive poses and water. Obviously, it is all in slow motion and set to music, but by now you know that already.

VERDICT

Tripe. This predates the slew of Diva tapes that clog up the release calendar in later years, and is the WWF's first attempt at encouraging sex-starved teen boys to part with their money so they can catch a glimpse of side boob and nipples through wet shirts. Is there anything of value on here at all? In a word, no. I am a staunch objector of the WWF/E "divas" because I think they damage and expose the business and take television time away from people with talent. If they were talented workers I would have no problem with them, but so very few of them are. Let's cut to the chase: the women in the WWF in 1999 were there because of their bodies, not because of their wrestling. They made some of them wrestle because they felt they probably had to, but no one, literally no one, wanted to see that. People wanted to see tits, and on a tape dedicated to those very women and thus those very tits, it needs to deliver in that one respect. It doesn't, so it is worthless.

2

BEST OF RAW VOL. 1

CAT NO: WWF236
RUN TIME: 62 minutes (approx)

Lee Maughan: Here we go with yet another *Best of RAW* compilation. This one would be entirely different to the *RAW: Prime Cuts*, *RAW Hits* and previous *Best of RAW* series, with three volumes instead focusing on the Attitude Era. Host is Michael Cole, who promises "great characters and storylines." So long, kayfabe.

Stone Cold Steve Austin
- From late 1997, Mr. McMahon demands Austin defend the Intercontinental title against the Rock, but Austin does what he wants, when he wants, threatening to whip McMahon's ass.

- We gloss over *WrestleMania XIV* and head to the next night on *RAW* as Austin surrenders the old winged eagle title belt in exchange for the belt more closely recognised with the Attitude Era. Mr. McMahon tells Austin he's proud to have him as champion, and arrogantly offers him the chance to do things the McMahon way. Nobody tells Austin what to do however, and he punctuates that statement with a Stone Cold Stunner, setting up the rip-roaring Austin vs. McMahon feud.

The Rock
- Cole informs that the Rock didn't get over until he joined the Nation of Domination in 1997 (although he says it much more diplomatically than that), which leads to an angle in which Rocky gives three $15,000 gold Rolex watches to Mark Henry, D'Lo Brown and Kama. Nation leader Faarooq is less than impressed at *his* gift - a cheap, framed portrait of the Rock. Later, during a match with Ken Shamrock, Faarooq refuses to allow the Nation to interfere when Shamrock has Rock caught in the ankle lock.

Skipping ahead, Rock smashes Shamrock square in the head with a brain melting chair shot before getting into an argument with Faarooq. Faarooq in turn calls Rocky out for a nose-to-nose and they brawl until the Nation can separate them. Marching up the ramp, Rocky throws up the eyebrow, giving the Nation the signal to attack Faarooq.

The Undertaker & Kane
- After continued threats from Paul Bearer, Kane finally arrived in the WWF in October 1997 at *Badd Blood* with his sights firmly set on the Undertaker. Initially, the Undertaker refused to fight Kane, with Kane beginning to show sympathy towards his big brother, even saving him from a beatdown at the hands of DX. However at the *Royal Rumble*, it was all proven to be a ruse as Kane chokeslammed the Undertaker into a casket and set it alight. Shortly afterwards, the Undertaker's corpse was wheeled out on the stage at *RAW* where it was hit by a lightning bolt, bringing him back to life. Yes, this really happened, and yes, because it was the Undertaker, people let the hokiness of it all slide. Finally accepting the challenge to fight, Undertaker pinned Kane at *WrestleMania XIV* following three tombstones.

D-Generation X Returns
- We skip the original Shawn Michaels incarnation of DX and instead head straight to the night after *WrestleMania XIV* as Triple H assumes control of the group and reintroduces Sean Waltman to the World Wrestling Federation. Sadly, Waltman's impassioned promo against Hulk Hogan and Eric Bischoff fails to make the cut here, but we do get a series of quick clips of DX driving a tank to *Monday Nitro* to declare war on WCW. Out of context though those clips may be, they're still tremendous fun to watch for anyone who lived through it.

Mick Foley
- Mick Foley entered the WWF as Mankind and frequently battled the Undertaker in those early years, but Mick had another side to himself that emerged through Dude Love, his alter ego and the character he dreamed of becoming as a teenager. His third character was the "king of the hardcore matches", Cactus Jack, who arrived in the WWF at Madison Square Garden in a memorable skit that saw all three personalities on screen at the same time.

- Cactus was soon reunited with Terry Funk (under the guise of Chainsaw Charlie) but the team were decimated by DX in a steel cage match. That leads to the following week where Mick cuts an absolutely *blistering* promo on the fans who chanted

VINCE MCMAHON

"Austin! Austin! Austin!" as he and Funk lay helpless in the cage:

"When I came here two years ago and I was Mankind, there were always people saying "You know, why don't you just be Cactus Jack?""Then I came out in tie-dye and some white boots and they said "Why don't you just be Cactus Jack?"Well I gave you Cactus Jack... I GAVE YOU EVERY GODDAMN BIT OF ENERGY I HAD! And when I was laying in there helpless, you chanted someone else's name. This is not a knock on 'Stone Cold' Steve Austin, hey, I'm happy he's the champion, and he may not admit it but we've known each other a long time and he's been my friend. But what you did to me and Terry Funk laying here in the middle of the ring was not only distasteful and disrespectful, it was Goddamn disgusting! And I'm gonna give you a chance to make it up to me, because I'm gonna accept a group apology right now. Well, I can finally say for the first time, after thirteen years of blood, sweat and tears, that it's not worth it any more. It's going to be a long time before you see Cactus Jack in the ring again."

D-Generation X

- A shift in attitudes (and fan responses) sees DX wage war with the Nation of Domination, leading to that popular late 90's wrestling staple: the costumed parody, giving us such classics as Triple H as the Crock, Road Dogg as B'Lo, and X-Pac as Mizark Henry, complete with unfortunate 1950s style blackface. Unfortunately, impressionist Jason Sensation's spot-on Owen Hart voice isn't included.

Val Venis

- According to Cole, Val's history of working in the adult entertainment industry was not considered an impediment to a successful career in the WWF. That would certainly change once the promotion went PG in July 2008.

- Val offers Kaientai a special look at his new skin flick, *Land of the Rising Venis*, in which he porks manager Mr. Yamaguchi's wife. Out for revenge, Yamaguchi forces his wife to undergo the "crawl of shame" through his legs as he prepares to spank her ass with a paddle. Val however steals the paddle, makes the save and rescues the damsel... I mean, slag in distress, so dreadful Asian stereotype Yamaguchi threatens to slice Val's dick off with a samurai sword. "I choppy-choppy your pee-pee! Ha ha ha ha!" It truly was a different time.

- The following week in a tag team match, Taka Michinoku

turned heel on Venis and joined up with Kaientai, a group he had previously been part of in Japan's Michinoku Pro Wrestling and ECW. The union made little sense in the WWF however, as the stable had initially been brought in as opponents for Taka in the ailing light heavyweight division. In one fell swoop, they killed that idea off completely, all for the sake of a dumb angle. And speaking of fell swoops, a camera bursts into a locker room just in time to see a bare-arsed Val with member spread out across the table, as Yamaguchi brings his blade down just as the lights go out. And that's it, no further explanation given.

McMahon and Austin

- In response to months of angles in which Mr. McMahon has Steve Austin arrested for his hell raising ways, Austin turns the table after tricking McMahon into admitting he assaulted him. McMahon's reaction to being cuffed is a classic, as he just hams it up a treat.

- Special guest refereeing a match later in the night, McMahon gets himself chokeslammed by the Undertaker before Kane arrives for a brawl through the crowd. Left alone in the ring, Austin arrives to dish out Stunners to stooges Pat Patterson and Gerald Brisco, before walloping a chair-wielding Dude Love in the face with a chair of his own.

- At *Breakdown '98*, the Undertaker and Kane simultaneously pinned Austin to render the WWF Title vacant. The following night on *RAW*, Mr. McMahon (armed with the old winged eagle belt for some reason) attempts to sort out the confusion, but before he can make his proclamation, Austin drives to the ring on a Zamboni to open up another can of whoop ass.

Mr. McMahon Gets Hurt

- Later that night, McMahon, having been attacked three times in the span of a week by 'Stone Cold', decides to renege on his deal to make either Kane or the Undertaker champion because: "As far as I'm concerned, it's like dealing with the handicapped! One's physical, and the other is mental." Undertaker warns Vince to watch his ass and not get out of line or he'll be the one who ends up handicapped. Unfortunately for Vince, the Undertaker catches him flipping the bird, so the brothers break his leg.

- Vince's injuries lead to some thoroughly unexpected results as, laid up in a hospital bed, he gets an unlikely visit from Mankind who presents him with a string of terrible gifts including a clown called Yurple, a collection of balloon animals, and a lousy puppet named Mr. Socko. Socko quickly takes on a life of its own, thanks in large part to Vince's deadpan disdain for it, and Mankind uses it administer the Mandible Claw for a victory over Mark Henry.

Austin and McMahon

- Back at the hospital, Mr. McMahon receives expert analysis from Dr. Austin, who pounds his broken ankle, zaps him with a defibrillator and smashes him over the head with a bedpan. Because this is Vince McMahon we're talking about, the skit ends with Austin shoving a tube up Vince's ass in an effort to "find out how full of shit you really are!", which surely should have gotten Austin done for sexual assault.

- On another live episode, Austin fills a wheelchair-bound McMahon's $50,000 Corvette full of cement.

- At *Judgment Day*, Austin was forced to referee a match between Kane and the Undertaker to determine a new WWF Champion, with a warning that if he didn't raise somebody's hand in victory that night, he would be fired. In one of the dumbest finishes to a match ever, Austin counts *both* guy's shoulders down, then declares *himself* the winner. Incensed, McMahon fires him, so Austin decides to take him hostage. Displeasingly, "Bang 3:16" and "I just pissed my pants!" are missing from this tape. Why show the first half of an angle and not show the conclusion to it?

The Undertaker

- Aggrieved at not winning the title the previous night, the Undertaker introduces his new look, having reconciled with Paul Bearer, promising that his Ministry of Darkness will unleashed a plague upon the World Wrestling Federation, with Faarooq, Bradshaw, Phineas Godwinn (as Mideon), Mabel (as Viscera) and the entire Brood all joining forces with the 'Dead Man'.

Austin is Reinstated

- Following Vince's kidnapping, Shane McMahon makes his debut as an on-screen character (after having previously been a commentator on *Sunday Night Heat*), signing Austin to a brand new contract as an act of rebellion against the father whose standards he could never live up to. The logic gap caused by Shane's heel turn on Austin a short time later at *Survivor Series: Deadly Game* would go quite some way to negating what a great angle this was, but in fairness to WWF writer Vince Russo, it didn't really have much place else to go after the first big reveal, so why not do the swerve turn?

VERDICT

Not a tape for anyone who's looking for actual in-ring wrestling action, but if you're after those "great characters and storylines", well, they're here in abundance. At just over an hour long, the tape absolutely flies by with some of the more outrageous and downright entertaining aspects from a time when it felt like everyone and everything was over with the WWF audience.

Throughout the course of our Complete WWF Video Guides, we've watched and re-watched so many Attitude Era events full of wall-to-wall boring matches and bad booking that we've often found ourselves wondering why we ever liked the late 90s in the first place. Watching so many classic clips back in this rapid fire format however makes it easy to see why people are still so very nostalgic for it. Taken in isolation and free of any of the storyline continuity problems that plagued Vince Russo's booking reign of terror, this tape is just pure, unadulterated fun, even if it does feel at times like you're watching an introductory promotional piece.

Very recommend for fans of the era with an hour to spare, *Best of RAW: Vol. 1* stands as the rose-tinted spectacles of Attitude Era VHS.

77

TEST

NO MERCY (UK)

CAT NO: WWF237
RUN TIME: 136 minutes (approx)

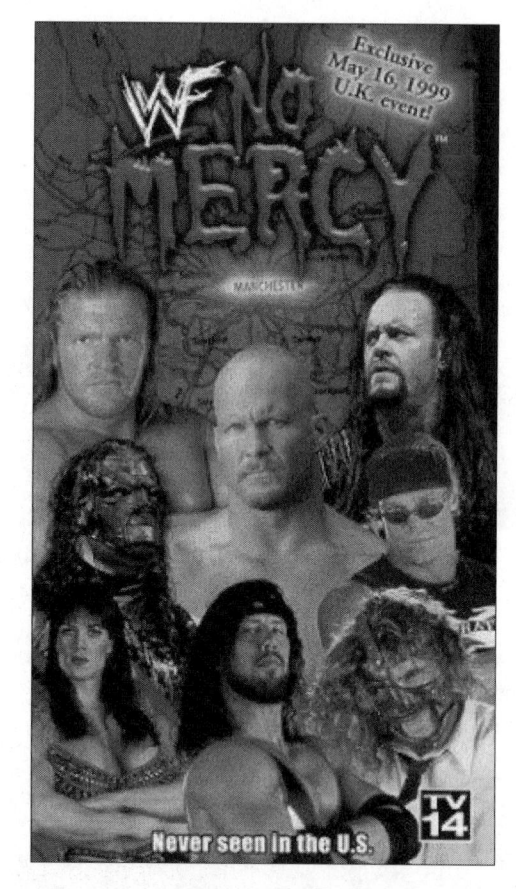

Lee Maughan: Hosted by Jim Ross and Jerry Lawler. Shane McMahon brings out the Corporate Ministry to kick things off with a bang, with a series of tiresome lines about showing "no mercy" to any of their opponents, bringing the damaged-beyond-repair European title "out of retirement for one night only" for his match with X-Pac, and revealing that tonight's main event will now be "governed under no holl barls... rules." Well that cleared that up.

Tiger Ali Singh vs. Gillberg
Another UK-only pay-per-view, another Tiger Ali Singh match. What did the good folks of the United Kingdom ever do to deserve this? And just like at *Capital Carnage*, he follows a long and mostly pointless McMahon promo with a long and pointless promo of his own. This one is notable for Singh's declaration that he's "more richer" than the fans who "think [he] should be driving a taxi cab." He follows that stunner by claiming "the only saving grace that England has is that it's populated by millions, and I mean millions, of my fellow Asian and East Indian people." That draws a round of boos from a minority of the crowd. Always good to know the "we're not actually racist" BNP are in the house. Interesting that those people would boo the idea of foreigners living in the UK whilst at the same time paying good money to attend a show that features not one British performer on the entire card. Oh, sweet irony.

Gillberg may have been a one note joke, but he was a pretty funny one, arriving with a plethora of security guards who all easily dwarf him. Not that they hired a squadron of beefcakes for the role, far from it, it's just that Duane Gill was so naturally unintimidating they could have put Rey Mistero, Jr. next to him and still made him look small. He coughs and splutters his way through a blast of fire extinguisher smoke as a bunch of runners wave some pathetic little sparklers around, and then it's time for action. And what action! Gillberg actually scores with a spear on Tiger but pauses to gurn at the audience, so Tiger kicks him in the calf twice and ends it with a neckbreaker at an exhausting 1:05. What a flier this show is off to! I can't call it a DUD thanks to Gillberg's amusing performance (as tiresome as it was already becoming by mid-1999), but Tiger was so piss-poor that he actually blew the finish, the only thing he had to do. Useless!
Final Rating: ½*

The Acolytes & Viscera vs. The Brood
20-minutes into the show, and it's finally time for a real match. The Brood get a very positive ovation from the crowd, far above the responses they were generally drawing back in the States, with Edge in particular receiving a whole bunch of screams from the females in attendance. With six guys in the match, you might think there's just enough talent to go around to make this a fun contest, and you'd be half right. The Brood do enter energetic performances when given a chance to shine, but most of the match is dominated by the Corporate Ministry team, who don't have enough in the tank to keep things interesting, even for just the 13:47 length of the bout. Case in point, Bradshaw, who starts repeating spots for an apparent lack of anything better to do (duck the clothesline, duck the elbow, crossbody, catch). To be fair to him, the first time he does it he drops Christian with a fallaway slam, but the second time, he gets hit with a dropkick to put Gangrel on top for a two count. Still, the lack of variety is really noticeable.

Eventually, Shane McMahon and Mideon come out, apparently confused as to why their monster team are unable to put the Lost Boys away, and Mideon drops Gangrel with a DDT on the floor, throwing him back in for Bradshaw to finish with the Clothesline from Hell. The idea is supposed to be that the Corporate Ministry are going to dominate the entire night, but putting the heels over in the first "proper" match of the night really deflates the previously hot crowd. A decent match, but one in which the heat segment went on for far too long.
Final Rating: **

Steve Blackman vs. Droz
And what a barnburner this should be, pitting a bloke with no personality against a guy who, even following a prior association with the Legion of Doom, still feels yet to have been established as anything more than a fetishist for tattoos, piercings and vomiting. To make matters worse, it's a completely cold match with no angle behind it. Consequently,

the crowd switch off completely. Even Ross and Lawler get bored with it, instead talking about the Monarchy and wondering aloud if Droz has had any penile modifications. It's a bit of a shame too, because it's hard to pick fault with any of the action, outside of its aching dullness. Blackman finishes at 8:01 with something of a triangle choke, and then everybody moves on with their lives.

Final Rating: *½

- Time now for a Beaver Cleavage skit! "Does mother's little Harry Beaver want some of mother's milk?" I've no idea why this was included here, as Cleavage isn't even on the card, and very few fans in the UK, especially amongst the WWF's target demographic at the time, would even understand the reference.

Promo Time: Mankind
Would you believe it? It's time for another in-ring promo! This one comes courtesy of Union leader Mankind. To give Mick Foley his due, he's a genuinely charming guy and at least cuts an amusing promo full of references to Manchester United, porn star Kay Parker and the British Bulldog, who the WWF were courting at the time after he found himself laid up in a hospital bed following the end of his WCW run. Mankind asks the crowd if they mind him using the word "ass" as he's already been told he's not allowed to say "wanker". He concludes by saying that while Billy Gunn may look good, anyone who's ever seen Foley in the shower knows what a real "bad ass" looks like.

- Now, I don't mind promos, even blatant filler ones, as long as they're entertaining. The previous Mankind interview was, but up next is quite the polar opposite - a string of pointless talking heads featuring the most awkward people on earth - pro wrestling fans going through a difficult puberty. Bad haircuts, acne, braces and bumfluff moustaches aplenty with nothing of note said, plus one actual grown up, chosen presumably because of her enormous funbags and low-cut shirt.

Kane vs. Mideon
Yet another on-paper match sure to make you glad you plonked your hard-earned money down on this pay-per-view in a string of them tonight, and one that lives down entirely to your expectations. I realise the WWF had done all they could with the Kane character during his initial heel run and felt they had little choice but to turn him babyface, and he *did* prove popular with fans, but this match still stands as an example of how fundamentally backwards it is to have an unstoppable monster in the hero role. When you've spent 18-months educating your audience to accept someone as practically impervious to pain, it becomes extremely challenging to engineer a situation where people could possibly feel any sympathy for him. His mask too, once a faceless symbol of fear, now makes it tough for him express any level of despair.

Worse yet, the guy trying to *get* the heat has just spent the best part of the last three years being portrayed as a dopey pig farmer, and all of a sudden he's supposed to be accepted as a legitimate threat to this deadly machine that towers over him. The upshot is yet another completely heatless match that manages to make its slender 4:38 running time still feel like it went on about 4:30 too long, and the icing on the cake comes when the Corporate Ministry runs out for the lousy disqualification, because God knows Dennis Knight needs protecting on a card only people in the UK can even see. But there's more! X-Pac runs in to help his big buddy out, and that's enough to scatter the ENTIRE heel group. Shane McMahon fleeing from X-Pac? Yes. Mideon fleeing from X-Pac, after he's just wrestled Kane? Sure, why not. Shane McMahon, Mideon, 500-pound Viscera AND the Acolytes fleeing from little X-Pac? Credibility shattering. So much for ensuring the Corporate Ministry dominate tonight, because they just looked like the biggest pussies to every step foot in a ring.

Final Rating: DUD

- This past week on *RAW*, gigantic pain in the arse Sable tore off Debra's evening gown during a defence of her Women's Title, only for commissioner Shawn Michaels to declare Debra the winner on account of her being the one left standing in her bra and panties. The look on Sable's face as Michaels hands the title over to Debra and declares her the new champion is absolutely priceless, as this was actually a legitimate screwjob finish that WWF management completely blindsided her with on her way out the door. Consequently, she's making her final appearance tonight, but the title match is obviously off. Not only that, but the Sable vs. Tori match is off too, explained as Sable having a cold. Yet another bait and switch on a UK-only pay-per-view. Years later, I've still to figure out why the WWF treated the burgeoning UK pay-per-view audience with such contempt.

Nicole Bass vs. Tori
Bass finishes with the chokeslam in 31-seconds. What, you thought Gillberg-Singh was going to be the shortest match on this wretched show? Mardy arse Sable couldn't even be bothered to stick around to see it. "Tori, completed outmanned" notes JR. "Don't you think? No pun intended." He follows that outburst of sexism by labelling Bass a "shemale", to which Lawler threatens to grass Ross up. "I said *she*-male!" retorts the then-48 year old JR, as if that somehow justifies his pathetic, uneducated schoolyard "banter" (Hey! Let's all laugh at the new kid because they're new and talk different than us so clearly they must be a freak and thus, made a figure of fun!), but which actually just serves to confirm that he knew exactly what he was saying, which pretty much outs him as either massively naive, or massively homophobic. How deeply vile and unpleasant of him.

Final Rating: DUD

WWF European Championship
Shane McMahon (c) vs. X-Pac
In further evidence of how shallow the talent pool is tonight, now we're presented with a non-worker defending a previously abolished title. Eat it up, Manchester, eat it up. Obviously there isn't much Shane can do, so they dress the early portion of the action up with a surprise run-in from stooges Pat Patterson and Gerald Brisco, who as Mr. McMahon's right hand men, had been fired by Shane on *RAW*, Vince having yet to have been revealed as the "Higher Power" that the Undertaker had been worshipping to. I suppose it's probably best to just presume that they weren't in on the big secret, otherwise their blocking Shane's attempt to get counted out wouldn't make any sense in hindsight. Not that any of that whole stupid angle made a lick of sense anyway.

The presence of Patterson and Brisco draws out Chyna for a pair of low blows, as Lawler begins to fixate on a man in the crowd dressed like her, and Shane hits the chinlock. He does follow with a suplex and an elbow however, which at least puts him above IRS in the excitement stakes. The shortcuts continue as the referee gets bumped, allowing Chyna to deck X-Pac with the European title belt, but Shane misses the broncobuster and eats an X-Factor. Chyna trips the referee and goes up but gets crotched, but that creates an opening for Triple H to slide in (oo-er) and blast X-Pac with a Pedigree to

RHYNO

rightfully so kayfabe-wise too.
Final Rating: **¾

- Over at ringside, 'Uncle Jerry' pokes a child. In the eyes I mean. Which is still something I didn't expect to see, quite frankly.

- To the back now for yet *another* promo… and it's with Mankind, who's already had a promo out in the ring tonight! That is absolutely maddening on a pay-per-view, to wheel guys out multiple times because the roster you've brought over is so piss-weak that you can't even throw a full card together. Anyway, the purpose of this is so the Corporate Ministry can attack him and "injure" his knee, which was already legitimately hurt at the time and in dire need of surgery.

Billy Gunn vs. Mankind
Believe it or not, this is really the semi-final for tonight's card, with a guy who's leg is so bad he can barely move against a perennial midcarder who has only just recently turned heel on his tag team partner of the previous 18-months (was it really only that long?) to begin his long-awaited singles push. In fact, his heel turn is still so fresh that he actually gets a knee-jerk babyface pop when his music hits, only for fans to quickly realise he's a baddie now.

Billy bases most of his offense around Mankind's injured wheel, which is one of those weird wrestling things because it does make sound psychological sense, but it really can't be doing much for the state of Mankind's actually knackered knee. As a result, Mankind can't really do a lot, but he does take a big bump over the guardrail which is actually worse here than when he usually does it

give Shane the win at 8:29, as the Corporate Ministry administer yet another beat down. Kane eventually makes the save with JR actually covering for his late arrival by suggesting he was "sequestered" backstage, but how he'd have that sort of information I have no idea.

For the second UK-only pay-per-view running, X-Pac appeared to be one of the few guys on the card not to treat his match like a night off, entering a very commendable performance. Shane also deserves credit for taking some hellacious bumps over the top to the floor, something a man in his position didn't really need to do. Overall, the match had enough going on to be moderately exciting, although it was pretty blatant how much they had to work around Shane's obvious limitations, and

because the ring is parked on an elevated platform. That platform incidentally was the same set-up that saw, at a post-*WrestleMania XV* house show in Newcastle, England, Triple H slip and get his leg trapped under the guardrail while jawing with the fans at ringside, just in time for the lights to go out for the Undertaker's grand entrance. Seeing Hunter wriggling, worming and panicking to get free in the dark, lit up only by a series of flashbulbs going off, is a memory that will stay with me forever. Eventually Chyna had to come to his rescue and drag him free, concluding one of the great "lost" wrestling botches, witnessed by just a few thousand folks in the arena that night, now gloriously immortalised at long last via the gift of the printed word.

34

Escaping a figure four, Mankind brings a chair in and lands a Kobashi Driver before applying the Mandible Claw. Billy counters that with a drop toehold and lands a piledriver on the chair, which referee Teddy Long counts as a three, but then calls a two as the bell rings. Oh boy, just what this show needed. Billy drops Mankind with the Fameasser on the chair as Long calls for the bell... then rushes over to make the real three count. What a mess that was. And why wasn't Gunn disqualified for using the chair anyway? The match was okay up to that point, but Foley was really struggling at times, and while I'm not one to advocate the sort of bait-and-switch we witnessed earlier, I think in the case of a legitimate injury, changing the card up here and pairing Mankind off with Shane would have been to everybody's benefit. That way, Mankind could have been disguised in the smoke and mirrors match in the same manner as Shane was (and indeed, they could have even used the Brood to take some of the bumps for Mankind), while X-Pac could have given his same performance against Gunn in what likely would have been a better match.
Final Rating: **

- And now we start to lay it on *really* thick and Ross and Lawler send well-wishes to Davey Boy Smith who was still recovering from the spinal staph infection he suffered after WCW's *Fall Brawl '98*, an injury that almost paralysed him and left him in a hospital bed for six months. They put Davey over huge as a "great, former WWF superstar" who has "experienced a lot of personal losses in his family in recent months." Sadly, there'd be much more family tragedy to come just one week later. The WWF's continued pursuit of Smith and resultant insistence once they did sign him to go on a PR campaign absolving them of any blame over the death of Owen Hart was every bit as exploitative as Vince McMahon shoving a camera in Melanie Pillman's face on *RAW* the night after her husband Brian was found dead in his hotel room, making sure to broadcast to the entire world the her confused, emotional responses to Vince's less-than-subtle line of "There's other things to blame for this than the WWF, correct?" questioning. You stay classy, Vince.

WWF Championship
Steve Austin (c) vs. Triple H vs. The Undertaker
If Hunter and the Undertaker are both part of the Corporate Ministry, why doesn't one of them lay down for the other on the promise of the first crack at the title? Presumably because neither could agree on who would do the honours. If only Kevin Nash were around...

Undertaker attacks with Austin's belt to start but barely grazes him, so they repeat the spot... except this time he misses completely. From there, all three brawl around the building like every Steve Austin main event you ever saw after he came back from his neck injury. Punch kick, punch kick, punch kick, and so it goes for literally about eight minutes before Austin actually uses a wrestling move, suplexing Triple H on the floor.

As you may have guessed, WWF main event brawls are not my favourite kind of matches, but the crowd do go crazy for it so c'est la vie. Hunter tries to use a chair on Austin so referee Earl Hebner grabs it away from him, but then allows Austin to use it on both Hunter and the Undertaker. I smell cahoots!

Undertaker and Triple H eventually get into their inevitable shoving match over who gets the rights to stomp the daylights out of Austin, like two Psirens wiping each other out over who gets the rights to suck a lone victim's brain out through a straw. Hilariously, Paul Bearer threatens Chyna with his mad Mr. Miyagi skillz out on the floor, and then it's back to more brawling. Helmsley and Austin actually team up briefly to try to eliminate the Undertaker, but Triple H quickly turns on 'Stone Cold'. Before long, the finishers start getting teased, Undertaker attempting a Tombstone, Triple H going for a Pedigree, Undertaker landing a chokeslam on Triple H and Austin dropping Undertaker with a Stunner. Triple H also gets a Stunner for his troubles, but the Corporate Ministry hit the ring and destroy Austin. Why isn't that a disqualification? This match is no holds barred (or "no holl barls", anyway), but they never said anything about it being no DQ. And anyway, if it's no DQ, what were they even waiting for? Christmas?

The presence of the Ministry is enough to bring out X-Pac, Kane, Mankind and the Brood for a gigantic brawl, which is actually a pretty neat payoff to all the lousy finishes so far, and everybody fights to the back, Undertaker included, leaving just Austin, Helmsley, Chyna and Shane, with Chyna eating a Stunner before Triple H tastes another one for the pin. Incredibly, the match went more than 25-minutes, which I think was more down to the fact the show was running so short, rather than any great need to get so much brawling in early on.
Final Rating: **½

Post-match, Shane tries to scarper but runs headlong into X-Pac, who sends him back inside for a Stunner and a Bronco Buster. He also hits Triple H with a Bronco Buster, then gives one to Chyna too, just for the hell of it. It wouldn't be the last time he shoved his dick in her face. Austin and X-Pac share a beer (with Hebner joining in, just as he'd done back at *Capital Carnage*) before Austin hits Triple H and Shane with a double Stunner. Not to be outdone, X-Pac hits Shane with another X-Factor, then Austin offers Triple H a beer as a peace offering before blasting him with yet another Stunner, his fourth of the night. And then X-Pac gives him yet another Bronco Buster, so Austin tops him by giving Shane another Stunner, and the crowd just eats it up. That still doesn't forgive the previous 2+ hours though.

VERDICT

Without question, one of the worst pay-per-views of the 1990s, that fortunately few people will have ever had the misfortune to see. Make no mistake though, there would have been outrage if the WWF had tried to pass off a card like this for one of its home-grown PPV shows. Useless, directionless matches with no reason for even existing, two outright squash matches, the heels going over in no less than five of the eight bouts, and the entire event clocking in at just 2 hours 16 minutes. The live crowd might have reacted well, but coverage from fans and critics alike in the UK wrestling press following the event reacted with fury over such a paltry, pointless offering. Still, it could be worse - the VHS box art for this show actually threatens a running time of THREE HOURS for this. I don't think I could have taken another 45 seconds, let alone an additional 45 minutes. I think that's one instance in which we can all be thankful for false advertising.

30

ANDRE THE GIANT - LARGER THAN LIFE

CAT NO: WWF238
RUN TIME: 44 minutes (approx)

Lee Maughan: In the pre-DVD era, the WWF was largely unwilling to admit it even had any history, despite prefixing many New Generation era broadcasts with the slogan "For over 50 years, the revolutionary force in sports entertainment!" There were largely two reasons for this; Firstly, many of the WWF's legendary stars of yesteryear were on very bad terms with the promotion (Bruno Sammartino, 'Superstar' Billy Graham), or were working for the opposition (Hulk Hogan, Randy Savage, Roddy Piper). Secondly, the WWF was always about the now, about what was current and what was happening. Who cared about Don Muraco or Pedro Morales anymore? The promotion figure most of its fan base was made up of young children who wouldn't even know those names anyway, and as such, it wasn't worth wasting any airtime, video tape or magazine print on them at the expense of current superstars.

The one notable exception was all-time legend and McMahon loyalist Andre the Giant. A special attraction booked out by Vince McMahon Sr. to promotions all across the country, Andre was one of the few guys of the 70s and 80s known nationwide from more than just magazine coverage. His size precluding him from staying in any single area for much more than a week at a time lest he lose his appeal, Andre would bump around from territory to territory, usually making annual or bi-annual appearances for special supercards, blowoffs where the babyface needs the ultimate tag team partner, or for special battle royal attractions (the regular claim that Andre was the winner of more battle royals than anyone else in history was likely not just typical pro-wrestling bluster.)

With André advancing in years (exacerbated by his Acromegaly), he was never going to be a serious candidate for a jump to WCW once the regional territorial system began dying out, and his death in January 1993 from congestive heart failure resulted in the WWF creating its Hall of Fame specifically to honour his memory and, somewhat cynically, allowed them to celebrate his legacy safe in the knowledge that for sure he wouldn't show up on opposition TV. In the absence of Andre (as well as Hogan and Sammartino), Jimmy Snuka would become the WWF's go to legend, but Andre was the first guy the notoriously stubborn WWF were openly willing to mythologize as a Babe Ruth-type figure for wrestling.

This tape is actually a break from the norm as the documentary was originally produced by A&E for The Biography Channel in 1999, with the WWF later cashing in by giving it an official VHS release. Despite the somewhat independent nature of the production, there's still plenty of hyperbole to be found, as an unrecognisably thin Gorilla Monsoon calls André "the most recognisable sports figure of the 20th century, along with Muhammad Ali." Gorilla was grade A bullshitter right to the end.

Ominously, our tale starts with this corker - "In the summer of 1986, 92,000 people filled the SilverDome in Pontiac Michigan to see Hulk Hogan wrestle Andre the Giant for the World Heavyweight championship. It was the largest audience ever assembled under one roof for a sporting event." The voiceover announcer goes on to "educate" us that "Throughout a 20 year career, the Giant had never been defeated", which is about as accurate as claiming *WrestleMania III* took place in the summer of 1986, that it drew 92,000 people, or that it was the largest audience ever assembled under one roof for a sporting event. Close perhaps, but no cigar. Hogan's victory that night is declared an "upset" despite repeated assertions that André was "past his prime" (also a bizarre instance of a non-WWF produced documentary actually keeping kayfabe and ignoring the predetermined nature of the outcome.)

André René Roussimoff was born on May 19, 1946 in the French farming village of Moliens (not Grenoble, as commonly repeated), the third of five children to Boris and Mariann Roussimoff, a couple of Belgian and Polish ancestry who emigrated to France prior to World War II. At birth, André weighed an astonishing eleven pounds, although his brothers and sisters were all born and grew to "normal" sizes. It's believed that André's paternal grandfather had been 7'8, but none of the family still living have ever been able to confirm that claim.

André was a good, quiet student who particularly excelled at math, and spent much of his spare time playing soccer, usually as a goalkeeper. André's brother Jacques recounts that as children, their parents allowed them much freedom, but that they were also poor and had to work a lot to make ends meet. By the time he was 16, André was already over six feet tall, and weighed over 240 pounds. Eventually working the harvest with his father, André quit school, deciding he didn't need an education to spend a lifetime working in a field that was not his own. A two year woodwork apprenticeship brought him as much hope for the future as farming did, as did a stint working in a factory building hay bailers.

Continuing to grow, André was invited to join a local rugby club, but declined as he much preferred soccer. By the time he was 18 however, news of his existence had spread to Paris, and a local wrestling promoter soon showed up at the Roussimoff household with big money promises of turning André into a special attraction. From a mid-80s episode of *Tuesday Night Titans*, 'Lord' Alfred Hayes recalls collecting a teenage André and taking him to Porte de Versailles, but André's parents weren't entirely happy with his decision to leave. Moving to Paris, André took a day job as a mover and spent his nights training in a wrestling gym, but he found it difficult to adapt.

The ill-informed voiceover man calls wrestling "90% performance, 10% competition", which is one of the oddest estimations I've ever heard, but has a point in noting that pro wrestling appealed a lot more to those who found amateur or Olympic grappling "boring", dubbing the pro game "sports entertainment". Hey, if you want the WWF to give you access to video clips, sooner or later you're going to have to bite the bullet and let them put their idiosyncratic spin on things.

Back home in 1965, André was drafted into the French peacetime army, but he was deemed unfit for service as the army had no shoes big enough, beds long enough or trenches deep enough to accommodate him. Back in Paris, André began training with legendary French-Canadian star Edouard Carpentier who taught him how to bump, and told him to get as much in-ring experience as he could in preparation for Carpentier bringing him to the United States.

French promoters billed André as 'Geant Ferre', the name of a legendary French lumberjack, and he spent the next few years wrestling throughout Europe and Africa, in arenas and on the carnival circuit. It was on the carnival shows that André would challenge audience members to fight him. He never lost, and he was quickly the centre of attention. His trips home were highly anticipated, and a sign that read "Moliens, Population: 27" would be changed to read "Moliens, Population: 30" whenever André was back in town for card games with his friends.

By 1969, Carpentier was ready to bring André to the States, but André had already signed a contract to wrestle in Japan as 'Monster Roussimoff'. It was over in Japan where André was examined for the first time by a prominent doctor, who diagnosed him with a rare glandular disorder known as Acromegaly, a condition which caused his body to continue secreting growth hormones. André literally could not stop growing, and he got bigger and bigger with each passing year. Unwilling to see another doctor for treatment despite being told he wouldn't live past 40, André ignored the issue and never spoke a word of it to his family. Long-time friend Arnold Skaaland believed that was always in the back of André's mind, and was what was led to his drinking in such great excess. 'Classy' Freddie Blassie on the other hand felt the drinking came about because André was lonely. "When you're as big as he was, people look at you like you're a freak, and you resent that eventually. And I'm sure he did, because he had feelings just like you or I."

After his tour of Japan André headed to Montreal to hook up with Carpentier where, as Carpentier had predicted, he was an instant hit with fans. The problem was that before long, the novelty wore off as promoters were unable to find opponents to match up with him. Looking for a solution, Carpentier called Vince McMahon, Sr, who proposed a constant road schedule where André would never outstay his welcome as an attraction in any given area. McMahon also suggested a name change, as Jean Ferre meant little to American fans. From that point on, he would simply be billed as 'Andre the Giant'.

In 1971, McMahon became the (real life) manager of André, and he once again found himself an instant hit with fans in McMahon's World Wide Wrestling Federation. During this period, André developed a taste for fine wine, in addition to consuming copious amounts of food that few could keep up with, enjoying a full five course meal every single night. Notes André's long-time friend, travel companion and WWF referee Tim White in a completely serious tone: "The legend that travels around with André, the food, the drink... He could do this, he could do that, he ate sixteen steaks, twelve lobsters, drank a case of beer, ten bottles of wine and finished it off with a bottle of Jack Daniels. Well, I'm here to tell you, it's all true." More legendary than his eating were the tales of André's drinking. The most famous is the oft-recounted story of the night he drank over a hundred bottles of beer in one sitting, and on many occasions, would down multiple bottles of blended whiskey before dinner, several bottles of wine during it and polish it off with cognac for dessert, but exact numbers are hard to corroborate as his drinking partners would usually be unconscious long before André crossed the finish line. Even more amazingly, André was always the designated driver after his gargantuan drinking sessions, usually because most of his friends would end up sick.

Skaaland continues with his sad tales of André's loneliness - "He used to tell me sometimes, he said "You know Arnie, I'd like to see a play. You know, I heard so much about these plays on Broadway, I'd like to go." I said "Well André, I'll get some tickets and we'll go." He said "No Arnie, I can't. I couldn't go to a play. First of all, I can't fit in the seats, and if I could find a seat I'd be blocking everybody off. Everybody would be looking at me..." "He really felt bad because he couldn't go see a play."

André also felt he didn't need to keep himself in shape because nobody could match up to him in the ring anyway. Frenchy Bernard, the manager of André's estate recalls that he never jogged or ran, and never used any of the weightlifting equipment or treadmills that he bought. Killer Kowalski still praises André as "exceptionally good" in the ring, and Bernard puts André over for always looking after his opponent in the ring more than himself, which is standard wrestling etiquette.

André frequently made light of his inconveniences, he struggled daily with discomfort and indignities, routinely sitting on the floor in airplanes unable to accommodate him even in

ANDRE THE GIANT

first class. White recalls that he would regularly be swamped by the public before going to hotel rooms and finding the beds to be too small. He would also be unable to dial the telephone to reception because his fingers were too large ("like bananas" notes Blassie) and he would frequently be chased around the hotel by fans who would call his room all night, causing him to up sticks and change hotels in the middle of the night after it got to be too much. One night in a bar, a group of guys started poking the sleeping bear by telling André he might be big but he wasn't strong. Pushed to his limits, André gave chase and the four guys bailed to their car. Unable to unlock the doors, André simply picked the car up and turned it completely over, the four guys still inside it. André was gone before a group of police officers arrived, confused as to how the guys had gotten into such a predicament and sceptical of their drunken tales of an angry giant being responsible.

Nearing 30, André was finding himself a mainstream celebrity, thanks in large part to his status as one of the first travelling "superstars" of wrestling, at a time when all but the NWA World Champion would stick to one geographical region at a time before moving on after several weeks, months or years. Vince McMahon, Jr. thinks the appeal of André lay in his status as a real-life fairy story, noting that everybody growing up reads *Jack and the Beanstalk*. He also recounts that Andre had girlfriends in every town, but that there were two women very special to him, aside from his mother. Rene Goulet mentions that he would have married the first of those women, had he not been on the road so much. The second was a daughter from the Seattle area whom he rarely ever spoke of. According to White, André wanted to bring her to his ranch and get to know her, but problems with her mother prevented that from happening, which hurt him quite a bit.

By the end of the 70s, André was over 400 pounds and still growing, but his indulgent lifestyle and the rigours of constant wrestling were taking their toll. By the early 1980s and into his mid-30s, he was told by doctors that he wouldn't reach 40. Instead of taking the news as a death sentence, he put it to the side and took it as a reminder to live life to the fullest. As the mid-80s rolled around and the WWF was becoming a national powerhouse, André's body was quickly beginning to break down. A broken ankle was credited to Japanese-born Mongolian stereotype Killer Khan, but in reality the injury had happened when he simply got out of bed one morning. The recovery was a slow and painful process, made all the harder by the lack of crutches long enough or strong enough to support him.

Before long, his Acromegaly started to catch up with him. Unable to physically grow any more, he began aging rapidly, his joints unable to handle the stress of his weight, causing him to slow down significantly as he began to look like a completely different person. Gone was the washboard stomach and giant-yet-proportioned limbs, replaced by a stooping, hunched ogre of a man. In his younger years, he had turned to drink but as he got older, the pain in his back and knees were too much to take and he could no longer mask the pain.

In 1986, André travelled to England to undertake arguably his most famous role, and certainly the one most non-wrestling fans would recognise him from, portraying Fezzik, the gentle giant in Rob Reiner's beloved romantic fantasy adventure comedy *The Princess Bride*. Gorilla recalls that André loved doing the movie and that he considered it one of the greatest things he ever did in his life. While in England, André opted to have surgery to ease the pain in his back, but his anaesthesiologist was terrified about what dosage to give him. He was scared that too much would kill him, but also fearful that André would wake up with his back laid open if they didn't give him enough. All they were able to equate it to was his drinking, where André suggested he needed around two litres of vodka just to get a buzz. The operation was considered a success, but all it did was create another problem; André was no longer able to bend over, resulting in more difficulty, and more pain. "I would say after his surgery on his back, he was never the same" says Bernard, sadly.

André was soon back in the ring however, matching up with Hulk Hogan in the main event of *WrestleMania III*. André's (admittedly few and mostly forgotten) previous losses were ignored, and the match was sold on one simple premise: Could the Hulk beat the unbeatable Giant? McMahon recalls that Hogan was extremely worried about the match, and couldn't believe what André was going to do for him and for the business. He also gushes with praise for André setting the example for all other wrestlers to follow in how to do the right thing and give back to the business that made his fortune, even allowing Hogan to bodyslam him on his surgically repaired back.

Passing his 41st birthday and no longer wrestling's star attraction, André was aware he was living on borrowed time, but he never stopped wrestling. He signed on for several rematches with Hogan, but fans quickly caught on to the fact his skills were rapidly diminishing. In truth, the once-agile Giant had deteriorated so quickly he could barely move, even with assistance. He soon began seeking peace and refuge from the spotlight on a ranch he'd bought in Ellerbe, North Carolina. Away from the spotlight, André was finally able to relax, playing cards, barbecuing and drinking with only his closest friends. His favourite recreative was riding around on an ATV, checking out the longhorn cattle he raised, and he enjoyed watching TV late into the night on a specially-made recliner, before sleeping all day long.

In December 1992, André wrestled his last match (a six-man tag alongside Giant Baba and Rusher Kimura against Haruka Eigen, Motoshi Okuma, and Masa Fuchi). By this point having swelled to over 550 pounds, every movement required painful effort. One night he told Frenchy that if he died, he wanted to be cremated and his ashes scattered on the farm. It was a subtle hint that André realised he was dying, though not from his disease, but of a broken heart. He missed wrestling that much.

"The end was like the way he lived it" says White. "He never, ever complained. I had stopped at the ranch, it was just before New Year. André at that time was on crutches and his condition had taken over him. I was in tears because he was hurting so bad, yet he was so happy that I stopped through that he was telling jokes. Matter of fact, I told him "Boss, I'm going to leave at about 8 tomorrow morning." This is something he never did when we were on the ranch, he goes "What time? I'm gonna get up, we'll have something for breakfast and then you can go." He never would do that. When I drove away, I knew something was wrong and it just killed me because... you know, he was just the greatest, and it really hurt. That was the last time I saw him."

Just after New Year 1993, André got a call to come back to France. His father had passed away. For days after the funeral, André hung around in his village, playing cards with his old friends. Every night, he would drive back to Paris and sleep in a hotel. Then, on the night of January 27, 1993, André finally went to sleep, and never woke up. His chauffeur found him in the morning, and his death was attributed to congestive heart failure from a build-up of fluid in his body. At the time of his death, he was 530 pounds, and had surprised confounded doctors by living until the age of 46. As one of his village friends notes, "He was a very simple person, a person who loved his village, loved the people he was around… He died too quickly. He deserved a better destiny."

As André had requested, his body was returned to North Carolina where it was cremated two weeks after his death. More than 200 of André's friends attended the funeral including Vince McMahon, Jr., Hulk Hogan, Randy Savage, Rene Goulet and Mad Dog Vachon. After the ceremony, Frenchy rode a horse around the ranch to spread Andre's ashes. Unfortunately, a touching documentary ends how it begins, with another ridiculous voiceover: "Andre the Giant was modern wrestling's first and only international attraction. On his broad shoulders, wrestling rose from its status as questionable sport to become big business and, some might argue, performance art." Oh, boy.

VERDICT

Aside from a few spurious claims from the voiceover scattered at the beginning and end of the production, this is an engrossing, fascinating and touchingly sad tale of not just Andre the Giant, pro wrestling icon, but of André Roussimoff, loyal friend and gentle giant. The only real complaints you could make about it are the brief running time owing to its status as a TV production, and the lack of talking head appearances from some of his other contemporaries such as Hulk Hogan, Bruno Sammartino, Harley Race or Bobby Heenan (who in other interviews has told the hilarious story of André asking an air hostess for a screwdriver and her bringing him an actual screwdriver rather than a drink - "He's a drunken giant, we're on an airplane, don't bring him tools! What would you have brought over if he'd said 'Bloody Mary'!?"), or from his celebrity friends like Rob Reiner, Cary Elwes and Arnold Schwarzenegger (who also has a hilarious story of his own about André's vast generosity, with Schwarzenegger attempting to secretly pay for dinner one night while filming *Conan the Destroyer* in Mexico, only to find himself being lifted up by the armpits by André and basketball great Wilt Chamberlain, carried out of the restaurant and gently sat down on the hood of his car with André declaring "No! You make me very angry Arnold!").

It's too bad that even in the nostalgia-fuelled DVD biography era of the mid-2000s, WWE never felt compelled to recut this documentary into a feature length piece, or indeed produce an entirely new documentary of their own, instead choosing to cheaply re-release an old Coliseum Video feature on Andre that they had previously released in the mid-80s. Perhaps that owes in large part to the fact that most of the useable footage of his matches they have in their vault comes from his waning years, but his life story is much more interesting than most, and would more than make up for a lacklustre second disc of mostly bad matches. Still, the Ultimate Warrior was hardly a wizard of the ring wars, and if he can get a three-disc DVD set, then the iconic André is certainly deserving of similar coverage.

95

IT'S OUR TIME

CAT NO: WWF239
RUN TIME: 64 minutes (approx)

James Dixon: The title might not make it obvious, but this is a profile tape for new WWF Champion Triple H and his sidekick / girlfriend / workout buddy Chyna. The title references Triple H's "seagulls" music that he was using at the time, you see. Much like the snitch on *Harry Potter: The Deathly Hallows Part 2*, we "open at the close" with Triple H's recent (and first) WWF Championship win over Mankind on *RAW*. It should have been at *SummerSlam* the night before, but for various reasons that didn't happen. Of note from the *RAW* match is Chyna's reaction to Hunter winning the belt, as she appears to have a little orgasm. Anyway, Michael Cole narrates the tape. Why? Why is it always Michael Cole?

Three days after the win, we catch up with Hunter and Chyna riding in the back of a car, and Trips claims that: "The people who work in our office don't even understand what we do" as pertains to the schedule, and then outlines what it entrails with the eating, travelling, etc. He says he would love to take some of them on the road with him for a month to experience the lifestyle. Maybe *that* is why he hooked up with Steph. Hunter says he judges cities not by how they look or any other criteria than where the gyms are and how easy it is to find something good to eat, and that he always looks for a Gold's or World gym. Sounds thrilling. He adds that he fell in love with working out, which is not a revelation, and he gets cranky if he doesn't go to a gym for a few days. But it is SO boring though. He brings up Ted Arcidi, of all people, who introduced him to Killer Kowalski's wrestling school. We then see footage from his early days in the WWF when he was a snobby blue blood and a frankly tedious worker.

We go to a shoot style interview on *Sunday Night Heat* with JR. He talks about having residual anger left over from the way he was treated after the Kliq Curtain Call, because all he was doing was saying goodbye to his friends. Yeah, and pissing directly in Vince's backyard at the same time by violating kayfabe for a public goodbye, when it could have been done in the locker room. Hunter says Vince told him: "I gotta punish somebody, and you're my man" and that "Every day it's eating a hole in my fucking stomach JR", which isn't bleeped out. JR tries to calm him down, to which Hunter responds: "You want me to fucking shoot?" and that "Nobody in the office had the balls to punish anyone else." Erm, like who? Kevin Nash and Scott Hall were gone from the company and Shawn Michaels was the WWF Champion and new face of the company. Who the hell else could they punish? He talks about the burial he received and the office doing "everything they could to screw with me" such as putting him in the ring with bad workers, giving him no angles, jobbing him every week and such like. This is true, but then he got rewarded with the Intercontinental Title and a few months later was the *King of the Ring*. He says he found Chyna and that made the difference in turning things around for him, though the punishment was already over before she came in. Talk turns to Chyna essentially forcing her way into the WWF, with Vince initially resistant because he didn't see the value in a monster woman because he couldn't see a spot for a character like that, but eventually he succumbed to the pestering. He was right to acquiesce, because the Chyna bodyguard character was excellent. When she later became what amounts to a rhino dressed as a peacock; not so much.

Talk turns to the original incarnation of DX, and Hunter claims the WWF were trying to keep him and Shawn Michaels apart both onscreen and backstage, though he doesn't say that it was because they were such colossal assholes at the time when they were together. He talks about the WWF giving them warnings about not saying certain things because they would get thrown off the air, and says they were getting letters from USA Network telling them to stop. In response DX made a mock press conference speech where they promised not to say certain things, but in the process said *all* of those things. When Hunter says they will have to make less dick references, Shawn responds "Ah, shit!" and Hunter tells him "Hey man, watch your fucking mouth". All of this is uncensored too, making this one of the most potty-mouthed tapes out there. Staying with DX, though this time the new rebooted version, we see footage of X-Pac's WWF return. He says he is back to "rip ass", which is delightfully ironic given the arsehole tear he suffered years later on an indy show. Trips says he likes working with his buddies, not that nepotism runs rife or anything. Hell, his buddies are the only ones he would ever put over. Chyna then comes out with a real humdinger, claiming: "He's always been held back, but he's a nice guy so he won't say anything". Christ. Chyna tells a story of a pre-*WrestleMania XIV* rally in Boston, where some jerk in the crowd threw batteries at Shawn Michaels, which prompted a hissy fit from HBK, who stormed off. Man, he wouldn't have lasted 5 minutes in the 70s. HHH had to improvise and cut the promo himself, which apparently won him some plaudits. The thing is, he shouldn't have had to be the one who was building the main event of the most important show of the year when it didn't even involve him. Chyna wishes he wouldn't be so business orientated and would do more for himself. Well shit, he sure listened to THAT advice from 2000 onwards!

To the DX-Nation feud, and the immense DX parody of the Nation (with Hunter as "The Crock") and subsequent brawl on *RAW*. To highlights of the ladder match at *SummerSlam '98*, which I attest is a classic, despite Furious' underplaying of it elsewhere. I rated it highly in *The Complete WWF Video Guide Volume #4*, and I stand by that. I think it is psychologically sound and historically very important, which adds to its allure. It made both guys, much like a ladder bout did for the Hardys and Edge & Christian the following year. Hell, you could even claim it established Shawn Michaels firmly as one of the best in the world after *WrestleMania X*. Yes, this suffers from "ladder selling", which is similar to "cage selling", in that it involves staying down for ages from innocuous moves and very slow climbing, but hey they had both taken a pounding. I prefer some slow climbing to a multitude of spots that mean nothing and lead nowhere. It's a shame that instead of showing this properly, they put the least fitting music in history over the top. It is a jarring mix of jaunty panpipes and whistles, with a hint of Japanese techno sounds like it was gleamed from the leftovers of video game *Mirror's Edge*. Obviously it wasn't because that game came out a decade after this release, but that's what it sounds like. This tape is honestly worth seeking out to hear how completely baffling this music is alone. Trips actually downplays the match and says it could have been even better if he was 100% fit.

We take a look at how Hunter injured his knee during a match with Jeff Jarrett, and it was one of those silly freak accidents from an innocent looking move, with his leg just getting stuck while planted and his knee twisting out. This was the first of three major leg injuries that caused him to miss extended periods of time out over the course of his career, with him tearing his quad in 2001 and missing eight months, and then doing the same thing again in early 2007. Regarding the 1998 knee injury featured here, Hunter says he was worried about it when he came back, with Chyna bollocking him for coming back too soon, before launching into a diatribe against the practice in the business of guys coming back sooner than they should from injury so they don't lose their spots, which she rightly says is "very unhealthy". It's perhaps the most insightful thing she has ever said on camera.

Tangent: Within this section, Triple H says that Vince McMahon thinks anyone in the WWF could be the next Steve Austin, meaning he expects people to fight for their spots and opportunities, and then grab the brass ring with both hands. Now, that may have been true in 1999, but as I write this many years later, there is just no way. Since WWE became the only show in town in 2001, there is far too much fear in the locker room, with too many guys scared of losing their spots if they speak out and suggest something for themselves rather than just going with the flow. Plus, everything is badly and boringly scripted to the hilt anyway by writers who don't know the business at all, so everyone just has to do what they are told and follow directives and sound like carbon copies of one another as they churn out fake sounding dialogue. The few who didn't just sit there quietly and take what they were given were the ones who got over, but post Attitude the WWE made far fewer genuine money drawing stars than it should have done given the monopoly it had. Over the years in wrestling, it is always the guys who have gone slightly against the mould and done something fresh and new that have gotten over. That's never going to happen when everyone is being written by the same people. Why could WWE not see that? Why is this relevant to this tape? Well, Triple H is someone who was given exactly that opportunity to go against the grain and get over in his own way (with DX), so he should know better than anyone what works best in wrestling from his own experiences of being allowed to let loose. The fact he became head honcho in the 2010s and didn't implement a change back from overly scripted to natural and free-flowing, continues to annoy.

After Hunter returned, he donned some really ugly bright green tights and was booked in a WWF Championship match with The Rock in an "I Quit" match on *RAW*. We get a couple of highlights, including an idiotic Corporate Elbow onto a ring bell placed over Hunter's face. It would hurt Rock way more! Trips says "suck it" instead of "I quit" and then comes back and pounds on Rock, but each time he could have it won he says he is not done and carries on with the kicking. The Corporation come out and threaten to break Chyna's neck if Trips doesn't quit, so he does. Then, because this is deep into Vince Russo's reign of (t)error, Chyna turns heel on him. It's retarded. Like, the dumbest friggin' booking ever, because after the payoff a few months later, none of it makes ANY sense at all. None. Hunter and Chyna reunited in a few months and it was all a ruse! For more on this, check out Lee's phenomenal breakdown of the booking for this angle in *The Complete WWF Video Guide Volume #4*. Trips tries to make sense of it all and defends Chyna turning on him, trying to kayfabe it a little, even though the rest of the tape hasn't been kayfabed at all. Hunter points out that: "You gotta connive way ahead of the other connivers", which was like his mantra as his career progressed.

We move back to Chyna, who was rejected from everything else she tried because of how she looked, but wrestling was obviously a perfect fit for her. Trips sums up her major flaw as being her focus and drive to better herself, which seems like a strange criticism but it actually makes sense because as he points out, as soon as she has reached a goal she doesn't celebrate her achievement but instead focuses on the next target, and thus can't enjoy her success. Curiously enough, that same thing ended up being a problem for her behind the scenes as well. Having being pushed to the moon, allowed to hang in the ring with the guys and even have an IC Title reign, she started to get greedy and want more and more. Instead of the WWF Championship that she coveted, she got shunted back down to the women's division, which she wasn't happy about, and then in 2001 when she demanded Steve Austin type money to sign a new contract, the WWF balked and let her go. Architect of her own downfall...

Back to the Hunter-Kane feud and them taking turns throwing fire at each other, as if that is just a normal thing that people do to each other. Michael Cole shines as usual, saying that: "Kane suffered superficial burns to the exposed parts of his body". So, his arm and eyes then. What a terrible comment to completely cheapen the impact. We get highlights of their dull match from *WrestleMania XV* with more completely unfitting music. This one doesn't have panpipes, thankfully, but sounds identical to a track from *F-Zero X*. Why does everything sound like a video game?

Back to Hunter and Chyna's interview, and this time the muscular couple offer up relationship advice! "If the trash is nearly full, empty the bag" says Hunter. Well thank you very much. Freddie Blassie's "advice to the lovelorn" this ain't. Chyna says the couple are all about wrestling 80% of the time, and there is not much difference between their personal and professional lives. I guess 80% ended up not being enough for Trips, who wanted wrestling 100% of the time and dumped her for Stephanie McMahon so he could be fully engulfed by the industry. Good on him, I say.

Trips defends his 1999 heel turn and calls wrestling "a friendless business". He has that right. As one old-timer once said: "Do you want to make money? Or do you want to make friends?". Hunter says that no one wanted to see him wrestle Steve Austin for the WWF Title as a babyface, though neglects to mention that they didn't particularly want him to as a heel either. He says it was time to get serious and that he dropped everything he had been doing for the last two years such as his catchphrases, the people around him, his look, etc. I agree with this decision, and guys like Tatanka and others who turned but remained identical in every regard should take note. Back to the pre-*SummerSlam* Jim Ross interview from *Heat*, and Trips goes on and on about how "it's about me". By the time the match came around he was like a broken record and everyone was sick of hearing him talk. The WWF pushed him to the top too hard, and he was forced down everyone's throats so much that it almost didn't stick. But the WWF were determined and stubborn. It was like they were saying to the fans: "This guy IS going to be a top star and you ARE going to accept him, and we are going to keep featuring him in key spots and putting him over everyone until you do".

A Strap Match at *Fully Loaded 1999* against the Rock features next, as Hunter continues to be put over everyone in sight. It did EVENTUALLY work (though it took a few months for fans to accept him as top dog, and he was helped by Steve Austin being out injured as 1999 drew to a close), but it shows the WWF could push people properly and elevate them with booking when they were determined enough. On this occasion fans weren't quite ready, but the WWF persisted. What a marked contrast to WWE and its stop/start even-steven booking and constant derailing of pushes, or refusals to pull the trigger on guys when they were hot. I mean, again, Hunter as the guy in charge there should have been looking at his own push as an example of what works and how to make a star. Well, right up until the final few weeks before the big payoff show that is, but we will get to that in a minute.

Back to Chyna, who qualifies for the *King of the Ring* tournament by virtue of a win over Val Venis on *RAW*. This was the start of a dark run, with Chyna going over far more talented opponents and getting a push to the IC Title because she was a gimmick. I make my feelings clear on this elsewhere, but I disagreed with the whole thing. Not even entirely because she was a woman either, more that she was clunky and her selling was a shambles. Her match with Road Dogg at the *King of the Ring* PPV is shown, which Road Dogg wins after having protected his plums from a Chyna low blow by using a metal cup. Chyna says that sometimes she cries about not being able to do some things. What a mark.

With Triple H having won the long-winded strap bout at *Fully Loaded* to grab a title shot at *SummerSlam*, Vince Russo then interjected his colossal fat head and overbooked the build to the August spectacular to buggery, chopping and changing the advertised main event week after week until no one gave a shit any more. It starts with a promo on *RAW* between Hunter and guest referee for the proposed Austin-Hunter match; Jesse Ventura. This is your typical Triple H shouty and overly punctuated promo, as are the majority which set up the bout actually, which as noted changes a dozen times. I went over this in detail last volume, but the short version is that after being protected and booked like an unstoppable force for months, Trips then does a couple of jobs to Chyna and a double fall with Mankind in the weeks before the show. The only positive about any of this is the FANTASTIC DELIVERY from Linda McMahon when she shuffles the bout into a three way and calls it "the triple threat compromise". That phraseology is layered with double meaning and tickles me every time I hear it. This time the highlights of the match in question are set to something from *Streets of Rage*, as our video game trend continues. And then Mankind wins, as the strongly pushed handpicked would-be WWF main event star fails to win the big one at the PPV, in a moment of choking that Lex Luger would be proud of. Yeah, great stuff. Kept us all guessing though, right Vinnie Ru? Erm...

The next night Trips threatened to break JR's arm if Mankind didn't give him a title shot. Mankind came out and agreed, but then Trips went ahead and broke it anyway. Mankind still gave him the shot, which rendered the whole thing as pointless, and made everyone out to be a liar. Surely as Mankind you would fight him but not put the title on the line if you were just wanting to avenge your buddy. Nonsensical booking aside, we end where we began with Hunter's title win, before he closes out the tape by once again giving us his advice about emptying the garbage.

VERDICT

It's a strange mix of good and bizarre, with the behind the scenes interview actually engaging and a genuine insight into the man and woman behind the characters. And then they go and kayfabe things, thus cheapening what has already been said. I have no problem with a kayfabe tape if that's purely what it is designed to be, but mixing the two together for profiles like this just doesn't work. Contrary to some of the best wrestling storylines which marry the two together so that people believe everything about the angle. It's Jerry Jarrett booking 101. The best bio tapes the WWF has put out are the ones that take you behind the character and combine it with exciting footage, and this half does both of those things. As mentioned too the highlights are all set to wildly inappropriate music, which makes for a galling viewing experience at times. Worth checking out for sure, but perhaps not worth going out of your way to see due to some of the poor editing choices and occasionally out of place comments.

60

HULK HOGAN

AUSTIN VS. MCMAHON

CAT NO: WWF240
RUN TIME: 78 minutes (approx)

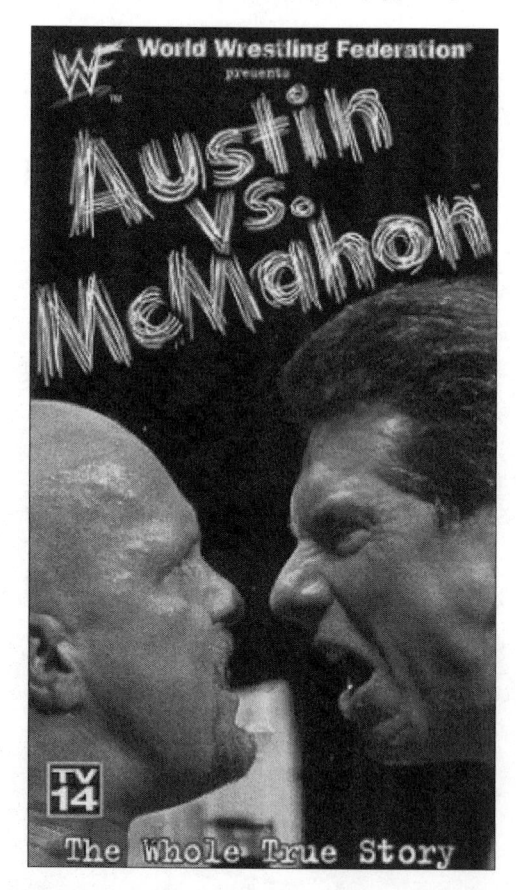

Lee Maughan: The whole concept was so incredibly simplistic that it's actually amazing no promoter ever thought to do it (at least on such a grand scale) before. The oppressed, speak-his-mind, blue collar everyman, against the snooty, arrogant, pompous billionaire owner. It was every working man's fantasy come to life - telling the boss to kiss your ass, while you simultaneously kick his. It was a masterstroke. It was a touch of genius. It was Austin vs. McMahon.

With three decades in the business, Jim Ross calls the feud "the hottest, most emotional feud that I've ever been apart of." Earl Hebner meanwhile thinks the two "don't get along at all". What is this, *Austin vs. McMahon: The Whole Kayfabed Story*? And the idea that he merely suspects they might not get along when he's been in the ring with them on plenty of occasions just speaks to what a complete cretin he must really be. Then again, he and twin brother Dave managed to get themselves fired from their lifetime jobs with the company in 2005 for allegedly selling unlicensed merchandise, so that perhaps shouldn't come as any kind of surprise.

"Vince McMahon is the most successful practitioner in sports entertainment" notes the voiceover. That may well be true but you still can't help rolling your eyes when hearing such verbiage on a McMahon-owned and approved release. He bought "a modest North Eastern professional wrestling circuit" from his father and began broadcasting his television nationally, initially serving as an announcer with only "wrestling insiders" aware that he actually owned the company. A devoted family man, Vince's wife and children also work for the WWF, though none are explicitly named here. I wouldn't worry about it, they'll all be headlining *WrestleMania* soon enough.

Steve Austin (no mention of his real name) was born in Victoria, Texas, and his career in wrestling began with little fanfare. "I was working on a freight dock, loading and unloading trucks. I saw a little ad for a wrestling school on TV, a few months later I had my first match. That match [paid] $40. I paid my dues." No mention is made of his trainer ('Gentleman' Chris Adams) or his first opponent (Frogman LeBlanc). Continuing to gloss over things at a breakneck pace, Austin tore his tricep in Japan and got fired by WCW over the phone. TV producer Kerwin Silfies skirts around the Ringmaster character, but admits that he didn't think Steve wanted to do it. No shit. Silfies thinks Austin's insistence that he put the black boots and black trunks back on was the beginning of 'Stone Cold'. Really? I thought it was the beginning of Ice Dagger. Austin soon started dropping announcers and officials with Stone Cold Stunners so McMahon demanded he give up the Intercontinental title or face the consequences. "A lot of viewers looked at Austin, and lived through Austin voyeuristically" claims JR. I think he means "vicariously" there, "voyeuristically" suggests that people liked spying on the guy with the big bald head as he slapped around his, erm, big bald head.

Quizzed on if he really wants to see Austin as WWF Champion, Vince says it would be one thing if he changed his ways and allowed himself to be moulded, but that Austin as he is now would be "a public relations corporate nightmare." Vince tops it with an "Oh, hell no!" and warns Austin "That's the bottom line because Vince McMahon said so!" Austin later takes umbrage with McMahon calling Mike Tyson the "baddest man on the planet", but no footage is shown of the integral Austin-Tyson confrontation, presumably to save on royalties. Still, much more important to get some cutting insight from Michael Cole on film, right? At *WrestleMania XIV*, Austin Stunnered his way to the WWF Title with a victory over Shawn Michaels. The next night on *RAW*, McMahon proudly introduced Austin in order to present him with a brand new title belt, the one more closely associated with the Attitude Era than the 'Winged Eagle' that Austin had claimed the previous evening. McMahon claims to be proud of Austin and tries to butter him up by suggesting that if he paired up his physical prowess with McMahon's mental prowess, Austin could one day become the greatest superstar of all time. Austin responds by promising to cause chaos and give Vince grey hairs. Vince gives Austin a choice of doing things the easy way or the hard way and 'Stone Cold' chooses the hard way, dropping Vince with another Stunner to confirm his selection. A classic promo to be sure. In another memorable moment, Vince brings Austin out in a suit and tie as his new corporate-approved champion, but Austin arrives without the agreed-upon Gucci shoes and sporting an Austin

3:16 baseball cap. Vince browbeats Austin for some of his fashion choices, so Austin tears the suit off, punches Vince in the balls and takes a photograph of a doubled Vince. If only Twitter had been around in 1998 that picture would have been a classic. April 13, 1998 proves to be a pivotal day for the WWF in the vaunted Monday Night War with WCW, as the premise of an Austin vs. McMahon match on free TV gives *RAW* its first ratings victory over *Monday Nitro* in 83 weeks. Before the two can clash however, Dude Love assaults Austin, setting up a match between the two at *Unforgiven*. There, McMahon's interference backfires and Austin gives him a brain busting chair shot across the noggin for good measure. Looking for redemption, Vince baits Dude Love into destroying his friend and mentor Terry Funk to "prove" his worth for a rematch with Austin at *Over the Edge*.

As the weeks pass, McMahon and lieutenants Pat Patterson, Gerald Brisco and Sgt. Slaughter attempt to make Austin's life a misery, with McMahon bragging about assaulting 'Stone Cold'. Austin returns fire by calling Vince "the world's dumbest son of a bitch", and getting Vince's hired police protection to arrest him for the admission. At *Over the Edge*, special referee McMahon eats another brain cell-reducing chair shot before Austin forces him to make the three count on the Dude. Changing direction, McMahon forces Austin to defend the WWF Title against Kane at the *King of the Ring* in a first blood match. Austin loses, but only after accidentally being struck in the head with a chair by the Undertaker. Kane promises Austin a rematch the next night on *RAW* where Austin wins the title back. Skipping Austin's title defence against Undertaker at *SummerSlam* (and the introduction of Austin's personalised 'Smoking Skull' belt), McMahon puts Austin in another against-the-odds clash, this time in a triple threat against both Kane and the Undertaker at *Breakdown*. The brothers manage to pin Austin simultaneously, and the next night on *RAW*, Vince invites Austin to the title presentation ceremony. That would be the night Austin famously rode a Zamboni into the arena to attack McMahon with.

From there, a "fired" Austin kidnaps McMahon, ties him up, and threatens to shoot him with a pop gun, giving the world "Bang 3:16" as the catchphrase du jour for a week or so. The threat of a bullet to the head causes Vince to quite literally piss himself in the ring before Austin reveals that he's been signed to a new contract, courtesy of Vince's son Shane. That leads directly to the 1999 *Royal Rumble* (as both *Survivor Series: Deadly Game* and *Rock Bottom: In Your House* are ignored completely, as is the silly swerve that Shane only re-signed Austin to screw him over) and Vince winning the Rumble match, but forfeiting his designated WWF Title shot at *WrestleMania*. Not to worry though folks; he'd win the title from Triple H just a few months later anyway. With Vince out of contention for *WrestleMania*, Commissioner Shawn Michaels designates Rumble runner up Austin the new number one contender, but 'Stone Cold' promises to give his shot up… if Vince can beat him in a cage match at *St. Valentine's Day Massacre*. That match would see Vince take one of the roughest bumps you'll ever see, plunging off the side of the cage and landing directly across the edge of the announce table at ringside, which barely gives way. The other notable incident that night saw the debut of McMahon's secret weapon, Paul Wight, who broke through the ring and threw Austin against the cage with such force that it actually gave way, allowing him to escape for the victory. Wight would of course go on to assume the more familiar Big Show moniker.

Following the famous beer bath angle on *RAW*, Austin won his third WWF Title from the Rock at *WrestleMania XV*, a fitting conclusion to the whole entire saga. Only it isn't, as the WWF starts going to ridiculous lengths in an attempt to milk the issue for all it's worth, leading to Vince's terrifically underwhelming reveal as the 'Higher Power' and leader of the Corporate Ministry, after months of feuding with Undertaker. Undertaker's "Where to, Stephanie!?" quote during her abduction still raises an unintentional chuckle, as does some snappily edited footage of Austin's profanity - "Austin 3:16 says that's bullshit, you jackass, son-of-a-bitch little bastard! I just whipped your ass!" Vince's wife Linda, understandably upset with her husband and son for plotting to abduct their daughter just so he could wind up Austin, opts to install Austin as CEO of the WWF, as opposed to anything sensible like, you know, getting a divorce. Austin's first act is to book himself in a handicap match against Vince and Shane at *King of the Ring*, which Vince changes to a ladder match. Austin looks to have the match won but the briefcase containing Austin and Vince's rights to a management position in the WWF is mysteriously raised out of Austin's reach, but lowered to allow Shane an easy victory. The identity of the culprit would infuriatingly go unrevealed.

That somehow leads to Austin squaring off with the Undertaker in a first blood match at *Fully Loaded*, which Austin wins, forcing Vince out of the WWF as per a pre-match stipulation, contradicted just seconds later by a talking head from JR in which he states "He *is* the boss! He *does* own the company! He's not an actor playing Vince McMahon, he *is* Vince McMahon. So he's playing himself, but it's him!" Kerwin Silfies finishes with a strong suspicion that, deep down, the two of them really like working with each other.

VERDICT

Undeniably, the clips on offer here remain wildly entertaining, just as they were at the time, but things do get a little repetitive given the nature of the rivalry, and once you get past the real "blow off" of Austin beating McMahon in the cage, winning the title back from the Rock and into the lousy 'Higher Power' stuff, it really begins to fall off a cliff. Not only that, but the late 90s were actually a pretty weird time for the pro wrestling autobiographical video tape, presenting something of a murky grey area as an increasing core of fans began to grow smart to the business thanks in large part to the internet. The upshot saw certain interviewees discussing the business for the work it really was, while some of the more staunch veterans were unable to shake off the glory days of kayfabe, continuing to push that what you're seeing is actually real. Consequently this tape, along with others like *Lita: It Just Feels Right* and WCW's *Superstar Series* line all came with a very odd mix of what one might term as "shootfabe", with frustratingly contradictory statements often made as one party tries to push an issue as real, with another talking about what great chums everyone involved is. At the time, it was actually fascinating for hardcore fans to hear so many well known on-screen personalities talk openly about the business, especially on official releases such as this, but just a few years later the shoot interview market went into overdrive thanks to the likes of RF Video, Highspots, Ring of Honor and Kayfabe Commentaries, quickly dating these tapes as out of touch for an audience that was finally able to hear the *actual* whole true story.

57

REBELLION 1999

CAT NO: WWF241
RUN TIME: 143 minutes (approx)

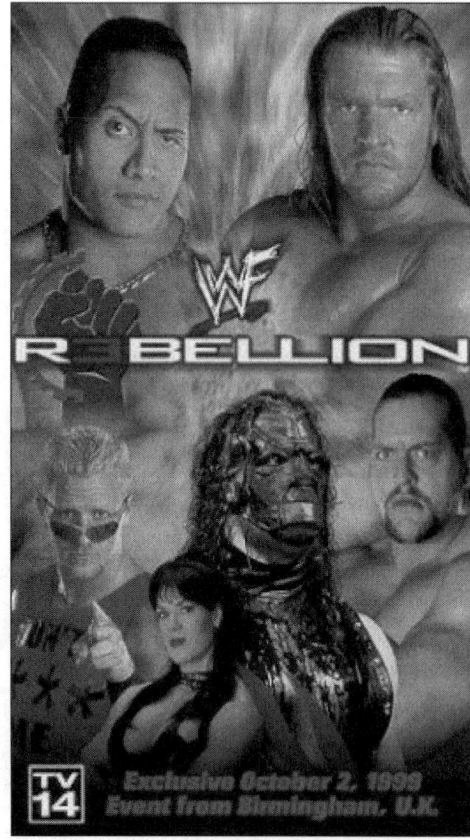

James Dixon: Held live in Birmingham, England on October 2nd 1999, this is the second UK exclusive pay-per-view event of the year, following the woeful *No Mercy* in May, and the similarly crappy *Capital Carnage* in 1998. In fact, the WWF's track record on British shores had been pretty dire prior to those also, with the likes of *Mayhem in Manchester* and *Battle Royal at the Albert Hall* as well as the host of *UK Rampage* shows, all failing to deliver a quality experience for WWF fans across the pond. Only *One Night Only* in 1997 and the excellent *SummerSlam '92* have impressed, so expectations are not high here, especially in a year that has seen the WWF's PPV output at home come up seriously short in the quality stakes. Glancing through the card on offer hardly inspires confidence either. One notable thing regarding the show is that it is the last to be polluted by Vince Russo and his particular brand of horrible booking, as he and Ed Ferrara both upped and left the company three days later. Ding dong, the witch is dead! Nearly...

Jim Johnston's cobbled together track *'Rebellion'* plays us in, and it just sounds like the backing track in the Rock's theme on a loop. The crowd is red hot and there is a sea of signs as far as the eye can see. Jim Ross and Michael Hayes host...

Promo Time: Jeff Jarrett
Jarrett gets big heat due to his recent misogyny, and he comes out with a vacuum cleaner. He cuts a promo, saying how women belong in the kitchen and are only good for making babies. He asks any woman in the crowd to come and accept his £1000 challenge, which is cleaning up oatmeal with the vacuum. A plant comes in and attempts it, and does a horrible job, before Jarrett pushes her over and puts her in the figure four. The attempts at selling from the chick are mind-blowingly bad. Chyna charges down to make the save and they have some awkward exchanges before Chyna clotheslines Jarrett out of the ring, and then leaves to her music. What a horrible way to start the show.

Jarrett stays out because he is in the first match, and a coin toss decides whether Jarrett's Intercontinental Championship or D'Lo Brown's European Championship are on the line. Naturally with us being in England, the IC Title wins out. What is the point of the European title if it can't even get some focus when the WWF are actually *in* Europe!?

WWF Intercontinental Championship
Jeff Jarrett (c) vs. D'Lo Brown
D'Lo runs through Jarrett easily and causes the champ to attempt to bail, but D'Lo brings him back. Jarrett goes right to a sleeper when we return to the ring, and they do the dropping the arm fight-out spot right away, which is far too early in the bout. D'Lo uses a nice stalling suplex but gets caught coming off the top with a Jarrett dropkick, as the champ continues his beating. He gets inventive with an arm breaker from the middle rope, but gets caught with a dodgy looking D'Lo powerbomb, which JR wrongly calls the Sky High. He always calls that move wrong. Three days later, D'Lo permanently paralysed poor Darren Drozdov with the very same move. If only Jarrett had took him to task backstage over how high he landed from the bump here. D'Lo continues his house show comeback, in that it is fairly basic. He does throw in a superplex though, and then they go back-and-forth at the end and refrain from resting at all. Mind you, they only go a paltry 6-minutes so nor should they. Jarrett gets tossed allowing his valet Miss Kitty to jump on the apron and distract D'Lo in the standard "dumb babyface falls for the foxy woman" scenario, and Jarrett levels D'Lo with the vacuum cleaner from earlier to score the dirty pin. Like on seemingly every UK show, the crowd gets a heel going over first to deflate them, though at least the action was fairly solid and entertaining while it lasted.
Final Rating: **

The Godfather vs. Gangrel
It's that age old classic battle between pimp and vampire, presumably because the vampire keeps biting the hos. Only in wrestling, huh? Speaking of the loose ladies, Godfather gets booed when he first comes out because the hos are not with him, but he is just teasing, and out comes a selection of Birmingham's finest street rats. On the ho scale, they are about a collective 3/10. Not the best. Both of these guys fall very firmly into the bracket of gimmick far outweighing the talent, and the action in the early going is fairly messy. Godfather bounces Gangrel into each buckle before getting caught with a

DDT, with the use of the move as a transitional hold particularly frustrating what with Gangrel's finisher being a variation of the same move. Why kill your own finisher because you are too lazy to do something different? The crowd completely dies for this, because having seen the Godfather do his pre-match spiel and having caught an eyeful of the hos, there is really not much more to see. Lots of clotheslines, not a lot else. Michael Hayes has fun chugging along to the Ho Train, and the Pimp Drop finishes this in just over 4-minutes. JR's claims of this having been a "hard fought victory" are pushing it a little.
Final Rating: ½*

Backstage, Michael Cole does his typically bad job interviewing Chyna, who says she is going to mop the floor with Jeff Jarrett later on. The British Bulldog shows up and plays heel, telling Chyna that no one cares about her and that he demands a WWF Championship match tonight. Why are they making their most marketable asset in the UK a heel? Yes, I get that he is a heel in the US, but come on, this is the Attitude Era! Since when have things like that mattered?

Val Venis vs. Mark Henry
Val cuts his usual tiresome, innuendo-laced promo before the match, comparing himself to the game of rugby because it is played with balls, gets rough and the object is to score. Val was a decent hand in the ring, but his gimmick was a one-trick pony. Mark Henry here is doing his 'Sexual Chocolate' gimmick, and one could rather reason that it is illogical that these two would want to wrestle each other, because surely their gimmicks align quite well and they would more likely be friends? I guess neither man wants to share. Henry is still very rough around the edges in 1999, and he has a lot of edges. His attempts at selling are rather woeful, and the general structure of this bout is shoddy. There is just nothing to it other than moves for the sake of moves for 3-minutes, before Val cleanly wins following the Money Shot. This was like a squash, though if you saw this on paper now you would never assume that it would go in favour of Val.
Final Rating: ½*

Backstage, Davey Boy charges into the McMahons' locker room and as promised, demands a title shot from Vince. Vince points out that Davey already had his title shot, but Davey dismisses it as unfair because the Rock was the referee in the bout. Vince tells him to calm down, but Davey does the opposite and hurls a metal bin across the room, which accidentally smashes Stephanie in the face (off camera, unfortunately) and knocks her out. "Get me a medic! A medic, dammit!" yells Vince in an audition for ER. Incredibly this turned out to be fairly important historically, as Steph supposedly got amnesia, which led to her forced union with Triple H, the McMahon-Helmsley era and Steph and Hunter dating in real life as life imitated art, changing the course of the company for real behind the scenes forever.

Four Corner's Match
WWF Women's Championship
Ivory (c) vs. Tori vs. Luna vs. Jacqueline
This is one of those dumb matches that makes no sense at all to have a title defended in, because of the fact the belt can change hands without the champion even being involved. As far as WWF women's wrestlers go, there are some pretty solid girls in there. All of them are actual wrestlers, rather than the later convention of putting models in the ring and asking them to work. They take it upon themselves to go with tornado rules for this, with all four girls in the ring at once. Ivory takes a header and decides to watch for a while, smartly letting them beat each other up while she rests. It is a tactic I have employed in multi man matches on wrestling console games many times. The crowd is dead again for this, so they decide to try and wake them up by doing midget wrestling spots. One example is a four way sleeper spot that ends with all four girls down when they do a collective jawbreaker, and another sees referee Tim White get landed on by a different girl after each attempted kick out. Glad to see they are taking this seriously. After just 3-minutes of combat, Ivory clonks Jacqueline in the head with her title belt and covers her for the win, retaining the title. Shame we saw essentially that exact finish already in the Jarrett match earlier on. This was so brief that it was never boring, and I appreciated the attempts at humour. It just all feels somewhat pointless.
Final Rating: *

We get a recap from what happened 10-minutes ago with Davey Boy, in case anyone watching had forgot. What is the point of showing something like this twice on a PPV? It's not like RAW where you might tune in halfway through. If you ordered the show, you saw it happen already. Steph gets carted away by paramedics, and the bonus for her is that treatment is free on the NHS. Michael Cole, who looks like he has been squeezed and then stretched, so thin is his face compared to circa 2008 onwards, interviews Davey Boy backstage. Davey refuses to apologise for what happened, trips over his words a bunch of times and harps on some more about his title shot. I still don't get why he is heel.

Road Dogg vs. Chris Jericho
The thing with Attitude, is that every guy has to do a promo prior to their match, which may well have been fun for the live crowd to sing along to, but watching it back is frustrating. There comes a point when you just want them to get on with it. Dogg jumps Jericho in the aisle and they brawl into the crowd, which is another of those live crowd-pleasing shortcuts that is not particularly exciting to watch. Road Dogg was a strange choice to be one of Jericho's first storyline promos, because his style doesn't mesh very well with Jericho's strengths at all. The action is all rather predictable and uninspired, with the WWF having done a wonderful job in turning Jericho into just another face in the crowd after a memorable debut. Jericho's bodyguard, the worst performer on RAW in 1993, Curtis 'Mr.' Hughes turns the tide for Y2J, who then proceeds to wear down Dogg with a series of interest-sapping rest holds. The standard Attitude ref bump rears its head when Dogg accidentally clocks the ref, which is a spot vastly overused. How many times have you seen the ref get accidentally clobbered in MMA or boxing? Almost never, yet it happens in the WWF seemingly every other week. Dogg hits his jiving elbow, but Hughes comes in with a chair to the skull for a Jericho near fall when the ref recovers. Dogg fights back, but Hughes distracts the ref and Jericho wins it thanks to a Marc Mero special: a punch to the cock. When discussing this card with others I was surprised how many enjoyed this match far more than I did, putting it at around *** or even slightly higher, but I thought it was lazy, clunky and even fairly boring.
Final Rating: *¾

Chyna vs. Jeff Jarrett
Double duty for Double J, as these two continue their feud from the last few months. This is Jarrett's penultimate WWF PPV appearance, with his next one being the infamous Good Housekeeping match, prior to which a contractless Jarrett demanded in the region of $200,000 to put Chyna over before leaving the company to join his buddy Vince Russo in WCW. The WWF could have saved themselves a lot of headaches if

FURIOUS ABOUT: RIKISHI

It speaks volumes about Rikishi's big "push" that despite having the biggest year of his career during this book, I still opted to give him one of the shorter bios. Rikishi had worked as one half of the Headshrinkers before attempting several failed singles pushes (Make a Difference and the Sultan). He was rebranded as a sumo wrestler, who danced. He spent roughly a year getting crazy over as a dancing babyface until turning heel by confessing he ran over Steve Austin. In what should have been a career making turn, he soon played second fiddle to Triple H. Rikishi managed a few main events out of this run, including the Six-Pack Challenge at Armageddon 2000. After a brief, failed team with Haku, Rikishi switched back face and promptly missed half a year with a shoulder injury. He returned but gained weight and was released by the WWE in 2004.

they had put Chyna over here for the IC Title, but it is not even on the line. In fact it is barely even a match, as the British Bulldog interjects himself after around 2-minutes and decks Chyna with the running powerslam for the DQ.
Final Rating: Not rated

No Disqualification Match
The Big Show vs. Kane
Is Big Show a babyface or a heel this week? Who knows, it's impossible to keep up. Big Show is grimacing so I will assume he is the heel. At least for once Kane can generate some sympathy in the face role due to giving up so much weight, but my God I have seen this match and every variation of it approximately 1,004 times. There is literally no difference between the early ones and those from a decade and a half later. Well, other than the size of Big Show's gut. Does this match really need this stip? The announcers barely even mention the "No DQ" thing, and for the majority of the match the guys just whale away on each other, not doing anything that would usually be illegal. Hell, the referee even counts Show when he chokes out Kane with his boot in the corner. Show's calling here is VERY noticeable too, because it is so damn loud. It's not like you have to look for it, you can just hear him bellowing out spots. Neither guy has any discernible tactic other than just hitting, though Show does try a Boston crab at one point, and Kane an enzuigiri! They finally remember the No DQ rules at the very end when Show brings a chair into play, but it backfires when Kane boots it into his face and then finishes him with a slam. Yes, a slam. So, the stipulation was utterly pointless as it turns out, existing only so they could repeat the same weapon assisted finish as in two of the previous matches, but with it this time being legal. This was hard work, but I have seen them do worse.
Final Rating: *

X-Pac vs. The British Bulldog
Davey returns to Birmingham, the scene of his darkest career hour in September 1997 when he was caught up in a vicious political game involving Bret Hart, Vince McMahon and Shawn Michaels, and was forced to lose his European Championship to Michaels despite having promised his dying sister that he would come through for her. According to many who knew him, Davey's passion for the business died that day, and he was never the same again. Because he is so used to being loved in his home country he just can't help himself when a fan shows him some support, and he returns a grateful wink. He might have done everything possible this evening to make Birmingham despise him, but some fans just don't want to boo their national hero. Michael Hayes comments that Davey looks to have never been in better condition, which is a laugh. If anything, Davey has never been in *worse* condition, with his back on the verge of completely destroyed. You can see him noticeably favouring it when he walks around, never mind takes bumps. I never quite understood why he wrestled in jeans during this run either. I assume it was related to his back somehow, but when he first arrived he was still in his tights, so who knows. It was probably just another piece of WWF creative "genius", with them thinking that like the Big Bossman and the Legion of Doom before him, Davey needed an Attitude makeover. They have changed his music too, and now the classic strains of *'Rule Britannia'* have been replaced by a sly Jim Johnston reworking of Kona Crush's theme, only slowed down and featuring barking dogs. Not his best work. The WWF asked so much of Jim in 1999 with constant repackaging of talent and wanting themes for every show, that he probably just got sick and decided to churn out any old shite. I am struggling to think of a single theme from 1999 that is as memorable as some of his earlier (and later) work.

To the match then, and this would have been a hell of a contest half a decade ago, when Davey was still supremely talented, quick and mobile, and Sean Waltman genuinely was one of the finest workers on the planet. Despite his injuries, Davey does try his best to work through them, bumping around for Pac's armdrags and using his strength to catch Pac on a spinning heel kick and then again to execute his famous stalling vertical suplex. A chinlock follows, for far too long considering the match only goes 5-minutes, but such are the limitations of Davey. While it is disappointing to see him in this shape, the fact he is here at all is pretty remarkable when you remember he was in a hospital for six months when he first injured his back after *that* bump onto Warrior's trapdoor in WCW. Davey catches Pac running into the corner and crotches him, then hits the powerslam for the finish, and boy he looks shattered.
Final Rating: *¼

Tag Team Triangle Match
Edge & Christian vs. The Acolytes vs. The Hollys
This is elimination rules, and is apparently for a shot at the tag titles. The action is fast and furious to begin with, and none of the teams get an advantage as they trade suplexes and shots. Poor Crash gets taken on by a vicious Bradshaw Clothesline From Hell, and the Hollys are gone after just a couple of minutes. This then becomes a regular tag match between the former Ministry members, with the Acolytes controlling Edge before a lukewarm tag to Christian. He doesn't do particularly well either, getting caught by Bradshaw with a fallaway slam and then kicked around the ring by Faarooq, who then goes to a bearhug. The crowd plays along, but Christian's fight back is quickly quelled by a big spinebuster and then a double team version. Christian continues to show plenty of life, until Bradshaw nearly moves the ring by giving him a hard posting in the corner. Faarooq makes a mistake in putting his head down, and then avoids the Dominator and hits a DDT, finally getting the hot tag to Edge. He is all fiery with dropkicks and clotheslines, but he gets drilled with a Clothesline From Hell for a near fall, with Christian saving. Edge fires back with a Tornado DDT on Bradshaw, and surprisingly that is enough for the win. Decent enough throwaway tag match, though it would have benefitted from the Hollys lasting a little longer.

Final Rating: **

Steel Cage Match
WWF Championship
Triple H (c) vs. The Rock

My oh my, the Rock is over. Like, combine the reactions for the rest babyfaces on the roster and it still doesn't come close. "This is amazing!" says JR, in a sound bite that was used for years in the WWF's signature opening splash. The WWF Title has already changed hands an unprecedented ten times this year, which is more than in the first 20-years combined. Usually there would be no chance of the company switching the belt on a UK-only card, but in the current trigger happy climate, fans sensed that it was possible. A lot of that was down to the lack of any real belief from fans in Triple H as champion, with many still viewing him as an upper midcarder in an elevated position. As Arnold Furious will outline elsewhere, it was Mick 'Cactus Jack' Foley that truly "made" him. Rock on the other hand, was riding an incredible peakless wave, and it was assumed that he would be embarking upon his fourth title reign soon, but it would actually be another seven months before he lifted the gold again. Prior to the bout, Rock cuts his standard promo, but it is the Rock, so it is typically entertaining. He does his "Finally..." spiel for the Birmingham audience, and he is not lying either, having worked in the city twice before. Once just a few weeks after his TV debut in November 1996 where he defeated TL Hopper, and then again earlier in the year where he teamed with Ken Shamrock in a defeat to Steve Austin and the Big Show on a house show card as part of the company's annual overseas post *WrestleMania* tour.

To the match then, which is contested in the classic blue bars cage, though painted black with us being in the Attitude Era. Black must be edgier, or something. The rules are escape only, so there are no pinfalls or submissions here. They go back-and-forth with brawling early on, exchanging shots and a number of elbows. Rock attempts to scale the cage first, but is cut off and then caught with a gut shot when he comes off the ropes with a double axe handle, throwing in the Ted DiBiase sell in the process. Hunter sets about wearing Rocky down with his methodical knee and fist based offence, but Rock fires back with punches of his own and a swinging neckbreaker, then tries to leave again. This time Hunter pulls him off and he takes a big overblown bump in the same manner as when he takes a Stunner. Is he trying to channel Curt Hennig tonight or something? Hunter uses the cage, smashing the back of Rock's head into the steel, but he soon gets caught with a Samoan drop that leaves both guys down. Rock's comeback is only fleeting, with Hunter once again taking charge with a clothesline and finally mounting his first escape attempt. Rock recovers and they jockey for position, then Hunter takes a big silly Ric Flair style bump from up top. Credit to these guys for effort on a show where many performers have gone through the motions. The climbing and blocking comes thick and fast now, with Rock exciting the crowd by coming close, before they battle up top and end up crotching themselves simultaneously. Nice spot. Hunter goes for a double axe handle but gets caught with the Rock Bottom, but Rock climbs too slowly and is easily thwarted when he tries to leave, as Hunter connects with a back suplex. Each move is now met with subsequent "cage selling" from both, with moves like powerslams keeping them down for far longer than they usually would if the cage wasn't a factor. They do a nice sequence with Hunter escaping another Rock Bottom and connecting with the Pedigree, which has the crowd rightly worried. Hunter crawls for the door, but Rock just stops him by grabbing onto his leg for dear life. Hunter finds a chair on the outside but Earl Hebner oversteps his mark, as usual, and takes it off him. But, it's no disqualification, that much has been made very clear. In the context of the match a chair is as legal as a punch or a slam, so Earl has no business getting involved. Triple H decides to belt him for his insolence, and shortly afterwards Rock escapes and thus wins the title, but obviously the ref is out. Why wouldn't another ref come out and call the decision?

Hunter escapes too and they brawl around the building, in a cage match, and then return to ringside where Rock busts Hunter open with a hard chair shot and then stops off for a spot of commentary. "He is oozing monkey piss!" says Rocky. Rock lays Hunter on the cheap English announce table and comes off the cage (about five rungs up, not from the top) with an elbow. Back in the ring and Hunter takes header after header into the steel and then eats a Rocky DDT. For some reason, Rock decides to climb the cage rather than escape through the still open door. This brings out the British Bulldog, who stops Rock leaving and throws him back into the cage with one hand. Shane McMahon flies down the aisle to avenge his sister, but he eats a running powerslam on the outside. Pat Patterson and Jerry Brisco are next to try and stop Davey, but he disposes of both of them easily and then turns his attention to the combatants in the ring. Davey stomps away at both but gets taken out, leaving all three guys down. The interference continues, with Chyna, a big babyface earlier in the night, running down and slamming the cage door onto Rock's head. This is no heel turn, she is still aligned with super heel Helmsley on television, despite her playing babyface when competing in matches. What a ridiculous company. Rock stops Hunter leaving but faces 3-on-1 odds and can't fight them for long, meaning Hunter escapes and retains his belt. In the ring, Davey hits Rock with the powerslam, but Vince McMahon comes charging down the aisle with a chain. He locks the cage door, then gives Davey the middle fingers and very audibly yells "FUCK YOU!" to him. I guess you can get away with that more in the UK. Rock hits the Rock Bottom and People's Elbow to get his heat back and end things on a babyface high for the crowd, and that wraps up the match and the show. This was so overbooked that it couldn't be boring, especially in the final ten minutes, and the presence of blood also adds to the drama. A pretty good match to end a pretty drab show.
Final Rating: ***½

VERDICT

As ever with a UK exclusive PPV event, it fails to achieve a standard that would be acceptable back in the States. Then again, the majority of the shows in 1999 were pretty poor so perhaps it is no more or less than was expected. At least there is something redeeming about the card, with the main event almost giving fans their money's worth. But when you then consider that this card cost the best part of £15 on PPV and that the superior *No Mercy 1999* two weeks later was free to Sky Sports subscribers, and featured the epic Hardy Boyz-Edge & Christian ladder match, it is hard to believe that anyone watching at the time was satisfied. As a video tape it is more acceptable, but outside of the chance to see Rock and Hunter go toe-to-toe in the fresh surroundings of a pretty good but not brilliant cage match, this is not worth your time.

33

SURVIVOR SERIES 1999

CAT NO: WWF242
RUN TIME: 156 minutes (approx)

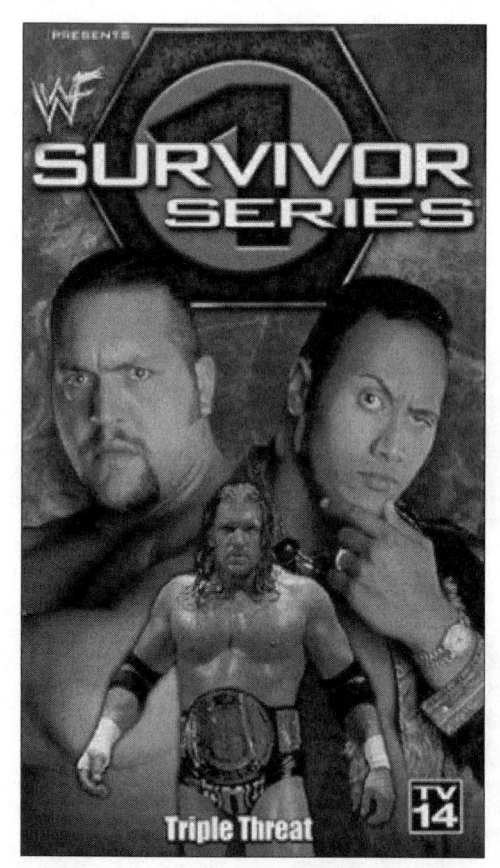

James Dixon: The last few versions of this show have been pretty monumental. The previous year was the "Deadly Game" tournament to crown a new WWF Champion, which The Rock won after a heel turn and a night where there was next to no wrestling worth shouting home about. The year before was the infamous Montreal Screwjob, about which enough has been written already. 1996 saw Sycho Sid dethrone WWF Champion Shawn Michaels to thunderous applause, while on the undercard Steve Austin and Bret Hart assembled a bona fide classic. 1995 and 1994 both saw title changes too, with Bret Hart winning the title from long time champion Diesel in '95, having lost it to Bob Backlund in a very long and mostly boring bout in '94. Plenty to live up to then, and this show will be remembered long into the future too, but for something stupid and idiotic rather than monumental...

Survivor Series Elimination Match
The Godfather, D'Lo Brown & The Headbangers vs. The Dudley Boyz & The Acolytes
Everyone on Team Godfather is dressed like a pimp, and the Headbangers look pretty damn ace. It tickles Godfather big time, who rolls around on the canvas laughing. Wait and minute... THE HEADBANGERS!? Man, those guys were well past their sell-by-date in 1997! This is early into the Dudleys' WWF run, and they are still clad in their tie-dye garb, having not yet made the switch to camo gear in order to make them a WWF branded creation. Bubba still stutters too, and wants a piece of the "h-h-h-h-h-hos". "N-n-n-n-n-no" says the Godfather. The Headbangers both wear big Scouser perm wigs as part of their pimpin' attire, and attempt to work the match in them until spoilsport Bubba rips Mosh's off. The opening exchanges between Bubba and Mosh are actually very lively, with Mosh looking better than he has in years. Thrasher's hair is massive, and seeing him fly around the ring with it atop his head is richly comical. It doesn't last long either, with Bradshaw hitting Thrasher so hard that it falls off his head. The pace continues to be electric, and then BAM, Thrasher is murdered with the Clothesline from Hell. So long. 4-3 heels, the way it should be. Bradshaw brings Godfather in with a middle finger, but it turns out to be a dumb move because Faarooq had Mosh beat, but the ref ended up distracted. Mosh lasts a little longer and continues to impress me with his kinetic energy, before succumbing to 3D. 4-2. D'Lo comes in for the first time with Bubba, but then gets absolutely annihilated by Bradshaw with a chair. Realising he has been disqualified, Bradshaw decides to drill Bubba with it too just for kicks, and boy does he ever. God, I love Bradshaw! Faarooq and D-Von can't get it together after that, and fight each other when they can't decide who pins D'Lo. They fight to the back and both get counted out, leaving us 2-1 babyfaces. Sky High gets a two count, but Bubba keeps fighting, which is backwards really with him being the heel. They go up top and D'Lo looks for a superplex or a rana, but you can't do that shit to Bubba, and he hits his vicious top rope Bubba Bomb, but it only gets two. Hey, this is *Survivor Series!;* That's a three count and then some! D'Lo gets the hot tag and Godfather finally gets in the match, which is smart booking because he is easily the worst of all the guys and obviously all sizzle and no steak. He hits the Ho Train and D'Lo comes off the top with his frog splash, and this time Bubba is done. I enjoyed this; it was a really fun opener and was non-stop for the duration of its 9-minutes. That along with the amusing attire of the babyfaces and the extra effort from the Headbangers, as well as the sheer bastardry of Bradshaw, made this a surprisingly good watch.
Final Rating: ***

Shawn Stasiak vs. Kurt Angle
An historic moment then, as this is the PPV debut of Shawn Stasiak! Oh, and Kurt Angle too... In less than a year he will be WWF Champion and one of the best workers AND characters on the roster. Angle that is, not Stasiak. He is a heel, but acts like a clean-cut 80's style babyface. "This is a different style of WWF competition than we are used to seeing, quite frankly" says JR. Yes, because he actually *wrestles*. As Nirvana said: "I know, I know: a dirty word". The Attitude crowd doesn't give a flying damn of course, because they just want to see tits and weapons and hear catchphrases. Stasiak is not a good opponent for Angle, because he is tedious. He also gets a good deal of this match, which is ass backwards. Angle resorts to a clothesline and stops off to cut a promo on the crowd, berating them for booing an Olympic gold medallist. Then he gets back in the ring and Stasiak goes back to a chinlock, a move he has used for the majority of this match. Unforgivable

really, as the whole thing only goes less than 6-minutes. After getting battered for most of the match, Angle hits the Olympic Slam and that is that. Boring match, but things will get better for Kurt, a man I consider to be one of the greatest in-ring performers of his generation.
Final Rating: ½*

Survivor Series Elimination Match
Val Venis, Mark Henry, Gangrel & Steve Blackman vs. The British Bulldog & The Mean Street Posse

What on earth do any of Val's team have in common? Well, Val and Henry are both lovers of the ladies of course, but they were fighting each other just last month on the UK-exclusive PPV *Rebellion*. Speaking of last month, the British Bulldog was mixing it up with the main eventers on that same show, but now he is reduced to teaming with the Mean Street Posse. The Posse are the drizzling shits in the ring, but their music is sensational. If this was two years ago then Bulldog would have been able to carry this to something worth seeing, but with the condition of his back now, there is no chance of that. JR mentions the last time Davey Boy was at *Survivor Series* and how it was something of a big deal, and indeed his last appearance for the company in that run. Jerry Lawler attempts his favourite trick of trying to get his co-announcer to say something they don't want to say by asking why that show is of relevance, and JR calls his bluff and outlines the whole thing. Meanwhile in the ring, this match is already dragging. Pete Gas goes first thanks to Blackman, then Rodney comes in and embarrasses himself with a horrible elbow drop. "Let's see what Gangrel can do with Rodney here" says JR. Nothing, JR, nothing. Joey Abs accidentally hits Rodney in the face when aiming for Gangrel, then Rodney eats the Impaler DDT and off he goes. 4-2 to the babyfaces then, and the crowd are apathetic to the max. Mark Henry comes in with Abs, who is actually a wrestler unlike the other two, but Henry barely is at this stage and their exchanges are bordering on disastrous. JR amuses himself by saying "Sexual Chocolate" in various different ways, and then Mark Henry splashes Abs to get rid of him. Bulldog is left alone and takes a really horrible looking bump from a Mark Henry splash, which looked painful for a regular guy, never mind someone with a recently seriously injured back. Bulldog then takes his own foolish bump when he hits Gangrel with a superplex, which eliminates him from the bout. Bulldog gets rid of Blackman soon after with a fisherman's suplex, but he can't fight the odds for long. After another minute or two of laboured exchanges, Henry hits his big slam and Venis connects with the Money Shot ("a penetrating move" - JR) for the win. It's the exact same finish as in the opening elimination match! This was a real slog. It was almost the same length as the opener, but felt like twice as long. The Mean Street Posse had no business being involved in actual matches. They were fine as a nepotistic Shane McMahon hire to act as his protectors, but actually wrestling? No!
Final Rating: ¼*

"Oh, *I'm sorry*" says Michael Cole after walking into the girls locker room uninvited and catching an eyeful of Terri's nubbins. You know Michael, you are supposed to knock and then WAIT,

---

FURIOUS ABOUT: THE BIG SHOW (1999-2002)

Paul Wight is a strange beast. Given his size and the WWE's obsession with size, it's curious he's had such an underachieving career. This was especially true of his first 3 years in company. He debuted against Steve Austin in a main event and the suggestion was that he'd be catapulted right into main event storylines. But the WWF already had their WrestleMania planned out so he found himself working against Mankind in the background. His attitude to wrestling was decidedly sloppy and half-baked, which came about because nobody in WCW had ever thought to correct him and get him to actually put some effort in. So the WWE locker room looked down upon the giant as a lazy, good-for-nothing WCW slacker. Show ended up bouncing around the midcard until getting inserted into the title picture, somewhat out of the blue, at Survivor Series '99 where he won his first WWE title. Interest in his reign was low though and his title matches were nowhere near the top end. He was merely a placeholder until Triple H won the belt in January 2000. After a brief feud with The Rock and a WrestleMania main event where he was hardly involved, Show moved on to Shane McMahon and his first involvement with the Undertaker. Show's lack of effort became so palpable, combined with huge weight gain, he found himself dumped into Ohio Valley Wrestling to regain his mojo. A move that must have been embarrassing for a multiple time world champion, Show came back overweight but with an improved attitude. As was true during his entire run in wrestling, Show frequently flipped between face and heel during this 3 year stint. Going from a bully to a joker and back again. Despite criticisms Show won his second WWE title in 2002.

---

not knock and then just charge in like a wide-eyed pervert. The women show him some attention anyway, and hot chicks touching him freaks him out apparently, so he hightails it out of there.

Sudden Death Match
Mae Young, The Fabulous Moolah, Tori & Debra vs. Ivory, Jacqueline, Luna & Terri

The WWF have been smart about this, and one fall ends it rather than us having to sit through the rigmarole of eliminations. The entrances last longer than the match. Far longer, actually, as the whole bout goes under 2-minutes. The pop that greets Debra's music is disheartening. I just don't get it with her. Yeah, her busty bazongas are massive, but they are not real. You might as well strap two bags of sand on your chest and get yourself all excited over that. There are a lot of unattractive women in this match, and then there is Terri, who is at the bottom of the pile. Yes, behind Mae and Moolah even. The pensioners attack Ivory is the aisle, and JR says it "may not be classic". Jacqueline shows why by mistiming a DDT so badly that the crowd let out a huge collective sigh of disgust. A weak ass double clothesline from Moolah and Mae takes down WWF Women's Champion Ivory, and actually keeps her down for the pin! Oh right, it's *Survivor Series*. That's fine then. Every single one of the 110 seconds that this went were horrific.
Final Rating: -*

X-Pac vs. Kane
This is personal, as it is a battle of former partners. The WWF of course added a bunch of fluff to the story as it progressed

and ended up making it too silly to care about, but here it still makes sense. Pac stabbed Kane in the back, and Kane wants revenge. Backstage earlier on, Michael Cole interviewed Kane and his love interest Tori, and the latter cut a really good promo that was both subtle and engaging, getting across the point in just a few words. That's all they needed! Just let things play out organically rather than over seasoning everything with crap. Tori also makes a remark about X-Pac's "little hose", which readers can observe for themselves by watching his porno with Chyna. "Hos? Like the Godfather's hos?" asks Lawler. "Hose! S...E" responds JR. "Ahhhhhh" says Lawler, who finally understands. Kane does his usual ring post fire gimmick, but Pac knows the drill to a tee and jumps Kane during it to try and gain an advantage. It doesn't work for long because Kane is just so big. "These guys were partners for a long, long time" says Lawler, as "a long, long time" is redefined in the WWF as meaning "a few months". Remember when teams would be together for years, sometimes decades, and sometimes, just sometimes, NOT turn on each other!? They trade the advantage while not really doing much, before Kane catches the Bronco Buster and then hits a tilt-a-whirl backbreaker. Kane is starting to dominate, and a chokeslam would finish before the screamingly predictable interference from Road Dogg breaks it up. Kane deals with him but gets caught with the X-Factor, but he kicks out. Pac comes off the top but gets caught in the Tombstone, which brings out Triple H with a belt shot for the DQ. DX put a 3-on-1 beating on Kane, which brings out Tori for the... save? What is she gonna do!? What she ends up doing is spinning X-Pac around, but on instinct he turns around with a reactionary spin kick and accidentally wipes her out. This INSTANTLY revives Kane, and DX scarper. The timing on that spot was exceptional though, so much credit for that. A decade later, the involvement of Triple H in this match would have probably led to a PPV title shot for Kane, but that opportunity never comes. It was just interference for the sake of dragging out another match or two between the former tag partners. At least their next bout is in a cage, which does make sense. The match here was crap and didn't have a finish, but that post-match kick spot really was great.
Final Rating: *¼

Backstage, The Rock starts into a promo but gets jumped by Triple H, and they end up having a pull-apart brawl.

Handicap Survivor Series Elimination Match
The Big Show vs. The Big Bossman, Prince Albert, Mideon & Viscera
The leanest guy in the ring of five is Mideon... Mideon! And boy does my favourite wrestler ever look the part tonight, bedecked as he is in loose fitting sweats and with badly applied face paint adorning his fat redneck mush. He looks and acts like a 5-year-old playing dress-up wrestler. Video Control goes wild with clips, showing us the Big Bossman reciting a poem about Show's deceased father, and then stealing his casket at the funeral. Distasteful, inconsiderate crap. It's just an example of the WWF doing something for the sole purpose of getting a reaction. Did it make anyone want to pay to see Bossman-Show? No. Nothing could. Finally we see Show destroying his own team of the Blue Meanie, Taka Michinoku and Sho Funaki as Meanie pleads "we're on your side" as he gets hurled into a wall. Show wants to do this thing alone. Wow, can you imagine a superb worker like Taka in there with Phineas Godwin and Mabel? Show is looking lean and mean here and he obliterates the opposition in record time. Mideon goes after just 18-seconds from a chokeslam and Albert follows with still less than 30-seconds on the clock. The crowd goes crazy for Show slamming and chokeslamming Viscera out before a minute has even passed, and then Bossman legs it and gets counted out. The whole thing lasts less than 90-seconds! It's the second wise decision that the WWF have made tonight regarding match times. This show (pardon the pun) of complete dominance is exactly how Show should have been booked in his WWF run. It is one of the few times he has felt like a monster, and the crowd reacted to him like he was a star. It's too short to even rate, but I actually enjoyed what they did here. It made sense.
Final Rating: Not rated (too short)

Backstage, something quite important occurs. It starts with Triple H and Steve Austin having a brawl while Road Dogg creeps around, clearly up to mischief. Austin searches for Hunter in the arena's parking garage and then he becomes the victim of a hit and run, as a car ploughs into him. Vince McMahon, Stephanie, Shane, head of security Jim Dawson, Test and EMTs quickly arrive on the scene, and JR leaves the commentary desk to go and check on his friend. DX show up and deny any involvement, and Vince slaps Hunter in the face and calls him a son-of-a-bitch. "It's not something we do" says Hunter as they leave the area.

Tangent: Okay, let's discuss this. Unquestionably the WWF did the angle well and it is believable and handled smartly with the feel of it being a shoot, but obviously no one buys that it is, because it's the WWF and it was a HIT AND RUN. It's just too far over the top for anyone to believe that it is anything but an angle. As far as the question of bad taste, there is no doubt that this does cross a line. Hundreds of thousands of people lose their lives every day from car accidents, and if you subscribe to the widely held opinion that wrestling should exist as a form of escapist entertainment, then you do not want to be reminded of such horrible real life things as having lost a loved one or a friend in a manner similar to this. So why do it at all? Well, the problem the WWF had coming in to this show was that Steve Austin was still suffering the after effects of Owen Hart's botched piledriver at *SummerSlam '97* and his neck was now bothering him to the point where he could no longer delay surgery and had to take significant time off. Of course, doing the angle at the PPV itself is basically taking people's money and then not giving them what they thought they had bought, but the WWF have a history of that sort of thing. If they were doing this angle at all, they would have been better served doing it on free television and announcing that Austin wouldn't be at *Survivor Series* in advance. At least doing it that way engenders some good will to counterbalance the distasteful angle. Surely there was a better way of writing him off television for the best part of a year than this though. As far as Austin goes, this for me is the end of his run as a babyface megastar. He came back in 2000 but the WWF wasn't the same place, and he had been surpassed in the popularity stakes by The Rock, and the style of the main events had changed from his brawling punch-kick stuff to workrate and wrestling. Austin for the first time felt like just another guy, and turned heel in early 2001 in an effort to revitalise his character. He turned babyface again at the end of the year, but by early 2002 he was gone from the company after "taking his ball and going home" and then he retired after a match with The Rock at *WrestleMania XIX* following a very brief comeback. So yes, this was pretty damn important indeed...

WWF Intercontinental Championship
Chyna (c) vs. Chris Jericho
Despite the uninspired booking, Jericho is still over huge with the crowd tonight. I guess the sight of their babyface hero of the last three years nearly getting murdered hasn't affected

THE BIG SHOW

them too badly. I have written elsewhere in this tome about my feelings on Chyna being Intercontinental Champion, and to sum it up I agree with Jericho's assertion that it is an embarrassment. I mean, she just goddamn sucks as a wrestler. The fisticuffs brawl they have at the start is poor, and nothing Chyna does feels or looks natural, it's like she is carefully thinking about every pre-planned spot. There is an amusing moment where they do a waistlock switch and Jericho mule kicks Chyna directly in the cunt, but she just looks at him as if to say: "Yeah? And what is THAT gonna do!?". Well, he probably assumed like most of the rest of us did that she was actually a dude. Chyna follows that with a rana that more closely resembles her being powerbombed, and then she takes Triple H's wild bump in the corner over the ropes, and actually does it well. She is yin and yang. Jericho starts to boss things, which means Chyna has to sell. She is very hit and miss with that too. Chyna eventually tries to fire back with her wild haymaker punches, and the girls in the crowd cheer, but the males start to turn on her, and they pop Jericho big when he belts Chyna back to the ground. Jericho starts taking the piss and strutting around, and Chyna is gassed from being in the ring for more than ten minutes so doesn't show any fire in response. To give her a rest, Jericho gives Miss Kitty a kiss, right in front of Jerry Lawler, then snapmares her on the outside to almost no response. Years ago that would have been an inquest, a suspension and months off injured for the femme in question. Hell, Roddy Piper did the same thing to Cyndi Lauper to set up the historic *The War to Settle the Score*. Chyna recovers enough to go into the next round of the pre-discussed routine and gets the better of Y2J on the outside, but back in the ring takes a big powerbomb, which she nearly botches by jumping wrong. Thankfully for her, Jericho is a veteran by this point and knows what he is doing, so saves her from a broken neck. Chyna fires back again, slowly, then connects with her impressive springboard elbow and a DDT for a near fall. JR and Lawler discuss Jericho's pre-match promise to get a sex change if he doesn't win the title, but thankfully the WWF didn't hold him to that one. In 1999, would you have put it past them to do so? Jericho hits Chyna with the IC belt which should obviously finish, but Chyna is nailing Triple H so she gets to kick out. Chyna responds with a Pedigree, but Jericho kicks out of that and now the crowd is raucous in support of Jericho. The Walls of Jericho gets a HUGE pop, and they boo like crazy when Chyna reaches the ropes, apart from a few shrill cheers, of course. That might not seem like much of a big deal reading this now, but Chyna was super-over as a babyface in 1999 and was genuinely one of the top stars in the company as far as reactions go. For a while at least, until the WWF pushed her too far and pissed off the fans who had being accepting of her competing with the guys, but who were not on board with her winning titles. After a sloppy and slow start, this has got good and has built really well. They go up top and Chyna hits Jericho in the nuts, then sets up a friggin' PEDIGREE FROM THE TOP. Jesus, I can barely look. Thankfully she lets go way early and lets Jericho take his own bump, making it look pretty sloppy but at least it is safe. That is of course enough for the win. Dave Meltzer only gave this a single snowflake, which I think is outrageously harsh. It was clunky at first, but Jericho showed why he was one of the best in the world at this point and dragged Chyna to a very watchable match, made all the more entertaining by the superb reactions from the crowd, which alone make this worth seeing.
Final Rating: ***

Backstage, Triple H continues to deny all involvement in the hit and run, but like a bastard he asks Shane McMahon if tonight's match is now just a straight-up singles bout against The Rock.

Survivor Series Elimination Match
The Hollys & Too Cool vs. Edge & Christian & The Hardy Boyz
Having fought tooth and nail in an epic ladder match last month, Edge & Christian and the Hardy Boyz are now teaming. Obviously. Everyone in this is solid and capable of plenty of effort and energy, and with so many guys in there this could be very good indeed. And plenty of effort and energy is exactly what we get in the first few minutes, though the crowd are surprisingly quiet, clearly burned out from the last match. Matt Hardy takes a vicious slingshot powerbomb on the outside from Grandmaster Sexay, which starts a series of dives and Jeff getting backdropped over the ropes onto everyone in another crazy spot. Sexay hits a bulldog on Christian and stops off to put some goggles on, but misses whatever he was going for in the corner and wipes out the camera man. Edge goes spear crazy and wipes everyone out, including, inadvertently, his own partner Matt. Jeff then gets sent into Edge, and Hardcore rolls him up for the three. Immediately afterwards Scotty comes in with a sudden death DDT from the top on Matt, and that is him out of the match too. The heels are bossing this. Not that the Hollys or Too Cool are particularly heelish mind you. Scotty does the Worm before it was over, and Too Cool drill Jeff with a spike powerbomb, but he kicks out. Sexay channels the Divas division with a hairtoss, as Lawler refers to the rainbow haired Hardy as a "hippy" which prompts a verbal battering from JR. The announcers then get into a good natured and richly entertaining verbal sparring battle, when JR asks: "Brian Christopher or Grandmaster Sexay. How do you spell that, anyway? S-e-x-y? or S-e-x-a-y? You ain't got a clue, forget it, you're talking about hippies here!" Lawler responds in equally amusing fashion, telling JR: "I don't know, I don't go around asking people how they spell their names! I'm more interested in where they played football..." The latter comment obviously being a reference to JR's obsession with football and guys' sporting backgrounds. I enjoy King and JR when they bicker and argue. Things in the ring then break down horribly when Hardcore and Crash start arguing, and Terri gets on the ropes to distract Sexay. Too much going on at once and nothing actually happening at the same time. Then suddenly Jeff hits a 450 splash and that's the end of Scotty. Christian and Jeff try Poetry in Motion, but it doesn't come off and the Tennessee Jam finishes off Jeff. Sexay immediately follows thanks to Christian's DDT, leaving us with the Hollys against Christian. The crowd still doesn't care, unfortunately. Christian manages to survive and gets rid of Crash with the Unprettier, but seconds later Hardcore drops down on a victory roll attempt and scores the win. Lots of moves and spots happened, but it was all a bit messy and disjointed for my liking. It could and probably should have been way better, but as it is it was only decent.
Final Rating: **¾

Backstage, Shane updates us on Austin's condition and confirms that he is out of the triple threat. Well, duh.

WWF Tag Team Championship
The New Age Outlaws (c) vs. Al Snow & Mankind
Despite being heels and having potentially just been involved in a hit and run, the Outlaws still do their sing-a-long entrance and seek crowd approval. Wha? That is idiotic. Jerry Lawler quite rightly points out that Billy Gunn hasn't been seen at all tonight, and that all signs point to him as being the driver of the car that ran Austin down. Yep, it certainly would have made more sense than Rikishi, that's for sure. "Mankind gave Al Snow head last week on *SmackDown!*" says JR, and it is hard to tell

if knew he what he was saying or if he just fuddled into it. We are now entering the twilight of Mick Foley's career as an active full-time performer, and boy does it show. His look is the worst it has ever been (to this point, I hasten to add, because it gets worse) and here he wears a dirty white shirt and tie, sweatpants and white sneakers. He is also looking fairly big, and he hobbles around, struggling badly with his knees. Compare this to the past few years where he was one of the premiere performers on the roster, and his efforts in this are fairly noticeably lacking. I guess it is not his fault given the injuries, but it is tough to watch his decline. How he managed to then turn things around so quickly and impressively two months later when he was reborn for two immense PPV matches against Triple H as Cactus Jack, is beyond me. You don't go from lumbering and crocked to career best performances in that short a timeframe, you just don't. This match is insufferably boring, and it goes a draining 14-minutes! Which sicko's idea of a joke is this? The crowd are silent, they just don't care at all. The Outlaws just run formula for an age on Al Snow before the tag to Mankind, which must be really unsatisfying for a creative performer like Mick Foley to be involved in. Suddenly stuff does start happening, with Dogg getting a near fall on Mankind after a Gunn Fameasser, and then the challengers getting some near falls of their own. Dogg trips Mankind on the outside, and a spike piledriver puts him away. Billy Gunn looks positively livid about the victory, or perhaps he is just being reflective and pensive because he has just ran down Steve Austin (in storyline terms). I strongly suspect that Gunn being the driver was in fact the plan, and he was directed to play things this way. Well that, or he is just appalled with himself for having being involved in that dog of a match.

Final Rating: ½*

WWF Championship
Triple H (c) vs. The Rock vs. The Big Show
The Rock was perhaps the favourite coming into this, as many fans expected him to end Triple H's run with the WWF Title here, especially with the amount of title switches that have occurred in 1999 already. The third man is unannounced until the Big Show heads out, and he is a pretty good choice after the strong reactions to him earlier, but he is not Steve Austin and certainly not comparable to him. The Rock's reaction to Show's music is brilliant; he looks like he just smelled something awful. Rock and Trips immediately team up to try and take Show out, but he responds with a flying double clothesline and then dominates both with his size. The WWF rather booked themselves into a corner here in a way, because Show was at his best when he was running through people, but obviously he couldn't do that against these guys in the main event. Can you imagine the fan backlash if this only went a few minutes? Instead Show has to work the best part of 20-minutes, which doesn't play to his strengths at all. He is in good shape here and his conditioning far superior to the 2010s when he became a semi-mobile tub of lard who would blow up after a few minutes and moved around the ring like a crippled hippo, but it still doesn't help him look as impressive as he could be. Him wrestling the match in a t-shirt is annoying too. The solution to the problem is shortcuts, and they soon take to brawling around the arena. I guess no one else has done it tonight so it is not too bad, which is in marked contrast to some shows this year where seemingly every match would venture outside of the confines of the squared circle. During the brawl Hunter takes a really pointless bump through a random table thanks to a Rock slap, and in a horrible spot Rock uses a fire extinguisher on Big Show and misses by about a foot. Show sells it anyway. The brawl continues, with Rock taking a back suplex in the aisle from Hunter and Show sending Triple H hard into the steps. JR claims he must have banged his nose because it is swelling up and huge. Ha, amusing! Things get silly as Rock uses the ring bell on Show, and it is barely sold and garners no reaction. That's desensitisation for you. Rock and Hunter team up again to suplex Show through the Spanish announce table, giving him a nice rest and keeping him out of the way so they can brawl into the stands. They haven't been in the ring for a good ten minutes now. I hate matches like that. When they do make it back to the ring, an Irish whip reversal causes an accidental ref bump, which is a spot I hate as I have said elsewhere. Rock hits the Rock Bottom and Shane flies down the aisle to act as referee, because God forbid a main event in 1999 doesn't have McMahon family involvement. Rock hits it again, and Show pulls Shane out to prevent the count. Show takes Rock out on the outside so he can have a prolonged selling and resting session, and then gives Triple H the "biggest damn biel" that JR ever saw. He has been excessive in putting over Show's size in this, rather telegraphing that he is going to win the thing. Trips takes issue with Shane and drills him with the Pedigree, then gets taken out himself. DX run in to brawl with Show and Rock, and the crowd start to loudly chant for Austin. Sorry folks, not tonight. Vince McMahon then heads down the aisle and swings the WWF Title at Hunter, but misses, then connects the second time he tries before Show nails the chokeslam and Vince counts the three for Show's first WWF Title. "Vince screwed Triple H" yells JR, because it is *Survivor Series* and we have to reference Montreal every year. Show breaks down in tears as he celebrates his win and we go off the air. The match was full of shortcuts, lots of "walking brawling" where they don't do a whole lot but pretend that they are, and an overbooked finish that people weren't quite 100% sure was official because Vince made the count. It was not bad, but as a match it was instantly forgettable other than the title change, and Show dropped the title back to Hunter within a few weeks anyway and was soon shunted back down to the midcard after a few months as a top guy. It would be a pattern that he continued to follow for the rest of his career.

Final Rating: *¾

VERDICT

It's a very middling show at best, but the Steve Austin angle makes it memorable, though for all the wrong reasons. Advertising a main event PPV match and then changing it during the show is not acceptable practice, and the WWF are lucky there wasn't a bigger adverse reaction to them for doing that. The two best matches on the card are good but with flaws, and many of the others just flat out sucked. This is par for the course in 1999 though, and when you watch back the cards the WWF were putting on, it is amazing to see just how well they were doing in every aspect of the company with regards to television ratings, live attendance and PPV buys. They had all that success, and yet the product pretty much sucked. There is nothing on here worth going out of your way to see, so this is not recommended viewing.

34

ARMAGEDDON 1999

CAT NO: WWF243
RUN TIME: 170 minutes (approx)

Arnold Furious: 1999 had been a rocky year for in-ring and the December PPV has always been a bit of a downer. The WWF often struggled to think of things to fill the dead space with between the twisty *Survivor Series* (this year headlined by a surprise Big Show title win) and the inevitable Road to *WrestleMania* beginning in January. 1999 was no exception and this PPV was headlined by Triple H and Vince McMahon, doing battle over the future of Stephanie. Almost a battle for control of her soul. The rest of the card contains little of historical value.

Tangent: the main event of *Sunday Night Heat* was Al Snow beating Test. If the WWF had any belief in Test he'd have main evented the PPV, as he was most obviously wronged by Triple H stealing his fiancé and pre-marrying her before their *RAW* marriage. Vince would have been better served to corner Test here and gain another main eventer rather than once again having a McMahon headline. I think the fans began to turn on McMahon presence on TV around this time and quite rightly so. It was becoming too much.

We're in Fort Lauderdale, Florida. Hosts are Jim Ross and Jerry Lawler.

Tag Team Battle Royal #1 Contendership Match
Participants: The Dudley Boyz, Edge & Christian, The Mean Street Posse, The Headbangers, The Acolytes, Too Cool, Mark Henry & The Godfather, The Hardy Boyz

The Dudleys were hot off a ridiculously heat generating run in ECW but are somewhat sheared of personality by not being able to swear or use most of their carnage spots. Luckily their violent interactions with pretty boy teams like E&C and the Hardys helped. The 'Bangers have come back after Thrasher's knee injury and Mosh's idiotic Beaver Cleavage angle. The Hardys have Terri in their corner after winning the Terri Invitational, but she doesn't opt to join them at ringside. The line up for this match should tell you that tag team wrestling was back on the agenda in the WWF and a division that had been largely dead for years was reviving. Sadly this is a battle royal rather than a *Survivor Series* style elimination match, which would have better served the talent involved. The Posse cheat with Rodney getting dumped and replaced by Joey Abs. He gets tossed too and Rodney sneaks back in. Pete Gas looks a bit like Colt Cabana. Eventually all three of them get thrown out and that's one of the few filler teams gone. 'Bangers follow, their best days long behind them. The APA team up to dump Henry and that leaves five genuinely decent teams. E&C outsmart Too Cool and throw them both out and in a rare piece of coherent 1999 booking the top four teams remain. D-Von heads to the floor to drag Edge out of the ring. That's perhaps a surprise as I'd argue E&C were the top team of the era. The Dudleys use the "Wazzup" headbutt before it had a name or shouting. Jeff gets double teamed but Matt throws D-Von out while he's celebrating. Jeff busts out an Arabian press, which pops the hell out of the crowd while both Matt and Bradshaw topple out. Bradshaw landed first but the ref was nowhere near it and had no idea. The Acolytes opt to kill Jeff, but he dumps Faarooq out. The ref, blind Jimmy Korderas, manages to miss that too. They tease some interesting finishes, with both Bradshaw and Matt hanging on for dear life until Jeff gets backdropped clear over everyone and the Acolytes win to noticeable heat. The Hardys' high risk offence made them big fan favourites. As far as tag team battle royals go, this one is pretty good. I persist that an elimination match would have worked more effectively. Also I'd rather have seen two of the top four compete for the belts at the Rumble rather than the weakest of the four teams against the Outlaws. But hey, those other teams will have their day in the sun.
Final Rating: **

Backstage: Kurt Angle gets to put himself over and blame Steve Blackman for their teams defeat to the Dudley Boyz on *SmackDown!*. Kurt claims the fans in Florida would appreciate a true American hero like himself.

Kurt Angle vs. Steve Blackman
Angle's debut against Shawn Stasiak had been a muted affair. Angle thought he was a babyface (kayfabe) but was alarmed to hear the fans booing his arrogance and his three I's. He briefly formed a team with Blackman but that ended a few days before this when they lost to the Dudleys. The crowd aren't quite sure

what to make of Angle at this point and he doesn't have the kind of heat you'd think he would. He already gets wrestling though and his charisma comes through in spades. When matched with bigger stars with more experience he'd immediately look like a goddamn megastar. He tries for a moonsault here but misses, allowing Blackman to hook a sloppy Oriental crossbow. Blackman wasn't a great technician and should have focused on his striking. The fans chant "USA" almost insinuating support for the Olympic gold medallist. Florida, seriously lacking in patience, then start to chant "boring", which is insulting considering the lack of rest holds they're employing. Some of these Attitude fans were impossible to please. I'm glad to see the back of them. Angle works hard and loads the match with spots, constantly hitting either strikes or suplexes. He is a workrate freak. If anything he needs to slow down a bit, which shows the idiocy of the "boring" chants. Angle manages to plant Blackman with a German suplex for the win, which is in keeping with the same disjointed vibe the entire match had. It never felt like it was building to anything, but they both worked hard and this was much better than the fans gave it credit for.
Final Rating: **¼

Backstage: Michael Cole gets all flustered by BB's enormous knockers. BB was originally named "Barbara Bush", but I suspect Vince's Republican leanings changed that. Or inspired it...

Evening Gown Pool Match
WWF Women's Championship
Ivory (c) vs. Miss Kitty vs. Jacqueline vs. BB

BB used to work at Hooters so this is up her alleyway. BB shows her timing by dragging Kitty into the pool when neither of them are on camera. This kind of thing makes a mockery of women's wrestling and has no place in the business. It'd be ok if it was just no-talents like BB and Kitty working each other with no title involved, but genuine workers like Jacqueline and Ivory are just being embarrassed. The WWF's intention here was surely to flash some titties and everyone figured it'd be the buoyant BB who exposed herself. Both she and Jacqueline are eliminated though and despite a lengthy tease BB escapes with her bra in tact. Kitty strips Ivory off and wins the women's title. This did not belong on a wrestling show. I like tits as much as the next man, but they should have kept an actual title out of the titillation.
Final Rating: -***

Post Match: Kitty promises to get naked and her first act as Women's Champion is to expose her bosoms to a hearty pop. Sgt. Slaughter quickly covers her up with a towel, but those were honest to God boobies on PPV. Mae Young tries to kill all the young boners that arrived during the unveiling scene by stripping off herself, but luckily Sarge is still nearby with a handy towel, thus saving everyone's eyes.

Backstage: Rikishi, who's not quite found a niche and only debuted a few weeks ago, prepares for his match with the Hollys. He claims to represent "all the healthy fat people out there". Oh, boy, that's just wrong. Rikishi was yet another gimmick for the unfortunate Fatu and it seemed doomed from the start. Luckily for him he formed an entertaining three man unit with Too Cool shortly after this and became a healthy fat guy who danced, which gave him significantly more substance and made him fun.

The Hollys vs. Viscera & Rikishi Phatu
Rikishi's lack of overness is palpable. He beats down the Hollys by himself while Vis just stands around watching. Lawler, like the child he is, continues to bang on about Miss Kitty as if his girlfriend exposing herself to the world made him proud. Crash's purpose in this match is to take a load of bumps while Hardcore picks his spots. The Hollys working over Vis is horribly boring but the crowd seem to enjoy it because they like big fat guys more than Olympic wrestling heroes. Attitude. Rikishi's hard Samoan head allows him to no sell a DDT and he starts popping off stuff like elevated cutters and sitout piledrivers! Vis miscues on him though, and the Hollys get the upset win.
Final Rating: ½*

Post Match: Vis is all "that may have slightly been my fault" but Rikishi's aggression about it causes a pull apart ruck. The crowd completely ignore it.

Backstage: Val Venis hits on Lillian Garcia while claiming the European Championship will be a gateway for him to go and sex up Europe.

WWF European Championship
The British Bulldog (c) vs. D'Lo Brown vs. Val Venis

1999 Davey Boy Smith makes me sad because he's so badly deteriorated. Seeing as the European Title meant almost nothing by this point, Bulldog was given it back despite his condition. Amazing to think just two years earlier he was one of the best workers in the business. The WWF's bizarre storytelling has Davey wrestling in jeans and he's got the Mean Street Posse in his corner. Or he would if Teddy Long didn't send them to the back. The lack of interest in the title is somewhat offset by D'Lo's popularity, and to a lesser extent Val's. Brown hits a nice dive in the early going, which allows Bulldog to lie around selling for ages, a typical issue in three-way matches. He returns and D'Lo spends a while just standing around doing nothing. Eventually Val gets double teamed as these guys aren't creative enough to do three-way spots. D'Lo botches a springboard, which was an issue with Brown where he felt the need to insert more dangerous spots to make himself more entertaining but in ability terms so much of it was beyond him. As if the match didn't suck enough, Bulldog badly botches his bump on a double hip toss. Again the three way match falls to pieces as Bulldog just stands around doing nothing while the other two work. You couldn't have thought up more triple spots? Bulldog's bumps look so much worse because of how good Brown's are alongside them. Bulldog will take a terrible bump then D'Lo a great one. I know Davey had a bad back but if it was so bad he couldn't take bumps, why's he not doing something else? The horrors of old wrestlers. D'Lo should win with the Lo Down but Val hits both guys with the Money Shot (eww) to win the belt. The crowd were very pro-Brown and he was the easy choice to win, as he was synonymous with the European Title after Bulldog's departure. Naturally they put the strap on Val, who didn't need it and didn't suit it. Given its lack of importance, the European belt stayed around Val's waist for two months until strap collecting Kurt Angle won it. The match suffered from the usual threesome pitfalls (bad selling, nonsensical storytelling) with the added bonus of several key botches.
Final Rating: ½*

Backstage: X-Pac gives us details of stipulations with the forthcoming Kane cage match. Kane can only win by pinfall but Pac can escape. He goes on to disparage Kane's "old lady" for calling his hotel room late at night. This was when Tori was hanging around with Kane.

CHRIS JERICHO

Steel Cage Match
Kane vs. X-Pac
Tori was an interesting choice to sex-up the Kane character. People tend to forget what she did and how much she was involved with top end guys. The timing of the heel DX reunion rather scuppered an excellent Kane-Pac tag team storyline. Pac has recently entered into his "X-Pac heat" run, as people started to genuinely hate him. He's still a decent worker, which people really tend to forget. The idea behind this match is that Kane is too powerful and dominant for Pac to win under any normal circumstance. Even Pac's slanting of the rules to suit him don't help when Kane is throwing him around like a rag doll. Kane's freaky strength allows Pac to basically jump at him from any angle and Kane can just catch him. Even when Pac has the advantage he can't get anything close to a pin. Their counters are a little bit sloppy, but only because of the size difference with Kane finding it hard to take bumps for the smaller man. You could argue Pac shouldn't be attempting moves like DDTs on the big man, but if he doesn't hit impact stuff he has no threat. The New Age Outlaws run out here to cut the lock off the cage and Mr. Ass slams the door into Kane's face before throwing a chair in for Pac. He hits the X-Factor on it before handcuffing Kane to the cage. This is just too much for Kane's girlfriend and Tori jumps in there to stop Pac escaping. Pac spits right in her face and hits the X-Factor on a woman, which draws less heat than you'd expect but was a scuzzy move. Kane snaps the handcuffs and walks out of the cage to stop Pac from winning, as he'd already climbed over, and follows with a top of the cage flying clothesline (hell of a spot for a big man). Tombstone finishes. The difference between the tiny X-Pac and the massive Kane should have turned Pac face, but it's testament to his sleaziness that it didn't. Kane gets a happy ending, but it won't last. Surprisingly good match. One of Kane's best singles matches to this point.
Final Rating: **½

WWF Intercontinental Championship
Chyna (c) vs. Chris Jericho
The WWF somewhat screwed up by debuting Jericho as a top star and then throwing him in with Chyna. Jericho should have gone over her at *Survivor Series* to begin a long IC Title run. Miss Kitty corners Chyna, looking like a mini-version of her, complete with smaller title belt. Chyna is horrendously sloppy in the early going, making a hash of all her strikes. Jericho shows remarkable disdain by hurling Chyna womb first into the announce table before she dropkicks a chair into his face and he flings it over his shoulder, narrowly missing Mark Yeaton. Chyna's sloppiness continues with a handspring back elbow and an ugly DDT. She's in over her head in big singles matches. Just because she could organise a tag match and work coherently through bouts didn't mean she was a candidate for a big push. It should have been enough she was wrestling against men. Jericho makes a point of working over Chyna's injured thumb that he hit with a hammer in the build up to this match. He even nails the thumb with a dropkick, which is precision dropkicking. Chyna improves as the match continues, hitting her spots cleaner and taking better bumps. Jericho is nonplussed by the whole thing and just works a standard match, which is both good and bad. Good that he's able to hold Chyna's weaknesses together and bad because the match doesn't feel special. At least until nearer the conclusion where the crowd start to love and hate Jericho in equal measures. Jericho takes a few tasty bumps and gets a solid counter out of the Pedigree into the backslide. They make a hash of a back superplex with Chyna landing awkwardly across Jericho's face. The nasty landing makes it a more realistic near fall though. Chyna tries a roll up out of the corner but gets strapped in the Walls of Jericho and has to tap out. The crowd's reaction is raucous and reflects Jericho's arrival as a top tier star. The match is loaded with mistakes, but the result makes it seem better. I still think the WWF flubbed the Jericho push after nailing his debut. Luckily he's always been jobproof (in that it doesn't matter if he wins or not, the crowd reaction is still strong for him), but imagine how much bigger he would have been if the WWF had actually gotten behind him from day one and made his main event matches about him. The crowd know he's a star and that Chyna will never amount to any more than this. This is her glass ceiling, while Jericho is championship material. I persist Jericho should have won the WWF Title in 2000. Strike while the iron is hot!
Final Rating: **¾

Backstage: Chris Jericho gets interview time where he claims he's restored the IC Title to its rightful position. Chyna shows up to shake Jericho's hand as a mark of respect. JR calls it a classy move, which it is. It kept Chyna babyface after dicing with forced heeldom here. Sometimes you just run into someone who's better than you. Hell, Jericho knew that from day one when he was outshined in Wrestling Camp by Lance Storm, the only other competent guy he trained with.

WWF Tag Team Championship
The New Age Outlaws (c) vs. The Rock N' Sock Connection
Seeing as Triple H was the focus of the WWF, despite Show being WWF Champion, Rock found himself paired with Mankind and going after the tag titles that, despite the tag team division's revival, were way beneath him. The Outlaws get a sing-a-long arrival but are soon drowned out by Rocky chants. The basis of this match is that Al Snow was jealous of the Rock's popularity and resents Mick picking Rock over Snow for this title shot. As Mick explained, Rocky gets a bigger "pop". Mick's health was failing him in late 1999 and he was considering retirement. His broken down body still looks pretty slim compared to how big he'd get just a year on from this, but it's his knees that are knackered. I never cared for his switch to sweatpants in 1999 though; it makes him look like a slob. The Rock tagging in gets a massive pop, which shows you where he's at from a popularity standpoint. Rock looks in top condition. The improvement he made in terms of movement and technique since debuting in 1996 is amazing. All the things that looked clunky in 1996 are smooth here. All his bumps are clean. It's almost a pity that Rock got so big, so fast that he was bigger than the sport and went into movies. I feel like we may have missed out on some quality matches. With this bout, there are a great many disappointments. Given the collective popularity of all four guys they coast by on that alone. The only guy who ever looks like switching it up is Rock. His bursts of offence are the best thing about the match. Mick's stuff is noticeably less kinetic. He has good spots worked out though and they run a clever ref bump ahead of a tidy piledriver on Road Dogg. Double arm DDT should finish, but with no ref Mankind resorts to the Socko Claw. Al Snow runs in to whack Mankind with Head but Rock saves the pin and goes after Snow in the aisle. The Outlaws use the opening to ding Mankind with the ring bell, but he kicks out of that. Rock gets a hot tag and pops off spots on both Outlaws. Billy eats a Rock Bottom, but Al Snow runs in for the title saving DQ. Unsatisfying finish aside they were building nicely towards a conclusion. A better finish might have elevated this to good. Snow takes the Rock Bottom and a People's Elbow as punctuation and a reminder who the real star is here. Some snazzy formula was offset by a lack of creativity from a few participants. Gunn was especially bland, alarmingly so, perhaps due to his continued frustrations over a failed singles

TORI

push.
Final Rating: **½

WWF Championship
The Big Show (c) vs. The Big Bossman
Somehow Bossman is number one contender for the title, having scored a major upset win over the Rock. Seeing as he was in the midst of a, frankly ridiculous, feud with the champ that sort of makes sense. Not that anyone wants to see Show-Bossman on PPV and certainly not for the big strap. Bossman's behaviour (making fun of Show's dad and a cancer angle) was beyond despicable and this is one of the WWF's most unpleasant angles. For me, death is off limits unless you've got a great angle. This angle was just sick. I know some fans found the coffin riding to be suitably silly that it made the whole thing a joke, but not me. Prince Albert is in Bossman's corner to take a chokeslam through the announce table in the early going. It's a shame the WWF basically used this match as an excuse to take the belt off the lazy giant champion, as Bossman was pretty much useless at this point in his career. Show takes a bump on the floor and the crowd get very bored, this time with good reason as Show just lies around doing nothing all match. Show does insert a nip up, which freaks JR out, and finishes with a chokeslam. The match was 3-minutes and still felt too long. Bossman had no business being in a PPV title match and this could easily have been resolved on *RAW*. What was resolved on *RAW* was the title, with Hunter beating Show between this PPV and the *Royal Rumble*, thus ending a damp squib of a run for Show as champion.
Final Rating: ¼*

No Holds Barred
Triple H vs. Vince McMahon
This came about because of Vince feuding with yet another WWF Champion. Hunter reformed DX to protect his title and Vince didn't take too kindly to that (also, Vince suspected DX

were involved in the hit-and-run on Steve Austin), interfering at *Survivor Series* and costing Hunter the belt. Hunter considered the title to be his and his alone and resented Vince for his interference, going on to ruin Stephanie McMahon's wedding by announcing he'd pre-married her when she was unconscious in Vegas. I'm still not sure that counts. But this is one of those times where the eventual turn made everything seem more legit. What could have been a daft heel turn made the whole storyline click into place. So the stipulations are as follows: if Vince wins the marriage is annulled. If Hunter wins he gets a title shot and the marriage remains. Hunter punctuated his abuse by throwing Shane off the ramp on *SmackDown!* and making out with Steph. Interesting to note this match takes place after Vince had been "banned from WWF TV forever" about six months ago. He's actually had a WWF Title run since then. Only in wrestling.

I remember being shocked by Steph's heel turn as she'd been utterly useless as a babyface but she took to the role like a duck to water. It's just a pity Hunter and Vince decide to have a dick measuring competition first as they go 30-minutes. 30-minutes! What madman thought that would be good fun? Vince isn't a wrestler and doesn't have any spots. Hunter, with all due respect, has never been adept at carrying people of lesser ability. It's a recipe of disaster and the match is a humongous waste of PPV time. Seeing as Vince can't wrestle at all they fill the match with brawling. Unlike when Austin-McMahon headlined a PPV it's not filled with moments that excite. The difference with that match was, as a heel, Vince was getting his comeuppance (in spades). With this match it's just brawling for the sake of it. Yes, it is a personal feud but Hunter, as the wrestler should dominate, and he does, but why unlike the showboating Austin, does he not go for the finish quickly? He doesn't want to punish Vince, he just wants to win so he can go back to what really matters; the WWF Title. The match is dying a death so Mankind wheels out a shopping trolley full of weapons for Vince. His "use these bad boys" instruction makes me chuckle. Hunter at least inserts psychological common sense by washing his eyes out about 10-minutes after a powder shot from the chairman of the board. As if to say "I was only losing because I couldn't see". Mick's hardcore weapons make the match marginally more interesting, but it still drags something fierce. Why did they go 30-minutes again? What was the logic behind that? There's no wrestling at all and the garbage is just that. Did I mention it's 30-minutes long? Madness. It boggles the mind that the WWF won the wrestling war with PPV main events like this. It goes to show just how awful WCW was at the same time.

Tangent: WCW's December PPV, unlike the WWF's, was their biggest show of the year; *Starrcade*. The 1999 version of the show suffered from a case of the Vince Russos however. He managed to insert thirteen matches onto the card, thus depriving everyone of time to tell a story. At least they had a match that cracked *** with Benoit-Jarrett in a ladder match for the US Title, but in typical WCW form they billed it as a MOTY when it was merely the best match on a bad show. The main event saw Bret Hart suffer a concussion from an errant Bill Goldberg kick that ended the Hitman's career. Incidentally the actual 1999 MOTY *was* from WCW and was given away on free TV when Bret Hart and Chris Benoit worked each other on *Nitro*. The ladder match was around ***¼.

Hunter gets creative with the props and uses a machine gun (yes, really) to knock Vince down. Vince manages the same with a flap from a helicopter, as the set for *Armageddon* features several military vehicles. The weird thing about all the garbage shots is the lack of selling. Various objects are bounced off Hunter's head, then off Vince's head, rinse, repeat. When that gets boring Hunter just flat out disappears. As in we head to the parking lot and he's nowhere to be seen. This is the month after the hit and run on Steve Austin and Hunter tries a similar trick on Vince, but McMahon hops over a rail to survive a badly lit, badly shot attack. A replay shows how close Vince came to serious injury. After that they resort to the same deal; bouncing heads off objects over and over again. To mix things up they add in a silly bump with both guys climbing a tower by the entranceway before Vince falls off onto a safety landing mat. That's deemed worthy of a "holy shit" chant from the same crowd that chanted "boring" at Kurt Angle. Betcha feel stupid now! Vince blades from the bump, which makes little sense. The match contains shit for the sake of it. It needs blood so Vince just bleeds. It doesn't work like that! Hunter stops off to cut a promo in front of Steph before grabbing Sledgie, his trusted Sledgehammer. Vince kicks him in the balls, steals the hammer and Steph leaps in the ring to demand her own vengeance. Hunter takes the hammer off her and wears Vince out with it for the pin. Steph's initial reaction is of horror, which is her first official good acting performance. Hunter threatens a hammer shot on Steph before the twist in the tale; Steph smiling and hugging her husband. It's almost worth waiting for as the sly grin appears on her face. It wasn't the best executed of turns, but I'm quite fond of it. The McMahon-Helmsley faction took over after this and bossed the WWF for months with Hunter on top. It made for good TV. Eventually Steph's screechy voice and constant appearances wore as thin as her old man's had, but this was a moment where the WWF went in a new direction, though admittedly still with the McMahon's as the focus. They needed something big to fill the Austin void. Who knew Steph would be it? As for the match, it's a never-ending hardcore mess with way too much garbage and no actual wrestling. At least they never lost the crowd, apart from me, so it stays out of negative snowflakes. But it's a chore to sit through and I don't recommend it.

Final Rating: ½*

VERDICT

On paper it's a poor show. There's nothing over *** and for a PPV that's just not good enough. You could argue Jericho-Chyna is pretty good and it is, for a Chyna singles match, but it's not great. Jericho's title win is the biggest deal about the show, despite Steph's heel turn, and that's worth checking out. The rest of the card is forgettable. At least the Show-Bossman angle got blown off here, but as far as PPV title matches go, it's low down on the scale. Very low. There are other positives; you won't see many more competent Kane singles matches than the cage bout with X-Pac and at least the storylines that began here went on to logical conclusions; Steph's turn set up months of programming and Jericho's win catapulted him up the card. That was the benefit of having Chris Kreski as head of creative after Vince Russo's departure. He used storyboards and actually planned stuff out in advance, creating one of the best years of TV and PPV in the process before leaving, citing burn-out, and was replaced by Stephanie McMahon. Sadly he died of cancer in 2005.

25

ROYAL RUMBLE 2000

CAT NO: WWF244
RUN TIME: 166 minutes (approx)

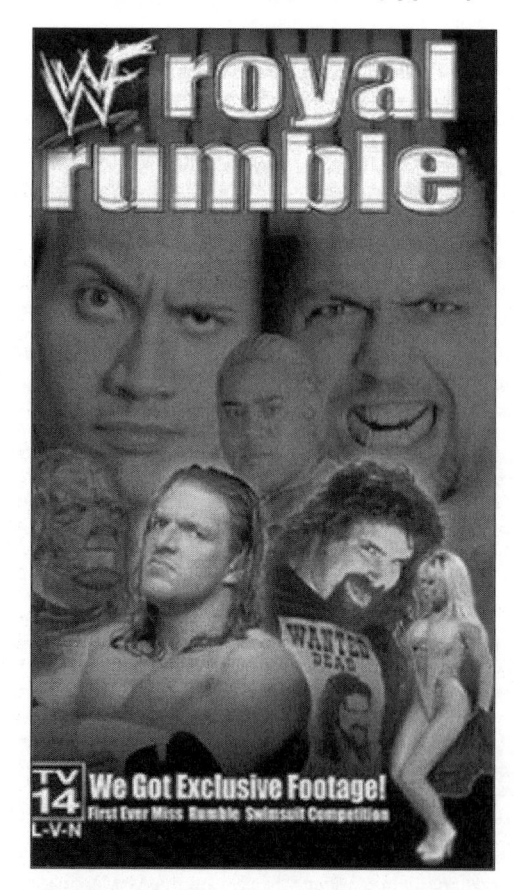

Arnold Furious: I remember when this show aired I proclaimed it to be my favourite PPV of all time. While that may not be the case now, it's certainly still a quality show. Mainly because of the epic Cactus Jack vs. Triple H match that *made* Hunter as a main eventer and a WWF icon. So, we have Mick Foley to blame for that. As we progress I'm sure you'll fondly recall this show as I do. We're in New York City at Madison Square Garden. Hosts are Jim Ross and Jerry Lawler.

Kurt Angle vs. Tazz
Normally mystery opponents are a total downer (usually Savio Vega) and some people suspected Angle would just get someone to squash here. However the WWF signed Taz away from ECW, added a Z, and made themselves a new star. Or they would have if they hadn't then gone and signed Chris Benoit, Dean Malenko, Eddie Guerrero and Perry Saturn, thus crowding their midcard with taller superstars than Tazz, and his career floundered. But here we get to see the Tazz that was imagined. A machine. Angle stops off to run down the crowd, New York sports teams and points out he's undefeated. The crowd chants "we want Taz". It actually got to the point where the WWF went on WWF.com and stated the mystery opponent would not be Taz. But of course it is.

Tazz's arrival still gives me chills. Even though the WWF let ECW run around in their rings in 1997, they flat out signed Tazz, the human suplex machine, to a long term contract. This provokes a lengthy and loud "ECW" chant. The signing of Tazz showed a marked change in recruitment policy for the WWF. For years their hires were specifically big guys who looked the part. Tazz was a fat orange midget... but he was great to watch. Angle decides to show Tazz a few suplexes including one on the floor. Head and arm super Tazzplex! Angle barely survives that thanks to a foot on the ropes. This becomes an absolute suplex-fest with Tazz escaping the Olympic Slam with a release German before hitting a few suplexes that confuse JR with their complexity, before the Tazzmission finishes. The match shows the initial intentions of the WWF regarding Tazz and he must have been totally bummed out when this initial mega-push faltered. For one night at least, Tazz had arrived in the WWF and in sensational fashion. A new year meant new stars and a crowded roster left Tazz directionless before a hopeless feud with Jerry Lawler killed what little heat he had. I like to watch this every now and again to see what might have been. A Tazz that beat Kurt Angle in 3 minutes could have been a contender.
Final Rating: **½

Backstage: Terri gets left backstage by the Hardys because of the violent nature of the forthcoming table match. "Tonight we're gonna put the Dudleys through tables or we're gonna die trying" says Matt.

Video Control gives us an exclusive comment from newcomer Tazz who runs his usual ECW spiel claiming he'll "run right through this company". Not quite, but at the time it must have felt like it.

Tag Team Table Match
The Dudley Boyz vs. The Hardy Boyz
The more ECW guys the WWF stole, the more entertaining the show got! Mainly because the Dudleys now get to work against teams that can sell, they become a top commodity with superior workrate to other big guy teams. The Dudleys open up here with a pre-match promo where Bubba professes his love of baseball pitcher John Rocker, which draws enormous heat. Rocker had gotten into hot water the previous month by making inflammatory and ill-advised comments during an interview, which offended... just about everyone. He took shots at pretty much every ethnic minority and insinuated New York was full of gays with AIDS and 20 year old single moms with four kids. He was particularly vilified in New York for his remarks and in MSG the Dudleys were wary of getting popped for their ECW connection. That little remark cut off their pop in 3 seconds flat. The whole set up allows the pretty boy Hardys to get popped and cheered in New York, which wasn't easy. This is one of the reasons why the Dudleys were one of the top tag teams in wrestling.

The first thing this match has going for it is a total lack of tags. No weird scenarios with guys standing around on the apron; we get right into it tornado style. The Duds get a table and try

to backdrop Jeff through it only for Matt to shove the table out of the way. The spot looks incredibly dangerous and is totally reliant on Matt's timing. They continue to tease table spots while Jeff hits a suicide dive and nails Bubba with a chair shot to set up his railrunner spot… and Bubba smacks him with a table. The levels of action and excitement are just wild here, like they saw themselves as the hot opener, despite going on second. As if the tables weren't enough Matt pulls out a ladder, thus upping the ante and making the TLC match a future inevitability. Bubba gets tabled at ringside, with Matt legdropping off a ladder and Jeff jumping over the camera from the ring to make it a double team. Jeff's sudden arrival in shot is amazing. That's worthy of a "holy shit" chant and 2000 saw a clear increase in wild and crazy high spots. Instead of being one-offs they became the norm. Both Hardys miss D-Von in an attempt to repeat the first table spot with D-Von dodging both, one after another. Both spots looked incredibly painful. The Dudleys start moving furniture and set up a table across the ring steps, in the ring, and superbomb Matt through it. Even the bits in between big table spots are sickening as there are stiff chair shots everywhere. The big finale involves Bubba setting up a table stack in the entranceway, which is MADNESS. Bubba intends to throw Jeff off the balcony, which the crowd oblige by moving out of the way. Jeff goes low and chair shots Bubba off the balcony through all the tables! Not content with that Matt chucks D-Von onto a table and Jeff hits the Swanton to win it. This match is total carnage. The combination of high risk and hardcore changed the game. ECW had been running hardcore matches for years but the top wrestlers, the technicians, steered clear of them. The WWF decided to have hardcore matches with good wrestlers in. A luxury of an international company with tonnes of talent. The bar was raised, quite significantly, by the tag team madness of 2000.
Final Rating: ****

Backstage: Kurt Angle, woozy, isn't sure if he won or not and tells EMTs that if Tazz used a choke he's still undefeated as it's illegal.

Miss Rumble 2000
Jerry Lawler is MC and an assortment of veterans are hauled out to officiate, including Fred Blassie. Participants are Ivory, Terri, Jacqueline, BB, Luna Vachon and WWF Women's Champion The Kat (formally Miss Kitty). Ivory can't be bothered. Terri bounces on the ropes for additional pop. I never quite understood why Jacqui didn't get the pops considering her bootilicious bod, plus she always gives it her all. BB relies entirely on appearance with little effort involved. They should have just kept her as an EMT. I much preferred her with her clothes on. Her bikini wearing diva personality was incredibly bland but having a sexy EMT made for a better show. Like Chelsea's first team doctor Eva Carneiro. Luna threatens violence and refuses to undress. Kat's bikini is made of bubble wrap causing Lawler to mess his tights. Of course the WWF can't just do a bikini contest without a "Mae Young is ancient and likes to take her clothes off" bit. So yeah, Mae comes out and disrobes. Luckily my eyes are saved by a post production CENSORED sign until Mark Henry runs out to cover up his lady's wappers. Mae is proclaimed the winner and gets her tits out again. I do like Terri's reaction of "Really!?" aimed at the judges, as if the whole thing was a shoot. This is a horrendous blight on an otherwise brilliant PPV.

Video control takes us to WWF New York in Times Square where Coach tries to talk about the venue, but is mobbed by marks.

Backstage: Chris Jericho and Chyna argue about who gets to wear the IC Title to the ring as they're co-champions. Earl, or more likely Dave Hebner takes the belt as essentially the title is now vacant, as there are no DQ's in a three-way. Tonight we get to see who's the actual champion.

WWF Intercontinental Championship
Chris Jericho (c) vs. Chyna (c) vs. Hardcore Holly
I'm not sure why Holly is involved seeing as the dispute doesn't involve him. Late in December a match between Jericho and Chyna ended in a double pin. The belt should have been vacated, ideally. Jericho gets the biggest reaction of all three by some distance. He cuts a nonsense promo about New York throwing a Jericho celebration party when he wins, which is still greeted with huge support. Jericho and Holly exchange slaps only for Chyna to get involved and booed. I think people were getting a wee bit tired of her babyface act at this point, though New York is traditionally ahead of the curve on hating babyfaces. The fellas throw Chyna to the floor and just work each other, which is pretty good. Jericho would have it with the Walls but Chyna saves. Chyna has a few moves that look like they belong to a rookie, like an air shot clothesline. It's awful. Jericho pops the crowd with his springboard dive and Chyna responds with her handspring back elbow, which is jeered. Holly throws her out again so we can get a good one-on-one. Typical three way matches tend to involve one guy selling for ages but they alternate pretty well here. Chyna's timing is lacking in her big spots and this isn't the environment for her. It's too complicated. Jericho takes one in the plums and Chyna Pedigrees Bob, but Holly kicks out. It was a sick looking Pedigree too with Bob pretty much faceplanting himself. The interaction between these three is a lot better than you'd think due to Bob's curmudgeonly behaviour, Jericho's high spots and Chyna's ambition. They even work in a series of believable near falls that make each person a viable winner. There are better triple threat matches out there but considering those involved, it's really solid. Chyna lifts the Walls of Jericho to heat but Jericho bulldogs her and hits the Lionsault to claim sole possession of the IC Title. This is one of those matches that proves Jericho can make anything good. On paper it looked bowling shoe ugly, but it's actually a decent match.
Final Rating: ***

Backstage: The Rock cuts off Michael Cole so he can listen to the millions… and millions of the Rock's fans chanting the Rock's name. Finally he's come back to New York City! Rock is asked who he's worried about in the Rumble. Rock singles out Crash Holly and Headbanger Mosh as potential threats, popping the hell out of the crowd. "If the Rock can get by those two he might just have a shot". Cole brings up Big Show only for Rock to order him a "big tall glass of shut up juice". Even when the Rock screws up a line he still makes it fun. This promo is electric and Rock guaran-damn-tees victory in the Rumble. New York smells what he's cooking.

Video Control gives us an exclusive chat with Chris Jericho who says it was a gruelling match but he's now undisputed IC champion. He dubs the belt "the InterChrisenental" championship. Jericho is a total dork but I love him for it.

WWF Tag Team Championship
The New Age Outlaws (c) vs. The Acolytes
This is a bit of a nothing match, as the WWF had little interest in putting the titles on the Acolytes, and it really only exists so Road Dogg can do his pre-match sing-a-long with the champs bit. The WWF had made it clear with the tables match what the future of the division was. Highlights here include Bradshaw

treating Billy Gunn like a cruiserweight jobber and Faarooq doing Road Dogg's shaky dancing routine. Billy takes the Clothesline from Hell and Faarooq should finish with a spinebuster on Road Dogg. Gunn saves the titles by pulling the ref out of the ring. Double powerbomb on RD and X-Pac runs in to once again save the belts. Faarooq gives him a spinebuster too only for Billy to catch Bradshaw with a Fameasser to retain. Very quick filler match, but all good fun and constant action.
Final Rating: *½

Video Control gives us Road Dogg's exclusive rhyming promo about getting their asses kicked but still being the C-H-A-M-P. After that we move onto shilling the WWF Title match, starting with Hunter beating Big Show with a Pedigree for the title. Next up the McMahon-Helmsley faction fire Mankind, so the Rock gathers the entire locker room together to have him reinstated. Hunter promptly beats the crap out of Mankind and Pedigrees him through the announce table. Not a good build for a PPV? Having the challenger get squashed every time out? Quite. But Mankind wasn't getting the shot. "I think the fans deserve a substitute in that match. I think you know the guy (takes mask off) his name is CACTUS JACK". God, I love that moment. Mick's characterisation and switch from the feeble minded Mankind to the hardcore icon Cactus Jack is a thing of beauty. It only worked because of how well Mick had constructed the two characters.

Street Fight
WWF Championship
Triple H (c) vs. Cactus Jack
Interesting that they don't bill Cactus as being from Truth or Consequences, New Mexico as Foley was from New York (Long Island). Plenty of "Foley is God" signs out there. To this point I feel Mick's best match in the business was his classic with Shawn Michaels at *Mind Games*, despite the lack of finish. That's about to change. The only beef I have with this match is that it should have gone on last, after the Rumble. Mick jaws away before the bell, which Foley said in his book *Have a Nice Day* was actually him asking about Hunter's cologne. He does it very aggressively though. Foley was so broken down by 2000 that it's a minor miracle he can move around with the athleticism that he does. I guess he knew he had two matches left, so he could leave it all in the ring. This is reflected in his *WrestleMania* performance, when he'd been retired for a month and his body had fallen apart. This match though is all about progression and building. They start out on the floor brawling and Cactus takes a shot with the ring bell, which was enough to put Mankind down. But Cactus Jack isn't Mankind. Not anymore. He's gained a mythical power that lifts him above that. Hunter grabs a chair so Jack demands a shot with it and Hunter delivers. Cactus goes down like a sack of spuds, but he gets back up! They don't do much wrestling, they don't need to, but Cactus inserts swinging neckbreakers and backdrops on the floor, as if to pay homage to wrestling in an unusual setting. They insert a much maligned crowd brawl (in that I hate all crowd brawls) but it's merely to get to a New York style alleyway part of the entrance. This leads to Hunter taking a suplex on a pallet. Much to Hunter's horror, he discovers a piece of wood stabbed him in the leg during that spot. Not for the last time, Hunter just carries on. Lots of blood from that and it's right in the calf. That would hinder the mobility of a normal man. For all the flak we've given Hunter, he sure knew how to man-up and work with pain. In order to push the envelope Cactus grabs his 2x4 wrapped in barbed wire, which gets a massive pop. As per usual Cactus bringing a weapon in backfires, as Hunter nut shots him and uses the 2x4 on Jack.

It's vicious. The WWF has seen nothing this violent beforehand. Double arm DDT, but in a rare moment of weird selling, Cactus stays down for too long before pinning. Hunter rolls his shoulder while the ref is hiding the 2x4. "Where's the bat?" screams Cactus at Earl Hebner. Mick lays out Hugo Savinovich for not giving him the bat from under the Spanish announce table. Hunter then takes a 2x4 shot right in the noggin. It's a beauty. Hunter kicks out and the fans are already biting on the near falls. Also Hunter is bleeding like a stuck pig from the head and the leg. He's having to earn this title in blood, sweat and tears.

Like his hero Ric Flair, Hunter's blond hair is turning a shade of red as Cactus beats at his bloody head. It's a crimson mask! Cactus remembers his last match with Hunter and goes for a piledriver on the announce table to replicate that famous MSG win from *RAW* in 1997. Hunter feels it coming and backdrops out, breaking the table before the main event. It's at this point that JR spots the puncture wound in Hunter's calf and sells the hell out of it. He's been working with that for 10-minutes! Hunter sets for the Pedigree and unfortunately does it in line with the buckles, rather telegraphing the reversal. Hunter then face bumps onto the barbed wire… for 2. Hunter has juiced so much that the fans buy everything as a near fall now. Cactus Clothesline sets up Cactus to take a hip toss onto the ring steps. Cactus follows that with yet another knees-first bump into the ring steps, which makes you wonder if he was planning on walking after this match, let alone wrestling a main event the following month. Hunter, always the cerebral assassin, takes out Cactus' leg. This allows him to grab handcuffs and cuff up Foley. People get depressed at the sight of Cactus getting cuffed as it brings back memories of the Rock's brutalisation of him at the Rumble in 1999. It also ends the fans' hope that Cactus can win the title. Hunter goes after the ring steps but Jack manages to drop toehold him, in a superb piece of defensive wrestling. Hunter then wears him out with a chair, which creates a great visual as part of the chair breaks off and flies towards the crowd. Sometimes props can magically help you create a better visual. Hunter is far safer with his chair shots than Rock was a year earlier. As Cactus starts begging Hunter to hit him properly, the Rock runs out and chair shots Hunter so the cops can unlock Jack's cuffs. Now it's a fair fight again and Cactus's first call of business is to hit that piledriver on the table. The Spanish table does not oblige and stays in one piece. Because it's not falls count anywhere Cactus has to take it back into the ring, and on the way picks up a massive bag of thumbtacks. Stephanie McMahon can't take it anymore and runs out to appeal to Cactus's sense of fair play. Hunter takes the opening and backdrops Jack into the tacks. Great sell from Stephanie on that. PEDIGREE! ONE-TWO-THR…NOOO! KICKOUT! This was outstanding business as the Pedigree was death and nobody ever kicked out of it. Hunter's one-legged complaint to the ref is brilliant, but as soon as Cactus is up a second Pedigree on the thumbtacks gets the job done. A brutal ballet that had a ridiculous escalation of violence for the WWF. It was a massive breakthrough for hardcore wrestling to see the WWF Title defended in such a manner. I know some purists aren't keen on this, but I love Mick Foley as a talent and this was his moment to shine in a way that no one else could. The match with Shawn Michaels was a demonstration of how brilliant he could be in the WWF's PG-13 environment. This is a demonstration of what was possible when the rulebook gets thrown out of the window. Hunter's selling and bleeding made the match, and the match made him.
Final Rating: *****

Tangent: One issue I have with this match is that the bar was set so high with the violence that everything that followed was trying to live up to it. And they shouldn't have. Luckily the WWF acquired a host of technical marvels during 2000 and changed their in ring style in the process. I'm probably more of a garbage fan than the other guys so this match is more important to me. As an avid ECW fan, seeing the 18-rated violence cross over to the WWF was a thrill. I must admit, since then I've been more inclined to love technical wrestling and more old school stuff, but I think that's a natural progression as a wrestling fan.

Video Control takes us to WWF New York where Coach asks Linda McMahon how she feels about Steph and her actions of late. Linda promises this will be handled "the McMahon way". In other words, all of them will saturate TV for the next two months.

Royal Rumble Match
#1 is **D'Lo Brown**. #2 is **Grandmaster Sexay**. This is a real downer coming off the WWF Title match. No offence to these guys but they're midcard at best and the fans don't want to sit through 90-seconds of them. As I said earlier, I think the WWF Title should have gone on last. #3 is **Headbanger Mosh**, complete with enormous furry tits, like an acid flashback from *Fear and Loathing in Las Vegas*. Kaientai run in to attack Mosh, possibly sent by The Rock, intimidated by Mosh's potential threat. D'Lo bumps on Mosh's ankle, thus injuring him. Look on the bright side Mosh; you haven't got a bit of wood stuck in your calf. #4 is **Christian** and someone finally gets a pop. Christian was hugely underrated as a wrestler in his early days and in my opinion he was way ahead of Edge, pretty much until he left the WWE and stagnated somewhat in TNA. #5 is **Rikishi** and despite his total lack of reaction at *Armageddon*, he gets a huge pop here. He starts cleaning house. Mosh goes. Christian goes too, clearly seen as disposable at this point in his career. D'Lo finds himself no sold and gets dumped with the Rikishi Driver. That leaves Rikishi and his buddy Grandmasta Sexay. #6 is **Scotty 2 Hotty**. In order to break up the Rumbleness of the Rumble we break it down and everybody dances. And thus Fatu finally gets over. Rikishi makes the curious decision to eliminate both of Too Cool, instead of waiting in the ring and having a 3-on-1 advantage over everyone else! What a fat idiot. The fans cheer him anyway. I love Scotty's hair by the way. It's like twelve *Something About Mary*'s. #7 is **Steve Blackman**. The crowd hate him because he's not fun and he doesn't dance. Blackman eats the Rikishi Driver and gets thrown out in short order. Rikishi already has six eliminations. #8 is **Viscera**, following on from their brief team and feud. Big Vis halts Rikishi's momentum, but Rikishi barges him out anyway and gets his 7th elimination. #9 is **the Big Bossman**. He brings some seriously old school stalling by not entering until #10, which is **Test**.

#11 is **the British Bulldog**, who is still wearing jeans instead of tights. #12 is **Gangrel** as the match slows down and the ring fills up. Kaientai run in again and this time Taka takes a massive unprotected bump over the top, landing badly on his shoulder. #13 is **Edge** and he gets the biggest pop so far. One of the major issues with the Rumble is a lack of star power and therefore a lack of believability when it comes to potential winners, so you have to make it entertaining instead. The

VISCERA

WWF gets that, sometimes, and #14 is **Bob Backlund**. I get the feeling this was a late decision as he's wearing red shorts instead of gear. Everyone gangs up to throw Rikishi out thus ending the entertaining opening segment of the match. #15 is **Chris Jericho**, who gets a massive pop, even bigger than when he won the IC Title earlier. He throws Backlund out to get going. #16 is **Crash Holly**. "Stranger things have happened" says JR and Lawler points out that Rock singled Crash out as a threat. Oh, Uncle Jerry, you are a muppet. #17 is **Chyna** who goes right after Jericho with weak forearms before suplexing him out from the apron, which is not a popular decision. Bossman knocks Chyna out to add to the misery of the situation. The Rumble needs big names and with those two gone there's not much happening. #18 is **Faarooq**. The Mean Street Posse run in to attack him and Bossman throws him out. I'm not sure why the Posse decided to go after the Acolytes. #19 is **Road Dogg**. I love that the fans sing his entrance for him. The crowd, drifting, chant "we want puppies". It's a sign of the times. An entrant every 90 seconds isn't keeping the crowd's attention and the middle section of this Rumble isn't up to much. #20 is **Al Snow**.

Road Dogg eliminates Bulldog in the battle of the dogs. Still seven guys in the ring and it remains crowded and slow. #21 is **Val Venis**. Funaki runs in again, this time solo because of Taka getting his shoulder bust up last time out. Road Dogg develops a new tactic of hugging the bottom rope, thus making sure he can't be picked up and can't be thrown out. #22 is **Prince Albert** whose arrival coincides with Edge's elimination. No star power at all there now and no potential winners; just a bunch of scrubs. The crowd's silence reflects that as the hugging continues. #23 is **Hardcore Holly**. You'd think he'd team up with Crash but they end up in opposite corners. Just as the match is losing the crowd out comes #24… **The Rock**. The match desperately needed him. He throws Bossman out immediately with his patented spit punch. "He's just a jabroni" comments King of the departed Cobb County prison guard. #25 is **Billy Gunn**. He goes after Rock, following up their 1999 feud. Everyone moves to one side to allow Rock to DDT Crash and eliminate one of his "biggest concerns". Road Dogg is still hugging the bottom rope. Every now and again someone kicks him. #26 is **The Big Show**. "Business is going to pick up" states JR. Show would be better off if he didn't keep flip-flopping between face and heel. Less than a month ago he was a face, now he's heel again. Show lobs Test and Gangrel out for starters before going after the Rock. Hardcore saves Rock and Show presses him… into the ring. Why not over the top? That's just nonsensical. #27 is **Bradshaw**. This brings out the Mean Street Posse again. They get less joy against Bradshaw, who beats the crap out of all of them before the Outlaws put him out. Wonderful clothesline on Rodney in the midst of all that. #28 is **Kane**. Val goes after him and gets thrown out. Kane and Rock try to have a brawl but Albert interjects and beats both men down in the corner. Albertamania is running wild! He is the man! #29 is **the Godfather**, complete with Ho Train. Kane puts Albert out so the Prince can get a closer look at the Hos. Not that he needs to pay. He is all that is man. Funaki runs in again, to get a look at the Hos, and gets thrown out as Lawler gets his chuckles watching Taka's elimination for the fourth time on split-screen replay. #30 is **X-Pac**. Nine guys in there and one of them is going to *WrestleMania*, but only Rock, Show and maybe Kane are realistic contenders. Holly goes out first to no reaction. Godfather follows, courtesy of Show. Rock pops off a Samoan drop on Al Snow and throws him out. Billy throws Road Dogg out, which makes no sense and Kane eliminates him right afterwards with no one watching his back.

Final Four: The Rock, The Big Show, Kane and X-Pac. Rock does a great dodge on Pac's spinning heel kick and tosses him out as Kane brawls with the Outlaws on the floor. Considering the DX faction had three of the last six guys, they fared remarkably poorly. Seeing as the refs were watching Kane, Pac's elimination is missed and he sneaks back in. Need more refs. Pac took a massive back bump too. He gets that spin kick on Rock at the second attempt. Kane and Show go at it in one of their patented slugfests. Kane manages a slam on Show but Pac spin kicks him out. Broncobuster for Show! That's a bad idea. Show presses X-Pac clean out of the ring for it. The fans erupt, realising Rock is on for the win if he can dump Big Show. Spinebuster! People's Elbow! Show survives though and hits the chokeslam, deflating the crowd. Show goes to javelin Rock over the top but somehow falls out himself, and Rock uses the ropes to stay in. As far as Rumbles go, it's middling. The stuff with Rikishi started the match off right and everything after the Rock came in was good. The middle of the match was quite dull, but the right guy went over. Rock's celebration is cut off by the returning Big Show, thus setting up the February PPV.
Final Rating: ***¼

Addendum: It would be revealed that Rock botched the finish and his feet touched before Show went out. Rock response to the campaigning Show? Nobody cares! Video Control gives us Rock's reaction to winning the Rumble before we see what's left of Hunter. "Go in the crowd and tell my parents that I'm okay". Seeing the after effects and the doctors working on Hunter's leg and stitching it up gives us an extra slap in the face of realism as we finish the tape.

VERDICT

Obviously the show is special because of the title match, but aside from that it's very enjoyable throughout. Jericho finally got the IC Title solo, the tables match was tremendous entertainment and Tazz's debut was sensational. The Rumble itself is okay but is largely overshadowed by the title match. It's an honest to God match of the year candidate and will compete for best match in this book's awards, easily. I don't think Hunter has ever topped this level of awesomeness. The only match that even comes close is the often overlooked and underrated Three Stages of Hell with Steve Austin at *No Way Out 2001*. The reason I tend to look at this as his best work is because it made him. Before this match he was WWF champion but he wasn't over for his wrestling, he was over for his dickish behaviour. This match changed fan perception of him and he went on a great run of main events afterward, dominating the 2000 awards and was proclaimed wrestler of the year by most people. It all began here.

100

THE BRITISH BULLDOG

NO WAY OUT 2000

CAT NO: WWF245
RUN TIME: 172 minutes (approx)

Arnold Furious: We're in Hartford, Connecticut. Hosts are Jim Ross and Jerry Lawler. The whole show is built around Mick Foley putting his career on the line to get a shot at the WWF Title and his childhood dream of main eventing *WrestleMania*. That match, against Triple H, will take place inside the demonic Hell in a Cell.

WWF Intercontinental Championship
Chris Jericho (c) vs. Kurt Angle

Kurt gets a customary heel promo pre-match where he sucks up to Hartford by saying unlike the Hartford Whalers he's going to come back some day as a role model for all the fans. Upon arriving in the WWF, Angle immediately made a point of talking, extensively, in order to make fans notice he wasn't just a technician. Chyna joins us at ringside, complete with her firework bazooka (penis envy!), to ruin the match at some point. She's supposed to be here as Jericho's friend. Having finally seen Chyna off for the IC Title, Jericho is now lined up to job the belt. Of course Angle, or Kirk Angel as Jericho calls him, is an absolute megastar in the making so it's all good. These guys naturally have decent chemistry, as Angle is brilliant with anyone and Jericho is way above the average guys he was having okay matches with. The match is loaded with counters and Angle's fast improving sportz entertainment stuff. Jericho throws in an insanely dangerous moonsault off the ring steps as a counter for being whipped into them. If he'd not put his hands down he'd have landed on his head. Jericho continues to innovate with a Tiger Backbreaker. Jericho was always very inventive, he just had issues with not being able to hit his crazy new moves clean. Angle switches gears on his usual match tactic by going after the arm, although to be fair this is prior to his ankle lock finisher so it's okay. Jericho sometimes upsets me with his lucha stuff, like loose Irish whips and other crap that ruins lucha matches, but then he did work for EMLL for a few years. Jericho manages his double powerbomb, despite the injured arm. Not sure that was the right spot. Angle counters out of the pin into an armbar, making me wish Ken Shamrock was still around to work Angle in a shoot-style match. Angle's early finisher the Olympic Slam shows off how lame it is, with Jericho kicking out of it despite Angle only debuting a few months ago. Angle, frustrated, goes after the belt, but that allows Jericho to hook the Walls of Jericho. Angle, being a wrestling machine, should wrestle out but uses the ropes instead. There are definitely kinks in the game plans of both guys. Angle goes after Chyna with the IC belt and that causes her to get bumped. The ref checks on her thus allowing Angle, in a creative spot, to waffle Jericho with his own belt in mid-Lionsault for the pin and the title. This was Chyna at her most feeble and weak. As she got better looking, the booking of her fell off. The match is not without flaws but they were creative and talented enough to work around them.
Final Rating: ***¼

Backstage: The Dudley Boyz mouth off to Michael Cole about putting people through tables and taking what they want.

WWF Tag Team Championship
The New Age Outlaws (c) vs. The Dudley Boyz

This represented a passing of the torch as the Outlaws had gotten extremely stale and were done as a tag team. The Dudleys had set the world on fire with their actions outside the ring and their matches in it. Along with Edge & Christian and the Hardy Boyz they were taking over the division. The Outlaws were too busy relying on formula and Road Dogg's pre-match spiel. Road Dogg works most of the match due to Billy having a torn rotator cuff and Gunn would actually miss most of 2000 because of it. I feel bad for Road Dogg who the WWF were never keen on pushing in singles, for whatever reason; presumably his physique. He was always really solid and sometimes good in the ring. He was a great seller and demonstrates that as the Duds give him a beating for five minutes straight. Billy shows his limitations when he's tagged, totally unable to use or even move his left arm. He still manages a Fameasser before Bubba smacks him with a lead pipe. You can see Billy covering up, terrified of the pain he's about to be in. Bubba then hops into the ring and the 3D finishes. This was a changing of the guard with the Outlaws being finished as a team after this, until being reunited in TNA as the James Gang and then, incredibly, for another tag title run in WWE in 2014! The match is brisk and one dimensional but the right team went over and the division was great from this point on.

Final Rating: *¼

Mark Henry vs. Viscera
This is not a good idea. It stems from Mark Henry having gotten 76-year-old Mae Young pregnant (?!?) and Vis deciding that the angle needed Mae being splashed by a 500lbs fat guy clad in garbage bags. JR points out that if "rated on the star system" this may not rate highly. It goes even lower when Vis manages to completely miss an axe handle. Henry had just about gotten the hang of taking a bump after four years as a pro, but he wasn't improving at an acceptable rate and the WWF actually sent him to OVW not long after this. The crowd chant "boring", because the match is, and that brings down Mae Young. Oh the humanity! Vis goes to repeat his splash but waddles into a Henry slam for the pin. JR was right about a lack of snowflakes. This gets none and likes it. Henry would actually revive his WWF career by winning the 2002 Arnold Strongman Classic competition and returned to the WWF later that year. Eventually he even became a half-decent worker too. He certainly wasn't here.
Final Rating: DUD

Backstage: Lillian Garcia asks Jericho about his title loss, trying to blame Chyna. Jericho blames Angle for belting him and warns him to stop celebrating his victory. Elsewhere Billy Gunn gets treated by EMTs, saying he can't move his shoulder at all. See you in October, Mr. Ass.

The Hardy Boyz vs. Edge & Christian
You can tell the tag division is back as this is non-title between two regular tag teams and it's not only on PPV but it has heat. Rightly so too. The APA come down to ringside as Terri purchased them to watch her back, this being after the Dudleys had tabled her. This was both teams' opportunity to prove they could work a match without gimmicks attached. Which they can, because they're all decent workers and Jeff has a lot of sizzle. Christian wrestles circles around him and works some tidy spots in with Matt. Jeff's high risk stuff is all over the place. He hits Poetry in Motion but a springboard set up, needlessly convoluted, for the Arabian press causes him to splash Christian's knees. Matt spends most of this match completely forgetting he's a babyface and mouths off at Christian whenever possible. He then tries for a Razor's Edge, countered into a neckbreaker by Christian. Maybe Matt was being heel as they were working heat on Christian. Hot tag to Edge and Jeff botches another high risk spot, landing in completely the wrong place from a backdrop. E&C get a spell working heat on Jeff and it's not as effective as the Hardys' heat although I put that down to Jeff being less capable than Christian at selling. Edge straightens him up with a jumping piledriver. Of course that's not a finish, but it should be. Jeff keeps trying to get a tag, after his big spots, so Edge straightens him out again with a sitout powerbomb. That was also of the jumping variety, because Edge is a total bastard. While Jeff's selling is patchy, I have no complaints about his bumping. He looks like a rag doll in there. Edge decides it'd be fair if he took a few licks as well and Jeff gets to cut off his missile dropkick with a dropkick. Hot tag to Matt and like Edge's hot tag, it's rather heatless, as the fans don't buy into formula anymore and both teams are babyfaces. Christian gets double-teamed and Edge shows great timing to break the fall. Timing was one of his specialities. The Hardys go for Poetry in Motion but Edge stops that with a mid air spear. Terri decides to turn heel by shoving Jeff off the buckles and weakly slapping Matt. That sets up the Unprettier and E&C claim a tag title shot. Shame the Terri angle overwhelmed the finish, but neither team needed to take a clean job. Matt gets pissy with Terri but she hired the APA so they murder the Hardys to collect payment, leading to a short-lived union between Terri and E&C.
Final Rating: ***½

Backstage: Edge & Christian are happy to go to *WrestleMania* as top contenders and claim the Hardys would have taken the win any way they could as well. Elsewhere Big Show whinges about how he won the *Royal Rumble* match and asks for footage of the Rumble finish. Rock's feet do indeed touch first and Show should have gone to 'Mania. Show doesn't behave like a heel, but the fans don't care for whinging and Rock is the bigger star. Although tonight's booking won't reflect that.

The Big Bossman vs. Tazz
This is not quite what Tazz had in mind for his second PPV match, working a washed up veteran and his pierced sidekick Prince Albert. Given Tazz's diminutive stature they needed to book him against and over big name talents quickly to establish him as a real threat. Beating Angle was good, but he needed someone who could bump for him here. Bossman isn't it. He's not even that old, at 36, but his career began so long ago that his style just doesn't fit into Attitude. I never got his persistent WWF run during the era and he'd routinely be in bad matches. Tazz has it won with a very quick Tazzmission, but Albert jumps in for the DQ and subsequent double teaming, which makes Tazz look like a total punk. Tazz keeps fighting back so Bossman breaks his night stick over Tazz's head. That shuts the crowd up in a hurry and Tazz blades off it. He comes

---

FURIOUS ABOUT: RAVEN
I've always liked Scott Levy. In WCW, in the early 90s, he was an entertaining cruiserweight. In the WWF he was the hilarious upper class fop called Johnny Polo, endearing himself to the HoW offices with his ridiculous claims and wonderful relationship with "Uncle" Gorilla Monsoon. His career took an astonishing turn when he signed for ECW. He stripped away his colourful WWF façade and turned to the darkness as Raven. A grunge rocker gimmick, Raven delivered outstanding promos that cut other ECW talent to the core and in particular he had amazing feuds with Tommy Dreamer and the Sandman. Taking two personalities and fleshing them out with extraordinary psychological warfare. Turning Sandman's wife and son against him was a work of pure evil. Raven's two-year run in ECW changed perception of him and made him famous enough that WCW threw cash his way in 1997 and brought him into the fold. Raven was a misfit in WCW but he knew that and formed The Flock, taking a bunch of other misfits and making them into something useful. Raven's WCW run was full of highlights, like him passing out in the Crippler Crossface and smiling as he did so, the Raven's Rules hardcore matches, the feud with DDP and Saturn's destruction of the Flock. Vince McMahon wasn't a fan though, and when Jim Ross hired Raven he was met with criticism from the boss. Raven had a few good matches in the WWF, including an excellent hardcore match with Rhyno.

fighting back again but tenacity wasn't Tazz's main reason for being over, it was the trail of destruction he left. He should have at least suplexed one of these guys on their head.
Final Rating: ½*

No Holds Barred
Kane vs. X-Pac
Pac turned on Kane, after saying they were "bros", and then stole Kane's girlfriend Tori. I know they felt the need to pile it on thick with X-Pac's heel actions, but Tori went from being an interesting character to another bitch diva. The WWF was obsessed with turning its ladyfolk heel. Pac rather upped the ante by launching a "wall of fire" at Kane on *SmackDown!*. It's all about the psychology of Kane being burned as a child. It's credit to X-Pac that Kane had some of his best singles matches, to that point, against the DXer despite them being rather short. Kane pretty much no sells everything X-Pac does until Pac uses the ring bell. Pac tries for a chair shot but Paul Bearer lays him out. When you get knocked down and beaten up by Paul Bearer, you know you're small fry. Kane continues to beat the crap out of X-Pac getting massive pops for doing so until a chokeslam brings Tori in. Kane wriggles her off his back into a Tombstone, provoking JR into yelling "TOMBSTONE TORI". She was one of the original recipients of the famous "jezebel" insult JR liked to throw around because old-timey swearing can be fun. I'm disappointed he never calls her a harlot or a shrew. Kane grabs the ring steps but Pac kicks him into his face and jumps on top for the upset win. There's something to be said for X-Pac in 2000, and indeed 1999, for making Kane, previously a one-trick pony, into an entertaining character. He's not quite sunk into X-Pac heat yet, although the moment is getting closer. Here he was still a viable commodity.
Final Rating: **¼

Backstage: The Radicalz are interviewed about their WWF PPV debut. Malenko and Benoit are sorely lacking in personality.

Too Cool & Rikishi vs. The Radicalz
Eddie is still out with a busted elbow, but he's at ringside to offer moral support (in the form of a metal bar). Rikishi steals the bar and bashes Eddie in the elbow to eliminate that "support". It's not the first time Eddie has been incapacitated by a bar. Considering how the WWF lucked in to four readymade top stars in the Radicalz, it's amazing how many jobs they managed to endure in their first couple of months. As if Vince couldn't resist killing something WCW branded. It's easy to forget that under all that gimmick Too Cool are both decent wrestlers. The histrionics are rather overwhelming, which is a pity because it makes the Radicalz look like a pack of assholes. Benoit even takes a Stinkface. For a moment I'm sure he was wishing he'd stayed in WCW, seeing as he'd be World Champion instead of nose deep in a Samoan's ass. There's one guy who can't be made to look stupid though; Dean Malenko, because he's so goddamn good it's just impossible. Malenko may be the best technician in modern wrestling history. On the other side of the ring Rikishi has a bad ankle, which limits his participation and makes the match a lot better than you'd expect. Saturn tends to stay out as well, leaving two regular tag teams having a good tag team match. 2000 was a renaissance year for tag team wrestling. The Radicalz run formula heat on Scotty and they are great at it. All of them. Even Saturn who pops off ranas and slingshot hilos. He's a decent flier with some muscle to back it up. Malenko is just perfect, but Benoit alongside him also shows a tonne of aggression. Benoit's ability was to make things look realistic and his selling was unparalleled. Rikishi gets the hot tag and kills Saturn with the Rikishi Driver. The match promptly goes to hell as Too Cool are more interested in getting Scotty to do the Worm than actually competing and being realistic. Welcome to the WWF, fellas. Enjoy playing second fiddle to two goofs and a dancing fatty. Saturn handily re-positions himself for the Hip Hop Drop, seeing as Grandmasta Sexay didn't bother checking to see where he was before heading up top. Saturn does an amazing job of moving into position without making it look like he is. Compare that to Kane moving for Chris Jericho's Lionsault later in the year (at *Survivor Series*) and it's no contest. That's what the Radicalz brought to the dance. Rikishi Driver for Malenko and Rikishi squashes him in the corner for another Radicalz job. They really should have gone over here. You shouldn't need to rebuild your best workers and new hires after a few weeks of booking. Regardless, the Radicalz were terrific here and that's without their top asset; Eddie Guerrero.
Final Rating: ***½

Tangent: Seeing as this is my first show with Chris Benoit on, I guess I should probably address the child murdering elephant in the room. I've come to terms with Benoit's crimes and I can sufficiently differentiate between Benoit the bastard and Benoit the wrestler. I still enjoy his work, although less than before, even if his legacy as a man is despicable. Basically I'll be judging his matches and angles based on how good they are rather than his reprehensible behaviour.

Backstage: Kurt Angle's IC Title celebrations continue! He's been celebrating for the entire show.

The Big Show vs. The Rock
Winner gets a title shot at *WrestleMania*. Rock won the Rumble but as we have seen his feet blatantly touched first, so Show has a valid claim. This is one of those matches that only exists so the WWF Title challenger has something to do on the February PPV. Because the Rock winning outcome was so obvious the WWF decided to switch gears, which would lead to a shitty four way title match at 'Mania that Triple H won. Basically, what nobody wanted. Apart from me, at the time, as I was a big fan of heels. Rock tries to take the match at his usual breakneck pace, which Show struggles with. Rock still pops off his floatover DDT even if Show counters out of everything else with sheer power. Both guys take meaty bumps on the floor, Show's is especially impressive for a big man. Show was actually trying in early 2000 and it wasn't until later in the year that he got lazy and demoted to OVW. Rock has his work cut out regardless of that and soon finds himself repeating spots. Show wasn't great at long singles matches. That really wasn't his thing. Also, as a heel, he's not exactly clever when it comes to pacing and Rock has to frequently insert comebacks where they don't belong to make the match less boring. Ref Earl Hebner is bumped, Show hits the chokeslam and Rock blatantly starts looking out for Tim White with one eye. Earl Hebner pulls Timmy out causing a ref argument. Shane McMahon comes out to stop that and leaps into the ring to tattoo Rock with a flying chair shot. Awesome timing from Shane. Show throws an arm over Rock and Tim counts the three. The only other possible reason for putting Show over was to try and convince people that Mick Foley might beat Triple H and head to *WrestleMania* as he'd be facing a heel.
Final Rating: **

Backstage: Kurt Angle continues to celebrate, which pisses Jericho off enough that he beats the IC champ up and throws him into the boot of his own rental car. Chyna's purple velour tracksuit is very distracting.

Hell in a Cell
WWF Championship
Triple H (c) vs. Cactus Jack

Mick is so desperate to beat Triple H and go on to main event *WrestleMania* that he's put his career on the line. If Hunter wins, Mick has to retire. This match was not an easy feat for either man as they had to try and one-up their terrific match at the *Royal Rumble* (as well as the Hell in a Cell from *King of the Ring '98*). Hunter pays Mick tremendous respect by coming out first, despite being champion. What happened to this guy? The respect makes this one of the all-time best filler feuds for a champion before *WrestleMania*. As the Cell lowers, Cactus discovers the door is covered in locks to prevent him from taking this to the top of the cell. Stephanie helpfully yells "there's no way out", thus mentioning the name of the PPV. They open with brawling, mirroring the Rumble match. Next comes Jack's search for weapons, this time opting for a chair. As per usual that misfires for him. Next is Cactus taking sickening bumps into the ring steps. I know he had bad knees and that's why he was retiring, but that doesn't mean he needs to take ridiculous bumps on them. It's as if he though retiring from wrestling meant he'd never use his knees for anything again. Hunter takes the Double Arm DDT on a chair, which should finish and would in any normal environment. Seeing as it's a retirement match, Hunter kicks out and nobody even worries about it. They run a great spot where Hunter is punched into a set up chair, then Jack charges him for the knee strike and Hunter slips off into a drop toehold into the chair. That's how you combine environment and moveset to make something special happen. Hunter takes a catapult into the Cell and drops under the apron for a really obvious bladejob. Hunter went through a phase where he seemed to enjoy bleeding. It wasn't even a harsh looking bump to set up the gigjob. Stephanie breaks out some more top notch selling to react to Cactus hitting a chair assisted elbow drop off the top rope to the floor. Cactus throws the ring steps at Hunter and it goes through the cage wall, which draws an enormous pop and the fans realise Cactus can get out of the Cell thus opening up the possibility of insanity. Both guys take vicious bumps through the busted section, Cactus busting his arm wide open in the process. Cactus goes for his patented piledriver on the announce table, the only move he's got that can beat Hunter. Apart from the big elbow... off a cage.

Cactus tries to climb but Steph drags him back down. That irks Jack but then he remembers he stashed a 2x4 wrapped in barbed wire at ringside and grabs it. Hunter takes it full in the forehead and that would have been a good spot to bleed off. Hunter wants to escape the barbed wire and climbs the Cell to do so, and Cactus follows. The fans start to lose their minds at this point. Cactus makes the mistake of bringing his 2x4 with him and Hunter rakes it across his face causing Cactus to drop through the Spanish announce table. "Mick is hurt" shouts JR and I'm not surprised because the monitors weren't moved or anything. This mirrors the original Mick Foley Hell in a Cell bump and in a bit he'll mimic the other one too. Cactus is busted wide open and decides to throw a chair onto the top of the Cell. Hunter's reaction shots are great. He stands back, wary of the chair but bleeding profusely and a mix of scared and anxious. He still has the 2x4 though so nails Cactus with it. The barbed wire shreds Foley's shirt and they work in more vicious barbed wire shots than at the Rumble, but the fans are already a little desensitised to it. Hunter makes the dubious decision to take a massive back bump on the top of the Cell and almost goes through the corner, which isn't over the ring or anything. Cactus, nutcase that he is, hits the Double Arm DDT on the Cell. What would have happened if the roof gave way on that spot? Cactus didn't only stash the 2x4 wrapped in barbed wire, he stashed fire on the top of the Cell too and lights that 2x4 up. The fans go crazy for that and Jack wafts the flaming 2x4 in Hunter's general direction. Cactus wants a piledriver on the fire but takes a backdrop, the Cell gives way and Mick goes through the canvas. "Holy shit" – the crowd. "Holy shit" – Triple H. "Yay" – Stephanie McMahon. "Uuueerrauuuughhh" – Cactus Jack. Cactus does an epic sell job even though the landing was much safer than at *King of the Ring '98* as they gimmicked the ring this time. Interesting to note the set up chair in the corner almost comes back to haunt Mick, just like the one at *King of the Ring*. This time he gets lucky. Hunter is totally freaked out by the whole thing and slowly approaches Jack's corpse, but Cactus starts moving. I love Hunter's reaction to that too. Cactus manages to get to his knees so Hunter pummels him back down. Pedigree! Cactus has nothing left, after taking two massive bumps, and stays down for the career ending three count. Hell of a way for Mick Foley to go out and during his last two matches he left it all in the ring. The match has a similar vibe to the Rumble one, but it felt like less of an achievement as they'd already done the match once. This one had bigger bumps and bigger emotion, and yet somehow feels slightly less satisfying.

Final Rating: ****½

Post Match: EMTs come down to stretcher Mick out but he refuses their help. He looks absolutely destroyed, physically and emotionally. The crowd chant "Foley" while JR puts over Mick as a person, pointing out how many assholes there are in the business and how genuine Mick is. Mick staggers out to a standing ovation. His final salute as he walks through the curtain is so sad, but at least he went out on his own terms. Well, until next month when he came back and wrestled at *WrestleMania*. Mick's return slightly taints this match too, and without his participation at *WrestleMania*, and indeed all the matches since, especially in TNA, I could consider going up to full board on the snowflakes. At any rate, it's one of the best Hell in a Cell matches, only really bettered by the first one with Taker and Shawn. And this one has a decisive finish. Another must see bout and if you're reading this you've likely seen it. The good news is, it still holds up.

Backstage: The Coach brings us an exclusive wrap up for WWF Home Video. Not exactly how I'd end the tape, as Mick's farewell was so perfect. We see interviews with a load of the participants done by Coach.

VERDICT

They crammed a few too many matches in here, but there were some tremendous highlights. Hunter-Cactus II delivered with an emotional farewell for Mick Foley. It's not all about that match, despite it being fantastic, as the Dudley Boyz won the tag titles, Kurt Angle won his first major title by becoming IC champ and both the tag division and the singles division got big boosts from Edge, Christian, the Hardys and the Radicalz. Even Kane and X-Pac was pretty good. As a show it flew by and had very few weak points. It comes pretty highly recommended.

77

WRESTLEMANIA 2000

CAT NO: WWF246
RUN TIME: 215 minutes (approx)

Arnold Furious: Coming off two stellar PPVs (both headlined by epic Hunter-Cactus matches) the WWF was revved up and ready for *WrestleMania*. I was too and I think my level of expectation for this show was completely unmatched and unparalleled by any other show, ever, in the history of wrestling. That might be overselling it a bit but I was ridiculously excited for it at the time, hoping for an amazing event, packed with great wrestling. It didn't quite pan out that way and of the three shows that start 2000 this is the weakest, which it shouldn't be as *WrestleMania* should always be in the running for the best PPV of the year, yet in 2000 it wasn't even close.

We're in Anaheim, California at the Arrowhead Pond, home of *WrestleMania XII*. Hosts are Jim Ross and Jerry Lawler. The crowd's muted reaction at the beginning of the show is a bad sign, and *WrestleMania* has actually suffered quite a few dead crowds over the years. Lillian Garcia sings the American national anthem. I still don't agree with the American bollocks that permeates the WWF at times. As a global company it should behave like one.

**The Godfather & D'Lo Brown
vs. The Big Bossman & Bull Buchanan**
Godfather gets rapped to the ring by Ice T constantly rapping "pimpin' ain't easy". I'm amazed Ice T can contain his language and only let's slip two "bitches" and absolutely no "motherfuckers"! I'm startled. D'Lo was going through a spell as a pimp in training while his "opposite" Bull Buchanan is Bossman's protégé. Buchanan had previously been Recon in the Truth Commission. Oddly enough both understudies would form a tag team in Pro Wrestling NOAH and were GHC tag champs, for all of a week. Brown vs. Buchanan isn't a bad match, though Bull isn't over enough to be working *WrestleMania*. This is also not good enough to be a hot opener, again, especially at 'Mania. Get things off with a bang, not a whimper. Bull manages his one sensational spot; leaping to the top rope and flying off with a back elbow, which is impressive athleticism for a big man. He has no personality though, which is death in the WWF. If you can't name a single characteristic of a guy, if you can't describe him without mentioning his appearance then that guy is never, ever going to get over. He's big, he's bald. Does he look like a bitch? That only works if you've seen *Pulp Fiction*. Anyway, the match just plods by and some asshole, some absolute tool, decided to give it 9-minutes. 9-minutes! They have maybe 3-minutes of stuff. Later on Benoit, Jericho and Angle only get 13-minutes for two falls. D'Lo at least inserts a fan friendly super rana even if the set up is incredibly clunky. Godfather hits the Ho Train only for Bull to save Bossman from the Lo Down. D'Lo runs right into the Bossman Slam and Bull adds a mahoosive leg jam for the pin. The opposite of a hot opener and *WrestleMania 2000*'s first big stupid mistake.
Final Rating: ¾*

Backstage: Hunter and Stephanie kick back and enjoy the moment as they're both World Champions and in the storylines have just put on the biggest *WrestleMania* of all time. JR speculates that Hunter is very relaxed considering he's defending his title against three guys later and thinks it's psychological warfare. Well, he is the 'Cerebral Assassin'.

**Battle Royal
WWF Hardcore Championship**
Participants: Crash Holly (c), Tazz, Viscera, Rodney, Pete Gas, Joey Abs, Hardcore Holly, Taka Michinoku, Funaki, Mosh, Thrasher, Bradshaw, Faarooq

This match has a 15-minute time limit and pins are legal during the whole thing, with no eliminations. Whoever holds the belt at the end is champion. The Hardcore Title being defended 24 hours a day was an interesting gimmick although they could have taken it even further. Anyone who's a fan of Japanese promotion DDT will understand what I mean by that. They took the hardcore concept and cranked it up to 11. Former DDT Ironman Heavymetalweight champions include a monkey, a dog, several stuffed dolls, three different ladders, a poster, a chair, a beer, a stuffed doll of wrestler Jun Kasai (two-time champ) and Misutero, who is an invisible wrestler. The match where a dog beats a ladder is on YouTube. Fill your boots.

Tazz manages to isolate Crash in the early going and pin him with a capture suplex for the belt. Now Tazz is the defending champion for the remainder of the match. Vis crushes Tazz against the ring post and then squashes him with a splash on the floor for the title. In between pinfalls everyone just brawls around the ring using assorted crap as weapons; Bradshaw nails someone with a phone, Crash bleeds all over the place to show how hardcore he is, Vis ends up a tough nut to crack and manages to hold the belt for half the match. Bradshaw seems to enjoy this environment more than most, given his size, power and viciousness. He goes on an absolute rampage, nailing everyone with plunder. Pete Gas bleeds a gusher, which must be worrying for a rookie. At least that should take the edge off any *WrestleMania* nerves. Poor Rodney and his shock of blonde hair gets rough treatment from half a dozen guys. Bradshaw murders Taka with a powerbomb, which he nailed. The APA go after Vis and beat the crap out of him but throw Funaki on top for the pin suggesting they didn't want a bull's-eye on their back for the rest of the match. Taka was on top too and gets steamed with Funaki getting the belt. Funaki decides discretion is the better part of valour and RUNS away. The Posse go after him and Rodney manages a title reign of a matter of seconds before Joey Abs hits a gutwrench suplex for the belt. Thrasher runs Abs into a roller shutter for the title as it rapidly changes hands. Thrasher takes such a pasting backstage that he heads back to the ring where there are still a few big hitters remaining. Pete Gas doesn't let him get that far and tags Thrasher with a fire extinguisher for the title. Gas is bleeding all over his sweater. He's Hardcore! Tazz dumps him on his head with an exploder suplex for another title run, his first being about 40 seconds. He lasts longer during his second run until he, Crash and Hardcore Holly battle it out in the ring with time expiring. Everyone else remains ringside bashing each other in the noggin with crap. The Hollys take it in turns to try for the belt and Tazz is so dopey from head shots he keeps going for pins that don't do anything. Crash nails Tazz with a metal sheet to reclaim his title but Tazz immediately chokes him out with the Tazzmission. Crash holds on but Hardcore hits both men with JR's candy jar and takes the title with a second remaining. I think they botched the finish as Crash runs off with the belt. Seeing as it's the Hardcore Title and no-one cares about title changes, Hardcore Holly ends up with the belt by mistake and Crash wins it back on *RAW* the next night. Crash would go on to hold the belt 22 times. This was fun crap, with the last couple of minutes being the most creative.

Final Rating: **½

Video Control gives us footage from the *WrestleMania* weekend and everything that was attached to 'Mania in 2000. There are tonnes of signings, actual wrestling matches and cool stuff. I think 2000 was the first year they really nailed the Fan Access weekend and it's been gold ever since.

Backstage: Al Snow is interrupted in his preparation for *WrestleMania* by tag team partner Steve Blackman. It seems Al has a surprise for his Head Cheese buddy. Elsewhere Trish Stratus' boobs walk. The left one is called Test and the right one Albert.

Head Cheese vs. T & A
Al introduces us to Chester McCheeserton, a midget dressed as a block of cheese who's going to play "let's go Head-Cheese" on his ass cheeks. Head Cheese was the first time Steve Blackman got over as a face but for some reason the WWF thought it didn't work and stopped the silliness. Trish Stratus is the star of the T&A team, without making it into the ring. She's way more popular than everyone else, even the silly Head Cheese team. JR's headset packs up leaving Jerry to spend the match drooling over Trish's cleavage. Not that there's a match worth talking about. As much as I love Albert and his impossibly big head, he was always a second until going to New Japan and learning how to work. It got to the point where Albert was having genuinely awesome singles matches with top Japanese talent. While you'd never think that at this stage of his career, here he's still a guilty pleasure of mine. The most entertaining part of the match is the camera catching Chester checking out Trish at ringside. Can't say I blame him. Trish is ridiculously hot at this point her career, and most points after it, and is one of my favourite divas, ever. It's a pity she's not wrestling as she ended up a better in ring talent than Test and Blackman. That's not even a joke! JR calls the match ugly just as Snow hits an Asai moonsault on Albert to shut him up. It really is a mess though. The tags are all over the place and nobody seems to want to lead. T&A have slightly better teamwork. Blackman gets distracted by Chester one time too many and Albert slams him ahead of a Test Savage Elbow drop. JR pretty much buries the match by claiming "neither team got it on track". The match was a mess and everybody knows it, but at least they tried and you certainly couldn't call the work lazy. Post match Al says it's time to cut the cheese and turns heel on poor Chester.

Final Rating: ***

Backstage: The Kat prepares with Mae Young for tonight and objects keep covering up her nudity in a spot lifted from *Austin Powers*.

Elsewhere: The Dudley Boyz accuse the WWF of screwing with them by putting them in a ladder match at *WrestleMania* when D-Von is afraid of heights. Bubba points out they're ready to take the ladder match to a "whole new level of violence".

Triangle Ladder Match
WWF Tag Team Championship
The Dudley Boyz (c) vs. Edge & Christian vs. Hardy Boyz
This match is deliberately slanted to steal the show with these guys basically reinventing the possibilities of a ladder match. It's also the opportunity for tag teams to do the business on the biggest show of the year, which is new for the WWF. All three teams had been working decent matches with each other stemming from the E&C vs. Hardys ladder match at *No Mercy '99*. It's hard to imagine it, considering the Duds are the champs and the Hardys have held the straps, that Edge & Christian have not been the WWF Tag Team Champions to this point. Jeff starts the match aiming to steal the show, which is exactly what he did at *No Mercy* and he hits a few flying spots in the early going. This culminates in him missing a 450 Splash on a ladder with Bubba moving. His shins! Bubba follows with a senton bomb with a ladder in play. As the match continues everyone starts taking those Jeff-level bumps involving ladders. Every spot looks painful. Bubba works the old Terry Funk spinning ladder spot for a dash of comedy sauce to break up the brutality. Christian is the first to come off the ladder hitting a dive onto Bubba and Matt at ringside and that garners a "holy shit" chant. But better is to come! Jeff climbs the ladder in search of belts and Edge spears him off it by diving off the top rope. Matt takes Edge off the ladder with a sit out Razor's Edge and he absolutely PLANTS Edge with it. They get clever by setting up a ladder each, thus giving us three set up and organically arriving at a silly spot. The first one is Bubba giving Christian a cutter off the top of the ladders. Both guys are screwed from that. The Hardys both climb ladders to splash/legdrop Bubba. But he was already dead! E&C suplex D-Von over the top of a ladder and every spot is met with "OOOOOOHHHHH" from Anaheim who are loving

every minute of this.

They up the ante with everyone climbing on duelling ladders and both Jeff and Christian take massive bumps over the top rope. This is a career shortening environment. The Dudleys are left standing alone and Christian staggers back inside into a ladder sandwich. 3D on Edge! Bubba goes nuts and the Dudleys get the tables! Their determination to murder people through tables rather derails their title aspirations. At the point where they grab the tables everyone else is down and they have the match won, but feel the urge to build a load of furniture and platform under the belts with a table. It's a big storyline flaw as they stop to set up a spot instead of just winning. It's something I feel happens too often in the famous TLC series and it's very evident at this point in this match. Matt takes a vicious powerbomb through a table but D-Von misses with a splash on Jeff to do the same to both Hardys. Jeff tries a follow up railrunner on Bubba but he'd picked up a ladder and throws it in Jeff's face in mid air. Another storyline crack sees Bubba set up a ridiculous ladder in the ramp and a table under it. He grabs Jeff by his hair. Time to die, Jeffykins! Christian saves with the ring bell allowing Jeff to go up top and destroy Bubba with a batshit crazy Swanton Bomb off the stupidly tall ladder. That just stuns the crowd and eliminates both men from the match. Matt and Christian head up but Edge shoves Matt off through a table in the most dangerous spot of the night and E&C claim the tag titles. Years of similar silly matches with contrived bumps have hurt the reputation of this one. It has lots of wild bumps in it and at the time people were calling it a MOTYC. It's certainly good fun but not MOTY by any stretch of the imagination.
Final Rating: ****

Backstage: Mick Foley with a haircut and sudden weight gain gets interviewed with the thoroughly boring Linda McMahon. Mick says he wants people to talk about this match for the next 10 years. They won't, unfortunately. Certainly the two matches in the months prior had already left Mick with a good legacy, though he did finally have a "*WrestleMania*" moment" years later with Edge, courtesy of a spear through a flaming table.

Cat Fight
Terri vs. The Kat
The winner is the person to throw their opponent out of the ring, which is a stupid stipulation. The referee is Val Venis, presumably because he's a pervert. His referee towel is a cute touch. Terri floated into this useless feud by turning heel on the Hardys because she was holding them back. Both girls have old fossils in their corner. Terri has Moolah while newly bleached blonde Kat has Mae Young. Both wrestlers make out with the referee to try and gain an advantage. Val gets distracted by Mae, the most worthless second in history, while Kat throws Terri to the floor. Mae then goes after Val like a horny bitch and Kat wins again, which Val misses because of Mae. Moolah drags Kat to the floor and Terri wins via stupidity. This was an absolute heap of shit. A total abortion. They should have gotten rid of everybody involved in it. I can't fathom why this was on the *WrestleMania* card and I can only assume it was done because both of them were relatively comfortable with nudity. Not that there's any nudity in the match, but their willingness to strip off equated to a 'Mania pay day and we all had to sit through it.
Final Rating: -****

Backstage: Eddie Guerrero is bit smitten with Chyna, which ticks off Saturn and Malenko. Eddie promises to lay all his Latino Heat on Chyna. In the babyface locker room Chyna voms in her mouth a bit.

Eddie Guerrero, Dean Malenko & Perry Saturn
vs. Too Cool & Chyna
Great to see Eddie recover from an elbow injury to make his *WrestleMania* debut. This may be personal bias but Eddie is one of the best wrestlers of his generation and was my favourite wrestler from the point where Bret left the WWF to Eddie's death. Chyna does a bit of dancing with Grandmasta Sexay and she's pretty good. Eddie dominates in the in-ring proceedings whether he's taking heat or delivering spots on Scotty, who makes a good punching bag. Eddie is kinetic and at one point goes from dancing to laying Chyna out to taking a monstrous suplex to the floor in a 10 second spell. Saturn does a pretty decent Shawn Michaels impression doing his superkick/Savage Elbow bit, only he gets more height on the elbow than Shawn and does them the other way round. The match builds with Eddie avoiding Chyna until Chyna hits handspring back elbows and double nut shots on Malenko and Saturn. Eddie jumps her from behind but Chyna escapes a powerbomb and hits Eddie with her own. Her pants nearly fall down in the process. Chyna had switched from sensible to sexy wrestling gear and this particular outfit is rubbish. Chyna puts Eddie away with a sleeper slam and the Radicalz lose yet again! Astonishing booking. As someone who believes Malenko should have been main eventing, this kind of booking baffles me. Decent match but the finish takes the edge off it somewhat.
Final Rating: **¾

Video Control gives us a quick interview with Shane McMahon where he puts the Big Show over before we see Kurt Angle slapping the Crossface chicken-wing on Bob Backlund for causing the double title defence for him tonight. Elsewhere Vince McMahon says he will be a factor in the main event, but believes the Rock doesn't need his help. He guarantees to "make it right". Meanwhile Triple H says none of this matters as he won't allow himself to lose the title because he is "that damn good". Steph gives a little "woo" after that as she was feeling it.

WWF Intercontinental Championship
WWF European Championship
Kurt Angle (c)(c) vs. Chris Jericho vs. Chris Benoit
Angle comes in with both titles but they'll be decided in separate falls, so the first fall is for the IC Title then the second for the European Title. You'd think it'd be the other way around but such is booking in the WWF sometimes. Jericho cuts a pre-match promo, which is as daft as he is but causes crowd adoration. Three way matches are usually a bad idea as they have kooky selling and weird psychology. Luckily all three of these guys are great workers so it's less of a mess than it might have been. The selling is still odd. Benoit goes to the floor early and spends a little too long there. It's all a bit disjointed and they might have been better off having Angle wrestle Jericho first, then Benoit or vice versa. Jericho takes the first big bump off the match, off the top rope and into the announce table in the same bump Foley will later take in the main event… only Jericho lands it. I like how Lawler notices that Jericho wrestles like a heel because he's spent most of his recent career as one. It's like Ventura pointing out Hogan's flaws, only Lawler is less creative. Angle demonstrates an issue with his finisher when he hits a back suplex and it looks remarkably similar to the Olympic Slam. The match is a mess but at least everyone executes their spots clean as a whistle, seeing as they're all top guys. Angle's suplexes are a thing of beauty and his learning curve is amazingly steep. It puts the Rock's improvement from 1996 into 1997 to shame, which is

saying something. They run a nice counters spot in the corner as all three guys get onto the same page. Moments like that would proliferate later, better, triple threat matches (like those from TNA featuring A.J. Styles, Christopher Daniels and Samoa Joe). Chicken-wing on Jericho and he passes out leaving Benoit to save. Benoit tosses Angle into the crowd, Jericho is still out so Benoit finishes him with the Swandive headbutt for the IC Title.

Benoit goes immediately for another pin and Angle has to sprint back in to save his European Title. Angle goes up for a moonsault, Jericho crotches him and Benoit back suplexes Jericho off, freeing up Angle for the moonsault, which misses. Good sequence. Jericho gets the Walls on Kurt but Benoit saves. Jericho just about hits his double powerbomb on Angle but Benoit interrupts the pin with the rolling Germans. As the natural fatigue selling kicks in, they're able to structure a better match. The selling is more consistent. Timmy White eats a flying forearm off Jericho but Chris turns into the Crippler Crossface and taps out. There's no ref or Benoit would have been a double champion. Benoit's attempts to revive the ref crack me up. "Ref. Ref. Ref. REF. REF. REEEEEFFFF. REEFFFFFFF!" As if he's only staying down because he's hard of hearing. Benoit misses the Swandive on Angle and Jericho hits him with a Lionsault for the European Title, thus jobbing both titles off Angle without him losing either fall. The match got better and smarter as it progressed.
Final Rating: ***¼

X-Pac & Road Dogg vs. Rikishi & Kane
DX's new entrance music, as if they needed it, is rapped by Run DMC. They have Tori in their corner. Tori slaps Paul Bearer but he no sells it. What was with Bearer in 2000? First he's picking fights with X-Pac and now he's not selling! Rikishi gives Road Dogg an early Stinkface. Tori finds herself in trouble right after that as she escapes Kane by jumping into the ring but X-Pac saves her from an ass in the face. Road Dogg gets painfully no sold by Rikishi, which demonstrates why he never got a big singles push despite being a legitimate talent. Both he and X-Pac take slick bumps for the two big men and generally salvage what should be a mismatched mess. It is a nothing match though, intended entirely as a placeholder before the main event. It's full of filler spots like Tori taking the Stinkface and it ends quickly with Kane hitting a Tombstone on X-Pac to finally get his revenge. A pity the revenge is hidden away in a corner at *WrestleMania* instead of getting a more meaningful chunk of a less important PPV.
Final Rating: *½

Post Match: Too Cool run down for a big *WrestleMania* dance and the San Diego Chicken follows. Kane looks at him funny, like Jason Voorhees aiming to murder a teen. The fans are desperate to see Kane dance but that's outside his comfort zone. The chicken joins in the dancing while Kane stares a hole in him. Pete Rose jumps in behind Kane hoping to get his revenge on the burned up monster. Rikishi cuts him off, as if he needed to, and Kane hits a chokeslam. Stinkface follows as the WWF continue to have a good laugh at the expense of Pete Rose.

Backstage: The Rock stops off Kevin Kelly so he can address the millions… and millions of the Rock's fans. Rock cuts a dynamic promo saying this show isn't about the McMahons or even Mick Foley's final match, it's about the WWF Title. We head to ringside and see a few celebrities including Michael Clarke Duncan and Martin Short. When they zoom in on Martin he assumes they're looking at someone else, and behind him,

FURIOUS ABOUT: DEAN MALENKO

Malenko is one of the finest technical wrestlers to ever lace up a pair of boots. He began to get noticed working in Japan in the early 90s but had been in the business as far back as 1979. He even worked for the WWF in the 80s as a referee, something we pointed out back in Volume #1. He formed a team with his brother Joe and they worked for AJPW. ECW picked the brothers up but quickly discovered Dean was the horse to bet on and paired up with Eddy Guerrero in a series of terrific wrestling matches in 1995. Too good, in fact, as WCW signed them both immediately and Malenko began a career of being overlooked yet considered a great worker. His WCW career largely consisted of midcard/cruiserweight feuds without much emotion but with tonnes of hard work. The peak of this being the Benoit feud, which resulted in a match at Hog Wild '96, which would easily have been ***** with a better crowd. He had another memorable feud with Chris Jericho where the Canuck mercilessly belittled him and his family. He joined the WWF with the rest of the Radicalz but retired in 2001.

thinking everyone is looking at him is Dustin Diamond, aka Screech from *Saved By the Bell*. I don't know which is more tragic; Martin thinking he's not famous or Screech thinking he is.

WWF Championship
Triple H (c) vs. Mick Foley vs. The Big Show vs. The Rock
A McMahon in every corner; Steph with her husband, Linda with Mick, Shane with Show and Vince with Rock. The McMahon gimmick only exists so Vince can turn on Rock at the end of the show and this match really should have been HHH vs. Rock as it was the biggest match in the company. Did the WWF get cold feet regarding Rock and Hunter's ability to carry the main event? Or was Foley getting such ridiculous love for the first two PPVs of the year that they felt he belonged here, and Show ended up along for the ride? This is no DQ and is under elimination rules, which is the first smart piece of booking surrounding the match. Vince tries to mess with Hunter by standing where the Tripper normally does his water spit. They start off by pairing up; Hunter vs. Mick and Show vs. Rock. Foley looks in poor condition having left most of his career splattered over the ring at *No Way Out* last month. Show dominates with his size including a wicked biel on Hunter halfway across the ring. They all begin to realise that Show's power and size is something they must eliminate and all three guys team up to get rid of Show. This puts Show well and truly in his place. Rock Bottom finishes him off after a Foley chair shot. He flopped back face after *WrestleMania*, which is typical of his whole career. A mixture of underachievement and an inability to define his role.

Lawler, an old school heel, thinks that Hunter is shit outta luck here (as it's two faces versus one heel). Hunter offers to team with Mick who shakes his head, so he goes to Rock instead who agrees and sucker punches Hunter in the back of the head. Of course Mick and Rock were a regular tag team during 1999 as the Rock N' Sock Connection and Rock rallied against the Helmsleys to get Mick reinstalled when he was fired. Foley brings his usual idiocy by giving Rock the ring bell to hit Hunter with and, as per usual, the weapon backfires on Mick as Rock miscues. Foley goes for the barbed wire 2x4 and Hunter's sell is tremendous; the memories of the last two months coming flooding back as he topples over backwards. Naturally, as Mick brought it into play, it backfires on him. Double Arm DDT sets up Mr. Socko, as Foley, wrestling as himself, can use all his personality stuff. Rock belts Hunter to set up the People's Elbow and Mick sees an opening for the Mandible Claw on Rock. You idiot! Just eliminate Triple H first! The crowd gets conflicted and a mesh of "Foley" and "Rocky" chants ring out, which is probably why they didn't finish with Foley-Rock, but honestly they probably should have done. Although I'm conflicted as Hunter going over here made him a dominant heel champion, something the WWF had never had. Man, booking is hard! Rock kicks out of Foley's Double Arm DDT. To be fair to Mick, he really tries hard here even if he's in rough shape. Mick gets a lot of heat for teaming with Hunter, thinking he has a better shot at beating Hunter than he does Rock. Which is a bit perverse as, based on historical results, the opposite was true. Hunter sets Rock on the Spanish announce table for Foley to elbow drop him through it. Foley, with his knees knackered, can't make it and lands sternum first on the edge. Hunter has a hell of a match with the Spanish table, finally jumping off the rail to break it. Pedigree for Foley but Mick kicks out again, making the previously killer finisher ever so slightly fallible. Chair shot. Pedigree on a chair and Foley is toast. I seem to remember a few people picking Foley to win the title here but that was based on his performances over the previous two months and what remained of Foley was never going to win. At least he gets a nice send off from the fans as they chant "Foley" as he hobbles out holding his chest. He can't quite resists nailing Hunter with the barbed wire 2x4 on his way out.

You'd think that would set up Rock to take the title. Meanwhile Rock has been down selling a blown spot for about 4-minutes while all this was going on. Hunter was left alone for so long he has time to blade. "Finish that sucker" – Michael Clarke Duncan. Seeing as (Hardcore Title aside) the matches tonight have mainly taken place by ringside, Hunter and Rock head up the entranceway for a Main Event Brawl. It allows JR to deliver one of my all-time favourite calls as Rock goes to bash Hunter with the ring steps and Triple H hits the steps with a chair. JR: "Jesus Criminey". He is just desperate to avoid blaspheming and it makes me laugh every time. Hunter hits a piledriver on the ring steps and Rock keeps kicking out. They work in a few obvious finisher counters including HHH setting for a Pedigree right by the ropes, just like Scott Hall used to do to telegraph a counter. Dear opponent, kindly counter this move by backdropping me to the floor, yours sincerely HH Helmsley Esq. They follow that was a customary crowd brawl as the main event rapidly heads downhill. If there's one thing I can't stand it's two guys doing fatigue selling for measurably long spells. So when Rock hits a spinebuster both guys lie around for ages afterward. Main event of *WrestleMania*, fellas. They do a spot right after that where Rock suplexes Hunter through the announce table and that's worthy of a double down, but following on from one dead spot with another dead spot is poor. If they don't have the cardio to keep going without putting in rest spots they shouldn't go 40-minutes!

Vince gets himself involved by attacking Hunter, which brings Shane back out to brawl with his pops. This is reaching the point of ridiculousness as Rock spends an eternity down selling nothing. He's just lying in the ring while Vince and Shane brawl. The only worthwhile thing about all this is Steph's facial reactions. She had a spell of being a tremendous heel and this is bang in the middle of it. The McMahon's continue to brawl so we all now know what this main event is really about. Vince blades off a chair shot and still Rock and Hunter are just lying in the ring. Rock suddenly finds some energy, which he built up by lying around doing nothing for five minutes. That's that Main Event Style that some people don't know how to work. The match continues to rumble on as they've got to wait for Vince to come back out here and he has to sell the bladejob before that happens. Not content with that Shane gets in the ring and they run a convoluted spot where Rock catapults Hunter into him. Rock Bottom and suddenly that energy disperses again and both guys lie around doing nothing. Who booked this shit? Vince comes charging back down, lays out Shane with a terrible worked punch and chair shots Rock. Again, the only good thing about this is Steph's stunned reaction. It's brilliant. For some reason they book Rock to kick out of the first chair shot so Vince hits him again and Hunter pins to retain in one of the all-time crowd deflating moments in WWF history. Hope you're proud of that one fellas. The match is way too long and when it ends Vince and Stephanie hug it out in the ring with no wrestlers present just so we know what it was all about. I quite like the first half of the match, until Foley goes out, but the second half is so goddamn awful it defies belief. A bunch of soap opera bullshit and bad selling. Rock comes storming back down to break up the McMahon family reunion. Rock Bottom for Shane. Rock Bottom for Vince. Stephanie gets all pissy in Rock's face about it. "I don't think he'll do it King (Steph slaps Rock)… ohhhh, he might" – great call from JR. Rock Bottom for Steph! He adds in a People's Elbow, which Steph has no idea how to sell so she just lies there and takes it (ahem). At least Rock abusing McMahons sends the fans home slightly happy, but that doesn't excuse the 20-minutes of crap that occurred directly before it.

Final Rating: **¼

VERDICT

Where do you even start with this show? It's totally all over the place. The opener was dreadful, the hardcore match was silly yet entertaining, T&A vs. Head Cheese had no business being on *WrestleMania*, the tag team ladder match was enormous fun despite all the set up processes, but that was immediately followed by Terri vs. The Kat, which was just horrid. It's like the show was continually flopping between rubbish and great. Sometimes in the same match, as evidenced in the main event. Although I couldn't recommend this in good conscience, as everyone involved has done better elsewhere, all *WrestleMania* shows are still required viewing. This one shows the WWF's balls at the time, because with WCW faltering they could have taken the easy route out of their main event situation and booked The Rock to win the title. Instead they did the hard thing and stuck with a heel Triple H. It had never been done before, certainly not to this degree. Putting Triple H over this big was a vindication of his monster push and the WWF's desire to see things through with him as *the* man. Not recommended, but probably still worth seeing once.

34

TERRI RUNNELS

BACKLASH 2000

CAT NO: WWF247
RUN TIME: 174 minutes (approx)

James Dixon: Following on from the badly booked mess that was *WrestleMania 2000*, one of the most disappointing PPVs of the year, comes this show, and it has a mighty reputation...

WWF Tag Team Championship
Edge & Christian (c) vs. X-Pac & Road Dogg
But first, out comes Debra after six months off our screens, and she is the guest ring announcer. They couldn't have picked a worse job for her to do, because she is absolutely awful at it. Screechy and uninterested is a polite way to put it. I can't quite work out who the heels are because DX do their sing along entrance and seek out crowd pops. But then again, X-Pac is involved, and before it became cool to boo the babyfaces who annoy you (see: John Cena), there was X-Pac heat. He gets plenty of chants here of "X-Pac sucks" and as the match progresses the crowd continues to harass him. It's a shame his legacy will probably be this unwanted heat, because he was still a good worker when he was getting those reactions, and prior to that in the early 90s I would count him as one of the best performers in the entire world. He shows what a horrible little toe rag he is here though by spitting at his opponents, which JR calls "spatting" to my amusement. I always enjoy it when JR stumbles over what he meant to say and comes out with something like that, because it makes him seem more natural and human, rather than automated and generated by a corporate machine. He comes across like a curmudgeonly old uncle, but one with a warm heart and pleasant disposition. On screen at least. I tried watching this show with my wife, but all she could go on about was Edge and Christian's constant fiddling with their hair and how shiny Edge's tights are, so she was asked to leave. I worry at first that they are going to settle into formula, and for a little while they do as DX run heat on Christian, but thankfully outside of a brief Road Dogg chinlock they keep it interesting. After a double falling reverse DDT, Christian makes a hot tag to Edge and he sets about being a house of fire, before hitting X-Pac with a powerbomb for the first in a sequence of near falls. The crowd buys into them, and it looks to be over when X-Pac hits the X-Factor on Edge, but Christian sneaks in and belts Pac with the ring bell while the ref is distracted by Dogg and DX valet Tori, and that is enough for the champs to get the win. X-Pac bleeds like a stuck pig afterwards to heighten the impact of the bell shot, but did this match really need such an excessive finish or the use of blood, especially after the bout? Of course it didn't. A pretty good opener once they got going, but they alternated between not doing much early on and then doing too much at the end.
Final Rating: **½

WWF Light Heavyweight Championship
Dean Malenko (c) vs. Scotty 2 Hotty
I am thrilled about getting the chance to cover Dean Malenko, who I think is one of the most criminally underrated performers in the business. He is a masterful technician and a true artist of his craft, and considering his complete lack of personality and diminutive stature, he did incredibly well for himself in a big man industry. Scotty at this point is super over as a flamboyant babyface wigga, and not really known for his classic mat wrestling clinics, well not at all in fact, but that is exactly what he is forced into assembling here. Malenko bosses the match at his pace and with his style, and Scotty is capable so manages to look good in there. Malenko targets the leg, mercilessly, and just dismantles it slowly but surely, or methodically as JR puts it. Usually that is commentator slang for "slow", and while the pace is hardly breakneck, at the same time there is zero wasted motion from Malenko and every single thing he does has purpose and meaning, so it is not boring. Some of the crowd think it is and chant as such, but only a small ingrate minority. After getting outclassed for the majority of the contest, Scotty finally makes his comeback, only to get hit with a superplex, but that leaves Dean down too. They pace quickens with Scotty scoring a near fall from a backslide and Malenko responding by going for his cloverleaf finisher, only to get cradled for another close count. Malenko goes for the powerbomb, but Scotty hits the bulldog and that is of course the set up for the ridiculous Worm. Scotty then undoes all of his good work in selling the injured leg by doing the hopping section of the Worm on his bad wheel! What a complete moron. That has killed this match for me now, because it renders everything Dean did to soften him up as completely pointless. Dean kicks out and gets a near fall of his own using the ropes (the same thing he did to beat Scotty on *SmackDown!* recently) but this time the referee sees it and

stops the count. A sitout powerbomb from Malenko follows for two, and a powerslam garners the same result. Scotty is still fighting, and recovers enough to go for a superplex, but Malenko reverses it in goddamn mid air into a phenomenal DDT, and this couldn't be more over. Holy shit, what a ridiculous and brilliant finish. This was a technical wrestling master class from Malenko, but the Worm really ruined it for me. It's still a very good match though, and easily the best of Scotty's career.
Final Rating: ***½

Bull Buchanan & The Big Bossman vs. The Acolytes
I could be wrong, but I don't expect this to feature quite as much mat wrestling as the previous encounter. The term "slobberknocker" was invented for this kind of match. They start quick enough though, and mini-Bossman (Buchanan) shows some impressive athletic ability before Bradshaw smashes through him. The heel duo get more success against Faarooq, briefly, before a meaty clothesline bumps the Bossman. The Acolytes take charge for a while, but they are the babyfaces so at some point have to take heat, and that inevitably kills the crowd and thus the match, because both of them are just so badass that you can't build sympathy on them. It's the same problem Hulk Hogan had in the 80s when they tried to run house show loops with him. He never looked in peril and never lost, so the crowd had no interest in return matches against the same opponents, which is why he would do programs with various different guys. Few managed to get a run of matches in the same venues against him outside of Randy Savage. The heat here comes on Faarooq, but nothing really happens and it is brief, and thus the decibel level doesn't change at all when Bradshaw tags in. Things break down with Faarooq and Bossman brawling on the outside, then Buchanan hits a big superplex on Bradshaw for a near fall. Meanwhile, Bossman and Faarooq continue to brawl. Bradshaw hits the Clothesline From Hell on Buchanan but Bossman breaks it up, then gets nightstick happy on the Acolytes before Buchanan finishes Bradshaw with a scissor kick from the top. Impressive stuff from Bull, but the match was nothing.
Final Rating: *¼

Backstage, the Hardys warn that they will not take it easy on one another in the next match. In a different locker room, Crash Holly has the opposite idea and wants cousin Hardcore to team up with him, but Hardcore slaps him and walks off.

WWF Hardcore Championship
Crash Holly (c) vs. Tazz vs. Matt Hardy vs. Jeff Hardy vs. Hardcore Holly vs. Perry Saturn
There are six talented guys involved in this, considering it is a scrap for the Hardcore Title. The rules are that the match ends if Crash pins any of the other five guys, but those five can only pin him, which also ends the bout. Essentially it is a 5-on-1 handicap match. Everyone takes turns beating on Crash and breaking up falls at first, so Crash legs it and tries to escape up the swinging pendulums that are part of the *Backlash* set. Matt follows him up and kicks Crash down, and poor Elroy gets stuck upside down in the structure. Matt pops the crowd by following that with a dive onto all five guys from on the pendulum, before Saturn shows what a vicious bastard he is when he drills Crash through another of the pendulums. Not to be outdone, Jeff uses the swinging implements to get leverage for a rana on Saturn and then the Hardys run Crash back to the ring to finish things, only to be smashed in the skull by a tray-wielding Tazz. This is utterly chaotic and frantic, but in a good way. Things do calm down a little as everyone starts selling, so Tazz takes it upon himself to try and remove Crash's head from his shoulders with a clothesline. Hardcore brings the plunder in the form of a road sign, and drills his cousin, but can't put him away. Poor Crash tries to take a breather on the outside but everyone zones in on him like a pack of wolves. "Crash, just give them the belt, hell!" says JR, summing up his predicament. This is actually a really smartly booked match, because unlike the mindless chaos and silliness at *WrestleMania* last month, this has structure and the unique rules tell a very easy to follow story that makes sense. Everyone wants the title and there is only one man they can beat, but that means they still have to fight each other in order to win. It is almost like *Battle Royale*. More brawling occurs before the Hardys decide to bring kitchenware to the, erm, table, and drill everyone with tray shots. Everyone starts flying around as the director struggles to keep up, then Tazz tries to murder Jeff with a cord yelling "choke, choke" at him while he does. Nice. Things meander a little, but Hardcore wakes people up with a Falcon Arrow onto a chair on Crash, but still no dice. Jeff Hardy goes to his strength and brings a ladder into the ring, which is met by the pop of the night so far. The crowd knows what a ladder and Jeff Hardy together means, and he doesn't disappoint, coming off the top with a Swanton bomb onto Crash. Matt tries to sneak a pin from that, so Jeff slaps him and then the brothers argue, before Tazz wipes them out with a double clothesline. The crowd goes nuts for the Tazzmission, but Saturn stops that, literally as it turns out, by using a stop sign. The Hardys recover and hit stereo dives onto Saturn and Hardcore, and Crash drapes an arm over Tazz to score the win and retain the title, having absorbed an absolute kicking all match. I disagree with jobbing out Tazz, especially in a throwaway match like this, but I had a lot of fun watching it and there were only a few down moments, which were then quickly forgotten when the next big spot or weapon shot came along. Like I said in the review of the *Hardcore* tape, I rate these matches almost on their own separate scale, and this one was a very fun one indeed.
Final Rating: ***

The Big Show vs. Kurt Angle
This comes during Big Show's short lived gimmick of being an impersonator, with him dressing up as other performers such as Val Venis, Roddy Piper and The Godfather. Six months ago he was winning the WWF Championship and was presented and pushed as a monster. The WWF just had no idea how to use the guy for so long. It's funny really, because Vince McMahon would often joke about WCW's misuse of him and gloat about how he would make him into the next Andre the Giant. Yeah, not quite. Angle cuts a promo pre match to get himself a ton of heat and have the crowd begging for him to get his comeuppance, and then Big Show comes out dressed as Hulk Hogan, or "The Showster" as he is known tonight. The get up is tremendous, with Show looking all the world like a big fat version of the Hulkster. The pop he receives shows that the crowd still love Hogan though, even if the WWF are playing it off as ironic cheers. Show's Hogan impression on the stick is dead on. Angle jumps him and Show immediately starts Hulking Up. "The old no sell" says JR. The crowd eats this up and pops huge for the big boot and leg drop, but Angle thankfully kicks out. "Nobody ever does that, do they!?" quips Lawler. Quite. Angle tries to ground the Showster by taking out his legs, as the crowd LOUDLY chants "Hogan". Show gets pissed off with Angle and chops the piss out of him, before a huge chokeslam finishes Kurt off in under 3-minutes. Unfortunately Show's short-lived rap version of his theme plays him out of the ring. It's dreadful. The match, while brief, was a lot of fun and the live crowd loved the nostalgia, but jobbing out one of the most promising guys on the roster in a silly comedy match was not great booking. Thankfully Angle continued his

meteoric rise in spite of setbacks like this, so I can't rate the match down because of that. Harmless fun, as it turns out.
Final Rating: **

The Dudley Boyz vs. T&A
Bubba is currently going through a phase of getting orgasmic pleasure from powerbombing women through tables, and Trish Stratus is his current target, but he keeps failing to get wood because he is infatuated and keeps going into a trance when he sees her. Somehow he is a babyface in this scenario, because putting women through tables is obviously a thing to be cheered vociferously. Bubba chases Trish around the ring and gets wiped out with a Test clothesline to start, and then the match kicks in. The problem is that no one cares, because all they want to see is Trish getting put through a table. "I'm gonna get you, you little bitch" yells Bubba. Wait a minute, backstage but five minutes ago he couldn't drag himself away from a monitor that she was on, but now in her presence he is able to overcome his issues? It's all bollocks really, isn't it? The match meanders on for eleven worthless minutes, which is at least twice as long as it needs to be. The crowd gets bored and begs for tables, with JR mocking them for chanting for an inanimate object. They try all the standard tag team wrestling tricks to get the fans into it, such as the missed hot tag spot, but it doesn't work. Nothing they could do would work, because like I say, there is only one thing this crowd wants. The heat on D-Von lasts forever, and a day, before the hot tag finally comes. The Dudleys hit a double neckbreaker, which JR screams is "3D! 3D!" and is shocked when Test kicks out, claiming they didn't get all of it. Yeah, they didn't get any of it, because it's a different move. They call for the real 3D and JR says "one more time" like a goofy pet coon (that's the phrase, right?), but Bubba stops mid move because Trish is on the apron shaking her ass. Test takes advantage and kicks Bubba in the face, and T&A score the somewhat surprising win. In the aftermath, Bubba finally gets his hands on Trish, as the crowd roar in favour of the man-on-woman violence. Bubba holds Trish in place but she tries to escape with the old lip lock. It appears to work, but then Bubba grabs her by the hair and the crowd can barely contain their excitement. A particularly vicious top rope powerbomb through the table follows, and in the aftermath Bubba sits grinning maniacally, with JR suggesting that someone should "get him a cigarette". The response from WWF fans to this kind of thing is borderline disturbing, but taken in the context of purely entertainment, it is a good payoff to a fairly wretched feud. The match sucked though.
Final Rating: ¾*

Trish does a stretcher job to sell the effects of the powerbomb, and gets carted off in an ambulance. At the same time, Eddie Guerrero and Chyna arrive fresh from prom, and are told to head to the ring right now for their match or Eddie will be stripped of his European title. Eddie drives straight through into the arena, and he has to change out of his tuxedo and into his wrestling gear out of the trunk of his car. I like that Eddie didn't just turn up with his gear already on, which is something that always annoys me in wrestling. Guys in real life don't walk around in their gear just in case they need to wrestle suddenly.

WWF European Championship
Eddie Guerrero (c) vs. Essa Rios
Eddie doesn't have his tights with him, so wrestles the match in his dress pants and bowtie. He looks outstanding. They immediately cut a furious pace with a bunch of quick switches that are impossible to keep up with. The WWF employs "creative editing" as Essa makes a mess of an armdrag sequence, and the tape release of the show cuts away to Chyna. So if you simply MUST see Essa botch a spot, you will have to acquire a bootleg. The match is really exciting, with flip planchas, slingshot sentons and other lucha moves aplenty, but for whatever reason the crowd are just not into it. How can you not be into a guy as entertaining and talented as Eddie Guerrero and as high-octane as Essa Rios!? Eddie takes an wild bump right across the ring and onto his head from a monkey flip, folding up like an accordion. On the outside Chyna belts Essa and Lita tries to get involved when Eddie goes for a powerbomb, but Chyna pushes her off the ropes and into the announce table... just. The distraction is enough for Essa to backdrop out of the move, and he follows up with a quebrada, nearly wiping out the announcers and their table in the process. Not a happy landing. They go back into the ring, very briefly, and then Rios hits his ridiculously dangerous but thrilling to watch tope con hilo over the post, which does at least get a polite response from the crowd. What's annoying is that they have gone ape-shit for a parody act and a brutal attack on a woman, but have barely paid lip service to two great wrestling contests. Assholes. Back in the ring they trade the advantage some more, before Eddie catches an opening when he gets his knees up on Essa's beautiful moonsault, and he puts this to bed with the Gory Special into a spinning neckbreaker. JR calls it an airplane spin, as he continues to have a right old time naming moves tonight. I enjoyed many aspects of this, from the graceful flying to Eddie working the entire thing in his prom gear, but the rotten crowd really hurt it. Worth seeing for sure, but if the crowd was there it would be close to another star.
Final Rating: ***¼

WWF Intercontinental Championship
Chris Benoit (c) vs. Chris Jericho
There are an awful lot of titles on the line tonight, and as of yet none of them have changed hands! Toto, I've a feeling we're not in 1999 anymore! Jericho gets a nice pop and cuts a brief pre match promo running down Al Gore for being a robot, though without naming him. The first couple of minutes are wonderful, as they just beat the snot out of each other without reservation, chopping viciously before turning to suplexes. It's my favourite kind of wrestling to watch. Benoit then backdrops Jericho over the ropes but misses his tope and crashes hard into the barrier and floor. It looked brutal. They fight on the outside, with Jericho hurdling the steps when Benoit tries to send him into them, only for Benoit to dropkick them into his legs when he turns around. It's a great use of the surroundings. Benoit takes over for the next few minutes, slowing things down a little to give the crowd chance to recover from the quick and violent start. Jericho continues to show plenty of fire though, and manages to catch a breather with a tackle and the Lionsault. They take a double down before Benoit goes back to meaty, loud, and cutting chops. He is just VICIOUS with them. Jericho responds in kind and catches a two count from a cradle, then they fight over a suplex with Jericho winning and hanging Benoit over the ropes, but he misses his springboard dropkick. Benoit, because he is a master, brushes it off rather than selling it anyway. They improvise an alternative, which ends with a Jericho back suplex from the top that Benoit half reverses in mid air, meaning they both land hard. Jericho comes back with powerbombs, but Benoit catches him in the Crossface and very nearly taps him out, but Jericho makes the ropes. Benoit goes for it again but Jericho blocks it and counters into the Walls of Jericho, only for Benoit to escape that. Great stuff all of that there; this is shaping up to be a classic. Unfortunately the next spot sees Jericho accidentally drill the ref with a flying forearm, in that accidental ref bump spot I hate so much. Benoit looks to take advantage with a belt shot, but Jericho kicks out. Super speedy recovery from Tim

White, though as his repeated onscreen suicide attempts showed, he has incredible powers of recuperation. Benoit comes off top with his flying headbutt, but Jericho uses the IC Title to block it and the ref calls for the bell, calling a DQ. Urgh, what a terrible finish to a great match! How immensely frustrating. Jericho snaps and attacks White, placing him in the Walls, which JR says is "very uncharacteristic of Chris Jericho". Clearly, he wasn't watching WCW in '98. This is a really, really good match, but the finish has to lose it some points. What a shame. Given another 5 minutes of near falls and a decisive finish, it could have gone down as one of the all-time greats.
Final Rating: ***¾

WWF Championship
Triple H (c) vs. The Rock
This match is loaded with extracurricular stuff, with Vince and Stephanie McMahon accompanying Triple H (hey, remember when Vince and Hunter were embroiled in a blood feud four months ago?), Shane McMahon serving as the referee and Steve Austin in the corner of The Rock. The problem is, Austin hasn't arrived yet and everyone is worried. It's an extra layer of drama on top of an already heavyweight feud. Rock has been chasing the WWF Championship for months and all of this should really have come to a head at *WrestleMania,* but at least the WWF are trying to right their wrongs tonight, and so far have done a great job with all the other matches, some dodgy booking aside. From around 2012, WWE got into a habit of referring to matches as having a "big fight feel", when more often than not they had nothing of the sort and it was just a desperate attempt from the company to try and make some bouts feel more important than they actually were. This though, has exactly that. I actually have no problem with the WWF overbooking this to the hilt, because let's face it we have seen these two go at it dozens of times over the years, and have seen everything they have to offer. There are unlikely to be many surprises, so adding new elements keeps it fresh and interesting. Just before the match, Vince gets on the mic to tell the crowd that the card is "subject to change", really hammering home that 'Stone Cold' is not here. They don't believe him, and chant loudly for Austin. It doesn't take long for the additional players to get involved, as Vince sends Rock into the post while Shane makes fast counts and ignores Hunter's cheating. The odds are firmly stacked against the challenger here, which is again good booking because the babyface should be in as much peril as possible prior to making a big comeback. Triple H continues to cheat, using his feet on the ropes while applying a chinlock, which Shane purposely ignores. Rocky keeps trying to come back, but Hunter stays in control. Rock finally gets back into it when he drops Hunter nose-first on the buckles, and a double clothesline keeps both guys down. When Rock recovers, Vince smashes Rock with the WWF Title belt and a super quick count from Shane on the subsequent pin nearly ends it. The crowd don't like that at all and once again chant for Austin. Rock continues to defy the odds and sends Hunter into the ropes for his dangerous corner bump that he loves to take, and they briefly brawl outside again before a Rock DDT back in the ring should finish, but Shane refuses to count. Rock is not impressed so belts Shane in the mush. Back to the outside and Trips goes for the Pedigree on the table only for Rock to escape with a low blow and set up the Rock Bottom. Shane gets in the way to block it, so Rock grabs him to and delivers a DOUBLE ROCK BOTTOM through the table. Holy shit, that was brilliant. Perfectly timed and executed too. It's not one of those things that sounds better on paper than it looks, if anything it is the opposite. Vince and Steph's reactions are superb too.

Vince has seen enough and attacks Rock, but that ends as well for him as you would expect, before Trips saves him with a low blow. The Pedigree would finish but Shane is still out, so Vince signals for Pat Patterson and Gerald Brisco, both dressed as referees, to come and make the count. They do, but Rock kicks out. The Stooges stomp away at Rock and hold him in place for Hunter to beat on him so more, then Steph gives Vince a chair. Hunter holds Rock, who DOESN'T move, and thus gets laid out by Vince. This is seemingly academic now, but then Steve Austin's music hits and the building nearly collapses from the response he gets. Austin comes out, for his first live appearance in six months (other than a brief backstage segment on *SmackDown!* when he blew up the McMahon-Helmsley bus) wielding a chair and looking rather rotund. I guess he had nothing else to do but sit at home and drink beer while he recovered from his neck surgery. Austin proceeds to tear through everyone other than the Rock, belting them in the head with chair shots that ricochet around the quaking building. My God, what a reaction and what an interjection from 'Stone Cold'. Linda McMahon then turns up with Earl Hebner, who in the storyline had recently been fired, and she pushes Stephanie out of the way on route to the ring. Rock hits the People's Elbow, Hebner jumps in to count the fall and Rock is the new WWF Champion. It is just a wall of noise inside the arena now, it's unbelievable. Steve Austin returns in his truck after Rock has had chance to celebrate a little, and they share a beer with not a Stunner in sight. What an incredible, perfectly booked piece of sportz entertainment this was. The rest of the show has featured a number of really good wrestling matches and some other entertaining pieces of sizzle, but this trumps all of them for its sheer immensity and epic nature. Truly one of the greatest examples of how to book WWF main events and give the people EXACTLY what they want.
Final Rating: ****½

The tape doesn't end on that perfect high note, instead featuring Coach presenting the *Backlash* wrap-up. This features is a poor addition to these tapes, because they are so unnecessary. What we get are promos from the likes of Crash, Malenko and Angle, none of which add in any way to my enjoyment of what I have just seen. Coach's pronunciation of the word "escape" as "eck-scape" is incredibly ack-nnoying too. The sooner they scrap this "exclusive" the better.

VERDICT

You can see where this show gets its reputation from. From start to finish it is loaded with quality and entertainment, from the wonderful wrestling in the IC, European and Light Heavyweight title matches to the throwaway fun of the hardcore division and Big Show doing the nostalgia act. Even without the main event, there is something for everyone already. When you factor in the main event as well, this goes from being a very good show to one of the best that the company has ever put on. Five matches were above *** (a couple well above) and even the stuff that wasn't quite so good was never actually bad, it was just there. An absolute triumph then, and this unsurprisingly comes with the highest recommendation. It is also the second WWF PPV of the year already to receive a perfect score, and this was only April! 2000 was a wonderful year to be a WWF fan.

100

JUDGMENT DAY 2000

CAT NO: WWF248
RUN TIME: 174 minutes (approx)

James Dixon: We start, like every good paid event should, with a backstage segment featuring the McMahon clan. Vince sends Jerry Brisco to go and get everyone coffee, while running down tonight's card with his DX buddies and Shane McMahon. Unfortunately for Brisco he is the current Hardcore Champion, and thus he doesn't manage the journey for coffee because the Headbangers attack him. We then see Shawn Michaels, the referee for the main event Iron Man Match tonight, walking down the corridor clad in incredibly tight fitting shorts. This should all have happened later on, or on *Heat*.

Kurt Angle, Edge & Christian vs. Rikishi & Too Cool
Kurt talks on his way to the ring to generate his usual heat, and introduces the rest of Team ECK: Edge and Christian. They do a promo too, with Christian calling Louisville "lewis-vill" and Edge announcing the debut of a new 5 second pose, this one mocking Kentucky natives, complete with big goofy teeth and silly hats. The babyfaces are super over, far more so than you would ever imagine. Perhaps WWE was right in 2014: crowd reactions don't equate to drawing money. This starts with all six men in the ring and a babyface triple team spot on all three of Team ECK, before a tag match breaks out. Scotty and Christian pair off for a while, and Too Cool do a clever spot where Scotty is getting sent into the corner so Sexay jumps in front of the buckle to pad his landing and allow him to reverse. Edge tries to copy the innovative spot for Christian, but Scotty reverses the whip and Sexay comes in and kicks the hell out of Edge. I liked that. The crowd chants for Rikishi, loudly, but instead they get Grandmaster Sexay getting his groove on so hard that his trousers fall down mid dance, exposing his tighty whities. Scotty thinks the whole thing is a riot. Too Cool are a lot of fun. Rikishi finally enters the fray and cleans house, but he misses an attempted butt splash on Angle. Rikishi isn't down for long because there is no way he is taking the heat, which starts when Angle prevents the Worm with a big clothesline on Scotty. Edge & Christian use fake tags and Demolition beat downs, but Scotty shows plenty of fire against Kurt, and indeed the heat is pleasingly brief, with Scotty getting the tag to Rikishi after an alley oop into the ropes. The crowd is absolutely electric for this entire match, screaming and hollering as much as any crowd you will ever hear. Rikishi uses his size to dominate and throws in the Stink Face on poor Kurt, then no sells a double DDT because he is Samoan. Edge manages to take him down with a spear and then tries an intentionally horrible Worm, but Scotty bulldogs him midway through and hits the real Worm on him and then on Edge for good measure. Rikishi goes for the Rikishi Driver on Edge, but Christian uses the ring bell to seemingly seal the victory, only for Sexay to come off the top with Tennessee Jam and get his team the win. The crowd goes apeshit for that. Too Cool and Rikishi do their majorly over dance after the match, and they remain my favourite dancing gimmick characters of all time. These guys were fantastic fun, and this match was nonstop and entertaining throughout. Great start to the show.
Final Rating: ***½

Backstage, Michael Cole and his frosted hair talks to Shawn Michaels. Michaels dismisses his "asinine" questions, and then condescendingly slaps him and walks away. Cole rolls his eyes like a complete gimboid in response.

In the parking lot earlier tonight on *Heat*, Dean Malenko did his best Christian Bale *Batman* voice, telling Chyna to stay out of the Radicalz's business. Perry Saturn turns up and shows the charisma and promo ability that made him into a megastar too. Eddie Guerrero aside, the Radicalz were all horrible at promos.

WWF European Championship
Eddie Guerrero (c) vs. Perry Saturn vs. Dean Malenko
This could be very good indeed, because while they might not be great speakers, they are all great wrestlers. Jim Ross throws out the incorrect facts early, claiming that the last two times the European Title has been defended on pay-per-view the champion has left beltless. It's the other way around; Eddie defended the title against Essa Rios last month at *Backlash* and again earlier this month on UK-exclusive PPV event *Insurrextion 2000*, this time against Chris Jericho. The early going sees all three remain in the ring and work spots that incorporate everyone involved rather than two guys going at it while one stands around or sells. It makes for a much better match, but it is almost like it is in front of a different crowd than the opener. There is plenty of innovation to keep me happy

though, such as Saturn suplexing Eddie onto Malenko's shoulder where he follows with an atomic drop, only for Eddie to throw out a mule kick and get both guys in the nuts, or another where Eddie goes for his tilt-a-whirl head scissors, only for Malenko to catch him midway through with a sidewalk slam. All very nice, but for some reason the fans just don't care. Malenko and Eddie briefly pair off, with Malenko hitting the sitout powerbomb and then going for another, only for Eddie to go right through into a sunset flip, but Malenko counters again into the Texas Cloverleaf. The Ring of Honor crowd or Japanese audiences would love all of this. There are so many clever almost barely noticeable things that they do, but they are lost on the audience. They do at least react to Malenko's always impressive top rope gut buster, and then Saturn gets all cheeky and uses the frog splash on Guerrero and the Cloverleaf on Malenko; their own moves. Guerrero and Malenko don't approve of that, and Eddie decks him with his own brain buster before Malenko puts him in the Rings of Saturn. Another excellent spot follows as they hit an innovative triple German suplex (which you could also call a triple back suplex if you want, because they all moved to the side to avoid clashing heads), and then Chyna gets involved with her apparently deadly bouquet of roses, drilling Saturn in the head with them on the outside. Back in the ring she tries the same on Malenko but gets caught, so she trips him causing a face-first bump onto the flowers, and Eddie catches him with an Oklahoma roll for the popular win. Ah, seems the deadly flowers were loaded with a lead pipe. Shitty crowd reactions aside, this was a great piece of entertainment too. Completely different to the opener, but just as entertaining in its own way. The WWF really did have something for everyone in 2000.
Final Rating: ***½

Video Control show shows us how Jerry Brisco won the Hardcore title on *SmackDown!* a few days ago by pinning a sleeping Crash Holly. We go backstage at the PPV and see Brisco sneaking around in a bathroom, shitting himself at the sight of his own reflection and punching the mirror like a goof.

Falls Count Anywhere
Shane McMahon vs. The Big Show
Last month the Big Show was busting out the comedy as a Hulk Hogan impersonator, the month before he was in the main event at *WrestleMania 2000*, now he is stuck in a midcard feud with a non-wrestler and back to his lumbering self. Has anyone suffered from the WWF/E's infamous start/stop booking as badly as the Big Show? Shane tries diving on Show to start, but gets caught and beaten up, then Show literally kicks his ass while talking trash to him. Show looks for the chokeslam, but the Big Bossman jumps in with a nightstick to the leg. Show quickly disposes of him with headbutts and a powerbomb, so Test and Albert run down with chairs to help Shane, only to get them punched right back in their faces. Trish Stratus takes a turn at interfering, punching Show in his big bollocks, but gets chokeslammed out of the ring and onto T&A. Show chases Shane up the aisle and hurls him way high into the *Judgment Day* set, then rips some of the set apart and goes to crush him with it. Shane goes all ninja and uses the set to get leverage to boot Show away, then T&A come to his rescue. Show gets drilled with a makeshift battering ram, but doesn't sell it for long before he goes back to hurling T&A around like children. Bull Buchanan gets involved and pulverises Show with his nightstick, then Shane channels *Royal Rumble '99* and shoves some electrical equipment onto Show, which lands on his leg and traps him. From there Shane finds a friggin' cinder block and breaks it over Show's head for the win. Well, it was a little bit overbooked and silly, but I guess that was the idea. At least it is different to everything else on the show. Why Shane had to go over a guy who was WWF Champion less than six months ago who also went over The Rock in February, I cannot answer. It's a shame for Show really, because he was booked to look very strong and impressive here prior to counting the lights.
Final Rating: **

Backstage, Show gets helped to an ambulance by Sgt. Slaughter and Tony Garea, while crying and whimpering like a giant pussy. Who would cheer for a big cry-baby? No wonder he has always struggled to really get over.

Meanwhile, Jerry Brisco heads into the referees' locker room looking for sanctuary, but when he dozes off the refs try and get in a sneaky pin on him. Brisco wakes before the plan reaches fruition and he yells at them for trying him. Tough night for poor Gerald.

Elsewhere backstage, Triple H and Shawn Michaels do some catching up, with Hunter imploring Michaels not to wear his shorter-than-short shorts. For once, I agree with him on something.

Submission Match
WWF Intercontinental Championship
Chris Benoit (c) vs. Chris Jericho
These guys have traded the Intercontinental title between themselves since their solid outing last month at *Backlash*, rather cheapening the belt with the hotshotting in the process. To add to the drama, Benoit had his leg done over by Hardcore Holly and a steel chair on *SmackDown!* a few days back. Shouldn't it be the babyface who comes in with the disadvantage? They start here in a similar vein to *Backlash* with violent, loud chopping and early submission attempts. They trade Tombstone set up switches before Benoit hits a shoulder breaker, already looking to weaken Jericho for the Crossface. He follows that with his diving headbutt onto the shoulder and then continues to target the body part like a Terminator. Jericho is equally smart with his work and goes for the hurt knee of Benoit, as well as trying to soften up the back. They stop off from the submissions to have another brutal chop fight, seemingly just for their own amusement, then Jericho misses a blind charge and smashes his shoulder into the post. Benoit targets it again, they twat each other with more chops, and then right back to the focused assaults. This is so smartly and logically worked, and the stuff they do so tight and intense, that it is hard to believe that this is the same company that later pushed loose and lazy robots like John Cena and Randy Orton. Jericho realises he needs to up his game because his shoulder is suffering, and he rips Benoit's knee brace off and whips him with it. He does it hard too, so Benoit gives him a receipt with a kick to the face. Jericho is undeterred and puts Benoit in a tarantula version of the Walls of Jericho in the ropes, but Benoit uses tenacity to fight out. The announcers are dumbfounded by that one, they have no idea what call it. Jericho fights for the Walls but Benoit bashes him with the brace and locks in the Crossface. Jericho nearly makes the ropes so Benoit drags him to the centre of the ring and puts it on again, then when Jericho escapes he locks it on once more, but this time around the throat rather than the face, choking Jericho out and forcing ref Tim White to call it via stoppage. This flew by, to the point that when it finished I was actually shocked it had ended so soon, only to then discover they went nearly 15-minutes. From start to finish it was super stiff, super intense, intelligently worked, full of spot-on psychology and didn't slow down at all. I actually think the only thing that hurts it slightly is that it probably could

TOO COOL

have done with another 5-minutes of submission attempts and counters, but that is a minor quibble and doesn't take away from another brilliant encounter between the two. What a show this is so far.
Final Rating: ****¼

Backstage, Michael Cole interviews Gerald Brisco, who is completely unaware of two vendors in the background plotting to take the belt. Brisco eventually catches them in the act motioning about his title, so he kicks the coffee out of their hands and belts them with popcorn before scarpering.

Tables Match
X-Pac & Road Dogg vs. The Dudley Boyz
The rules here are that both members of a team must go through a table for the match to be over. Last week on *RAW* Bubba suffered the ignominy of being splashed through a table by DX's valet Tori, and he has revenge on his mind. For no conceivable reason, this starts out as a regular tag with Bubba and X-Pac on the apron. It makes no sense at all to work it like this. Because of the rules, the crowd doesn't get into anything while it is structured this way, because all they want to see is table stuff. It's like when guys do random bits of technical wrestling to kill time before going into the main body of a match; it means nothing. Finally things break down as they should with all four guys brawling in the aisle. Bubba gets the better of X-Pac and then spots Tori, but he thinks better of exacting revenge on her just yet. And then... it becomes a normal tag match again with DX working heat on D-Von. Urgh. At one point Bubba tries to come in but gets stopped by the referee because he didn't tag, with Jerry Lawler pointing out the silliness of it all and rightly noting that there are no DQs because there is only one way to win. They even do the fake hot tag spot, and again Bubba lets the ref prevent his entry into the match. What are DX achieving by working D-Von over anyway? They need to put him through a table, not wear him

down for a pin. Eventually the hot tag comes and Bubba cleans house and NOW we get some tables brought into play. But it is DX who get the first elimination, with Road Dogg sending D-Von headfirst into the steps and then drilling him through a table on the outside with a pump handle slam. Thankfully D-Von stays around rather than disappearing to the back, which I wouldn't have been surprised if he had done. X-Pac and Bubba fight over a table in the ring, then X-Pac stupidly goes for a rana and inevitably gets powerbombed through the furniture. What an idiotic move to try. Bubba and Road Dogg argue, and the ref for no reason tries to stop them so they team up to hiptoss him through a table in the corner. Jerry Brisco shows up as the Dudleys hit 3D on Road Dogg through the table, but there is now obviously no referee. Brisco pulls Dogg out of the ring as Bubba goes to powerbomb Tori through another table, but Brisco blocks it and X-Pac hits an X-Factor off the top through the wood while Brisco revives the ref who calls the match. Brisco makes the mistake of staying around and mocking the Duds, so they 3D him through a table. Continuing with the logical chasm that has been this whole match, nobody pins Brisco to win his Hardcore title, even though everyone has been trying to attack him all night. There was nothing wrong with the actual execution of anything, but I hated this for the sheer stupidity of it all. Whoever road agented this match should be ashamed of themselves.
Final Rating: *

60-Minute Iron Man Match
WWF Championship
The Rock (c) vs. Triple H
These two had an incredible match with a super feel-good ending at *Backlash*, but I admit to having apprehensions about sitting through 60-minutes of them going at it. Like last month they have to follow some tremendous undercard matches, but once again they are given a helping hand from outsiders, with Shawn Michaels serving as the referee. Triple H comes out with the McMahons, but sends them to the back because he wants to do things tonight by himself. It's a total babyface move, but it gives them the chance to come back later and inject some excitement if the match needs it.

First Fall: They have an intense stare down to begin with and then lock up to a thunderous response. They come over all Goldberg-Lesnar with a long lock up, but don't get pissed on like those guys did. Rock goes to a side headlock, as Lawler rightly points out that they can't make the mistake of cutting a quick pace, and notes that Rock's longest match to date is 30-minutes, against the same opponent two years prior. Rare insight from the King! When he doesn't make puerile jokes and talk about puppies, he offers a lot to WWF broadcasts when alongside JR. Rock does a lot of running as he hits tackles and goes for various pinfall attempts, but Trips bails plenty to waste some time and give both guys a breather. Michaels shows impartiality, and continues to count Hunter out when he tells him to stop. The pace remains methodical, as it has to, with Rock working a headlock and Hunter opting for punch-kick and a top wristlock into an armbar. The hold is almost certainly going nowhere, but as Lawler points out; they are using controlling holds and making their opponent expend energy. Rock fires back with punches as we pass the 10-minute mark with very little having happened, and then from nowhere he hits the Rock Bottom to score the first fall.
Score: Rock 1, Hunter 0.

Second Fall: There is no rest between falls, so Rock stays right on Hunter as the second fall starts, and they take things to the outside for a brawl in the aisle. They go back-and-forth, with both using the crowd barrier to their advantage, but Rocky remains the aggressor, suplexing Hunter back in the ring and then wrapping his leg around the post and bashing it into the apron and ring steps. Taking out the wheel is good strategy from the champ, though it does mean we are going to see either 45-minutes of selling the leg from Hunter or him ignoring it as the match progresses. Rock is now essentially working heat on Hunter, but again the match type necessitates alternating periods of control. Rock puts a figure four on, but Hunter, like a babyface, refuses to give up. The face/heel roles really do feel reversed at the moment, and the crowd are pretty quiet throughout this period. Hunter continues to play babyface when he spins the figure four around, but Rock reverses it again and they end up in the ropes, so Michaels breaks it up. To the outside again and Rock gets caught with a desperation clothesline, and then they take a shortcut with a brawl through the crowd. A brief one mind you, as if they thought better of it once they got out there. Over a decade later, another fan called Ronald Basham III sued the WWE, Rock and Triple H, claiming he was seriously injured in the brawl when a fan was pushed onto his leg by one of the wrestlers. He played football in high school on his "seriously injured knee" mind you, not that we are implying anything... Twenty minutes on the clock now, and the crowd become distracted by something in the crowd in the same place as where Rock and Hunter were just brawling. Perhaps it is Basham doing a stretcher job. Back in the ring, Hunter hits a couple of elbows and keeps going for covers, but Rock gets out. Hunter biels Rock out of the ring when he starts fighting back, but Rock responds by sending Hunter into the steps. Rock continues to target the knee and goes for the figure four again, but Hunter catches him with the Pedigree to even the scores.
Score: Rock 1, Hunter 1.

Third Fall: Hunter chokes Rocky, but Shawn pulls him off as he continues to be impartial. Rocky is groggy, and Hunter catches him with a cradle almost immediately to take the lead. Smart booking, though he probably should have gone for the cover immediately after the fall started.
Score: Rock 1, Hunter 2.

Fourth Fall: Rock shows some fight with punches, but Hunter throws him to the outside. Rock sells being dazed and confused and wanders around with little purpose or direction, but has enough about him to send Hunter into the set. He tries for a suplex, but Trips reverses into one of his own and both guys are out in the aisle. Shawn counts, though I am not sure why because a double count out achieves nothing, and if he is counting because they are both down like if they were in the ring, what difference would one guy getting up make anyway? Trips tries to return to the ring, but Rock hits him with a back suplex in the aisle, and they are both down again. Rock is starting to get his shit together and backdrops Hunter, still in the aisle, as Shawn Michaels relays the message to the announcers that he isn't going to call any "bullshit count outs". Why was he counting them both earlier then!? The pace is now very laboured as both guys sell the effects of the past 30-minutes, and then from nowhere Trips hits a piledriver and scores another fall. "Piledriver always works" says Lawler. He should cast his mind back to *RAW* in 1997 where seemingly every guy on the roster used it as a transition.
Score: Rock 1, Hunter 3.

Fifth Fall: Hunter is bossing things now and the situation looks bleak for Rocky. He shows the crowd he is still alive by exploding out of the corner with a clothesline, but gets quickly taken back down. Hunter makes a dumb decision and goes up

top, the opposite of the defensive strategy that Lawler implores him to employ, and Rock gives him the Flair bump. Both guys are down, and when they get back to their feet Rock takes over with punches. He tries a cradle and nearly gets a fall, then Hunter gets a near fall of his own immediately in response from a high knee. Hunter goes to the sleeper, which is a more sensible strategy, using the ropes for leverage in the process. He gets caught by Michaels and kicked off, which gives Rock chance to capitalise on the distraction, and he does with more punches and a belly-to-belly suplex. Hunter kicks out of that. Back to swinging, and Rock hits a DDT after a messed up floatover (though, well recovered) for the three.
Score: Rock 2, Hunter 3.

Sixth Fall: Back outside we go, and Shawn Michaels prevents Hunter from using a chair, but happily watches on as Rock sends Hunter into the steps. Back in the ring Hunter uses the chair and instantly gets disqualified by Michaels, and now we are even.
Score: Rock 3, Hunter 3.

Seventh Fall: Rock, who is busted open, is hurt from the chair shot, so Hunter covers him with his feet on the ropes and retakes the lead. Smart booking, though Ricky Steamboat and Rick Rude did something very similar in their ***** Iron Man bout at *Beach Blast '92*. Still, I appreciate the homage.
Score: Rock 3, Hunter 4.

Eighth Fall: Rock's blade job is not the best. He is hardly wearing a crimson mask here. Hunter goes back to the sleeper and Rock fights out, but Hunter catches him with it again and this time Rocky's arm drops three times. Yes, he jobbed to a sleeper! Brutus Beefcake must be beaming with pride.
Score: Rock 3, Hunter 5.

Ninth Fall: Hunter tries to hold on to the sleeper but Michaels drags him off by the hair and makes him break it. The crowd comes to their feet as the two have a shoving match, but it doesn't go any further. Rock fires up again with more punches and sends Hunter into the corner for that big backwards bump over the top that he likes to take. Finally the fans are starting to get into this a little more, having been sat on their hands for a lot of it. It's easy to understand why; they have been fed instant gratification Vince Russo inspired crash TV booking for the last few years, and only in the last couple of months have the WWF began the switch from over-the-top excess and swerve booking to workrate. 60-minutes for one match in this era is almost incomprehensible and they are just not used to it. Ten minutes remain as Hunter again foolishly scales the buckles, and again it backfires for him as Rock bounces into the ropes and crotches him. Rock keeps trying for a superplex but Hunter knows what he is going for and fights him off. Rock is undeterred and finally connects with it, and once again both guys are out. They certainly have epic selling nailed in this, that's for sure. Rock makes the cover, but Hunter gets out, and Rocky only has 8-minutes to make up two falls. Rock connects with a tired elbow and clotheslines Hunter to the outside, where they again have a brawl. Hunter sends Rock into the steps and then clears the monitors off the announce table as he sets up a Rock Bottom on it, but Rock reverses into a Pedigree, but the table doesn't sell. It never sells for Triple H; it's the only thing in the company that can get away with it. Hunter gets counted out, and Rock is back in the game.
Score: Rock 4, Hunter 5.

Tenth Fall: And with 3-minutes left on the clock, here come the McMahons. Hunter is now bleeding as well from the Pedigree, and Michaels counts him out again, but he makes it back in the ring just before the ten count. Rock hits a DDT and then stops off to drill both Shane and Vince on the apron, then hits a spinebuster to set up the People's Elbow. Michaels stands in a VERY suspicious position, as if he is about to hit Rock with the superkick after he hits the second set of ropes, but he doesn't and Rock connects with the move and evens us up!
Score: Rock 5, Hunter 5!

Eleventh Fall: Two minutes are left of the clock, and an irate Shane pulls Shawn out of the ring, so Michaels drills him and Vince. DX come down and take out Shawn, then lay a beating on the Rock as a nursery rhyme plays on the screen. It is of course the signal for the return of the Undertaker, who has been out injured for months. But it is not the Undertaker as we know him, but rather a new version: the American Badass. That horror is not fully clear just yet though, and the fans are thrilled to have Taker back. He sets about demolishing DX, Shane and then Vince, before drilling Trips with a chokeslam and Tombstone as the time expires. Just as this happens, Michaels recovers and calls for the bell, and Fink announces to the aghast crowd that Hunter won the sixth fall via DQ and is the new WWF Champion. Louisville is not impressed and they hurl stuff at Shawn, who high tails it out of there and pleads his case to Taker. I think he called it spot on. Some think the finish is disappointing, but it makes a lot of sense because it doesn't hurt the Rock, sets up Hunter as a beatable champion and creates various issues for the future.

What of the match then? Well, I know some of my fellow writers rate this very highly, but I personally found it a little slow for my tastes. I understand that it had to be because of the length, and there is no doubt that it is very well worked and well booked, I just think there are other matches that are as long or close that are better than it. A few featuring Ric Flair spring to mind, as does the Lesnar-Angle Iron Man from *SmackDown!* a few years later. I do think it is better than the Iron Man between Bret Hart and Shawn Michaels at *WrestleMania XII*, and I am pleased that after that damp squib 0-0 draw they went for the exact opposite here. So very good, without question, but for me it's not one of the true greats.
Final Score: Rock 5, Hunter 6.
Final Rating: ****

VERDICT

From top to bottom, this is one of the finest cards that the WWF have ever produced. I said the same thing about last month's *Backlash* show too, and Furious felt much the same about *Royal Rumble* in January as well, which all serves to highlight what a tremendous year this was for the company in the ring. Personally I found *Backlash* slightly better, because I enjoyed the main event more, even though the undercard here is stronger. Almost perfect, but not quite, thought still obviously a very, very highly recommended show.

98

SHANE MCMAHON

KING OF THE RING 2000

CAT NO: WWF249
RUN TIME: 157 minutes (approx)

Lee Maughan: Hosts are Jim Ross and Jerry Lawler.

King of the Ring Tournament, Quarter-Final
Rikishi vs. Chris Benoit
Chris Benoit has made it to the quarter-finals thanks to a pinfall victory over the Road Dogg and a submission win against X-Pac, while Rikishi is here after a disqualification win over Shane McMahon and a pinfall victory against occasional partner Scotty 2 Hotty. Rikishi has also just beaten Benoit three nights previous on *SmackDown!* with a banzai drop to win the Intercontinental title, and Benoit is out for revenge. So much so that he just wallops Rikishi in the face with a steel chair after 3:25 of time-filling action, administering a beat-down post-match for good measure. What a lousy start to the show.
Final Rating: *

King of the Ring Tournament, Quarter-Final
Val Venis vs. Eddie Guerrero
Val went over Al Snow and Jeff Hardy to make it to the quarter-finals, whilst Eddie beat Matt Hardy and Chyna. Eddie also has Chyna in his corner, whilst Val is accompanied by Trish Stratus. Val if you'll recall, is a guy who slept with Jenna Jameson, Mrs. Yamaguchi, Terri Runnels and Ryan Shamrock, but here they're trying to push that he only wants a "business relationship" with Trish. Eddie has also chopped off his mullet at long last, making him look like a carbon copy of his older brother Hector.

The match is pretty much nonstop action throughout, with Guerrero going lucharesu early on with a Mexican surfboard into an awesome modified dragon sleeper. He follows with a huracanrana, but misses a frog splash off the top and runs into a spinebuster from Val. Guerrero though gets the knees up on a Money Shot attempt and catches an Oklahoma roll. Val tries to steal a pin with his feet on the ropes, so Guerrero goes back to the huracanrana, this time off the top, and that's enough for Trish who gets up on the apron to distract the referee. Chyna blocks that and bonks Val who goes after her (not in that way), giving Eddie a chance to roll him up for two in a great nearfall that everybody figured was the finish. The real finish comes a few moments later when Val pops back up and drops Eddie with a fisherman suplex for the pin.

Good match, as both guys looked to have their working boots on for this one, but the WWF just seemed to be pushing the wrong guy here as Val wasn't particularly over at this point whereas Eddie was, and the result only served to hurt Eddie more than it helped Val.
Final Rating: ***

King of the Ring Tournament, Quarter-Final
Crash Holly vs. Bull Buchanan
Crash made it through with a 90-second pin on Albert and a disqualification victory over his cousin Hardcore Holly, and Buchanan has earned his berth with victories over Steve Blackman and Perry Saturn. Crash is currently in the midst of his push as a "super heavyweight", but he can't do any of his goofy hardcore comedy here and Bull Buchanan just isn't over, so the crowd completely switch off until the inevitable - Bull dominates almost the entire match but misses the scissors kick and gets rolled up for a fluke pin, meaning Bull looked like an idiot, and Crash only advanced because he got lucky. Very poor booking choice there.
Final Rating: *

King of the Ring Tournament, Quarter-Final
Kurt Angle vs. Chris Jericho
Angle rolled over Bradshaw and Bubba Ray Dudley to make it here, and Jericho boasts victories over fellow Canadians Test and Edge. It's too bad this isn't the finals because it feels wasted here, especially given who else has already gone through, but Jericho is feuding with Stephanie McMahon-Helmsley (and Triple H by proxy) so we just *have* to get involvement from her here instead of letting Angle go over with a clean pin. Sure enough, she runs out just as Jericho has Angle trapped in the Walls of Jericho, which distracts the referee long enough to miss Angle tapping out. Also distracted, Jericho gets shoved into the referee who takes a bump, but Stephanie's attempted belt shot on Jericho misses, and she clobbers Angle instead. Jericho grabs her for an unwanted makeout session (which is surely grounds for a sexual harassment lawsuit, though you have to ask where Triple H

was during all of this), but Kurt recovers and hits the Olympic Slam to advance at 9:50. Match was doing just fine before all the shenanigans at the end, but it wasn't as spectacular as you might expect for Jericho vs. Angle.
Final Rating: ***

- Mick Foley is live at WWF New York with Ivory tending bar, largely as a reminder that WWF New York still exists. Foley has a brand new buzzcut and some interesting news about a meeting he'll soon be having about his role in the company going forward.

Elimination Match
WWF Tag Team Championship
Too Cool (c) vs. Edge & Christian vs. The Hardy Boyz vs. T&A
Even if you're not paying attention or you don't have much of a memory for these things, you can still tell this is the peak of popularity for Rikishi and his crew, since not only is he the Intercontinental champion, into the semi-finals of the *King of the Ring* tournament and feuding on TV with Val Venis, but Too Cool are actually the Tag Team Champions as well, having knocked off Edge & Christian on *RAW* at the back end of May. Too Cool's popularity notwithstanding, the title change was seemingly also done for a couple of other reasons, as the involvement of Kid Rock's hype-man Joe C in the finish of that match certainly attests to (and we all know how much the WWF/WWE loves to take advantage of even the slenderest of celebrity involvement). Besides whatever precious column inches using a rapper's sidekick could generate, it was also starting to feel, just as with the New Age Outlaws before them, that Edge & Christian were beginning to completely overshadow the entire tag team division, with the short-term change going someway to make sure they weren't completely dominant.

This would actually be Lita's pay-per-view debut with the Hardy Boyz after splitting from Essa Rios, and it's her team who work the entire opening portion of the match with T&A. That's no exaggeration either, as after Trish all-but repeats her interactions from earlier in the night (but with Lita in the role of Chyna), Matt pins Test after Jeff nails him with a senton off the top at 3:42. They might as well have just done a regular match there.

Scotty 2 Hotty comes in next, but otherwise the entire second portion of the match is strictly Edge & Christian against the Hardy Boyz. Lita too, who catches Edge with a huracanrana. It wouldn't be the last time she'd wrap her legs around his head like that... Matt escapes an Impaler and hits a Twist of Fate for two, but Edge blocks a senton from Jeff and evades another of Matt's Twist of Fate attempts, and that leads into Christian hitting the Impaler at the second time of asking for the pin.

Grandmaster Sexay comes in with a missile dropkick on Edge but stops to jiggle like an idiot, leading to JR wondering aloud what his parents must think. "Why don't you ask them sometime?" remarks Lawler, as we've clearly regressed to pretending Lawler isn't his father despite having already publicly let the cat out of the bag three years ago. Scotty takes a cheapshot as the heels take over with some old school spots, including the always popular "accidentally headbutt your partner in the groin" bit. They even get in a flapjack which JR actually references as shades of the Midnight Express (who they were essentially a modern day version of, with the Hardy Boyz as the updated Rock n' Roll Express and the Dudley Boyz as something of a fresh spin on the Road Warriors,

FURIOUS ABOUT: APA
During an era where tag wrestling was flying high, one of the top teams were the Acolytes, which morphed into the Acolyte Protection Agency in 2000. The gimmick changing from devil worshipping crazies to hired guns who liked to drink beer. It was a lighter gimmick, the same way most of the Ministry lightened up in 2000; Edge & Christian turning into goofy comedy guys and Dennis Knight becoming Naked Mideon. As the APA, Faarooq and Bradshaw were less involved in major tag team matches and more popular as characters. The various protection angles started out quite seriously but soon they were playing poker every week, drinking beer and mucking about. It was around this time that the WWF noticed how Faarooq was deteriorating but Bradshaw was improving. The no brainer was to split them up when the brand extension kicked in and push Bradshaw as the wrestler. It didn't take and the APA were back in business in mid 2003 for a final run. Ron Simmons retired in 2004 allowing Bradshaw to switch gimmicks to JBL and take off on a proper singles career. He would win the WWE title shortly afterward and held the belt for 280 days.

gimmick aside.) They take out Grandmaster and mockingly go for the Worm, but Scotty drops them both with a mistimed bulldog and hits the Worm for real. Too Cool then look to finish with the Veg-o-Matic (a combination Demolition Decapitation/ Alabama Jam top rope legdrop, both invented and popularised by those lads again, the Midnight Express) but Christian nails Grandmaster with a belt to regain the titles at 14:11.

The crowd was dead throughout most of this, but then that's what you get for booking a four-way instead of a straight tag match. Because you instead had to book essentially three separate matches, none of which had adequate time to develop, and with two babyface teams in there, you leave the crowd somewhat unsure of who to cheer for. Some cheer both, some pick sides, and some choose neither. Here, most chose neither.
Final Rating: **¾

- Backstage, Michael Cole can't believe Crash Holly has made it this far in the tournament, counterproductively confirming what a fluke he is.

King of the Ring Tournament, Semi-Final
Rikishi vs. Val Venis
With a little rejigging and some fan-friendly booking, we could have seen Benoit vs. Guerrero and Angle vs. Jericho in the semi-finals. Or Angle vs. Benoit and Jericho vs. Guerrero. Or Jericho vs. Benoit and Angle vs. Guerrero. Instead we've got Angle vs. Crash Holly and this. Rikishi and Venis were actually in the midst of quite a violent feud that had seen Rikishi superkick and splash Val off the *SmackDown!* stage and slam him through the announcers table, before Val returned fire by ramming a television monitor in Rikishi's head and walloping him with a gigantic unprotected chair shot.

Unfortunately, despite those issues, they work a fairly routine match. Val does employ the Divorce Court (another Midnight Express special, later employed by Nigel McGuinness) to work over Rikishi's already-injured arm, but the crowd don't particularly care about any of this. Val wraps Rikishi's arm around the post to add further damage before coming off the top… right into a belly-to-belly suplex for the completely out-of-nowhere pin at a paltry 3:16. Finally it gets violent as Rikishi goes for a banzai drop on Trish, but Val makes the save and drops the steel steps on Rikishi's arm, then whacks it with a chair for good measure.
Final Rating: *

King of the Ring Tournament, Quarter-Final
Kurt Angle vs. Crash Holly
What a semi-final this is, pitting a complete fluke against a bloke who already tapped out and by rights, shouldn't even be here. Angle breaks out some nifty amateur influenced rolls early and Crash fires back with a tasty Northern lariat and a missile dropkick, but the outcome is so overwhelmingly predictable at this point that the crowd just doesn't care. Angle puts everyone out of their misery with the Olympic Slam at an epic 3:58.
Final Rating: *

Evening Gown Match
WWF Hardcore Championship
Pat Patterson (c) vs. Gerald Brisco
And now for a complete travesty. Brisco had won the Hardcore title after blindsiding Crash Holly with a 2x4 on *RAW*, only for Patterson to double cross him at the victory party, pouring champagne over his head that somehow managed to blind him then rolling him up for the pin. This was of course still during the period where the title was being defended under 24/7 rules, which made for some amusing skits at first but had already started to feel tired and worn out. Naturally fearful of a revenge attack, Patterson took to dressing in drag (you know, because in real life he's a homosexual so he must be into cross dressing, har har har, how my sides do split) and began hanging out in the women's locker room. Discovering this, Brisco also began dressing in drag so he could sneak up on Patterson, and in the midst of all this chaos, Mr. McMahon ordered the two to settle it in the WWF's first ever "Hardcore Evening Gown match". And here it is. Lucky us.

Brisco comes out to Hulk Hogan's old '*Real American*' theme music, the gag being that he actually is a "real American", being of Native American heritage. Patterson comes out to some Las Vegas showgirl music because again, he's a gay and thus flamboyant. So they start brawling pathetically and ripping each other's dresses off until Patterson pulls a sanitary pad out of his knickers and rubs it into Brisco's face, at which point the crowd being booing *vociferously* in disgust at what they're being presented with. Patterson follows by hoisting his skirt up and attempting a Stinkface but the crowd just hates this insulting, unamusing garbage and lets them know. That doesn't stop them continuing to rip each other's gowns to shreds, leaving them both in their undergarments as Crash mercifully returns and destroys both guys with a garbage can to kick off his 10th reign as champion.

How anybody could have envisioned that this would be even remotely amusing is beyond me, and although they sportingly went along with it, the whole thing just served to really tarnish the legacy of two long-time wrestling greats. A truly rotten waste of pay-per-view time. A truly rotten waste of *any* time, quite frankly, and one of the worst matches in wrestling history.

Final Rating: -****

Tables and Dumpsters Match
The Dudley Boyz vs. X-Pac, Road Dogg & Tori
This was during the period where Bubba Ray Dudley was practically having orgasms every time he powerbombed a woman through a table, and Tori was on his hit list. That streak of violence against women somehow made they Dudleys de facto babyfaces against fellow heels DX, who were on their last legs after a rotator cuff injury put Billy Gunn on the shelf and Triple H began spending more and more time with the McMahons. Even a brand new remix of their theme from RUN DMC isn't enough to stop the rot.

The rules here are that to win, DX have to put both Dudleys in a dumpster, or the Dudleys have to put all three DXers through tables, those gimmicks being the "speciality" of each team. Yes, the dumpster is the speciality of D-Generation X, despite Road Dogg being the only guy on the team to have ever been in a dumpster match, a match incidentally that he lost. But let's not allow semantics to get in the way of good, silly fun. For some reason, both teams are also abiding by regular tag rules, which they predictably drop halfway through the bout anyway. Things start to get really wacky when the Dudleys hit the as-yet unnamed Wazzup Drop on Tori but D-Von refuses to get up, making sure to get himself a good deep lungful. DX actually "win" the match by shoving Bubba and D-Von into the dumpster, but the referee is too busy checking on Tori's pudding to notice, so the Dudleys crawl out of SECRET DOORS on the sides of the dumpster. That allows for an amusing spot where DX bring the referee over to show them their handiwork only to find nobody in the dumpster, the escaped Dudleys crawling under the ring before popping up on the other side to level them from behind with steel chairs.

The next nutty spot comes when the Dudleys move the steel steps into the ring and Bubba stands on them, giving Road Dogg a standing Awesomebomb over the top to the floor, crashing through two stacked up tables as he goes. Absolutely bonkers. X-Pac tries to return fire by splashing D-Von through a table, but Bubba Ray crotches him on the top and D-Von gives him a superplex through the table instead. That just leaves Tori, who jumps into the dumpster on her own volition, but it's all a ruse as DX attack the Dudleys from behind with chairs, knocking them into the dumpster for the win, something of a surprising result given the Dudleys were on the rise at the time with DX being yesterday's news, but then this show has been rife with questionable booking decisions. Tori it should be noted, seemed to suffer a genuine injury when Bubba fell on her in the dumpster, because she holds her arm completely limp for the post-match shenanigans which see Road Dogg and X-Pac eat a 3D each and Tori taste a superbomb through a table. Big spots + amusing psychology = fun match.
Final Rating: ***¼

King of the Ring Tournament, Final
Kurt Angle vs. Rikishi
Speaking of questionable booking decisions, why did the WWF book a guy with a limited skillset and obvious cardio issues like Rikishi to work three matches in a single night? Why did they also have that same guy carry a show-long arm injury, further limiting his range? And why did they book such a predictable climax in which the result was never in doubt? Hell, why did they bother booking the entire tournament to have an average match time of just 5:30 on the night, and a paltry 3:52 including TV matches? How can anybody take seriously a tournament with such a scant amount of time devoted to it? Half of Rikishi's

matches have been disqualification victories too, which is like a step below winning a game of football on a penalty shoot out!

With all that taken into consideration, the crowd still don't care about this tournament, waiting out Rikishi's Samoan drop and Ace Crusher (with the supposedly injured shoulder I should add) until the inevitable. Angle goes low to avoid the Stinkface and hits an Olympic Slam but only gets two. Rikishi avoids a sunset flip takeover with a sit-down splash for two, but no matter how hard they try to make this final seem epic, the crowd just won't bite. Rikishi goes up top (I know as a Headshrinker he used to deliver top rope splashes, but he's significantly heavier here and very fatigued) and Angle finally takes it with an impressive belly-to-belly superplex. King Kurt is crowned in perhaps the least exciting manner possible, and to top that, the ceremony isn't even taking place tonight. No, you'll have to tune in to *RAW* for that.

I know Angle was the outstanding choice here even before the tournament began, but Benoit and Jericho could both have legitimate cases made for them winning, while Guerrero might have been something of an outside chance but wouldn't have upset anyone by claiming the grand prize, so why one of them couldn't have been give the nod to reach the finals I don't know. The presence of any of those three would have provided a much better match to go out on, and offered some genuine drama regarding the outcome.
Final Rating: *

WWF Championship
Triple H (c), Mr. McMahon & Shane McMahon
vs. The Rock, The Undertaker & Kane
Speaking of questionable booking decisions, here's the WWF Title being defended in a six-man tag, where the heel champion has two non-wrestlers on his team. I suppose to some extent, stacking the odds against the champion is a way to guarantee a title change without actually guaranteeing it, but the fact a change appears to be such an obvious outcome, coupled with the knowledge that the babyfaces likely won't be able to decide between them who gets to take the pin, manages to throw the result somewhat up in the air. It's such confused psychology though, especially as Triple H, the lead heel, is the one who's up against the odds, especially in light of the fact that neither of his partners are actually wrestlers. The babyfaces meanwhile manage to look like idiots, bickering over who gets to win the belt so much that they wind up robbing each other of sure-fire chances to win it, when in reality the opposition should be easy prey. As a result, the live crowd don't really cotton on to any of this convoluted nonsense, with some of them seemingly unable to tell if the babyfaces have turned heel on each other or not. At one point they seem to go the whole hog with Kane helping Triple H, only to turn on him a few seconds later. Whatever happened to just having a good old fashioned pro wrestling match?

Now while I do stand by those arguments for why the match is so flawed, I will say that it does at least create a dynamic you otherwise wouldn't normally have, which does allow for a certain level of intrigue that wouldn't otherwise be there. Credit also goes to Shane McMahon for taking one of the most ridiculously dangerous bumps I've ever seen, a chokeslam off the top through the ringside announcers table. Remember, this isn't a wrestler trying to get noticed and make a name for himself, this is a company executive destroying his body for your entertainment. Also a source of great fun, albeit unintentionally so, is JR's muddled assertion that the Undertaker "came to become the WWF Title", which conjures up an amusing set of mental images that see Undertaker wrapped around John Cena's waist, slung over Randy Orton's shoulder and hung above the ring as a bunch of guys attempt to scale a ladder and claim him as their own.

Eventually, the inevitable happens, as Vince tries for a People's Elbow but gets caught with a Rock Bottom to give Rock his fifth WWF Title and sparing Triple H from doing the job. That would also be the third consecutive pay-per-view in a row that the title has changed hands, although 2000 doesn't quite match up to 1999 in that regard, where the belt switched hands on average more than once a month. Overall this match wasn't too bad, and for all the aforementioned problems caused by the dumb rules, they did at least create a modicum of interest that wouldn't otherwise have been there. It's not the sort of match you'd want to run more than once though, not after having seen it play out in all of its overbooked daftness.
Final Rating: **½

VERDICT

Aside from the blindingly obvious low point of the evening, *King of the Ring* wasn't such a bad show by 1999 standards. Unfortunately for the WWF, it wasn't 1999 anymore, it was 2000, a year largely noted for an awesome run of in-ring performances and a general lack of Vince Russo-style silliness. This show sadly harkens back to those bad old days, with an overload on the bad booking front and just few decent performances scattered throughout.

As for the Patterson-Brisco debacle, some may be wondering what the justification is for a -**** rating, as opposed to a full -*****. Simply put, while I do consider it an affront to the paying customer and a real stain against the legacies of both men, it only lasted a handful of minutes (a handful too many, sure) and was never intended to be anything more than comic relief (misguided comic relief, sure). 1999's Kennel from Hell match between Al Snow and the Big Bossman is something I consider -***** because it was intended to be a serious blow-off, and while you can't always know for certain if something that sounds funny on paper will actually *be* funny in front of a paying audience, I think anybody with half a brain could have guessed that including actual dogs in the match was just a bad idea. Then there's WCW's notorious Doomsday cage match from *Uncensored* '96, which was on overly-long, action-less burial of all the promotion's top heels in a ludicrous scenario that saw two men triumph over eight, masquerading as a pay-per-view main event. Held against those, the Hardcore Evening Gown match didn't perhaps plummet to those depths… but boy, did it ever come close.

33

FULLY LOADED 2000

CAT NO: WWF250
RUN TIME: 168 minutes (approx)

Arnold Furious: My wish list for this book was basically as follows: *Royal Rumble 2000*, *No Way Out 2000* (for Mick Foley's farewell double shot) and *Fully Loaded 2000*. Those were the three shows I was really eager to review. For those who don't recall, this is a fine show. A snapshot of the year. It features a triple main event as the WWF took their three most promising midcard talents (Kurt Angle, Chris Jericho and Chris Benoit) and threw them against their three most established top card talents (Undertaker, Triple H and the Rock). It was an attempt to examine the glass ceiling to see if any of them belonged above it. By all rights Jericho should have been above it already, having beaten Hunter for the WWF Title only to have the decision reversed when Earl Hebner admitted a fast count. Like James has stated elsewhere, I thought it was Jericho's time and striking while the iron was hot could have given him a massive boost as a talent. 2000 may have been the Rock's year but him not winning the title at that point wouldn't have been an issue as he was already monstrously over and it wouldn't have hurt him at all. Whereas Jericho winning would have taken him to another level and the WWF would have gained a main eventer.

Tangent: This was the third and final *Fully Loaded* PPV. An event that debuted in 1998 and a spin-off of the DX push, featuring Hunter crotch-chopping on the poster. *Fully Loaded* was replaced in 2001 by the *InVasion* PPV, with the title being too wishy-washy to promote a massive WWF vs. WCW storyline. When the 2002 schedule rolled around *Fully Loaded* had disappeared for good, replaced by the even more generic *Vengeance*. Not that *Vengeance* retained its PPV status for that long, replaced in 2008 by the *Night of Champions*, which sounds a bit lame (like an SMW special), before briefly reappearing in 2011 to fill a gap. We're in Dallas, Texas. Hosts are Jim Ross and Jerry Lawler.

T&A vs. The Hardy Boyz & Lita
A mixed gender tag match to open and I think this shows the difference between a coherent and popular team like the Hardys and a slapped together comedy team like Head Cheese, as T&A got nowhere at *WrestleMania* against Head Cheese but here thanks to Trish's popularity and her rivalry with Lita, T&A are suddenly worthwhile. I love Trish Stratus but she completely changed professional wrestling forever in a negative way. The WWF went in for her looks but then found out she was eager to wrestle and let her, which created this image of a WWF Diva; a good looking woman who was fit and able to compete. It's what the WWF has looked for in every single female recruit ever since, which has been a detriment to their product. The versatility of Trish eventually made the likes of Ivory, Molly Holly and Jazz a thing of the past. The ladies really add to the popularity of the match here with their actions and a *gasp* over and competitive feud. Albert shows his abilities by taking an opening shine off Matt and for a big man he was frequently able to get over smaller guys. The contrast with Test, who can't take anything convincingly, is noticeable. Despite his flaws the match still works tremendously well as size and power versus risk taking and teamwork. It's a simple story but excellently executed. Who'd have thought Test & Albert would figure into a trademark hot opener? Lita gets her name chanted, which shows you how far she came in a short time. She started out as a Spanish speaking valet for Essa Rios before eclipsing his popularity in no time flat and getting teamed up with the Hardys instead. The ladies can wrestle the men so Trish tags in to slap Matt but then gets picked off with some excellent heel miscues into a triple suplex spot! Awesome stuff. Albert then presses Jeff clean over the top rope in a devastating spot. The action continues at a breakneck pace, which makes you wonder why Test & Albert were not that good every week but then immediately notice the Hardys uncanny ability of making almost everyone else look good. The result is T&A's greatest moment in wrestling, courtesy of some terrific and creative counters from the brothers. Lita hits a flying DDT on Test and adds in a crossbody to the floor on Albert as the fans go INSANE. Test staggers back up into a flying rana from Lita and the crowd completely lose their shit. Test recovers to hit a powerbomb and Trish comes in for the pin only for Lita to manage a last gasp kickout. Trish shows she can wrestle a bit by hitting a bulldog, which pops JR; always good news for a young wrestler. Trish's strikes leave a little to be desired but they set her up to take a goddamn superplex off Lita, which shows both girls' natural ability. That sets Lita up for the moonsault and the faces go over in a great opening match.

A perfect way to start any PPV. Lita and Trish's feud was the backbone of the women's division for the entire time they worked in the company, with both eventually retiring a few months apart.
Final Rating: ***½

Backstage: Mick Foley, with new buzzcut, gets informed that Christian has food poisoning. Elsewhere: the Underbiker arrives and chases Kurt Angle around on his motorbike.

Tazz vs. Al Snow
Tazz came into the WWF as a hot babyface but got injured and when he came back they turned him heel, for some reason. The WWF figured Snow would be a good guy to get Tazz over as they'd worked together in ECW (Snow's ECW debut match was opposite Taz). They'd be wrong. Snow's career once again faltered after his brush with main event stardom failed in 1999. Here they make the dubious decision to give Snow most of the match, including a stupid moonsault just one match after Lita used it to finish. Tazz ends up looking like a total punk who has to rely on Snow's fixation with a mannequin head for an opening. The way these guys insert spots feels like I'm watching two kids have a match on the Playstation. Eventually they do work a decent spot as Tazz gets the Tazzmission and Al tries to hip toss out only for Tazz to hold on and get the submission. The rest of the match was rubbish. JR references Tazz's "path of rage", which seems to involve him looking like a chump for four minutes before exchanging spots and then getting a finisher off a defensive counter.
Final Rating: *

Backstage: a doctor confirms that Christian is really sick.

Elsewhere: Triple H and Steph hang out making fun of Christian's illness. An enormous amount of flowers show up and Hunter points out they're not from him. Turns out they're from Kurt Angle and Hunter gets a raging case of jealously. I hate Stephanie McMahon's obsession with love triangles. This is wrestling missy, not a bloody soap opera.

Tangent: During 2000 Steph found herself constantly at the centre of angles. As the WWF Champion's wife she contributed quite nicely, but then found herself kissed by Chris Jericho and the object of Kurt Angle's affections. Not that she was fantasy booking herself into her own programs or anything. The annoying thing is that Steph got over on her own merits and then proceeded to force herself down the public's throat. She'd already done the hard work but insisted on forcing the issue long after she needed to. As a viewer it became enormously frustrating. What's worse is that as time progressed Hunter became even worse than her, forcing his agenda and making sure the show was focused entirely on him when here, at his peak, that wasn't the case. At least not in the matches, where he'd routinely go 50-50 in the booking. Take the Jericho feud where he jobbed on TV, albeit to have the decision reversed, and let Jericho kick his ass before the match before just barely eeking out a win. Compare that to Triple H feuds from 2003 and the difference is alarming.

WWF European Championship
Eddie Guerrero (c) vs. Perry Saturn
This started out as a weird stalker angle where Eddie thought Chyna was hot and went after her, only for Chyna to reciprocate and turn on Jericho to allow Eddie to win this strap. The involvement of the ladies broke up the Radicalz good and proper causing Saturn to gain a valet in Terri. Saturn was a tremendous talent when he was "on", but he's not "on" at all here and Eddie has to carry the match, with Saturn botching all of his bumps. It's testament to what a phenomenal talent Eddie is that the match remains passable. Saturn is absolutely all over the place though, at one point hitting a powerbomb, which involves no impact on him at all, and then lying around selling afterwards. What are you doing, man? So Eddie takes over again and pops off spots with Saturn managing to bust his head open by taking a DDT wrong. By contrast Eddie is sharp and nails everything, constantly covering for Saturn's shortcomings. The crowd dies on them though because of Saturn's visible issues and his timing being so out of whack. A powerbomb sets up a moonsault, which looks awful and misses. Saturn can't get his shit together and takes another horrible bump to the floor before knocking Chyna through an announce table in a terrible spot. Terri decides this is a good time to run down, kicks Eddie in the cojones and Saturn finishes with a Savage Elbow. I feel bad for Eddie who was awesome here but just couldn't carry a sloppy opponent and both valets to a good match.
Final Rating: **

Backstage: Mick Foley rumbles Christian for fake the vomiting by pouring a substance from a bucket into the toilet. The tag title defence is on.

Elsewhere: Undertaker talks smack about Kurt Angle before spotting the Olympic gold medallist hoping on his bike. This leads to a chase sequence to be continued later.

WWF Tag Team Championship
Edge & Christian (c) vs. The Acolytes
Edge & Christian's heel promo before the match is one of my favourites of all time. Seeing as the setting is Dallas they opt for making fun of the JFK Assassination. Tragedy + time = comedy. "If JFK had spent five more minutes in Dallas he'd have committed suicide anyway" – Christian. Being a big rangy Texan, Bradshaw takes exception at the cheap heat and cuts an astonishing promo about Dick Murdoch and the Freebirds. It's so incredible that it makes you wonder how it took the WWF another four years to give him a serious push. He always had that ability inside him as is evidenced here. After delivering excellent promos apiece the match is unfortunately something of an underwhelming experience. The Acolytes basically just pound E&C until they realise the match desperately needs heat and awkwardly transition into it. Christian takes both finishers until Edge runs in with a tag belt and makes sure the ref sees him hit Faarooq with it for the cheap DQ. This was in keeping with Edge & Christian's tag title reign and how they'll do anything to keep the straps, but the match itself doesn't quite live up to the hype and at 5.29 is the second shortest match on the card.
Final Rating: ¾*

Video Control takes us to WWF New York where the Big Bossman checks IDs. It's probably a better role for him than wrestling.

Backstage: Triple H and Stephanie continue to argue about flowers.

Elsewhere: Taker continues to stalk Kurt Angle only for the Olympic Hero to set him up and nail the Dead Man in the knee with a wrench.

Steel Cage Match
WWF Intercontinental Championship
Val Venis (c) vs. Rikishi

Rikishi won the belt off Chris Benoit in a mysterious piece of booking that only serves to reflect Rikishi's popularity in early 2000. A snapshot of that moment. Seeing as he was feuding with Val, over a *King of the Ring* result, the belt switched hands (thanks to a random attack from Tazz). Trish is back out here as manager of Val, the idea being that she could take his career to another level. Evidence of that being his IC Title win (albeit his second). The cage match has lost some steam after the introduction of the Hell in a Cell in 1997 and thus this bout has no heat at all. I'm not really sure how it went wrong for Rikishi as he went from being a monster babyface to getting smaller and smaller reactions until a weird heel turn, where he was revealed as the driver who ran over Steve Austin. Val goes low to avoid the Stinkface and they blow a bulldog follow up called "somewhat of a bulldog headlock" by JR trying to cover for the blown spot. Val's work was usually quite tight but losing his hair and then losing his gimmick resulted in him being dispatched into mediocrity. So both these guys are on the cusp of not being big stars anymore. I think the lack of content in this cage match rather reflects why neither ended up as main eventers. You have to take your chances when they come round. Cage matches are among the hardest to work effectively and a lot of younger fans were not able to relate to the violent nature of them as there were many more violent matches as the years went by. Back in the 80s the cage match was it! By 2000 the match concept was all but dead. Trish smashes the door into Rikishi's head, which brings out Lita to a massive pop (to show who the real stars are) to give Trish a receipt for some earlier belt shots. It makes Trish a non-factor and also intensifies the already hot Trish-Lita feud. It looks as if Rikishi will therefore regain his IC Title and the big man has a big spot planned too. With Val and the ref down Rikishi climbs onto the top of the cage and SPLASHES VAL FROM ON TOP OF IT! Even in an age of ridiculous bumps, seeing someone of Rikishi's size hit a splash off the top of a cage is amazing. That really should finish but the WWF somewhat errs by having Tazz run in to hit Rikishi with a camera again (causing audible groans from the crowd) and Val retains. So they lifted a finish from free TV for the PPV match? Lazy. Bad finish aside the match was okay and the big splash off the cage sticks in the memory.
Final Rating: **½

Backstage: the love triangle drama continues as Triple H goes in search of Kurt Angle, instead running into Chris Jericho, who's been mucking around with the flowers all night. Jericho leaves Hunter lying, which shows you how close he was to being the man in 2000. So close, yet so far away.

Promo Time: Shane McMahon
Shane comes out for a mid-PPV chat. He decides to call out the Rock for a match right now, although not for the WWF Title as "Chris Benoit will be winning that later". Rock comes out to respond and calls Shane a pussy. Rock knows it's a set up so he wants to know where Benoit is hiding, suspecting "up your candy ass". Instead Benoit pops up on the Titantron to promise victory by submission or pinfall, referencing that a DQ causes a title change. Benoit tears up all the Rock's personal effects to show him he means business.

Kurt Angle vs. The Undertaker
This is a burial. I'm not sure why the WWF decided to book this way as Kurt began clumsily upsetting Taker and then made things worse with half-hearted apologies. This leads to a match up where Taker gets most of it and Angle comes out looking like shit despite having had one of the hottest debut years in the entire history of wrestling. Luckily Taker couldn't hold him down and Angle eventually came out on a par with the 'Dead Man'. Although the stupidity of the booking here helped to tank Angle's first title run. Taker even pulls Angle up on a few covers to give him an extended beating. Idiocy. Taker even has an out for losing here, with his knee having been assaulted not once but twice with a wrench. That's the only way Angle gets any offence because Taker is a mark for himself. Mark by name, mark by nature. He's slowly wandered away from his zombie gimmick too. Not only with the leather vest and the lack of hair dye (leaving him ginger) but also by wearing comfy slacks, like Mick Foley on his day off. At the time I probably marked harder for the Underbiker than for his zombie gimmick but that's just because I hate the zombie gimmick. As if to make matters even worse Taker starts banging away on the mat like he's tapping out, as if he needs encouragement from 16,000 Texans to get the job done while simultaneously behaving like he's working in front of 200 fans at a state fair. He does occasionally limp to sell the damage to his knee but then hits a chokeslam with one arm for no good reason. Last Ride finishes. Angle luckily bounced back by not working with Undertaker. This was during a stage in the Undertaker's career where getting a passable match out of him would have been a minor miracle, and yet he apparently had the temerity to complain that various WCW guys "couldn't work" the next year.
Final Rating: ½*

Last Man Standing Match
Triple H vs. Chris Jericho
This is the peak of Jericho as a babyface in the WWF as he's shown as an equal to Triple H and this isn't long after he briefly beat Hunter (via fast count) for a phantom WWF Title run. The opening shine sees Jericho beat the crap out of HHH and if there's one thing Hunter did well in 2000 it was getting other people over. Something he's totally failed to follow up on ever since. You look at the respect he gives Foley, Rock and Jericho in 2000 and you can see how it made them. Having people go over on your big stars is how you make new ones. Jericho got over because he beat Triple H up. Triple H didn't lose any popularity and if anything he got over even more because the smart fans respected him for doing the hard work. As for the marks, he'd have them forever because he's got a cool entrance and a cool finisher. It almost pains me to watch Hunter in 2000 because he was such a tremendous talent and yet he deliberately stopped being so. Jericho has an out, like Taker did, as Hunter injured his ribs with a sledgehammer prior to the PPV and HHH works that area. Like a bastard. There's a bit where Hunter rams his shoulder into Jericho's ribs in the corner relentlessly. It shows both his cardio and his aggression. He's a beast. Jericho takes such a beating on the ribs that you feel he's done, which is a huge turnaround from the opening shine. Jericho gets a series of hope spots culminating in the Lionsault, which gets knees into the injured ribs. Because Jericho can't catch his breath he can't stand. Hunter goes to finish with the Main Event Sleeper, eager to capitalise on the situation he's created. Jericho does a great job of selling how close he is to being finished with his rubber legs and his begging Hunter to kick his ass, if he can. Jericho manages a weak crotch chop; Pedigree!

The crowd loved the crotch chop. That should do it, given that the match has been suitably brutal, but Hunter played the cerebral approach and did the work. As Jericho starts to stir Hunter bails for a chair, pissed off that Chris won't stay down. He even chair shots the ribs, continuing his unrelenting focus. The escalating violence was a trademark of Hunter's best matches. Hunter figures a Pedigree on a chair will do it but Jericho goes low to save himself. Jericho comes back with a

chair shot and Hunter bleeds a gusher off that. It's hideous, a massive cut and loads of juice from it, with Hunter once again sacrificing his own wellbeing for the good of the match. Now it's a total reversal as Hunter has the weakness and Jericho, like a shark, smells the blood. But those ribs are always a weakness for Hunter to exploit too, so the match goes back-and-forth with one aspect countering the other. The match had previously worked on a "periods of dominance" strategy. This new back-and-forth creates an exciting conclusion as the match is wide open. They duel with monitor shots but both survive the 10 count. Pedigree is countered into the Walls of Jericho and Hunter taps out but that's not in the rules. Jericho just wants to cripple Hunter's legs so he can't stand. Hunter gets into the ropes then realises there's no DQ so the ref can't break it. Steph realises that means she can interfere and jumps in there only for Jericho to slap her in the Walls of Jericho and Hunter has to save. The timing of that is a bit weird as Hunter has to recover his legs way too quickly, but then wouldn't you to save your wife? Hunter pulls out the sledgehammer but misses and he gets catapulted into the post. Jericho gets in one of those sledgehammer punches to set up a table spot. Hunter goes low to block it and back suplexes Jericho through the announce table. Jericho's defence for losing is that his head hits the floor after the table, and Hunter gets up, just, and Jericho stays down. Great match. Another classic from Hunter's 2000 run and Jericho's defining moment as a WWF wrestler, in that he was good enough to mix it up with the main eventers but ultimately he wasn't better than them. He was so, so close. Don't even get me started on his eventual title run where he took backseat to Stephanie and Triple H having marital issues!
Final Rating: ****½

WWF Championship
The Rock (c) vs. Chris Benoit
There's a strange stipulation here where if Rock loses on DQ the title changes hands. Which rather begs the question; why doesn't Shane McMahon just run in and hit Benoit as soon as the match starts? Having these guys work together had a twofold bonus; it helped Benoit to understand "sportz entertainment" and what he needed to do in main event matches, and also improved Rock's in-ring because as WWF champion he simply had to measure up to Benoit. Rock's explosive in-ring is complemented well by Benoit's uncanny in-ring skillset. It makes for a wonderful beginning where Benoit and Shane bounce all over the place for Rock. Benoit's ability makes it easier for the Rock to hide his shortcomings as a wrestler and it creates a very good title defence. Shane's presence is a slight distraction and he sets up a Benoit belt shot for a near fall that you feel he doesn't need. With Benoit being a technical master, he could just outwrestle Rock. Indeed he seems to counter pretty much everything into suplexes before hooking the Sharpshooter. Rock makes the ropes but Shane interferes again by lowbridging Rock to the floor. The timing was flawless on it with Shane leaping into position at the last half second. Rock responds to the leg work with his own and a figure four. Mirroring has always been a good wrestling strategy but Rock's approach is more like "an eye for eye" keeping himself creative in the process. The Rock's energy combines well with Benoit's workmanlike approach and this is a great main event because of it.

Hunter had introduced violence into the main events and blood to distinguish his stuff from Austin's arena covering brawls. Rock distinguished his main events by having them take place at frenetic pace and actually delivering in the ring, not around it. Rock has a few moments where spots appear to be on the verge of going wrong because of the complexity or the difficulty levels involved, but everything ends up working. Chalk that up to Benoit being a ring general. It makes you wonder why WCW never pushed him like this. Benoit can't talk and has very little charisma but he's a machine in the ring so he's suited to facing off with charismatic babyfaces like the Rock. Spinebuster sets up the People's Elbow but Shane distracts the ref on the pin and Benoit kicks out. As the spots continue you can see Benoit slowly coaching the Rock into the bigger spots, making sure nothing goes wrong and yet keeping the pace of the match high. It's masterful stuff and Rock really does a terrific job of keeping up. It's smart, hard work. Benoit brings a chair in but Rock steals it. Shane sneaks in and bashes the ref in the back, making the ref believe the Rock did it, which is again well-timed stuff from all involved. Rock gets the Crossface on Benoit but the ref calls for the bell. Rock thinks he's won by submission but the ref announces Benoit wins via DQ and is the new champion. Benoit celebrates with Shane and the belt and, like Jericho before him, there's a bittersweet moment where he thinks he's the champion. The WWF sure liked messing with these guys in 2000. Rock blades after the bell, courtesy of a Shane chair shot, but out comes commissioner Mick Foley to straighten everything out and he orders the match to continue. The fans who'd been pelting the ring with Styrofoam cups are able to settle down again. Benoit gets the rolling Germans to set up the Crippler Crossface but Rock survives. The timing on Rock dragging himself into the ropes wasn't right at all. It didn't feel like there was any tension behind it despite Rock bleeding all over Benoit's arm. Rock Bottom out of nowhere wins it and rather takes away all the hard work of the previous 20-minutes. However it was still a hard fought contest and one of Rock's best singles matches to this point.
Final Rating: ****¼

VERDICT

It's incredible that Triple H went over here with no title on the line. You could argue that 2000 was the year that made Hunter a main event star and the WWF must have felt he needed to stay strong. If that wasn't enough, Rock and Taker went over in their respective matches too. To recap; they pushed three undercard guys against three established guys and all of the established guys won, which was an issue with the WWF for some time: the fabled "glass ceiling". As if to apologise for it, the WWF put the title on Kurt Angle immediately only to have his run turn into a bit of a joke, with his *real* big push coming a year later as a babyface hero against Steve Austin, so they could turn around and say "see, told you". I still think Jericho should have won, and you could argue Benoit on this show could easily have won the belt without ruining the WWF's plans too.

Despite the results, this is a great PPV with two killer main events and a strong opening match all delivering. It does have the unfortunate downside of Angle-Undertaker, but the Last Man Standing match and the WWF Title match compensate for it. HHH-Jericho is a genuine MOTYC although not my personal pick for the best match of 2000 in the WWF. Rock-Benoit could be arguably an outside contender for MOTY too. When you have a PPV with two outstanding matches on it like this one, it's impossible not to like.

85

SUMMERSLAM 2000

CAT NO: WWF251
RUN TIME: 170 minutes (approx)

Lee Maughan: From the Raleigh Entertainment and Sports Arena in Raleigh, North Carolina. Hosts are Jim Ross and Jerry Lawler.

Right to Censor vs. Too Cool & Rikishi
This is Right to Censor's pay-per-view debut, but they don't have Val Venis with them yet. Rikishi and Too Cool do have two of the renamed Goodfather's hos with them though, one of whom you'll know as Victoria, later to become the valet of Stevie Richards, oddly enough. Like most pay-per-view undercard matches of the day, this was pretty short, just a shade over five minutes in fact. The babyfaces still get to do most of their trademark stuff, namely butt splashes in the corner and dancing like goofballs, but as Scotty 2 Hotty looks to finish with the Worm, he eats a Steviekick from Richards for the pin.
Final Rating: *½

X-Pac vs. Road Dogg
Welcome to the WWF's answer to the nWo B-Team saga, as these two are basically fighting it out over the rights to DX (which they actually already did back at *Fully Loaded* '99), even though the group is basically just them at this point. Good thing the WWF put them over the Dudley Boyz back at *King of the Ring*, eh? The crux of this match is that what started out as a "friendly rivalry" has escalated after X-Pac "accidentally" headbutted Road Dogg off the ring apron through a table on *RAW*, and Dogg abandoned X-Pac during a handicap match four nights later on *SmackDown!*.

The crowd are pretty split on X-Pac, but they take to Road Dogg 100% as a babyface, which is the direction the WWF wanted anyway. X-Pac's heel work is subtle enough that you can tell he's the heel, but you can still pretend there's some ambiguity there if you're prepared to suspend your disbelief just a tad. What's harder to suspend your disbelief over is JR's absurd claim that many fans consider these two to be one of the best tag teams of all time, when in reality they'd only been teaming semi-regularly since Billy Gunn tore his rotator cuff against the Dudleys at *No Way Out*.

Early on they play around with some comedy spots, like Road Dogg kicking X-Pac in the ass and X-Pac selling it like Ricky Steamboat selling a Ric Flair chop after 45-minutes of a 60-minute match. X-Pac also begins gloating after landing the Bronco Buster at the second attempt, thus sending out stronger signals about his status as the heel, finally confirming it with a low blow on Road Dogg's attempted pumphandle slam that sets up an X-Factor for the pin. Post-match, X-Pac wants to make friends after proving who the better man was, so Road Dogg kicks him in the gut, simulates anal sex with him, and gives him a pumphandle anyway to officially end DX.
Final Rating: **

WWF Intercontinental Championship
Val Venis (c) & Trish Stratus vs. Chyna & Eddie Guerrero
JR actually has the audacity to call the stipulations here "a first" despite this coming only two months after Triple H had to defend the WWF Title in a six-man tag match at *King of the Ring*. And, like that match, the defending heel champion has a non-wrestler for a partner. You'd think the stipulations would set up a Guerrero heel turn with him "robbing" Chyna of a victory on a blind tag or something like that, but there isn't even a hint of that here. Instead, Eddie and Chyna take turns wiping the floor with Val, even breaking out a Midnight Express-style flapjack. Trish, still green as grass here, only really comes into play towards the end, getting immediately caught out by Eddie as she tries to claim a pin in the place of the knackered Val, and he passes her on to Chyna who gives her the gorilla press for the three and title. Not to fear, Eddie would take the belt a couple of weeks later on *RAW* by "accidentally" pinning Chyna in a triple threat match after Kurt Angle laid her out with a belt shot.
Final Rating: **¾

- Earlier tonight on *Sunday Night Heat*, Kurt Angle refused to answer any questions regarding his kissing Stephanie McMahon on *SmackDown!*

- Meanwhile, back in the makeup chair, Stephanie lets slip that Kurt is a good kisser. Uh-oh.

Jerry Lawler vs. Tazz
So having spent the best part of three and a half years as a badass killing machine in ECW and entering the WWF to much fanfare and positive audience response back at the *Royal Rumble*, Tazz in the space of eight months has been reduced to feuding with a couple of commentators. The match came about after JR called Tazz "a piece of garbage" on TV, which Tazz took exception to, with Lawler standing up for JR's honour. That led to an angle where Tazz abducted Ross, left him in a rental car and smashed the windows in, causing broken glass to embed itself in JR's eye. That was preceded by a distasteful line from Tazz regarding JR's issues with Bell's Palsy - "I'd love to slap you across your face but it looks like God already beat me to it!"

As one might expect, there's very little to the actual match as they race through their spots in the limited amount of time they've been berthed, with Lawler throwing a dropkick early and Tazz missing a senton of all things. Lawler then pulls the strap down after a gruelling four minutes but Tazz no-sells the piledriver and throws Lawler into the ref, bumping him. Then, with the Tazzmission locked in deep, JR rises from the announce table and smashes a huge jar of candy into Tazz's face, shattering it in a spectacular visual that draws a huge pop from the crowd, and Lawler gets the pin off that a few seconds later.

Not much of an actual match, and a very backwards booking decision to have the still somewhat new guy lose to the part-timer, but a tremendous payoff to the angle. Tazz would go on to beat Lawler the following month at *Unforgiven* in a strap match that saw the Raven character debut in the WWF, and in an odd bit of synergy, Tazz would choke Lawler out at *One Night Stand* 2006 following interference from another announcer, Joey Styles.
Final Rating: *

WWF Hardcore Championship
Shane McMahon (c) vs. Steve Blackman
Shane won the Hardcore title from Blackman on *RAW* with the aid of Test, Albert, Edge, Christian, a kendo stick and the 24/7 rule, and now Blackman's out for revenge. Shane tries to hightail it through the crowd but Blackman gives chase, dumps a trashcan over his head and plays him like a drum with a pair of karate sticks. Test and Albert quickly run-in and get some heat on Blackman to prevent the match from being entirely one-sided, but Blackman survives a top-rope elbow drop from Test and all four brawl up the aisle, where Albert accidentally wipes out Test after Blackman pulls him in the way of a kendo stick shot.

Shane, still looking to escape, decides the best course of action is to clamber up the Titantron, but Blackman takes out Albert and gives chase, smashing Shane in the legs with repeated kendo stick shots until he plummets backwards off the scaffolding and crashes through the stage below. Blackman follows with a flying elbow from about 20 feet up to add an exclamation point to that, although the camera angle on the landing reveals a significant amount of padding, somewhat lessening the impact. Still a couple of nutty bumps to take, especially for Shane who went off backwards from about 30 feet in the air. A decent match capped off with a hell of a visual, and kudos again to company CEO Shane for attempting to cripple himself in the name of entertainment when he really didn't have to.
Final Rating: ***

Best 2 out of 3 Falls
Chris Benoit vs. Chris Jericho
In typical WWF fashion, the full-on nature of this feud was somewhat tainted by the usual rotten "comedy" the promotion has so frequently liked to crowbar into things over the years, with Jericho rhyming like Dr. Seuss as badly photoshopped pictures of Benoit sailing boats, riding goats and playing baseball flashed up the screen. What a way to follow up Benoit trying to crush Jericho under a garage door that was.

First Fall: Quick first fall as Jericho gets posted on the outside and Benoit counters a Tombstone piledriver into a shoulderbreaker. He then avoids a Lionsault with the knees and locks on the Crossface to go 1-0 up.

Second Fall: With Jericho's arm still hurting, Benoit immediately goes back into the Crossface, but Jericho makes the ropes so Benoit rams the shoulder into the ringpost three times and counters Jericho's return fire with rolling German suplexes. Jericho manages to wheelbarrow roll his way through the third one and catch Benoit in the Walls of Jericho to tie the score in another quick fall.

Third Fall: They trade off on powerbomb reversals and Jericho attempts a piledriver but he can't deliver due to the injured shoulder, so Benoit counters with a dragon suplex. Benoit looks for the diving headbutt off that but Jericho catches him up top for a super huracanrana that only gets two. The Lionsault hits at the second time of asking but Jericho comes down hard on his shoulder, so can't make the cover, and Benoit counters Jericho's last-ditch schoolboy with a roll-up of his own, grabbing the bottom to ensure the three count.

Good match, although it felt like they were trying to deliver something epic and they just didn't have enough time for that. Ultimately, the match would have probably been better served had it just been one fall. The psychology was very sound, and the bout was very action-oriented, but they'd have a much more spectacular outing at the 2001 *Royal Rumble*, that time with a ladder involved.
Final Rating: ***½

TLC Match
WWF Tag Team Championship
Edge & Christian (c) vs. The Hardy Boyz vs. The Dudleys
If Shawn Michaels and Razor Ramon set new standards for spectacular gimmick bouts with their ladder matches together in 1994 and 1995, then Edge, Christian, the Hardy Boyz and the Dudley Boyz raised the bar to previously unimaginable heights at the turn of the century with their incredible table, ladder and chair-based stunt festivals. Unofficially kicking off in October 1999 when doubles ladder match put Edge, Christian and the Hardys on the map at *No Mercy '99*, the Dudleys were added to the mix for a sensational triple team ladder bout that stole the show at the otherwise meek *WrestleMania 2000*. Since then, the Dudleys have introduced regular table-smashing to WWF audiences, while "chair expertise" has been crowbarred in as the speciality of Edge & Christian, giving each tandem a foreign object-based gimmick. And now, for the very first time, those elements are about to come to a head, and the results are *spectacular*...

One of the many great things about the match is how it escalates in nuttiness, the spots getting bigger and bigger and bigger as they go. For example, they throw chairs at one another before the ladders even come into play, and when they do, nobody goes crashing through any tables for a good little

> **FURIOUS ABOUT: JERRY LYNN**
>
> The New F'N Show was a big star for ECW, even if he was RVD's jobber. He began his career in the late 80s and was catching the eye back in 1991 in Global working the Lightning Kid. While Sean Waltman got signed by the WWF and got made into a star, Lynn went to WCW and didn't. He spent two years there under a hood working as Mr JL. Like many others he developed a grudge against WCW, and Eric Bischoff, as he was fired while injured. ECW picked him up in 1997 and they struggled to find him something to do, bouncing him around their midcard before discovering, in 1999, that he had an almost telepathic understanding with TV champion Rob Van Dam. RVD was a big talent but ECW had a hard time finding people who could hang with him. Lynn could and the two developed a storied rivalry with Lynn never quite able to score a win. He finally bested RVD at Hardcore Heaven 2000, with outside help, before claiming the ECW title at Anarchy Rulz later in the year. Lynn lost again to RVD to headline ECW's final PPV and quickly signed for the WWF.

while. It's perfect that way because you "Ooh!" and "Ahh!" at each spot slightly crazier than the last, but they never feel like they're regressing at any point. Christian for instance takes a full nelson bomb off a ladder which draws very audible gasps from the audience, a reaction it might not have enjoyed had the tables already been in play. Jeff then gets pushed onto a ladder balanced atop another, creating a see-saw effect that whacks Matt in the face. On the one hand that's a great spot, because unlike a lot of ladder-based spots, you just don't see it coming. On the other hand, it's the same spot that caused Joey Mercury's nose to explode in disgusting fashion at *Armageddon 2006*, so I certainly wouldn't recommend it to anyone with a ladder match in their immediate future.

The tables are then brought in with Christian eating a 3D through one, usually a sure-fire match-ender, but not here. The Dudleys then stack two tables side-by-side atop two other tables, but Edge cuts them off with a chair before they can do anything with them. That's yet another great thing about this match because so often in these types of matches you'll see someone set up a table only to crash through it seconds later in the most blatantly contrived manner possible. Sabu was notorious for it in ECW, but here it makes total sense since they had success with a similar set-up just two months ago at *King of the Ring*, where they powerbombed Road Dogg from the ring through two stacked up tables, and the fact they get cut off by Edge means you completely forget the tables are set up in that manner anyway, making their eventual impact that much greater.

I also think six guys across three teams is probably the perfect number for this kind of match, because it allows for two to four guys at a time to rest and/or stay out of the way (under the pretence of selling of course) while those left standing perform their next high spot. When you have more guys in the match (such as later Money in the Bank ladder matches with ten wrestlers in there), you'd see guys drop to the floor and play dead for lengthy periods after just a couple of minutes, having taken moves that weren't particularly impactful-looking, and it hurts the credibility somewhat. You don't get that here because you also have the advantage of passing off somebody's lack of involvement as taking a respite if their partner remains active. Simply put, the tag team format of the match allows Jeff Hardy to spend a few minutes selling the pain after missing a senton off a giant ladder through a table (on the outside, mind you), but also spend a few extra moments catching his breath even after recovering as big brother Matt goes to war in the ring. I also loved that Bubba moved on that senton since he got nailed with it once before, in the aforementioned *WrestleMania 2000* match. Progressive psychology at its finest.

Remember those four tables the Dudleys parked on the outside of the ring? Bubba clambers up the giant ladder (now firmly planted in the ring), but gets pushed off sideways by Edge and Christian, sending him flying over the top, through the tables, and ending up a broken heap on the floor. Absolutely insane, and how he never blew his shoulder or elbow (or both) out doing a stunt that risky, I'll never know. And that's not even the most ridiculous bump of the match! Lita runs in and returns fire by pushing Edge and Christian sideways off the ladder, resulting in them both landing balls-first across the top rope, and then Matt begins to climb the ladder in what pretty much everyone had pegged as the big hometown hero finish. Not so. D-Von recovers just in time to tip the ladder from the opposite side, sending Matt over the top through two ringside tables BACKWARDS. He could easily have broken his neck doing that, especially if he'd come down across the ringside barrier. Just absolutely bonkers.

You'd think that would be it for the nuttiness, but Lita goes to check on Matt so Edge blasts her with a stiff spear, her head landing barely an inch away from the cold, sharp edge of an errant ladder laid across the floor. You think about how sore everyone in this match must have been for a month afterwards, but they're playing with such narrow margins that even watching it back years later you can't help but grimace at how close they all came to doing permanent damage had they just been a couple of inches either side off target. Finally, Jeff and D-Von, the last apparent survivors of this whole incredible car wreck, climb up and each grab a belt, but Edge and Christian pull the ladder out from beneath them, resulting in an impromptu game of Hang Tough. D-Von suddenly falls flat on his back, leaving Jeff alone with the belts for the second false finish as the crowd just absolutely explodes… but he can't get enough purchase to unhook the belts, so Edge and Christian SWAT him down with a ladder, then climb it to retrieve the belts.

Just absolutely incredible stuff that built and built and built to the finish with the spots getting riskier and more intense as they went along, and just when you thought they couldn't top themselves, they did over and over again. Perhaps even better than that was that not a single spot was missed, nothing felt out of place, everything was completely organic, it ebbed and flowed like any great pro wrestling battle should… Obviously there'll be some who feel a stunt show like this shouldn't compare to a technical classic, but wrestling has many forms, and as far as those stunt shows go, this one was damn well perfection.

Final Rating: *****

- Backstage, Triple H wants an explanation from Stephanie on how she could let Kurt kiss her, and warns her to stay away from Angle in future.

Thong Stinkface Match
The Kat vs. Terri Runnels
And from TLC to this. Still, you can't argue this show hasn't delivered a little bit of something for everybody thus far. This came about after the Kat had Rikishi give Terri a Stinkface, and Terri returned the favour with one of her own at WWF New York. Kat's also lost her black wig and mini-Chyna dominatrix leathers, which is a shame. They actually strip off before the match, instantly removing any of the clothes-tearing suspense they might otherwise have enjoyed, so instead need to fill the first couple of minutes by… well, I'm hesitant to call it "wrestling" in the traditional sense. The Kat's attempt at a spear is absolutely horrendous, and her bronco buster isn't much better. The referee inadvertently takes a headbutt to the nuts, and the Kat polishes things off by pulling a wedgie then sticking Terri's nose up her brown hole. Not sure I can really rate this as any kind of a match, but they basically promised that for your pay-per-view money one girl would stick her ass in the other girl's face, and that's exactly what you got.

The Undertaker vs. Kane
The angle here is that Kane turned on the Undertaker because he's "a monster", which is WWF code for "We need a match for *SummerSlam*." Still, the two were feuding when the Undertaker left in 1999, so the fact they were suddenly friends again when he came back at *Judgment Day* didn't make much sense either. The difference between their match here and the multitude of others they've had in the past is the Undertaker is now deep into his 'American Bad Ass' phase with blue denim shirt, while Kane is debuting his new sleeveless look. Otherwise, it's entirely the same, uninspiring punch-kick-punch-kick festival their matches usually are. In an attempt to spice things up, they start hurling the steel steps around at each other, and Undertaker pulls Kane's mask off… which inexplicably results in his music suddenly playing as Kane walks away, no decision having ever been rendered. JR's belief that "I don't think this match ever started, I never heard a bell!" only adds to the anticlimax. As Johnny Rotten once said as the Sex Pistols disintegrated on stage at the Winterland in San Francisco back in 1978: "Ever get the feeling you've been cheated?"
Final Rating: *

- Backstage, Stephanie gets a call from Kurt but lies to Hunter about it, telling him it's her mom Linda. That makes things a little bit awkward when Hunter asks if he can say hi to her.

WWF Championship
The Rock (c) vs. Triple H vs. Kurt Angle
Before the match starts, Kurt openly declares that he wishes he'd kissed Stephanie sooner, so Triple H comes marching out to do some serious damage. And serious damage is accomplished when he attempts to Pedigree Angle on the Spanish announce table, only for it to go into business for itself and give way before the planned spot, causing Angle to fall head-first to the floor, legitimately knocking him out cold before the Rock has even been introduced. The thud with which his head smashes against the broken table is just sickening, and sure enough, he has to be stretchered out as Rocky finally arrives and gets into a brawl with Hunter. Shockingly (albeit somewhat through hindsight), Triple H actually catches up with the stretcher, wheels it back down the aisle, and starts punching Angle in the head, hardly the optimum thing to do to a bloke who's just suffered a concussion.

With Angle out of commission, Rock and Triple H have to improvise most of the way, but given how frequently they've clashed over the past three years, that isn't really a problem. Stephanie comes out to get yelled at by Hunter, but the lack of Angle lessens the impact of that, and Hunter has to call new spots for her. She winds up accidentally lamping him with a really weak belt shot, and Sgt. Slaughter soon shows up to get her out of there, which is probably for the best given how completely lost she looks in this unscripted environment. Presumably Slaughter was feeding her new instructions as she catches up with Kurt and begs him to return to the match, which he does, only to break up a pin attempt by Triple H.

The re-emergence of Angle allows them to go to the scheduled finish, with Triple H accidentally belting Stephanie with his sledgehammer before Angle takes it and uses it on Hunter for two. Rock then dumps Angle and finishes Triple H with the People's Elbow, to somewhat surprisingly retain the title, despite basically appearing to be the odd man out in the entire storyline. There is of course the booking school of thought that the guys with the angle don't need the belt while the guy without the angle does, because now you've got the Triple H-Angle grudge match going forward, plus Rock can defend the title for a main event double-header, rather than just putting the belt with the angle and leaving Rock with no direction. Kudos as well to Rock and Hunter for holding the whole thing together as the WWF's best laid plans almost go to waste, although years of research since 2000 into the effects of concussions makes the whole experience of watching Angle "gut it out, old school style" somewhat unpleasant.
Final Rating: ***½

VERDICT

Whilst *WrestleMania 2000* was something of a washout (despite that awesome triple team ladder match) and *King of the Ring* was a damp squib, most of the WWF's pay-per-view output in 2000 was absolutely stellar, and *SummerSlam* was no exception, which makes its status as something of a "forgotten show" all the more puzzling. Perhaps it's the fact the main event was one small stop on a continuing storyline, perhaps the fact the stunning TLC match was followed by another on a much grander scale at *WrestleMania X-SEVEN*, or perhaps the fact that Chris Benoit and Chris Jericho bettered their technical masterclass with a superbly intense ladder match at 2001's *Royal Rumble*. Whatever the case, it feels like *SummerSlam 2000* over the years has been overlooked by many fans for the stellar show it really is. Storylines, angles, title changes, payoffs, insane bumps, and good old fashioned wrestling; Yes, this show has it all. And butts too, can't forget about the butts. In fact, watching *that* particular round of titillation (or should that be assillation) back, it's hard to believe the WWF ever got away with it, as sleazy and gratuitous as it was. I mean, you could practically see what those girls had eaten for lunch!

84

UNFORGIVEN 2000

CAT NO: WWF252
RUN TIME: 172 minutes (approx)

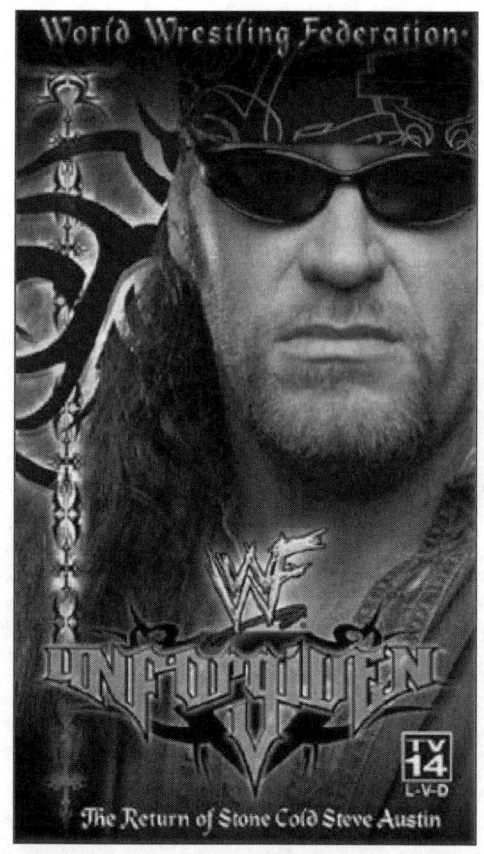

Lee Maughan: From the First Union Center in Philadelphia, PA. Hosts are Jim Ross and Jerry Lawler.

Right to Censor vs. The Dudley Boyz & The APA
Very basic eight-man here as everyone bar Steven Richards takes a brief turn on offence before the heels get the heat on D-Von, which is about as thrilling as it sounds when you consider that the RTC squad is basically just made up of guys who never really caught on either as workers or personalities in their previous gimmicks (the Godfather for example was extremely over but pretty much sucked in the ring, while Val Venis' big push over the summer as a serious wrestler saw him go absolutely nowhere, even with Trish Stratus by his side and the Intercontinental Title around his waist). In all fairness, you'd hardly waste useable talent on such a limited gimmick that exists entirely to grind Vince McMahon's axe, when lukewarm bodies will do.

Inevitably, it all breaks down into a big eight-man brawl until Richards pops in from behind and levels Bubba with the Stevenkick, giving Val the pin. Annoyingly, the Dudleys and the Acolytes then get all their heat back by killing Richards, polishing him off with a superbomb through a table, thus negating the story of the match entirely, that being everyone wanting to get their hands on him and him being too cowardly to get in the ring. What a pointless way to blow your load so quickly on Richards getting his comeuppance, which is what you'd expect the ultimate payoff to the whole RTC thing to have been.
Final Rating: *½

Strap Match
Tazz vs. Jerry Lawler
To illustrate just how far Tazz has fallen down the pecking order since his WWF debut back at the *Royal Rumble*, we're in Philadelphia tonight and *nobody* cares about him. That's a truly shocking indictment of the WWF's booking of the guy, given that he was basically God here just over a year ago. Fortunately, the crowd does react to another ECW alum here; the debuting Raven, who blasts Lawler with the Evenflow after Tazz no-sells three piledrivers and kicks the referee in the nuts. Tazz chokes out Lawler with the Tazzmission to finish, which makes absolutely no sense since this was a strap match and Lawler spent part of it trying to touch all four turnbuckles, but whatever, it's not like it was any good anyway. Sadly, Raven's WWF stint would go on to be about as useful as Tazz's was.
Final Rating: *

- Meanwhile, Steve Austin arrives with intent to find out who ran him down at *Survivor Series*, and he punks out Kevin Kelly. Double meanwhile, Michael Cole replaces Lawler on colour commentary. Oh thanks a lot, Raven.

Hardcore Invitational
WWF Hardcore Championship
Steve Blackman (c) vs. Perry Saturn vs. Crash vs. Al Snow vs. Test vs. Funaki
This is basically a tornado rules match with unlimited falls until the 10-minute time limit is up, although it isn't quite made clear whether you have to pin the champion to win the belt or if you can just pin anyone. Man, what's with these goofy rules tonight? Blackman starts by smashing a trash can lid over Saturn's head on a suicide dive attempt, a spot Chris Benoit and Chris Jericho would famously repeat with a steel chair at the 2001 *Royal Rumble*, then Trish Stratus and Terri Runnels both get hit with Head. Test then bumps off a Head shot from Snow despite their being no visible contact.

Saturn comes off the top with a moonsault to the floor and heads backstage with Funaki, allowing Crash to steal a pin on Blackman off a trash can blow from Test, and that gives him the title with six minutes to go. JR points out that it's smart strategy to go after the guy who is recognised as champion, which suggests that you have to beat the champion to become the champion, which is better than beating someone who *isn't* the champion to win a title, but just makes the match completely convoluted. Why don't the five guys team up and take out the champion? Yeah, they'll have to fight each other eventually anyway, but why waste your time on Funaki when Blackman is the man to beat? Crash tries to leg it with the belt but Saturn returns from backstage and smashes him with yet another trash can to win the title.

They waste some time brawling through the crowd before Saturn and Blackman get into a stick duel in the ring. Blackman wins that then wipes everyone out with a Singapore cane, and smashes it over Saturn's head to win his title back with 50 seconds on the clock. Blackman tries the Crash method of pegging it down the aisle and finally all the guys go after Blackman at once, but none of the idiots think to try for a pin, and the time expires as everyone piles on. What the purpose of any of this was, I have no idea. Totally uninspired brawling and an overabundance of trash can shots, but Saturn at least looked motivated.
Final Rating: *

- Speaking of idiots, Tony Garea asks where Kurt Angle got his gold medal, then Steve Austin arrives and kicks Angle's ass. Why yes, Angle *is* co-headlining the pay-per-view tonight, thanks for asking.

Chris Jericho vs. X-Pac
This is actually a rematch from last year's *Unforgiven*, which was Jericho's WWF pay-per-view debut, although the heel/face alignment has since reversed for both guys. This time, the match has come about thanks to X-Pac attacking Jericho with various martial arts weaponry, though what his motivation was remains unclear. I'll just pretend X-Pac harboured resentment over Jericho beating him for the WCW Cruiserweight Title on that *Saturday Nitro* house show back in '97. Hey, it's more of an explanation than the WWF could be bothered to think of.

X-Pac is still decked out in his best green and black DX clobber, despite that group having officially died at *SummerSlam*. Ross suggests X-Pac may be trying to prove a point (what that point is also goes unexplained) and that it may be time for the "sidekick" to become a leader, foreshadowing (*groan*) X-Factor. Sadly, he spends a portion of the match killing time with a sleeper, which is very disappointing to see from a match with enough on-paper potential to steal the show. Then again, Jericho was doing jobs for Viscera around this period, so perhaps not.

Jericho gets the Walls of Jericho and X-Pac escapes before a Lionsault hits the knees, but X-Pac jumps into a second Walls of Jericho for the submission, which is X-Pac's first major loss in quite some time. It was that booking protection (along with his status as Triple H's real-life chum) that partly led to such online fan resentment towards him and the resultant term "X-Pac heat". It didn't help that the guy still had plenty of talent but put on underwhelming matches like this, especially with an "internet darling" like Jericho. X-Pac of course gets all his heat back after the match, battering Jericho with a pair of rubber nunchucks, setting up a cage match for next month.
Final Rating: **½

- Back in Commissioner Foley's office, Angle tells Mick he'll be okay for the match tonight because when he won the gold medal in '96, he had a mild headache the day before and irritable bowel syndrome during the match, so a beating from Austin won't have any effect. Foley decides to make the match No Disqualifications.

- In an odd segment, Austin bumps into the Rock, who's rental car it was that ran Austin down at the *Survivor Series*. Despite this, and despite the fact that the two have been bitter rivals in the past, Austin somehow knows it wasn't the Rock who was responsible, despite suspecting everybody else on the planet, and the pair shake hands. I guess logic has to go out the window when your previous top heel has since become your interim top babyface and you don't want to jeopardise that. Joe interrupts the love-fest with news about Austin's assailant. Joe who? Just Joe. Austin kicks Just Joe's ass because he "looks kinda stupid", which isn't just felonious assault, but also completely counterproductive too. Way to go there, Sherlock Austin and Doctor Rockson.

Steel Cage Match
WWF Tag Team Championship
Edge & Christian (c) vs. The Hardy Boyz
This is tornado rules with all four guys in the ring at once, but it's also got those dumb "first team out the cage wins" stipulations, where one guy escaping means his partner faces a 2-on-1 disadvantage. There's yet another lack of communication in getting that point across however, as Jeff climbs out of the cage early and neither Ross nor Cole is able to explain what's going on, or whether Jeff can get back in the cage or not. In fact, their on-air speculation sounds like an attempt at getting clarification from somebody backstage on the headsets. JR eventually settles on the idea that Jeff can get back in the cage if he wants, so of course he attempts to only for the outside referee to contradictorily block him off. All of these minor plot holes creeping in and the lack of consideration put into the details are really indicative of someone suffering from burnout, and indeed, head writer Chris Kreski would soon find himself replaced in November by Stephanie McMahon. It's too bad because the WWF had been on fire for most of 2000, but everyone hits the wall sooner or later.

Jeff shoves a chair into the ring but Christian clonks him on the noggin with the cage door before he and Edge try for a Conchairto on Matt. Matt ducks and climbs up the cage with Christian in hot pursuit, but Jeff meets Christian with a ladder and delivers Whisper in the Wind off the cage. Christian attempts to get back in using the ladder but Lita predictably runs out mid-match (her usual role in these big gimmick matches) and blasts him with a huracanrana off the ladder to a big reaction. Edge goes up but the Hardys meet him there with a Conchairto of their own using the chair that Jeff had thrown in earlier, sending Edge crashing down to the mat and giving the Hardys chance to escape together and claim the titles.

I like that they tried to build the psychology of the match around the cage and work in some highspots off that, but at the same time the cage felt more like a hindrance than a help, limiting the kind of spots these two teams usually like to do and never really feeling like the slugfest a good old fashioned cage match is supposed to. The early part of the bout was pretty dull, and at times it felt less like a cage match and more like they were trying to figure out a way to use the cage to do a ladder match without the ladder.
Final Rating: **¾

- Backstage, Stephanie McMahon-Helmsley is so happy to see Austin that she's got a present for him - the hat he was wearing the night he got ran over. I guess that's kind of interesting given where the angle eventually went, but Austin doesn't care, displaying an enormous lack of aptitude for sleuthing only previously seen in buffoonish detectives like Frank Drebin, Ty Lookwell and Inspector Gadget. Stephanie tells him that Shane McMahon has video evidence of the culprit.

WWF Intercontinental Championship
Eddie Guerrero (c) vs. Rikishi
After Eddie "accidentally" won the Intercontinental Title from Chyna in a triple threat match with Kurt Angle on *RAW*, Chyna had begun accusing him of using her just to get his hands on

MAE YOUNG & THE FABULOUS MOOLAH

the belt. Eddie denied this, demanded Chyna support him like he'd supported her when she was champion, and tore up a locker room in frustration. After he apologised for his actions, Chyna agreed to stick around... only for Eddie to blow up again when she announced that was going to be appearing nude in *Playboy*. Chyna again tried to leave Eddie until he suddenly asked her to marry him, to which Chyna agreed, showing how emotionally unstable she was even back then. The only problem was a deeply jealous Eddie decided to take it upon himself to try and book an audience with *Playboy* impresario Hugh Hefner for a heart-to-heart and have the pictures pulled, which is about where we are with things here. Needless to say, there's a trouble brewin'.

Chyna actually gets involved in the match in the weirdest of ways, as Rikishi catches Eddie with an avalanche in the corner off a missed Frog Splash, but his pin attempt off the Banzai Drop is blocked by Chyna... who scurries into the ring and very politely asks the referee not to make a count before scooting back to the floor. It looked like she might have been out of position there because she had to run all the way across the ring to get there in time, which just didn't look right at all. Rikishi naturally goes after Chyna and decks her with a crescent kick, drawing the disqualification after six completely useless minutes. Why didn't Chyna get disqualified for jumping in the ring? Just another head-scratcher on a show full of them I guess. Rikishi gives her a Banzai Drop to add the exclamation point and tease his impending heel turn, and then Eddie, in a very amusing piece of characterisation, rushes over not to check on Chyna, but to grab and cradle his precious title belt. Rubbish match though.
Final Rating: *

Triple H vs. Kurt Angle
I'm sure you all know the story so far, but to recap: Kurt and Stephanie were "just friends" until Stephanie took a knock to head and Kurt made out with her, to which she reciprocated. Kurt played dumb but her husband Triple H naturally didn't take kindly to it, and vowed to kick Kurt's ass. Nothing was settled at *SummerSlam* however, so with Kurt still denying any relationship Hunter baited him into another match by accusing him of being gay, because even though this is 2000, it's also the WWF and homosexuality is still something to be sneered at and made fun of.

Triple H has heavily taped ribs here, stemming from a sledgehammer attack at the hands of Angle on *SmackDown!*, and not only is his wife believed to be having an affair with his opponent, but the man he retired earlier in the year, Mick Foley, is the special guest referee. Man, how will he ever overcome odds as stacked against him as those?! Duh, with a one-armed Pedigree, stupid! Six months of slow build and 17 tedious minutes of combat, all for the least intriguing finish imaginable, as Stephanie kicks Kurt in the groin and Hunter pins him right in the middle. True, Stephanie still appears concerned about Kurt, but the status quo has largely been restored, Foley barely got involved making his presence all but worthless, and Triple H gets to force a kiss on his missus to show everyone what a manly man's man he is, unlike that big drape-shopping daisy Angle.
Final Rating: **¼

- Shane McMahon, still aggrieved at Steve Blackman for having the temerity to kick his ass after Shane had stolen Blackman's Hardcore Title, tries to blame the 'Lethal Weapon' for the hit and run on Austin, using video footage of Blackman running down Ken Shamrock as proof. I'm not sure I'd want to call back to such a heelish act when the guy responsible for it is now solidly a babyface, but Austin's a much bigger star than Blackman anyway, so it doesn't really matter. And that leads to Austin's grand in-ring return, complete with a horrid nu-metal interpretation his theme. He gives Blackman a Stone Cold Stunner then shares a few brews with Shane before dropping him with three Stunners too.

WWF Championship
The Rock (c) vs. Chris Benoit vs. The Undertaker vs. Kane
Ah yes, the classic case of having a pay-per-view that needs a match, as opposed to having a match that needs a pay-per-view. The solution? Throw two separate feuds together in a muddled four-way, and chuck in a false finish to give the illusion that the whole thing isn't just a giant placeholder to fill a B-show. In this case it's Benoit who gets the "honours", dropping Undertaker with a chair and pinning him in the ropes, only for Commissioner Foley to restart the match moments later, marking the third time in seven months that Benoit has won a World title and had it immediately taken away (WCW *SuperBrawl 2000*, *Fully Loaded*, and here). Given that this was the second time this exact thing had happened to Benoit in the WWF, and that Foley was also responsible the last time it happened, one could be forgiven for thinking a Foley-Benoit feud may have been on the cards long-term, at least until Chris Kreski's demotion and the departure of Foley from the Commissioner role in December 2000.

Forced to trudge back to the ring, Benoit gets triple-teamed by the other three, until it all breaks down again into the same old "hit a move, pull the guy off, hit another move, pull the other guy off" routine that multi-person matches often lazily degenerate into. Benoit grabs another chair and starts blasting Undertaker and Kane with it, once again exposing the logical flaws that seemingly nobody bothered to think through tonight. Why not just announce it as no disqualifications and save yourself the headache? And then in another really dumb spot, Rock hits Benoit with a Rock Bottom and goes for the pin, but instead of breaking up the count, Kane decides his best option is to prevent Undertaker from achieving that very same goal, thus screwing himself twice in one go! That might not have been so bad if at any point it had been made clear his motivation was simply to prevent Undertaker winning the title, but it was never presented that way so it just made absolutely no sense. Logic aside, the action was fine, and this was probably the best match of the night, though that isn't saying much.
Final Rating: **¾

VERDICT

Unforgiven 2000 might be one of the worst WWF pay-per-views I've ever seen. Not because it's bad, because it really isn't, but the show is plagued with logical flaw after logical flaw after logical flaw, and absolutely nothing delivers what it promises on paper. The main draw for the show is Steve Austin returning to find out who ran him over at last year's *Survivor Series*, but not only does he not find answers, neither do the paying customers watching at home. Similarly, nothing at all is either resolved or advanced in the Triple H-Kurt Angle match, pushed as the payoff to several months' worth of angles between the two.

Nothing else on the card offers any sort of blow-off or satisfying conclusion, and nothing serves to set up anything interesting going forward either. At a push you could argue the title change in the cage match was the lead-in for Edge & Christian to begin dressing as Los Conquistadors in an effort to get their belts back, but then you'd have to admit that in purchasing this PPV or VHS release, that you just paid money to see a cage match set up a goofy comedy angle, and are you really willing to do that?

All in all, very little on the show delivers. The aforementioned cage match doesn't (nor could it) live up to previous gimmick matches between the two teams, and the Chris Jericho vs. X-Pac match which was an on-paper sleeper turned out to be a much more literal interpretation of that; a real snoozer. The best thing on the card, the main event, was entirely predictable, typically routine, and terribly illogical. A Rock vs. Chris Benoit singles match would have been preferable, perhaps a Best 2-out-of-3 Falls bout to play off their previous meeting at *Fully Loaded* earlier in the year.

This was the absolute definition of "filler", and, were it not for the tag team title change, could very easily have been confused with any number of similarly uneventful UK-only pay-per view events. Yes, 2000 was mostly a brilliant year for the WWF, but like WCW in 1998, once September rolled around, the cracks were beginning to show.

33

NO MERCY 2000

CAT NO: WWF253
RUN TIME: 164 minutes (approx)

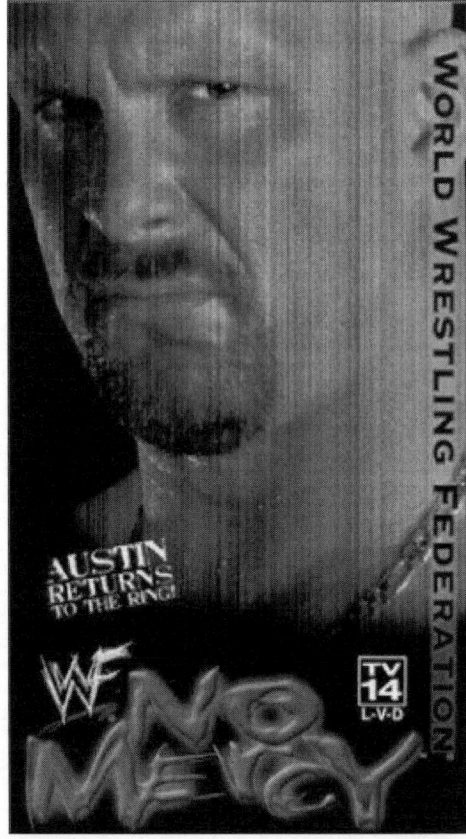

Lee Maughan: From the Pepsi Arena in Albany, New York (the same building incidentally that hosted the 1992 *Royal Rumble*, and 2006's *New Year's Revolution*.) Hosts are Jim Ross and Jerry Lawler.

The Dudley Boyz Tag Team Elimination Table Invitational
This is tornado rules with two teams in the ring at a time, and a new team enters when one team is eliminated by having a member of that team put through a table. Imagine sort of a Royal Rumble/Survivor Series hybrid. Too Cool are team #1, a pair of hip hop white guys, dancing down the aisle to some techno pop tune, table underarm like some sanitised Saturday morning cartoon incarnation of Public Enemy. They're followed at #2 by a duo making their collective debut on a WWF pay-per-view (although they were actually teammates at last November's *Survivor Series*), the thrown together Lo Down of D'Lo Brown and Chaz. The plain tracksuit bottoms they sport are incredibly lifeless, giving the team a distinctly jobberish look, and the lack of a singlet for D'Lo really exemplifies why he wore one for almost the entirety of his career. Not a good look for him at all. Unfortunately, this first "mini-match" of sorts has absolutely nothing going for it, then Chaz gets shoved off the top on a superplex attempt as D'Lo simultaneously misses a frog splash, both crashing through tables, and that's it for them. Thanks for coming, guys.

Team #3 are Tazz and Raven, disappointingly enough. I say disappointingly because if you'll recall, Raven only debuted in the WWF last month at *Unforgiven*, and already he's been placed in a thrown-together team with Tazz, a guy who's hardly been on a roll himself having just come off an announcer's feud with Jerry Lawler, the team being presented as also rans in a throwaway gimmick match opener. Furthermore, Raven is already being systematically stripped of his identity, appearing here in a plain black t-shirt rather than a cool band shirt, and his jean shorts aren't as ripped and tatty as they usually are. Before long, he'd be coming to the ring not to the suitably disaffected punk and grunge tunes that accompanied his ECW and WCW runs, but a Jim Johnston generic rock chugger complete with actual raven calls, and he was soon sporting a clean white shirt and black leather shorts like some kind of Bizarro World Raven. What a criminal misuse of talent that would prove to be, though according to Raven himself in a shoot interview years later, he had been told by a writer that Vince's first words at one booking meeting upon hearing the news of his signing were "Who the *fuck* hired Raven!?" Jim Ross was the responsible party, by the way. The only reason I can find for Raven to have even been paired up with Tazz at this point is that they both had a connection to ECW, although they actually crossed paths very rarely in the land of Extreme. Still, as we're in New York tonight and as either of these guys alone have more personality than D'Lo and Chaz combined, this portion of the match garners a much bigger reaction than the last, and is infinitely more interesting. The crowd also get more into it as Too Cool start breaking out their signature stuff, in particular Scotty 2 Hotty doing the Worm under a table, and a surprisingly vibrant "You fucked up!" chants kicks up when Grandmaster Sexay tries a sunset powerbomb to the floor, only to smash a ringside table to pieces with his feet. That Scotty eats a double superplex through a table moments later suggests they could have just gone home early or called an audible and explained that both members of the team needed to go through tables to be eliminated (especially in light of the fact that both members of Lo Down had suffered the same fate), but JR blathers around in an attempt to conjure up an explanation before settling somewhere along the lines of "it was an accident, so it doesn't count". So take note, footballers; Next time you score an own goal, just protest that it was only an accident and the boffins at FIFA will no doubt have your transgression stricken from the record!

The crowd absolutely explode with the arrival of team #4, the Dudley Boyz themselves in case you couldn't guess, and that gets the "ECW!" chants going. Tazz quickly takes a Bubba Bomb and Raven is the lucky recipient of tonight's Wazzup Drop, before Tazz makes a minor comeback with a T-Bone Tazzplex. "Minor" is certainly the key word there as the Dudleys immediately take back over, and D-Von puts Tazz through a table with a Dudleyville Jam. Our final team are of course Right to Censor, here represented by Bull Buchanan and the Goodfather. Bull wipes out the referee with a lariat, which given its accidental nature shouldn't count, according to JR law, which should immediately tip you off to the finish. And

104

indeed, Bubba Ray powerbombs Bull through the table, but Goodfather smashes Bubba in the head with a steel chair and lays him amidst the wreckage, dragging Bull out just in time for the referee to revive and call it for RTC. A second referee quickly arrives, explains the situation, and a quickie restart sees Goodfather go through a table courtesy of a 3D for the real finish. Taken as a series of individual matches as some may view them, these were all fairly sub-*SmackDown!* standard TV throwaways, but when viewed as a single narrative, which is the way the whole thing was actually booked, it's not bad. No one segment particularly outstays its welcome, the shortness of some of the individual bouts is a help rather than a hindrance owing to the structure of the piece, and the whole thing builds in an increasingly exciting manner. Too Cool save their best spots for their second match, then the guys more associated with hardcore get involved, then comes the team the match was designed for, before it all ends with the big showdown against the annoying heel group, complete with a silly Dusty finish to keep RTC somewhat strong, whilst still giving the crowd what they want. I can't really complain about any of that.
Final Rating: **½

- Out in the parking lot, Rikishi waits on the arrival of Steve Austin whilst slowly stroking his giant tool. It's a sledgehammer. If you've ever heard the term "sledgehammer of plot", this is the most literal interpretation of it. If you'll recall when Austin returned at *Unforgiven* last month, Stephanie McMahon-Helmsley presented him with his baseball cap from the night he was run over, and now Rikishi is walking around carrying the signature weapon of Triple H. Hmm, I wonder who could *really* have been behind that hit and run assault?

- Elsewhere, Trish, Test and Albert plan to let the tits fall where they may, which is the same strategy I employed the last time I got dragged along to the Little Black Book lap dancing club for a mate's stag party.

Trish Stratus & T&A vs. Lita & The APA
This might read like an odd match on paper but the Hardy Boyz are tag team champions and have a defence coming later tonight, so Lita is teaming with the APA who have prior with T&A, stemming from a poker game in which T&A lost all their money and started gambling with Trish's clothes. Needless to say, the APA beat T&A for the T n' A. Of course, this is wrestling, so it all escalated into brawling rather than boobies, setting up this match. Only, there isn't a match, as the camera cuts backstage to find Bradshaw under a filing cabinet and Faarooq getting his skull caved in by Test and Albert. Lita heads back to investigate, only to meet T&A head-on and get jumped from behind for an ass whupping from Trish. T&A soon set about her too, and that brings the Hardys out for the save. Ordinarily, I'd complain about such a blatant bait-and-switch on a per-per-view, but this one meant I didn't have to sit through two still-green girls catfighting and four big slugs clubbering on each other for five minutes, plus I got a good old-fashioned 'rasslin angle into the bargain to boot, all of which I consider a big win. Given all that, they probably should have considered renaming this show WWF *Small Mercy*.

- In the locker room, Christian waxes lyrical about holding Edge's nuts as he blew chunks last night. It turns out it wasn't their peanut platter but rather a short-term virus that kept them from accepting the Dudleys' invitation into the elimination tables match earlier tonight, and not at all because they're secretly masquerading as Los Conquistadors in an attempt to claim back the tag titles they lost to the Hardys last month..

Steel Cage Match
Chris Jericho vs. X-Pac
Jericho's pre-match promo completely buries X-Pac and the entire concept of D-Generation-X as passé, drawing particular attention to his hair and increasingly stale black and green tights. To that end, X-Pac arrives sporting a new black and silver with red trim design, but he's still coming out to his DX theme, despite the group being dead and buried ever since *SummerSlam*. It kind of reminds me of when Tito Santana used to wear those tights with the Strike Force logo emblazoned on the arse cheek, long after Rick Martel had turned heel on him at *WrestleMania V*. Cage matches always strike me as somewhat odd when they're being contested between two guys who you could still realistically label as cruiserweights. The whole blood 'n' guts nature of concept matches screams for carve-em-up brawlers like Bruiser Brody, not high fliers like Jericho and X-Pac. In truth, their styles would better suit a ladder match, but since Edge, Christian, the Hardys and the Dudleys have already started taking those bouts to the next level, it's perhaps for the best that this isn't one. That said, the initial crux of the feud was X-Pac beating Jericho from behind with nunchucks, and how that equates to a cage match is anybody's guess. A ladder match where you have to grab the nunchucks would have made more sense, or even just a good old fashioned street fight. Worse still is that the very idea of a cage match, once the ultimate issue-ender in all of wrestling, has become increasingly passé, thanks in no small part to the emergence of the Hell in a Cell gimmick. The fact the cage match is only third on the show tonight is a testimony to that.

Still, they make good use of the steel, Jericho at one point climbing the turnbuckles to give X-Pac a superbomb off the cage in a thoroughly nutty spot. X-Pac's super slow crawl to the door hurts the suspense a little, but back up top he gets crotched on the cage where Jericho somehow works him into a Walls of Jericho to a big reaction. From there, it's Jericho's turn to take a ridiculously oversized bump as X-Pac kicks him in the buttocks, causing him to flip bump off the top of the cage and into the ring. X-Pac sees an easy escape from there, and actually stands on the cage door for leverage, only for Jericho to his a last-gasp dropkick on the cage, causing X-Pac to slip and crotch himself on the door! Credit where it's due; that was awesome. Jericho simply walks out the door for the win, making sure to swing it open as hard as he can so X-Pac bumps his noggin on the side of the cage in the process. Much better than their lethargic outing at *Unforgiven*, with some very creative spots thrown in for good measure.
Final Rating: ***¼

Right to Censor vs. Chyna & Billy Gunn
This was supposed to be Billy challenging Eddie Guerrero for the Intercontinental title, but Eddie suffered a hamstring injury while defending the title against Chris Jericho on *RAW* last Monday, so we get this instead. Lucky us. Although not as big as the one he received in 1999, Billy is actually on something of a renewed singles push here, but the fact he's less over at this point than Chyna (whose current popularity has in large part been siphoned off Guerrero's charisma the previous few months) should clue you in on how well the whole thing panned out. Indeed, it's Gunn who gets the snot kicked out of him here with Chyna taking the hot tag, though that in part comes down to the fact Billy is known to be coming off major shoulder surgery, and perhaps also to the fact that Chyna was a pretty rotten worker for the most part. Then of course there's the theory that the way she was so strongly booked was to overcompensate for the insider knowledge that her real-life boyfriend, Triple H, was already secretly knocking off

Stephanie McMahon at this point, information to which Chyna was not yet privy. Billy cleans house and hits the Fameasser on Richards but Bull Buchanan and the Goodfather arrive for a mass brawl, and that allows Eddie to sneak in from behind and smash a lead-piper loaded bouquet of roses over Chyna's head, giving Val the pin.
Final Rating: *¼

- In the locker room, Triple H refuses to allow Stephanie McMahon-Helmsley to accompany him for his match with Chris Benoit later tonight, so she gives him a mystery tape of Benoit applying the Crossface, and tells him there's "something interesting" about it. She then says she has to leave to help Kurt Angle get ready for his title match with the Rock, so Hunter warns her that he'll hold Angle personally responsible for her safety tonight.

No Holds Barred
Steve Austin vs. Rikishi
You might think this is pretty early in the show for what should be a major blowoff, and that alone should tip you off as to the outcome. The match is the payoff to a rather lousy angle cooked up by the WWF last year when, fearful that they would harm their own buyrate with honesty, they opted to advertise Austin for the *Survivor Series* main event despite knowing a whole month in advance that he wouldn't be able to wrestle due to his neck injury. One of those angles where the promoter comes up with an initial idea and goes for it without having figured out the payoff, poor old Rikishi was drafted in to play the culprit, claiming "I did it for the Rock... I did it for the People." The whole turn seemed like such a waste of a supremely popular act, but in fairness, Rikishi's whole dancing Samoan gimmick was strictly a mid-card act with a limited shelf life, so sacrificing him for the role wasn't that big of a loss. Unfortunately, he's still dressed in his quasi-sumo outfit with Hawaiian muumuu, continuing to look every bit the comedy character that was his station, and not the evil badass he needed to be. That just gets emphasised as Austin kicks his ass all around the building, choking him out with a rope, busting him open with a steel chair, then driving him out of the arena on the back of his truck.

Out in the parking lot, Austin dumps Rikishi up against a wall and attempts to mow him down in cold blood, only to drunkenly crash into a police car. He decides to ram the cop car again, and then, mere seconds later, an entire fleet of squad cars appear out of nowhere and arrest Austin, in one of the dumbest finishes to a pay-per-view match that I can ever recall. See, that's the problem with these B-shows, as they force you into delivering matches you aren't ready to. Case in point here, as Austin needed to get revenge in his big comeback, but they didn't want to immediately job out the freshly-turned Rikishi, and the upshot was the new monster heel being treated like a complete and total jobber, all topped off with a deeply unsatisfying non-finish.
Final Rating: DUD

WWF European Championship
William Regal vs. Naked Mideon
And from one mess to another, behold Naked Mideon. Thankfully, Commissioner Foley has agreed to Regal's demands that Mideon should actually get dressed for this match. Unthankfully, that becomes the story of a truly useless tussle, as Regal outwrestles Mideon to the point that he gets so frustrated, he pulls his pants down and jiggles. Mideon that is, not Regal, though I can't imagine the alternative would have been pleasant either. And then Mideon makes out with Regal. Where's Lou Thesz when you need him? Couldn't this big, sloppy, naked snog have been saved for Trish and Lita? Egads! Regal crotches Mideon on the top (my deepest sympathies to whomever the WWF's towel boy is tonight) but refuses to apply the Regal Stretch for fear of accidentally getting a boner mid move and penetrating the former hog farmer's slop-fuelled anus. A neckbreaker instead finishes this unfunniest of comedy matches in merciful fashion. And who the hell thought the pasty, blubbery redneck threatening to take his clothes off would make for a babyface gimmick?!
Final Rating: DUD

- Earlier tonight on *Sunday Night HeAT*, Kurt Angle pulled a 'Weird Al' Yankovic special when he "interviewed" the Rock, using some very selective editing to pull together an obviously fake series of sound bites in which he managed to implicate Rock in the running down of Austin. It's absolutely amazing to me that the same promotion responsible for this kind of creative sketch also figured Naked Mideon would provide giggles aplenty.

WWF Tag Team Championship
The Hardy Boyz (c) vs. Los Conquistadors
For some reason, despite being arguably the most successful tag team of the entire Attitude Era, Edge & Christian have apparently "run out" of rematches for the titles, having lost them in a cage last month to the Hardys. Looking to find new number one contenders, a tag team battle royal was held, surprisingly being won by the returning Conquistadors. Only it wasn't José Luis Rivera and José Estrada, Sr. under the hoods; this slimmer, lankier version actually bore more of a physical resemblance to… well, Edge & Christian. The whole gimmick was actually a fun little way to breathe some life into a feud that was increasingly being driven into the ground with endless rematches, but while the silly gold lamé suits made for amusing TV skits, on pay-per-view they just make for one of the dullest matches these two teams ever had. The Conquistadors' sub-lucha tumbles might be amusing one or twice, but over the course of an extended match it quickly grows tiresome, and the heels are hugely handicapped by the fact they can't work in any of their signature spots, lest they give the game away. We're supposed to know it's really Edge & Christian in there, but to make the angle work they have to pretend like it's not really them, so they can only really dish out a bunch of wrestling school basics and silly comedy.

Here in the HoW offices, we've long held a theory that certain WWF gimmicks were so overwhelming that they actually overcame a wrestler's talent, and this appears to be another case of that. Dos (Christian) does hit his usual springboard crossbody, which he can get away with as a lucha-style move, and a spot on the floor sees Matt accidentally wipe out Jeff with a dive off the top, but it's not enough to rescue the previous eight-odd minutes of blandness and crowd apathy. Matt hits the Twist of Fate on Uno (Edge) and tears his mask off, revealing… another mask, and that opening allows Dos (Christian) to sneak in from behind and hit the Sin Más Bonita for the pin and the titles.
Final Rating: *

Triple H vs. Chris Benoit
This came about when Benoit stuck one on Stephanie's nut on *RAW* during an argument with Kurt Angle. The next week, Stephanie slapped Benoit across the chops so Benoit retaliated by costing Triple H a number one contenders match against Angle, and the two have been smashing each other with steel chairs ever since. The match starts out as an odd "Bizarro World" mirror match of sorts, with Hunter completely

outwrestling Benoit at every turn, working over his knee with a Mutalock of all things, before Benoit turns the tables Triple H style and throws him into the steel on the outside. Surprisingly, that doesn't bust Triple H open even though he covered up like he was going for the blade, and had bled on TV to build heat. Back inside, Benoit targets the arm with Divorce Court, a sick hammerlock suplex, a Northern Lights suplex and a snap suplex into an armlock. It's all great stuff, but there's kind of a vibe to it like he's going slower than usual with his spots. It's all Benoit's stuff, but it's at Triple H's pace. Hunter shows that he's still alive by grabbing a small package after a diving headbutt and starts throwing out suplexes of his own, but Benoit blocks a Pedigree with rolling Germans. Hunter in turn blocks those so Benoit counters with a dragon suplex and locks in the Crippler Crossface, which Hunter powers up from to deliver a Death Valley Driver. How he or Stephanie figured that out from a tape of him being trapped in the hold on *RAW* I'm not quite sure, but that's the cue for Stephanie to run out and slap Benoit's mush yet again.

They start going for finishers with the other reversing them until the referee stops to admonish Stephanie for no reason in particular, and that opening allows Hunter to go low and land the Pedigree for the pin, ending both Benoit's flirtation with the main event scene (for three-and-a-half years at least, save for a brief dalliance in the summer of 2001) and his own status as the number three babyface in the promotion (behind Austin and Rock), becoming the more preferable number one heel after the revelation that he was the mastermind behind Rikishi's hit and run on Austin last year. Of course, Austin himself would supplant Hunter as the top heel in April, much to Triple H's legitimate annoyance, but hey, he got six months out of it and went down with a brutal quadriceps injury in May anyway, and there's only so many spots to go around. Very good Japanese-style match built around holds and counter holds, sprinkled with some US-style sports entertainment shenanigans towards the end that at least fit the context of the feud. On the negative side of things, the crowd weren't particularly noisy for the pure grappling portions, and it felt pretty slow compared to everything else on the show, but this was still another fine match to add to Triple H's excellent 2000 run.
Final Rating: ***¾

- Backstage, a noticeably out-of-breath Edge & Christian bump into the Conquistadors and celebrate their victory tonight, before warning them they'll do battle for the titles tomorrow night on *RAW*. So Edge & Christian had used up all their shots at the Hardy Boyz but were automatic number one contenders to any other team that won the belts *before* the Hardys could get their rematch in? I guess you can't ever let logic get in the way of a good story, even though you could easily have gone with a Conquistadors-Hardys rematch on *RAW*, then done the Conquistadors-Edge & Christian match the next week. The Conquistadors here by the way were played by Aaron Aguilera as Uno (later known in WWE as Jesus, bodyguard of Carlito Caribbean Cool) and Christopher Daniels as Dos.

No Disqualification
WWF Championship
The Rock (c) vs. Kurt Angle
As noted, Kurt won a number one contender's match against Triple H on *RAW* to get this title shot, and, since Triple H labelled Stephanie a "liability" after she accidentally cost him that match, he's also invited Steph to be his full-time manager. They start with your usual WWF Main Event Style™ brawl, Kurt jumping Rock at the bell before the fight down the aisle where Rock throws Kurt through the *No Mercy* set. Back to the ring they finally start throwing in some wrestling moves, Rock landing a dragon screw leg whip and locking in his typically lousy Sharpshooter, but Stephanie distracts the referee and he doesn't see Angle tap out. That sends Rock in hot pursuit of Stephanie, allowing Angle to cut him off with a belly-to-belly suplex, and he blasts Rock with the title belt as Stephanie provides a completely pointless distraction in this No Disqualifications match. Rock comes back with a superplex but Angle, on this suplex-heavy show, returns fire with a German, only to disobey Steph's orders and resultantly miss a moonsault off the top. Rock lands a DDT but Stephanie jumps in to break it up so Rock gives her a Rock Bottom, and of course that brings out Hunter. He decks Angle for allowing Stephanie to get hurt, then blasts Rock with a Pedigree for putting his hands on her, and carts her off to the back. Angle's cover only gets two in a heart-stopping near fall, and then super-heel Rikishi waddles out to really confuse the issue, attacking Angle so that Rock can snap off another Rock Bottom. The crowd seem completely confused about how to react now, as Rikishi is a heel but trying to take out Angle (a heel) for the benefit of the Rock (a babyface), despite the Rock having made it clear that he wants nothing to do with him. I like how layered it all is, but for the casual pro-wrestling audience, particularly a WWF one that's largely into seeing superstars much more than great matches and interwoven storylines, the lack of a clear black and white narrative really clouds the issue. Rikishi goes for an avalanche in the corner but Angle pulls the Rock in the way and they both get squished, so Rikishi tries to make up for it was a thrust kick, only for Angle to duck at the last second, causing him to again blast the Rock. What a clown. Angle then takes out Rikishi with the Olympic Slam before landing one on the Rock for the pin and the title to a significantly loud babyface reaction. So, with less than a year on the main roster, and indeed, less than a year of major league exposure *anywhere*, Kurt Angle completes a meteoric rise to the WWF Title. Of course, with Triple H's impending heel turn and the continued push of Rikishi, that meant the title was now on the third string main event heel, but sometimes, egos just have to be stroked. Really good sports entertainment style match, and a great alternative to the technical wrestling of the Triple H-Benoit match, although I could have lived without all the Steve Austin-level walkabout brawling at the start.
Final Rating: ***¾

VERDICT

And thus ends the era of WWF pay-per-views helmed by Chris Kreski, replaced at the top of the pecking order shortly thereafter by Stephanie McMahon herself. Not coincidentally, the creativity and intrigue in the WWF's product dissipated almost immediately after the change, exacerbated by the lack of understanding and chip-on-the-shoulder booking of the invasion angle a few months later. Still, this was pretty fine show to go out on for the most part, starting decently enough, completely bottoming out in the middle, but redeeming itself with two choice main events. You may want to skip ahead through the crap if you do ever decide to revisit this card on the WWE Network or wherever, but it does come mildly recommended, at least if you're headstrong enough to live with all the "Stephanie McMahon - wrestling savant" stuff.

53

THE ROCK - THE PEOPLE'S CHAMP

CAT NO: WWF254
RUN TIME: 90 minutes (approx)

Lee Maughan: Hosted by the Rock himself, which is a rather pleasant surprise when you're expecting the likes of Michael Cole or Jonathan Coachman...

...But as if this tape somehow knew, we start with comments from who else, but Michael Cole. His wisdom is quickly followed by another of the WWF's go-to talking heads, Steve Lombardi, offering up such platitudes as "What that Rock is, is the man that found the answer." That's for clearing that up, Brawler. Jerry Lawler at least offers up some actual insight into what makes the Rock so great; "He has it all. Good looking guy, great body, great wrestler, tremendous amount of charisma and as good as anybody ever has been on the microphone." Hardcore Holly thinks: "If it wasn't for him, we wouldn't have the crowds we have. I think he's got the best promo in the business, bar none." That's a hell of a compliment, though you wonder if Steve Austin might have had something to say about such claims!

What follows next is highly amusing compendium of Rock's greatest catchphrases, and I will say that, having watched this tape back-to-back with *Austin vs. McMahon*, the Rock certainly offers a lot more variety than 'Stone Cold' continually flipping the bird, threatening to whip someone's ass and dropping authority figures with Stone Cold Stunners. Not that that's a knock on Austin in any way, indeed it goes without saying that his act was a runaway success, but in terms of a profile tape, Rock's material takes a lot longer to start wearing thin.

The action picks up in mid-1999, not exactly a banner year for wrestling in North America, with Rock challenging the Undertaker to defend the WWF Title against him at *King of the Ring*. Corporate Ministry leader Mr. McMahon agrees but only on the condition that Rock can win a special stipulation match on *RAW*, which turns out to be a triple threat match against the Undertaker and Triple H. A typically overbooked WWF main event sees Chyna accidentally trip Undertaker from the outside, in a repeat of the same miscommunication between Jeff Jarrett and the Road Dogg at *In Your House 2* back in July 1995. Rock ends up pinning Triple H after Hunter and Undertaker get into a shoving match, but the impact is somewhat lessened when you consider that Undertaker had already verbally accepted the *King of the Ring* showdown *before* this convoluted mess was even booked.

To the *King of the Ring* then, where Rock gets a visual pin on the Undertaker while the referee is laid out. The rest of the highlights package on offer here makes the match look moderately exciting, but such is the magic of selective editing. For reference, Arnold Furious only scored the match at *¾ in *The Complete WWF Video Guide, Vol. 4*, and I'd be inclined to agree with him. Indeed, it's actually much better viewed in the music video-lite format you get here.

Recycled weekend TV fluff crowbarred in next as Rock throws out the first pitch at a Pittsburgh Pirates game, promising to deliver either a "roody poo fastball" or a "candy ass curve." He declares the pitch "electrifying" then buries the production crew for standing around playing pocket pool all day. This segment shouldn't have been anywhere near as entertaining as it was but that's the Rock for you. Much less charming is a sequence of nerdy fans doing rotten Rock impressions. Strictly fast forward material there.

Lawler heaps more praise on the Rock by saying he's one of those special guys who can draw you into a match, and get you on the edge of your seat guessing who's going to win, and those are the kind of matches he loves. No wonder the 'King' lost all interest once he started calling all those John "foregone conclusion" Cena matches!

On *RAW*, Rock beats Triple H in a cage match, though absolutely no context is provided as to why the match even happened, like it was just done for the sake of it. More than that, you can tell cage matches were becoming passé when the tired old "heel manager slams the cage door on the babyface's head" spot gets used as a mid-match false finish

TAZZ

rather than a way to set up a new feud, as it did the first time it was used on Christmas night, 1982 at Reunion Arena in Dallas, when Freebird Terry Gordy slammed the door on Kerry Von Erich's head as Von Erich was just moments away from claiming Ric Flair's NWA World Heavyweight Championship.

The tape the suddenly turns into a Saturday morning magazine show, complete with late 90s background dance music, as Rock drops a bunch of guys with the Rock Bottom and cuts in-ring promos with a bunch of local sporting celebrities. What a pointless little filler segment this was.

The Triple H-Rock issue rumbles on to *Fully Loaded* where interference from Billy Gunn gives Triple H victory in a very punchy-kicky strap match (awarded **½ in Volume 4). That puts Rock and Gunn on a collision course for *SummerSlam* but before that, Rock visits Miami to get his hair cut and buy some garish shirts, which was as thrilling to watch as I'm sure it is for you to read. The feud for Gunn was the WWF finally pulling the trigger on his long-awaited push to superstardom but he was clearly outmatched in every single department by the 'Great One'. His poise, his timing, his ring work, his talking ability; Gunn was just completely out of his depth against a real main eventer, as their "Kiss My Ass" match (*¾ in Volume 4) only served to underline. It was to be Gunn's first and only real flirtation with breaking into the headliner club.

Rock says that if you don't want to be the WWF Champion and the absolute best you can be, then you shouldn't be in the WWF, a philosophy worth applying to almost any aspect of life. Talk returns to Triple H and Rock threatens to shove the WWF Title belt up Hunter's ass. He also suggests he'll do the same with his $600 shoes. You see what I mean? Steve Austin never offered that sort of variety, especially when it came to anal discomfort. Rock and Hunter square off yet again on *SmackDown!* for the WWF Title with Shawn Michaels as the special guest referee, teeny weeny cycling shorts and all. 'HBK' blasts Rock with Sweet Chin Music as Rock goes for a People's Elbow, setting up an all-time dream match that would sadly never come to be.

Rock heads back to Miami to hang out with the Hurricanes, where one awkward teen brags about hanging out in the "rain, sleet and snails, all for the Rock." That's not a typo either. I know wrestling fans are a weird bunch at the best of times, but snails?

Yes! With nothing better to do, the Rock joins forces with Mankind to form the outrageously entertaining Rock 'N' Sock Connection, dropping a double People's Elbow for a tag team title victory over the Big Show and the Undertaker. That's followed by months of Mankind stealing the Rock's catchphrases and Rock growing increasingly frustrated with him until they drop the titles to the reunited New Age Outlaws.

Mankind's method of apology is to organise a special edition of *This is Your Life* on *RAW*, a thoroughly ridiculous, entirely improvised 25-minute in-ring comedy that accomplished absolutely nothing yet was so charmingly wacky, it actually popped a colossal 8.4 television rating, an all-time record that still stood some 15 years later. Unfortunately, it was exactly those kind of numbers that served to fuel Vince Russo's idea that fans cared more about dumb skits than actual wrestling, which missed the point entirely that they actually cared about well defined characters with strong personalities. Mankind brings out Rock's old highschool sweetheart (with Lex Luger's old Narcissist theme dubbed over the top) and Rock recounts a story of how she cut him off at second base before telling her to "poontang your ass on out of here!"

Mankind gifts Rock a specially made Ribera Steakhouse-style Rock N' Sock Connection jacket and introduces the specially airbrushed "Mr. Rocko" before dedicating himself to the team, but miscommunication during a *SmackDown!* match with Val Venis leads to Rock blasting Mankind with a Rock Bottom before he "wipes his ass of this team" and promises his only partner from now on will be "the People". He goes 2-on-1 against Bull Buchanan and the Big Bossman but Mankind makes the save when Rock finds himself in trouble.

Lawler talks about what a stroke of genius it was for Rock to only refer to himself in the third person, and the unique options that opened up for him on promos that nobody else was able to replicate. He talks about his philosophies as a heel commentator, nothing that "The Rock is like the only "quote" good guy that I can't say anything bad about because I have to put over his sense of humour because I like it. I would really look like a complete idiot if I went out there and tried to say something bad about a guy that's talking about poontang pie, it's just too funny and it's just too cool to not like. When he really started adding that element of humour, that's when I thought that that was gonna push him right over the edge."

As Mick Foley would later reveal, his idea behind the Rock 'N' Sock team had been twofold. Firstly, he openly admitted that his body was breaking down and had intended to retire in October 1999 until he found out that Steve Austin would be out of action for around a year with neck problems, and opted to stick around and lend a hand. The team with the Rock would be a way to have fun without having to do anything too physical. Secondly, he saw the team as a way to "soften" the Rock's character, who was still acting selfish, stuck-up and arrogant despite now being cast as a babyface. Foley's intended direction for the partnership was to have Rock begin to take a begrudging shine to Mankind, adding an element of compassion to his character. However, as the weeks and months passed, Rock's character continued on without change, and Foley gave up on the whole idea. That leads to angle with Foley's real-life pal Al Snow becoming jealous of Mankind's relationship with the Rock, and growing increasingly annoyed with Rock's constant dismissals of him. The leads to a cage match on *SmackDown!* which Snow wins. Not really; Rock kicks his ass, and that's that.

Rock heads to Tower Books in New York to sign copies of his literary masterpiece *The Rock Says...*, where he talks about his life around the business. More content like this wouldn't have gone amiss, or stories about the Rock as a child on the road with his wrestler father Rocky Johnson and promoter grandmother Lia Maivia. Sadly, it's only mentioned in passing as the feature heads back in time to the night after *St. Valentine's Day Massacre*, where a heel Rock asks Mr. McMahon "Who is this roody poo?" and does everything in his power to belittle the WWF's newest signing, Paul Wight. It's an entirely counterproductive interview, emasculating the giant right out of the gate, and that somehow leads to Rock and Big Show's collision at the end of the 2000 *Royal Rumble*. Famously, they blow the ending, as they both go over the top together and Rock's feet actually hit the deck first, meaning Big Show should have won. Usefully, the WWF was able to play that into a pre-*WrestleMania* angle with Big Show seeking his revenge. Unfortunately, it also helped justify the WWF's decision to put Big Show (and Mick Foley) into the *WrestleMania* main event, a super-lame four-way along with Rock, Triple H and "a McMahon in every corner." Yechh!

VERDICT

As noted, 1999 wasn't a banner year for the WWF, or for North American wrestling in general, and the same can be said for the Rock as he meanders around from filler feud to filler feud, rumbles with guys distinctly below his station, and catches up with his old nemesis Triple H. Again, like other profile tapes of the era, there's a curious mix of work and shoot on offer from the talking heads, with Michael Cole in particular adding nothing of value, although *SmackDown!* announcing partner Jerry Lawler does offer up some interesting discussion by delving into his psychological mindset on why the character is so successful and how he opts to present that from the broadcast booth.

Sadly, much like many of the feuds covered on this tape, most of the material feels like filler. Rock is unquestionably an extremely charismatic man, but how many times does one need to sit through footage of his personal appearances and blubbery praise from the sort of wrestling fans whose on-screen presence is enough to make you wish you weren't one? While these spots did serve to break up what otherwise might have been a monotonous collection of extended music videos recounting around seven months of Rock matches, it didn't go unnoticed that they also served to drag this tape kicking and screaming to a 90-minute duration. Given the relatively brief time period covered and the lack of real insight into the man himself, this feature would have been served at no more than 60.

All in all however, this tape does come someway recommended if you were a major Rock fan at the time, as many were, and a DVD re-release comes with another 30-odd minutes of extras if you're the sort of person who really can't get enough of the guy, although many of them are simply extended versions of the same promos culled from the main feature.

58

LANCE STORM

MICK FOLEY - MADMAN UNMASKED

CAT NO: WWF255
RUN TIME: 45 minutes (approx)

Arnold Furious: When I first started to explore wrestling outside of the WWF I homed in on guys I knew and understood from the WWF who'd worked elsewhere. One of my first forays into the world of tape trading came in 1997 when I picked up some tapes from a guy in the States. Having seen footage of Mick Foley working in the famous IWA: King of the Deathmatches, that was one of the first tapes I picked up, along with another detailing the best of Mick Foley in Japan. By the end of the tape trading era I had more "Best of" Mick Foley tapes than of anyone else knocking around my house. Largely because the WWF had also been releasing Foley tapes and his crossover appeal allowed me to explore the various different areas of his wrestling history such as WCW, ECW and the brutal matches in Japan. Like anyone who watched wrestling in 1997, I felt a connection with Mick. He was a fan, an everyday shlub who didn't look great and didn't have a wrestler's physique but he was a big star anyway. The WWF capitalised on the connection with the fans and released quite a few Foley tapes and DVDs over the years. Not as many as they did for Steve Austin and the Rock, but you could at a push call Foley the third biggest shifter of merchandise during the same era. Mainly because he also wrote books that everyone bought, thus dispelling the myth that wrestling fans didn't read.

Like a few other profile tapes this one comes from the Biography Channel. I had it taped off TV for years along with the Andre the Giant and Steve Austin bios that also got WWF tape releases. You can tell it's not a straight up WWF production because The Undertaker is billed as "Mark Calaway". We start off with a few talking heads and clips of Mick getting bashed with stuff and taking sick bumps. The voiceover guy confirms my earlier statement by telling us Foley is a "money making machine".

We move on to an outside the ring interview with Barry Blaustein, director of Beyond the Mat, so you know for sure it's not a WWF production. As a kid Mick liked cartoons, sports and the Chicago Bears. Mick's Dad, Jack Foley, talks about Mick getting kids from the neighbourhood and having a baseball league. Mick's brother John, rarely seen on TV, talks about how competitive Mick was. Mick tried a few sports but became obsessed with professional wrestling because of the showmanship and the ladies. He wasn't sure how to go about a career in wrestling though and joined the amateur team in school. Mick talks about losing an amateur match and how humiliating it was. We get clips of The Loved One where Mick eats dog food while doing push ups. Childhood friend Danny Zucker points out Mick was nuts and didn't wear protective clothing when he played lacrosse. Mick found himself getting frustrated with the ladies in high school so he'd try harder and harder to do crazy stuff to get himself over with girls. That ended up driving them further away.

The origin of Dude Love came from a date Mick had with a girl, that he thought was going well until the goodnight kiss when she called him by the wrong name: "Frank". Mick wrote his own film based on the events called The Legend of Frank Foley before doing a sequel about a wrestling champion, the aforementioned The Loved One where Mick first played the character "Dude Love". The finale of this movie enterprise was Mick jumping off Danny Zucker's roof in an attempt to emulate Jimmy Snuka. This was on the back of Mick hitchhiking to Madison Square Garden to see Snuka wrestle Don Muraco, which was also the point where Mick decided to become a wrestler. Amazingly the take of Mick's stunt now available on video was the second take, as the cameraman missed the first one. The lack of linear storytelling is somewhat jarring here as they mention the Snuka love and then go back in time to Mick travelling to MSG.

Supportive brother John says he never thought Mick would make it and constantly told him to give it up, but promoter Tommy D saw The Loved One and asked Dominic DeNucci to train him. DeNucci told Foley he'd train him if he stayed in college, sensing his enthusiasm was great but his body was not. Mick was working on a communications degree in upstate

FURIOUS ABOUT: RHYNO

There have been few transitions from the hardcore world of ECW to the mainstream of the WWE than Rhyno (Dudleyz aside). He came in hot, having been booked strong for 2 years previously in ECW, and aligned himself with an another hot act in Edge & Christian. His popularity was soaring thanks to Paul Heyman's on-air calls of "GORE, GORE, GORE" to describe his finisher. His heel status was solidified during the Invasion as he teamed with the Alliance, only to lose a year of his career with a neck injury. By his return in 2003, the character had lost a lot of traction with the fans and his chance to impress had passed by. A shame really, as when he went out injured he'd developed a cult following and management were high on him. He left the WWE in 2005, having peaked as US champion in the Alliance angle.

New York but DeNucci's wrestling school was in Pennsylvania. I think everyone thought Foley would just give up when he realised how much travelling would be involved in pursuing his dream, but instead he would drive for five or six hours and sleep in his car. DeNucci points out Mick never complained even when it was below freezing. "He realised I was terrible" says Mick of DeNucci, but Dominic really appreciated his commitment. We get a little footage of Mick training at DeNucci's school. He really is terrible. Mick puts DeNucci over by saying he never hurt him but made sure he understood the business and respected what the guys went through to become wrestlers. We get clips of Foley being used as enhancement in the WWF and hitting an awful back elbow on Davey Boy Smith, who ignores it. Mick talks about Dynamite Kid beating the hell out of him and says he couldn't chew food for a month afterwards. His mom hasn't enjoyed wrestling ever since.

We move on to Mick working the indy circuit with Shane Douglas. The footage is quite rare and it's all trainee indy stuff. Mick needed a better character and changed his name to Cactus Jack, which was his Dad's nickname. Mick points out his life improved a lot when he met his wife Collette. She wasn't a wrestling fan and didn't know who Mick was. Collette drove him to improve his matches and work on his offensive moves. Mick talks about changing Cactus Jack to make him scary and intimidating. We skip over his WCW career as Mick says he felt "trapped" and left without telling Collette. Foley went into the indies and we get clips from ECW where he felt he built a better reputation for himself than he did in WCW. We move on again to Japan where Mick worked against Terry Funk in a barbed wire match. The clips include the legendary fire chair. That's it for the pre-WWF stuff and we skip ahead again to 1996.

His year on the indies in 1995 got the attention of the WWF. Vince McMahon talks about seeing the footage and Vince figured Mick was insane so he was doubtful whether he'd work out in the WWF. We get the famous Vince speech where he told Mick he wanted to call him 'Mason the Mutilator'. Mick came up with Mankind instead because he didn't want to be called Mason and Vince went with it after Mick talked about the double meaning and how good the promos could be. We skip ahead again to the sit down interviews with Jim Ross, but hardly see any of that either. Foley puts over wrestling as a circus and that he's the guy that gets shot out of a cannon. This leads into the Mandible Claw, which in turn leads into Mr. Socko and his debut as "the worst ventriloquist act of all time" with Vince McMahon in his hospital bed. Mick says the whole thing was an accident. Taker suggests the sock was because Mick lost his leather hand covering.

We switch gears and go to 1998 and the triple Foley characters, but that doesn't go anywhere. Voiceover man tells us Mick wanted to do something no one would never forget. Vince tells us Mick had told him he wanted to "try something different", which made him nervous. They're talking about King of the Ring '98 and the Hell in a Cell. Voiceover man points out the bump was planned but still stunned everyone. Taker says he thought the match was over and Mick's career was probably over too. We get the footage of Mick getting back up and charging back down to the Cell. Taker puts over the second bump as being even more violent than the first one and suggests the panel wasn't supposed to break. Jerry Lawler reiterates that and says it's a worse bump because it was so unprotected. Vince says he was worried about Mick being dead but he just went ahead and got back up. Mick couldn't remember the rest of the match and asked Taker if he had used the thumbtacks and Taker told him to look at his arm, which was full of tacks. Vince went up to Mick afterwards and told him "never again". Foley calls it his defining moment.

Mick took two months to heal after Hell in a Cell and his kids were worried. Voiceover man talks about injuries and how his body wasn't as good as it used to be. Vince says Mick could do whatever he wanted, if that was acting or game show hosting or being an agent in the WWF. Whatever he did, he'd be the best at it. Taker points out he never liked Dude Love and thinks Mick didn't like it much either, which is weirdly out of place. Mick waxes lyrical about his career and is happy with what he's achieved. Vince puts him over and says not many people get to live their dream like Mick has. "The dreams don't stop". Mick describes himself as having a thimbleful of talent but a truckload of intestinal fortitude. The tape then abruptly ends.

VERDICT

It's not easy to fit an entire career into 45-minutes and this doesn't do Mick justice at all. It skims over so many great moments and barely touches upon most of his big achievements in the business. They do linger on a few things, like Hell in a Cell, but his family is only mentioned in passing and we don't even see his kids. ECW is reduced to a few seconds of footage against the Sandman and WCW less than that, which is the issue with a 45-minute run time. It's not a bad watch, because Mick is so likeable as a person, but if you're any kind of wrestling fan you know everything that's said here. Also if you followed wrestling at the time you probably saw it for free on TV when it first aired. Frustrations over brevity aside, it's an easy watch. There is some rare footage included of Mick growing up, DeNucci training him and indy stuff that you don't normally see, along with the oft seen footage of Mick diving off a roof and the Hell in a Cell. It's an interesting mixture and it won't take up a lot of your time, so is probably worth seeing once.

49

EVE OF DESTRUCTION

CAT NO: WWF256
RUN TIME: 45 minutes (approx)

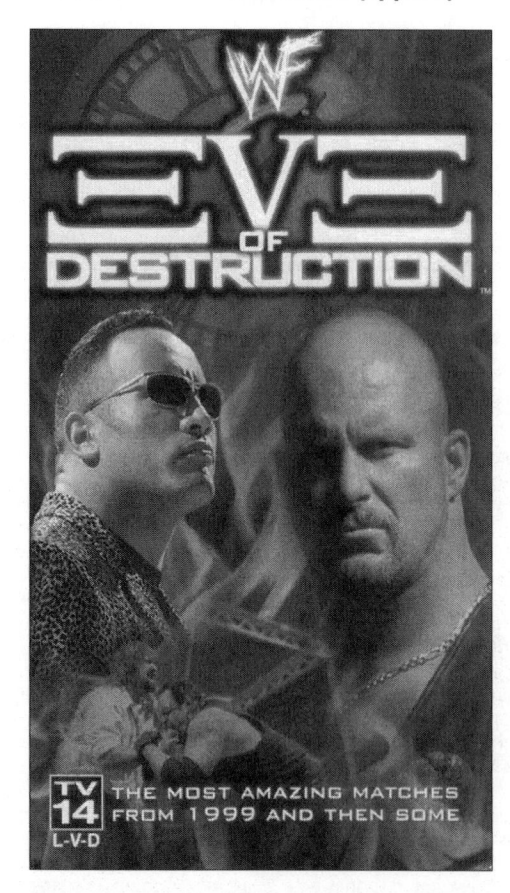

James Dixon: This is a taster tape highlighting some of the WWF's most brutal matches from the past 18-months. None are shown in full but rather in highlight form, mostly set to music, with talking heads from the roster offering comments and analysis.

Hell in a Cell
The Undertaker vs. Mankind
[King of the Ring 1998 - 06/28/98]
Mick Foley speaks first, talking about how he realised he and Taker were going to struggle to live up to the incredible standards set by Shawn Michaels and the Undertaker in their 1997 match of the year at *Badd Blood*. It was a task made even harder by Undertaker having a broken foot. "The possibility of stinking up the place was high" says Foley. Taker kayfabes and says he knew he needed to do something drastic to counter Mankind's usual brutality, though in reality he was uncomfortable with the big bumps and had to be pestered by Foley until he was worn down. The Big Bossman chimes in and claims he was worried when he saw the bumps, which is odd given he didn't return to the WWF until October, some four months after the show. D'Lo Brown and Steve Austin say how scared they were when they saw the first fall; "It was devastating" offers Stone Cold.

Taker couldn't believe Foley returned to the ring, but anyone who knew Mick Foley probably wasn't really all that surprised. He is good crazy, with the art coming first in his mind ahead of his own wellbeing. Road Dogg saw the second bump, the one through the cage, and thought that was the end of Mick. Wrestlers know the truth; *that* was the really painful one. Foley counters that and claims it wasn't all that painful when it happened... because he was unconscious.

We break from the talking heads and the accompanying footage that matches what is being said, to see random highlights of the rest of the bout set to a typically soulless and weak song from God-botherers P.O.D. Jeff Hardy then calls it the best match he has ever seen, which is why he will always be remembered as a stunt guy ahead of a wrestler. It was a remarkable spectacle, sure, but it was far from a great match in the traditional sense. "I feel like I have done more" says Mick, clearly disappointed that from his entire body of work, his career will be defined by two silly bumps. More half hearted nu-metal dirge follows as we see the same bumps again, only this time slightly slowed down and with the soundtrack attempting to change the tone to a reflective sobriety. It doesn't fit at all.

Steel Cage Match
Steve Austin vs. Vince McMahon
[St. Valentine's Day Massacre - 02/14/99]
"I had the butterflies in my stomach" says Vince in a rare out of character interview, while the rest of his roster discuss how little chance he had going in to the bout as he was "a suit against an athlete". We go back-and-forth between Steve and Vince discussing their strategies, while more popular alternative music from the day whirs away in the background. This is a very odd presentation. The talking head stuff is relatively non-kayfabed and insightful, but the highlights to the music make it feel like an MTV music video. The Hardy Boyz enjoyed Vince's nasty table bump, but Edge says it was "ugly", which it was. Vince bounced on the no selling table first before it decided to break. Shane McMahon says that everyone in the back was worried and begging for him to get up, which is only half true because it was all part of the show, even if the bump was more nasty than expected. The match continued, with Vince taking a pasting and constantly defying Austin with "sign language", and then taking a further kicking for his insolence. That is, until the lumbering behemoth Paul 'The Giant' Wight, later the Big Show, made his WWF debut by coming through the ring, Undertaker style. He instantly established himself as a giant goofball by hurling Austin into the side of the cage, only for it to swing open allowing Austin to drop out and win. The sombre music returns, but trying to tug on the emotional heartstrings for an Austin-McMahon confrontation is just never going to work.

Last Man Standing Match
WWF Championship
Mankind (c) vs. The Rock
[Royal Rumble 1999 - 01/24/99]
This is another bout from the series of violent encounters these

> **FURIOUS ABOUT: SATURN**
>
> Perry Saturn was an outstanding wrestler in ECW. So much so WCW signed him and not his tag team partner, John Kronus. Saturn was head and shoulders above him, and much of the ECW roster. He spent three years grinding away in the WCW midcard before joining WWE as part of the Radicalz. The WWE clearly only wanted Benoit and Guerrero and Saturn found himself in a string of pointless tag team matches. After smacking around jobber Mike Bell, Saturn found his push stalled further as he was saddled with a gimmick where he'd suffered too many concussions and entered into a relationship with a mop. He'd been teamed with Terri as a valet beforehand and she became jealous of the mop, leading to an angle where Raven fed "Moppy" into a wood chipper. Shortly afterward Saturn was sidelined with a serious knee injury and left the company in 2002.

two had in early 1999. It follows their controversial outing at *Royal Rumble 1999* where Rock took liberties with Foley's health and welfare by drilling him with a series of sickening and hard to watch chair shots to his unprotected skull. This is less violent, though still features some meaty bumps, and is presented like a post-modernist Japanese influenced movie what with the music used, the subtitles in between spots and things cut all over the place out of sequence. It's like Quentin Tarantino's handy work. Two of the highlights, at least according to the tape, are Mankind attempting the worst People's Elbow in history and Rock taking a seat and doing a spot of commentary. Michael Cole turns up as a talking head, and good lord he looks like a crack addict. Honestly, the difference between him here and in later years when he became the unwelcome "voice of WWE" is astonishing. Michael, just what did you change your diet to? Dianabol and pies? Another moment featured sees Rock taking another break from the action to sing an out of breath rendition of 'Heartbreak Hotel'. Edge thinks he shouldn't give up his day job and Mick says he thought he was off key. In the context of the match he shut him up with a Mandible Claw, but the finish soon followed and turned out to be a damp squib draw, with the title change coming the next night on *RAW* instead. Obviously.

WWF European Championship
Shane McMahon (c) vs. X-Pac
[WrestleMania XV - 03/28/99]
To the second best match from *WrestleMania XV*, which says more about the show than it does the quality of this bout, which was only average. Shane shows that being the bosses son he can get away with whatever he wants, including stealing moves from the real workers, as he tries the People's Elbow. X-Pac says it bordered on a felony, which Shane laughs off as "all entertainment". I guess taking Rob Van Dam's Van Terminator and making it his own two years later falls in the same category... I would be interested to hear how he defends taking a pasting and no-selling it and then mounting a comeback, something he has done many times. Highlights from the bout continue to roll, including the ending that saw Triple H turning heel on X-Pac to render the prior three months of storyline completely nonsensical. No one saw it coming through, right Vinny Ru? Shane sums things up by talking about what an honour it was to compete at *WrestleMania* and that some guys never get there. The fact he was only there because his surname was McMahon and him being on the card took a spot from someone more deserving who had worked for years to get a shot, is naturally not mentioned.

In an interlude, Cyprus Hill's unappealing blend of rap and metal, without being listenable as either, blares out as Steve Austin dicks around in some vehicles, which was one of his favourite extracurricular pastimes. The usual Austin footage of him commandeering and utilising a monster truck, a cement truck, a zamboni and a beer truck follows. Austin says there were no safety harnesses in any of the vehicles, so he just had to improvise and hope for the best. Yeah, there is nothing quite like putting your most marketable and money making star in potential danger each week by having him play amateur stuntman. This is quite a fun little segment though, with Austin joking about inadvertently ribbing himself when he tried to take a drink from the beer hose used in the famous "beer bash" spot, not realising how powerful it was, while Mick Foley makes the funny and says he wants Austin to prove how tough he is by coming out on a moped. He is right, that would be a blast.

Terri Invitational Ladder Match
The Hardy Boyz vs. Edge & Christian
[No Mercy 1999 - 10/17/99]
Along with the Hell in a Cell, this is probably the most important match on the tape historically, because of the importance to the participants. Actually I would say that it is even more important than the famous Cell encounter as it made three future World Champions... and Matt Hardy, rather than just one. There is good reason too, because the bout is a master class in stunt-filled spots, with thrills and innovation around every corner. All four guys were on the bottom rung prior to the bout, and while they weren't nobodies, they were fairly close. Talk about grabbing the brass ring with both hands; the performance from all four was so sensational that not only did they receive a standing ovation from those in attendance at the Gund Arena that night, but also the following night from the *RAW* crowd in Columbus, Ohio. Edge tells an often repeated story about how Mick Foley, one of the WWF's genuine main eventers and all around nice guys, came up to them after the bout and praised the work, telling them they had earned their spot. He is absolutely right. I remember being blown away by this when watching it live, and it still holds up as one of the finest ladder based encounters in the history of the business.

VERDICT

It's not very long, but you get plenty of bang for your buck with this tape. As an introduction to some of the WWF's most celebrated stunt bouts from the Attitude era, it does a pretty great job. The music is not to everyone's tastes though, well anyone's actually. I love heavy metal, but the tosh accompanying the clips on this tape is obscure, flat and dull. Who has EVER liked P.O.D? That aside, the interviews are varied and fun, and relevant, and the general pace of the presentation keeps things moving at such a speed that even if the matches weren't good it wouldn't be boring. The fact that they all range from good to great makes this a recommended offering for someone merely wanting to see what all the fuss is about.

80

CHYNA FITNESS

CAT NO: WWF257
RUN TIME: 45 minutes (approx)

Arnold Furious: Given the WWF's constant attempts to reach a crossover market, it's almost a surprise they don't have a whole line of keep fit video releases. And yet if you type "WWF fitness" into Play.com the only wrestling related entertainment that comes up is Triple H movie *The Chaperone*. The only exercise you'd get from that movie is quickly rushing to eject the DVD as soon as it starts to save yourself 103 minutes of painfully unfunny Triple H dramedy. So this VHS release is the only attempt to crack the fitness market.

This tape is subtitled "More Than Meets the Eye", which was also the marketing terminology used for *Transformers* toys back in the 80s. I'd rather spend the following 45-minutes watching old *Transformers* cartoons. I'm not entirely sure what they're getting at there. Chyna, when looked upon, is a muscular bodybuilding woman. So how is she "more than meets the eye"? I guess they must be referring to her personality, but it's a fitness video!

Host is Chyna, obviously, and she opens by discussing her role in wrestling and how she considers being "the top superstar wrestler that has ever been" a fortunate career. She talks more about how sexy she feels than how talented she is, which is a bit odd. We get a few talking head interviews with WWF superstars who say Chyna works harder in the gym than they do. Hunter gushes about her form, comparing her to a Greek statue and virtually creams his pants in the process. Chyna has a chat with a few wrestlers about their workout, which leads to Big Show doing jumping jacks while Chyna shoots the shit with Stephanie McMahon. This would be before Steph made off with Chyna's boyfriend, presumably. Show is actually hilarious and makes me wonder where his videotape is. '*Big Show Fitness*' would be awesome. It'd involve chain-smoking cigarettes and eating cheeseburgers, but he's a funny guy so it'd be good TV.

In order to do Chyna's workout you need three sets of weights, a jumping rope. And 40 spare minutes. Chyna promises to work "every single of inch of your body". So get warmed up folks, get up off your sofa and start punching! Chyna presents her face as a target. Is this the Sean Waltman exercise tape? "Kane, Rock, Triple H" she shouts as if she's punching out main eventers. Next up is squats. Feeling the burn yet readers? "Rome wasn't built in a day" she philosophically advises while giving us an eyeful of her cleavage. Next is the jump rope, which she claims can be done anywhere. Anywhere with a high enough ceiling! If I tried to jump rope in front of the office TV, three things would happen: 1. I'd fall over my feet because I'm uncoordinated. 2. The rope would get tangled up in the ceiling fan. 3. James' black coffee would get knocked over and he would become very grouchy indeed.

ROUND 1! I wasn't aware we were working a round system, but we head into some strength training as Chyna lies on her back, positioning the camera to look straight down her top for the second time. She goes to the heavy weights first before switching to medium weights for bicep curls. "You need a licence to carry these guns" says Chyna. No wonder they didn't let her talk for the first year of her WWF run. Third set is light weights lifted out to the shoulder. "Like Val Venis and D'Lo Brown" suggests Chyna, though each weight is tiny. From those reps we go right into the cardio and knee lifts. Just a quick reminder: this tape costs as little as $2 (though more like £6 for UK readers!). After a few vigorous knee lifts we go into recovery, which isn't the foetal position but rather puffing your chest out, so the viewers at home get a good solid look at your jugs for the third time in 10-minutes.

ROUND 2! Chyna and her massive hooters encourage us into Round 2 where we'll be blasting our triceps. My triceps need a good blasting, I don't know about yours. I swear Chyna is advertising her availability as a porn star even here as she moans, grunts, imagines everyone sweating and does a lot of bending over in tight clothing. I do enjoy the various cutaways where Chyna stresses how these exercises help you press various WWF superstars. Two sets of reps take us into cardio #2, which is lunges. I can't even watch a lunge without thinking of Joey Tribbiani, but thankfully Chyna adds in uppercuts at groin level to show how this exercise has benefitted her wrestling career, interspersed with footage of her nut-shotting dudes on TV. In case everyone is getting too excited, we need to stretch and warm down again.

ROUND 3! Chyna teases doing girls push ups before delivering the real deal, adding that you can do a push up anywhere. Well, not on a high wire. Or in the cockpit of a fighter jet. Don't lie to the viewers, Chyna. After that Chyna goes to town on her abs before mentioning her "nice firm buttocks". Exercise freaks are just weird people. I'm glad Arnold Schwarzenegger is around to motivate people, because if we were stuck with Richard Simmons, Cher, Mr. Motivator and all those other weirdoes, nobody would work out at all. Chyna moves on to squat thrusts and I almost wish I was doing the workout instead of writing about it as I might actually get something out of the tape. Chyna yells "you can do this" as she continues the routine, as if sensing my curiosity. I really couldn't! Not without remodelling my office.

ROUND 4! Chyna poses in between rounds, and ahead of Round 4, as if to build it up as the most intense, decides to get her chest bollocks out and pose with one hand across them. Back to the good old bicep curls, sitting down this time and Chyna points out her left arm is weaker than the right. "They don't call me the 9th Wonder of the World for nothing" says Chyna before encouraging us to become the 10th, 11th and 12th. Is she talking directly to the three writers of this book, I wonder? That Lee Maughan, he's the 11th Wonder of the World, they'll be saying. Maybe. More weights lifted and this time it's behind her head, which apparently helps her to get armdragged by Kurt Angle as that's the footage that accompanies it. Back to cardio with more squats and standing jumps. "Hard work makes a great body" preaches Chyna. Meh, it sounds too much like hard work.

ROUND 5! Thankfully Chyna doesn't follow through on the stripping and opts for a "most muscular" pose as a tribute to Ravishing Rick Rude. At least that's how I'm interpreting it. He is simply ravishing and they were in the same stable. More vertical lifts to the shoulder with the light weights. I'm not the best person to describe all this as I don't do much working out, unless lifting heavy pint glasses counts. "My butt has to look good" says Chyna before disparaging the rear end of Rikishi. He's Samoan, it's genetics. Although putting mayonnaise on everything probably doesn't help. Back to the cardio with a weird crabwalk thing. I call it the Gran Naniwa. "Woo, I'm pooped" says Chyna before we head into…

ROUND 6! After all that intensity Chyna balances on her elbows and toes and just stays there. My abs hurt just watching. She continues with abdominal exercises, citing that good abs are the basis for everything else. One thing I've really liked about this workout is the variety but this 6th round is a vicious assault on the abdominal region, which is a really easy place to do muscle damage if you go in unprepared. If I was doing the workout while watching this I would skip most of Round 6, but then my abs suck. I have one large circular ab, full of beer. The last round focuses entirely on blasting those abs and contains no weights at all. I'm not going to argue with Chyna's technique as she's the one with the incredibly muscular body. She says she wanted to be an inspiration to others and that's the workout done.

FURIOUS ABOUT: CHRIS BENOIT

Before Chris Benoit defected from WCW at the turn of the millennium, with fellow Radicalz Guerrero, Saturn and Malenko, he was WCW's biggest star. His work with Bret Hart and Jeff Jarrett in 1999 had cemented his place at the top of the card. WCW were aware he wanted to leave and put the WCW title on him, only for Benoit to leave anyway. Benoit's in-ring excellence wasn't matched by his persona however and joining the WWF was a big risk. Just because he could work ***** matches and had the physique and athleticism the WWF liked, didn't mean he'd be a hit. His "Mr Roboto" behaviour was indeed one of the first things Chris Jericho made fun of him for during their 2000 feud. In the ring, he was almost unmatched, except by Kurt Angle, and whoever he ran into proceeded to have their best matches. In particular The Rock had an excellent title defence against Benoit in the kind of match Rock didn't have; it was technically superb. Benoit's technical excellence had been built up over many years; mainly through working the best junior heavyweights in the world in Japan (Liger, Kanemoto, Eddy, Ohtani, Sasuke) before working slick midcard matches with the best North America had to offer in WCW (Eddy, Malenko, Jericho). When he arrived in the WWF his in-ring was near perfect. In this three year period he had great matches with The Rock, Jericho, Triple H, Angle and Austin. Matches we're still talking about today, despite what happened to Benoit later in life. While there's no escaping Benoit's tainted legacy, the list of great matches he left behind are worth considering. Those matches shouldn't be wiped from the face of the Earth and there has to be a disconnect between that Benoit and the killer.

VERDICT

It's a workout tape and they really trim the fat around it. There is a five minute introduction, which is the most entertaining bit of the tape and then a 40-minute workout. It's no better or no worse than other workout tapes that are available. A point I made at the start is the lack of fitness tapes and such from the WWF. I can only assume this didn't sell very well, and the whole ICOPRO deal was a bit of a set back too. Either that or the WWF looked at the audience and thought they didn't have the capacity for self improvement. I hear ya, WWF, self improvement is hard. As an instructor Chyna comes across okay. I'm not overly keen on fitness instructor types who spend their lives telling genetically inferior people to try harder and being all bouncy and enthused, but Chyna is no worse than the rest. If you're planning on watching this for the sake of completionism, you really don't need to. The opening five minutes are good for a laugh, mainly because of Big Show, but the rest is just a workout. I like how they tried to tie it into wrestling, but seeing as the tape is intended as a workout, the cutaways had to be quick and it doesn't allow for much of a viewing experience. Or you could bust out the jump rope and three sets of weights and burn off some fat, tubby.

25

INSURREXTION 2000

CAT NO: WWF258
RUN TIME: 140 minutes (approx)

Arnold Furious: Normally when writing these books I deliberately do everything in order. It's not because I have OCD or anything but I like to reference myself and earlier events. It helps me to mentally catalogue the history of wrestling. When I do stuff out of order, I frequently find myself referencing future events, which I don't like doing. So when I deliberately skipped over *Insurrextion 2000* when I was doing my 2000 quota for this book it wasn't an easy decision to make. I feel that UK PPVs are hard to watch when lined up against the American equivalent from a month, or even a week, beforehand. The quality of wrestling never matches up and it'll always feel like a lightweight version of a proper American PPV. So I skipped *Insurrextion* and decided to watch it as a standalone show, with no real frame of reference for how good things are compared to the shows around this one. I'm hoping it'll be a more rewarding experience, seeing as 2000 had lots of great wrestling and great shows. Instead of feeling like a subpar 2000 show, it should just feel like a good show. If that makes sense.

The card for this show is one of the most loaded cards you'll see on a UK-only PPV too. You've got Angle-Benoit, Guerrero-Jericho, Hardys-E&C and the main event is Rock vs. HHH (& Shane). We're in London, England. Hosts are Jim Ross and Jerry Lawler.

Too Cool vs. Perry Saturn & Dean Malenko
Too Cool get a massive pop, which was always the way when a "proper" star name came out at the start of an overseas show. Malenko is the Light Heavyweight champion and this is an extension of his feud with Scotty. We get a clip from Malenko's win over Scotty at *Backlash*, which is a superb match, a genuine **** classic and one of Dean's few PPV outings in singles in the WWF. Dean does an incredible job of making Scotty look like a legitimate threat to him and also of bringing the kind of counters very few wrestlers were capable of at the time. I think Malenko is probably the most underrated wrestler the WWF have ever had. His timing is immaculate. Dean can even make the goofiest Scotty spot look like gold. Too Cool can get away with a minimal amount of effort and indeed GMS basically just stands on the apron for most of the match, having recently recovered from knee surgery. GMS stands around until it's time for the hot tag but even that merely serves to set up Scotty's infamous double Worm. Saturn accidentally mashes Malenko with a lariat, Malenko accidentally headbutts him in the groin (as you do) and GMS finishes with the Hip Hop Drop. Fun opener, albeit on the short side. Malenko held the whole thing together and I'm still perplexed as to why he didn't get a serious WWF push. Even WCW pushed him!
Final Rating: **¼

Backstage: The Kat and Mae Young prepare for tonight's match. No hints of nudity or anything.

Promo Time: Vince McMahon
He runs a little cheap heat and tells us Triple H, in a fair world, would still be WWF Champion. He blames Linda, Earl Hebner and Steve Austin for conspiring against him. Vince guarantees a new champion as there's no Linda, no Hebner and no Austin tonight. Vince promises the new champion will be a "McMahon family member". Typical time-wasting mid-PPV promo from Vince. He didn't actually say anything other than stir the pot regarding Hunter and Shane coexisting. So basically he created distrust that wasn't there and discord from his family's relative harmony. From a character standpoint it makes him look like a moron. Worse still, his appearance reminds the fans the main event is really far off and it hurts the crowd reactions for the next match.

Bull Buchanan vs. Kane
Now *this* would be a typical UK-only PPV outing. The idea being that the WWF wants to get a look at Bull as they think he has a shot at being a long term star, but they don't trust him to work this match in America where people might see him being mediocre. They want to give him a try… but not anywhere he might be seen. You either trust him or you don't. Bull has great agility for a big man and back in the 80s he might have been perceived as a star. During Attitude there was a clear switch from big guys to small guys with personality though. Bull is now just a skilled monster for Kane to slay. He shows off his whole moveset with a lot of flying until he jumps into a chokeslam.

Bull didn't look out of place but the normally noisy crowd didn't give a crap about him.
Final Rating: ¾*

Backstage: Triple H and Stephanie hang out. Hunter is pleased to be termed a "McMahon family member" until Steph points out that Vince might have been talking about Shane.

Road Dogg vs. Bradshaw
Tori is in Road Dogg's corner, which allows her to jump about in lime green hot pants. I approve. It's a bit sad that *this* is DX now; Roadie and his valet. He does the whole DX spiel including a modified Outlaws introduction and some bonus rhyming. Faarooq comes down and joins commentary until he blatantly interferes and gets kicked out. Thanks for coming, Ron. Man, the WWF had a load of airline tickets spare in 2000. Business was good. Regardless of assistance Bradshaw spends the match beating Road Dogg up. Oh, and also getting caught on camera calling spots. Not from ringside, mind you, but from the hard cam. Does he think they don't speak English in England? The clues in the name, mate. Road Dogg gets in his crowd-pleasing offence but eventually just walks into the Clothesline from Hell. Tori distracts to prevent a pin and Road Dogg suddenly pops up like he's fine. Amazingly Road Dogg hits the Pumphandle Slam and goes over clean. There isn't the pop you'd expect but rather a stunned silence. The selling was terrible here and the match was just filler.
Final Rating: ½*

Backstage: Fabulous Moolah puts over Terri, the little 'She Devil', as a legitimate wrestling threat. Lawler knows better and asks the crowd "are you ready for some puppies and kittens?" Indeed.

The Kat vs. Terri
This is an arm-wrestling contest. Terri should know what she's doing here as she worked the babyface part of this deal back in 1997 against Sunny. She starts stalling before Lawler introduces anything. The crowd does not care about the bullshit though and start chanting for "puppies". "Caaahmmm on, Jerry, do somethin'" yells Kat. I realise with the way I've written that it reads like Cockney, but it's supposed to be a Memphis drawl. Lawler can't bring himself to abuse the babyfaces though as he's dating Kat. They finally hook up, Terri spits water in Kat's face but Mae pours water over Terri's head, thus creating a wet t-shirt contest, and Kat wins. Let's face it, these two are only on the show because of their willingness to get nekkid. Kat almost obliges that as her tits get exposed, briefly.
Final Rating: DUD

Backstage: Crash Holly finds Showkishi hilarious.

The Dudley Boyz vs. Rikishi & Showkishi
For those who don't remember, Big Show turned face after *WrestleMania* and started impersonating other wrestlers (and Conan the Barbarian). Rikishi found this so endearing that they formed a team, with Show playing Rikishi. It's funny, because this is the laziest impression Show ever did. He's just wearing Rikishi's spare tights. The gimmick was quite simple: Show would come out having fun and then someone would piss him off and he'd kill them. The gimmick worked for a while until he just turned heel, yet again. Seeing as D-Von annoys the giant during the introductions, that kills the fun before we get going. Apart from on commentary where Lawler details how the Stinkface is effective. "He always has one in the departure lounge at all times" before mentioning a "chocolate hostage", which JR plays along with beautifully. Part of the issue here is that the Dudleys are babyface so while they cheat a bit they don't draw any heat. Double Stinkface connects as departure lounges are presented to both Dudleys. Edge & Christian come down for a "run in", called a "run on" by a confused Lawler. Bloody marks. Bubba takes a spear so he has an out when Show chokeslams him. As if he needs one, with Show being a former WWF Champion and Bubba being a midcard tag team guy. Too Cool run down to do the dancing gimmick after the match. Everyone dances. Much fun is had by all. The whole segment is almost worth it to see Bubba Ray Dudley bust out his moves. Massive Rikishi heat stealing pop for that, to the point where I wonder how over the Dudleys would have gotten if they'd got a dancing gimmick as well as the tables gimmick! The pop would still be ongoing.
Final Rating: ½*

Video Control shows us Kurt Angle checking out London. "Nice jacket. Hi, Kurt Angle, Olympic hero".

Backstage: Chris Benoit, sporting a massive shiner from an errant Jericho belt shot days earlier, says Kurt Angle is in the wrong place at the wrong time.

Kurt Angle vs. Chris Benoit
Angle seems to get a decent pop everywhere he's gone so he runs a bunch of cheap heat, mainly by saying England's kids should learn to speak the real universal language: "American". "Let's not forget World War II, where we saved you from the Germans". Because Benoit can't see this ends up being cut short at only 6-minutes long, which was a huge gyp at the time and a big disappointment considering the talent. Crash Holly pops down to commentate, seeing as he's got nothing else to do. JR chides him like someone's angry granddad. "That's enough out of you, young man". Anyway, in the ring Angle goes after Benoit's eye. The slow pace suggests a long match with Angle building a lot of heat, not the 6-minute match it is. I'm guessing Benoit really couldn't see, which makes you wonder why they had the match in the first place. Benoit does manage the rolling Germans and the Crossface but Angle thumbs the eye, with the ref's hand, to escape. Swandive headbutt misses, which exacerbates that eye injury. Benoit swings wildly but gets hit with the Angle Slam. Considering one of the guys couldn't see and it played second fiddle to Crash Holly, this was okay. The psychology surrounding the eye led to virtually every near fall and the finish itself. Smart work.
Final Rating: **½

Backstage: Shane McMahon thinks Vince is favouring him and he'll walk out WWF champion tonight.

WWF Hardcore Championship
Crash Holly (c) vs. The British Bulldog
During the previous match Crash had been complaining of a lack of Englishmen to challenge for his title, so Davey comes out with a ref to compete. Davey retired about three weeks after this so it really is a career concluding turn. A pity the fans don't know that and thus don't treat him with much respect. His 1999 run showed how deteriorated he was as a worker and it's sad to see him this broken down. The hardcore situation lets him take it easy with a bunch of plunder shots. They don't do anything you'd call "good" and Davey finishes with the running powerslam for one last time nostalgia pop in England. Looking back, it's really sad to see. Knowing he'll never appear on another PPV and indeed will be dead just two years later, makes this rather tragic viewing.
Final Rating: ¼*

JERRY LYNN

Video Control takes us to Edge & Christian earlier, charging youngster Frank £5 for an autograph before getting more cash from fans for photos. Michael Cole takes exception as Christian calls this "easy money". What's remarkable is how many American wrestlers actually came over to England and genuinely charged money for everything. I think there are guys out there who treated the UK like a licence to rip the fans off. Cole taking umbrage shows the WWF taking the high road. Credit where it's due; the WWF has always treated the fanbase with at least a modicum of respect. Although, I suspect that's mainly because PR is so important to them.

WWF Tag Team Championship
Edge & Christian (c) vs. The Hardy Boyz
These guys all busted their asses in 1999 to get themselves noticed but the level of effort is noticeably lower here. You can't really work full-bore forever in wrestling and very few have even tried, but a little effort goes a long way. They run some good tag team stuff, albeit stuff every die-hard wrestling fan has seen many times over. Like protecting your partner from the turnbuckle and then having the heel get outsmarted. Matt seems the most energised of the guys and instigates a brawl with Christian before hitting the yodelling legdrop and setting up double teams. Jeff and Edge manage a great counters sequence, which finally gets a reaction from an unusually quiet London crowd. I think part of the problem is the crowd having to sit through subpar action and then having to be dragged back up again. To their credit, despite taking it easy, neither team rests or inserts chinlocks. Edge vs. Jeff is particularly good, which is surprising considering how great Matt vs. Christian used to be just a year beforehand. This is around the time when Edge and Jeff started to equal and even surpass

their colleagues. The Hardys seem to have better teaming. Christian gets picked off for Twist of Fate and the Swanton bomb. It's over so Edge grabs the ring bell and runs in for a blatant DQ. Everyone seemed a touch sluggish, though the match had its moments. A slow Edge & Christian vs. Hardys is still better than most tag team efforts. The Dudleys run in afterwards to hit the 3D on Christian and Bubba powerbombs Edge through a table.
Final Rating: **½

WWF European Championship
Eddie Guerrero (c) vs. Chris Jericho

This is after Chyna turned heel and relented to Eddie's Latino Heat. "I don't like being your champion anyway, man" says Eddie. Did he just address an entire crowd as "man"? He threatens to kick London out of Europe. Jericho is the IC champion but that's not on the line here, thanks to a Timmy White pre-match coin toss. Jericho gets by far the biggest pop on the show to this point. The difference between the opening in this match and the last one is amazing. They go absolutely FULL BORE, 100mph, and counter at ridiculous pace. Eddie slows things down with heel psychology and threatening to walk out. That allows them to resume just as quickly. They run the same deal again but with Chyna getting involved. It's good psychology as it allows them to work hard but get rest periods in without resting. It gives the crowd a sense of them never stopping. They get in a simplified version of the Guerrero-Malenko near falls sequence as Jericho struggles with complex switches in direction, and I'm surprised it doesn't get better pops. After that the heart goes from the match and the pacing slows a little. As if they went out to steal the show and got up to that point and thought, "that'll do". They work the Gory special and somehow Jericho reverses it only for Eddie, who obviously knows the move better, to escape and for Jericho to dump him on his face. Another superb counter after that with Jericho going for a powerbomb, Eddie countering into to rana to the floor and both guys taking a nasty bump. With the ref checking Eddie, Jericho eats a DDT off Chyna. Jericho kicks out and gets the double powerbomb. Lionsault scores but Chyna distracts the ref and Jericho springboard dropkicks her off the apron. Jericho turns into a belt shot from Eddie though and Guerrero retains. Cheat to win, holmes! An easy winner of best match on the show and one of the better UK-only PPV matches.
Final Rating: ***½

Backstage: Shane McMahon gets all excited about winning the title tonight and Triple H points out he's going to be the champion. Steph turns around and says "What does it matter who the champ is?" "It matters to me" say both guys at once.

Elsewhere: The Rock absorbs the adoration of the UK populace. He runs through catchphrases and the crowd eats it up.

WWF Championship
The Rock (c) vs. Triple H vs. Shane McMahon

Vince accompanies Shane out here and Steph corners her husband. If Hunter and Shane were smart they'd double team Rock out of the match and then one guy would lie down for the other, therefore winning the title and getting it off the Rock. I guess that's why they had to have a backstage quarrel between all the McMahons to set up that not happening. I like how Hunter initially orders Shane into the corner. Quiet now, adults talking. They establish a rip-roaring pace in this one too, content that with three guys out there they can afford to have one of them taking a break to rest. It's not Rock though, who seems to be involved in every spot, every moment and every bump. That's the price you pay as champion. To be the man you've got to work harder than everyone else. You've got to be better than everyone else. Triple H brings the comedy by doing the Ali Shuffle, to mock Shane. Hunter and Shane's competition to see who can do the most elaborate punch is actually a lot of fun. As if 2-on-1 wasn't enough Vince interjects with choking on the ropes. Hunter gets a sleeper, which is the first rest spot of the match and it drags on and on. But if you don't like never-ending sleeper holds then you don't know how to work and you don't understand wrestling. Allegedly. It does pick up as Rock catches Shane in a sleeper, while in a sleeper, and Shane has to jawbreaker out thus jawbreakering Hunter too. It's a funny spot but the lack of crowd reaction shows how "indy" it is. "What the hell was that?" bemoans Vince. It was funny! Shane breaks up a Hunter pinfall, which causes their relationship to fall apart. Shane gets in a great missed moonsault where he lands on his feet. Wonderful athleticism. A DDT follows, although you'd know that without looking as Hunter yells "DDT" to Rock as he moves in. I know calling spots allows them to connect right but at least try to disguise it. Like fellow locker room leader Bradshaw, Hunter gets caught calling spots on camera, thus exposing the business. They run some more comedy sauce with Shane being unable to hit a Pedigree on account of a lack of strength. Rock continues to fight the odds until Hunter waffles him with the belt but there's no ref, thanks to Mike Chioda taking a comedy bump. Jerry Brisco runs in to replace him and he allows Shane to use a chair, which hits Hunter by mistake. Vince flat out runs into the ring after that, as we get a lot of leeway in the rules. Hunter goes low; Pedigree! The fans think they'll see a title switch but Rock just calmly kicks out. I've never seen a less dramatic kick out from the Pedigree. Hunter thinks Brisco counted slowly and knocks him out (what?) Another Pedigree and Vince pulls off Brisco's ref shirt to appoint himself the official. This brings out Earl Hebner, to the kind of pop refs shouldn't get, to pull Vince out of the ring. Overbooked? A bit, yes. Vince chases Earl around the ring before running into the Rock Bottom. Hunter falls to the floor in a convoluted top rope crotching, and Shane gets laid out with a spinebuster. Following all this? People's Elbow for Shane and Rock retains. Hunter's stupidity at having Rock beaten clean and blaming his own ref for the kick out led to all the other problems for the McMahon's. Although if Shane just got onside from the get-go the belt would have switched. Anyway, Rock overcomes the odds and despite the ridiculous overbooking it was a fun contest. Not sure about some of the selling in the last five minutes though.
Final Rating: ***¼

VERDICT

They tried to keep this show bright and breezy for the UK audience. It doesn't measure up to the better UK PPVs (like *One Night Only*) but at least it's worthwhile. The overbooked but entertaining main event is worth seeing, ditto the European Title match. The rest of the card I could probably live without, but a UK show with two good matches on it still stands out as being pretty decent. There's still an awful lot of rubbish on the undercard but at least the main events delivered. Flash forward two years and that will not be the case at *Insurrextion 2002*. For a UK show, this is slightly recommended.

42

TLC - TABLES LADDERS CHAIRS

CAT NO: WWF259
RUN TIME: 55 minutes (approx)

James Dixon: We start inauspiciously, with the voiceover man declaring: "This video tape is not really about tables, ladders and chairs". Well, pardon me for expecting it might be given the title and all. He drops another belter moments later, talking about how the three teams that this tape is actually about (as if you hadn't figured it out already; the Hardy Boyz, Edge & Christian and the Dudleys) have a "love of sports entertainment that goes back to their childhood". Erm, wrestling? It's when used in context like this that the WWF/E's silly company speak is brought into sharp focus and made to sound ridiculous. Who grows up and says they love sports entertainment? No one. Plenty grow up loving wrestling of course, but we can't say that. Or can we now? I can never remember. I guess it depends on which athletic commission we are trying to hoodwink or which broadcaster we are trying to squeeze for every penny...

We get the same footage of the pre-teen Hardy Boyz pretending to be wrestlers that has featured on a couple of other tapes, as we briefly touch upon each of the guys' backgrounds. Bubba says he went to wrestling school (shouldn't that be "sports entertainment school"?) and got trained the proper way, then learned the business by working with and being around guys like Terry Funk. Christian talks about never losing sight of his goal, while Edge says he never had any doubts in his mind about making it. We see the Hardys' WWF debuts from *RAW* back in 1994, with Matt working Nikolai Volkoff in only his seventh match (with the addendum of: in a hard ring, because Matt and Jeff had been putting on backyard shows using trampolines for years) and Jeff getting a kicking from Razor Ramon. Jeff claims he got such a kicking that he wanted to leave the business and do something else, but a match with the 1-2-3 Kid the next night was much easier on him and "cleansed his soul". I am not quite convinced that this is entirely true, because I have seen that match against Scott Hall and he doesn't stiff him at all. In fact, according to Kevin Nash, Jeff was one of Scott's favourite guys to work with and he would often put him over behind the curtain to those who mattered. That could well be just Nash giving the Kliq credit for "discovering" the young Hardy early, but someone's story doesn't add up somewhere.

Whoever scripted the voiceover man's lines continues to shine, as he delivers this humdinger: "In sports entertainment, respect for the past is held in high regard". Oh, there is MUCH to say about that! In the PG Era, WWE ritualistically cheapened its own rich history because it was ashamed of it one way or another. The Golden Era of the 50s (which was prior to the WWWF being around, but the point remains valid) was considered too small time and came with the WWE enforced stigma of being contested in "smoke filled halls", the 80s stuff was too cartoony and overblown to take seriously (look how WWE mocked the involvement of Cyndi Lauper, Roddy Piper and Wendi Richter in making the company mainstream during a segment on *RAW* in 2012), the Attitude Era they couldn't show because they did some pretty disgraceful things unsuitable for a PG environment, guys who helped build the company were buried if they were not in the good books at any given time, title histories were doctored and changed to suit rather than being factually accurate, the list goes on. Nevertheless, despite being deep into the Monday Night Wars when this was released (though admittedly, they are almost over and WCW are no longer even a factor), the Dudleys still put over the likes of Hulk Hogan, Roddy Piper and Ric Flair as influences. Matt takes a different route, sucking up to creative team writer and onetime manager and tag partner Michael Hayes, before rightly crediting Mick Foley as having played an important role in the team's WWF development by putting them in his *Three Faces of Foley* tape and earning them a bit of extra cash through royalties. I have said it elsewhere I am sure, but Mick Foley was and is a credit to the wrestling business.

Voiceover man returns to tell us that: "innovation came from reinterpreting the past" (isn't that something of an oxymoron?) as we see the brilliant Shawn Michaels-Razor Ramon match from *SummerSlam '95*, which all of the guys on the tape put over. What about the *WrestleMania* one?! I personally prefer *SummerSlam* but the general consensus, certainly within the WWF, is that the first one was the game changer. Well actually it was, but the second one still squeaks it, but usually the WWF forgets it existed. Anyway, Jeff says that when he watched the match, he decided: "That is the future of professional wrestling" That rather explains a lot. It is still kind of strange that they don't show any of the *WrestleMania* ladder match at all, or any footage from any other ladder bouts except for this one, what with them building up "the past" for the purpose of setting up the next segments.

Edge and Christian talk about the Brood, which Edge says made him feel more comfortable as a performer because of the cool entrance and the blood bath gimmick, as well as having guys alongside him and a purpose. We see Gangrel turning on Edge, Christian siding with the latter and the ill-fitting New Brood with the Hardys, which led to their excellent and career changing feud. Matt says the turning point for all of their careers was the ladder match at *No Mercy 1999*, which of course is absolutely right. Talking head JR then refers to ladders as both inanimate and unpredictable, but I would argue from a physics point of view that something inanimate is entirely predictable, actually. Terri calls the match a nail-biter, acting as if she really had a genuine interest in the outcome. Pure kayfabe. Highlights follow, with the footage interspersed with comments from the guys involved. Edge puts over the quite excellent camera above the ladder that was used for the first time in that bout, because it showed the silly heights and gave a new dimension to the action. It added a lot to the spectacle. All the main spots from the match are here, but seeing them out of context doesn't really do the bout full justice. It was more than *just* spots, as good as they were. It was about the innovation, the change in crowd response from uncaring to enthralled and the joy of watching four guys go from wrestlers to stars in sixteen glorious minutes. A lot of these comments and stories also feature on *Eve of Destruction,* such as how Mick Foley put them all over backstage after the match and how they received a respectful standing ovation on *RAW* the next night. The latter is pretty impressive actually, and shows that WWF fans do appreciate serious levels of effort.

Those two teams alone probably could have gone a long way towards revitalising an ailing tag division, but the arrival of the Dudleys added a third, larger and more brutal element that was absolutely key in helping tag team wrestling scale new heights in the company. Few actually thought that the Dudleys would get over in the WWF, with many expecting them to go the way of Public Enemy and other former ECW alumni before them, where a gimmick that worked in a bingo hall didn't translate to international television. But instead they were given a gimmick that suited them (tables) and given the chance to be themselves (in character terms), rather than stripping them of what got them over elsewhere in the first place like has happened to many others. Bubba recognises that, with D-Von openly admitting that he thought they would have obstacles to overcome in order to repeat their success from ECW. We get footage of the Duds and the Hardys taking turns putting each other through tables in inventive ways, before we see the start of Bubba's obsession with doing the same to women, starting when he assaults EMT B.B. It starts off with Bubba seemingly injured and getting stretchered out, with D-Von asking him: "Does it hurt?". "No! It doesn't hurt!" says Bubba, who then gets up off the stretcher and attacks poor B.B, hitting her with a vicious top rope Bubba Bomb through a table. Bubba's delightfully maniacal facials helped make this stuff work. Edge and Christian try and run the Dudleys off afterwards, but Bubba sits up like a psychopathic horror movie villain and D-Von kills them with chairs.

We briefly stop off to tackle the age old question: is it fake? All of the guys talk about being asked by fans what the weaponry is *really* made of, and they go on the defensive, with the

LOS CONQUISTADORS

Dudleys inviting people into the ring with them to see how physical wrestling really is. The thing is, anyone who thinks the props are gimmicked is not going to believe otherwise no matter what you say to them, and real wrestling fans don't particularly care either way, they just want to be entertained. I think anyone with half a brain can see that the chairs, tables and ladders are all very real, so this whole piece is somewhat redundant. Matt rounds things off my saying how: "If it's a chair I got coming, I want it coming hard!". Yeah, and that is why you went completely nuts.

Next stop is the richly entertaining tag team tables match between the Hardys and the Dudleys from *Royal Rumble 2000*. If the *No Mercy* ladder match made the guys in that, then this match went a long way towards solidifying the Dudleys's spot and sending the Hardys into supernova. That it took place in the hallowed ground of MSG helped a lot as well, because if something is over in the Garden it is over everywhere. This match has effort levels you rarely see from an undercard match. It's not just guys sleepwalking through tired spots and going through the motions while reeling off a few catchphrases to please the crowd, but rather four young and hungry guys who want to make names for themselves and establish their spots. The best tables match ever? Almost certainly. The editing here is very good too, with cuts between the Hardys' pre-match promo backstage and Bubba's in the ring building the tension, and then the match itself sped up and slowed down where appropriate, with different angles used and high tempo (and for once, fitting) music in the background. Again, showing lots of spots one after another doesn't quite do it justice, but you still get the idea.

We see the angle from *RAW* where the Hardys have the tag titles won, only for the Duds to prevent the fall and take out both of them with 3D. The Dudleys are fixin' to put the Hardys through a table, but then their useless manager Terri does a dumb thing and gets in the ring. Bad move. D-Von grabs her and goes to hit her, but Bubba rollicks him "Whatcha gonna do? Punch her in the face!? Why would you punch her in the face, when you could put her through a table!?". And then, they do, as Terri folds like a tiny little accordion. Again on *RAW*, Mark Henry beats D-Von in a singles bout, but the real story comes afterwards. The Duds take out Henry with 3D and then put Mae Young through a table!!! She was 127 years old at the time! It's not an easier bump or anything, it is still the Bubba Bomb from the top, and it's not even close to as super safe as the Terri bump either. Make no mistake though, that is down to the tough as nails Mae rather than Bubba. Mae would have kicked his ass if he had taken it easy on her. The crowd doesn't quite believe it is going to really happen as they are setting it up, and JR and Lawler both add incredible gravitas to the act with their announcing. When Bubba comes off the top the crowd realise that this IS happening, and they go wild. Bubba's euphoric trance afterwards is excellent, and was totally ripped off years later by Festus. The Dudleys follow that up with something even more crazy: putting Mae through a table OFF THE STAGE. Can you imagine that getting green-lighted in the PG environment!? Mae was batshit crazy for agreeing to take all of this. The same thing happens again on *SmackDown!* to Lita, before our tour of Bubba Ray's acts of wood based misogyny concludes at *Backlash* with the famous and very popular decking of Trish in the same manner. At least this time he had a motive, though I really loved the character trait that he was just addicted to notching up women for his "wood list", as twisted and wrong as it might be. Trish gets DRILLED on her bump, big time. Why did they never do it to Steph? That, I would have enjoyed. We then see Bubba powerbomb Christian through Edge onto a table, which destroys Edge's face.

At *WrestleMania 2000* they took the *No Mercy* bout and added the Dudleys to the mix, and the results are much the same. It's another tremendous bout, though not quite career defining in the same way, but still another in a long list of stunt matches featuring the teams that is definitely worth hunting out. The highlights package follows the same format as discussed earlier, and the slight criticism remains the same. The continued innovation of the ladder match continues with this effort, and the addition of two extra bodies makes for some great spots, such as Bubba's three stooges helicopter impression with the ladder, a sequence towards the end where all six guys climb for the belts and take wild bumps, and then the brilliant "table mountain" spot at the end with a table set up over two ladders. It's a shame we don't get comments from the guys during this too, going over the bumps, spots and generally craziness, but that doesn't matter, it's just something I would have liked to have seen is all. Bubba says HBK was the first man backstage behind the curtain waiting to shake everyone's hands and put them over, which is a rare touch of class from Michaels prior to him finding the big man upstairs. We see all six guys hugging and thanking each other backstage, as Jeff talks about the pressure they had going into the bout because of what they had to live up to. Edge calls the finish a "dream sequence" and Christian mentions that when they were kids they used to pretend to be tag champions, and that it became reality. Their story is among the better feel-good ones out there.

VERDICT

This is a fun journey through a six month period that turned perception of tag team wrestling in the WWF on its head. The three duos featured took the opportunities they were given to shine with both hands, and changed a piece of the industry. With one generation of fans, ladder matches will always be associated with the six guys featured here, and their matches will always be fondly remembered, as they should be. Of course there are negatives to all of this too: Edge was forced into early retirement due to injuries caused in these bouts, Jeff and Matt both became drug abusers, probably because of the pain of the bumps catching up to them and Christian had plenty of injury problems too and missed a lot of time later into his career. The Dudleys fared better, with Bubba a decade later going on to become one of the top heels in the world and TNA Champion, with D-Von remaining relevant well into the future. Though, the Dudleys did take less risky bumps than the other guys, and they had a little more padding to protect them too. The tape is not the end of the TLC story for these six against each other, as they had two bouts that were actually dubbed "TLC" at *SummerSlam 2000* and then again at *WrestleMania X-Seven*, this time incorporating chairs and tables into the equation officially. They too are some of the finest stunt matches of all time, and the entire series between the three duos stands the test of time as one of the best of the Attitude Era. This tape does a really good job in capturing the essence of the beginning of it. Recommended.

72

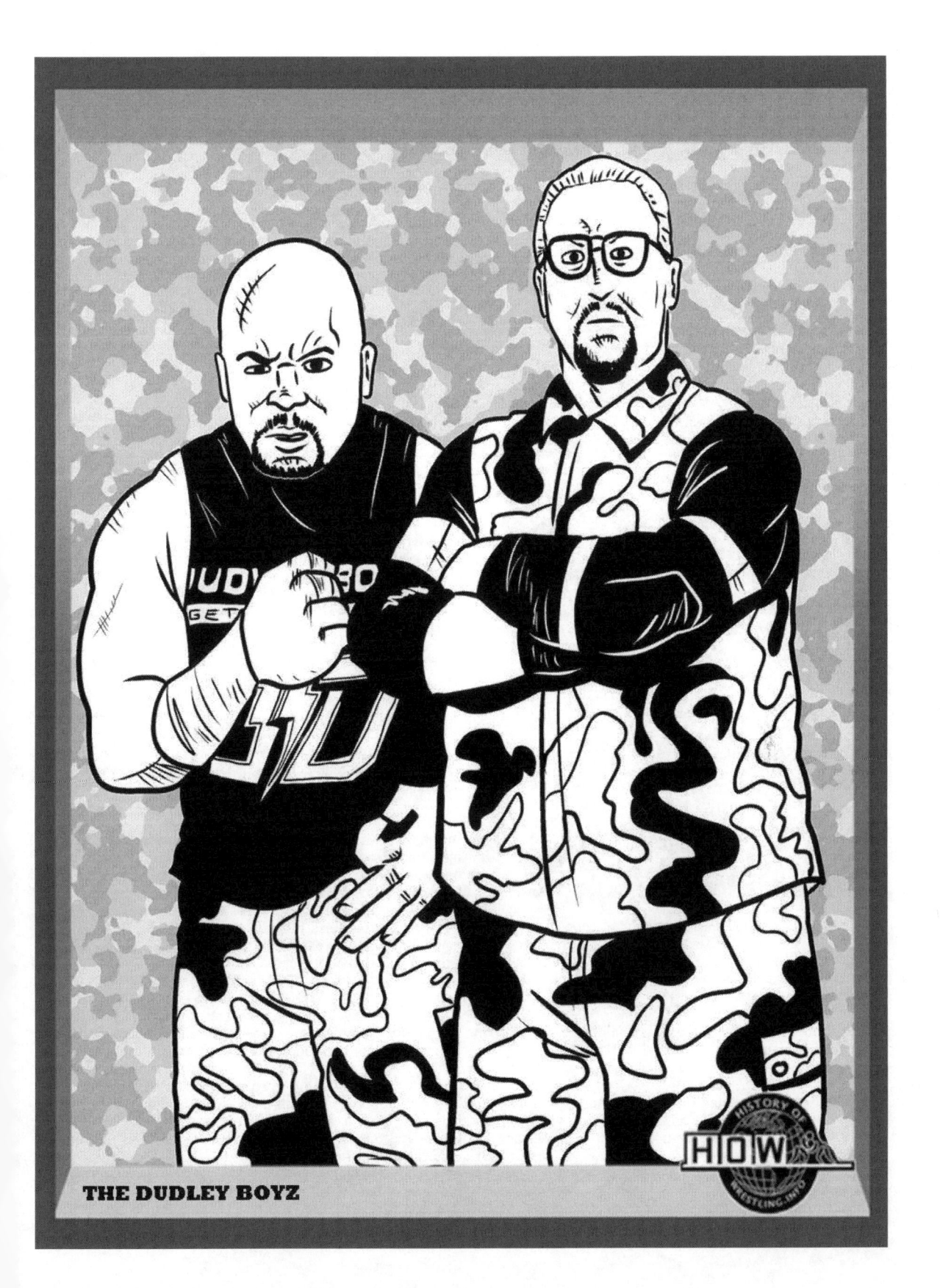

THE DUDLEY BOYZ

STONE COLD STEVE AUSTIN - LORD OF THE RING

CAT NO: WWF260
RUN TIME: 45 minutes (approx)

James Dixon: Yes folks it is yet another Stone Cold Steve Austin tape, the third in this book out of a remarkable five, which is stunning for a two-and-a-half-year period. That's not to mention the handful from the previous book. Stone Cold has nearly as many bio tapes than Hulk Hogan did (actually 8 to Hogan's astonishing 13, and that is only in VHS format). This particular outing is a little different, as it is a direct-to-VHS port of an A&E piece that was screened in November 1999, that goes behind the scenes of Austin's life and career.

Authoritative voiceover man tells us how Austin is a different person behind the character, as in-ring footage with cartoony enhanced sound effects rolls in the background. We get the revelation that Steve Austin is, get this, not even Stone Cold's real name! We hear about him growing up, which is the usual enhanced-reality, idealist American tale. You know the drill; good kid, focused on studying, had success at football, always seemed destined for success. "He took care of his body by eating right and working out, even when he didn't have to" says the V.O. He also used to shit diamonds and burp in beautiful falsetto... presumably. Austin's sister drops him in the shit by telling a story about how he used to be so shy that he couldn't talk on the phone and order his own food, so she had to do it for him. She gets a kick out of telling that story she says, not that she is envious of her brother's enormous success or anything.

Austin says how he used to love watching wrestling from Texas when he was younger, which would be Fritz Von Erich's WCCW promotion, though his sister claims she doesn't even remember him watching it at all. Why must she undermine him at every turn? Austin decided to get into the business and his high school football coach worried about his chances, but Steve went ahead and did it anyway, training with World Class star Chris Adams. Mick Foley recounts a story that he also told in his book *Have a Nice Day* about watching the guys train to get a kick out of how bad they were, but that he noticed one guy called Steve Williams who looked like a natural. He was also at the Beatles' first gig at the Cavern in 1961 too, don't you know. Michael Hayes puts over Austin's work ethic compared to some guys in the business who were just bodies, before we turn to Vince McMahon for his take on what wrestling is:

"Part talk show, part action adventure, a little bit of comedy thrown in there, or perhaps I should say humour, as compared to what some people may think; of two people in their underwear, in a squared circle somewhere..."

And that folks, is why Vince McMahon calls it Sports Entertainment instead of professional wrestling. Did you notice, he didn't mention athleticism or, you know, sport!?

Steve Austin recalls how he went from Steve Williams to Steve Austin, with a promoter (Dutch Mantel, though he is not mentioned by name) changing his surname and telling him he had 15-minutes to come up with something better. What is omitted is that he only had to change his name in the first place because of 'Dr. Death' Steve Williams being a fairly notable name in the business at the time. Steve says he hated the name at first and he didn't want to be Steve Austin because he didn't want to rip off the character with the same name in *The Six Million Dollar Man*, but he couldn't come up with anything better and it stuck. Who could have predicted then that the name Steve Austin would become far more synonymous with the wrestler than the television character, who himself was insanely popular once upon a time.

We move to WCW and the 'Stunning' nickname, which Austin also didn't like because he didn't think it fit his persona. "I'm only okay looking, actually" he says modestly. The WCW stuff is covered only with stills rather than video, and predictably very little positive is said about his time there. "Steve was fired over the phone" offers the voiceover man, as we go to Austin's brilliant but brief ECW tenure. Vince tells some porkies about "spotting Austin's talent" and hiring him away from ECW, and we then see him as the Ringmaster. Yeah, great eye for talent

FURIOUS ABOUT: THE DUDLEY BOYZ

Making the transition from ECW to WWF wasn't easy but the Dudleyz achieved it through two simple moves. Violence against women and the use of tables. Those two elements turned a tag team with a cool finisher into superstars. The Dudleyz originally wore tie-dye gear but the WWF wanted to rebrand them and switched the gear to camouflage, which gave them a distinctive feel while retaining the core of what made them the Dudleyz. With their tag team rivals using ladders, the Dudleyz differentiated themselves by using tables. The escalation of violence made it hard for them to have normal matches as the crowds would demand 'wood'. Initially the Dudleyz were heels and their women-tabling ways focused on babyfaces until Bubba took a shine to powerbombing heel women through tables, like Trish and Tori and that was enough to switch the Dudleyz face. They took part in several high profile TLC-style matches, elevating the tag titles in the process before turning heel during the Invasion and joining the Alliance. Before coming to the WWF, the Dudleyz were eight time ECW tag team champions and before leaving the WWE, they'd amassed a further ten sets of tag titles (8 world, 1 WWE and 1 WCW). They've since added two IWGP tag titles, the NWA tag titles and TNA's tag titles, twice. The sheer volume of belts makes them one of the most successful teams to ever grace a wrestling ring and they were PWI's tag team of the decade for 2000-2009.

---

there Vince, just superb. "The Ringmaster was a bad move" says Hayes. NO FUCKING KIDDING! The story of Austin's change of persona is told, though not the actual one. Apparently the WWF thought it would be good for business to have a badass in their ranks, though the truth is they lucked into 'Stone Cold', as he came up with the character and made it work, the WWF just happened to be the company he worked for who enabled him. When the WWF tried to contribute, they came up with some truly awful ideas, and amusingly the horrible "Ice Dagger" name that was proposed by some imbecile on the writing team is mentioned, though the even better "Chilly McFreeze" is not. I would love to know who exactly it was that came up with those.

"This is the quality that would make Steve Austin a millionaire" says the voiceover man of Austin's hell-raising blue-collar babyface character. Hmm, that rather kills his everyman persona, doesn't it? Vince defends the depth of the Austin character, despite the swearing and the sign language, which is right. He was far more than just an on-the-nose purposely offensive character, he was well-rounded and relatable. Austin tells the story of how one day the office asked him if he could come up with a different hand signal than his middle fingered salute, to which he responded resoundingly: "No" What other hand signal could he *possibly* have used? More controversy from Steve came when he coined his famous and insanely over "Austin 3:16" catchphrase at *King of the Ring '96*, which sparked outrage amongst religious do-gooders. Despite that, Austin has a chuckle over the fact that priests and other religious folk frequently ask him for autographs when they bump into him. Amusing.

We see Austin's career-changing injury at *SummerSlam '97* thanks to Owen Hart's foolish inverted piledriver, and Austin says how since then he has avoided anything that involves him taking bumps on his neck. Since those days of course, the WWE has adopted a company-wide ban on all moves like that due to their danger and potential for causing injury. It is the wise thing to do, because ultimately the health of the performer should come ahead of any spot. Just think how much longer Austin's career could have been if that had been the case in 1997. He might have had another decade in the business at least.

We see more segments and skits from Austin between 1997 and 1999, with his unparalleled success outlined by the voiceover guy who mentions how the business exploded as his popularity increased. The true reach of the Steve Austin juggernaut is then outlined, with the narrator claiming he earns $5-$10million per year from wrestling, which again makes it difficult to get behind him as a working class hero, but then this tape is very out of character anyway so I guess it doesn't really matter. It is aimed at a different audience than his usual merchandise. Speaking of merchandise, the mass of Austin licensed products available is also covered in detail. Austin talks about how hands-on he is with anything bearing his likeness, and that he gets involved in every aspect of his own marketing. There have been some pretty shoddy Steve Austin cash-grab releases over the years (including, if you can believe this; talking soap!), so maybe he is not involved in *everything*.

Steve's family turn up again, with his mother saying how she wouldn't have let her kids watch a character like Steve Austin, and his bitchy sister saying that she doesn't always agree with or approve of the stuff he does on television. The man behind the character is further portrayed as a down-to-earth, humble guy with strong family values who never forgot his roots, though his 1999 divorce from wife Jeanie Clark is brought up. Austin chalks it up to experience, and says he won't make the same mistakes next time. Yeah... In closing, Vince compares Austin to Babe Ruth, as a man who has transcended the medium he is famous for, but Austin thinks people "shouldn't get all worked up about it". We need more guys like Steve Austin in the wrestling business. It would be a much better place for it.

VERDICT

Well, it is not a wrestling tape, that is for sure. If you are looking for anything resembling a Steve Austin highlight package then pick up one of the countless other Stone Cold releases, because there is none of that here. Instead it is more akin to a Biography Channel piece, and it is a fairly good one at that because the nonsense and hyperbole that usually permeates these things when they are wrestling related, is almost entirely absent. Some facts are withheld, but not to the detriment of the piece. If you are interested in finding out more about Steve Austin and the man behind the bluster, then this is a pretty good look at his story.

50

DIVAS - POSTCARD FROM THE CARIBBEAN

CAT NO: WWF261
RUN TIME: 52 minutes (approx)

James Dixon: Hosted by Shane McMahon's wife Marissa Mazzola-McMahon, oddly enough. The tape is based around a RAW Magazine shoot from in the Dominican Republic, mostly set on a beach, featuring Trish, Tori, Terri, Ivory and Miss Kitty. Terri shrieks like a banshee as she splashes in the waves and Tori says she loves what they are doing. I can believe that. Trish talks us through a typical day, getting up at 5am to get dolled up, which is something that reminds Ivory that this is work and not all fun in the sun. Yeah, tough break. According to Ivory, the "work" is rewarding and everyone brings something different to the table. The only difference between them that I can see is how much they are willing to take their clothes off, with Miss Kitty being at the sluttiest end of the scale.

Trish teases by promising nudity, but Marisa quickly interjects that this doesn't happen, though points out that the beaches are so secluded that it could. A few of the girls do get their bazongas out, but obviously cover them up. They should have taken them to somewhere like Spain, where all the girls have their funbags out on the beaches over there. The amount of fake smiling on this tape already is nearly on a par with the amount of fake tits.

Miss Kitty
"I'm really not a wrestler" says Kitty, before adding: "Two girls wrestling each other? I don't think that's what people really wanna see". Well, that about sums her up, doesn't it? God forbid people want to see wrestling on a wrestling show! Marissa describes Kat as having a "carefree attitude", which means she is easy and open to showing off all of her assets while her future husband knocks one out under the announce table. The clichéd sexy video follows, with slow motion highlights of Kat doing such thrilling things as... nothing at all, actually. She just stands there looking into the distance like a vapid idiot. We see the travesty of Kitty winning the WWF Women's Title in a swimming pool match at *Armageddon*, as great pioneers of women's wrestling the Fabulous Moolah and Mae Young look on. Horrible. After the match Kitty promised to strip, and she did, whipping off her shirt to reveal her pert little boobies. She is one of very few examples of honest to goodness titties that the WWF has delivered on. Kitty says that Miss Kitty is playful and the Kat is more vicious, but in real life she is more the former. Oh she is playful alright, just ask Jack Dupp. Another fascinating slow motion video follows, which features Kitty standing up in a pool and then... closing her eyes. To the infamous *Royal Rumble 2000* swimsuit competition, where the girls did everything but strip completely naked while Jerry Lawler hosted and acted like a giddy undersexed teenager. We see all of the girls involved (Ivory, Terri, Luna, Jacqueline, BB) and then Kat's outfit, which is just bubble wrap covering her treats. And then because it is the WWF, Mae Young came out and showed "all her fans her puppies" and won the contest. What the hell was this? "Images of the Kat get the imagination going every time" says secret lesbian Mazzola. Then to wrap up Kat's segment, exactly what we needed: another slow motion video. Marissa says she wants to be involved in a cat fight because it looks fun to roll around... Ookay. Repressing anything there, love?

Ivory
Ivory's voice is pretty damn annoying. Her character is supposed to be, but she sounds like that when she sits down and talks normally too. "New is good" she says, and talks about liking new experiences, describing one from this trip that saw a dude climb a palm tree barefoot and acquire some baby woodpeckers. You wouldn't expect this on a wrestling tape. We see some in ring footage of Ivory, with her feud against Tori covered and highlights from their crap match at *SummerSlam 1999* shown. "Wrestling is like a good dance, timing is everything" she says. Oh man, the irony! Especially after highlights from that match where they made a mess of various spots. Next we see the really fun women's hardcore match between the same opponents that also features on the *Hardcore* tape. It goes too far at the end, with a mirror smashed over Tori's head and Ivory branding her with an iron,

but Tori does the whole match in a very revealing thong, so as a red blooded male I can't complain too much. And now, another video set to music, though with less slow motion stuff than in the Kat one because Ivory is far less of a willing stripper and poser. Her feature gets wrapped up quickly, and it is around half the length of Kat's. If that.

Tori
According to Tori, seeing the sun rise and feeling the rays on her body is "a gift". She is easily pleased. Her bio starts out with the slow-mo video, which is just swell. She also calls being "part of the WWF machine" a gift. Every day is Christmas to her it seems. We see the angle from *SmackDown!* where Tori turned heel on Kane and joined forces with DX, because the writers all had issues with women that they wanted to cathartically resolve on screen through others. Tori puts over her acting ability when Kane has her by the throat for a chokeslam, and then we see the 'Big Red Machine' drill her with a Tombstone. Marissa puts her over as being as tough as the men, and we see her splashing Bubba Ray Dudley through a table to emphasise that. Tori talks about her passion for yoga, which she does for three hours a day rather than spending much time in the gym. "Each curve is carefully crafted" says Marissa with more than a hint of lust, then calls her body a work of art. We see the bizarre practice of all-over body painting that she partakes in, which is just too strange for words. The appeal is completely lost on me. Tori discusses the balance she looks to strike between muscled and aggressive and being too intimidating, as Marissa puts her over some more. Boy, does she want to be on that beach.

Trish Stratus
Eventually Trish became a very competent in-ring performer, but here she was still just eye candy. She is fantastic eye candy though, and by far the most attractive girl on the tape. Her slow-mo video provides plenty of shots of her clad in revealing thongs, erotically holding her hair and pouting. And then she talks about her love of comics... Yes, as well as being stunning she is also a geek, making her even more desirable. Ah the old classic, the hose pipe on the white t-shirt, with plenty of nipple action going on here. We see the silly Bubba Ray Dudley-Trish feud, where Bubba became infatuated with her and unable to "get wood" and put her through a table as he desired. During this Trish cut a very odd sensual promo describing her passion for tables, getting turned on by "long ones" and "rubbing them down after use". Instead of seeing the top rope powerbomb through a table payoff, we get Marissa purring over her and yet another video -yes it is slowed down- this time featuring lots of sand and animal references. It goes on forever.

Terri
Oh man, not Terri. "She's got a smokin' body" says Marissa, no longer trying to repress anything. Terri says she doesn't see herself in any grand light, but that she knows people like her

> **FURIOUS ABOUT: TRISH STRATUS**
>
> Trish's transformation from valet to WWF women's champion is one of the companies greatest female success stories. Trish, despite being a wrestling fan, began her career as a model for muscle magazines. She looked great and that was enough for the WWF to take a shot with her and she was hired in late 1999. The WWF fast-tracked her onto TV and she began her managing career in March 2000, taking charge of Test & Albert and pairing them as a tag team before also managing IC champion Val Venis. Her managerial career lasted about a year before she got too over to be around undercard guys like Test and got bumped up into an angle with Vince McMahon. Portrayed as Vince's lover, she rankled Vince's daughter Stephanie and the two had a shockingly good match at No Way Out 2001. Vince ended up dumping Trish and Stratus found her way into the women's division. Despite an ankle injury derailing her early push, she won the women's title at Survivor Series '99. It would be the first of seven titles. Initially undeserving of title attention she grew into the role and is remembered as one of the best women's champions.

ass, but she thinks it is too bubbly. Cue the video and more from Marissa: "It's what's on the inside that counts, but looking at Terri it is easy to forget". Terri reveals that she is naturally a ginge! No wonder she calls herself the "she-Devil". We get a few clips of Terri getting involved in matches, and Bubba putting her through a table, very safely. She admits she is not a wrestler and doesn't want to be one... and then she worked the women's match at *WrestleMania 2000*. Astonishingly, it is the only singles match on the show, and we see highlights from it here. It only goes a couple of minutes but it is a disaster. "The hardest thing for me is the waiting" she complains about the paid vacation to the Caribbean where she is pampered beyond belief.

Marissa talks about the RAW Magazine photo shoot, implying that the guy who has to go through all the pictures knocks a cheeky one out while he is pouring over them. We meet him, and he talks us through the finer points of picking the right photo for the magazine cover. So, how does one go about getting his job...?

VERDICT

This is definitely not a wrestling tape, that much is for certain. There is almost no wrestling on here at all, but there is plenty of footage of five sun-kissed women splashing around in pools, pouting at cameras and beaming big fake smiles, all while Mrs. Shane McMahon allows her "experimental" side to be revealed to the world. Guys who bought this looking for more than the WWF shows on television will be left sorely (literally) disappointed, while I can't any reason girls would want to watch this, unless they want their self esteem shredding. So really, the whole thing is a completely pointless affair. Then again, they churned out dozens of these things over the years so obviously someone was buying them, I just can't quite work out who. From my perspective though, this is not recommended at all.

10

CHRIS JERICHO - BREAK DOWN THE WALLS

CAT NO: WWF262
RUN TIME: 60 minutes (approx)

James Dixon: We open the profile tape deal with a bunch of fans (each subtitled "Jerichoholic" and then a number), who talk about how much they love Jericho. I feel the focus group used may be slightly biased. One of the marks says how they like Jericho because of his "charasma", which about sums up the bunch that were interviewed.

The best place to start is... the start. Or at least Jericho's WWF start, with his much anticipated debut on *RAW* covered extensively and accompanied by talking heads the Rock, a jealous Edge ("Damn!" he thought, when hearing the reaction Jericho got), a tired looking Michael Cole and of course Jericho himself. For those unaware, Jericho's debut was hyped for a month with a mystery "Countdown to the Millennium" clock which didn't mention him by name, but pretty much everyone had it figured out. It was Jericho's idea, one he got while in a post office when he saw a real countdown to the Millennium clock on the wall, and thought it would be a cool way to bring someone into a wrestling company. He was absolutely right; the idea and debut is absolute genius because it builds anticipation, gets people talking and has an exact time and place that people can write in their diaries to make sure they tune in and don't miss it. The countdown just happened to climax during the middle of a Rock promo, and the pop for the word "Jericho" appearing on the Titantron is something else. It is one of my favourite crowd reactions ever. Jericho's subsequent promo is decent, but he does an anti-WWF gimmick which was clearly going nowhere because there are too many holes in what he was saying. He makes outlandish claims such as the WWF's ratings and buyrates plummeting, which all the fans knew was bullshit because the company was on its hottest streak in years and interest in the group was through the roof. Perhaps the idea was that he was delusional or something, but that was always doomed to failure. Rock counters Jericho's proclamation of being the "Y2J problem" by talking about his "KY Jelly solution", which of course involves a boot in the ass. The pervert. Automaton Michael Cole thinks the best way to make an impact in the WWF is to interrupt the Rock, but Rock actually ended up promo-schooling Jericho with his retort, which rather undermined him from the off. Within a few weeks Jericho was shunted into the midcard working a feud with Road Dogg, as he quickly became yet another example of the WWF's inability to use talent correctly and to the best of their abilities. Don't get me wrong this is a fun promo from both and a wonderful way to debut, one of my favourite debuts ever in fact, but it should have propelled Jericho to the main event right away and it just didn't do that. It would be two years before he won the WWF Championship and even then he was treated as something of a joke champion, playing second fiddle to Stephanie McMahon and Triple H. It wasn't until his WWF return years later and program with Shawn Michaels that he finally became accepted as *the* man, briefly, and given the respect his talent deserves.

We go back to the start of Jericho's career, and he tells a cute story about meeting Ricky Steamboat at a convention and asking him how tall he was. When he found out they were the same size, he realised he had a shot of being a wrestler, though he was some 70lbs short of his weight. Jericho went to train at the Hart Brothers' school in Calgary, where he and Lance Storm (who is not mentioned) were the standouts. Jericho says how pleased he was that he came through a good school that taught him the proper values of the business and also beat him up day after day to see if he had the heart for it. A far cry for the WWF Development Center then, which churns out manufactured, cookie cutter robots. Jericho's career in Japan and with ECW is touched upon very briefly, with Mick Foley giving himself credit for recommending Jericho to Paul Heyman, having seen him work for WAR in Japan. WCW is not brought up at all.

From there we cut abruptly to Jericho's feud with Chyna, a battle based around misogyny but that echoed the views of many fans. Chyna as Intercontinental Champion was a disgrace to the rich history of the belt. She was an average at best worker by WWF women's standards, never mind compared to some of the finest workers of a generation. Guys should fight guys and girls should fight girls, it just isn't realistic for a women, even one like Chyna, to beat a highly trained male athlete at the top of their game. There is a reason that literally every other physical sport in the world separates the two genders. Could Chyna beat up some random dude on the street? Sure, but that is different. I thought this whole feud was lame and the matches were invariably poor. It was a waste of Jericho and a bastardisation of a once great belt.

We once again delve into Jericho's personal life, as his discusses his father Ted Irvine, a former hockey player for the New York Rangers in the NHL. Hockey continues as the focus, with a bunch of actors talking about a charity hockey game that Jericho played in. I couldn't give two shits about hockey, so let's move on...

...Unfortunately moving on proves to be tough as the hockey thing last forever. Honestly, the segment has been going a legitimate ten minutes now. I thought this was a wrestling profile tape!?

Next up Jericho's strength; his promos. Chris watches a promo of his from 1990 on a lavish big screen in his house, and mocks his accent and cheesy babyface nature. It's pretty terrible. We cut to modern times, with Jericho mispronouncing everyone's names on purpose. Kirk Angel (Kurt Angle), Raisin (Raven) and countless others feature. Jericho is a funny guy. He then tells Vince McMahon he has a small penis.

We continue with Jericho's excellent feud against Chris Ben-oyt (Benoit), which featured some brutal matches full of manly striking and reckless abandon. One such bout profiled is from *Backlash 2000*, which clocks in at ***¾. We get extended highlights set to an upbeat, high-tempo, generic rock track, which encapsulates the action and drama nicely. The finish is a disappointment, with Benoit going over on a DQ when he goes for his flying headbutt and Jericho belts him with the IC Title. Benoit got his nose legitimately broken and bloodied from the shot, and on *SmackDown!* a few days later where Jericho finally won the belt, his nose juiced another gusher. Watching these matches back the difference in the tightness of the work and the level of intensity and execution compared to flailing limb specialists like Kofi Kingston or our favourite target, the faker than fake John Cena, is striking. The feud between Jericho and Benoit continues into *SummerSlam* and their slightly underwhelming by their lofty standards 2/3 falls bout. Again we get highlights, though thankfully this time we are spared the bad music. At first anyway. We join things at the end of the first fall with Benoit tapping out Jericho with the Crossface, and then trying to do the same thing instantly, only to end up caught in the Walls of Jericho and tapping himself. 1-1 then and now the music and sped-up footage kicks in, all made to look more exciting with clever editing that repeats the key spots, before Benoit finishes with a cheeky pin.

Back to Jericho's massive home, and Christian is randomly there watering his plants like a house boy. Jericho shows off his self-mark wall, which has a bunch of magazine covers framed that feature him, including two covers from TV Guide that he marks for big. He then shows off his CD collection and kayfabes about Fozzy, acting like he is just a big fan rather than the lead singer. Jericho puts over Fozzy lead singer Moongoose McQueen (himself), and that leads to a Mick Foley esque split personality spot and an interview from Moongoose. My wife loves Fozzy, which about sums them up. Personally, I think they are the drizzling shits. I love heavy metal, but Fozzy are neither of those things. Man, this is like Jericho's second book *Undisputed*, where he spent half of it droning on about his crappy rock band instead of wrestling, which no one reading cares about. This is now just a *Behind the Music* parody, with Moongoose purposely acting like a clichéd rock star diva asshole. From what I have heard from some people who have met him, it's no act.

Finally back to wrestling, and Jericho's vicious barbs at Steph McMahon that resulted in a classic bout between Y2J and WWF Champion Triple H on *RAW* with the belt on the line. This is out of sequence mind, but sure, let's go with it. This was Jericho's night, with a rabid crowd firmly behind him in his quest to smash through the glass ceiling and lift the gold. And that is exactly what he did, pinning Hunter to a huge pop after Hunter and replacement referee Earl Hebner had a shoving match and Earl got knocked on his ass, causing Jericho to catch a pin and Earl to count quickly. Unfortunately, two-faced pussy Earl got forced into reversing the decision, and the result was stricken from the record. Poor decision, WWF. This was the time for Jericho, the proverbial iron was hot. Once he had pulled a Lex Luger and missed out on his big shot, it took him an age to rebuild his status. In fact, I would be tempted to say this was the most popular that Jericho was at any time in his WWF/E run. The Triple H feud carried on, with Jericho continuing to verbally humiliate Steph gleefully, leading to a sledgehammer beat down from evil DX that left Jericho bloodied. The blow-off came at *Fully Loaded 2000* in an epic Last Man Standing match. It is bloody, brutal and intense, and in 23-minutes they assemble a highly physical encounter that often gets forgotten about, but is one of their best outings opposite each other. There was just so much that was good in 2000 that it became hard to differentiate between the plethora of ****+ matches on offer seemingly every week. Once again no full match here, but the highlights are done well again and sum up the action nicely. Triple H is modest about the bout, calling it a match of the year candidate. Not that he has a major ego that needs stroking constantly or anything.

Jericho closes out the tape by saying he is here to entertain, and then bedecked in a suit, jumps into his pool.

VERDICT

This is an excellent profile tape about Chris Jericho's early WWF career, though anyone looking for anything deeper that covers his pre-WWF days is looking in the wrong place and would be better off seeking out his 2010 *Breaking the Code: Behind the Walls of Chris Jericho* DVD. This tape offers plenty of entertainment during its 60-minutes of runtime though, with the majority of the wrestling on display ranging from stellar to superb, and the stick work from Y2J always entertaining, especially that killer debut. I could have lived without the tedious hockey and Fozzy segments, but the top quality action more than makes up for it. As far as WWF bio tapes go, this is one of the better ones.

70

KURT ANGLE - IT'S TRUE! IT'S TRUE

CAT NO: WWF263
RUN TIME: 72 minutes (approx)

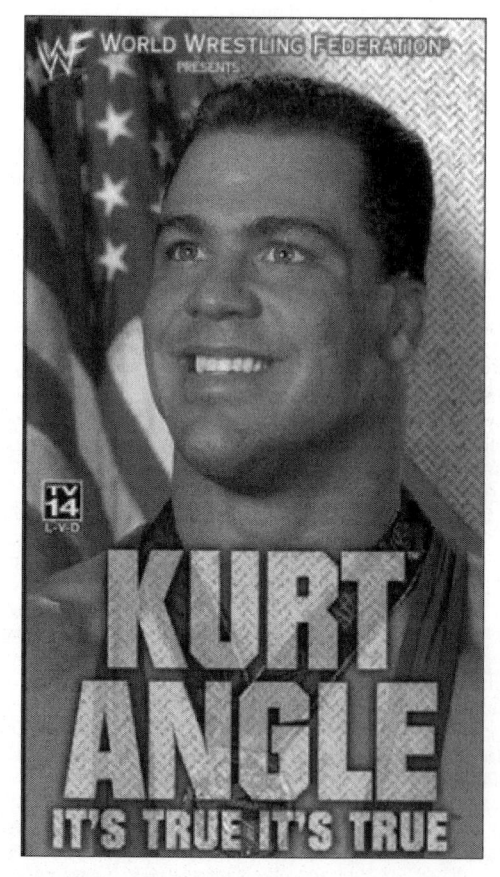

James Dixon: The bio starts on the set of a commercial that Angle is apparently filming, with him acting like a prima donna in an attempt to get over his character as that of an asshole. Is he in character or is it real? It's hard to say, because the real life Angle is pretty off the wall and at times appears to be borderline insane. Unfortunately, all of Angle's interviews for this tape are 100% kayfabed, which thus makes everything he says utterly worthless. Jerry Lawler puts over Angle's gold medal that he won at the 1996 Atlanta Olympic Games. The WWF loved that little fact of course, because it added legitimacy to their product to have not only an Olympian (which they have of course had before), but a genuine gold medal winner. It rather puts them championing Mark Henry's 16th place finish at the same games into perspective. Stevie Richards, in full RTC gimmick, puts over Angle's strength of character, while Rikishi gets a kick out of him because he is funny. Angle remains in full-on character mode and claims he was hired because of his "three I's" and then we see his WWF introduction vignettes, which are not really any different to his exclusive interviews for the tape. We see Angle's debut promo at *Survivor Series*, where he got booed essentially for being an 80's style babyface. The difference between him and say Rocky Maivia, is that he was supposed to get that reaction. Vince McMahon is a smart guy some of the time, and he realised that a clean-cut all-American babyface was exactly the antithesis of the company's current modus operendi. It worked a charm. It does lead one to wonder just what the hell Vince Russo would have tried to do with him. He probably would have made him into a cross-dresser or something. Steve Blackman, Angle's often forgotten about tag partner from his early weeks, talks about Kurt being a pain in his ass, which led to a match at *Armageddon*. Angle and Blackman both talk about the program in character, which makes this whole thing feel like a promo piece produced by non wrestling folk who think it is all real. I guess kayfabing should be commended, but you expect something more from these tapes now.

We see Tazz's sensational WWF "debut" the *Royal Rumble 2000* (in reality he worked "ECW *RAW*" back in February 1997), with Angle protesting that he didn't know who he was facing and that he lost to a choke, which was an illegal hold. "The next night" says the video when footage from *SmackDown!* taped two days later (and airing four days after the Rumble) airs, with Angle attacking Tazz. The pace continues at a scatterbrain pace with no time to pause for breath or indeed take anything in, as Angle rips off the Rock on *RAW* to set up a match between them, which he lost. That loss somehow made him the number one contender to the European Title, which he battled champion Val Venis for on *SmackDown!* ten days after the Rock defeat. Brief highlights are shown set to the dulcet tones of Michael Cole and with basic rock rumbling in the background. It sounds like Jim Johnston knocked it out in about 15-minutes. Angle wins with the Olympic Slam and celebrates like he just won another medal. Overblown performances like these are what endeared Kurt to not only the fans but the office as well, because he clearly "got it" as far as the sports entertainment aspect of the business, and he managed to ascend the ranks in record time because of that.

We go back to the set of the phony commercial, with Angle complaining about how long a shot is taking and telling the director to speed it up. The director shows why he got into the business of movie making rather than acting, because the exchange is completely hokey and unbelievable. Even Chris Jericho gets in on the kayfabing, repeating Blackman's sentiments about Angle being a pain in the ass. We go to their feud and the match for Jericho's Intercontinental Title at *No Way Out 2000* that Angle won, and the generic backing track returns as we see various moves from the match out of context, including a spot that highlights Kurt's inexperience when Jericho tries a silly Asai moonsault from the steel steps, but misses by a mile. With a few more months under his belt, Angle probably would have compensated for Jericho coming up short. The match isn't as good as you would expect when hearing the names Angle and Jericho, but for a guy with three months experience it was pretty sensational.

Back to the set, and Angle continues to act like a diva, complaining that the director said he had made a mistake in a previous take, before whining about the following scene taking an hour to set up. This whole segment is pretty much a complete waste of tape. More complaining follows, this time back in the WWF with Angle unhappy about having to defend both of his titles in a three way at the singles match bereft *WrestleMania 2000*. "The first fall will be for the European Title, the second fall will be for the Intercontinental Title" says Cole in the build up, which as ever with Cole is wrong. In his defence, that was certainly the logical assumption, but for whatever reason they did it backwards with Benoit pinning Jericho to win the IC Title, then the match immediately continuing with the second fall for the almost worthless European Title. It's another decent encounter, but again fails to thrill in the manner you might hope given the talent. There are plenty of big suplexes and fun spots to make it worth checking out still though, including the debut of Angle's beautiful technique moonsault, which of course misses. The second fall comes when Jericho pins Benoit following the Lionsault, meaning Kurt lost both belts without getting beat. Still in character, he says the experience taught him life was unfair and he learned from it. What tosh.

Oh Jesus friggin' Christ; Steve Lombardi is here to pollute yet another bio tape with his verbal tripe. Lombardi's insightful offering this time out? He thinks Angle's gold medals are not real and are made of "chaw-ko-layte"... So either he is in denial that the 1996 Olympics existed or he thinks the whole thing is a work. Either way he is a fucking mook. Jerry Brisco calls Angle arrogant and hard to get along with, which is rich from a two-faced stooge, and then Harvey Wippleman calls Angle hard to get along with too. This from a man who washes his clothes by putting them at the bottom of the basket and figuring that after weeks in there, they will probably be clean. Rikishi tells Kurt to shove his medal up his ass and then we see Kurt getting a Stinkface. "What does a Stinkface actually do!?" asks Kurt quite rightly. He says he wasn't humiliated by the experience. To the *King of the Ring* and the final seconds of his tournament matches, including the qualifiers, which basically consists of Angle doing the Olympic Slam then winning over and over again. Not thrilling. The final gets a little more airtime at least, with two of the new flavours of 2000, Angle and Rikishi, meeting in the showdown encounter. It's not much of a match, and really Rikishi was a poor choice to work with Kurt both stylistically and in terms of stature, because no one thought he was going to win the thing. The WWF got things right with the Angle push, for the most part, and he warranted and justified his place at the top of the card, but Rikishi was a novelty act and a fad who got over for his dancing."I don't look up to him, I think he's a piece of gawbayge" says Lombardi. Urgh.

Meanwhile, Tazz is pissed off that Angle stole his towel while he was taking a shower. It's like preschoolers bickering. We get some more fake behind the scenes footage, this time of Kurt taping off a small square area of the locker room as his own so that everyone else knows not to enter his personal space. If he did that for real, he would have had the piss beaten out of him and would be forced to endure the infamous wrestler court. Back to the infernal set, with more made up nonsense that is supposed to somehow put Kurt over, but just makes him look like an ass. Okay, his gimmick might be that he *is* an ass, but do we need a tape, an eternal documentation of a performer, blighted by a waste of time like this? If they had dropped this, then instead of the schizophrenic highlight reels, we could have seen one or two, you know, MATCHES! But no, and the next blink-and-you-will-miss-it feud to get airtime is Angle's program with the Undertaker, which was a bad idea. The build up was decent enough but the 7-minute match at *Fully Loaded 2000* was crap, with Angle's momentum dealt a major blow by his clean and decisive job here.

To the really tremendously booked Angle-Hunter-Steph love triangle from summer 2000 next (read elsewhere in this book for more on this), as Steve Lombardi calls Angle "poison" and says Triple H was justified in being annoyed with him and wanting to take him out. The story had incredible momentum and fans latched onto it in a big way, but then the WWF went and had Kurt lose, again and again, and killed it stone dead. This was the first, last and only time I have ever found Stephanie compelling and interesting viewing. Usually I find her to be as enjoyable as and similar sounding to nails on a chalkboard. What we see of the build up is just the same video that was used to promote *SummerSlam*. The feud was all about the love triangle, but the match was a three way also featuring WWF Champion the Rock, who was the spare wheel afterthought here more than at any other time in his career. Angle got taken out of the match with an injury after Hunter Pedigreed him through a table, but later made a miraculous recovery and a Stampede comeback when Steph begged him to return to the ring to help Hunter. After fighting valiantly, he got pinned by the Rock and then carried a hurt Steph to the back while Hunter was out cold.

The blow-off came the following month at *Unforgiven*, and again we see the same video that aired countless times on free TV, and then more brief highlights from the actual match, with Triple H pinning Kurt. It was an incredibly flat ending to what had been a wonderfully crafted story. This was probably one of the first instances of the internet beginning their backlash against Triple H for holding someone down and going over when he didn't need to. Of course, it wouldn't be the last. This being the WWF where wins and losses don't matter a jot, consecutive defeats over the last three PPVs are enough to garner Angle a WWF Title shot against the Rock at *No Mercy 2000*. This is the first match that actually gets a decent amount of airtime, and as well it should because Angle shocks the world and completes the most successful rookie year in history by capturing the belt after interference from Rikishi and an Olympic Slam. That is still not enough for Lombardi, who decides he just doesn't like Angle. Well you know what, Lombardi? I don't particularly care for you either. Is there a more pointless person in all of wrestling? "I don't want them to know the real Kurt Angle and what's inside" says Kurt in conclusion. Yeah, I figured that from sitting through an hour of this completely pointless tape!

VERDICT

What do you get when you take a guy who only has a year in the business and try to do an hour profile tape on him without offering any insight or behind the character interviews? Boredom. Complete boredom. Kurt staying in character throughout the tape really hurt it, and the talking heads playing along and kayfabing everything ruined it further. Kayfabe is fine, but this is an era where excellent bio tapes are being released that delve further into the person behind the guy on the screen, so there is no excuse to not do the same with this. What it boils down to is a tape full of highlights and hype videos, with little substance, few threads holding things together and nothing new at all. Entirely missable.

25

REBELLION 2000

CAT NO: WWF264
RUN TIME: 140 minutes (approx)

Arnold Furious: With these UK-exclusive PPVs the WWF essentially filmed a glorified house show and then charged Sky Box Office customers cash for it, while UK viewers were getting the major US shows for free. They did this over and over again. The only good thing about these shows is that they provide an interesting snapshot of a certain time. This one happens to fall in between *Survivor Series 2000*, where Steve Austin got a measure of revenge on Triple H for the hit and run attack the year prior, and *Armageddon 2000*, where all the WWF's top tier guys fought in a Hell in a Cell for the WWF Title, with the title becoming more important than Austin's need for revenge. According to the back cover of *Rebellion 2000* it "set the stage for *Armageddon 2000*". The only way that can be is if Undertaker vs. Chris Benoit on this show was considered a "decider" as to who would join the six-man main event at the show. The other four competitors, plus HHH, were the same guys in the main event here.

We're in Sheffield, England. Hosts are Jim Ross and Tazz. Video Control takes us backstage to see Mick Foley and Debra arrive via black cab. The crowd is incredibly hot and greet us with a sea of signs.

Promo Time: Mick Foley
He lists off the participants in tonight's four-way main event with both Rock and Austin getting huge pops. Foley points out Triple H wanted in that match causing Mick to do a spot-on Hunter impression before telling us he's stayed at home in protest. Foley goes on to muse over Kurt Angle possibly getting disqualified to retain his title, which never happens in four-ways anyway, announcing the match as no DQ and no count out. Well, Debra does, thus earning her plane trip to the UK. This brings out a steaming hot Kurt Angle to complain and run cheap heat, but Foley insists his decision is final. Foley was funny but this was only here to kill time and make the event feel like something more than a house show.

Elimination Tables Match
T&A vs. Edge & Christian vs. The Dudley Boyz
The WWF opt for a hot opener with one of the crown jewels of 2000; the tag team division. All these teams are over, although T&A do rely quite heavily on a superstar manager in Trish. Despite the only way to win involving tabling your opponent, it starts out as a by-the-numbers tag. I'm not sure why anyone would bother adhering to the rules. Albert gets a lot of early stuff and bosses the match with his size. The crowd are desperate for tables, which they would be even if it wasn't a tables match, so the Dudleys oblige and Albert attempts a suplex though one only for E&C to double powerbomb him through the table. Trish was a non-factor, which is weird considering she isn't working tonight bar a backstage skit later. You'd think they would use her. With T&A gone we resort to a standard Dudleys vs. E&C encounter, including bizarre heat on D-Von. Why would the ref stop Bubba getting the tag? It's a tables match, there are no DQs anyway. It's a massive logic flaw that cripples the match and allows them to coast by on formula. E&C try for the Wazzup headbutt but Bubba reverses the pin, causing a miscue and then they hit their own Wazzup headbutt. The crowd knows that's the lead in spot for "Get the tables". Christian prevents the 3D on Edge but Bubba just jacks him up instead and a 3D on Christian finishes. This was typical house show fodder with two big bumps inserted. The weird refereeing really hurt the match. You have to credit the WWF though; during Attitude they had an uncanny knack of making nothing matches seem important.
Final Rating: *½

WWF Women's Championship
Ivory (c) vs. Lita
Steven Richards accompanies Ivory representing Right to Censor. Stevie criticises the *Full Monty* before pointing out that all nudity is wrong, adding that having pubs everywhere is wrong too, before eventually turning on the monarchy, blaming them for letting all this happen. Ivory rounds on Lita and her underwear showing over the top of her trousers, urging her to cover up or get slapped. This is a rematch from *Survivor Series*, which was a horrible match. This is slightly better as they've developed a smidge of chemistry. Lita's dropkick sure is atrocious though. To give the match more substance they involve Stevie and Lita has always been at her most popular when laying out male wrestlers. At least they have something approaching a plan here compared to *Survivor Series*, but Lita's spots are remarkably sloppy, such as a quarter pace tope

onto Stevie. He didn't even do anything! Ivory blocks a sunset flip and Richards grabs her hands to help out for the pin. Spots like the Twist of Fate were rough around the edges but the WWF must have known this would be poor and only gave it 3-minutes. It was fairly inoffensive, considering the abortion at *Survivor Series*.
Final Rating: *

Backstage: The Rock milks his reaction before finally returning to Sheffield. Rock slightly modifies his promo to replace "ass" with "bum". "Hehehe, bum" – Tazz. He promises Kurt Angle an early Christmas gift of an ass kicking, if you smell what he's cooking.

WWF Hardcore Championship
Steve Blackman (c) vs. Perry Saturn
They didn't bother flying Terri over, showing how important she was to the Radicalz's act. Keep in mind the WWF was red hot and could afford to do whatever they liked; hence Trish flying over to corner a tag team in the opener who worked for 4-minutes and she did nothing. Plus Debra coming over here just to stand next to Mick Foley and botch her lines. Tazz puts over both guys and says this will be a "rocketbustah". "What's a rocketbuster"? asks JR. "What's a donnybrook?" replies Tazz. He had his moments. The idea behind this Blackman Hardcore Title run was that he himself was a weapon. It was a subtle way to tone down the division a bit. Unfortunately the violence was all the Hardcore Title had going for it, aside from the 24/7 stipulation. Given the martial arts abilities on show they're able to structure a clever little match full of dodges, ducks and dips. No dives, though. Oh wait, Saturn goes for a dive only for Blackman to nail him with a metal shelf. I've seen that spot a few times and it works better with a chair, but kudos to them for inserting it into a nothing PPV. Blackman lifts Raven's drop toehold into a chair, which leads to the champ wearing Saturn out with sticks. "He's fast as a pet coon" shouts Tazz, possibly trying to break JR and definitely making me chuckle. Saturn goes for a chair shot but Blackman kicks it back in his face for the pin. Energetic little hardcore match with much more wrestling than you'd expect.
Final Rating: **½

Backstage: William Regal gets a decidedly mixed reaction for appearing. The WWF want him to get booed in his own country, presumably because they want uniform reactions to their talent across the board. Regal tries to get a bit of cheap heat by calling Prince Naseem Hamed "worthless", which would be true a few years later. I hate that they resort to cheap heat at the end with Regal criticising Britain's "dental hygiene". You're from England, mate, you know that's fiction. His disingenuous behaviour is aimed at turning the crowd on him for his title defence. The same way the WWF deliberately had Davey Boy Smith act like a twat before appearing on the *Rebellion* card a year earlier. I can only assume the WWF were desperate for a "Bret Hart situation" to not arise again where a guy would be cheered in one country and booed in another. It'd be too confusing for the viewing public of sheep and imbeciles. Every time a British guy came home on a tour, the WWF seemed determined for them to get heat. I don't get it. Surely you take whatever pops you can get!?

WWF European Championship
William Regal (c) vs. Crash Holly
Molly Holly gets a trip to England too, courtesy of being able to do spots. Despite all the efforts to get Regal booed he still walks out to a mixed reaction. Take THAT WWF! Regal manages to sell it as heel heat but there's an actual "Regal" chant. There's a big "welcome home Regal" banner too. "He ain't no Hugh Grant" – JR. "Who? Who'd he ever beat?" – Tazz. There are times when Tazz cracks me up. I know he's not technically a good announcer but if a colour guy makes me laugh then he's doing his job. Regal gets another interview where he claims to be better than Steve Austin and The Rock and proclaims himself "the pride and joy of this country", which finally drags heat out of the audience only to be countered by another loud "Regal" chant. You can't force fans to make decisions sometimes, WWF. Big props to those Sheffield fans for not being told what to do. Regal counters Crash's explosive and speedy offence with European style. Seeing as nothing else is getting him hate Regal goes to a chinlock. In a five minute match, sir! Cheap heat via restholds! If Crash thought this would be an easy ride he soon finds out different though as Regal suplexes him square on his neck, All Japan style. Regal shows a lot of ass on cheeky roll ups before dropping Crash on his face for the three but Crash has his foot on the ropes. Molly gets in there to protest, hits a missile dropkick and Crash gets the cheap win for the strap. The fans pop the title change. Regal gives both Hollys a kicking afterwards and takes the belt anyway. Well, you deserved that Molly.
Final Rating: *¾

Backstage: Kurt Angle points out title changes do happen in England, appealing to Chris Benoit to watch his back. Seeing as Benoit is wrestling the Undertaker tonight, he suggests it won't happen.

Eddie Guerrero & Dean Malenko vs. Chyna & Billy Gunn
This is right off the back of Eddie cheating on Chyna with the Godfather's Ho's so it has decent heat. Billy plays second fiddle to Chyna despite being the IC champion, a title he won by beating Eddie; the most over guy in the match. Gunn's limitations are covered nicely by Eddie, who's an exceptional in-ring talent. He plays this match a little cartoony though, walking on tippy toes to sneak up on Billy before begging off instantly when Gunn turns round. Malenko wrestling Chyna is a bizarre situation as Malenko, a gent as always, basically throws himself into the counters and still makes it look believable. It's like he's wrestling himself and it makes Chyna look like a competent technical wrestler. That's how great Dean was at the technical stuff. If you looked bad wrestling Dean Malenko, then you were in the wrong business. There's not that much of an in-ring story, with Chyna taking heat and trying to sell a bad leg. Meanwhile Billy plays up to his strengths by standing on the apron waiting for a hot tag. If standing around waiting for a hot tag counted for anything Billy would be a world champion. During Billy's cleaning house sequence, Eddie makes an amazing save where he goes from grappling Chyna in the corner at the two count to saving the match in the blink of an eye. Malenko survives the Fameasser due to another remarkable Eddie save but Gunn takes it with the One and Only instead, which is the Sleeper Slam he started using when he adopted a new nickname. Decent match, irritating finish. Only the WWF seemed to see value in putting someone as untalented as Billy Gunn over someone as talented as Eddie Guerrero. But Eddie kept his heat, so I guess they knew what they were doing.
Final Rating: **½

Video Control takes us to a roving English reporter called Dan and a woman from Birmingham shames my home town by shouting "wazzup" when she's interviewed. Nice one, love.

Kane vs. Chris Jericho
Word has it this feud was a tester to see if Jericho could be a

KURT ANGLE

legitimate main eventer as he'd need to wrestle against big super heavyweight guys if he was the champion. How'd that work out? Well, Jericho wrestled in the opening match at *WrestleMania*. I think that about sums it up. It's basically an excuse not to push him into the main events and his momentum was gone, thought Jericho is still hugely over and gets enormous pops for his pre-match verbal assault on Kane, so naturally he's jobbing. I figure with Angle going over in the main event they'd need to book one big face win and this should be it. The WWF probably reasoned that Jericho needed to lose all the matches until the big blow-off at *Armageddon*, in his specialist Last Man Standing match, but it creates a real downer here as three of the last four matches have heels going over, bar the Undertaker against Benoit. But that's a given, because it's the Undertaker. At least this match is shorter than the one at *Survivor Series*. That's about all the good I have to say about it. These guys have almost no chemistry, no interesting spots and just fill the match with punching. It's not what you want from a Jericho match but that's probably his attempt to work the fabled "Main Event Style". After plodding through 8-minutes of this Kane finishes with a chokeslam. Jericho had already lost some of his heat by being demoted to working X-Pac but at least those were good matches. The ones with Kane were rubbish. They try like hell to get Jericho over after the match by having him nail Kane with a chair and actually, honest to God, tap him with the Walls of Jericho, one of very few times that Kane has ever submitted.
Final Rating: *

Backstage: Lita pours herself a drink while Trish Stratus makes fun of her failure to win the title tonight. Lita takes exception and they brawl around backstage, thus justifying flying Trish over. UK PPV's have a history of nudity but none occurs here despite both Trish and Ivory being reduced to their bra and panties in a locker room scuffle.

WWF Tag Team Championship
Right To Censor (c) vs. The Hardy Boyz
RTC is the Goodfather and Bull Buchanan and I don't understand them being booked as tag champs given the strength of the division and their relative weakness as a team. Like a lot of workers who treat the UK shows as a day off, they work a basic size vs. speed storyline here and Jeff gets picked off for heat. Hot tag sets up a Goodfather belt shot miscuing and Val Venis, still rhymes with penis, makes the save. This leads to heat on Matt. Way to go, guys, run that formula into the ground. Hot tag to Jeff and he starts popping off mistimed high spots. It all looks a bit clumsy, though not Lita levels of clumsy. Perhaps they all stayed up a bit too late last night on the ales. Jeff gets a Swanton but the ref is distracted and Val hits the Money Shot to allow a reversed pin for the finish. The problem with tag team formula is it's been done to death and it's been done a whole hell of a lot better than this. RTC are still a dull tag team, with tiresome heat sequences dominating the 8-minutes.
Final Rating: *¼

Backstage: Angle looks for backup again, asking Edge & Christian, who are a little banged up after their tables match. Christian describes his table bump as "way harsh". Once again Angle gets no joy.

Elsewhere: Undertaker walks so the Radicalz kick his ass 4-on-1 and destroy his knee. The shoulder would be a better target for the Crossface, but Taker had an ongoing knee injury.

Chris Benoit vs. The Undertaker

Taker fails to appear first time out so Benoit points out he got "a little too lippy" and left his badass back in America. Benoit demands a forfeit victory. Taker makes it out on his third entrance music, hobbling down on one leg. Why didn't he ride his bike down? That would have been easier on the knee surely? JR claims anyone that's had success against Taker has gone after the legs. Like who exactly? I know Bret Hart once beat the Undertaker after employing a similar tactic, but it was with outside interference and the legwork went nowhere. Taker's selling of the knee, the whole focus of the match, is sporadic. In that he moves around normally but then gets reminded of the knee with a kick or such and limps for a bit. Then it doesn't effect his spots until he hits the Old School ropewalk and then he's hurt. It's not the best selling you'll see. It's an issue just about anyone faces while trying to tell a body part injury story. It's hard to develop consistency and keep it entertaining. Considering Benoit should run the match, thanks to the injury, the opposite is true with Taker bossing things with power moves and even inserting his own heat spots like a bearhug. It's all backwards but then Taker did suck something fierce during his 'American Badass' era. Benoit tries like hell to bring psychology to the match and almost everything he does focuses on the knee. The problem with Benoit grinding away at limb holds is that the match comes off the back of the tag title match, which was all heat. It doesn't matter how technically competent Benoit is, his stuff just isn't that interesting. So on one hand you've got selling inconsistencies and on the other you've got quite dull technical stuff. And after some 12-minutes of this Taker grabs an inside cradle and wins. I get they wanted to put Benoit over by having him beat Taker up so bad he couldn't do any of his big offensive stuff (chokeslam, Tombstone, Last Ride) but then Taker outwrestles him. That's a big strange. Despite all my complaints the structure of this, inconsistencies aside, make it the best wrestling match on the show.
Final Rating: ***

WWF Championship
Kurt Angle (c) vs. The Rock vs. Steve Austin vs. Rikishi

Angle comes out second, after Rikishi, to really put over how out of his depth he is. The message here is clean and simple; Rock and Austin are the stars and they'll be main eventing *WrestleMania*. The biggest disappointment about this show is the main event. They wheel out a load of time-killing midcard crap only to gyp the main event of time; giving it less than 9-minutes! Rock gets a decent pop but Austin's is enormous. Absence makes the heart grow fonder. Austin is focused and goes right after Angle. They have magnificent chemistry from the get go. After taking a kicking off Austin and Rock, Angle goes to leave, which isn't a clever move considering anyone can pin anyone. When Rock chases after the champ, he leaves Austin alone with Rikishi, which is a massive risk. One Stunner and it's over. Given the short run time of this match all four guys go full tilt for the entire contest. Rock nut shots Rikishi to avoid a Stinkface and the spinebuster sets up a People's Elbow, weirdly facing the Titantron not the hard cam. Everyone fights over the pin thus denying Rock the title. The heels clear out and the crowd gets excited about Austin vs. The Rock and them duking it out gets a big reaction. As per usual they nail the sportz entertainment stuff. Stunner! Angle has to save his title and everyone gets a near fall in quick succession. Austin stomps a mudhole in Angle but turns right into the Rock Bottom! They've exchanged finishers. Rikishi pulls the Rock out and Angle lays Rock out with the Olympic Slam but the ref is still outside so Rock kicks out. Edge & Christian show up to help out Angle, which is enough to distract Austin. Rock Bottom on Rikishi but Edge saves the title, although he was late and Rock had to jump off his own cover at 2½ to avoid an accidental belt change. The Radicalz run down next. Stunner for Rikishi but the Radicalz save the title. It might be overbooked but this has been constant action. Rikishi staggers to his feet and Angle downs him with the Olympic Slam to retain. I hated this back in 2000 and hadn't seen it since, but despite the overbooking it's enormous fun. To send the fans home happy Austin and Rock pop off finishers on the Radicalz. This match is electric, despite a very short run time. Knowing going in that it'll only be 9-minutes long makes it easier to enjoy. In typical house show fare the show ends with Rock and Austin threatening violence on each other before they drink beer. Rock looks like he's getting a buzz as he actually drinks instead of pouring beer all over his face. Good job he didn't have a beer drinking gimmick or he'd have ended up a functioning alcoholic.
Final Rating: ***

FURIOUS ABOUT: RTC

The RTC came about to parody to the PTC, the Parents Television Council, which had openly criticised the WWE for violence and sexual themes. The group's secondary purpose was to take some of the more offensive characters, a porn star and a pimp, and turn them into goody-two-shoes censorship fans. The group was comprised of Steven Richards, who'd previously wrestled as an impersonator of gimmicks, as leader. Also Ivory, Bull Buchanan, Val Venis and the Go(o)dfather made up the numbers. The group won a few honours, despite being roundly hated by the fans. Ivory was women's champion, thanks to a feud with most of the diva's over their appearance and Buchanan & Goodfather were tag champions. RTC began to fall apart at WrestleMania X-7 where everyone lost. Not long afterwards the group splintered and disbanded in May. Undertaker doing the duties by beating them in a 4 on 1 match.

VERDICT

UK PPV's are generally a write-off but this one is a fairly easy watch. A couple of the undercard matches are decent (Radicalz tag and the hardcore match) and the last two matches end the show on a high. Taker-Benoit is the best wrestling match on the card but the main event is enormous fun. The interaction between Austin and Rock was worth seeing the match for and I'd actually recommend tracking it down. It's the two biggest babyfaces in the industry enjoying their company and competition. For a UK show, it's just about a thumbs up, though if they'd run a 9-minute main event in America people would be demanding refunds.

44

SURVIVOR SERIES 2000

CAT NO: WWF265
RUN TIME: 170 minutes (approx)

Arnold Furious: For all my praise of 2000, and the booking, it does suffer from a sour aftertaste where the storylines went somewhat off the rails toward year's end. This is mainly because of a change in creative where the outgoing Chris Kreski, blaming stress and overwork, was replaced by in-house ideas person Stephanie McMahon. While I'm writing this I can actually hear your collective groan while reading it in the future. That's how powerful it is, people. Steph's ideas mostly circulated around love triangles and world famous wrestlers being infatuated with her and her family. The booking on this show is so irritating it may be a rough ride for both me, the viewer, and you, the reader, as we both have to tolerate a series of half-baked ideas and booking disasters. Oh, and Triple H is the centre of the wrestling universe. But you knew that already.

We're in Tampa, Florida. The opening PPV plug, normally a collection of snippets, promos and shills, is a Triple H promo and that's it. That about sums up Steph's creative focus. Hosts are Jim Ross and Jerry Lawler.

Test, Albert & Trish Stratus vs. Steve Blackman, Crash Holly & Molly Holly
Trish is trying to get herself taken more seriously by wearing more clothes. Boo? She's still hot. Molly only debuted a few weeks ago and is rocking a country bumpkin gimmick. Not sure why Hardcore Holly isn't teaming with the rest of his family and instead has a European Title shot later. T&A had a fantastic hot opener with the Hardys back at *Fully Loaded* so they've been given the opening slot again to pop the crowd, which they do, but Crash and Blackman are hardly on the Hardys' level. To be fair to Crash he tries to be and inserts crowd-pleasing face spots and takes a hiding from T&A. Trish doesn't have the same chemistry with Molly that she has with Lita and the spots look really awkward when the ladies are in there. Trish would become a solid worker but she only shows flashes of that here and she's basically the focus of the match. Molly catches her with a sunset flip for the duke. A brisk, crowd-pleasing opener. The T&A six-person matches were actually a lot of fun. I wish there had been more of them but unfortunately Trish quickly got to be the star of the team and moved up the card solo. Her learning curve was suitably steep that's it's not unrealistic to call her a female version of The Rock.
Final Rating: **¼

Backstage: Edge & Christian make excuses for not helping Kurt Angle out. Christian thinks he might have mono (which would certainly explain his performance later tonight). Angle says it's okay because he's got the Undertaker's number and he just wants to celebrate later.

Video Control takes us to earlier where Lo Down aren't on "the list" so they're not allowed backstage. Poor D'Lo. How the mighty have fallen. I can understand the security guy not recognising jobbers like Tiger Ali Singh and Mosh, but D'Lo is a former IC champion!

Road Dogg, K-Kwik, Chyna & Billy Gunn vs. Chris Benoit, Eddie Guerrero, Dean Malenko & Perry Saturn
3 Live Kru get an early team up as Road Dogg and K-Kwik formed a team with a rapping gimmick. They were "getting ROWDAH". Ron Killings is making his PPV debut. Chyna and Billy were teaming up after Gunn stood up for Chyna when Eddie mistreated her. He's also known as 'The One' Billy Gunn. The one what? The one guy who can't get over in singles? The one guy the WWF keep trying to push although nobody gives a shit about him? The Radicalz are back as a unit after Eddie's heel turn but they are wasted here. The match exists to prove Billy is a big singles star, getting Chyna's blessing in the process, and he's due to dominate proceedings. Chyna gets a spell on offence where they almost do something fun as Saturn grabs a waistlock to block the handspring back elbow and he's about to hit a release German suplex that would have popped the hell out of me, but Chyna counters with a low blow which misses by about a foot (unless Saturn is enormously well blessed and is missing a leg). A ruckus follows so Eddie belt shots Chyna to dump her out of the match. The Radicalz pick off Road Dogg and it seems like only a matter of time before they win the whole shebang. And they should. Seeing as Eddie starts hitting slingshot hilos on specific body parts, like some sort of wrestling God, that should be enough to put Road Dogg away and make it 4-on-2. They could even give Billy a pinfall over Saturn and still have the Radicalz go over.

They needed to push these guys hard and just forget the WCW connection. Let's face it, the WWF didn't have too many guys on the same level technically as the Radicalz. Instead Billy gets a hot tag and finishes Eddie with a Sleeper Slam. Boo! Killings gets a tag and Malenko makes him look like a main eventer before they blow a spot and ruin everything. If I got to work Benoit, Malenko and Guerrero I'd look like a star too. Killings is a decent talent but Benoit plants him with a German suplex to leave it three Radicalz vs. New Age Outlaws. Naturally Road Dogg gets picked off for heat. Saturn puts him out with a Northern Lights suplex and that leaves Billy 3-on-1 so he can do his Superman bit (they really did try to give Billy the Hogan/Cena push, but nobody was interested). Meanwhile the normally assured Radicalz get to look like bumbling idiots. Luckily Malenko can make anything look realistic but I get peeved when he's forced to stumble into Billy's Fameasser. He makes it look right, but in the process he looks like a tool. Billy hits something vaguely resembling a Jackhammer on Saturn, showing that's he's already blown up as he's used to working for 30 seconds at the end of an Outlaws match. Billy kicks out of the Swandive headbutt but then Saturn yanks his legs away and Benoit drops on top for the pin. Survivors: Chris Benoit and Perry Saturn. A massive waste of an awesome collection of heel talent, specifically designed to try and get Billy Gunn over... again. Did they not learn from his previous two aborted singles pushes? Unfortunately Benoit got stuck in a feud with him, which killed his momentum. Benoit's momentum. Not Billy's. Billy has no momentum.
Final Rating: **

Backstage: Chris Jericho ridicules the spilt coffee feud with Kane, before spinning it on its head by talking about his own burning rage which is desperate to escape. Kane's reasoning for the feud being that he's a monster so he's going to destroy something beautiful. No wait, that's Tyler Durden.

Chris Jericho vs. Kane
So Stephanie's watch has already cut the legs off Benoit's big push and jobbed Eddie to a midcarder's secondary finisher, now we see why Jericho lost all his main event momentum toward the end of 2000. A pointless feud with Kane, literally over a spilled coffee, that put him in a situation he couldn't win. The WWF seemed to have genuine intent to push Kane as a monster heel but then switched him face as soon as this feud was finished. By the time *WrestleMania* rolled round Jericho found himself jerking the curtain. A ridiculous idea just a few months before this in mid-2000 when he was regularly competing against the main eventers and getting 50-50 results. Jericho is slightly sloppy at times but when he's working talented guys you don't notice. Kane isn't one of those guys who can cover stuff up, so when Jericho barely scratches him with a dropkick he just bumps it over the top rope. Jericho is a confidence guy and that must dent it as his next big play is blowing a dive to the floor. I know Kane is limited in the ring but Jericho's tactic should surely be to take a load of bumps, like X-Pac, to get the contrast over. They do get a few bumps in there but Kane doesn't seem particularly interested or able to get anything over. They just don't have any timing or chemistry. Frustratingly the match gets 12:32, almost exactly the same length of time as the preceding match! Why didn't they let that go longer and chop five minutes off this? They normally didn't bother giving Kane PPV time because he sucks. Around this time the shine seemed to come off Jericho too. He started making silly little mistakes and it hurt him in my eyes. Kane survives a stint in the Walls of Jericho but as he kicks Jericho off, Chris takes a lousy back bump. It looks totally out of place. The worst is yet to come as Kane falls into the wrong spot for the Lionsault so helpfully rolls into position for it. Urgh. It's all a set up for Kane finishing with a chokeslam. This feud killed Jericho as a face. It killed all his momentum. The match was awful, especially for Jericho, who'd been on fire since his debut a year earlier.
Final Rating: *

Backstage: Terri tells the Radicalz that Triple H will meet up with them later, and Benoit does something resembling laughter.

WWF European Championship
William Regal (c) vs. Hardcore Holly
Regal returned in September 2000 after a failed second stint in WCW. He was a magnificent character in the WWF though and is currently enjoying a run as the WWF's "Goodwill Ambassador". Bobcore is back after having his arm broken by Kurt Angle but he's obviously not good enough to be in the WWF Title picture so he takes out his frustrations on Regal. Regal sees the arm as a target and assaults it methodically. Regal's in-ring was a little out of date as he was still using a lot of technical stuff without the striking, but would later add in layers of a variety of styles that he knew. Here his body part working is largely ignored by the Florida fans. Not that Holly is a sympathetic guy to get heat on. Regal inserts little bits of European style only to be met with a smashmouth southern approach. The proverbial "clash of styles". The commentators get bored and start talking about the electoral process. "I ain't for no monarchy" says JR like a total hick. It's so bad that even Lawler sits there laughing at him. Holly gets pissed off and nails Regal with the European Title for the DQ. Match wasn't much of anything other than a demonstration of Regal's skills.
Final Rating: *½

Backstage: Super slutty Trish asks Kurt Angle about his career and wonders if he needs "special assistance". Angle doesn't get it.

The Rock vs. Rikishi
This was a real brainfart. The WWF painted themselves into a corner by having someone run over Steve Austin to put him out of action for a year, then left it wide open as a big mystery, making fans throw out guesses about what amazing swerve the WWF had up their sleeve. Then it was revealed as Rikishi and because the WWF knew he couldn't draw they got cold feet about it immediately, so chucked him in against Rock here to do the job and finish the angle. Luckily this match still has some heat because Rock could generate heat against everybody. He comes in like a house on fire and the fans eat it up. The psychology is twofold for the match. Firstly the Rock has injured ribs from a sledgehammer assault on *SmackDown!* and secondly Rikishi has known the Rock for a long time, as they're from the same Samoan family, so he feels he can get into Rock's head. The Rock's energy is sufficient for the match to deliver. The ref gets bumped and Rikishi considers a sledgehammer shot. Rock's timing in punching him is perfect. Rock Bottom but Rock stays down hurt and the ref is still on the floor anyway. I think the WWF figured Rikishi would get over from kicking out of the Rock Bottom but the delay on the pin was enormous. After that spot the match picks up a bit and Rock runs into a Samoan drop. There is genuine effort to get this over but it's an uphill struggle. Not because Rikishi is a bad worker, because he isn't, but rather because the initial reveal on who ran over Austin is such a disappointment. Rikishi actually gives Rock a Stinkface, which is another big rub (pun intended) for 'Kish. That serves to piss Rock off though and he explodes out of the corner with a lariat, hits a spinebuster and

K-KWIK

finishes with the People's Elbow. Thanks for coming Rikishi. Enjoy tagging with Haku, getting injured and turning back face. It must be depressing considering the Rock takes just as long to pin after the People's Elbow as the Rock Bottom, but this time Rikishi stays down counting lights. Rikishi tries to get a little heat back post match by hitting a thrust kick and a few Banzai Drops, but I wasn't buying it then and I'm not now. The "Who ran over Stone Cold?" angle should have been red hot. This match was not.

Final Rating: **¾

Video Control takes us to WWF New York where Raven is just hanging out observing the rubes. He doesn't even say anything. He just stands there staring at people. I'm not sure what that was supposed to achieve. Raven was never going to get a push because Vince McMahon didn't like him.

Backstage: Triple H watches as Steve Austin arrives, only for

Mick Foley to stroll in ban the Radicalz from ringside in the Austin-Hunter match (keep that in mind) and make it no DQ. Triple H doesn't care. Way to sell those stipulations, champ!

WWF Women's Championship
Ivory (c) vs. Lita

Ivory has joined Right to Censor, with their hideous music (it's a dirge), so she looks a schoolmarm. RTC took exception to Lita's thongs. There were people out there in the PG Era who claimed that the WWE women's division used to be so much better "back in the day" and cite the likes of Lita as being responsible for this. They clearly weren't referring to this match, which is an absolute dog. It's almost unbearably sloppy and Lita manages to get herself opened up hardway above the eye. This causes Ivory to deliberately work soft for the rest of match, making it even worse. Every spot looks very pre-planned, even basic things like clotheslines. Lita pops off a few really sloppy high spots including a snap rana where Ivory lands square on the top of her head. Steven Richards strolls out to help catch Lita on her big dive, which is one of the few spots that's actually clean although largely due to Stevie being able to just stand there and take Lita flying at him. Lita ducks a horrendous missed belt shot but moonsaults into Ivory's knees and Ivory retains. I think the finish was supposed to be a belt shot but it sure missed, the same as 95% of the match. Lita bled an absolute gusher but the accident was the only convincing part of the entire thing. I love how she deliberately pulls her hair back as she walks out so she can show off the juice though. Lita was best in short bursts; those tags with the Hardys being a perfect use of her in the ring. Any kind of sustained match at this point in her career just exposed how messy she was. Ivory later compared her to Gumby (the claymation stick figure, not the Monty Python character).
Final Rating: DUD

Backstage: The Coach tells us Rock is coughing up a lot of blood. Elsewhere Jericho jumps Kane with a chair to try and get some heat back from jobbing. He beats the crap out of Taker's baby brother but the match wasn't booked that way. Elsewhere the Undertaker tells us the "golden boy" is going to take his Last Ride.

WWF Championship
Kurt Angle (c) vs. The Undertaker

Angle is celebrating his one year anniversary in the WWF by defending the WWF Title on PPV. Meteoric rise! Kurt asks us to take a silent moment to reflect on a favourite Kurt Angle memory of year one. Of course Angle comes out first to demonstrate who the real star is, although you'd never know it from Taker's ring attire. He's wearing the worst trousers in wrestling history. They never reappeared so I assume someone took him to one side and said "I know you're a legend and all, but you look like a tool". He looks like someone's confused granddad who was in a motorbike crash in 1984 and ain't been the same since. When your ring attire undermines the quality of the match, you know it's bad. Taker pulls the same bullshit as he did at *Fully Loaded* against Angle, by pulling him up on covers. He treats Kurt like such a joke that the phrase "transitional champion" pops into mind, but he's only a quarter of the way through his reign, which makes Taker's burial all the worse. Sure, Taker has treated other well established wrestlers with equal contempt but the key word is "established". This is Angle's first big run and sticking him in with Taker does him no favours at all. He'd move on to have three successful title defences on PPV after this and yet all of them involved shenanigans before a job to the Rock in February. I know Angle is a heel but Triple H beat Mick Foley clean and it made him. Angle beat nobody clean until Steve Austin the following year when he finally got over as a main eventer. The match gets worse and worse as Taker makes Angle tap to an armbar, instead of wrestling out, and the champ needs Edge & Christian to distract the ref and the Undertaker to save the title. Angle tries to work a smart match and assaults Taker's leg to slow him down. Taker's trousers may have magical powers though as he kicks his way out and bails to punch Edge & Christian. As the ref escorts E&C out Taker hits a chokeslam and that's twice Taker has had the match won clean only for Angle to be saved with interference. It'd be a good story (like Benoit and Shane against The Rock) if they were working hard, but they're not. Angle at least uses that leg attack to build to bigger spots like the figure four. No matter what he tries, he can't get one over on Taker and I get the match they're going for but that doesn't make it any good. Mainly because Taker only sells when he feels like it and the leg injury doesn't stop his mobility at all. Angle wins major brownie points for what appears to be an impromptu ring post figure four. He isn't quite sure how to apply it, but being a savant he just does it anyway. Kurt goes for a powerslam or something similar and gets countered into a Tombstone only to counter himself into the ropes. The set up is for Angle to crawl under the ring. Taker hauls him out, hits the Last Ride and wins the title. That is until the ref notices; that's not Kurt Angle! It was actually his brother Eric. As Earl Hebner is pointing that out to Taker, the real Kurt slips into the ring and gets a sneaky roll up to retain his title. The match didn't perform like they were hoping for with Taker's false hope spots and the finish came off as flat, mainly due to Eric failing to jump for the Last Ride at the first time of asking. It's an okay match and it's way better than the burial at *Fully Loaded*, but still nowhere near what they were capable of and would do better later.
Final Rating: **½

Video Control gives us a shill of the Fanatic Series and the first one is Austin's *Hell Yeah* tape. I'd be pretty pissed off if I'd paid to see *Hell Yeah*. Wait a minute… I did!

Edge, Christian, The Goodfather & Bull Buchanan vs. The Hardy Boyz & The Dudley Boyz

Right to Censor's team are the tag champions, which is ludicrous considering how many great teams exist in the WWF in 2000. The Dudleys obsession with putting people through tables has them as faces, along with the baby blue-eyed Hardys. Despite the three best tags teams in the company being on show, nobody gets going, which is a bit disappointing. They're running through spots at half speed, knowing full well the match has been inserted as a buffer between title match and main event. They do have a quadruple DDT spot before the Hardys reveal grey camo undershirts for solidarity, but that's where the fun begins and ends. RTC member Val Venis runs in to lay out Matt and Edge debuts the Edge-o-matic to dump the elder Hardy. The match still lumbers a touch and has no heat. D-Von walks into the Unprettier and heels are up 4-to-2. Now we have an interesting scenario as Bubba and Jeff are forced to form a mismatched team. There is some terrific camera work as Edge gets dumped on the ropes and I swear his hair hits the lens. Edge accidentally spears Bull and Bubba pins him. Edge turns into the Bubba Bomb and Christian splashes Edge for some reason. It's put down as a miscue but it was a botch. That dumps Edge leaving us the weird combo of Bubba & Jeff vs. Christian & Goodfather. Bubba gets picked off with Goodfather's DVD. I get why they had mismatched partners as it kept the match unpredictable and eliminated predictable teamwork, but it also eliminates fun. Christian gets dumped with a Swanton leaving it 1-on-1 and the eliminations

have felt extremely close together with little action in between. RTC miscue and Jeff drops on Goodfather for the pin. Survivor: Jeff Hardy. Jeff gets a kicking post match so Matt runs in and hits two Twists of Fate. 3-D for the Goodfather. Wazzup headbutt for Val. Bubba orders everyone to get the tables and Stevie Richards eats a superbomb through the wood. At least they got around to pleasing the crowd after the match, but the bout itself was strangely dreary.
Final Rating: *¾

Video Control gives us a recap of why Austin is angry with Triple H. Basically the Game revealed himself as Rikishi's accomplice pointing out he benefitted the most from Austin being out injured for a year. I guess that makes sense.

No Disqualification Match
Triple H vs. Steve Austin
Hunter comes out to a remix of his music with all the lyrics removed thus making him seem quite boring. I guess they wanted to remove anything that made him look like a face. Austin also has new music, which absolutely sucks. An issue with WWF merchandising is they always want something new to sell so they did a load of new wrestler themes with "more Attitude" not caring how they'd sound as actual entrance music. Considering Austin has been out for a year you'd think he'd be quite angry but he can't get that across in the early going. So they just punch each other… for ages and ages and ages. I'd grown tired of Austin's "brawl all over the arena" main events before his year off so the way this match turns out is a disappointment. Especially considering Triple H's huge advancements during 2000. A match like the *Royal Rumble* one with Cactus Jack or *Fully Loaded* with Chris Jericho would have been gold. Slowly escalating violence. Austin waffles Hunter with a monitor so the Tripper can go for a really, really obvious bladejob. At least he doesn't get caught on camera. Austin lets him bleed a while so he can enjoy a cold beer. Well, it's a Budweiser (in a can) so I guess it almost qualifies as a beer. It backfires as Austin slips over on the water he spilt all over the floor when picking up his cooler, before yelling "clear that shit up" to one of the guys at ringside. If you didn't want water all over the floor you shouldn't have tipped water all over the floor, jackass. They work in a tidy counter where Austin goes for a Stunner and Hunter counters right into a neckbreaker.

Mid Match Tangent: It occurs to me that some people don't care for Austin's *WrestleMania* heel turn but I'm completely in favour of it. At this point, November 2000, Austin was played out as a face and bored the hell out of me with his one-dimensional matches. The heel turn not only gave us a series of phenomenally funny interviews in 2001 but also changed Austin's in-ring to a mat game. His stuff with Angle was better than anything he did while he was on top in 1999. The Benoit, Jericho and RVD stuff was all good too. If a poorly judged heel turn at 'Mania was the price to pay for all those quality matches and funny skits, it was a price worth paying.

Back to the match and Hunter sets up another obvious, about to be countered Pedigree that's so obvious you can see a technician trying to remove the remaining monitor from the announce table, getting Earl Hebner to do it instead and Hebner giving Hunter a signal that he can't get the monitor out so Hunter should watch out for it on his bump. Then the Pedigree is countered into a backdrop through the announce table, for the three people in the arena who weren't aware it was going to happen. Why don't we just stop the whole damn match and explain to the crowd what's about to happen shall we? As if that's not dumb enough Hunter yells "hit me" at Austin in their next exchange. I'm all for calling it in the ring as it creates organic matches that respond to the crowd's interest in the match but calling is an art form. Triple H's calls were frequently too loud. Stunner! The match is over but Austin decides to Pillmanize Triple H's ankle, which is a nice touch as it shows how far Austin has gone in his search for revenge that he's reverted to heeldom and tactics he used against wrestlers in 1996. When Hunter escapes by rolling out of the ring the crowd has seen the last of the match. They head out the back and the Radicalz attack Austin (as they were barred from ringside, not attacking in the back). Hebner can't do a damn thing about it as the match is no DQ. A flotilla of referees arrive as Hunter jumps into a car. Benoit baits Austin into the loading bay where Hunter waits in the aforementioned car. The whole thing becomes cinematic as we can hear Hunter talking very quietly inside his car and coughing. As Hunter continues to mutter, the scene makes for a good horror movie, but this is a wrestling match. Hunter gets picked up by a forklift, driven by Austin and eventually dropped. That's the end of the match and given the height, Triple H has to be dead. The whole thing is in very bad taste. Hunter showed remarkable powers of recovery by almost totally no selling the bump and returning to action a week later (whereas Austin merely got run over by a car and was out for a year). Presumably when the Grim Reaper turned up, Hunter told him he didn't know how to work WWF Main Event Style, promised to put him over later and nailed Death with a Pedigree. As for the rating; this was a lot better than Austin's main event skirmishes with Taker and Kane in 1998 because they had a few decent ideas that were well executed. My favourite being Hunter actually countering the Stunner by working Steve's bad neck. The ending leaves a bad taste in the mouth though, and ruins the PPV.
Final Rating: **

VERDICT

The traditional Survivor matches, inserted to satiate the old school members of the audience, were by-the-numbers affairs, badly booked and with quick and pointless eliminations. The Austin-Hunter main event is tiresome, badly booked and overly long with a terrible finish. Rock-Rikishi had pointless 50-50 booking (one guy wins, the other beats him up afterwards) despite Rock being miles above Rikishi on the card. Even so, it's still MOTN at **¾. The show bottomed out with a horrible Women's Title match, which could only have been saved by a babyface title win. Sorry to complain about the booking again, but that didn't happen. Steph took a while to realise that she couldn't have her cake and eat it. She couldn't push all her love story business AND push all of her future husband's hand-picked buddies. Unfortunately her whole run was blighted by an insistence at pushing the McMahon ideals on top of her own quirks. It all begins here. Fortunately the WWF's audience dictated what they wanted and the WWF were forced into pushing good workers, even if those pushes never seemed to be quite as long as the pushes for Triple H and his friends.

32

RIKISHI

ARMAGEDDON 2000

CAT NO: WWF266
RUN TIME: 170 minutes (approx)

James Dixon: This entire show is built around one single match, but what a mouth-watering prospect it is: Hell in a Cell featuring an incredible SIX guys. All of the big hitters in the company are involved, and Rikishi, as the WWF looks to up the ante for violence even further than ever before. Jim Ross and Jerry Lawler host, and we open with commissioner Mick Foley's promise earlier today on *Heat* that he would resign from his position if anyone was seriously injured in tonight's main event.

Elimination Match
The Hardy Boyz & Lita vs. Perry Saturn, Dean Malenko & Eddie Guerrero
The back story to this is that Dean had himself an unhealthy crush on Lita, so she led him on and they ended up in a hotel room together, where the Hardy Boyz beat the piss out of him. They are the babyfaces though, by the way. I am not sure why Eddie and Saturn feel so strongly about the issue that they need to be involved, but here they are. I also want to note that Eddie Guerrero has reverted to his WCW style attire with a singlet to go with his tights, which is a very midcard look for him. Things start as smoothly as you would expect from the participants involved, with Eddie getting plenty of heat and looking good early on. So obviously, he is the first guy eliminated from the match, suffering a Diamond Cutter from Lita before a Jeff Swanton finishes him off. That's a shame, because now the heels are not only a person down (though, whether having Lita on your team counts as an advantage or not is open to interpretation), but also bereft of personality. The logical way to rectify that? Having the babyface equivalent, Jeff Hardy, eliminated next thanks to a Saturn DVD. The booking here doesn't make much sense at all. Eddie and Jeff are the two most over guys in this, and the two most entertaining performers. We are soon left with just the key players in the feud, when Saturn eats a Twist of Fate and gets eliminated, leaving Dean, the heel remember, outnumbered against two of the people who attacked him. Other than going to bed with his socks on, what did he do wrong, exactly? Terri buys her team some time by coming into the ring and slapping Matt, which results in a Lita spear. Terri sells it by revealing her thong covered ass to the world, because her only purpose of existence is to flash that bubbly little money-maker. Dean takes advantage of all of this by shoving Matt into Lita and then rolling Hardy up for the three, leaving him alone with his would-be gal. So now we have one of the greatest mat technicians of a generation against a chick with two moves. What happens? Why, Lita dominates of course, flying around with head scissors, a tornado DDT and quick pin attempts. Dean sells for her like a champ, but finally cuts her off when she goes upstairs and he punches her then drills her with a superplex. Her bump is as typically floppy as ever, almost like she has no bones. The superplex would win it, but Dean wants to punish her for the humiliation, and rightly so, then gives her a battering before finishing with the Texas Cloverleaf. I don't understand almost all of the booking, but it was an entertaining enough opener for what it was.
Final Rating: **½

Backstage, Kurt Angle asks Lillian Garcia if she is Bulgarian. You had to be there.

WWF European Championship
William Regal (c) vs. Hardcore Holly
This could be a lot of fun, as both guys usually display a proclivity for stiffness. Prior to the bout, the wonderful snobby Regal character rips into Alabama (location of tonight's show and Holly's hometown), for not knowing what a handkerchief is, for never washing and for getting busy with their pets. Holly gets a polite response from his townsfolk, but there is more heat for Regal than there are cheers for bombastic Bob. The action is decent enough, but never quite makes it out of second gear, and with less than five minutes to play with they don't really have the time for the kind of brutal hard-hitting fight that got Regal rehired by the company in the first place (Regal worked Chris Benoit in a great match at the independent Brian Pillman Memorial show earlier in the year, in a match so good he was essentially hired on the spot, after previously having had a run as the 'Real Man's Man' in 1998 that ended due to "personal demons"). The match has far less heat in all than you would expect after Regal's verbal abuse and with Holly being the local boy, though there are a few meaty moments exchanged, just sadly not enough to get the juices flowing. The finish sees Raven appear from no-where, for seemingly no

reason, and plant Holly with his Evenflow DDT as Regal covers for the win. So, two heels going over in a row then, which kills this crowd right off the bat.
Final Rating: *½

Backstage, the once over dancing babyface turned drab heel Rikishi, talks about sacrificing everyone else in the main event tonight. Seems a bit excessive.

Chyna vs. Val Venis
If I could use an emoticon to describe my feelings about Right To Censor, it would be a big sad face. Chyna has irked the PTC-mocking group by posing for Playboy, who according to JR want to burn the pictures. Jesus, they must have burned an epitaph of her when they saw her porno... I know it is trite to keep bringing it up, but the jokes just keep coming to me! Plus, if you are going to go from tag teaming in the ring to being tag teamed in *your* ring, then you deserve a little mocking... I am sorry, I can't help it! Oh right, there is a match going on, or at least something resembling one. What it looks like to me is a series of moves being executed by an over pushed woman who fans are no longer all that interested in or tolerant of, and a guy who has lost all of his wacky charisma since turning heel and dropping his gimmick. Val misses the former Money Shot, Chyna nearly gets a fall but then gets distracted by Ivory and chases her around the ring. Back inside she gets caught by a Val fisherman's suplex and does the clean job. Remember when Chyna was protected in the booking? So for those keeping score, that is two of three matches that have featured women competing against men, and the third straight that has seen a heel go over. Did Vince Russo pop back over to New York for a day during his WCW hiatus?
Final Rating: ½*

The WWF basically promises a big bump tonight in the HIAC match by showing footage of Mick Foley doing very silly things within (and on top of) the same structure. Then in an interviewed conducted in the Cell while the arena was empty, the Undertaker talks about the rush he got from the Shawn Michaels HIAC bout, with accompanying footage shown. Then he rambles on about the Foley matches in the same setting, as this segment goes on for an unacceptable amount of time for a PPV broadcast. It is longer than both of the last two matches!

Promo Time: Vince McMahon
Oh come on now! Have we gone back to 1998? 2000 is the year where the in-ring wrestling rules all; we don't need ten minute story time with the Undertaker, or Vince McMahon cutting a promo that goes nowhere. Do your talking on free television, do your wrestling on the paid shows. This whole thing is meandering and tedious, with Vince turning into a television evangelist and asking for people to stand up and join him in rejecting the Hell in a Cell match tonight because it is so perverse. The way they are building this up, it should have ended someone's career in storyline terms, for a few months at the very least. It would have been a good opportunity to cancel the ill-advised Rikishi heel turn and have him take a few months off before coming back as a fan favourite.

Now, STILL no wrestling, as we get a long hype video for the uninspiring Kane-Chris Jericho feud, which was built around spilt coffee. Better than split milk I suppose, no sense crying over that...

Last Man Standing Match
Kane vs. Chris Jericho
This starts in the aisle, then suddenly BLACKNESS as they disappear backstage and the camera crew are not ready for it. They have a brief tussle backstage, purely so we can catch a glimpse of a truck filled with hay, because it will be important to a big spot in the main event later and would seem completely random when it was wheeled out otherwise. Crafty work, WWF, but I am on to you. Speaking of random, Mideon turns up while they are brawling, but is sent scurrying away from one Jericho punch. Okay then. Back to ringside and Kane hits a powerslam and then slowly works Jericho over. "This one will not last much longer at this pace" - JR. WHAT PACE!? This is strictly WWF Main Event Style slugging. Why do they like guys working this way so much? It is so immensely dull. Remember when Jericho was having pure wrestling blinders opposite Chris Benoit earlier in the year? Remember when he was beating Triple H for the WWF Championship (briefly) to an immense reaction on *RAW*? He should be in the Cell match, not sleepwalking through a midcard program with Kane. The crowd doesn't buy into any of the attempts at ending the match in the first ten minutes, because they know it is not going to end with something as simple as say a chokeslam. Jericho taking a five count from a barely connecting clothesline sums up the absurdity of the overselling. Things get more interesting when Jericho decks Kane with a chair, but then he goes back to his standard offence, at one point stupidly picking Kane up just so he can hit his bulldog set up that precedes the Lionsault. Why not just do it? I hate dumb stuff like that. They brawl to the outside again and this time towards the excessively decorated *Armageddon* set, which features knackered old cars, masses of stacked barrels and all manner of other props. Jericho tries to put Kane through a table with a bulldog, of all things, but unsurprisingly that doesn't work. Jericho then pushes over the very conveniently placed barrels, which land on a speaker stack and nowhere near Kane at all, and that keeps the 'Big Red Machine' down for the count. That finish was rotten, and the match preceding it was way too long and way too boring. What a horrible use of Jericho.
Final Rating: *

Over in WWF New York, Shawn Michaels offers some insight into tonight's Hell in a Cell match: "I've got no idea what's gonna happen". Right, fantastic.

Four Corner Match
WWF Tag Team Championship
The Goodfather & Bull Buchanan (c) vs. Edge & Christian vs. The Dudley Boyz vs. Road Dogg & K-Kwik
Just a few short months ago, the WWF's tag division was on top of the world following the incredible exploits of the Dudleys, the Hardys and Edge & Christian. Now, the insipid Right To Censor duo of the Goodfather and Bull Buchanan are the champions. Talk about taking a wrong turn off! Road Dogg and K-Kwik are not exactly remembered in the annals of history as one of the great teams either, with Dogg struggling to find his place in the WWF now that he is no longer paired with Billy Gunn, and K-Kwik shunted in as his tag partner because he also comes to the ring while yakking into the mic. This is not elimination rules, but rather one fall wins it, which is something I hate about multi-man title matches because it makes being the champion worthless and you can lose a title without actually losing the match. It just cheapens the prestige of everything. The action is entirely generic for the most part, though there is an excellent spot where Road Dogg and Bubba do stereo jabbing punches on Edge and Christian and begin to simultaneously dance to wind up a big one, but spot the other doing the same and punch each other out. The rest is bland because it is impossible to build heat in a multi man with so many guys involved, until Bubba comes in and ups the pace.

FURIOUS ABOUT: TAJIRI

Tajiri originally worked for the WWF in 1997 as part of their fledgling light heavyweight division. After a stint in Mexico he was signed by ECW and made his name there, thanks to an exciting series of matches, largely with Super Crazy but also for revolutionising tag team wrestling with Mikey Whipwreck. WWE signed him shortly after ECW closed, pairing him with William Regal as the commissioner's house boy. Tajiri managed to win the WCW US title during his first year in the company before finding himself in the cruiserweight division. He also won tag titles twice, with Regal and Eddy Guerrero. He turned heel after mistreating onscreen girlfriend Torrie Wilson, a bizarre couple. After three cruiserweight title runs, including taking the belt from Rey Mysterio Jr., Tajiri left the WWE aiming to become a journalist. He's since become a promoter in Japan where his WWE experience has been invaluable.

The crowd just want tables, they don't care about anything else, except they do go wild when the Dudleys do the Wazzup drop. Bubba finally calls for the tables, and they use one to clothesline Bull with, then hit the Doomsday Device on Edge. Bull comes back in and gets nailed with 3D, and Goodfather gets the same. The Duds continue to dominate, and use Wazzup on Christian too, but Edge smashes Bubba with a spear for a near fall. Christian then hits the Unprettier on Bubba behind the referee's back, and Edge pins him to win the belts to ZERO reaction. I don't think the crowd knew that this was single fall. Once Bubba got the hot tag and the Dudleys dominated, this became a fun match, but before that it was nothing. I still don't like that Edge & Christian won the belts but didn't beat the champions.
Final Rating: **

Backstage, Triple H shouts at Steph about how he is willing to sacrifice everything to be WWF Champion.

WWF Intercontinental Championship
Billy Gunn (c) vs. Chris Benoit

This is a bad period of Billy Gunn's career, as he embarks upon another disappointing singles run that ultimately goes nowhere. JR has an old codger whinge about him wearing earrings, saying he doesn't recall any other champions who wore them. He is aghast. He is also forgetting guys like Shawn Michaels, or even his good buddy Steve Austin, who had one briefly too. I would frankly be more upset about Gunn's glittery pink tights. Talk turns to Chris Benoit being the best technical wrestler in the WWF, and JR can only counter that by talking about how high Billy can jump. Well, that will help. Billy is way out of his league here, and he struggles to keep up with the intense tenacity of Benoit, who just keeps coming and coming, never letting Billy rest. Benoit dismantles Billy with consummate ease, damaging his leg and then targeting it, zoning in on the point of weakness like a Terminator. A lot of what Benoit did in the ring was Terminator-like, and not just because he had a robotic personality. Benoit switches tactics to his traditional mode of attack, nailing three German suplexes but missing the diving headbutt, giving Billy chance to finally mount some offence. Prior to this he has done nothing. A powerslam and press slam follow, then a jackhammer and Fameasser seem to have it won, but Benoit kicks out. Billy instead goes for a sleeper but Benoit switches into the Crossface, only for Gunn to reach the ropes. Billy makes a complete mess of a tilt-a-whirl, but covers it well by selling his knackered leg, then they have a nice long and audible chat about how to recover the spot. They opt for a boot in the corner, which gets a two count. Not a great choice, if I am honest. A back suplex gets another fall for Benoit, then Gunn nearly catches one with a roll up, only to immediately get caught in the Crossface, and that is the end of 'The One'. The knee work was all pretty pointless because it didn't factor into the finish at all, and Gunn looked so far out of his depth that it was at times embarrassing. If you ever want to see Chris Benoit coast through a match, this is "the one" to watch.
Final Rating: *½

Triple Threat Match
WWF Women's Championship
Ivory (c) vs. Molly Holly vs. Trish Stratus

Right To Censor for the third time! Spare me, please! Here we go again with the multi-person rules in a title match. Ivory just steps back and lets Trish and Molly go at it for a bit, but when Molly flips through a monkey flip she drills her with a clothesline in a nice spot. Pins attempts are broken up and unions formed then quickly broken, before Molly drills Trish with a powerbomb and Ivory steals the pin for the win. The whole thing runs just over 2-minutes. After the match T&A hit the ring to bully Molly, so Crash Holly comes out to save her and challenges the burly duo to a fight. They laugh at him, but then the APA music hits and they come down and kick tail, including Bradshaw thumping Albert with his delightful Clothesline From Hell. I love the APA in this role, they should have been used exclusively like this. Once they started wrestling and having to sell it unravelled, but as hired ass kickers they were cast perfectly.
Final Rating: ¾*

Now it is Rock's turn to talk about the main event, and he runs through his catchphrases before adding that he is walking into hell, but will come out as WWF Champion.

Hell in a Cell Match
WWF Championship
Kurt Angle (c) vs. The Undertaker vs. Steve Austin vs. The Rock vs. Triple H vs. Rikishi

Sesame Street sum up my feelings about the participants in this: "One of these things is not like the others / One of these things just doesn't belong / Can you tell which thing is not like the others / By the time I finish my song?" Joking aside, this really is one of the greatest collections of legendary WWF talent in one match that there is ever likely to be, aside from the *Royal Rumble* match I guess. The WWF have done a very good job of hyping this, really giving the Cell an incredible imposing aura, and building this up almost like someone in there is going to die. They really have laid it on thick. I question using the Cell for a second time on PPV in one year, though at least there is a strong storyline purpose for it, with WWF commissioner Mick Foley wanting all the madness (hit and run attacks, guys in cars getting dropped from forklift trucks, random attacks and assaults, etc) to stop and come to a head in one match. Plus, the concept of six guys in there at once is a very exciting one, and it is a little surprising that the WWF/E never did another one. I suppose it would have been too similar to the Elimination Chamber. Oh Jesus, get your boxers pulled up over your waistband and don yourself a baseball cap, because here comes the Undertaker to the chav-tastic tones of Limp Bizkit. How utterly horrid. We get a good insight into the WWF's opinion of champion Kurt Angle, with him coming out third rather than last. My only criticism of this match is that for

146

the third time tonight we have stripped the champion of their advantage because of the multi-man rules. Once was bad enough, but three times!? Overkill. If you want smooth mat wrestling exchanges then you are in the wrong place, because this is an all-out pier-sixer brawl right from the get go. Everyone pairs off, with so much going on that it is hard to keep track for both me and the director. Taker battles with Angle on the outside, Rock gets the better of Rikishi and Austin tangles with Triple H, before everyone switches partners and goes again. The director decides to treat this like a ladder match and focus on what is going on in the ring rather than the guys selling on the outside. Well, when possible at least, because sometimes nothing is happening in the ring and everyone is brawling on the outside. Austin rakes Hunter's face on the cage repeatedly and busts him open, though it doesn't rank very highly on the old Muta Scale, then drags him across the entire cage by his face. The close camera work continues to cause problems on this show by exposing the business, with Austin clearly asking "You alright?" and Hunter responding in the affirmative. Next up, everyone gets a turn to hit some big moves, with Hunter getting the Pedigree on Rikishi, only for Rock to save and hit a DDT. Angle breaks that up and hits the Olympic Slam, but Austin catches him with a Stunner before falling to an Undertaker chokeslam. Poor Rikishi, he got to hit nothing. Triple H continues to get well acquainted with the cage when Taker sends him into it face-first, while Rikishi and Austin have a ruckus in the ring.

Things take a turn for the bizarre when Vince McMahon and the stooges show up with the same hay-filled truck as we saw in the Kane-Jericho match earlier, and they attach a chain to the Cell door and rip it off. That makes sense, because Vince wants the match off, but the hay is a curious one in a construction truck. All will become clear soon. Vince wants the entire cage ripping down, but Mick Foley comes out and belts the stooges, then has McMahon dragged out by security. Of course, there is still the slight issue of the Cell lacking a door, and the participants take advantage of that and bail out to brawl around the arena. The sight of six guys brawling in the aisle and around the set is an exciting one, but logically it is a little flawed because you can only win the match in the ring. Anyone smart would have stayed in the cage while they all battered each other and then taken advantage. Triple H continues to be the MVP with some manly bumps, including one on the hood of a car when Austin sends a mounted camera into him. Hunter responds by putting Austin through a car window, and that makes this a double juicer, with Austin having himself a bleed. Rock and Hunter then fight on top of a car, with Hunter blocking the Rock Bottom and hitting the Pedigree. And now Rock is bleeding too! Triple juicer! I approve, because cage matches should always be blood-splattered, even if two of the guys are bleeding from the brawl in the aisle. The guys continue to have fun ramming each other into the various cars, with Austin slingshotting Hunter high onto a windshield. The whole thing outside the ring is one of the most fun arena brawls you will see, because there are just so many variables. The Undertaker and Kurt Angle take things to near the announce table, with Kurt smashing Taker hard in the face with a chair, which busts open Taker and makes this a quadruple juicer! Tremendous.

The decibel levels rise when Hunter and Austin climb the cage, with a big bump from someone almost demanded. Austin leathers Hunter and it looks like he will be the one to take the fall, but just as he is teetering on the edge, Hunter fights back to the centre of the cage. Austin hits a Stunner on top of the (reinforced) roof, and then Angle and Taker join the fracas up top. This is just complete and utter madness. Things get even more brutal when Taker busts open Angle on top of the cell by smashing his face into a support beam, making this an unprecedented QUINTUPLE JUICER!!! My God. Hunter and Austin do the smart thing and climb down, as Taker bullies the timekeeper into giving him a chair. He uses it to hit a home run with Kurt Angle's head, as Rikishi makes his way up the cage and uses the same chair on Taker. Kurt too makes the smart decision and climbs down the cage, leaving Rikishi and Taker up top. Rikishi is the only one not bleeding, and thus he drew the short straw of taking the big bump. They tease it for a while, then Taker grabs him by the throat and chokeslams him off the cage and into the truck full of hay. Well, fancy that just happening to be there, huh? Austin's facial reactions to the slightly underwhelming bump are great. Back in the ring, Rock and Austin have an electric Warrior-Hogan *Royal Rumble '90* type moment as they face off for the first time in the match, with the crowd reactions to their exchanges solidifying that bout as the number one option for the *WrestleMania* main event. Rock looks for the People's Elbow on Austin, but Triple H prevents it only to get dumped. Angle comes back and gets hit with Rock Bottom, then Austin drills Rocky with a Stunner. Triple H prevents the pin and hits a neckbreaker on Austin, as Kurt throws an arm over Rocky to get the super fluke pin. Austin gives Angle a last gasp Stunner afterwards to lay him out, with the ring just full of carnage. Weak booking of the lucky champion aside, this was a glorious match. I loved every single second of the 30 plus minutes it lasted, from the copious blood to the chaotic brawl in the aisle to the teases atop the cage. With six guys in there, it couldn't possibly be boring, and it never was, it was just war for the entire duration. I love this match, probably more than most, and to me it is almost the full boat. How could it have been any better? Sure the bump from Rikishi was a little telegraphed and he was well protected, but does that matter? Does someone have to seriously injure themselves for the match to be good? Of course not. This is 30-minutes of violence and blood and some of the best brawling you will likely see from some of the biggest names in the history of the business. For what it set out to achieve, it is very nearly perfect.

Final Rating: ****¾

VERDICT

The problem with the WWF putting all of the top guys in one match is a piss weak undercard that never completely sucks, but also never gets going either. Because of that this is purely a one match show, but what a match it is. Inevitably many will disagree with how highly I rate the bout, but that is fine, the enjoyment of wrestling is in the perception of the observer, and I *loved* it. The rest of the card you can ignore completely, but the main event is must-see viewing. It is the WWF at its most brutal and wantonly violent. Fans who later suffered through the John Cena Era will probably enjoy watching it back even more, because it feels like a completely different -and much better- company.

56

ROYAL RUMBLE 2001

CAT NO: WWF267
RUN TIME: 177 minutes (approx)

Lee Maughan: From New Orleans, Louisiana. Hosts are Jim Ross and Jerry Lawler.

WWF Tag Team Championship
Edge & Christian (c) vs. The Dudley Boyz
This match came about after Edge and Christian had made fun of the Dudleys' parents, belted them in the head with "Conchairto" chair shots on *RAW*, and driven them through tables on *SmackDown!*, all to no reply. Which, if you've followed wrestling for more than six months, should tip you off to the outcome here; another blip on the Edge & Christian reign of dominance where they kept dropping the titles for short periods so as not to completely overshadow every other team in the division, not to mention build up rematches. That's one of the key points of this neat little opener, as the ultimate goal was the second TLC match at *WrestleMania X-SEVEN*, with these two teams once again clashing with perennial rivals the Hardy Boyz.

A pretty good match here, dull chinlock on D-Von aside, with Edge and Christian at their new generation Midnight Express peak and Bubba Ray running wild off the hot tag. Amusing finish sees Edge and Christian attempt the Wazzup Drop but Bubba rolls through on Christian and Edge gets shoved off the top into a diving headbutt right on Christian's taint. That sets up the 3D to give the Dudleys their second reign as WWF Tag Team Champions. Several more would follow over the next couple of years.
Final Rating: ***¼

- Backstage, Triple H tells Stephanie McMahon-Helmsley that he doesn't want the heat between her and Trish Stratus to interfere in his match tonight. You see, Triple H was previously working an angle where Stephanie was the object of Kurt Angle's affections, but that just served to emasculate poor Hunter and make him the de facto babyface, all of it contradicting his status as Hunkiest Heel in This Damn Business™. Obviously that couldn't stand, despite how the storyline was firing on all cylinders, so Triple H beat Angle at *Unforgiven* and had it made that Stephanie only had eyes for him. It's all about the game, and how you play it.

Ladder Match
WWF Intercontinental Championship
Chris Benoit (c) vs. Chris Jericho
You may have noticed that between the first tag team ladder match at *No Mercy* '99, the triple team ladder match at *WrestleMania 2000*, TLC I at *SummerSlam*, this match, TLC II at *WrestleMania X-SEVEN* and TLC III a few months later on *SmackDown!*, the WWF had quite the ladder match fetish going on around the early part of the new century. Unlike all those spot-heavy, team-based ladder bouts I mentioned, which in many ways are the spiritual successor to the Shawn Michaels-Razor Ramon and Triple H-Rock classics of the 90s, this one feels a lot more like the natural heir to the Michaels-Bret Hart ladder match of '92. That's not to say that this match isn't without spectacular moments; early on, Benoit goes for topé suicida only to get belted square in the face with a chair shot from Jericho, on which Benoit has absolutely no way of protecting himself or falling safely, and instead just hopes for the best. But for the most part, the thrill is built around the chase.

Certainly, when watched in close proximity to those awesome TLC matches, the "car crash spectacle" element feels a little lacking, but the psychology, timing and realism are all there in spades. Not only that, but they also manage to achieve what for some may be the ultimate worker's goal - an entirely new move that nobody had ever seen before, in this case a Liontamer atop the ladder. Insane. Benoit also bumps around like an absolute maniac, taking full-on ladder shots to the face and throwing himself around (and out of) the ring, seemingly without a care for all the damage he's doing to his body. Sadly, it was the lasting effects of matches like this, and particularly spots like his utterly bonkers Swandive headbutt off the top of the ladder, that played a major part in his eventual meltdown. The knowledge of how it all ended for him makes this one very difficult to enjoy in hindsight, much more than many other Benoit bouts you could name, especially knowing that its overall quality came with such a heavy price tag.
Final Rating: ****½

- Elsewhere, Billy Gunn tries to talk Chyna out of her match with Ivory. The angle was that Ivory and the Right to Censor had broken Chyna's neck to set up their match.

WWF Women's Championship
Ivory (c) vs. Chyna
Chyna bumps Ivory around for a few minutes like the Ultimate Warrior on a hit of Randy Savage's special coffee mixture, but apparently suffers a stinger on a back flip handspring elbow in the corner, and that gives Ivory the pin at 3:33. She barely even made contact there and went down in the least believable manner possible, but far worse is the WWF's completely classless attempt to push the injury as legitimate. I mean it's not like Darren Drozdov landed on his neck during a match and ended up as a quadriplegic, is it? They carry Chyna out on a stretcher as JR puts on his solemn "Fans, this wasn't supposed to be part of tonight's entertainment" voice, setting himself up as the boy who cried wolf next time somebody gets hurt for real, and harkening back to the last time he got all choked up at the desk as Jerry Lawler ran to the ring to check on a felled wrestler. Considering Vince McMahon had just settled a multi-million dollar lawsuit with the estate of Owen Hart that pretty much destroyed the entire family, this was about as scummy and low class an angle that the WWF could have delivered at this point.

WWF Championship
Kurt Angle (c) vs. Triple H
Angle has Trish with him, who is currently knocking off Mr. McMahon while Vince's poor wife Linda is under sedation. And what a ridiculous sentence that is to write. That sadly means that most of the match here is just a backdrop to bitchy Stephanie bitching bitchily at bitchy Trish, as confirmed by the pre-match video package which all but ignores the actual wrestlers. And speaking of ignoring the wrestlers, JR tries to get Triple H's legwork over by referencing 'Nature Boy' Buddy Rogers to which Lawler, presumably being fed direction by Vince, tells him "enough of that 50s crap, nobody even remembers Buddy Rogers, let's talk about the 90s!" I'd call Lawler out on the fact that the 90s were also history by this point, but he manages to put his foot further in it just seconds later by going off on a rant about what he did to Andy Kaufman, which was back in the early 80s! If anyone was ever trying to pinpoint exactly when Lawler went from biting announcer to doddery old buffoon, may I nominate that little verbal exchange?

Of course, both guys spend the next ten minutes bashing each other's legs against the ringpost and applying Indian deathlocks, dragon screw leg whips, figure fours and the like, and one cannot help but wonder what the point of any of this is or why anybody should even care when the announcers have basically been told off for trying to get over the psychology behind it all. It's just utterly insulting to the guys in the ring, and everyone who's paid to watch this championship match. Sure enough, the second-fiddle nature of it all comes to the fore as Trish and Stephanie get into a catfight and Vince comes down to cart Trish away. Match? What match?

In deference to the extracurricular activity, it does draw the biggest reaction of the match so far, but then that kind of thing tends to happen when you position it as more important than the actual bout. Complaints ahoy - Angle uses an atomic drop on Helmsley, despite the damage that has supposedly been done to his leg, and Triple H low blows Angle in full view of the referee without even bothering to try and conceal it. That's just completely lazy. Angle's infraction at least didn't neuter the referee, and he *had* only been on the WWF scene for a little over a year, but Triple H really should have known better than that. The referee gets wiped out on the floor so Triple H goes for the belt and nails Angle with a Pedigree (because he has to get a visual three count before losing, you see), then Steve Austin runs in and drops Hunter with a Stone Cold Stunner in retaliation for Hunter admitting to have been behind Rikishi's running Austin over all the way back at the 1999 *Survivor Series*. Angle gets the three off that, and the stage is set for the divisive Austin-Triple H best Three Stages of Hell match at *No Way Out* that some people think is a masterpiece, while others view it as self-indulgent tedium at its worst. This match was pretty decent though, as Angle continued his slow transition from talented goofball to badass machine, even if he didn't actually win it on his own merit.
Final Rating: ***½

- Lawler asks for an update on Stephanie and Trish, who basically had a game of slapsies, but not for Chyna who less than 45-minutes ago suffered that potentially life-threatening neck injury. Sigh.

Royal Rumble Match
#1 is **Jeff Hardy** and #2 is **Bull Buchanan**. They're joined (almost) two minutes later by Jeff's brother **Matt Hardy** at #3. A double team Whisper in the Wind and a double clothesline puts Bull out, and the Hardys go at it. It's not exactly Demolition in 1989 for stature, but there's sure a lot more action. #4 is **Faarooq** in a tag team-heavy start to the match, but the Hardys team up again as soon as he gets in, which makes one wonder why they bothered wrestling each other. Jeff blows a second Whisper in the Wind but Matt hits a Twist of Fate and Jeff lands a Swanton Bomb and they eliminate Faarooq before going back to work on each other. #5 is *Whose Line is it Anyway?* host and future WWE Hall of Famer **Drew Carey**, in town to plug his own upcoming pay-per-view of improv comedy. He gets in the ring and parades around as the Hardys eliminate each other like a pair of complete idiots. They could have teamed up the entire match the way they were going, *then* fought it out. Cretins.

#6 is **Kane** as Lawler giddily reels off a bunch of celebrity magazine shows and newspapers like *Access Hollywood*, *Entertainment Tonight*, *The New York Post* and *E! Network*, as Vince McMahon undoubtedly slavers all over himself at the thought of all the publicity this could bring. #7 is **Raven** in something significantly less than two minutes as the previously unadvertised Carey eliminates himself in favour of high-fiving everyone in the front row. And that's how you get into the WWE Hall of Fame, folks. Oooh yeah, dig it?! **Al Snow** jumps the gun at #8 and brings a bunch of trash cans with him, turning the Rumble into an on-the-fly hardcore match, rolling a bowling ball in Raven's knackers. Continuing the theme are **Saturn** at #9 and **Steve Blackman** at #10.

#11 is **Grandmaster Sexay** but the brawling on offer is all rather tepid. It strikes me that this whole segment, which is a pretty fun deviation from the normal Rumble combat given the premium placed on hardcore wrestling at the time, even if the crowd aren't much into it, could have been elevated another notch had they done a couple of Hardcore title changes under the 24/7 rule here. Instead, Kane puts out Grandmaster and Blackman with trash can shots, chucks Raven over the top, boots out Snow and hurls out Saturn to end the segment, as **The Honky Tonk Man** arrives to shake, rattle n' roll at #12 in one of the Rumble's early "surprise returns". Honky sings his song until Kane takes his guitar and dumps him for his sixth consecutive elimination in a fun spot (and an easy payoff for

FURIOUS ABOUT: TAZZ

Tazz was an ECW Original. Joining the company in 1993 as the Tazmaniac, he refined his style and was built by Paul Heyman into one of the biggest stars outside of the WWE & WCW. On his path of destruction, Tazz had an excellent feud with Sabu and became ECW champion in 1999 beating Shane Douglas. Tazz held the belt until the WWE came calling in September 1999. Tazz debuted to great fanfare at the Royal Rumble, beating Kurt Angle, but soon faded into the background. 2000 saw a lot of new talent enter the WWE and Tazz found himself surplus to requirements. He returned to ECW to win their title, while still under WWE contract, before retiring and becoming a commentator. He returned again to partner Spike Dudley to the tag titles before retiring for good in 2002. His WWE-based "Path of Rage" never quite replicating the ECW one.

Honky). #13 however is former potential Honky protégé **The Rock**, and that means it's time to get serious. They trade clotheslines until Rock's former Nation of Domination teammate **The Goodfather** hits the ring at #14, and they trade fists until Rocky slaps him over and out. **Tazz** is #15, presumably for the comedy of seeing him square up to Kane, so Kane simply picks him up and swats him out like a fly. Remember last year when Tazz debuted to that spine-tingling reaction at Madison Square Garden then choked out Kurt Angle? Yup.

Halfway through and **Bradshaw** joins the fray at #16 and he wipes out the Rock with a Clothesline from Hell. #17 is **Albert** and he gets to throw his weight around because it doesn't matter in the WWF if you're talented like Tazz, just if you're big like Albert. #18 is **Hardcore Holly** who adds little, and would have been better suited to the hardcore stuff earlier. #19 is **K-Kwik** to almost no reaction. What's up? In a cool, unplanned spot, Bradshaw powerbombs K-Kwik at exactly the same time as Kane powerslams Holly, and **Val Venis** comes in at #20.

William Regal is #21 and **Test** is #22, putting nine guys in the ring until Test eliminates future Un-American partner Regal just a few moments later. #23 is **The Big Show** in another surprise, as he had been banished to WWF feeder league Ohio Valley Wrestling in 2000 in an effort to get him to lose weight. The fact he came back fatter than ever was a source of much amusement, but he eliminates Test and K-Kwik in short order before delivering chokeslams to Albert, Bradshaw, Venis, Holly and Kane. The Rock avoids a chokeslam of his own with a kick to the goolies before putting Show out with a clothesline, so Show rips out the ringside monitors and gives Rock a chokeslam through the English announce table as **Crash Holly** hits the ring at #24. Everyone in the ring gangs up on Kane until **The Undertaker** comes to his little brother's rescue at #25.

Kane adds Crash Holly and Albert to his hit list of eliminations as Undertaker dumps Bradshaw, Hardcore and Val, and **Scotty 2 Hotty** hits the ring at #26. JR calls him the "last chicken leg" and the Brothers of Destruction take turns dismantling him, dropping him with a double chokeslam before dumping him out. Are you watching this, Hardy Boyz? #27 is **Steve Austin**, but he gets battered from behind by Triple H before he can even hit the ring as Rock recovers from the chokeslam on the other side. #28 is **'The One' Billy Gunn** who sprints past a bloody Austin, and #29 is reigning WCW Hardcore champion **Meng**, once again known as **Haku** in a big surprise that nobody saw coming, marking the last major talent jump between WCW and the WWF before Vince McMahon bought the entire promotion out just two months later. #30 is the formerly red-hot **Rikishi**, now rendered something close to worthless after his nonsensical "I did it for 'da Rock… I did it… for 'da people!" heel turn in late 2000, and he gets popped in the chops by a resurgent Austin.

Austin dumps Haku and Rikishi surprisingly puts Undertaker out with a superkick before Rock kicks his blubbery ass. Rikishi fires back and goes for a Banzai Drop but Rock belts him in the plums to put him out, leaving the **Final Four**: Rock, Austin, Kane and Gunn.

Austin hurls out Gunn seconds later to little surprise, then locks eyes with Rocky as a fistfight breaks out. Austin avoids a Rock Bottom and lands the Stunner before nailing Kane with a Thesz Press. Rock gets his second wind and lands a Rock Bottom on Austin and tries to eliminate him, as Lawler declares that he's "been waiting years to see this, the Rock and the 'Rattlesnake'!" I think that pretty much confirms that this is the show where the 'King' finally lost his marbles. Kane sneaks up from behind and throws the Rock out for his 11th elimination tonight, a record that stood until Roman Reigns went one better in 2014. Austin whams Kane with a Stunner, three chair shots and a clothesline to put him out and win his record-breaking third Rumble match. Very good Rumble, albeit with just a little bit too much deadwood to really be considered a classic, along with a very anti-climactic finish. Perhaps if the final four had been Austin, Rocky, Undertaker and Kane there may have been more intrigue, but good fun throughout nevertheless.
Final Rating: ***¾

VERDICT

The *Royal Rumble* is a pretty tough show to screw up in many ways. There's a feeling that in wrestling, you should always aim to go out on a high, so as long as the Rumble match delivers, it doesn't really matter if the undercard sucks, it'll still be considered a good show. Here, not only did the Rumble match deliver, but the undercard was pretty damn rockin' too, notable black eye aside. Admittedly the Rumble suffered from a few too many dead spots, and it was hurt somewhat by the fact that it only had two logical winners, Rock or Austin, but on the plus side, it really felt like an unpredictable 50/50 toss-up between those two, which hasn't always been the case in other Rumbles. Very good show throughout, and highly recommended. Just make sure to pass the sickbag when Chyna goes down with her "neck injury".

98

HAKU

NO WAY OUT 2001

CAT NO: WWF268
RUN TIME: 160 minutes (approx)

James Dixon: With a month to go before the historic *WrestleMania X-Seven*, the annual February PPV *No Way Out* is there to set the stage and put all the pieces in place for that event. Going into the show the majority of the title holders were already in place, with Chris Jericho wearing the Intercontinental strap and the Dudleys reigning as WWF Tag Team Champions. Both of those are fine. It is at the top of the card where the WWF wants to do some shuffling around, with the talented but not (yet) significantly marketable Kurt Angle the current WWF Champion going against The Rock. Steve Austin had won the *Royal Rumble* match to earn a title shot at 'Mania, but first there is the small matter of Triple H to deal with, the man credited in storylines for masterminding the hit and run attack on him over a year ago. Tonight they go to war in a new kind of match: Three Stages of Hell.

WWF Hardcore Championship
Raven (c) vs. The Big Show
Jim Ross almost can't help himself sometimes, and erroneously states that Show made his debut two years earlier at *No Way Out '99*, which would be quite a feat what with it being a fictional show. He did debut two years earlier at the February PPV, but it was *St. Valentine's Day Massacre*. There was once a time in 1995-96 where these two guys were both considered among the most important performers in their respective organisations, with Raven tearing up ECW as Heavyweight Champion and Big Show working as simply The Giant over in WCW, where he was their World Champion. Now in the WWF, the place where Vince McMahon promises his famous "opportunities", they are both reduced to hitting each other with bags of popcorn and flimsy trash cans as they bicker over a comedy title. I would regard both as among the biggest individual missed opportunities that have competed in the WWF/E. Raven could have made a real impact if he had debuted as the man who drove the car to run down Austin, or at the very least had a minion do it, and instantly he would have been a headline star. Politics and Scott Levy's previous sins (in Vince's eyes) counted against him. This match is as big a farce as you would imagine, with random, meaningless weapon shots for a couple of minutes, before a popcorn vendor runs in and attempts to win the belt. It turns out to be Crash Holly in disguise, but it takes a good while for the announcers to realise that. Pretty soon the ring fills up with other guys, with division stalwarts Steve Blackman and Hardcore Holly getting involved, before Billy Gunn runs out and hits the Fameasser on Raven and wins the belt. Hardcore and Blackman aren't amused so team up against Gunn, who is then pinned by Raven for a title regaining fall. Raven's random ninja lady (Tori) wanders down to help him out, but she shows a distinct lack of the awareness you would associate with a ninja, and she gets decked from behind by Molly Holly. The ring clears and leaves Show and Raven, then Show hits a chokeslam on to a trash can, which was almost his hardcore division finisher such was the frequency with which he did it. That finally ends a completely useless match, that was literally just weak weapon shots and pinfalls that meant nothing. The hardcore division's day in the sun is well and truly up by now, but it rumbles on for another 18-months yet before finally being unified with the Intercontinental Championship.
Final Rating: ½*

WWF Intercontinental Championship
Chris Jericho (c) vs. Chris Benoit vs. Eddie Guerrero vs. X-Pac
Wow, check out the immense talent in this match. At various points in their careers, all of these guys could make realistic claims of being the best in the world. Unfortunately X-Pac is currently going through a career lull, with the fans rejecting him and just wanting him to go away. His performances since returning from a neck injury have been lacklustre to say the least. The only negative on paper here is the goofy set of rules that accompanies single fall multi man matches like this when a title is on the line, with the champ able to drop the belt without losing. I go on about it frequently, I realise that, but I will continue doing so until lazy promoters stop booking them! Benoit and Guerrero are partners so stick together here and beat on Jericho, with X-Pac getting in on the act too with a spin kick, and getting booed for his Crush-like martial arts poses. Benoit belts him and puts on the Crossface, but Jericho prevents the fall and brawls with Benoit on the outside. Back in the ring Eddie hits the frog splash on Pac to win it, but Jericho is alert to the danger again and stops it. The exchanges

between all four continue to be smooth and pleasingly intense, and a layer of storyline is added when the Benoit/Guerrero relationship breaks down and they start going to town on each other. Chris Jericho then makes the mistake of starting a chop war with Benoit, which is like pissing in a lion's face. Benoit mauls him with chops of his own in response. They are some of the hardest I have ever heard outside of Japan. The stuff between the two for the next couple of minutes is excellent, as it always is when they go toe-to-toe, and Jericho nearly gets the job done with the Walls of Jericho only for Eddie to come in to prevent it but get caught by the still alert Y2J. The same fate befalls X-Pac, but a Justin Credible appearance on the apron is enough to distract Jericho, and Benoit hits him with a sick dragon suplex. Eddie and Benoit go at it again, but the X-Factor duo pull Benoit out of the ring and hit him with a double superkick. Near falls aplenty now, most of them great and others involving X-Pac... Actually that's a little harsh, I am playing that one for pops. Pac has been fine in this. All four guys end up down in the ring and Benoit recovers first and hits the Swandive headbutt on Guerrero, only to be nearly beheaded by an X-Pac spin kick. Chop karma. Unfortunately for Pac, Jericho instantly catches him with a bridged O'Connor roll, and he retains the title. I had a good time watching this, because it didn't stop once, was filled with exciting near falls and there was plenty of intensity on offer. All of those tick my "win" column. It was a little short though, which prevents it from being a true classic.
Final Rating: ***¾

Backstage, Vince McMahon warns WWF commissioner William Regal to "do the ring thing" tonight in the upcoming Stephanie-Trish match. Regal was the one who came up with the idea to do the bout, and now he has to suffer the consequences. Regal is baffled about what to do. Over in WWF New York, Test is asked about the match because of his history with both women, and he says we will find out who the "biggest trash bag ho of the World Wrestling Federation is". Backstage again, Regal catches up with Trish as she is walking to the ring and tries to gleam an insight into her relationship with "good friend" Vince McMahon. She brushes him off because she is focused, and Regal continues to be perplexed by Vince's instructions.

Trish Stratus vs. Stephanie McMahon-Helmsley

Steph comes out with her "game face" on and it is hard not to laugh. She is like a much less intimidating and infinitely less talented Ronda Rousey. The storyline here is based around jealously, with Steph not amused about the Trish-Vince relationship/affair currently occurring. It's not down to taking her mother's feelings into account though, because Steph was a key component in sedating her and "removing" her. The suggestion is, at least to me, that Steph doesn't like being the number two woman in Vince's life, but there are definitely incestuous overtones. Regardless of that, the crowd is very much into this confrontation, though I have no idea who the babyface is here. Steph starts out more aggressively and shows that she has been getting some training when she hits a diving clothesline from the barricade! Her movement and selling are surprisingly good, which she deserves some credit for. She could have quite easily phoned in her in-ring "career", because there would obviously be no repercussions to her sucking, but that's just not the McMahon way. Trish mounts some offence with a bulldog and a well taken DDT and then tries to choke Steph out. This is the total opposite of what you might expect, and pisses all over the majority of "diva" matches that came both before and after. Steph gives Trish the Flair bump off the top and then batters her on the outside, before hurling a jug of water at her. Trish gets annoyed with that and ups her aggression, but gets caught on a rana attempt with a Steph powerbomb. The announcers can barely hide their surprise at how good this is, and then Steph gives everyone a treat by pulling Trish's pants down and spanking her thong covered ass. Yes please. The crowd are well behind Steph now, which is a little strange given what a complete twat her character is and her association with super heel Triple H, but at least they care. Regal makes his way out to interject himself when both end up down, but he can't decide what is best to do and changes his mind a couple of times, before giving up and stomping the ref in the head. Trish takes umbrage and slaps him, so Regal hits his neckbreaker on her and Steph covers for the win. This featured great storytelling and shockingly good execution, and was exciting and engaging for its 8-minute duration. Not a classic in the traditional sense, but one of the best women's matches that the WWF ever did from the Attitude Era onwards.
Final Rating: ***

Backstage, Vince is livid with Regal for not doing the right thing. He puts him in a tag match tomorrow night teaming with Steph against him and Trish. I do so enjoy it when the PPV is used to set up *RAW* matches.

Three Stages of Hell
Triple H vs. Steve Austin

This will be interesting. I remember watching this live and being thoroughly disappointed by it because it was slow and tiring, much like the over hyped Iron Man Match between Hunter and Rock at *Judgment Day 2000*. I later found out that most scribes considered it to be pretty much an all-time classic. I haven't seen it since then, but I am curious to see if my perception of the bout has changed as my attitude towards wrestling has evolved. Backstage, Michael Cole casually asks Austin: "Are you ready to enter Hell, next?" What a moronic question. The stipulations for this are that the match will go three falls (if necessary, though it obviously will be), with each fall different. The first is a straight singles match, the second a street fight and the third a cage match. Austin has been back and active for a couple of months now and his performances have been steadily improving as he gets his timing and wind back, and becomes more confident about his knackered neck and knees. He is hurt by the horrible reworking of his entrance music by Disturbed though, because it definitely reduces his pop.

First Fall (Single Match): They immediately brawl and the crowd comes unglued. The anticipation to them touching for the first time was cleverly built by the WWF introducing a "zero tolerance" policy into the storyline that prevented them from laying a finger on each other until the match lest they be fired. They should do things like that more often. Austin soon takes control by going after the arm and grinds at it for a while, but gets caught coming off the top with a perfectly timed boot to the mush, followed by a swinging neckbreaker. Trips hits another neckbreaker then drops knees on the surgically repaired body part, which is smart psychology because everyone knows that Austin's neck is screwed up. Austin gets back to his feet so Hunter shows why he is the 'Cerebral Assassin' when he hits a chop block to change focus to Austin's other weakness; his knees. Again, the crowd can instantly understand this because of Austin's well publicised track record of knee problems, and the two big stonking knee braces he is wearing offer a visual aid for those slow on the uptake. Trips goes to a figure four and uses the ropes for leverage, but Austin has the strength to pull the pair to the centre of the ring with the hold still applied to prevent the cheating, and then turns it around to reverse the pressure. Trips quickly reaches the ropes and drops an elbow on Austin's neck, continuing to impress me by working like a masterful mat technician. He uses the same blows to the knees, but gets caught by Austin when he procrastinates too long after one of them, and Austin leathers him in the head with his leg repeatedly. Austin hits the Thesz Press and elbow combo, then a clothesline when Hunter blocks the "kick" portion of the Stunner. JR covers for their noticeably loud calling by offering "These two have been talking to each other all match, but we can't repeat what they are saying". They go back-and-forth with near falls from roll ups, and then Austin catches the Stunner out of nowhere to win the first fall and beat Hunter clean. Strange for the babyface to win the first fall actually, but the standard rules and conventions don't always apply when the true big hitters go at it.

Second Fall (Street Fight): Austin has beaten Trips at what was claimed to be his own game in the straight singles bout, and now we go to what is probably more Austin's strength, the street fight, which again makes me wonder a little about the booking. They are seemingly setting Hunter up as the heroic babyface with it, even though he is the super-heel. Austin continues to dominate as the second fall starts, suplexing Hunter on the ramp and decking him with a monitor, before they disappear for a brawl into the crowd. Urgh, I really can't stand crowd brawls. They are lazy shortcuts for guys doing long matches who want to break things up a bit and rest. I understand their purpose and they are good for the live crowd, but not so much when watched back. There is very little variation to any of them so once you have seen one you have seen them all. Thankfully this one is super quick, and we return to the ring where Austin destroys Trips with a chair. He is merciless in leathering him over and over. It is very similar to what he does to Rock next month at *WrestleMania*, only to a very different response of course. That was a heel turn, this time it is justified revenge. Austin looks to escalate things even further when he retrieves a barbed wire covered 2x4 from behind the timekeepers table, but Hunter blocks and decks Austin with it, busting him open. Hunter continues his assault on the outside with a flurry of punches, but Austin reverses a Pedigree through the announce table with a backdrop through the Spanish table. Both guys are down and Austin recovers first, has a swig of beer and then smashes Hunter in the head with the can. The ref tries to pull him off when he is mounting Hunter and pounding him with punches, but Austin pushes him off and yells "get the fuck out of here". Quite right, it is a street fight! Back in the ring Hunter uses a desperation bell shot to the face of a bloody Austin, but it only gets two. A swinging neckbreaker onto a chair follows, as the pace begins to noticeably slow down due to both fatigue selling and actual fatigue. That's no discredit though, because they have gone pretty much all-out for the duration so far. Realising he is in trouble and has to win this fall, Hunter again goes after Austin's neck, then he does the horribly contrived spot where he sets the Pedigree up right by the ropes, which looks so unnatural, and shock of shocks he gets backdropped over the top. Back to the outside again then, and Austin smashes Hunter in the head with a chair to bust him open and then does the same again with the steel steps. A double juicer then, but that is hardly unexpected with the nature of the feud and the stipulations of the bout. Frankly it would have been wrong if they hadn't both bled. They continue to pound at each other and Hunter brings his sledgehammer into play, but Austin blocks it. Back in the ring Austin stomps a mud hole then goes for the Stunner, but Hunter pushes him off and decks him with the sledgehammer. The Pedigree follows and we are level pegging and going to the decisive third fall.

Third Fall: (Steel Cage Match): So it comes down to this, as if there was ever any doubt that it would. Even with the time it takes for the cage to descend, Austin still hasn't recovered from the second fall beating and Trips sends him into the cage, then uses the barbed wire 2x4 to grind his face. Austin counters with a chair, then finds a second wind and returns the favour with the wire. The crowd have been hot throughout the contest, but it is a long, long match and they are tiring, just like the guys in the ring. Because there is a cage around them, they decide to do some extended "cage selling" and now the pace has dropped considerably, and this is where I feel the match loses its way a little. Just because something is really, really long does not necessarily make it great or epic. Sometimes it just makes it boring. The rest of the match has been a triumph, but the cage portion to me is stretching things out just that little bit too far. We have already seen everything they have got, they have done all of their moves, they have hit each other with every weapon, and even the blood is starting to dry up. Triple H hits a Pedigree, but Austin is a megastar so he gets to kick out of it, but it leaves him struggling. Hunter grabs a chair and smashes Austin in the head with it, but Austin counters another Pedigree into a slingshot that sees Trips hit the cage. A tired Stunner from Austin only gets two, which doesn't quite shock the crowd as much as you would think. They both grab weapons, with Trips going for his trusty sledgehammer and Austin the barbed wire 2x4, and they drill each other at the same time, but Hunter lands on Austin and gets the unwitting pin.

It's a very strange piece of booking. Austin was going to *WrestleMania* to wrestle for the WWF Championship (and win), whereas Hunter's next task was putting over the Undertaker on the big show. What did beating Austin here actually achieve? Also, Austin was the babyface hero who lost a year of his career in storylines thanks to a Hunter orchestrated hit and run attack, so shouldn't he have avenged that and come out of this with justice having been served? A post match Stunner and the playing of his crappy new music doesn't exactly save face for him either. If *WrestleMania's* heel turn killed the character as far as him being an anti-hero for the masses, this result a month earlier certainly took some of the shine off him prior to that. The rating for the match is a tough call, because while the first two falls are great and really entertaining with superb psychology and mostly exciting brawling, the third is a chore. I understand that they were tired and that they went 40-minutes in total, but that doesn't make a difference. I am not rating them for their stamina and ability to wrestle for so long, I am rating them for how entertaining it was watching them doing it. The answer is "very", but with the addendum "for the most part", and for me this is definitely not the full boat as some have pegged it. Very, very good, absolutely, but not perfect.
Final Rating: ****½

Jerry Lawler vs. Steven Richards

From that hate-fuelled war of attrition we go to a battle over the right to see Miss Kitty naked. If Lawler wins she can bare all, but if Richards wins then she has to keep those puppies covered and join the RTC. Far more interesting than the five bland minutes on offer here is what happens in the days immediately following the show. Out of the blue, the unpopular Kittie was fired, with the excuse being that creative had nothing for her. Amusing really, what with her being in the middle of a storyline. The truth is that she had a horrible attitude backstage and wasn't well liked at all. Lawler, sticking up for his real life partner, walked out alongside her in protest, meaning he missed the entire crappy invasion angle. He wasn't gone long though, and returned at the back end of the year. In the interim

MISS KITTY

to show her support for Lawler standing by her, the deplorable Stacey 'Kat' Carter cheated on the King and left him. Classy girl. Tazz joins us for commentary here, which would be a sign of things to come in the future, as he ended up as an announcer on television and PPV shows for a number of years, then took up a similar role in TNA after he was released. Richards and Lawler assemble a basic match that doesn't interest anyone, and then they have one of the most disjointed and messy finishing sequences I have ever seen. The problem is Kat, who is out of position and misses her cue. What's supposed to happen is Lawler gets distracted by Ivory, while Kat tries to prevent Richards from taking advantage of that by hitting him with the women's title, only to miss and hit Lawler and cost him the match. A simple finish to a simple match. But no, Kat is so inept that things go horribly wrong. As planned Ivory looks to distract Lawler, and gets hit with a slam for her troubles. Referee Teddy Long spots her and tries to remove her from the ring, but she plays dead and won't be budged, so Lawler tries to assist. It is here that things break down. Lawler spends an age helping Long, as the sight of two fully grown men struggling to get a small woman out of the ring for what seems like forever becomes farcical. Richards tries to improvise by doing the belt shot himself, which Lawler clumsily blocks with a punch because he isn't expecting it, whereas Richards tries to hit him. Richards was on the other side of the ring and unable to communicate his new intentions, especially with the ref distracted and unable to relay information, so the whole thing is a mess to the trained eye. Richards bumps the punch and Lawler goes back to trying to get Ivory out of the ring, as things become even more unintentionally comical. Richards gets back to his feet and holds Lawler from behind in the same way you would if you wanted someone to hit him, only there is no one there to do so. Finally the Kat wakes up and comes charging in with a belt shot, but because of the way Richards is holding Lawler it looks like she is swinging for Jerry. So when she does hit the King, it looks more like a heel turn than an accident, which is what it was supposed to be. What a complete shambles.

Final Rating: -*

Table Match
WWF Tag Team Championship
The Dudley Boyz (c) vs. The Brothers of Destruction vs. Edge & Christian

Here we go again with shitty multi man stipulations in title matches. This time you don't even lose your belts if someone else gets pinned, but rather if they are put through a table. What happened to just having wrestling matches for wrestling titles, with singles belts defended in straight singles matches and tag belts defended in standard tag bouts? It's very hard to shake the feeling that the Undertaker doesn't belong here and was just shoehorned into the match to give him something to do. This would work much better if there hadn't already been a hardcore match and a bloody street fight on the show, but in this era the WWF frequently went with the more is more theory. Right away Taker and Kane dominate, throwing the Dudleys off the ramp and then dominating E&C, and are only slowed when the Duds return with chairs to the skull. Perennial foes the Dudleys and Edge & Christian get some ring time opposite each other while Taker and Kane oversell, and they do some pretty nice stuff, but none of it means anything because it is a tables match so the moves are just moves, there is no purpose to any of them. Bubba ducks a Conchairto and slingshots Edge, who is still holding a chair, into Christian, then the Duds hit the latter with the Wazzup drop. D-Von goes to grab the tables, but does so where Taker and Kane are, and they have recovered now so take him out. Back in the ring, the Brothers of Destruction decide to channel every pretty boy babyface duo from the 80s by hitting moves in unison on Edge & Christian, such as stereo powerslams and flying clotheslines. The BoD bring tables into play for the first time, but the Dudleys recover and fight back. The crowd, smart as ever, chant "we want tables". It's a tables match and there are already tables in the ring, you cretins! The vastly overmatched duos of Edge & Christian and the Dudleys combine to take out the Undertaker and Kane, and then table breaking attempts come into play. There are saves aplenty, and then the BoD decide it is time to dominate again and hit stereo chokeslams on everyone else. You know what works well in a match? Selling. The silliness continues when the BoD go for powerbombs on Edge and Christian through the tables, but instead out come Haku and Rikishi to brawl with the dominant duo to the back. For what purpose? No idea. It didn't lead anywhere, it was just an excuse to get Taker and Kane out of the match. A 3D through a table on Christian from the Duds soon follows, and they retain the titles. I thought this was mostly garbage. Taker and Kane didn't show any weakness whatsoever as they single-handedly tried to ruin the excellent tag team scene, and there was no thread holding anything together, it was just a bunch of stuff that happened and then the Dudleys winning. Completely throwaway.
Final Rating: *½

WWF Championship
Kurt Angle (c) vs. The Rock
Defying standard tradition, champion Kurt Angle is sent out first to really hammer home who the real star is here. Rock is such an overwhelming favourite that JR and Tazz have to try and desperately drum up some credibility for him. He shouldn't need it as WWF Champion, but he has been booked as such a fluke title holder that people don't take him seriously. They cut a furious hammer and tongs pace to begin with, exchanging blows and holds at speed. Angle goes for the ankle lock early, but Rock grabs the ropes to prevent it. Angle remains the aggressor with a brace of overhead belly-to-belly suplexes, but Rock comes back with one of his own. Tazz, a fan of suplexes, approves. A big clothesline from Rock is followed by his horrible, horrible Sharpshooter, but Angle quickly reaches the ropes. Why can no one except the Harts do that move right!? The explosive nature of the bout continues with Rock hitting a Samoan drop and Angle firing back with a back suplex, but he gets crotched on the top and hit with a superplex. They sure are busting out the big moves early. Angle shitcans Rock to buy himself some time, and Rock sells that he injured his leg on the landing to throw an element of doubt into the minds of the fans about who the victor will be. Angle gets too confident though and Rock hits a DDT to leave both guys down, and then Big Show's music hits... How wonderful. Show lumbers down and drills everyone in the ring, referee included, with a chokeslam then wanders off, again to his music. Erm, great, thanks for coming. What an annoying and unneeded interlude. Earl Hebner comes down to replace Mike Chioda as Kurt covers Rock for a visual win, but Earl and another ref, Tim White, are too busy helping Chioda to the back to notice. Earl eventually sees the pin attempt and jumps in, leaving Chioda to fall down in a moment of understated comedy, but Rock kicks out. Rock uses the title belt to try and get a cheap win, but Angle kicks out of that. That was a bit of a dick move from Rocky. Rock remembers his injured leg and stumbles towards Angle but gets caught in the ankle lock. Rock crawls to the ropes but Angle pulls him away and dials up the intensity, slamming Rock's leg into the mat and screaming at him loudly: "Tap out you son of a bitch! I'll break your fucking leg!" Rock reaches the ropes and tries to fight back, and they go back-and-forth before Rock hits a desperation spinebuster. The People's Elbow follows, but Angle kicks out in a very believable near fall that the crowd totally buys. Angle goes low behind the ref's back and he removes a turnbuckle pad, then counters a Rock Bottom attempt with a vicious elbow, before ramming Rock into the steel and hitting the Olympic slam for the... two. What a near fall that was. Everyone bought that as the finish, which is all the more impressive considering Angle was given no chance coming in. Rock rallies and Angle is introduced to the exposed steel, then the Rock Bottom seems to finish but the count is fudged and Angle is adjudged to have kicked out by Hebner. Angle's shoulders didn't move and the crowd knows it, so they loudly boo. What a shame for that to happen at the end of what has been a sensational match. Rock hits another and this time it counts, giving him his sixth WWF Championship reign and setting up a blockbuster match against Steve Austin at *WrestleMania*. This was tremendous from start to finish, ruined only slightly by the unwanted interference from the Big Show, and the really ugly botched count at the end. Don't let that put you off though, this is one of the most high octane main events of the era, and doesn't pause for breath once.
Final Rating: ****½

VERDICT

While there are a few pretty crappy things on here, they are mostly short and irrelevant and thus don't detract from an otherwise tremendous show. Four matches clocking in at over *** is not to be sniffed at, especially when the two biggest bouts on the card both deliver significantly more than that. After a lacklustre end to an otherwise excellent year 2000, the WWF rebounded with a trio of incredible PPVs in the first few months of 2001, and while this is the weakest of the three, it probably would have been a runaway winner of "show of the year" awards any other year. Highly recommended.

89

PERRY SATURN

WRESTLEMANIA X-SEVEN

CAT NO: WWF269
RUN TIME: 225 minutes (approx)

Lee Maughan: From the AstroDome in Houston, Texas. Hosts are Jim Ross and, appearing at a *WrestleMania* for the very first time, Paul Heyman. He was actually planned at various points to be on camera at the next three as there were initial plans to have him debut Brock Lesnar at *WrestleMania X8* (held off until *RAW*), to have him in Kurt Angle's corner at *WrestleMania XIX* (abandoned after he suffered legitimate injuries after taking a series of F5s from Lesnar, and was then demoted as head writer for *SmackDown!*, resulting in the writing off of his on-screen character three weeks before the show), and he was to return as Lesnar's manager for his match with Goldberg at *WrestleMania XX* (with Vince McMahon deciding not use Heyman after Lesnar and Goldberg both announced their intentions to leave WWE following that match). Consequently, Heyman wouldn't make his managerial debut on the show until he walked the aisle with C.M. Punk at *WrestleMania XXIX*, some 12 years after this.

WWF Intercontinental Championship
Chris Jericho (c) vs. William Regal
This match came about because Jericho pissed in the commissioner's teapot, the kind of gripping angle that would next year see Edge and Booker T scrapping over the rights to star in a Japanese shampoo commercial and Undisputed Champion Jericho squaring off with number one contender Triple H not just for the title, but more importantly for custody of Hunter and Stephanie McMahon's English Bulldog Lucy, which Jericho almost killed when he backed over it with a car. In case you couldn't tell, WCW was dead, ECW was dead, and the rot was already setting in. Jericho had also attacked Regal six days prior to this on *RAW* whilst disguised as Doink the Clown, in an angle lifted directly from WCW where La Park had unexpectedly pinned Randy Savage after a Diamond Cutter, only to then unmask as Diamond Dallas Page.

Jericho starts with a pescado, a back elbow off the top and immediately goes for the Walls of Jericho, which Regal counters out of, so Regal fires back by sending Jericho shoulder-first into the post twice and slapping on a wristlock to work the arm. That's actually some nice psychology which is probably lost on most people watching this show back without the context of the TV leading up to it, as it calls back to the previous edition of *SmackDown!* where Regal injured Jericho's shoulder by clobbering it with a fire extinguisher and locking on the Regal Stretch long after the referee had called for the bell.

Jericho tries to come back with a Lionsault but eats knee, so Regal blasts him with a release German suplex and then it's back to working the shoulder over with a series of stiff kicks, and Regal rips the turnbuckle pad off to do more damage in the corner. A student of the Ricky Steamboat school of showing there's still fight left in him yet, Jericho fires back with an enzuigiri and a missile dropkick, but makes the mistake of charging into the corner where shoulder meets steel again, and that allows Regal to hit a tasty butterfly superplex for two. Jericho then tries again for the Walls of Jericho as they pay off all the shoulder work, with Regal simply punching Jericho the arm to counter into the Regal Stretch.

Jericho makes the ropes off that and comes back with chops that turn Regal's chest red raw, so Regal kicks his face off in return. That however leads to Regal going face-first into the turnbuckle he himself exposed, although he lands out of position and Jericho has to throw in a momentum-killing suplex to reposition Regal for the match-ending Lionsault. That little error kind of made the finish look like it came out of nowhere, but while this didn't feel like an obvious choice for an opening match, it offered plenty in the way of action, stiffness and psychology.
Final Rating: ***¼

- Meanwhile, new WCW owner Shane McMahon arrives in a WCW-branded limousine. I think they missed a trick by not having him show up in a mysterious Hummer, but you can't win them all. Much as Shane's WCW would soon come to find out.

The APA & Tazz vs. Right to Censor
Right to Censor tonight are represented by Val Venis, Bull Buchanan and the Goodfather, with Steven Richards taking a pounding from Texas-native Jacqueline at the opening bell. You'd think the babyfaces getting their hands on Richards would be the post-match payoff, but not so. Instead, everyone

gets the chance to jump in, hit a big spot, and jump back out again (Faarooq lands a powerslam, Buchanan does his leg lariat off the top, Tazz hits a Tazzplex, etc) before another brawl breaks out, as JR compares Bradshaw to Dick Murdoch and "Little Stan Hansen". Buchanan powerbombs Bradshaw and Goodfather sets up for the Ho Train (a decidedly babyface-style move that he never gave up doing after going heel for whatever reason, perhaps due to laziness or a limited skillset), but Bradshaw recovers to blast him with the Clothesline from Hell for the pin.

This would have stood as perfectly acceptable blow off to the whole RTC gimmick had the Undertaker not already squashed all four of them in a handicap match on *SmackDown!* (not a complaint necessarily, as Undertaker was far more valuable to this show than the RTC were), and had they not stuck around for another couple of months before the invasion angle rendered them obsolete and rather surplus to requirements, having pretty much outlived their usefulness by then anyway. In fact, the original plan for Right to Censor was to set up a payoff where if they won, the Kat would have to join them, but if they lost they wouldn't be able to oppose her appearing nude in *PlayBoy*, which suggests Jerry Lawler may have been the fourth man on the babyface team here had he not quit in protest of Kat being released in February. The final payoff would have seen the Kat seducing Val and Goodfather back to their good old ways of pornography and prostitution. How she would have seduced Ivory remains unanswered, but I'm sure it would have made a hell of a home video.
Final Rating: **¼

- Elsewhere, Mr. McMahon's daughter, mistress and zonked-out wife plot tonight's strategy. I do love a good old-fashioned family reunion.

WWF Hardcore Championship
Raven (c) vs. Kane vs. The Big Show
"The Big Show has unlimited potential, but you can't make a living off potential, you've gotta get it done" notes JR during the entrances, in an obvious message to Big Show after his return from exile in WWF feeder promotion Ohio Valley Wrestling, where he was sent in 2000 to lose weight only to come back fatter than ever after breaking one of OVW's rings whilst running the ropes and managing to make himself sick from all the exercise.

Raven, ever the comedian, brings a shopping trolley full of plunder with him, including but not limited to a wacky Frankenstein mannequin and a shrub. It doesn't really come into play as all three immediately brawl through the crowd and backstage, where Kane flings Raven through a glass window after Raven had tried to choke him out with a hosepipe. Sadly they miss the obvious gag of squirting each other with it, but they make up for that when Big Show and Kane go crashing through a wall into some poor sod's office. From there, Raven commandeers a golf cart in an attempt to escape, but Big Show jumps on the back of it and Raven ends up crashing into a ditch. Ten years later, he would actually recount the story on his *Raven Effect* video blog:

"They actually came up with a pretty cool spot for me where they threw me through a plate glass window and were actually like "Okay, leave your leather jacket on for the match so you don't hurt" and I'm like "What? Don't be a pussy! I'm not wearing my jacket, just chuck me through it!" Didn't hurt a bit. What a bunch of pussies!

"Then they set up a thing where we were gonna have a chase, where I'm in the golf cart and Big Show's choking me out from behind while I'm driving, and I think what's supposed to happen is Kane's supposed to be driving [another cart] and he's supposed to chase us. And yours truly screwed the whole thing up. Not intentionally I mean, because that would have been like the greatest thing ever, 'cos the Astrodome was a big circle, the track we were on. So we're having this big chase scene and I'm trying to oversell it like Big Show's wrecking up the cart, and I'm trying to skitch back-and-forth, and there's this metal fence so I'm thinking I'll bounce off it, careen off it so it'll look really cool like in the movies. Unfortunately, the fence wasn't connected to the cement we were on, so we careened into it and it just fell off the earth, the two tyres went off the edge on the left side and I was so pissed! I actually tried to get out and pick the cart up to put it back on the track but Big Show was like "No! Just keep going!" but I thought it would have been cool had we put the cart back on track. But then I ran out into the middle of the road anyway and got run over by Kane, so that was pretty cool.

"But here's the interesting part, and this could have made WrestleMania history and could have made me, to some, the greatest man alive, but at the time possibly the greatest jackass of all time. [Where] I ran off the kerb, that's where all the wires were that ran to the show. I ran off the kerb and smashed through all the wires, and if I'd have gone another quarter of a centimetre I would have cut the power to the entire building. Yes, I could have ruined WrestleMania."

It's a shame we never got to see the madcap chase all the way around the Astrodome concourse, but Raven's crash just adds to the complete chaos of it all, before they brawl back out to the entrance stage. Big Show attempts to press slam Raven off the edge but gets a big boot right in the chops from Kane, which sends Show and Raven flying off the side and through a second stage on the floor. Kane follows with a giant flying leg drop off the side of the stage onto a big comfy crash mat (kind of killing the impact a bit) for the pin on Big Show to lift and his first (and only) Hardcore title. Kane would drop the strap to Rhyno a couple of weeks later, who would defend the title against Raven in a very fun match at *Backlash* but in many ways, this was the last big hurrah for the title as it was known, the mix of plunder and comedy jettisoned later in the year in order to reposition the belt as a vehicle for Rob Van Dam to do his ECW style matches, free from the confines of WWE's rigid rule structure.
Final Rating: ***

- Backstage, a stoic Kurt Angle rewatches videotape of himself tapping out to Chris Benoit's crossface, denying that it counted because there wasn't an official referee present to call it.

- Meanwhile, the Rock arrives to the show fashionably late. Who does he think he is? Bret Hart?

WWF European Championship
Test (c) vs. Eddie Guerrero
Eddie has Perry Saturn with him, sporting the most absurd furry top hat you've ever clapped your goggles on. Test shows off his strength advantage early, blocking a huracanrana from the top after landing a powerbomb, but sadly he also shows off his eternal goofiness, getting his foot caught between the top and middle ropes. Fortunately, the Radicalz are experienced enough to cover for it as Eddie uses it to stand on his bollocks before deciding to improvise and work over his leg. Really, he's lucky he wasn't in there with Vader, else he might have lost a

toe!

Test fights back with more power stuff, namely a tilt-a-whirl slam and a rotation powerbomb, but a blind charge leads to Eddie going low again, and with the referee distracted, Saturn slides in and hits the world famous Moss-Covered Three-Handled Family Gredunza, an awesome twisting fisherman buster that actually got its name from a skit Chris Jericho did on WCW *Monday Nitro* in 1998, where he declared himself "the man of 1,004 holds" (in reference to his then-nemesis Dean Malenko) before listing a variety of mundane arm drags, armbars and ridiculous made-up moves like the "Saskatchewan spinning nerve hold", the "shooting star staple superplex", the "Jericho screwdriver" and the "super blizzard." Saturn and Malenko both found the bit so amusing, they actually decided to invent a new move and name it after the most outrageously named one of them all, the aforementioned Moss-Covered Three-Handled Family Gredunza, the name of which was actually inspired by Dr. Seuss' children's book (and animated adaptation) *The Cat in the Hat*.

Eddie misses with the frog splash in his follow-up and Test gets a Niagara driver for two but opts to blast Guerrero and Saturn both with big boots, allowing Malenko to run for the distraction, and Eddie blasts Test with the title belt to pick up his second European Title. For some reason ("some reason" being his height), the WWF had a lot of faith in Test (at least until he blew it at the level they had him pegged for once too often), whereas Guerrero was actually the one who boasted all the charisma and the in-ring ability. This was a decidedly average match however.
Final Rating: **

Kurt Angle vs. Chris Benoit
They take to the mat early, trading holds and counter-holds amateur style, which Benoit eventually gets the best of as he goes for the Crippler Crossface, forcing Angle to go to the ropes to break the hold. Angle bails on another Crossface attempt and goes to the ropes again on a third, until he decides enough's enough and blindsides Benoit with a stiff forearm to take over. That turns it into a more WWF-style match with Angle sending Benoit into the steel steps and landing a snap suplex for two before a chop battle breaks out in the corner. "They wrestle, they brawl, they do it all!" declares Heyman, referencing an early ECW catchphrase.

They start breaking out more suplexes, Angle with two belly-to-bellys and Benoit with a Dynamite Kid-like snap suplex, a superplex and rolling Germans. Angles reverses into an ankle lock attempt but Benoit counters into one of his own, and a frustrated Angle gets caught in another Crossface but manages to reverse that and put the hold on Benoit instead, who makes the ropes. From there, the referee gets bumped as Benoit gets his fifth Crossface of the match, with Angle tapping out but nobody to call it. Angle comes back with the Angle Slam but Benoit gets the knees up on a moonsault and hits a diving headbutt for two. A desperate Angle then tries to go low, which leads to another mat-based reversal sequence, with Angle cradling Benoit and hooking the tights for the pin.

Some won't like that finish because they slowly build the match away from the technical wrestling and into a brawl, only to go back to the technical finish that makes it feel somewhat tacked on, but it does make sense in the context of them constantly trying to one-up each other with their holds. Others might not take to the ending feeling "cheap" but in fairness to the WWF, the whole point was to build to rematches between the two, and indeed, they followed up with an "Ultimate Submission match" the following month at *Backlash*, and with a pair of Best 2-out-of-3 falls matches at UK-only pay-per-view *Insurrextion* and *Judgment Day*. Not a classic by any means, especially as the mat wrestling didn't play so well to the stadium crowd, but if you're into slow building technical stuff, this is a worth a look.
Final Rating: ***¾

WWF Women's Championship
Ivory (c) vs. Chyna
The angle here is that Chyna posed for *PlayBoy* in late 2000, which Right to Censor took exception to, so Ivory broke Chyna's neck (although it was actually Val Venis who delivered the piledriver that did the damage) leading to Chyna vengefully going after Ivory's title. Interestingly, their angle at the 2001 *Royal Rumble* where Chyna re-injured her neck is completely ignored here, as it should be given the WWF's distasteful way of playing it up like a legitimate, career-ending injury in the same tone they used to announce the very real tragedy of the death of Owen Hart.

The upshot of all this is that Chyna "can't sue" anybody if she injures her neck again, but in return, Right to Censor are barred from ringside, making the outcome completely inevitable. JR describes Ivory's look as "Lilith Sternin"-like, and suggests renaming Chyna's clotheslines - "Maybe we could call that a "Chyna-line"... or maybe not." "Let's stick with "maybe not!"" replies Heyman. Chyna beats Ivory around like a ragdoll for a couple of minutes, destroys her with a powerbomb, pulls her up, and finishes her off for real with a Gorilla press. Problematically, since Chyna had been mixing it up with the male roster prior to this and had also held the Intercontinental Title, it was very difficult for fans to believe there was anybody on the Diva's roster who could actually beat her, and in fact, a contract dispute (or a firing, depending on who you choose to believe) resulted in her vacating/being stripped of the title without ever losing it. Still, at least this match was exactly as short as it needed to be.
Final Rating: *¼

Street Fight
Shane McMahon vs. Mr. McMahon
This one came about after Vince demanded a divorce from his wife Linda then drugged her all the way into constant catatonic sedation (the role she was undoubtedly born to play as her horrendously wooden acting actually fit the part perfectly) and began having it away with blonde bombshell Trish Stratus. This led to Vince's daughter Stephanie McMahon-Helmsley accusing Trish of being a homewrecker, leading to a match between the two at *No Way Out*. Stephanie won that match after Vince told Commissioner Regal to "do the right thing" and he chose the product of Vince's loins over his bit on the side. The next night on *RAW*, Vince called Trish his "little toy" and publicly dumped her before Stephanie poured slop all over her, and the following week she was made to earn Vince's forgiveness by striping down to her underwear and crawling around on her hands and knees, barking like a dog in a segment that was cut from broadcasts in the UK and Canada on grounds of taste and decency. Vince's son Shane naturally took exception to his old man behaving in this manner, so bought WCW six days before *WrestleMania* just to spite him, then announced Mick Foley (who Vince had fired as WWF commissioner in late 2000) as the special guest referee. So just a good old-fashioned pro 'rasslin angle then.

Shane gives a pre-match shout-out to his WCW squad up in a plush skybox: Lance Storm, Mike Awesome, Stacy Keibler,

Sean O'Haire, Chuck Palumbo, Johnny the Bull, Bill DeMott, Chavo Guerrero, Jr., Shawn Stasiak and John Laurinaitis. That's quite the crew Shane has bought himself there. He may as well have just stuck with the Mean Street Posse for all the good WCW did him. At least they wouldn't have cost him several million bucks. And what a way to introduce WCW on the biggest show of the year with a far away camera shot and an on-screen graphic identifying them as "WCW wrestlers". You'd think they could at least have figured out an angle for them... which may have been the original plan. Lance Storm picks up the story in a column at his StormWrestling.com website:

"The box seats were awesome [and] we had a small buffet of food and drink set up for us, as well as monitors and great seats... If memory serves, we got the call that we would be going only a couple of days before the event, and flew in [on] Sunday morning, I believe in hopes of keeping as low a profile as possible.

They flew us in, put us up in a different hotel [than the WWF talent] and had a bus booked to sneak us in the back door of the arena. We were even brought over a little bit late in hopes that all the fans would be in their seats and no-one would see us. Unfortunately, all these efforts to keep our WrestleMania appearance a secret were for nought because Shawn Stasiak did a radio or internet interview the day before and stooged the whole thing off. The office were furious, and many of us speculated that it might cost him his job. I was even told at one point the plan was to have us do a run-in on the Vince vs. Shane match, but Vince was so mad word had leaked that he killed the angle and almost sent us all home. Thankfully we got to stay and watch the show."

Vince is wearing a t-shirt underneath a workout sweater here, which I presume to mean that between buying WCW (for real), dealing with the faltering XFL and promoting a *WrestleMania*, he simply hasn't had enough time to get in the gym and buff himself up to the levels he was at for his matches in early 1999 and would again reach for his bout with Ric Flair at the 2002 *Royal Rumble*. Then again, he could also be wearing the shirt for protection from the barrage of kendo stick shots he suffers at the hands of Shane, the younger McMahon also getting in a spear, a series of elbow strikes and a baseball slide to the outside before working in his requisite big bump; driving himself though the Spanish announce table after missing a flying elbow from the middle rope.

From there, the soap opera kicks in as Trish wheels a comatose Linda to ringside, only to turn on Vince with a thunderous slap, not only asserting herself as an independent, free-thinking woman, but also turning herself babyface in the process. Angered by the betrayal, Stephanie jumps in for a catfight which Trish wins, and they fight all the way up the ramp as Foley tries to get Linda out of harm's way, only to get blasted atop the skull with a steel chair from Vince. Ever the sadomasochist, Vince decides to sit Linda up in the corner of the ring so she can watch him beat Shane into oblivion with an unsettling series of trash can shots to the head, but she suddenly rises from her zombified state (to an enormous reaction it must be noted) and kicks Vince right in the plums for her ultimate act of revenge. That's followed by Foley, who beats Vince senseless with a series of forearms to give him closure on all the previous wrongs he had inflicted upon him, and then Shane ends it with a match-topping coast-to-coast dropkick from one corner of the ring into a trash can-wielding Vince on the other.

Whilst some wrestling "purists" may see flaws with what they could consider as "overbooking" in this match, I don't think anybody could have reasonably expected the bout to be even half as good as it was considering the status of the principal participants as non-wrestlers, along with the age of McMahon the elder. Some may also argue that the bout loses points owing to the lack of context when viewed years removed from all of its build and surrounding angles, but wrestling has always been about delivering what the fans in a particular moment want and this delivered to them all sorts of turns, swerves and payoffs to months of angles, neatly bookended by two big bumps from Shane.

Did they mask the lack of actual wrestling with a bunch of shortcuts, like having Mick Foley work a portion of the match and diverting all the attention for Trish and Stephanie's confrontation? Sure. Was it a tawdry angle leading up to the match? Undoubtedly so. Was it a wildly entertaining goofball brawl fit for a stadium crowd? You'd better believe it, and while your mileage may vary in terms of any emotional connection to the action, for my money this remains a highly entertaining slice of the WWF's brand of sports entertainment silliness.
Final Rating: ***¾

- Yesterday at WWF Fan Axxess, Kevin Kelly met up with the Hardy Boyz during an autograph session. Matt's comments about their feud with the Edge & Christian and the Dudley Boyz that "This has been a two-year culmination and it's gonna end tomorrow. It has to" would prove stunningly naive in hindsight.

TLC Match
WWF Tag Team Championship
The Dudley Boyz (c) vs. Edge & Christian vs. The Hardy Boyz
Things follow the same basic formula here as with the previous TLC match from *SummerSlam 2000*, with the teams brawling to start and trading double teams early to make space in the ring before they bring in the gimmicks. Like the first meeting, the highspots also build progressively, as well they should. The first attempt at scaling the ladders, Edge gets pulled down by Matt, the second sees Edge clothesline Matt off in retaliation, and the third sees Jeff dropkick Edge off on his second climb. See how they start small, then every bump gets progressively bigger? Not only that, but the early bumps are all defensive, before they build to using the ladders for offense, Matt with a flying legdrop off one and the Dudleys with a Wazzup Drop off another. Similarly, they take their time before bringing the tables into play, with Bubba Ray powerbombing Jeff onto Edge through one in a great spot.

Also similar to the *SummerSlam* bout is Bubba stacking up four tables together on the outside for later use, but getting cut off, meaning they're in place for a key spot later on but it never feels anything less than completely organic, like it was set up intentionally, making for a spectacular payoff when they do finally come into play. Meanwhile, all six guys climb up three ladders in the ring and take bumps off them together, with Christian take a particularly nasty-looking spill over the top to the outside, which heralds the main variation between this match and *SummerSlam*, namely run-ins from each team's associates. Spike Dudley is up first, dropping Edge & Christian with a double Acid Drop, followed by Rhyno wiping out the Dudleys and the Hardys with Gores. Lita is of course the topper here, blasting Rhyno with a huracanrana before whipping off her top like Brandi Chastain at the 1999 Women's World Cup, only to eat a 3D from the Dudleys immediately after. Wrote Lita in her excessively titled 2004 autobiography *Lita: A Less Travelled R.O.A.D. - The Reality of Amy Dumas*:

"Before the match there was some debate over the order of the run-ins - some people wanted Rhyno to come out last because he was going to do the most damage, but Matt argued that my coming out last would provoke the biggest reaction. I didn't get involved in the discussions. I just sat there. "Tell me when you want me to come out," I said, "and what you want me to do, and that's what I'll do." It was decided that I'd be the third and final run-in. Matt was absolutely right - when I came down to the ring, I got one of the biggest pops of the night, which was very exciting.

Because of the size of the stadium, the WrestleMania ramp was super long. I didn't want to leave anyone hanging, so when the time came for me to hit the ring, I had to haul ass all the way. Edge was on the ladder, going for the belts, so I quickly slid into the ring and pulled him down. Watching the show later, J.R.'s commentary was inadvertently hilarious, "There's Lita, jerking Edge off the ladder."

Rhyno caught me right as I jerked Edge off. He was about to gorilla press me, but Spike came up behind him and hit him with a nut shot. I gave Rhyno a huracanrana then grabbed a chair and smashed it over Spike's head. I gave that chair shot everything I had. As a rule, girls give crappy-looking chair shots and I was determined to make mine count. I whacked Spike good - you could see the shape of his head in the way the chair was bent. I was really happy with the shot, but at the same time, I felt kind of bad. "Poor Spike" I thought, "I wouldn't want a chair bent over my head!" After the chair shot, I was on fire! I tore off my hot pink top and turned around to find the Dudleys, who got me with a 3D. That was it - I was done. No-one gets up from the 3D. Just ask Bubba."

After that, they ramp up the insanity with Jeff taking out Spike and Rhyno with a Swanton Bomb from a gigantic ladder through a table on the outside in a brutal spot, then he follows that by attempting to walk across three ladders in the ring like stepping stones to the belts. Sadly, the ladders heel on him and refuse to cooperate, ruining the spot. So there you go, Jeff Hardy is the guilty party for this not being a five star match. Points for effort though, as that would have been an awesomely creative spot and the ladder going off balance was just very unfortunate and not really his fault. He makes up for it with his next spot however, as he goes back up and hangs on to the belts, only for Bubba to pull his balancing ladder away (almost causing him to get ankles caught in the rungs, something which always makes me wince no matter how many times I watch this match knowing he avoided disaster) as Edge gives him a supersized spear off the top rope. Utterly bonkers.

Next, Bubba and Matt both climb opposite sides of the ladder, only for Rhyno to tip it over, sending the pair crashing through the four tables on the outside, a spot that was already dangerous enough when Bubba took the same bump by himself at *SummerSlam*. That leaves D-Von alone but Edge

EVIL EYE: GIMMICK BATTLE ROYAL

Let's see what everyone was doing between their last regular WWF run and this match: **The Bushwhackers** left the WWF in September 1996, astonishingly just a year before the onset of the Attitude Era. They worked some notable independents (sometimes billed as the Sheepherders, their old gimmick) as well as ECW, and had a stinker on legendarily bad PPV Heroes of Wrestling against **The Iron Sheik** and **Nikolai Volkoff**. Sheik ended his third run with the WWF (as The Sultan's manager) in 1997 after failing a drugs test. As well as the HOW debacle he also made infrequent appearances on indies, whereas Volkoff left in 1995 after a horrific run with the Million Dollar Corporation, and went into semi-retirement. **Duke Droese** left the WWF in 1996 citing burnout from the schedule, then did some shots from ECWA in Austria and future WWE feeder FCW out of Florida, where he as their Heavyweight Champion. **Earthquake** last competed as under the natural disaster gimmick in 1994 before joining Hulk Hogan and company in WCW, going through a series of ineffectual gimmicks (including 'The Shark') before returning to the WWF in 1998 as Oddities member Golga. His WWF tag partner Fred Ottman, today working as **Tugboat** left the WWF for a final time in 1994 after a brief second run following the WCW Shockmaster debacle, notable working Japan for WAR in some *very* curiously booked matches. **Brother Love, Jim Cornette, Hillbilly Jim, Michael Hayes, Kim Chee** and **Sgt. Slaughter** all worked for the WWF in some capacity behind the scenes anyway and dusted off the gimmicks as a one-off for his match. The **Doink the Clown** character appeared infrequently in the WWF and on various indies over the years, with a number of different guys playing the role. **The Goon** worked the indies under his more successful gimmick (and real name) 'Wild' Bill Irwin, having left the WWF in 1996 after just a few months with the company. Hector Guerrero, the man behind the **Gobbledy Gooker** gimmick bended bones for Smoky Mountain Wrestling, ECW and WCW following the welcome demise of the character in 1990. **Kamala** departed the WWF in 1993 and briefly left the business, before turning up in WCW as part of the Dungeon of Doom, as well as being a regular in the Memphis territory. **One Man Gang** also had a brief WCW run after leaving the WWF in 1990, holding the U.S. Title in 1995. He did a few shots for ECW too. **Repo Man** had a few spells in WCW too as Blacktop Bully and then under a golf gimmick!

holds on to him as Rhyno climbs the ladder with Christian on his shoulders, who grabs the belts to give him and Edge the win, their third straight in triple threat ladder/TLC matches, and their seventh (and sadly final) WWF Tag Team Title reign.

Before settling down to write this particular review, I conducted a straw poll of sorts asking readers of our books which of the first two TLC matches they preferred, and most selected the second one as their favourite. In truth, I also fell into that category but watching both back-to-back, I think that comes down to the fact this one played on a *WrestleMania* stage to a stadium-sized crowd, making it the more memorable and widely-viewed of the two, but objectively, I think the *SummerSlam* scrap takes it by a hair. The vastness of the Astrodome causes the audience reaction to feel delayed as the sound waves travel around the giant building (something many wrestlers believe is one of the negatives with working stadium shows), meaning the crowd reactions at *SummerSlam* feel bigger, despite that crowd being less than a third of the size of this one. I also think the first meeting has some slightly nuttier spots (namely Matt's back bump off a ladder, over the topes and through a table on the floor), and everything in the first match is hit to perfection, whereas Jeff misses his tightrope-like walk here, the only gaping flaw in the performance. Don't be mistaken though, this is still very much a five star effort from all concerned.

Final Rating: ****¾

Gimmick Battle Royal
Much like the "thong Stinkface match" at last year's *SummerSlam*, this is the buffer match after all the nutty highspots. To be fair, the only thing that could have topped those three teams in TLC would have been Captain Lance Murdock himself jumping over a tank filled with man-eating great white sharks, deadly electric eels, ravenous piranha, bone-crushing alligators, and perhaps most frightening of all, the King of the Jungle, one ferocious lion! Still, this is as good a second choice as any.

As a special surprise, 'Mean' Gene Okerlund and Bobby Heenan are the special guest commentators here, fresh from their runs in WCW (with scuttlebutt suggesting that Heenan was very disappointed not to get a job with the WWF after this), and your participants, in introductory order are: **The Bushwhackers** (without their camouflage pants to perhaps avoid a clash with the Dudleys' uniforms, ironic given that the Bushwhackers were introduced to ECW in 1998 in Dudley Boyz-inspired tie-dye for an angle with Tommy Dreamer and the Sandman), **Duke 'the Dumpster' Droese**, **The Iron Sheik** ("By the time the Iron Sheik gets to the ring it'll be *WrestleMania 38*!" jests Heenan, with Okerlund dryly commenting that he "moves like Carl Lewis"), **Earthquake** (who, out of WCW habits, Okerlund accidentally calls "John Tenta"), the **Goon** ("How would you like your kid to grow up and be called the 'Goon'?" asks Heenan, making reference to Okerlund's son Todd, a former right winger with the Springfield Falcons of the AHL, the New York Islanders of the NHL, and member of the 1988 United States Olympic hockey team), **Doink the Clown** (played here by Matt Borne and drawing a huge pop), **Kamala** along with Harvey Wippleman (the former Women's Champion, who elects to manage here rather than wrestle) and **Kim Chee** (Steve Lombardi, depriving the world of a Brooklyn Brawler appearance in a main card *WrestleMania* match), **Repo Man** ("About four years ago he got my mother-in-law!" jokes Okerlund. "About five years ago, everybody got your mother-in-law!" replies Heenan, quick as a flash), **James E. Cornette** ("The E. stands for 'Extra Effort'"), **Nikolai Volkoff** (bizarrely coming out to the Finnish national anthem, and who Heenan refers to as the "first Russian cosmonaut", no doubt unintentionally referencing the *Hulk Hogan's Rock 'N' Wrestling* episode *The Wrong Stuff* in which Nikolai is selected to go into space alongside the 'Hulkster'), **Michael P.S. Hayes** ("The man that taught Michael Jackson how to do the Moonwalk" and former World Class Championship Wrestling main eventer getting a fine welcome from the Texas audience as the classic '*Bad Street USA*' plays him to the ring), the **One Man Gang** (apparently having lost so much weight over the years that he was actually too small to fit into his more famous Akeem attire here), the **Gobbledy Gooker** (this marking the Gooker's only official match in WWF history with Héctor Guerrero sporting a much different costume than the one he wore back in 1990, his name tragically misspelt as 'Gobbly Gooker' on his on-screen graphic), History of Wrestling favourite **Tugboat**, **Hillbilly Jim** ("Living proof right there that Uncle Elmer had children"), and **Sgt. Slaughter**, whose entrance comes complete with a video package showing him firing a machine gun ("That was then, now he shoots blanks!").

Given the advancing years of many of the participants, there's even less to the match than usual for a battle royal. Jim Cornette actually told us a very funny story about how he and Bruce Prichard (**Brother Love**) intended to collect their *WrestleMania* payoff by standing in the corner out of harm's way, only for Prichard to immediately (accidentally) smack him in the eye. The eliminations come thick and fast (with Doink's elimination receiving a hearty round of boos from the audience), leaving a **final four** of Love, Slaughter (both long-time agents), Hillbilly (who for years did many personal appearances and on-sale dates for *WrestleMania* and the WWF in general), and Sheik. Love is the first to go, with Hillbilly dumping Slaughter from behind, and Sheik dumping Hillbilly in the same manner to win it, a result dictated by the fact Sheik was too fragile to take a bump over the top rope. Slaughter, whose weight often yo-yoed throughout his career and looking like a hot air balloon decorate in camouflage here, gets revenge for the good old US of A by slapping Sheik in the Cobra Clutch, despite nothing to complain about having been eliminated quite fairly by Hillbilly. I guess he was just getting himself some payback for the dissolution of the Triangle of Terror back in '91.

I don't really feel comfortable attaching any kind of rating to this because it was just a five minute diversion from the big matches, was all about seeing the old timers and hearing the entrance music anyway, played perfectly to the nostalgia crowd, and never outstayed its welcome. A fun little segment, as bad as the action inevitably was, but then it never promised any great wrestling to begin with.

The Undertaker vs. Triple H
Believe it or not, there was actually a time when the Undertaker had to call out his opponents for *WrestleMania*, and this is that time as Triple H had been bragging about beating every top guy on the roster until the 'Dead Man' let him know what a load of hot nonsense that was. Triple H initially refused the challenge, with Undertaker threatening physical violence against Hunter's wife Stephanie in order to get his way. What a petulant little child! Hunter's response was to destroy one of Undertaker's motorcycles with his trusty sledgehammer in one of those wrestling angles nobody outside of greasy chopper enthusiasts could ever care about ("Oh no! How will that poor multi-millionaire ever replace such a small element of the vast collection of crotch rockets we're continually told he owns?!").

Motörhead play Triple H to the ring, which is undeniably cool but rather out of place for a heel. It's just a shame they didn't have Limp Bizkit to play Undertaker to the ring until next year, because his entrance feels a little flat coming after a kickass live performance. JR claims this is the first time these two have met on pay-per-view, but it's actually the fourth: Undertaker, Henry Godwinn, Fatu & Savio Vega vs. Hunter Hearst Helmsley, King Mabel, Jerry Lawler & Dr. Isaac Yankem, DDS. (*Survivor Series, November 1995*); Steve Austin vs. Triple H vs. Undertaker (*No Mercy, May 1999*); Rock, Undertaker & Kane vs. Triple H, Mr. McMahon & Shane McMahon (*King of the Ring, June 2000*); and Triple H vs. Undertaker vs. Kurt Angle vs. Steve Austin vs. Rock vs. Rikishi (*Hell in a Cell match, Armageddon, December 2000*).

The match is your good old-fashioned brawl, with the replacement Spanish announce table rather amusingly getting destroyed, and Undertaker going for the old school ropewalk early only for Hunter to pull him off. They trade some big moves early too as Triple H hits two neckbreakers and a facecrusher, but referee Mike Chioda won't let him use his sledgehammer, allowing Undertaker enough time to block a Pedigree (bumping Chioda) and hit a chokeslam. Choida's count is of course slow after his spill, so Undertaker kicks him in the head and blasts him with an elbow, a thoroughly baffling move for a babyface. Triple H takes a pair of big bumps over the top to the floor and into the crowd, where they brawl over the hard camera rig and sound mixing area, a part of the set-up at televised wrestling shows you rarely ever see. That makes it a pretty unique place for them to slug it out, Triple H battering Undertaker with a series of full-on chair shots. Undertaker's response is another chokeslam, this time off the scaffolding. The replay manages to show the crash mat, rather lessening the impact of the spot, but the live crowd who didn't see it go nuts. Undertaker follows that up with an elbow from the scaffold, and then he beats up a group of EMTs. Man, what a total dick move that is! What did they ever do wrong?!

Back to the ring where one of the biggest flaws of the match becomes apparent, as Chioda is somehow still unconscious. You mean to tell me those EMTs were on the scene mere seconds after Triple H took that devastating chokeslam onto a piece of foam padding, but nobody stopped to say "Damn, that referee's been out cold for five minutes, and just from an elbow to the head and neck... Jeez, I hope he hasn't stopped breathing..."? Couldn't Undertaker at least have given him a Tombstone to have him down for that amount of time? I know they needed him to get wiped out so they could justify fighting through the crowd, but I find it entirely unrealistic that he wouldn't have revived by now, or that another referee wouldn't have come out to replace him.

Triple H lands a low blow then goes for a Tombstone, but Undertaker reverses it to one of his own. Reviving the referee (finally) he goes for a Last Ride, but Hunter bonks him on the head with the sledgehammer in an awesome spot that really should have been used a finish somewhere, but only gets two. Undertaker at least bleeds off that but Triple H makes the mistake of going for punches in the corner, and that's the opening Undertaker needs to get the Last Ride for the pin to go 9-0 at *WrestleMania*. Incidentally, this show is actually the first time his unbeaten record was seriously brought up, although it wasn't a major part of the storyline, more just a factoid thrown out by JR. Oddly enough, he was originally booked to *lose* this match as part of the ongoing superpush of Triple H, and the match was supposed to feature Shawn Michaels as the special guest referee with him costing Undertaker the match to set up his grand return to the promotion, only for Shawn to show up at *RAW* six nights earlier in the old "no condition to perform." Recalling the state of Michaels that night in his 2011 autobiography *Undisputed: How to Become World Champion in 1,372 Easy Steps*, Chris Jericho wrote:

"*I had just applied the intricate [Doink the] clown makeup and was waiting to do my run-in* (on William Regal) *when Shawn Michaels walked past me, gave a double take, and walked back.*

Shawn was one of my all-time favourites, and (along with Owen Hart and Ricky Steamboat) was my main inspiration to get into the wrestling business. I came to the WWE with the hope of working with him even though he was only with the company part-time at that point and still battling the demons that were holding him back in his life.

Shawn got in my clown face and gave me a Larry David-esque suspicious stare, and I noticed he was pretty wasted.

"What's going on, Chris?" he said, his eyelids drooping and his speech slurring. "Are you doing the Doink gimmick now?"

"No, I'm just doing it for tonight. I'm ambushing Regal."

"So you're gonna be Doink now?"

"No, no. I'm just doing it for one night as a way to surprise Regal."

"But why do you have to be Doink?" he asked again, slowly swaying back-and-forth.

"But I'm not Doink, Shawn, it's just for tonight."

"But why would they make you Doink?"

I felt like Abbott and Costello, except instead of Who's on First, the routine was Who's on Drugs, and it wasn't me.

"I'm NOT Doink. It's just an angle for tonight."

Shawn shook his head and waltzed away. "I don't like it, they should never have made you Doink."

He passed out in Vince's office later that night and was fired. Shawn eventually cleaned himself up and came back to WWE better than ever a few years later. When he did, I finally go to the chance to work with him and had one of the best matches of my career."

Anyway, this was a really good match for the most part as they made the absolute most out of what little they did (something they'd also do to even greater dramatic effect ten years later in their No Holds Barred match at *WrestleMania XXVII* when Undertaker's streak really was a big deal), but it did have a huge flaw in the ridiculous situation with the unconscious referee.
Final Rating: ***¾

- Meanwhile, Steve Austin is in the zone before his WWF Title match, staring a hole through himself in a mirror. Whilst the WWF production crew there probably just figured that made for a really cool-looking shot, there's actually a great deal of symbolism in Austin looking at a mirror image of himself, given what's about to go down.

No Disqualification Match
WWF Championship
The Rock (c) vs. Steve Austin
To recap, Austin won the *Royal Rumble* to become the number one contender to the title, while Rock beat Kurt Angle to become the champion. That's really all you need. Of course, the WWF writers just couldn't help themselves and added Austin's wife Debra as Rock's manager, really diluting the whole build until everyone realised how stupid that was and subsequently pretended it never happened, with Austin verbally writing her out of the storyline during a sit-down interview between he and the Rock. Austin's lines "I need to beat you, Rock. I need it more than anything you could ever imagine" would prove very prophetic.

Prior to the bout, Howard Finkel suspiciously announces that this is now a no disqualification match. Why would soon become apparent. As expected, they immediately begin brawling (foregoing what would have been a truly epic staredown) and start teasing Rock Bottoms and Stone Cold Stunners before Rock gets busted open on the outside. Austin, already working like a heel, goes after the cut, but Rocky's comeback is met with an overwhelming chorus of boos, which should have sent up a red flag that the direction this match is about to go in is the wrong one entirely. Rock's response is to deck Austin with the ring bell, allowing Austin to get colour of his own. Blading is such a double-edged sword to me because on one hand, I'm really not into the whole self-mutilation thing, but damned if the double juice doesn't add to the drama of it all.

An Austin Stunner attempt is blocked by the Rock and turned into a Sharpshooter, with Austin bleeding buckets a'la *WrestleMania 13*. A minor fault here, as Austin makes the ropes so referee Earl Hebner makes Rock break the hold. Why? It's no disqualification, what can he do about it? And then they repeat the spot, but with Austin applying the hold. From there, Austin really digs deep into the playbook and breaks out the Million Dollar Dream, allowing JR to reference Ted DiBiase. With the deeply religious DiBiase crusading against the WWF for their bad language and sexual content, he'd become persona non grata by the time Austin broke the hold out later in the year at *SummerSlam* against Kurt Angle, where JR made sure to reference it as a Cobra Clutch. They call back to *Survivor Series* '96 with Rock walling up the turnbuckles to roll through (a spot that in turn called back to *WrestleMania VIII*), but Austin kicks out.

A Stunner from the Rock gets two, and that's the cue for Mr. McMahon to hit the ring, as the major storyline for the year (or at least as was the plan) kicks in. Austin gets visibly frustrated at a two count from a spinebuster, allowing Rock to counter with one of his own and hit the People's Elbow, only for McMahon to break up the pin attempt, completely confusing the crowd. Rock naturally gives chase but runs into a Rock Bottom from Austin, but again he only gets two. Hebner then gets bumped which allows Austin to go low, and then Austin calls for a chair from Vince, which the crowd have absolutely no idea how to react to. Vince's chair shot on the Rock still only gets two, and Rock stays alive with a Rock Bottom on Austin but makes the mistake of going after Vince for a second time. That leads to a Stunner from Austin for a heart-stopping nearfall, so he blasts Rock with the chair himself but *still* can't put him down for three. "What's keepin' that montherfucker alive!?" he asks, before destroying Rock with a series of brutal chair shots as the crowd seem to be getting the idea of the heel turn... before realising that's not what they want at all, and giving an overwhelming babyface reaction to Austin when he *finally* pins Rock to regain the WWF title after 18 long months.

Austin and Vince share a beer to celebrate the victory and cement the heel turn, but the crowd don't care about that and cheer wildly despite the rather symbolic ending of the Attitude Era as they senselessly cut the balls off the one character the audience loved above all other. In later years, Austin admitted he was wrong to leave so much money on the table in his determination to play a heel character, regretting that he didn't just call an audible and drop Vince with a Stunner right there and then. Still, this was a superbly dramatic stadium-sized main event, even if it was coupled with arguably the dumbest heel turn in wrestling history.

Final Rating: ****¾

VERDICT

Over the course of compiling *The Complete WWF Video Guide* series, one subject that has cropped up continually is the idea of the "era". What era should a particular book cover? How can one reasonably justify a beginning and end point for an era? And just what *are* those points? In the past, we've spent many hours debating the subject. Where did the Rock 'n' Wrestling era end? Was it *WrestleMania V*, with the highest pay-per-view buyrate the WWF would draw in the eighties (and would draw for many years to come)? Was it *WrestleMania VI*, with Hulk Hogan and the Ultimate Warrior as the last stadium-sized dream match of that period? How about *WrestleMania VIII*, with the departure of Hogan, Roddy Piper and Jake Roberts from the promotion all in the span of one single afternoon? Or *King of the Ring* 1993, the last time the 'Hulkster' would appear on camera for the WWF in almost nine years, long after MTV, Cyndi Lauper, Mr. T et al were ancient history?

How about the New Generation? Did that begin when Bret Hart won his first WWF Title, or was it his re-ascension at *WrestleMania X* that underlined the passing of the Hogan/Lex Luger/Yokozuna years? Did it die with Scott Hall and Kevin Nash showing up in WCW? And did the Attitude Era kick off with Steve Austin's legendary promo at the 1996 *King of the Ring*, or was it closer to Bret uttering the words "This is bullshit!" on an episode of *RAW* in early 1997?

We can debate these arbitrary beginning and end points over and over, but in many ways, *WrestleMania X-Seven* stands rather symbolically as the death of the Attitude Era. Sure, Edge and Lita were offering up "live sex celebrations" well into 2006, but the second Steve Austin shook hands with mortal enemy Mr. McMahon, it was all over, an act of treason his character could never recover from, and a turn absolutely no fan was crying out for, no matter *how* good Austin was in the heel role. The one true blue-collar superstar who Average Joe could always count on to open a six pack of whoop ass was a corporate sell-out. 'Stone Cold' may have won the battles, but 'The Man' had most certainly won the war, and what a thoroughly depressing storyline conclusion that was. Worse still, the Rock was on his way to Hollywood, Mick Foley and Shawn Michaels had both retired, there was no chance at reconciliation with Bret Hart, and Triple H was about to go down with a quadriceps injury that resulted in him returning as bloated egomaniac who thought he was the second coming of Ric Flair, when he was actually closer to the second coming of Buddy Landel.

Perhaps fittingly, this last stand of the Austin glory years is a hell of a show too, one of the best (if not *the* best) that the WWF has ever done, with (mostly) clean finishes up and down the card, everyone busting their ass to put on great matches, and an awe-inspiring stadium setting. It's truly a card with something for everyone too, with storyline twists, angle payoffs, technical grappling, brawling, gimmicks, big bumps, stunts, blood... Really the only thing missing as a celebration and the culmination of the entire era was boobs, which the Kat would likely have provided had her career prospects not plummeted south a month earlier. Highest recommendation possible.

100

BACKLASH 2001

CAT NO: WWF270
RUN TIME: 165 minutes (approx)

Arnold Furious: Hot on the heels of *WrestleMania X-Seven*, the WWF's most creatively successful show of all time, comes this PPV. *WrestleMania* is widely regarded as the point where the Attitude Era came to an end and indeed the WWF's insanely hot three year run finished. After 'Mania interest in the product waned and with main events like the one on this show it's easy to see why. James mentioned elsewhere that the end of 2000 and start of 2001 saw a lot of major changes. Mick Foley was already retired but was now off TV, Austin turned heel, Rock went into movies and not long after this Triple H picked up his famous quad tear. The main event scene was decimated and the WWF paid the price for not promoting from within earlier. The likes of Chris Jericho, Chris Benoit and Kurt Angle now had to carry the company and hadn't been given the ball beforehand. So with the Rock off making movies the main event scene is compacted into one match: Steve Austin & Triple H vs. The Undertaker & Kane. I'd argue Kane isn't a main eventer, but at this point that's what they had. Everyone else had gotten a bit damaged. By the time they figured this out and actually pushed Angle and the Canadian Chris's, it was all a bit too late. I think the biggest flaw in all this is that Hunter was actually getting babyface reactions until he teamed with Austin and by all rights should have challenged for the title here, thus repeating the recent successes they'd enjoyed in singles but with the roles reversed. After all Austin and Hunter went from wanting to kill each other to teaming up. Presumably Hunter would have turned face at some point if he'd not gotten injured. I don't know what the long term plan was but I'd personally want to see a babyface Hunter challenge a heel Austin for the title at *Backlash*. It made good, logical sense. I guess Hunter wasn't interested in being a face, even though with Rock gone, he'd have been the company's top good guy.

Tangent: I'll be happy when we get into the DVD era. Some of my tapes have horribly deteriorated. I blame the WWF for putting them out on poor quality tape. My *Backlash* tape is the worst I've encountered so far, with most of my tapes from the 80s and 90s being in way better condition. Maybe they knew VHS was nearing an end and cut a few corners.

We're in Chicago, Illinois. Hosts are Jim Ross and Paul Heyman. One of the all-time great announce teams. Not quite up there with Gorilla Monsoon and Jesse Ventura, but not far off.

The Dudley Boyz vs. X-Factor
X-Factor; the group formed by X-Pac to prove he wasn't just a follower. By this point he was getting the fabled "X-Pac heat" in that people just didn't want him to be in the ring anymore. X-Factor sucked as a group for two reasons. 1. It was led by X-Pac. 2. It had the worst entrance music in wrestling history. And yes, I'm including RTC and Bastion Booger in that. If that wasn't enough reason to hate the group, they featured Justin Credible, the world's biggest jobber and most disliked ECW Heavyweight Champion ever. Not even Albert can carry all that baggage. The WWF planned this out as the hot opener so everyone works hard. There are really only two rules to a hot opener; 1. Pop the crowd. 2. Put the faces over. That doesn't happen. Why would you put X-Factor over? They constantly jobbed the Radicalz, who were a way more talented unit, but X-Factor go over? That just doesn't make sense to me. If you're a good heel group then jobs won't hurt you. The heel team work D-Von over for heat, which drags a bit. The hot tag to Bubba livens things up and it's not long before catchphrases are being popped off. JR has decided to call the Dudleys the "wizards of the wicked wood", which is okay by me because I love me some alliteration. Instead of getting tables Bubba gets double teamed and X-Pac, of all people, gets the pin just to really piss the crowd off. The WWF rather book themselves into a corner needing a big pop in the opener, so X-Pac takes 3D through a table after the match, thus giving us 50-50 booking that helps nobody. The Dudleys are still over, X-Factor still suck.
Final Rating: *½

Backstage: The Duchess of Queensbury arrives and is greeted by William Regal, who warns security to watch out for that scoundrel Chris Jericho.

Elsewhere: Kurt Angle warms up. Lillian Garcia questions his lack of nerves and Kurt says he's confident because he beat Benoit at *WrestleMania*.

Video Control gives us clips from *Heat* where Jerry Lynn defeated Crash Holly to win the Light Heavyweight Title on his debut. I'm really not sure why Lynn went wrong in the WWF because he was a terrific mat wrestler and should have slotted into the midcard somewhere. Aside from yet another classic with RVD, relegated to *Heat* again, he didn't get anything done. WWF's loss was TNA's gain and Lynn was the cornerstone of their hugely popular and different X Division where he routinely stole the show with the likes of Low-Ki and AJ Styles.

WWF Hardcore Championship
Rhyno (c) vs. Raven
Raven has gotten over, without the WWF system helping him, by just being cool. Interesting to note that we're three matches into the show, including *Heat*, and they've all been littered with former ECW talent. I count seven former ECW wrestlers. This is actually one of the better hardcore title matches as they go 100% into it and come up with creative spots that benefit both guys. An example; Raven is set up on a chair at ringside and Rhyno charges up the ring steps to attack him but Raven moves and Rhyno eats chair. That puts over the inventiveness of both, the aggression of Rhyno and speed of Raven all in one spot, and the match is full of other examples like this. Also the plunder shots are vicious, unflinching. The best spots involve the shopping trolley that Raven wheeled all his weapons down in, like a hardcore bag lady. First Raven lifts the trolley for his drop toehold spot, and it looks really unpleasant as Rhyno goes face first into the wheel. The spots in between tend to involve head shots with plunder but Raven is very deliberate about what he uses, picking metal signs that are lightweight but make a lot of noise. Less pain, more impact. Rhyno goes after the trolley again but Raven jabs him in the face with a metal bin and it falls on top of the champ. Great spot. The jab was a unique way to use that frequently used bin as an effective weapon. Rhyno sets for the Gore but Raven moves and Rhyno flies straight into the shopping trolley in an AMAZING spot. The way they set it up was perfectly organic too and the crowd LOVE it. Raven nails the trolley with a metal sink but can't get the pin and Rhyno Gores him to retain. Fantastic hardcore match with a great use of props. The trolley spot is one of the best executed spots I've ever seen in a hardcore match.
Final Rating: ***¼

Backstage: Shane McMahon reads out one of his childish rhymes, aimed at the Big Show, as they're wrestling each other tonight. Of course that makes sense; a giant former world champion vs. the promoter's son who isn't a wrestler. Michael Cole questions how sensible it is to mock Big Show, which brings Stephanie in to tell Shane he should apologise. He doesn't.

Elsewhere: Steve Austin arrives, dragging Debra behind him.

Elsewhere: The Coach tries to get the rules for the Duchess of Queensbury match from the horse's mouth. Regal stops her revealing the secrets and tells Coach to bugger off "to calling potato sack races in Kansas City". Which is funny because he's actually from Kansas City and used to be a local sports reporter. Nice of Regal to do his research.

Elsewhere: Vince McMahon warns Big Show to not hold back just because Shane is Vince's son. Vince seems to like that Show enjoys destroying McMahon's. Both guys do enormous fake laughs. I'm torn as to which one makes me smile more.

Duchess of Queensbury Match
Chris Jericho vs. William Regal
This match came about because of Jericho's disrespect for Regal's position as WWF commissioner. He even took a Jimmy Riddle in Regal's teapot. So Regal stacked the deck against him by demanding a Duchess of Queensbury rules match, where he didn't explain the rules of so he could screw Jericho. The whole name thing comes from the Marques of Queensbury rules, which govern professional boxing. Regal took it a step further by bringing out an actual Duchess of Queensbury. "I don't know which one of you looks more like a man" says Jericho, besmirching the good Duchess. "The poor woman is still mourning the loss of Princess Di" says Heyman, who seems to then be quickly shushed by the Gorilla Position. Jericho starts hard and fast before missing off the top. I'm surprised Regal didn't ban top rope moves as part of the stipulations. Regal grounds Jericho from there until he makes the mistake of going up top and gets picked off with a super rana. See, if he'd banned top rope moves that would never have happened. They work in a few nice counters like Jericho escaping the Regal Neckbreaker. Lionsault scores but the time limit for round one expires, according to the Duchess. Round two rapidly gets underway and Jericho takes a German suplex of the release variety. Regal Stretch gets applied but Jericho makes the ropes and counters into the Walls of Jericho. Regal taps out quickly but the Duchess informs us there are no submission in Duchess of Queensbury rules, which does make you wonder why Regal went for the Regal Stretch right beforehand. Jericho considers this sufficient provocation to go after the good Duchess. Regal nails Jericho with her sceptre and the ref calls for a DQ, but luckily for Regal there are no disqualifications. This match reminds me of the Quebec Rules match employed to screw with the Steiner Brothers back in the early 90s. Or, of course, the Vince McMahon approach to refereeing used against Steve Austin where he just changed the rules as it suited him. Regal works in a bit of comedy sauce by falling into her ladyship's groin. His reaction is incredible as he twitches and jerks around like a madman. Jericho decides enough is enough, lays out security and slaps the Duchess in the Walls of Jericho. Regal chair shots him down for the three though, thus defending the Duchess' good name. The match was all about Regal and how supremely entertaining he could be, as opposed to Jericho who could have been played by any random babyface. It's not much of a match, with very little competitive nature to it, but it's a fun exhibition.
Final Rating: **½

Ultimate Submission Match
Kurt Angle vs. Chris Benoit
Thirty minute time limit with the most submissions equalling the win. Angle calls all Chicago natives "fat, sweaty pigs" to endear himself to the crowd. Benoit immediately puts me off by wearing shiny lilac trunks instead of his normal ring gear. Both men are outstanding technicians, among the best in wrestling, and go right into amateur style counters on the mat, which is years ahead of its time. You can hear a very small minority popping the hell out of it. The amateur stuff is amazing as Angle tries to get the ankle lock by legitimate amateur means only for Benoit to control his head and stop it happening. It's like early UFC stuff only because it's a sportz entertainment match, not a shoot, they don't just lie around hugging each other. I'm looking at you Dan Severn. They trade on takedowns, which bores some of the audience so they insert little bits of pro stuff like Benoit chasing the Crossface to keep them involved. I'm glad I got this match because the UWFi style stuff is right up my alley. They spill through the ropes and Angle gets caught in the Crossface and taps out on the floor but that doesn't count. Angle feels the need to stall after that, which is sensible as Benoit smells blood. However Kurt

DEAN MALENKO

charges him, gets a kneebar and Benoit is stuck in the middle of the ring so he taps out to save himself for the second fall.

Angle 1 Benoit 0.

Now Kurt can go to that injured leg any time he wants and bizarrely it's the right one, not the left. Lucha-Angle! Kurt looks for a chopblock but Benoit catches his arm and gets a cross armbreaker for a submission.

Angle 1 Benoit 1

They played a smart opening ten minutes with back-and-forth mat stuff before both settling on a body part to work, both scoring submissions on body parts that they use their own patented finisher on. Benoit the arm for the Crossface, Angle the leg for the ankle lock. Benoit inserts a shoulderbreaker, the idea being that he works Angle's bad arm but also hurts his bad knee. But he does it on the left knee and immediately realises that's not the injured one. Oops. That's why we always work the left side Mr. Angle. Kurt positions the ref and hits Benoit with a chair to set up the ankle lock for a tap out.

Angle 2 Benoit 1

With Benoit down hurt from the previous hold, Angle jumps in and hooks the Crossface for another submission.

Angle 3 Benoit 1

I'm not overly keen on the Crossface working for Angle. Even with the injury stopping his movement, if there's one guy who knows how to get out of the Crossface it'd be Benoit. They spill outside again and Angle hooks the ankle lock on the floor mirroring the earlier Crossface and gets a tap out that doesn't count to match Benoit's earlier tap out that doesn't count. At the halfway point Angle starts working the arm, which I'd question after all the work done on the leg already. Maybe it's to keep Benoit off balance but the logical move would be to persist with the leg. As if to cement a different tactic Angle hooks an abdominal stretch, shades of the late Wilbur Snyder as I'm sure you all know, and therefore works the midsection too. He's trying to get an all over assault, so that if he catches any hold it could potentially score him a submission. Benoit tends to stay on the arm until he double legs Kurt into the Sharpshooter. That gets a lot of love thanks to Benoit's previous associations with the Hart Family. And he knows how to hook it right too. Angle gets countered into a half crab as soon as he makes the ropes and Kurt taps again. The way Benoit applied the half crab made it look more like half a Liontamer. Perhaps a wink to Chris Jericho.

Angle 3 Benoit 2

Angle has the common sense to roll outside when he needs a break, whereas Benoit stayed down in the ring. Which is why he's losing. They return to the countering but this time both of them drift into the ropes, using ring position to do the hard work for them, unlike the earlier part of the match. All the while, with Benoit hurting, the clock ticks down and Angle starts to look at holding on to what he's got. The final third of this match is a lot more disjointed than the earlier focused action, which had it on course for being a classic. The lack of action suggests both guys are a bit blown up and the crowd have lost interest. Kurt saves up enough energy for some suplexes. That seems to piss Benoit off into the rolling Germans. Angle tries to counter out and they save some terrific back-and-forth to set up a Benoit ankle lock, albeit slightly clumsy, and Benoit gets the tap out.

Angle 3 Benoit 3

The late submission leaves it even with 90 seconds left. Angle gets very defensive and gets caught in the rolling Germans again only to use it as a set up to go low. Ankle lock but Benoit cleverly rolls into the hold and gets the ropes. Back suplex sets up another ankle lock with seconds left. Benoit taps but the time limit has expired. The referee, one Mike Chioda, demands sudden death overtime, because America hates draws. They head back to the mat with Angle grabbing a grounded version of the abdominal stretch. Benoit counters out of it straight into the Crossface and Angle taps out. Benoit wins! Angle has an out by saying he tapped Benoit right after the time limit. I originally rated this at a sky high ****½, enamoured with the mat countering and the opening third, but in hindsight I've seen this type of match done better (in Japan) and the final third of this match isn't too good. Despite that I still think it gets underrated by Dave Meltzer and the like, but perhaps not by as much as I did at the time.
Final Rating: ***¾

Backstage: Triple H and Stephanie try to fill in a bit of continuity by talking about tonight's matches. It's the most awkward moment on the show.

Last Man Standing
The Big Show vs. Shane McMahon
This is the current angle the WWF have for WCW. Having planned out their storylines months in advance, a drastic difference to WCW who planned their shows about 30-minutes before they started, they only had space for one PPV outing. So they use WCW's owner, Shane McMahon, and set him up with an angle against Big Show where Shane tried to poach Show and Vince intervened. Essentially Vince promised Show he'd get a big push in exchange for shutting up his own son. I have a different take on Shane to most fans at the time, who seemed to consider him the "best" McMahon. I hate his promos and his work tends to involve one big stunt and everything else is horrible. He had great timing, as was evidenced when he cornered Benoit against the Rock, but that's about it. Shane pulls out every trick in the book to put Show down including kendo sticks, chairs and devil ether. It's all very stupid and the whole process just makes Show look bad. He even needs Vince to come down and save his gigantic ass from the ether attack. Show manages to pick Shane up and throw him around a bit before hitting the Final Cut and demanding a count out win. I'd be quite happy to call it quits at that but Show hauls Shane back up for a chokeslam. Show earns brownie points by screaming "kneel before me" like he's General Zod before hauling Shane up yet again for a Torture Rack, but Test runs in to save Shane. That's better booking as Shane needs the help because of the size difference. If there's one spot that shows what a poor worker Test was it's when he pulls a sign off the rail to hit Show with. Rhyno did the same thing in the hardcore match but he sold how tough it was to pull the sign off, thus making it seem like an achievement. Test just grabs it as he walks past. Way to sell it, Test! This sets up the finalé as Shane climbs the entranceway scaffold, which is an enormous metal structure. Test lays out Big Show on a safety airbag and Shane hits an insane elbow drop off the structure for the win. Test drags Shane to his feet to make sure he wins while Show can't be picked up by anyone so nobody bothers trying. Like all Shane matches it relied heavily on a big stunt spot, which would have been better employed getting over an actual active wrestler. The fall was about 20-25 feet but JR calls it 50 feet. Any way you slice it Shane wins by falling off something.
Final Rating: *

Backstage: Vince moans to Triple H about the outcome of the Last Man Standing match. Vince says he only has one son… Triple H.

Video Control takes us to WWF New York where Steve Blackman, minus personality, comments on Shane's dive. Grandmaster Sexay jumps in to liven the spot up. Back to JR and we replay Shane's dive. I'm not terribly comfortable with the WWF doing this sort of thing after Owen Hart's death. At least they didn't do this in the Kemper Arena.

WWF European Championship
Matt Hardy (c) vs. Christian vs. Eddie Guerrero
When wrestling other relatively small guys like Matt, it shows how tiny Eddie really was. It also shows that size isn't that important in wrestling as Eddie is one of the greats. The two challengers throw the champ outside, which immediately causes some wonky selling but allows a 1-on-1. All three of these guys are creative and clever so this becomes a template for later three-way matches as they seek to use all three guys, like Matt stopping a surfboard on Christian by sunset flipping Eddie. They don't quite get it right but the ideas are there. Eddie even gets to insert a pair of brainbusters, which you hardly ever see in the WWF because of the sharp drop on the bump. Eddie was the master of the brainbuster. As the match progresses it all makes good logical sense and it's a well put together contest. Edge runs down to spear Matt in the aisle. Eddie shoves Christian to the floor but Matt manages to kick out. Jeff takes umbrage and runs down to attack Edge. Unprettier on Eddie but Jeff hits (well, totally misses) the Swanton to break that up and Matt hits the Twist of Fate on Christian to retain. Good solid three-way spots without too much goofy selling. It looked like filler on paper, inserted between Shane's big ass elbow drop and the main event, but it just about delivered.
Final Rating: **¾

WWF Championship
WWF Intercontinental Championship
WWF Tag Team Championship
Steve Austin (c) & Triple H (c)
vs. The Brothers of Destruction (c)
If there's ever a match to demonstrate the WWF's creative failings after *WrestleMania X-Seven*, here it is. Austin needed a strong babyface challenger but the WWF felt they didn't have one (Benoit, Jericho, Hunter himself). This gleefully ignored Austin's history with Hunter and saw the Game settle for the IC Title. Does that sound right to you? At least Hunter is using Motorhead for his entrance music now. Austin is so freshly turned that he still gets a big pop. 2001 is not a good year for either Kane or Taker matches. Having them both together is bad news. It does not help that Austin decides to work this by doing as little as humanly possible. The opening five minutes is just Austin and Hunter standing around at ringside while the Brothers of Destruction hold the ring. Oh, Hunter gets punched off the apron twice but that's it. When the match gets underway Austin's character is so changed from the previous month that it scarcely makes sense. He begs off Taker in the corner but even as a heel Austin never showed fear like that. He just didn't give a shit. It was part of his appeal. Wasn't it enough that he was paired up with Vince McMahon? Both heels sell Undertaker's very appearance like death, with Hunter only offering to attack when the Dead Man's back is turned. The match works… for the Undertaker and all his marks because that's basically what it exists for. After the opening beating on the heels the match rapidly becomes insufferably boring. You have thought the WWF would have learned Kane isn't a main eventer by 2001 but here he is. Taker of 2001 isn't much better but at least he has exciting trademark spots. Flying DDT, Old School Ropewalk etc. Kane comes into this with an injured elbow and tries to work around it by only using his healthy right arm, whether he's in position to do that or not. Eventually the Two Man Powertrip work over Kane's bad left arm for the match's main heat sequence. Austin is more creative than Hunter in his assaults and uses both an armbar takedown and a chair shot to the elbow. The heat is merciless. Not because of the pain that's presumably etched across Kane's face, that we can't see, but rather how incredibly tedious it is. Kane's miserable comeback includes a botched clothesline. When you're botching clotheslines it might be time to consider a different career. Then he sandbags Austin on a back suplex and the match somehow deteriorates from boring to offensive. Hunter does stun me though by lining up a Pedigree bang in line with the ring post only to actually hit it! Maybe he felt it was becoming passé to have it countered every time. What follows is a convoluted series of spots where Hunter tags out in lieu of pinning and Austin walks right into a Taker chokeslam. The only person to get a pop during all this is Earl Hebner for shoving Steph off the apron. Taker clears everyone out, hits the Last Ride on Hunter but Taker isn't legal so the pin doesn't count. Austin then hits a sloppy Stunner on Kane and Hebner gets bumped. The match continues to rumble on, boring the hell out of everyone. Austin and Taker brawl into the crowd leaving it as Kane vs. Hunter. Steph runs in and Kane gives her a big boot, which pisses Vince off enough to run in. Hunter gets the sledgehammer off him and nails Kane in the elbow. Earl gets thrown back in and Hunter pins for the tag titles. This is not what you'd call a good match by anyone's standards. It's also 27-minutes long, which is way too long for Taker and Kane. Hell, Benoit and Angle, two of the company's top technicians, struggled to fill 30-minutes. Taker and Kane have a fraction of that wrestling ability. In the end the match worked around the same old deal; the McMahons. Vince's arrival turned the tide and the association with Vince is what makes Austin and Hunter the company's champions.
Final Rating: ¾*

VERDICT

The undercard is pretty decent. Even the matches that weren't good wrestling bouts, like the opener and Shane-Show, had moments of interest, like X-Pac getting tabled and Shane inserting one of his crazy bumps. The upside was the submission match, an excellent encounter between two of wrestling's best when they were both healthy and sane. Also the Hardcore Title match is one of the best for the title, combining Raven's ingenuity with Rhyno's aggression. I can't think of too many Hardcore Title matches that cracked ***. This one definitely did. The unfortunate downside of *Backlash 2001* is that people tend to remember main events more than anything else and the main event sucks. It's been a chore to sit through each time I've watched it. A marked contrast to the fun, clever and well-executed European Title match that immediately preceded the main event. Taker and Kane's tag team is a black mark on the entirety of 2001 and any time they appear bad things happen, the worst match of the year being a tag contest with KroniK at *Unforgiven*. But that's a story for another time and one that I'll also be telling. Lucky me.

55

WILLIAM REGAL

JUDGMENT DAY 2001

CAT NO: WWF271
RUN TIME: 160 minutes (approx)

Arnold Furious: Honestly, I don't know how it happened but I've ended up covering three straight PPVs after *WrestleMania*, all of which featured Steve Austin vs. The Undertaker or some combination of said match as the main event. It's a run of depressing and uncreative main event booking with dismal matches as a result. After the terrible main event of *Backlash* the WWF decided to split it into two matches here and have Austin-Taker and Hunter-Kane, therefore giving us two poor main events instead of just one. Luckily this is the show where they finally pulled the trigger on Chris Benoit's big babyface push, though oddly enough by having him lose. Even odder is that he picked up an injury around this time, which put him on the shelf for a year. Such is wrestling. Like Steve Austin when he was about to hit the big time, Benoit fell afoul of a serious neck injury, only Benoit couldn't exactly take the Austin route to recovery (staying on TV and knocking out authority figures). We're in Sacramento, California. Hosts are Jim Ross and Paul Heyman.

William Regal vs. Rikishi
Regal has vowed revenge on behalf of Stephanie McMahon-Helmsley who received a recent Stinkface. Rikishi's big heel run eventually petered out and he flopped back face like most big fat guys usually do. For storylines he was brought back from the darkside by Mick Foley. Regal has trouble working around Rikishi's limitations, using his facial ticks and personality rather than in-ring skill. Regal takes a Stinkface, which goes on for ages. Regal's selling is remarkable as the stench looks to have driven him borderline insane. If there's a guy with better facial expressions than William Regal, I've not seen him. Rikishi misses in the corner following up though and the Regal neckbreaker finishes a brisk 3-minute opener. Regal is a bloody mess after getting busted hardway off the ring steps, but luckily Michael Cole isn't on commentary so we can actually acknowledge the accidental blood.
Final Rating: *

Backstage: Edge & Christian debate the tag team turmoil match. Christian says they're a shoo-in for the Hall of Fame if they win, which makes me chuckle. They move on to Chris Jericho's mystery partner but Christian dismisses him as "shmuck sauce". Kurt Angle arrives to ask for advice on ladder matches, in the highly unlikely situation that he doesn't beat Chris Benoit in two straight falls. "Falling off sucks… so don't do it" advises Edge. These guys reek of awesomeness.

Elsewhere: 'The Game' and Mrs. 'The Game' arrive. Vince McMahon stops in for a chat and questions Triple H's judgement for messing with "the sanctity of marriage" as the Two Man Powertrip had targeted Undertaker's BOBFOC wife Sara. Hunter points out Vince is not exactly husband of the year, having had his wife committed.

2 out of 3 Falls Match
Chris Benoit vs. Kurt Angle
This is a match for Angle's gold medals. Unlike at the UK PPV *Insurrextion* the falls aren't straight up, but rather it's a "three stages" match. The first fall is pinfall only, the second fall is submission only and the third fall, if needed, is a ladder match with Kurt's medals hanging over the ring. Angle is much angrier here than in their previous bouts as he's been driven to desperation over the loss of his medals. His first move is to lift the rolling Germans off Benoit, which he absolutely nails. Angle had a very steep learning curve. He tries to steal the Swandive headbutt, which is how Benoit pinned him in England, only to miss and Benoit to lift the Angle Slam for the pin.

Second Fall: Submissions only. Benoit goes right into the Crossface, forcing Angle into the ropes to save his medals. They brawl outside to follow as JR points out Jack Doan is giving them leeway on the rules... but the only rule is submissions win! There's no DQ in a submissions match. They run a sensational counters sequence from ankle lock to ankle lock to ankle lock to Crossface. The skill level involved is extremely high. The counters continue as Angle goes for the belly-to-belly but Benoit recognises the set up and counters into the Crossface and when Angle blocks that, the cross armbreaker, which was one of the submissions in their ultimate submission match at *Backlash*. Another of those follows with Benoit hooking a vicious version of the Boston crab, a much more severe hold than the Walls of Jericho. It's so high up that Angle is able to squirm out though and that's a tip of the hat to another submission in the aforementioned bout. Benoit switches to a figure four as we get a tour of popular submission holds through the ages. Having adopted Flair's finish, Benoit starts to borrow liberally from his other work including a shinbreaker before using a Bret Hart-like drop on the ropes and then the dragon screw leg whip a'la Muta. He is busting out moves from all the leg-work greats, and Benoit has so much in his locker it makes for an interesting ride. And it's all clean as a whistle. Compare that to say, Shawn Michaels when he ventured outside of his comfort zone and tried various different moves far less effectually, and Shawn is one of the best of all time. That's how good Benoit and Angle are. Angle slam sets up the ankle lock and Benoit has to tap, taking us to the deciding third fall.

Third Fall: Ladder match. Angle starts out by grabbing a ladder only to discover it's really small and he can barely reach. It's like a midget comedy ladder. Benoit gets the real ladder and bashes Kurt in the face with it. The creativity and skill these two brought to the submissions section isn't as evident in the ladder portion of the bout. Angle tries a spot where he runs up the ladder in the corner only for Benoit to tip it over but he loses his footing and it looks dumb. The difficulty level attempted is really high again though. The problem they have is they set up the ladder, then do a spot on it, then set it up again and do a spot on it. The bumps are way harsh but there's nothing organic about them. Not like Bret-Shawn or even Shawn-Razor. That's the issue with the ladder match. After one such spot; a suplex onto the ladder, they manage to move from there to a seesaw spot where Benoit tips it into Angle's face. That's their best ladder spot as a second spot logically came from the first. Benoit slaps on the Crossface and Angle taps out but it's a ladder match so that counts for nothing. Edge & Christian run in to attack Benoit, and while they're doing so Angle pulls the medals down for the win. The middle fall is superb, an extension of the ultimate submission match, but the ladder match didn't quite click. Regardless it's top wrestling from two guys on form.
Final Rating: ****

Backstage: William Regal is interrupted by the Undertaker while getting treatment on his head. Taker demands No Holds Barred tonight by bullying the authorities. What a prick. "I'm not going to jail" he mumbles. MAAAAAAAAAAAAAARK!

Video Control takes us to WWF New York where Jerry Lynn, the Light Heavyweight champion, points out he should be at the PPV defending his title. He moans at JR that he's only got a promo and asks, mockingly, if it was ok. "I didn't book him in New York" says JR. Shoot!

WWF Hardcore Championship
Rhyno (c) vs. The Big Show vs. Test

The feud is Show vs. Test as Test helped Shane McMahon win a Last Man Standing match at *Backlash* and Show promptly cracked his ribs. Because that singles match would suck Rhyno gets inserted, as well as his Hardcore Title, to spice things up. They brawl around ringside a bit and when that gets boring they head into the back. Rhyno and Test team up to punch Show onto some pallets. You'd think they'd avoid pallets after Triple H's calf injury at *Royal Rumble 2000*. With Show down the other two brawl back to the ring. "The ring's this way" yells one of the fans. Quite. Rhyno and Test take it in turns to hit each other with plunder until Show strolls back down. Chokeslam for Rhyno and it's a release one so it's more vicious than Show's original chokeslam where he dropped to his knees. I never got that. Why make your finisher look softer than it is? The ring steps come into play as Rhyno uses them as a launch pad for the GORE, GORE, GORE! Show counts lights for Rhyno, believe it or not. Rhyno tried to get a bit creative with his spots but for whatever reason these three couldn't get it together. Rhyno looked enthused at least and Test was getting a decent push opposite Big Show, and Test would go on to feature quite prominently as a traitor in the Invasion angle, which somewhat damaged all the hard work that had gone into his face run here.
Final Rating: *¾

Backstage: Team Xtreme warm up as Matt puts over Lita. Eddie Guerrero shows up to offer help as Matt gets very overprotective of his girl. Foreshadowing. Elsewhere William Regal pops into Steve Austin's locker room to tell the champ the title match is No Holds Barred. Austin doesn't freak out and instead says "that's fine with me".

WWF Women's Championship
Chyna (c) vs. Lita

Chyna had turned slightly heel since becoming champion and basically destroying all opposition in the women's division. Backstage her contract was almost up and she demanded ludicrous money to re-sign. It couldn't have come at a worse time with WCW out of business and no competition knocking around. Chyna's value wasn't what she thought it was and she had nobody to play off. The WWF basically decided she wasn't worth the hassle and cut her loose. Chyna comes out dressed like a peacock, which about sums up her own overvaluation and increased sense of self worth. Despite being dumped by the WWF Chyna still had the longest women's title run since Alundra Blayze. As you'd expect this match is horribly sloppy. Lita spends most of it bouncing off Chyna and hitting lucky high spots. Chyna, not for the first time, has great trouble keeping herself in her costume, which is blatantly designed to make her look good rather than allow her to move. It prevents her being able to wrestle properly and ruins the match. Lita actually gets a bit creative around it, getting cheered for not looking like a doofus, and slaps on a cross armbreaker. Eddie Guerrero strolls out to take a look, making his last PPV appearance until *SummerSlam 2002*. He'd come back brighter. This is also Chyna's last PPV appearance. She wouldn't come back. The WWF created a monster with her. With Eddie they saved him from becoming one. Lita tries for the Twist of Fate but Chyna powers out and hits a powerbomb to retain. They'd have been better off switching the belt here but my guess is the WWF figured Chyna's wage demands would come down once she'd stopped to think about it. They didn't. The match is weird because Chyna's wardrobe issues overwhelmed proceedings and stopped them telling a story. Despite this Lita tried her hardest to get over the differences between them.
Final Rating: ½*

Backstage: Kurt Angle promises a ceremonial gold medal winning re-enactment on *RAW* tomorrow before stopping off to thank Edge & Christian. Edge is pleased that they don't have to listen to Kurt bitch about his medals anymore.

Elsewhere: Vince McMahon demands solidarity from the Two Man Powertrip. Everyone seems to be on the same page.

Chain Match
WWF Intercontinental Championship
Triple H (c) vs. Kane

I like that Hunter tried to elevate the IC Title by having himself as champion, after he'd been the WWF Champion, but it should have been to elevate midcarders (like he did with Jeff

FURIOUS ABOUT: TRIPLE H (1999-2002)

The 1999-2002 run of Triple H is one of the all-time great runs in wrestling, believe it or not. His background prior to this run was as follows: blueblood midcard heel, sidekick to world champion, leader of comedy midcard group known for catchphrases. Make no mistake about it, Hunter was elevated in a big way during the course of this book and never, ever looked back. His onscreen persona collected world titles, McMahon storylines and star ratings hand over fist. His dramatic run at the top began with a PPV headlining match against Vince McMahon in late 1999 before a three month long feud with Mick Foley over the WWF title that made him as a main event star. The Rumble street fight and the Hell in a Cell against Cactus Jack were both MOTY contenders in a year where Triple H produced a string of them. The McMahon-Helmsley faction took over the booking, both onscreen and behind the scenes, as he faced off against the top babyface in wrestling, The Rock. That feud and the love triangle storyline with Kurt Angle dominated 2000 and that's not even taking into consideration Hunter's barbaric feud with Chris Jericho! Nor his brief offshoot feud with Chris Benoit. Toward the end of 2000 Hunter was so good his in-ring skills were turning him babyface so the Cerebral Assassin cemented his heel status by revealing himself to be behind the attack on Steve Austin. The two entered into a violent feud, culminating in Hunter's victory over Austin in a 2 out of 3 falls match at No Way Out 2001. Yet another MOTYC. This time in a new year. After Austin's heel turn, Hunter joined forces with the Rattlesnake in a slightly dim booking decision. Hunter's match quality fell off a bit and he tore his quad working in yet another MOTYC against Jericho & Benoit on Raw. The injury cost him most of a year. When he returned he won the Royal Rumble, split from Steph, fended off Kurt Angle again and took the Undisputed world title from Jericho. He was The Game!

Hardy just before this), not working against Kane, who'd already been WWF Champion and was already well established. Plus this feud was pretty dull. Hunter is at his level best when someone is beating him up and Kane can't do that here because he's only got one arm. Hunter, ever the cerebral assassin, makes sure the chain is attached to Kane's bad arm so he can drag him around. The biggest issue with Hunter getting backstage sway was that his matches changed and he became significantly more dominant in them as he felt the need to remain strong as a heel. He became obsessed with it. The fact remains that heels are better when they do their job, which is to make the faces look good. I thought Hunter understood as his 2000 schedule featured him doing just that against all and sundry. Also his hero Ric Flair was never, ever, booked strong and he's one of the greatest heels in wrestling history. Kane drags Hunter into a chair and 'the Game' sneaks in a bladejob. Hunter seemed to think that bleeding equated to workrate for a while, again rather missing the point of Ric Flair's constant bleeding during the 80s in the NWA. The match is ugly. Eventually Hunter lines up a Pedigree but Kane powers out and goes low. The rest of the match is both guys punching each other, sometimes with the chain. It's emotionally lacking and creatively void. Chokeslam brings out Steve Austin for support. Kane boots him down and throws him out of the ring. He comes back with a chair but miscues and hits Hunter, with Kane almost botching the spot by not moving. Kane then drops on Hunter to win the IC Title in a bizarre booking decision. The only good thing about the title switch is that Kane would lose the belt to Albert, on June 28th, thus creating Albert Day. A traditional day of wonderment and heavy drinking. Also a cult that I lead called the Sons of Albert. If Triple H went over here, none of that would have happened.
Final Rating: *½

Backstage: Chris Jericho tells Coach he's going to be Y2J's tag team partner before pointing out he has a real partner. He calls his tag team partner a "real party animal".

Elsewhere: Triple H bitches about Vince McMahon not backing him up and losing the IC Title. Hunter would lose more the next night when the tag titles went and his quad followed suit. Had he not gotten injured I presume he'd have feuded with Austin during the summer months and Angle wouldn't have gotten his big title push.

Tag Team Turmoil
APA vs. Dean Malenko & Perry Saturn
This is an elimination match. Winner stays on until all the entrants have competed. Again Malenko is squandered on PPV, thrown into a nothing tag match. Saturn impresses by hitting an exploder on Bradshaw but he turns round into a spinebuster and the APA win.

APA vs. The Dudley Boyz
Spike is in the Dudleys' corner, as the crowd LOUDLY chant for tables and Paul E runs through the Dudleys' achievements. They were certainly the cornerstone of the ECW tag team division. Bradshaw takes over on D-Von as the crowd continue to LOUDLY demand those tables. Bubba makes the save and the Dudley Device connects. WAZZZZUP drop on Bradshaw. Bubba's wonderful delay on telling D-Von to get the tables is brilliant. As D-Von sets up the table Hardcore Holly runs out and puts him through it with the Alabamaslam. Bubba turns around to get clocked with the Clothesline from Hell and the APA win again. They had an interesting story with the Dudleys vs. Holly cousins as Spike had a thing for Molly, which was really cute. It became a Montagues vs. Capulets sort of deal. Forbidden love. That must have been a Stephanie McMahon angle.

APA vs. X-Pac & Justin Credible
Waltman is clean shaven and looks about 14 years old. He gets treated relatively well by the APA, who must have gotten to respect him during their 1999 business with Kane. Justin Credible on the other hand Bradshaw treats like a total bitch, which I agree with 100%. It doesn't help that Credible makes a mess of almost every spot he's involved in so the APA have to stiff him. Or is he making a mess of spots because he keeps getting stiffed? The match is a lot better when Waltman is in there. Bradshaw grabs X-Pac for a fallaway slam but Albert grabs his leg and holds it for X-Factor to pick up the big win.

X-Pac & Justin Credible vs. The Hardy Boyz
As all these guys are about the same size and have similar styles, apart from Justin, so it's a pretty decent encounter. X-Factor were underrated as a team but you can see why; the very presence of Credible is bad news, plus Pac was getting heat for being a bit of a knob and they had terrible music. If

they could have found someone better than Credible to take his spot that could have gone a long way to making the team work. Whatever he did in ECW to make himself "the man" he didn't bring to the WWF with him (we call that "Shane Douglas Syndrome"). Jeff misses the Swanton, by overshooting when he's supposed to connect. Albert pulls Matt out of the ring but Jeff nails him with a hilo. However Matt stumbles right into the superkick and X-Factor progress.

X-Pac & Justin Credible vs. Chris Jericho & Chris Benoit
Jericho's partner is Benoit, doing double duty (quadruple duty if you consider him working three falls already). Albert again interjects himself, as he's been the difference maker for X-Factor, allowing Benoit to get double teamed. X-Factor again play their role to perfection as they act like jackasses but don't threaten Jericho and Benoit all that much. Benoit slips out of the Broncobuster to show his speed and timing before Jericho tags in to dominate, but accidentally pounces the ref creating mayhem. A new ref comes down but Benoit prevents a spike piledriver. Double suplex for Albert when he runs in. Credible is then double suplexed onto Albert. Crossface and Walls of Jericho at the same time cause a double tap out and the Canadian Chris's advance.

Chris Jericho & Chris Benoit vs. Edge & Christian
Winner gets a tag title shot tomorrow night on *RAW*. Benoit is now in his fifth fall of the evening. Naturally this is an energetic contest as all four guys are very talented. Jericho takes heat off the former seven-time tag team champions. The match has some decent hope spots including a Lionsault that gets knees. Benoit comes in with his perfect timing and seemingly boundless energy on the hot tag. That works until Edge hooks a DDT but E&C decide to go for the Conchairto and get double dropkicked. Benoit gets set up for the Conchairto anyway but Jericho takes out Edge and Benoit counters Christian into the Crossface for the submission. Jericho and Benoit get a title shot on *RAW*, which would turn out to be one of the great *RAW* matches of all time as they virtually shattered the glass ceiling in a glorious switch in booking. But Triple H tore his quad and both Benoit and Jericho would end up coming up short in WWF Title bouts, before Vince switched gears and changed focus to WCW. For a moment there it looked as if the WWF were serious about restructuring the top of their card and the fans popped like crazy for it. This match merely served to set all that up. The whole turmoil ran about 30-minutes so I'll rate it as one big match.
Final Rating: ***½

No Holds Barred
WWF Championship
Steve Austin (c) vs. The Undertaker
Austin's non-reaction to this being made No Holds Barred earlier makes sense as that allows Triple H and Vince McMahon to come down and interfere on his behalf, and Vince even places himself at ringside before we get going. The typical Austin-Taker match is a basic common all-garden brawl. Normally, over the previous five years or so, they'd go 50-50 (even when Austin was a heel back in 1996) but because Austin is a freshly turned heel they have him get his ass kicked. Luckily he's an expert at that. So they brawl around ringside, then they brawl around in the ring. Austin is the first to take advantage of the rules by grabbing a chair but that gets him nowhere. Austin, having gotten nowhere, goes right after the Stunner and gets booted back down. Hell, son, that's like getting turned down for holding hands with a girl and asking for anal sex instead. Eventually Austin uses Vince as a distraction and goes after Taker's knee. This is the last vestige of a dying era as they desperately try to cling on to Attitude style. Paul Heyman makes a valid point on commentary by saying that Austin spent the previous four years saying "DTA; don't trust anybody" so why did we trust him? Austin slows the match right down by working the knee but the fans bite anyway and chant "Austin sucks". Anyone tuning in for the first time in a year or so would be somewhat confused. Out to the floor again and Taker chokeslams Austin through the announce table, thus wigging Vince out something fierce as he expects to be next. Taker's time wasting gives Austin a chance to kick out and plan his next piece of cheating. Although, given the No Holds Barred stipulation Austin can pretty much hit Taker with everything that's not nailed down and get away with it. Taker blades off one plunder shot as the WWF couldn't do a main event without blood during Attitude. Unfortunately for them Attitude is over. Austin's massive grin after punching at Taker's head gash is genius. Austin's heel run would be hard for him as he'd been such an amazing babyface, that keeping himself heel was tough. Heyman and Ross get into an argument over how Austin has changed with Paul winning out by reminding us that he used to manage both guys. Austin NAILS Taker with a chair shot and a massive "Austin" chant breaks out, demonstrating again how hard it was to keep him heel. Austin hauls Taker up; Stunner! Taker kicks out so Austin wears him out with chair shots. Taker goes low and hits the chokeslam before getting some receipts with the chair. Triple H runs in but gets a chair shot of his own. Think they're overdoing the chair shots yet? Taker has it won so Vince jumps in to break the fall. Taker kicks his ass too with Austin accidentally chair shotting the boss. Taker sets for the Last Ride but Hunter finally gets in a sledgehammer shot and knocks Taker out. Kane comes down to try and even the odds but Austin has already scored the pin to retain. This was a lot more fun than the other Austin-Taker-Hunter-Kane stuff as they cut loose the dead wood spots. They worked hard and had a decent brawl, on a par with most of their other big matches.
Final Rating: **¾

VERDICT

Like most WWF shows between *WrestleMania X-Seven* and the beginning of the big Kurt Angle babyface push, the show suffers from a number of issues. Like a stubborn reliance on the same old main event line up and a refusal to pull the trigger on the better workers. The following night however, and this is very important, Benoit and Jericho beat Austin and Hunter for the tag titles and for a brief moment it looked as though the hard working midcarders were going to take over the company. Only for Austin to see off every single one of them and the torch eventually get passed to, the as yet to debut, Brock Lesnar in the summer of 2002. The torch passing was done by the Rock, seeing as Austin had buggered off home by that point. In between you have some really serious misfires including a heel run for Jericho (overshadowed by Stephanie McMahon), a face run for Triple H (overshadowed by Stephanie McMahon), a heel run for the Undertaker (overshadowed by how much he sucked in the ring) and a bizarro-world babyface run for Hulk Hogan. If I told you any of this in May 2001 you'd think I was crazy, but the time's they were a changin'.

58

KING OF THE RING 2001

CAT NO: WWF272
RUN TIME: 167 minutes (approx)

Arnold Furious: 2001 was a year where a big deal was made of the WWF's glass ceiling and that certain wrestlers were doomed to a career of midcard efforts. It was very similar to the same situation that had held back the likes of Chris Benoit, Chris Jericho, Booker T, Eddie Guerrero and Dean Malenko in WCW. Perhaps it was pointed out to the WWF that they were going down the same road and employing the same main events over and over, and it forced their hand. So here, Jericho and Benoit found themselves elevated into the main event because the WWF didn't want to repeat WCW's mistakes. It was almost a wink to the recently defunct organisation to say "we learned from your mistakes". And yet they didn't. The WWF's initial attempts to push Jericho and Benoit came in 2000 and when those pushes faltered, due to an obsession with having the same four guys headline every show, it took the edge off their characters. If you're going to push someone do it properly first time around. The teased pushes only served to invigorate grass roots support for the duo but the masses saw both wrestlers as "nearly-men", wrestlers who were entertaining but were ultimately destined to not win the WWF Title. When their 2001 pushes came round the WWF had to create a scenario to get them over again; hence the big *RAW* win over Steve Austin & Triple H. But Hunter got injured in the process and the WWF had to decide which one, Benoit or Jericho, would get the big opportunity. As per usual they couldn't decide and gave it to both guys. Benoit actually had a serious neck injury so perhaps it wasn't the smartest of moves to involve him before having surgery but they'd already shot themselves in the foot with singles as both guys had come up short against Austin one-on-one. Again, questionable booking had wrecked a big opportunity. And that was nothing compared to the invasion angle. That kicks off properly here with DDP confronting the Undertaker. What should have been the first shot from WCW in the war ended up being a total burial. What else should we expect from a guy called the Undertaker?

We're in East Rutherford, New Jersey, which is too small to be acknowledged and instead the onscreen says "Continental Airlines Arena" because it sounds bigger. Hosts are Jim Ross and Paul Heyman. Before we get underway DDP runs down from the crowd.

Promo Time: Diamond Dallas Page
He says his sole purpose is to let the Undertaker know he's here. I don't get this whole angle as Page stalked Taker's average looking wife Sara when he already had a smoking hot wife at home in Kim Page. Kim was worth four or five Saras in terms of attractiveness. Why would he go after Sara? I get it's a ploy to piss Taker off but it doesn't work for me. Page goes on to say he's here to face Taker but reminds us tomorrow he'll be in MSG, the first ever WCW wrestler to do so. "I'm beggin' ya Taker. Make me famous!" DDP shakes hands with a few fans and sits ringside. The WCW overtones continue as Paul Heyman says there are rumours that either Jericho or Benoit may be negotiating with WCW and will jump tomorrow night in MSG. That really makes no sense to me as both left WCW under acrimonious circumstances. But since when has common sense gotten in the way of wrestling logic?

King of the Ring Semi-Final
Kurt Angle vs. Christian
Angle beat Hardcore Holly and Jeff Hardy to get here. Christian extraordinarily went over Kane and the Big Show! Naturally those weren't clean victories. Angle is going after the repeat KotR win, which would be another first. All four KotR semi-finalists are members of the same heel stable known as Team RECK. Christian has been helping Angle win matches for months! Christian is wearing his "Toffee Crisp" tights. Those are awesome. This is Christian's first big singles match since before E&C teamed up and he's eager to prove he can compete against a genuine star in Angle. The fans are clearly eager to cheer Angle and a "let's go Angle" chant starts up. You can't keep awesome workers heel forever. too many people love them. The technical stuff is good as Christian can hang with Angle and Kurt is becoming a real ring general. Two years into his career and he's easily in the top five workers in the business, albeit during a downturn in wrestling. Even in Japan the old guard were holding the fort and new stars weren't forthcoming. It wasn't until 2002 that ROH and TNA arrived and gave promising young workers like AJ Styles, Low-Ki and Bryan Danielson somewhere to showcase their ability. Angle uses suplexes to dominate, which brings down Shane

McMahon to get a look at the action. Perhaps he's scoping out potential WCW talent? Or perhaps he's just screwing with Kurt Angle who he's wrestling tonight. Angle misses a moonsault because of Shane's arrival and a series of teases follow where the crowd believe Christian will win. It'd make sense seeing as Angle is already doing double duty, but the Unprettier is countered into the ankle lock. Christian rather cleverly drags himself up the ref to get the ropes. Unprettier scores but Shane pulls Christian off the cover, to prolong Angle's evening and soften him up for the street fight. Christian gets Angle Slammed back into the ring and Kurt progresses to the final. Shane with an idiotic smirk on his face, heads to the back. Good wrestling even with the booking. The counters near the end showed how good Christian was. If it had not been for his poor run with Edge after this PPV he may have figured in the WWF's main event scene.
Final Rating: **¾

Backstage: Steve Austin gets very needy about Vince McMahon not being here. Austin stares a hole in Coach when he suggests either Benoit or Jericho might hop to WCW if they win tonight. I guess he just couldn't believe anyone would want to work there, following his own experiences. We head back to ringside where Heyman grabs an interview with DDP. He calls DDP "brazen". DDP calls it "balls", as in a move not lacking in testicular fortitude. We see footage of DDP from earlier on the Titantron as he orders lunch. Page gets freaked out and hypocritical about someone following him with a camera, which is exactly what he's done to Sara over the past few weeks.

King of the Ring Semi-Final
Edge vs. Rhyno
Edge beat Test and Saturn to get here. Rhyno went over Tazz and Tajiri. Both guys were getting a good level of support as Rhyno's smashmouth style had gotten him over in the midst of all the technical excellence. Rhyno, being badass, takes away from Team RECK by spitting in Edge's face. Rhyno's intensity allows him to transcend friendship when it comes to matches. There's a feeling he just hates everyone, even his friends. Rhyno wasn't just about getting in faces though and he takes a wicked bump off the apron, which looks really painful. These guys are good friends outside of the ring, maybe not as close as Edge and Christian, but close enough for Rhyno to realise he needs to be a contrast to get Edge over. Rhyno even accepts that what he needs to do is be boring as a contrast to Edge's flash, so he hooks a bodyscissors and works at Edge's ribs to set up the Gore. It's not particularly interesting but it does make sense. It's clear from this encounter that neither of these guys is on Angle's level technically but they're both quite creative. Rhyno goes for the Gore and Edge figures the best way to counter it is by throwing himself into a spear. Surely that would hurt Edge more as Rhyno has greater density. Another Gore misses and the Edge finishes with the Edgecution, the lifting DDT that JR keeps calling the Impaler. That was an okay match, if technically weak compared to the opener.
Final Rating: **¼

Video Control gives us a chat with Spike Dudley, who challenges the Dudleys for the tag titles tonight. His relationship with the cute-as-a-button Molly Holly was one of the nicer angles during 2001. Backstage, now, Spike says he's found a tag team partner. The Dudleys arrive to call Spike a disappointment. Elsewhere Tazz interviews Chris Jericho and asks about the WCW rumour. Jericho puts Shane over with a vague response about being aware of rumours, without actually denying them.

WWF Tag Team Championship
The Dudley Boyz (c) vs. Spike Dudley & Mystery Partner
The Duds won the belts a few days ago on *SmackDown!* when Austin nailed Benoit with the WWF Title. They had to get the belts off Benoit & Jericho because of Benoit's injury and were running out of time. The Dudleys were a sensible fix to the problem. Spike's mystery partner is Kane, which would become typical of the WWF's booking of the 'Big Red Machine'. He'd pop the crowd and wouldn't disappoint as a mystery guy but no one really rated him as a wrestler. This match is all about Spike, which is strange considering how small he is. I know there have been other small workers in the WWF but not ones that looked like him. He has no muscle mass, he just looks like a normal guy. I understand guys like Spike getting into wrestling but getting hired and pushed by the WWF? He's pretty much in a class by himself. The match is Spike getting roughed up by the Dudleys and Kane making a series of saves as Paul Heyman blames women for everything. Spike's main attribute is taking massive bumps, which makes Bubba look like a monster for big back drops and sitout powerbombs. That brings a wonderful contrast when Kane gets the tag and starts throwing Bubba around. Of course Bubba takes a wicked bump for a big man. The match itself is typical TV fare; established tag team vs. mismatched duo. The PPV spot is Kane throwing Spike over the top rope onto both Dudleys. It's not as extreme as the ECW spots involving Spike though, where Bam Bam Bigelow would throw him into the crowd. The Dudleys, now heel, refuse to do the Wazzup headbutt. D-Von gets a tidy counter out of the Acid Drop and Spike drops right into the 3D for the Duds to retain. This was a really solid tag team match. There was one minor botch where Kane had Bubba pinned and D-Von was late on the save but apart from that it worked. Post match the Dudleys get wood but Kane chokeslams Bubba through it. I love how Kane carries Spike out over his shoulder. He's a replacement for his little buddy X-Pac, only more loveable.
Final Rating: **½

Backstage: Christian offers good luck to Edge and hopes he wins *King of the Ring*. Back to ringside DDP gets further infuriated as footage appears on the Titantron of him being followed getting into his car. DDP rightly points out he's in the front row and isn't a hard man to find. Video Control takes us to WWF New York with Billy Gunn, former *King of the Ring* winner. Billy bitches about not being in the tournament and says he doesn't give a crap about who wins. Edge would reference Billy in his coronation speech, stating he wouldn't "Billy Gunn" his win. In other words, he wouldn't mess it up. Billy switched to heel pretty rapidly here because nobody cared about him.

King of the Ring Final
Kurt Angle vs. Edge
The tournament was steadily losing any kind of popularity and it concluding in the first half of the PPV about sums up where it ranked in terms of importance. After all Kurt Angle needs to get it out of the way so he can wrestle his actual money match with Shane McMahon. Kurt starts out by apologising to Edge and offering a handshake in regards to a disagreement they had last week. Angle then switches gears and says there's no way Edge can beat him so he should lie down and let Angle stay fresh for Shane. Kurt's superb line of "I think I know you" mimics Edge's own "you think you know me" entrance music. Like with the music, Angle is wrong and Edge punches him. I also love Angle's beatdown in the corner including a mudhole stomping, foreshadowing his face turn and feud with Steve Austin. It's not all about Kurt though and Edge takes a slick

DIAMOND DALLAS PAGE

having him win before he loses as it just takes the edge off Edge. Pun not intended. Shane runs in to lay out Kurt and Edge finishes with the Edgecution. They were shooting for epic down the stretch but the before stuff with Edge trying for some legacy selling on the ribs didn't quite work. Still, good match and the right guy went over. Edge didn't quite use this as a launch pad into the main events (upper midcard at best) and his push stumbled and faltered until 2005, his heel turn and the whole Lita deal. That pushed him over the top as a main eventer.
Final Rating: ***

Backstage: Edge says his win reeks of royalty. Christian pops in to congratulate Edge and heads off for balloons. "Now begins the era of awesomeness". Poor Edge, he was the only one who didn't see Christian's heel turn coming. I think that's another reason the fans didn't quite accept him as a big star right away. A really big star would sense potential deception, even from a long-time ally. That's not to take away from Edge who became a terrific addition to the upper midcard from this point onward and wrestled some excellent matches between 2001 and 2005, but it wasn't until later that he became a legitimate top card talent.

Elsewhere: Kurt Angle realises Shane helped him to beat Christian so he had an extra match. Doy. Angle goes off on a rant to yellow shirt security about WCW and tells them if anyone interferes in his match with Shane they'll never work in this town again.

bump over the top on a belly-to-belly. Edge came into this with bad ribs, courtesy of Rhyno's bodyscissors, which Angle targets. This deflects from his ankle lock and yet is entirely suitable to the Angle Slam, which focuses on the back/ribs. Logically working the back and ribs is the best tactic in any match as any impact move affects that area and deprives the victim of movement. A bad leg you can still hobble on. A bad back stops you moving. Indeed Angle's suplex-heavy moveset focuses a lot more on the spine than you realise. Edge does a top job of selling the ribs on each back bump. Just to remind the audience where the psychology of this lies. Edge and Angle had great chemistry based on Angle's technical skill and Edge's creativity and would go on to a series of terrific matches. This isn't one of their best. Indeed Angle's opener against Christian had better wrestling in it. Edge has big high spots though and hits a super rana. It's one of the safest super ranas you'll ever see but it's still a super rana. What's really amazing is when something goes wrong and Angle charges into something that doesn't happen and they manage to quickly switch to a backdrop. I've always said the best wrestlers are the ones who can make a mistake look like it isn't. They go to the finisher countering that Kurt would do with everyone good enough to wrestle that way. Edge has four finishers so that makes it all the more exciting as you're never quite sure what counter Edge is going to do. The ref gets bumped and Edge taps to the ankle lock. I'd question the need to protect Angle by

Light Heavyweight Championship
Jeff Hardy (c) vs. X-Pac

I know a lot of folks criticised X-Pac getting pushed in this division but he was still a good worker in 2001. People just hated him and there is a loud "X-Pac sucks" chant. Paul Heyman makes a point of putting Waltman over by saying he changed perception of the light heavyweight in the USA by busting his ass in the WWF in the early-mid 90s. I know Vince was desperate at the time, but it really did change the WWF forever when Waltman pinned Razor Ramon. People still talk about it! Jeff has a lot of flash but his moves are risky. The railrunner just about comes off and Pac makes a point of providing contrast by working a technically sound match and grounding the champ. Even when he hits something risky, and nails it, like the Jericho springboard to the floor the crowd still hate him. But he's better than Jeff! He actually hits all his moves. Unfortunately as a heel X-Pac also feels the need to slow the match down and a chinlock has no place in the cruiser matches, especially ones that run 7-minutes. Jeff's timing is somewhat lacking and when he dodges the Broncobuster it makes X-Pac look stupid because he moves so early. Compare that to Chris Benoit at *Judgment Day* where he slipped out at the last half second. Jeff absolutely fucks up a corner charge that Pac tried to jump over. The warning signs were there with Jeff. Pac tries to walk him through the next few spots and get the match back on track and Jeff becomes noticeably less showy. X-Factor gets three but Jeff just about gets his foot on the rope. X-Pac goes for another X-Factor blocked into a jawbreaker in a good spot. This match pains me because the structure is so good but the execution is so shoddy. Jeff eventually finishes with a Swanton. If you ever wanted a match from 2001 that demonstrated how good Sean Waltman was, still, while Jeff Hardy was a shambles, this is it. Waltman just about held it together but Jeff couldn't help himself and botched a few spots.

Final Rating: **

Backstage: William Regal, Tajiri and Steve Austin provide a few chuckles. Austin borrows the commissioner's phone (from 1981) to call Vince McMahon. "It's Steve... Steve Austin.... It's Stone Cold Steve Austin, the WWF Champion". Austin informs Vince of the rumours that either Benoit or Jericho will defect if they win. Austin tells Vince he needs him. Why would Vince McMahon not even be at the PPV? That never made sense to me. The plot was that he told Austin to get the job done by himself but surely, as owner, Vince should have been at the arena.

Promo Time: Diamond Dallas Page
There's more video footage of DDP arriving at the arena earlier. DDP gets impatient and demands Taker get his dead ass out here right now. More footage airs and reveals Sara had been taping DDP all day. The angle has already been incredibly stupid (why would Page stalk Taker's wife? Why would you put Taker's wife on TV? Why would you centre the first invasion angle around a man who has a legitimate grudge against WCW?) This should be an epic confrontation. A dream match of WWF vs. WCW the fans had wondered about for years. And yet it takes a few seconds for the fans to realise how WCW will get treated during the invasion, as their biggest name star (under WWF contract) gets absolutely pounded by Undertaker. I know Page is a guy who relied heavily on pre-planning to make anything look good, but that's no reason to bury him. Unless you're Undertaker. Sara strolls down to film it for her own amusement as a worker's wife gets to go over WCW's top draw. I think that about sums up the stupidity of the angle. Speaking of Sara; if she'd been debuted as a masked performer people would remember her as one of the hottest diva's of all time. Smoking hot body. This burial goes on forever and is one of the worst segments of the entire year. It kills the invasion dead before it even begins. The fans knew, after this, that no WCW guy was ever going to get over on the WWF hierarchy. This scuffle was 99% Undertaker and an embarrassment to Vince McMahon's business acumen. Let's run an inter-promotional angle where two companies collide but because one of them wasn't created by Vince it gets buried at every single turn. DDP doesn't even take a finisher before running away, merely a big boot. Seriously, this was a disaster. I can't believe Undertaker is stupid enough to not realise there was money to be made in an invasion angle. It's all about politics and protecting your spot, the exact complaint WWF workers had about WCW in the first place. The same reason why Taker never got a fair shake there (or Austin, or Foley, or Jericho, or Benoit, or Hunter, etc).

Backstage: Steve Austin asks one of the yellow shirt security guys how long it takes to get here from Greenwich. "I don't know, sir" so Austin asks again and magically the guy now knows it takes 90-minutes. Austin's persistence is admirable. He tells the stooge to come and get him when Vince gets here.

Street Fight
Shane McMahon vs. Kurt Angle
As a non-wrestler it's amazing how many matches Shane gets on PPV. What's even more amazing is how highly he's regarded. To be fair, this is Shane's best match. Largely because Angle could carry absolutely anyone at this point in his career, even in his third match of the night. Somehow Angle makes all Shane's goofball wrestling moves look competent. Shane meanwhile just has to take a load of bumps as Angle runs through an array of suplexes. Shane knows he can't win it in the ring so takes a risk by diving onto Angle over the announcing desk. Then it's party time as Shane wears out a kendo stick on Kurt's back and Angle finds himself opened up hardway as the weapons take over the match. It's a smart change of pace as the fans were getting bored by the one-sided technical match even if Angle was carrying it. Shane getting the ankle lock is ridiculous even if Angle is quick to kick out of it. Shane gets a sub-Rocky Maivia level floatover DDT, then he tries to figure out how to do a Sharpshooter and falls over like a twat. Shane is not a technical master. Shane follows that disaster with his dancing punches and somehow there's no counter at the end of it all. Angle just stands there taking it. I realise they have to do something to establish Shane as a threat but submission holds and striking isn't it because it's totally unbelievable. What he should have used was plunder, almost exclusively, as Kurt isn't used to a hardcore environment. Shane then bizarrely goes after a Shooting Star Press (!?!) that misses. I commend the effort but why would you even do a throwaway spot like that and not have it lead to a near fall? Put it like this: I don't even remember seeing an SSP on WWF TV to that point. Kidman had made the move popular in WCW, even if he couldn't hit the damn thing, but in the WWF it was a freak spot. I just don't understand the booking in this match at all. Then we get into the famous section of the match where Kurt Angle decides it'd be a good idea to belly-to-belly overhead suplex Shane through the plate glass entranceway. The first time nothing happens and Shane just drops on his head, so they repeat the spot, normally a sin, only for Shane to fly clean through it at the second time of asking. The result is both men get injured; Angle bleeding from the shoulder, Shane from the face. But Kurt isn't done and he tries for another belly-to-belly overhead suplex to send Shane back into the arena, and again the glass doesn't break and again Shane lands on his head. So they repeat the spot and... the glass no sells it again! This time Kurt has the common sense to just give up and just throw Shane through it. After all they managed one belly-to-belly overhead suplex through a plate glass window. Isn't that enough? The spot is so intense that Angle needs to drag Shane back into the ring, but McMahon still kicks out. Shane uses garbage shots to set up the Angle Slam. Naturally that's not the finish as the plate glass spot not finishing demands something ridiculous to follow it. Angle uses a piece of wood as a platform to set up an Angle Slam off the top, which gets a massive pop and shows that Angle was a genius. That finally finishes. I know this match gets monster ratings (Dave Meltzer of the Wrestling Observer went ****, so did James Dixon), but I have some pretty big issues with how even some parts of it are. Angle should dominate proceedings, especially with the technical stuff. Shane falling over trying to put on the Sharpshooter about sums his technical ability up. The glass spot is one for the ages, despite it getting botched three times, and the finish is great. It's Shane's best match, ever (we gave Test-Shane at *SummerSlam 1999* ***) and is part of the reason for his enormous reputation, despite a serious lack of skill.

Final Rating: ***½

Backstage: Chris Jericho walks. Elsewhere: Chris Benoit warms up. Walking isn't intense enough for him. Elsewhere: Steve Austin goes back to that yellow shirt and asks where Vince is. He's still not here, and Steve Lombardi orders Austin back inside because his match is next.

WWF Championship
Steve Austin (c) vs. Chris Benoit vs. Chris Jericho

Somewhere between *Judgment Day* and here something broke in Steve Austin's brain, and he went from being a generic heel, doing all his Attitude Era stuff to boos instead of cheers, to a mentally unhinged weirdo with intimacy issues and a rich streak of misogyny. His stuff with Vince, especially the "crazy hug" (you know the one I mean), showcased where the character was going. Losing Triple H to an injury was the best thing to happen to Austin's heel run. Benoit and Jericho start out on the same page, as if they'd decided to take out Austin and then decide the title between themselves. The clear face/face vs. heel approach is bad news for the quality of the match as it makes Austin the underdog, which is stupid, and Benoit has better chemistry with both Austin and Jericho than Austin and Jericho have with each other. If anything it would have been more interesting with the main conflict being between the two faces and the heel taking the opportunities that arose from that. Eventually they do fight each other but the structure of the match is horrible. You could see this is as a transition between the old Austin brawls and new age technical wrestling main events that would dominate the future. The match only gets going when Austin finds himself one-on-one with another guy, and only then can they start to wrestle. It reminds me how good Austin vs. Benoit (from *SmackDown!*) was, and even Austin vs. Jericho. Hell, the Austin vs. Benoit match was a MOTY candidate and I think that's what they were hoping for here. The Austin-Benoit encounter was only one week after the Austin & HHH vs. Benoit & Jericho tag from *RAW* that was even better. There's no doubt that the television was delivering during 2001, as it was not only unpredictable but also producing stunning matches and some great segments. Benoit shows his usual flair for being able to do anything as he lifts the Stunner. The ref is slyly bumped right beforehand, preventing a title change. Benoit grabs the belt and nails Austin with it for what should be a title change, only for Jericho to save his title opportunity. I'm sure Benoit would have given him a shot if he'd won. They probably should have worked that out beforehand. A common issue with three-way matches is that one guy normally lies around overselling for too long. Here Jericho stays down for minutes at a time and once he's back in, Benoit takes his turn to lie around while Y2J tries to get his finisher on. It doesn't make much sense and considering it was supposed to be these guys' big PPV break, because you'd think there would be more of a plan. It's not a bad match, but in terms of disappointments they don't come much higher in 2001, outside of the diabolical booking on the invasion of course. Jericho's stuff with Austin is mainly to blame as it's just, perhaps surprisingly, not very good.

It's even worse when you consider that Benoit is working at MOTY pace when he gets Austin alone, and he is doing it with a broken neck. The selling really irks me as Benoit takes about 3 minutes on the floor before Jericho has to dropkick him back down. Finally they sort that selling by having Benoit run in and chair shot Jericho, and it's a peach. That should keep him out of the match, but instead Austin hits Benoit with a Stunner and throws him outside. It's all backwards, especially as he hits his finish and then pins the *other* guy. Why wouldn't you pin the guy you hit the Stunner on? At least they work hard, but they certainly don't work smart. Maybe if Triple H hadn't injured himself we could have gotten Austin vs. Benoit and had them work that near ***** match on PPV instead. Not that I'm complaining about getting great matches for free, but I do when I then have to pay for a worse match. Benoit grabs the rolling Germans on his return to the ring. When they worked on *SmackDown!* he did ten in a row, but here it's only five. Austin goes low to make sure it doesn't carry on and they run a triple down. A triple down? Are you kidding me? I guess Austin had worked the whole match and probably needed a breather, but there's no rule in a three-way that the champion needs to be involved at all times. Walls of Jericho AND the Crossface get hooked and Austin taps out, but Earl Hebner doesn't allow it because only one guy can win, not both. At least they didn't book co-champions, I guess. Benoit realises this first and slaps Jericho in the Crossface, but Jericho slips out and finally it's Canadian Chris vs. Canadian Chris for the WWF Title before they run another triple down. This one at least sets up the arrival of WCW Champion; BOOKER T! He lays Austin out with an axe kick and dumps him through the announce table with the Book End. Austin was not too thrilled with that bump as it was totally unprotected and caused him to take some time off from working matches to recover. Yet another nail in WCW's coffin, and the invasion has barely begun. In the ring Jericho slaps on the Walls of Jericho, only for Benoit to make the ropes. The crowd got very excited for a moment, thinking they were about to see a title change. The Chris's continue to have a very solid match, without Austin, but they botch the Lionsault. You'd think Jericho would know how far away from the ropes he needs to put people for that move, but for some reason he sometimes struggled with it in the WWF. He manages a moonsault on Austin though, which he didn't do very often. Benoit stops the pin to hit a Swandive headbutt and Jericho saves the title. Benoit follows up with a back superplex on Jericho into another triple down. Then the most deflating finish, ever, as Austin just rolls over and pins Benoit. The actuality of the situation was that Benoit had a serious neck injury and could easily have been pinned if anyone hit a move on his neck, but the way it played out was weird and disappointing. The second half of the match has terrible selling and yet is great entertainment, whereas the first half has logical selling and terrible action. Compared to the recent clashes between these guys, the three-way situation just didn't work out.
Final Rating: ***

VERDICT

It's a solid show. Everything is good on the PPV, in terms of wrestling anyway, so it's well worth seeing. But if you've not seen the matches that set this PPV up, that's where the real money is. The Austin & Triple H vs. Benoit & Jericho match is one of the best of the year and the singles match between Benoit and Austin is right behind it. So get all that. If you only watch one Shane McMahon match you might want to make it this one too. His wrestling skill is pretty weak but the storytelling is good and their high spots are suitably epic. Kurt Angle has to be the MVP though; working three matches and delivering in all of them. The best of Shane's career and two solid ones with Edge and Christian, helping to establish them as singles guys after a few years of dominating tag team wrestling.

58

CHRIS BENOIT

INVASION

CAT NO: WWF273
RUN TIME: 161 minutes (approx)

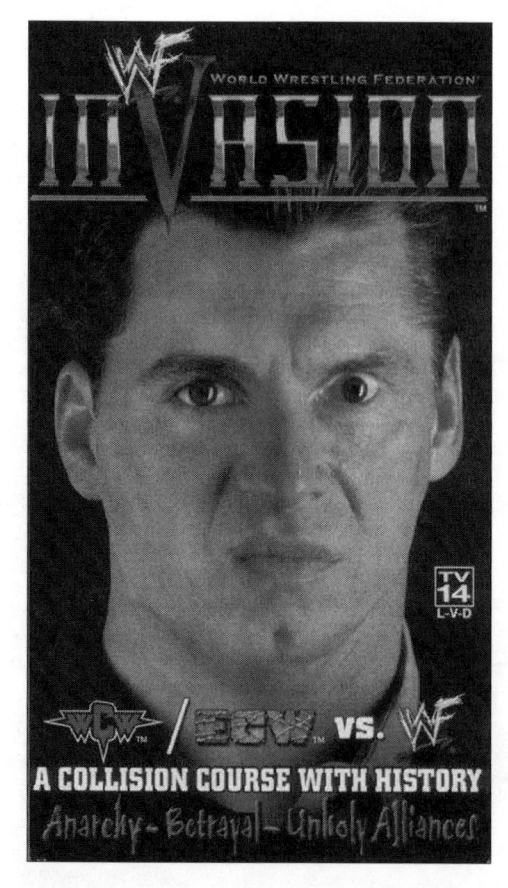

Lee Maughan: It was the one fans and pundits alike had salivated over for *years*. What if the stars of the WWF took on the stars of WCW? Who would stand supreme at the end of it all as THE dominant promotion in all of pro wrestling? Dream matches had been dreamt, fantasy supercards had been booked, but finally, for the first time ever, and with ECW added to the mix, the dream was about to become a reality...

July 22nd, 2001, from the Gund Arena in Cleveland, Ohio. Hosts are Jim Ross and Michael Cole, who sounds a lot more confident and assured than he did the last time he was on pay-per-view in early 1999, although he does have that annoying Bret Hart-like tendency of saying "the WCW" instead of just "WCW".

Edge & Christian vs. Mike Awesome & Lance Storm
Edge won the *King of the Ring* tournament last month and Christian has taken to jealously carrying his Stanley Cup-like trophy around like a newborn baby. Unfortunately for him, the whole invasion angle has pretty much thrown a spanner into the works of the WWF's plans to have him turn on and feud with Edge, as they're now needed as soldiers in the war against the Alliance. Not only that, but the inevitable outcome of his eventual turn was that it got lost in the shuffle of the main angle, and the resultant Edge vs. Christian blow-off never really scaled to the heights many had hoped it would achieve, outside of a very good cage match on UK-only pay-per-view *Rebellion* in November. Storm and Awesome meanwhile had previously partnered up as Team Canada in WCW, but were here as "ECW guys" after the big Alliance angle on *RAW*. Which makes it kind of weird that Storm was the first WCW name to invade the WWF, superkicking Perry Saturn during a match in Calgary, and Awesome was the first WCW guy to win a WWF Title, beating Rhyno (oddly enough, since he's in the main event tonight, also on the Alliance team) under 24/7 rules at the WWF's hallowed Madison Square Garden turf.

The match is pretty fun as Edge and Christian are able to run through their usual stuff, only as babyfaces now established at a much stronger level than they previously were as Brood members in 1999, although Christian does manage to get caught in the ropes on an elevated plancha attempt. Storm and Awesome have less continuity but hold things together well enough once they take over on offence, and they go into a fairly unpredictable back-and-forth finishing sequence, with Storm small-packaging Edge after Edge accidentally knocks Christian off the apron, but Christian rolling it over for two. Awesome then tries for the Awesome Bomb on Edge but Christian spears him mid-move to put Edge on top for the pin in what was a very all-action opener.
Score: WWF 1 - 0 Alliance.
Final Rating: ***½

Earl Hebner vs. Nick Patrick
Mick Foley is the special guest referee for this, as per a last-minute decree on *Sunday Night Heat*, and the match came about when Hebner got in Patrick's face over whose locker room space belonged to whom, and Patrick feigned a shoulder injury and refused to count any WWF pinfall attempts in a tag team match pitting Kurt Angle and Chris Jericho against Booker T and Diamond Dallas Page. Obviously this isn't much of a match, although Patrick, the real-life son of Jody 'the Assassin' Hamilton actually has in-ring experience as a wrestler, but the whole thing serves as a backdrop for all the referees getting into a brawl and Foley throwing them all out. Ah, the old switcheroo, wrestlers throwing out referees, dogs and cats living together, mass hysteria! Hebner hits a spear for the win, and Patrick argues the call so Foley puts him out with Mr. Socko. Call me crazy, but I thought this was terrific fun. The wrestler/referee role reversal, the scrappy intensity from both guys, and the crowd reaction to the novelty of it all made this an entertaining three minutes that never outstayed its welcome.
Score: WWF 2 - 0 Alliance.
Final Rating: *½

The APA vs. Chuck Palumbo & Sean O'Haire
This is WWF Tag Team champions vs. WCW Tag Team champions, but neither set of titles is on the line first time out. The story of the match seems to be that Palumbo and O'Haire have a ton of potential but they're completely outmatched by their WWF foes, which is sadly where the line ended up being drawn in this entire stupid invasion angle. Faarooq plays face-

in-peril for a while, but it's all very tokenistic as Bradshaw predictably takes over with a fallaway slam on Palumbo after Faarooq rocks O'Haire with a spinebuster. The champions (er... the WCW ones) manage to get in some superkicks to the APA but Palumbo walks into the Clothesline from Hell for the anti-climactic victory. Not a bad match, just a very average one in which the outcome was never in doubt.
Score: WWF 3 - 0 Alliance.
Final Rating: **

- Backstage, Chris Jericho tells Mr. McMahon not to fear WCW, but that ECW might be a threat under Paul Heyman. Hmm.

Kidman vs. X-Pac
This is another champion vs. champion match, as X-Pac is WWF Light Heavyweight champion and Kidman is the WCW Cruiserweight titlist. Not only that, but this is also the period where X-Pac was pretty much universally loathed by WWF supporters, so he gets booed out of the building despite batting for essentially the home team. X-Pac is a former WCW Cruiserweight champion in his own right (back in his days as Syxx), and actually squashed Kidman on an episode of *Saturday Night* back in 1997 with the Buzzkiller (his chickenwing/bodyscissors submission), although that was before Kidman found the flock, the wifebeater, the Shooting Star Press and credibility. X-Pac still dominates here because he's the heel (and tenured WWF guy), but Kidman does get to kick out of the X-Factor and block the Broncobuster, and he finishes with the Shooting Star Press in 7:13. Decent match with an interesting dynamic given the babyface was wrestling for the heel squad and vice versa.
Score: WWF 3 - 1 Alliance.
Final Rating: **¼

Raven vs. William Regal
The crowd doesn't seem to know how to take Regal, who's been the WWF's heel commissioner for months but is working like a total babyface here, and Raven gets something of a mixed reaction coming out to his generic rock and raven-calls theme that always stood as a glaring advertisement for how nobody in the WWF ever really seemed to "get" his disaffected Generation X grunge rock slacker character and just figured he was actually half-man, half-raven or something.

To say there's a clash of styles going on in this match would be an understatement, as Regal wants to wrestle whereas Raven wants to brawl, but they manage to hold it together well enough. It's just a shame they couldn't have just roasted each other instead, as they're two of the wittiest, funniest guys to ever grace the wrestling industry. Man, and special referee Foley could have emceed it! What a tragedy they had to wrestle instead. Raven goes for the Raven Effect (the much less cooler name for the Evenflow, again confirming the WWF's lack of understanding of the entire subculture that helped get Raven over in the first place) but Regal blocks it and sends him and the referee both out to the floor, allowing Tazz to sneak in and T-bone Tazzplex Regal before Raven recovers to finish with the Raven Effect.
Score: WWF 3 - 2 Alliance.
Final Rating: **

Hugh Morrus, Shawn Stasiak & Chris Kanyon vs. Billy Gunn, Albert & The Big Show
This is a pretty thrown-together excuse to get six guys all on the card in one go, as the WWF has Show-Gunns, the short-lived union of 'The One' Billy Gunn and the Big Show presented as a pair of loser underachievers who've both failed

---

FURIOUS ABOUT: SEAN O'HAIRE

The WWE tend to have a decent record when it comes to pushing people who are talented, as long as they're over 6 feet tall. At 6' 6", great on the mic and decent in the ring, you'd think Sean O'Haire would have gotten a big WWE push. You'd be wrong. The WWE couldn't quite get a grip on O'Haire and sent him to OVW. He spent ages down there, missing the entire Invasion and seeing a fleet of WCW talent get pushed ahead of him. When he finally made the main roster in 2003 it was with a Devil's Advocate gimmick that everyone loved. And the WWE still couldn't find anything for him, despite a series of killer promos. O'Haire found himself stripped of gimmick and Roddy Piper's student before a motorbike crash ended his WWE career. It still amazes me, that O'Haire never got a serious WWE push.

---

to reach their potential (a sure-fire way to ensure the team never got over) along with fellow heel Albert, card carrying X-Factor member, that useless trio now reduced to a duo after Justin Credible sought greener pastures with the Alliance (and subsequently managed to not get booked on this show, or on a single pay-per-view at all for the rest of the angle so well played there, Aldo Montoya.) The WCW team meanwhile is made up of Meat, Mortis and General Rection, hardly a triumvirate to cast fear into the souls of the WWF squad. Stasiak actually seems to be the captain of the team because they use his Mr. Perfect-alike theme for their entrance, and presumably because he used to be in the WWF before getting run out of town for covertly videotaping other people's private conversations.

The WWF guys all hit military presses to start, but it isn't pretty, and then they trade some moves because it's six guys all trying to get their shit in with only four minutes to do it. Albert seems to be getting the biggest push as he throws out his bicycle kicks and Baldo Bombs, and then everyone trades off their finishers until Stasiak hits the Meat Grinder on Gunn, and he and Morrus make a mess of the finish before Morrus takes control and gently lays his arm across Gunn for the sloppy pin. Afterwards, the WWF guys all lay the WCW guys out with their finishers, just to confirm that yes, both teams are complete losers.
Score: WWF 3 - 3 Alliance.
Final Rating: *½

Tajiri vs. Tazz
This is actually a rematch from an episode of *ECW on TNN* back in 1999, where Taz choked out Tajiri with the Tazmission. That was a different time however, and Tazz is no longer a badass killing machine, more a dumpy guy in a jumpsuit that makes him look rather rotund. In fact, before the match Regal categorises him as a "foul, miserable, toe-rag little gobshite", which is pretty accurate. JR calls him a "complex enigma" and notes him as "paranoid one moment, he's broadcasting the next, he's turning back on the WWF fans the next, I mean, he arguably is the most dominant ECW champion in the history of that organisation", which pretty much sums up the schizophrenic booking treatment he's received since arriving in the WWF at the 2000 *Royal Rumble*. Cole can't understand "why he's followed Paul Heyman yet again, giving up a brilliant

FURIOUS ABOUT: STACY KEIBLER

Like the song goes; "she got legs, knows how to use 'em". Stacy was one of WCW's hottest divas and also one of the youngest (just 20 when she signed for them). The WWE didn't quite know what to do with her but knew they wanted to use her. As revealed in her interviews she's a 'blank canvas'. Really pretty with stunning limbs but not interesting. She signed with WCW in 1999 as a Nitro Girl before being turned into valet Miss Hancock. Her WWE career was similar. Initially just a WCW pick up she became the Duchess of Dudleyville. She stayed with the WWE for five years, working with Test & Scott Steiner before becoming Super Stacy; another of Hurricane's sidekicks. She left the WWE in 2006 to be on Dancing With the Stars . After the show finished she tried for a Hollywood career and dated George Clooney.

---

career here in the World Wrestling Federation", confirming once more what a cretin he is.

Tajiri, presumably having not joined the Alliance so he can do the WWF's Japanese publicity work, gets a big reaction for a handspring elbow and the Tarantula. Tazz blocks some kicks though and counters with a capture suplex, but Tajiri blows the green mist in his face and finishes with the Buzzsaw Kick to put the WWF back ahead in a mostly dull outing.
Score: WWF 4 - 3 Alliance.
Final Rating: *¾

- Backstage, Matt Hardy is worried that Jeff Hardy might not be ready for Rob Van Dam, then gets decked with a chair shot from behind by RVD. Oh irony, you hilarious bastard.

WWF Hardcore Championship
Jeff Hardy (c) vs. Rob Van Dam

Earlier in the show, JR noted that tonight was "not about titles", which makes him a massive liar as Hardy is defending the Hardcore title here. This is actually the third time these two have wrestled, with Van Dam having beaten Hardy on a 1997 episode of *RAW is War* during the original ECW invasion angle of 1997, and pinning him in a tag match on an independent All Star Wrestling card on February 11th, 1998. Obviously the announcers can't reference his previous stint in the WWF because he was portraying an anti-ECW character at the time, with his defection credited to the absent Jerry Lawler.

Even with his relatively brief sojourn to the WWF, Van Dam is still largely new to the WWF crowd but there's already a noticeable groundswell of support for him from the vocal minority in a way none of the other Alliance names have enjoyed thus far. That vocal minority would become a vocal majority by the end of the match, the hardcore rules allowing for RVD to work in his usual outside-the-ring and chair-assisted offence that the ECW-like environment allows. Imagine that; a guy being allowed to play to his own strengths, unencumbered by the usual WWE siege mentality of forcing everyone to adapt to their "approved" method of working, and, *gasp!*, he actually gets himself over on his own merit. Who could have possibly predicted that?

The pair fight through the crowd, which is a lot more dynamic than when most guys do it because they use the guardrails to jump off of, as opposed to just brawling half-heartedly and throwing each other into walls, as so many wrestlers do in these frequently-tiresome situations, and before long, a ladder comes into play. Jeff climbs up it but RVD, from inside the ring, tips it over, causing Hardy to go flying off onto the ramp in a very nasty looking bump. That ramp can't have had any give in it whatsoever. "How do you learn to fall off a twenty foot ladder?!" asks JR, in a soundbyte that would accompany WWE DVDs for years to come, along with the line "How's he even able to stand is what I wanna know!", also muttered here. There's an answer that will score some serious points at your next pro wrestling trivia night.

RVD gets the Van Daminator to an enormous reaction and hits a chair-assisted running dropkick in the corner, but Jeff counters the split-legged moonsault and lands a DDT, giving RVD his first chance to work in the amazing pop-up head spike bump he always used to do in ECW whenever Tommy Dreamer gave him a piledriver. Jeff then goes for a Swanton Bomb after a backdrop suplex, but RVD rolls out of the way, smugly puts on the Hardcore title belt, and polishes Jeff off with the Five Star Frog Splash to win the title in the easy breakout performance of the night. Excellent match that was light-years ahead of the trashcans and kendo sticks synonymous with the Hardcore division in 1999 and 2000, and it even managed to set up a ladder match for *SummerSlam* too. Great stuff.
Score: WWF 4 - 4 Alliance.
Final Rating: ****

Bra and Panties Match
Trish Stratus & Lita vs. Stacy Keibler & Torrie Wilson

Trish and Lita weren't quite mortal enemies yet, but they were actually in the middle of a developing angle that largely got dropped so they could do this match. Trish at the time was sort-of dating/sort-of managing Jeff Hardy, which Lita didn't take kindly to, and Trish had also kissed Lita's boyfriend Matt Hardy after a match, in possibly the first recorded case of someone getting a taste of their own bitter medicine before even having sinned. Stacy and Torrie had also begun flirting with the Hardys in an attempt to get under the skin of Trish and Lita, so the WWF girls have put their differences aside to team up and defend the honour of the Federation. And how do you define the word "honour" better than with a tasteful bra and panties match?

Mick Foley is once again the special referee here, having only accepted the offer to helm the Hebner-Patrick clash in return for getting this gig, proving himself to be one of the smartest men in all of wrestling. I wonder if he's even bothered to sit down and consider what the actual rules are here because obviously the goal is strip both of your opponents of their clobber until they're parading about in their grundies, but what if, say, Torrie gets stripped but then never bothers to tag out, making it impossible for Stacy to lose? Can this thing go to a draw? Would Torrie be eliminated? Am I thinking too deeply about what essentially amounts to little more than throwaway titillation? I suppose somebody has to.

It's also quite possible that Foley's just in there to direct traffic, as Lita is actually the only fully-trained wrestler of the four girls at this point, with Trish still green as grass and the WCW contingent having been little more than eye candy for the entirety of their careers thus far. That wouldn't change. It shows too, as the action (what little there is of it) is awkward and scrappy, and then they pull each other's tops off before the

WWF duo take the duke after Poetry in Motion on Torrie and a bulldog to Stacy, and they're stripped of their bottoms. Unlike the other big gimmick match on the card, even with all the skin on show this totally outstayed its welcome.
Score: WWF 5 - 4 Alliance.
Final Rating: *

Inaugural Brawl
Booker T, Diamond Dallas Page, Rhyno & The Dudley Boyz vs. Kurt Angle, Steve Austin, Chris Jericho, Kane & The Undertaker
Once again, the underlying problems of the whole invasion angle are on display for all the world to see here, as aside from Shane McMahon heading up WCW and Stephanie McMahon-Helmsley leading the charge for ECW, the Alliance squad is only really made up of two "outsiders" in Booker and DDP, as Rhyno had already been in the WWF since February, before Vince McMahon had even bought the WCW trademarks, video library and contracts, and the Dudleys were just a few short weeks away from their two year anniversary in the promotion. Not only that, but the ECW contingent have never been presented as anything more than midcarders to the WWF audience, weakening their team right off the bat. Furthermore, DDP has already been saddled with a dreadful stalker gimmick and treated like a joke at the hands of the Undertaker at last month's *King of the Ring*, and incongruously, Booker doesn't even get top billing for his team, hitting the ring *before* DDP despite his current status as not only WCW World Heavyweight champion, but United States champion as well! Admittedly, that's because the match kicks off with Undertaker going after Page as soon as DDP makes his entrance, the whole thing turning into a giant brawl just in time for Steve Austin's arrival, but hey, while we're quibbling.

Austin's participation is another flaw in the whole setup, as he spends the entirety of the match beating the hell out of the Alliance guys, only to turn on Kurt Angle at the end and join up with them, which everybody could see coming from a mile away. In many ways, it was supposed to be the WWF's answer to Hulk Hogan betraying WCW at *Bash at the Beach* '96 and siding with the New World Order, but the difference there was Hogan didn't spend the entire match beating the living daylights out of Scott Hall and Kevin Nash before making the turn. Logically, there's no reason for Austin to spend so long fighting the guys he must already know to be his teammates. Why doesn't he just lay down for them right away and accomplish the same goal? Why doesn't he turn on Angle immediately? Yes, I know in a non-kayfabe sense the whole point was to cement his already ailing heel turn that nobody asked for and to set up Angle as a challenger for his WWF Title, but there are ways to do that without such gigantic gaps in logic.

Much subtler is something the announcers fail to pick up on entirely, making me wonder if it was just pure coincidence in the first place, but after Jericho's interview earlier in the night praising Paul Heyman, he wrestles here in purple tights emblazoned with a barbed wire motif. The keenly observant amongst you will note that ECW's logo at this point consists of purple lettering wrapped in a barbed wire motif. I appreciate the notion that this may have been Jericho's idea to throw people off the scent of the Austin turn, but no real tease is ever made so it's possibly it was all entire coincidental. I'm actually surprised he praised Heyman at all given the presence of Stephanie as the "owner" of ECW, and it's too bad Heyman wasn't used as an announcer for this show, given the chemistry he and JR had, and the dynamic it would have provided to have one representative from each side bickering throughout the show. But then, that's perhaps why they decided to avoid it. Still, it would have been preferable to Michael Cole, who unwittingly buries DDP even deeper by completely underselling Page's Diamond Cutter to Angle as a rather run-of-the-mill "neckbreaker". Nice one, you little twerp.

Eventually, the whole thing breaks down into an all-out brawl and, after a series of table-assisted high spots, Austin finally turns heel (again) after walloping Angle with a Stunner and dumping Booker T on top for the pin. Even credited with the victory, Booker's status as WCW World Champion has suddenly dropped with the addition of WWF titlist Austin, and his stock would only continue to fall until he was beaten into the ground by the Rock later in the year before the WWF finally decided to build him back up in their own image after "proving" their superiority over the apparently inferior WCW talent.

Final score: WWF 5 - 5 Alliance, although two of the WWF's victories came in non-wrestler matches (Hebner vs. Patrick and Trish/Lita vs. Stacy/Torrie). Still, I'm sure WWF loyalists would still claim a draw, so lets head back to *Sunday Night Heat* prior to the pay-per-view for the tiebreaker where Chavo Guerrero beat Scotty 2 Hotty, making it WWF 5 - 6 Alliance. Sorry, WWF; whichever way you slice it, you've lost your champion, you've lost your bragging rights (hey, there's a lame idea for a PPV in eight years time!) and you've lost this battle. But not to worry, you can just bury the Alliance at every turn for the next four months instead and prove your superiority, if not your booking genius.
Score: WWF 5-5 Alliance
Final Rating: ****

VERDICT

The Rock is flirting with Hollywood (though at this stage, it's more like heavy petting), Mankind has retired, Triple H is on the shelf, and Steve Austin is no longer the blue collar, working class everyman. The Invasion is in full swing, and the Attitude Era is dying a slow, painful death. Still, there was MUCH joy all around Titan Tower once news of *InVasion*'s buyrate came in, to the tune of an whopping 770,000 buys, a staggering number for a 'B-show' PPV, and at the time, the fourth most-bought pay-per-view in WWF history. In fact, well over a decade later it remained in WWE's all-time top 15 buyrates, the only non-*WrestleMania* show to achieve that status. Yes, more people paid to see the first ever on-screen clash between the WWF, WCW and ECW than any single *Royal Rumble*, *SummerSlam* or *Survivor Series* in history. More than paid to see Hulk Hogan vs. Andre the Giant at *WrestleMania III*, more than paid to see Hulk Hogan vs. The Ultimate Warrior at *WrestleMania VI*, and more than paid to see Steve Austin win his first WWF Title at *WrestleMania XIV*. And yet, just *four months* later, the angle was so cold that the WWF decided to pull the plug on it entirely at *Survivor Series*, in favour of a complete reboot. What an unmitigated *disaster* those months would prove to be, an unprecedented period of thoroughly rapid decline from which the promotion spent years struggling to recover.

65

SUMMERSLAM 2001

CAT NO: WWF274
RUN TIME: 162 minutes (approx)

Lee Maughan: From the Compaq Center in San Jose, California. Hosts are Jim Ross and Paul Heyman.

WWF Intercontinental Championship
Lance Storm (c) vs. Edge
If he can be serious for a minute, Lance would like to explain how he feels there's "no place for offbeat shenanigans in this business." Splendid. They work a fairly competitive back-and-forth match to start, with a flapjack, a flying crossbody and a rolling fireman's carry slam being the highlights, but Storm soon cranks on the abdominal stretch, much to my disappointment. One could argue that, within the psychology of the match he's at least attempting to wear Edge down for his finisher, but a rest hold is still a rest hold and it gives off the air that they're holding back somewhat since they're jerking the curtain.

They do ramp things up a notch when Edge catches Storm off a springboard and turns it into a powerbomb, and he also hits a tasty sitout powerbomb off a huracanrana attempt, but Storm comes right back and locks in the Canadian Maple Leaf. Edge makes it to the ropes and grabs a half crab of his own, and a few moments later, Christian appears, accidentally missing Storm on a charge and spearing Edge instead. The implication there is that he may have actually speared Edge on purpose, continuing the slow burn of Christian's heel turn, but Edge kicks out of Storm's pin attempt and counters a superkick into the Edgecution for the pin. Post-match, Christian grabs the belt and for all the world looks like he's about to deck Edge with it, which the crowd seem to expect, but they hug it out instead.
Final Rating: ***¼

- Backstage, Test cuts a pretty impassioned promo about why he betrayed the WWF for the Alliance, and manages to call Michael Cole a "bitch" along the way, so points for that.

Test & The Dudley Boyz vs. The APA & Spike Dudley
For those wondering, Spike is representing the WWF here because he started dating Molly Holly, which Bubba Ray and D-Von took exception to since they were feuding with Hardcore Holly and Crash Holly at the time. The APA are more or less just out there as the self-appointed defenders of all things WWF, but it's Spike who sees most of the ring time, getting absolutely hammered by the Dudleys, Bubba in particular.

Spike eventually avoids a diving headbutt from D-Von and gets the hot tag to Bradshaw who runs wild on Test with clotheslines and a powerbomb, then Spike looks to finish with the Dudley Dog only for Test to hurl him over the top and through a ringside table in a great visual. From there, Shane McMahon runs down and blasts Bradshaw between the eyes with a cookie sheet, giving Test the pin, a seemingly cheap finish but one they would actually pay off later in the night. Average match until the closing stretch, and you may have noticed a pattern in the booking so far tonight, at least in terms of outside interference...
Final Rating: **¼

- In the back, Edge is congratulated on his win by two of his best friends, Matt Hardy and Lita. Hindsight can be such a wonderful thing. Christian barges in to jealously announce that he's booked himself a shot at Matt's European Title tomorrow night on *RAW*, then calls his grandma to announce the good news. Unfortunately, grams only wants to speak with Edge, and hangs up when Christian takes back the phone. Guffaw.

- Elsewhere, Shawn Stasiak barges in on Debra without knocking, in what was surely an inside joke given the lengths they went to mention it, and he asks her for advice on how to impress Steve Austin. He complains about his pink, star-emblazoned tights ("I don't even know what 'Mecca' means!") so Debra tells him to go kick somebody's ass.

WCW Cruiserweight Championship
WWF Light Heavyweight Championship
X-Pac (c) vs. Tajiri (c)
This is the first, and in fact only, all-WWF bout tonight, with X-Pac looking to regain the Light Heavyweight title having recently lost it to Tajiri to set this reunification match up. They do some energetic, high-flying stuff, the kind X-Pac hasn't done in quite some time, and given the *SummerSlam* setting, that provides flashbacks to his outing with Hakushi back in '95.

Tajiri's in good form tonight too, hitting a nasty tree of woe dropkick and locking in the Tarantula. He follows with a bridging German suplex but X-Pac sends him to the outside and follows quickly with a topé con hilo. Back inside, X-Pac avoids a handspring elbow and hits the X-Factor but it only gets two, so X-Factor stablemate Albert (now teammate since Justin Credible joined the Alliance) comes out to run interference, making us three for three on that particular scorecard tonight. Tajiri catches him with red mist but the distraction is enough for X-Pac to hit a second X-Factor and re-link the two belts. Oddly enough, in a very un-WWF move, they would quickly jettison their own Light Heavyweight title but keep WCW's Cruiserweight crown, albeit with WWF branding. Solid match here, and it was nice to have the old Sean Waltman back for one night too.
Final Rating: **½

- Meanwhile, Perry Saturn is searching for the recently abducted Moppy over at WWF New York.

Chris Jericho vs. Rhyno
Rhyno is Stephanie McMahon-Helmsley's hand-picked monster in her continuing attempts to shut Jericho's mouth, though the impact of Rhyno Goring Jericho through the *SmackDown!* stage set is somewhat lessened when they cut to an angle that shows it basically consisted of a thin sheet of plastic and little else. This also comes from what you might loosely term the third "rut" of Jericho's WWF career, as he entered the promotion in 1999 to tremendous fanfare before quickly finding himself in the doghouse for apparently not knowing how to work "WWF style." He followed with a Chris Kreski-led resurgence in 2000 but found himself bouncing around the midcard once more come the autumn until another renewed push kicked in heading into 2001. By May, he and Chris Benoit were beating Steve Austin and Triple H for the tag titles in a killer *RAW* main event, but with Benoit's injury and the commencing of the invasion angle, he finds himself lost in the shuffle yet again. It's just too bad the WWF didn't go full circle a second time and book him against X-Pac at *Unforgiven* for the third straight year for a real chuckle.

Rhyno blocks the Walls of Jericho early but Stephanie grabs Jericho's leg when he goes up top, and the distraction sees him eat a Gore on the floor on the way down. Rhyno follows that with a flying body splash, which is one of the dumbest things he could conceivably do. His name is Rhyno and he's being pushed as the "Man Beast", he should be steamrolling Jericho head on, not taking to the skies. That's so ridiculously out of character. Jericho doesn't fare much better, badly blowing a Lionsault, then slipping off the top on a missile dropkick attempt and almost breaking his neck in the process. Worse still, he repeats the spot immediately, albeit from the middle rope, and for those of you watching the edited home video version, the removal of that botch is absolutely seamless.

Stephanie distracts the referee (four for four) so Jericho plants a big sloppy one on her, indirectly setting up their union in early 2002, and the Lionsault gets two but Rhyno fights back with a spinebuster and the Rhynotamer. Jericho makes it to the ropes so Rhyno sets himself for the Gore, but Jericho avoids that and finishes with the Walls. Decent match, blown spots aside.
Final Rating: **¾

- Backstage, Commissioner Regal bumps into the Rock, who admits he's hurting having been Bookended through a table last Thursday on *SmackDown!*, but this is *SummerSlam* and he's ready to go. The big joke of the otherwise serious promo is Rock taking a single step back as Shawn Stasiak barrels between the two and smashes into a wall before Rock steps forward again and finishes his speech to Regal. It was to become, quite literally, a running gag.

Ladder Match
WWF Hardcore Championship
Jeff Hardy (c) vs. Rob Van Dam
They start with some chain wrestling to establish parity, which I just find completely worthless here. Neither guy is even known for their chain wrestling, parity is already established by the fact this is a ladder match and you're only at a distinct disadvantage if you're 500 pounds or have no arms and legs, so the whole thing is such a transparent waste of time. Just go for the ladder!

Worse still is the fact that this is being billed as the "first ever hardcore ladder match", when in reality, it's not discernibly different to any other ladder match you've ever seen. I recognise that with the advent of the TLC matches, using tables and chairs would dilute that gimmick, but you'd think they could have dragged the 1999-approved trash cans and kendo sticks out of the mothballs for one night just to add a bit of variety and live up to the moniker. I get that the WWF would want to move away from the nutty highspots of said TLC matches, especially in light of the neck injury suffered by Chris Benoit after he wrestled in one on *SmackDown!* just a couple of months prior to this, but when you advertise a ladder match as "hardcore", you leave fans with a certain expectation that you can't deliver.

Eventually, they build to a spot where Jeff grabs the loop holding the belt but Van Dam pulls the ladder away, leaving him dangling there, so RVD swings Jeff from one side of the ring to the other, then attempts a springboard superkick on the rebound. I say attempt, because he actually misses, making himself look like a complete idiot on what would have been an incredibly cool spot if it had made contact. That's the nature of those kind of highspots though, sometimes you roll the dice and it comes up snake eyes.

FURIOUS ABOUT: TORRIE WILSON

Like Stacy Keibler, Torrie got into wrestling because her boyfriend was a fan of WCW. Her year long WCW career actually ended before the WWE bought the company out but the WWE were interested and brought her in for the Invasion. However after a matter of weeks they flipped Torrie face after pairing her up with Tajiri. After Tajiri turned heel and became controlling of her, Torrie broke free and engaged in a long and silly feud with Dawn Marie. The former ECW diva romanced Torrie's Dad Al Wilson, married him and caused him to die of a heart attack on their honeymoon with overly vigorous sex. Naturally this resulted in a grudge match on PPV. Only in wrestling. Torrie gained crossover popularity in 2003 after appearing in Playboy. In her later career Torrie even turned heel, relatively successfully, to feud with Ashley Massaro. She left the WWE in 2008.

Problematically, that leaves Jeff swinging around aimlessly, so he has to take a bump off nothing lest he accidentally pull down the belt that he's been booked to lose. He then immediately climbs back up using the ladder, thus making himself look every bit the fool RVD did, and Van Dam shoves him off it with Jeff taking a ridiculous flip bump into the ropes that saw his upper back land roughly on the mat, and looked like he could have torn both hamstrings *and* blown out both knees on the ropes to boot. For those unaware, pro wrestling ring ropes are extremely sturdy, not at all springy and elasticised as the work would have you believe.

From there, the result is academic, as Van Dam clambers up to claim his second reign as Hardcore champion. Though it may not come across as such in the review, I actually thought this was a pretty good match for the most part, and some of the big bumps were crazy, it just had a hard time living up to the bar the ladder and TLC matches had set over the previous couple of years.
Final Rating: ***½

Steel Cage Match
WWF Tag Team Championship
WCW Tag Team Championship
The Brothers of Destruction (c) vs. DDP & Kanyon (c)
What a disaster this is. As I'm sure you're aware, DDP had nonsensically revealed himself as the stalker of the Undertaker's wife Sara, despite every wrestling fan on the planet already being resolutely aware of his marriage to the smoking hot ex-Nitro Girl Kimberly. From there, Undertaker senselessly destroyed Page in a non-match "confrontation" at the *King of the Ring*, all but killing the angle stone dead. Despite that, their feud rumbled on for another two months with Page building a shrine to Sara and bringing his old New Jersey Triad buddy Kanyon into things, presumably so the WWF could kill off two careers in one fell swoop.

Undertaker and Kane are actually the WCW Tag Team champions here, having beaten Chuck Palumbo and Sean O'Haire on the August 7 edition of *SmackDown!*, while Page and Kanyon carry the WWF belts after beating previous champions the APA on the same night. And that's where parity ends, as the Brothers of Destruction just completely squash DDP and Kanyon, battering them from pillar to post, all while the Alliance guys try to flee in abject fear like the total cowards we all know everyone from WCW to be. Yeah! Show us your overwhelming superiority, WWF guys! That's what I've paid my pay-per-view money to see: an extended weekend TV squash match completely burying two guys who arguably could have been top players if not for this small-minded booking lark! Wooo! Last Ride his ass! Oh yeah, bang goes that People's Champ vs. People's Champ DDP vs. Rock main event so easy to promote that even Stevie Wonder could see it!

In fact, the only meagre offence DDP and Kanyon get the whole match is simply so Undertaker and Kane can work in a double sit-up spot, something which might have actually been effective if they'd actually shown some ass for more than 12 seconds first. They let Kanyon escape which leaves DDP alone with both of them, and Undertaker yanks him off the top rope with a chokeslam and finishes with the Last Ride to unify the titles in a travesty only topped by the Brothers' WCW Tag Title defence against KroniK the next month at *Unforgiven*. It's matches like this that resulted in so many smart fans growing to loathe the Undertaker during the first half of the 2000s, before his spectacular Lazarus-like rise as a super worker in the second half of the decade. Oddly enough, Undertaker and

FURIOUS ABOUT: WILLIAM REGAL
Regal is one of the most underrated and outstandingly talented men in all of wrestling. He debuted back in 1983 and worked in the UK for a decade before going to WCW. He had a six year run in WCW, which was quite successful winning four TV titles, before a failed WWF run in 1998, as the Real Man's Man, where a trip to rehab ruined him. After proving himself on the Indies, and back in WCW, Regal was hired by the WWE in 2000 where he became a Goodwill Ambassador and later WWE Commissioner. Largely competing as a heel, with a tremendous lexicon and even better facial expressions, Regal was a dominant force in the WWE's midcard for many years. He was twice IC champion and a four time European champion. His occasional drug issues aside, he's been a model WWE employee and has been a wonderfully consistent performer.

Kane would go on to drop both sets of belts in fairly clean fashion, the WWF straps to the Dudley Boyz and the WCW belts to Booker T and Test. Of course both of those teams were WWF-approved, unlike the DDP/Kanyon duo.
Final Rating: DUD

- In the medical room, a trainer attempts to tape up the Rock, but he won't allow it. He does however stop to take a step backwards and of course, Shawn Stasiak goes flying over a bench, with Rock once again failing to acknowledge his presence.

WWF Championship
Steve Austin (c) vs. Kurt Angle
With Austin turning heel at *InVasion* to lead the Alliance, the Rock flirting with Hollywood, Triple H and Chris Benoit on the injured reserve list and Chris Jericho bouncing around the midcard, Angle has recently found himself in the role of the WWF's lead babyface, with an accelerated month-long push into the realms of actually being a badass after more than a year as a goofball who just happened to be a great wrestler.

They meet in the aisle for Austin's standard match-opening walkabout brawl where Angle stomps a mudhole in Austin but fails to wipe it dry as they fight into the ring. Austin blasts Angle with three suplexes for a two count, so Angle returns fire with *seven* German suplexes and tries for the Olympic Slam, but Austin avoids it with a rake to the eyes. Over in the corner, they fight over a superplex with Austin getting it on the second attempt, adding a level of realism to the struggle that so few workers do. A Stunner out of nowhere gets a two count, visibly pissing Austin off, and a second one puts Angle on the floor where Austin shoves him into the steel post *six times* to draw blood, as he'd promised to do on *RAW*.

They brawl into the crowd where Austin suplexes Angle on the concrete, but Angle catches Austin with the ankle lock and actually drags him over the guardrail, up the steel steps, through the ropes and back into the ring without letting go, creating a visual reminiscent of the Austin-Bret Hart Sharpshooter spot from *WrestleMania 13*, only this time it's Angle who's the one basically bleeding to death. Back on the floor, Angle fires off suplexes of the belly-to-belly and backdrop variety, then heads back inside for a moonsault which actually connects, a move he'd legitimately broken Hardcore Holly's arm with previously. Running out of weaponry, Austin actually breaks out the Million Dollar Dream, allowing JR to make Ringmaster references, and they call back to the finish of the Austin-Hart *Survivor Series* '96 match, with Angle pushing off the top turnbuckle to roll into a pin. Austin's learnt from his past however, and keeps the hold applied to avoid defeat. Man, that's some *deep* psychology, right there.

Desperate now, Austin hits a third Stunner and still only gets two. He knows the end is near however, and smugly smirks before going for another one… only for Angle to grab his boot and counter with probably the most sudden yet super smooth counter into the Olympic Slam you'll ever see. Angle follows with another ankle lock attempt so Austin, now running on empty, punches referee Earl Hebner right in the face. Angle scores with a DDT so Mike Chioda runs in to make the pin but Austin kicks out and gives him a Stunner. That brings out third referee Tim White who blocks Austin's attempt at decking Angle with the title belt, so 'Stone Cold' blasts White with it instead.

Kurt hits another Olympic Slam and makes the cover, but with no WWF referees left, crooked WCW official Nick Patrick comes out… and disqualifies Austin for his referee abuse, ensuring the title stays with the Alliance. That's exactly the kind of finish you get when you've got a recently-turned babyface star whom it's too early to beat but an ongoing angle that requires you keep the title on the heel. Still, it did at least lead to a rematch the following month at *Unforgiven*, although real life would play a serious hand in the outcome of that match when America began looking for a national hero in the wake of the 9/11 terrorist attacks.

Interestingly, WWF writer Ed Koskey later revealed that the original plan was to have Angle beat Austin so badly that he needed to get himself disqualified to save the title, but that Austin changed the booking to what we actually saw. I presume that was because Austin didn't want to appear weak as the lead heel in the promotion, and didn't want the new babyface to be so aggressive as to draw sympathy for Austin. Either way, this match was absolutely awesome, even with the cheap ending.
Final Rating: ****½

**WCW Championship
Booker T (c) vs. The Rock**
The issue here is that Booker is basically being pushed as the Alliance's answer to the Rock, quite literally, being referred to as 'the Book' and putting more emphasis on the Bookend (Rock Bottom) as his finisher. You know, the Rock vs. DDP, People's Champ vs. People's Champ was right there, and instead they went with pushing a guy as a pale imitation of their own star. Just another nail in the coffin that was the invasion angle.

The match is pretty similar in make-up to the previous one, which can perhaps be explained by Austin's insistence on changing the structure of his outing. There's walkabout brawling to start before they fight into the ring, and then inevitably back to the floor before trading hot and heavy moves back inside, with Rock even breaking out La Majistral at one point. Unfortunately, where this match fails to compare to the previous one is with Booker slapping on a chinlock right in the middle of it, and Rock coming back with a Sharpshooter (Scorpion King Deathlock?) despite no previous legwork. Booker was always a talented guy, sure, and few workers have ever been as naturally good at performing as the Rock, but neither are holding a candle to Austin's performance tonight.

Rock catapults Booker into a turnbuckle exposed earlier by ringside cheerleader Shane McMahon (what cruel irony), and then because all WWF main event matches require it, there follows a gigantic dose of shenanigans as Shane lays out Rock with the WCW Title belt before getting his head completely ripped off by a vengeful Bradshaw, paying off Shane's earlier interference in the six-man. The Bookend gets two and Rock comes back with a flying lariat and a belly-to-belly before going into his usual finishing stretch with a spinebuster and the People's Elbow. A recovered Shane breaks that up so Rock gives him a Rock Bottom, only for Booker to land an axe kick and deliver the Spinneroonie to an overwhelmingly large reaction. JR's burial of it is a little hard to swallow, but then he is a WWF guy. Rocky of course pops right back up and ends it with the Rock Bottom to restore World Title parity that had been the Alliance's bragging rights for 28 glorious days. What a truly epic run of dominance.

Pretty good match in all, but it might be best viewed in isolation as it just couldn't follow Austin vs. Angle, especially given the layout similarities it bore, and while everything they did was perfectly competent, they just didn't have the chemistry to take it to the next level.
Final Rating: ***½

VERDICT

Despite a lot of the matches on offer here falling slightly below expectations (Edge-Storm, Jericho-Rhyno, RVD-Hardy, Rock-Booker), one match being a needlessly counterproductive waste of everyone's time (Brothers of Destruction-DDP/Kanyon) and one match suffering from a truly lousy conclusion (Angle-Austin), this is still a pretty darn solid wrestling pay-per-view overall. Sure, that could be said of just about any show from the invasion era, but it's certainly true here.

One final thought to leave you with: wouldn't it have been interesting, and certainly more beneficial to the promotion in the long term, if they'd turned the Rock heel and had him join the Alliance? In storyline, with two of the biggest stars defecting to the other side in a mirror of 1996, the WWF would have been forced to rebuild with younger guys like Jericho, Angle and perhaps even Booker and RVD on top. It certainly would have made sense from a business perspective with Austin on borrowed time following his neck surgery, Rock getting increasingly cosy with Hollywood and Triple H on the bench, but since the WWF were making money even in spite of themselves with the way they botched the invasion angle, that was never going to happen. Back in '96, they had their backs against the wall with a Ted Turner-owned, Eric Bischoff-led WCW bearing down on them. Here, they were the only game in town and long-term benefits or not, if it wasn't broke, they weren't about to fix it.

81

MICK FOLEY - HARD KNOCKS AND CHEAP POPS

CAT NO: WWF277
RUN TIME: 72 minutes (approx)

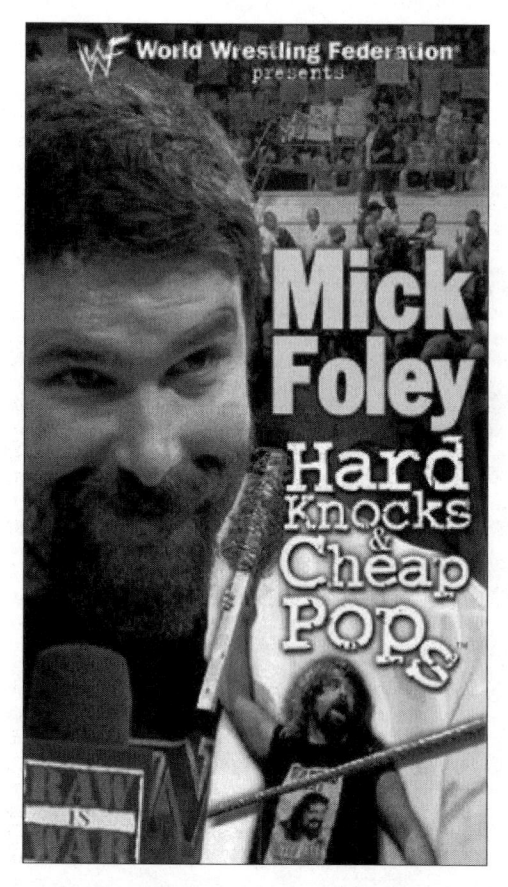

James Dixon: With Mick Foley having retired from active full-time competition in favour of a position as an onscreen authority figure, one much kinder to his battered body, this tapes covers the fun he had in that role as well as revisiting some of the tremendous performances he put in at the back end of his career. I have always been a big fan of Mick Foley, in terms of both his work and personality, as well as his books too. The last tape of his that I reviewed, *Three Faces of Foley*, scored a perfect 100 in *The Complete WWF Video Guide Volume #4*, so I am looking forward to this.

Host is Mick Foley himself, obviously. He starts out by talking about his favourite subject for ridicule; Al Snow. He discusses their relationship and brings up a match with Hardcore Holly where Al took a bunch of chair shots and decided to smile instead of sell them. The poor guy was just trying to play his unhinged character, but it garnered him some heat from the boys. At Mr. Socko's birthday party on *Sunday Night Heat*, Mick mocked Al by saying: "I'd first like to send congratulations to Al Snow for landing that lucrative endorsement deal with La-Z-Boy, which is surprising because Al doesn't usually sell chairs". Great line. Mick claims their relationship became strained because of his constant ribbing, and that his countless Al Snow jokes in his book *Have a Nice Day* were his backhanded way of apologising. People latched onto Mick in a big way after that book came out, and art imitated life on television as Al and Mick become onscreen best friends, and even tag champions. We see footage of the pair in Vegas, which leads to some fun segments with a planted fan pretending to be the Rock, who pesters them mercilessly. During a poker game, Foley states: "I've been dreaming about a hand like this all my life", to which Al quips: "You dream about your hand all the time." "Shut up, Al" barks Foley in response. The two had great chemistry.

Foley says that in 1999 his body told him to retire, but the money told him otherwise. At least he is honest. He says that's why he ended up teaming with the Rock, basically so he could coast by and do far less of a physically demanding style, instead relying on comedy, which he happened to be great at. The tandem had immense chemistry, they were perfect foil and a wonderful opposites attract partnership. They weren't together long, but had a host of fondly remembered moments together, and they delivered big time in the ratings. The segment with Mick throwing a "This is Your Life" celebration for his surly partner remains the highest rated in the history of *RAW*. Foley was on fire during the entire union, with his self-deprecating act winning him a lot of new fans, and producing some classic lines, such as a backstage interview where he says: "It doesn't matter what my name is, Michael Cole". Nobody was willing to "show ass" like Foley was. Unfortunately the duo didn't last, coming to an end when Mick found a signed copy of his book that he had given to Rock in the trash, and Mick cuts a vicious promo on his partner, getting angrier than he had been in years. Stupid airhead Divas idiotically gurning into the camera and delivering fake sounding scripted lines, this ain't. It turns out it was all a big misunderstanding though, and it was a jealous Al who had put the book in the bin. This results in a brief TV feud, with the match shown (in brief highlight form) ending when Rock belts Al with a couple of chair shots off camera, in what turns out to be his locker room.

We go to Mick's final program as a regular performer, his feud with Triple H, which is the meat of this tape. The rivalry is covered in detail, from Mick losing a Pink Slip on a Pole match to his big return a few weeks later. Trips batters and bloodies Mankind, resulting in him demasking in a subtle act of symbolism. Foley's full transformation from Mankind to Cactus Jack in a truly brilliant segment on *SmackDown!* (shown here set to the harrowing tones of *'O Fortuna')* is not so subtle, but then it was never supposed to be, and the crowd react to the metamorphosis brilliantly. Equally superb is the reaction from Triple H, who sells this better than he did anything else in his career. He puts the Cactus Jack character over as a main event title threat more with one look than he did with everyone he ever worked with, as he became a burial specialist down the years. I guess he knew Foley was retiring and thus wasn't a

FURIOUS ABOUT: TOMMY DREAMER

Dreamer WAS ECW. He defined the company in both style and attitude. He worked extremely hard to get over with the Philly fans and dedicated himself to hardcore. The Innovator of Violence worked in ECW from 1993 until it closed in 2001. He initially debuted alongside Rob Van Dam in a sensational switch in Invasion booking, albeit short-lived as Stephanie McMahon took over ECW in an idiotic move. While RVD's WWE career rapidly took off the aging Dreamer found himself in a secondary role before being shunted into HWA when the Invasion ended. He later developed a 'disgusting' persona where he'd eat garbage before returning to hardcore with 14 Hardcore title wins. Dreamer's knowledge of wrestling production, learned in ECW, held him in good stead and he moved into the office. In 2005 he was instrumental in the ECW reunion and the ECW Brand. Dreamer left the WWE in 2010.

threat to his position. Not that his position could ever possibly be under threat what with him NAILING THE BOSSES DAUGHTER! To his credit here, Trips downplays his role in making Cactus, saying that he was already a mythological being, and he just reacted to him. Mick rightly points out that if Trips had laughed him off when he in reality did little more than just take his shirt and mask off, it would have killed it. Taking angles like this seriously in wrestling makes a great deal of difference in generating interest in a contest. That is why long time fans got frustrated in the WWE PG-era, when everything was tongue in cheek, done with a wink and a nod or just downplayed as "part of the story". Wrestling was cool in 2000 because everyone was a badass, rather than everyone being a pretty boy with a tan and perfect hair. Can you imagine someone like The Miz or any of the stream of cookie-cutter generic sports entertainers working a feud like this?

We get footage from the epic and supremely violent *Royal Rumble 2000* match, which Trips says was brutal, but that they had already apologised to each other in the back so it was all okay. Goodbye, kayfabe. We see brutal chair shots to the face from Hunter, the sickening sight of a piece of wood from a broken pallet stabbing Hunter in the leg and the introduction of barbed wire into the WWF. Now, a note on that: when they first brought out Barbie, the wire was very real, and when Hunter used it on Cactus you could see it sticking in his shirt. As the match progressed, the old switcheroo was implemented by the Fink and the Spanish announce team, and the barbed wire bat replaced with a replica that featured rubber wire. The problem was that this bat looked new and fresh, whereas the old one has already began to unravel from getting stuck in Cactus' shirt. The change was made because Hunter was taking a bunch of shots to the face and understandably didn't want to risk losing an eye or ripping his skin open. I guess the question becomes: why didn't they just use that from the start? Mick didn't need to take any more brutal weapon shots to prove his toughness in this environment or to get another hardcore badge of honour. He already had plenty of those, and frankly no one would have known any different anyway if it had been gimmicked from the start. One thing they could not fake was the thousands of thumbtacks that Cactus introduced, and of course he was the one who took the bump into the pins. Hell, it

was his specialty. We get around 15-minutes of the tape devoted to this remarkable match, which is probably the greatest hardcore outing in history, coming it at around ****¾ in this writer's view.

I want to briefly stop off to mention the music that has been used on this tape. On a lot of other releases that I have covered in this book, the choice of music has been pretty crappy and generic, with everything from incessant techno noise to soulless throwaway half-assed nu metal dirge delivering an aural assault over the top of the footage. On this, it has been brilliant. Whoever was in charge of picking the accompanying music obviously knew what they were doing, because everything fits perfectly, and there is not a hint of P.O.D. in sight.

Even though Hunter went over at the Rumble, the feud between the two continues. What strikes me is that a lot of the angles and storyline progression came on *SmackDown!*, which is remarkable to me having gotten used to so many years where literally nothing at all happens on the show to move things along. Trips on *RAW* then challenges Cactus to his last shot at him or the title at *No Way Out 2000*, with the bout in question being Hell in a Cell with Foley's career on the line. This was the second match that made Triple H into a bona fide star, with Mick Foley once again putting his body on the line for the sake of his art and in an effort to help the career of his opponent. There are few as selfless in an industry full of bastards as Mick Foley. Mick talks about the tough legacy that he and Hunter had to live up to following their bout the previous month, and of course his own past shenanigans in the cell. "I didn't fancy my chances of winning, if you know what I mean" he offers with a winking glance as this tape continues to let the world in on the big (but really, not so big) secret. Foley mentions how he broke his own nose in the bout delivering a chair assisted elbow drop, and points out that it's a good job it wasn't Hunter's nose that got broken, or "we both would have drowned". Because it's enormous, you see. We see a spot where Cactus fell from halfway up the cage and through a table, which was a good bump and all but nothing compared to the one against Undertaker, and if you can't at least match something you have done already then why bother doing an inferior version? We see footage from the forgotten Hell in a Cell on *RAW* (why would you *ever* put the Cell on RAW!? Oh, right, Vince Russo was booking...) against Kane, where he took the same bump and missed the table by a mile, which looked hellacious. That begs another question: why would you take a bump like that again when it went so wrong the first time!? We don't get full highlights of this, but rather just the big bumps, with a flaming barbed wire bat brought into play, and then Cactus getting backdropped through the cage and indeed through the ring. The difference between this cage bump and the *King of the Ring '98* one is that this time, the cage was supposed to give way, and the ring had been played around with by the crew so that the bump was far more delicate. Again though, why try and recapture magic and run the same thing twice? That never works. Cactus was still alive so Hunter followed up with a Pedigree and that was it for Mick's fairly brief in real terms (four years), but still legendary WWF career...

...Only it wasn't, because he took the first step towards the complete and total bastardisation of his legacy by returning to the ring the following month at *WrestleMania 2000*. I don't blame the guy, because the promise of a *WrestleMania* payoff should always trump a kayfabed promise to the fans for anyone with any business sense, but at the same time it did retroactively cheapen the *No Way Out* battle. The pop that

COMMISSIONER FOLEY

Mick got for his return on *RAW* was something else, but the shape he showed up in was embarrassing. He was way heavier in just a month, which Foley claims was 20lbs, but it looks more like 30lbs at least. I have never seen anyone change shape so much in such a short space of time. In the 'Mania match, Foley shows that he has no sense again, repeating a spot from *Survivor Series: Deadly Game* where he made a mess of a flying elbow off the top through the announce table, severely and permanently damaging his knee in the process. It was one of the reasons he ended up having to retire early. In his infinite wisdom, Mick decided to repeat the spot again at *WrestleMania*, only with an extra tyre of tubbiness around his waist and the aforementioned jiggered knee. He came up short, VERY short, and smashed his chest into the table then bounced off in a heap, not even coming close to hitting the Rock. The silly bastard.

Now to a fun time in Mick's career, when he served as WWF commissioner. He was introduced by Shawn Michaels on *RAW*, complete with freshly shaven head and with a seriously crappy dress sense. Seriously, you think he looked scruffy in Mankind's later years? Just check him out in this role, with his baggy sweatpants, occasional charm necklace, t-shirt and sleeveless flannel shirt. He wouldn't have even got on WWE TV in the John Cena era, because the company was so cute about its own image. On the brief occasions he was involved on camera during that time, there was a strict directive to film him from the waist up. Hell the poor guy had been retired from full-time competition for over a decade, just let him eat his junk food and enjoy his life. He deserved any comforts he could get for what he had put his body through over the years. Annoyingly, one of the chief orchestrators of said directive was none other than one Triple H. I don't know if it was for the good of the company or Mick Foley's legacy, but whatever his rationale, he should show more respect to the man that made him into the top tier star he became. Back to the tape anyway, and we see the birth of the cheap pop during a promo with Triple H (with Stephanie nodding furiously in the background, completely out of synch with what is being said, making her look like a clueless imbecile), and then a collection of some of the better ones.

Foley continues his tradition of putting up and coming guys in his video tapes (he did the same thing for the Hardys on *Three Faces of Foley*) by featuring Edge & Christian. The two were at their absolute best as a doubles act around this time, and one of the segments shown that doesn't even involve Foley is the Kurt Angle birthday party, where they rile up the moody Triple H by wearing Teletubbies party hats, blowing streamers and playing theme songs on a kazoo. It's one of my favourite comedic segments in wrestling ever, and for me the peak of both Edge and Christian as entertainers. More so even than 'the Rated R Superstar' and more so than 'Captain Charisma' and his "peeps", I absolutely adored Edge & Christian as a team, because they left you wanting more each week. One segment of theirs also involving the kazoo that still cracks me up to this day is when they played Chris Benoit's theme while singing in monotone "Chris Benoit is here and he's really mad". It's utter genius.

We see more from Edge & Christian, who sit and talk with Foley about some of their finer moments onscreen together. Some of the wonderfully fun skits are shown, including an exchange backstage when the duo want their own locker room like the Rock, and Foley says how he never had his own locker room, and he was WWF Champion. Edge points out that: "You never change your clothes!" while Christian adds: "You just wrestle in what you are wearing!". The delivery from all three is perfect. They continue to shoot the shit, laughing about Foleys toy dog "Sarge" (named as a tribute to previous commissioner Sgt. Slaughter), Christian pretending to be sick to get out of a match, Christian trying to shed weight for a Light Heavyweight Title match by wearing a chicken suit, and Edge saying Mick is "full of poo" when he notices his Winnie the Pooh shirt. These interactions between the trio are one of the reasons that I enjoyed Foley in this role so much.

We stop off briefly to see Mick building Stephanie up with kindness before cruelly breaking her spirit, and then get some more amusing segments from his run in the role, including a doozey where he accidentally smashes Pat Patterson's hand with his gavel. Next a remarkably serious promo from atop a truck on Triple H, then onto the investigation into who ran over Steve Austin back at *Survivor Series 1999*. 'Stone Cold's' method of interrogation involved running through everyone with Stunners, which is probably the worst technique for gleaming information ever. I mean, they are all knocked out! Foley told Austin to stop interfering in matches, which he didn't, so Foley suspended him. That resulted in Stunners, obviously, and Mick in real life worrying about being a heel. We then take a brief look at Mick's children's Christmas book, as he sits down with the book's artist Jerry Lawler to discuss the kid that inspired the story, and to talk about some of the quirky art.

To the end of Foley's Commissioner run now, with Vince McMahon demanding that Foley resign from the role. William Regal speaking on behalf of the locker room requests the same, but Steve Austin comes to his defence and decks Vince, as Foley tears up the letter of resignation. But that was only a brief respite, because he was fired by Vince soon afterwards and beaten up by Edge, Christian and Kurt Angle. It was a shame. Foley leaving the screens was soon followed by Steve Austin turning heel, The Rock disappearing to make movies and Triple H getting injured. The glory days were over, and the WWF was a very different and much worse place in 2001 because of it.

VERDICT

Well, Mick opened up the businesses secrets in his first book, and now he spreads its legs on this video tape, delving deeper behind the curtain than anyone ever has previously. It's one thing to talk about things from the distant past in terms that make clear they were not so real, but to do it about feuds from a year prior seems a little strange. Kayfabe issues aside, the tape is constantly entertaining and has a very different feel to most other releases. You get the impression that this is exactly the tape that Mick wanted, and it does him justice both as a hardcore icon and as a happy-go-lucky, loveable entertainer. I don't think it quite reaches the heady heights of *Three Faces of Foley*, but there is plenty good on here to make it well worth your while. It brings back fond memories of a time when wrestling was still fun and not a corporate shell of its former glory. For that I can't do anything other than recommend it.

84

HARDCORE

CAT NO: WWF278
RUN TIME: 76 minutes (approx)

James Dixon: Having been a delightfully cheesy real life cartoon throughout the previous two decades of its existence, the WWF drastically changed tact in 1997/98 and decided to borrow liberally from the red hot ECW and embrace blood, guts and weapons. This tape is a celebration of all things hardcore from the WWF's infamous Attitude Era.

Tazz presents from a dilapidated building, and we start off with various WWF superstars discussing what the term "hardcore" means to them. Bradshaw thinks people enjoy it because they like to see violence whereas Christian takes on the question literally, and reads the Webster's Dictionary definition. Matt Hardy mentions injuries while his brother Jeff claims his dad is hardcore. This is not the tape for soppy nonsense and glowing soliloquies, Jeff. Even the Fink gets a few words, which tickles Tazz because of how out of place Fink is on a tape like this.

The tapes moves on to feature talent who have made the term hardcore popular, and naturally we start out with Mick Foley, one of the key perpetrators of the style in the company. Foley says he was doing hardcore matches in the WWF before the term became vogue, such as his slightly underrated and perversely entertaining Boiler Room Brawl from *SummerSlam '96* which was completely different to anything else the company was doing at the time. Highlights from Mick's various violent battles from over the years follow, including slightly extended footage from his wild brawl with mentor and best friend Terry Funk on *RAW* in 1998. As a thank you from Vince McMahon, the Mankind character was awarded the brand new Hardcore Championship, which was just an old winged eagle WWF Championship belt smashed to pieces with "hardcore" taped onto it. It was actually a really fun idea because it gave the plethora of otherwise fairly useless undercard guys a purpose and the chance to be entertaining, especially when the WWF introduced the wild 24/7 rules. For once the company didn't take itself too seriously, and it resulted in some memorable outings for guys who would have otherwise been afterthoughts. Like Al Snow...

No Holds Barred, Falls Count Anywhere
WWF Hardcore Championship
Road Dogg (c) vs. Al Snow
...Who is featured in this match from *RAW* against Road Dogg. Snow wrestles the match in a blood-soaked t-shirt, with the crimson coming from a Brood bloodbath two weeks prior. Al is at his most unhinged in this, hiding underneath the curtain prior to the bout and shooting crazed looks like a guy who has just drank all of Randy Savage's coffee stash. He takes some nasty bumps too, including a moonsault off the barricade through a table and some violent tray shots from Dogg, which he laughs about. The brawl heads all over the building and utilises all manner of comedic props along the way, including a potted plant. It's reminiscent of every backstage brawl you have ever seen, but it is still entertaining to watch. Why is it so fun to watch guys walking around taking the odd bump into something unusual? I have no idea, but it is! Al plays around with some metal poles and twirls them in his hands as he channels his previous one-off gimmick Shinobi, but Dogg fires back and they end up outside the building, where it just happens to be snowing heavily. How fitting. Dogg hits Snow with a snow shovel, which makes sense as a weapon to defeat someone called Snow I guess, and then pins him to lift the title after a piledriver onto a crate. That looked less than a barrel of laughs to take in that temperature! Both of these guys were really good at these type of matches because they were excellent at using their surroundings creatively, and this was no different. Hardcore matches I don't rate compared to actual wrestling bouts, I almost rate them in their own category because they are so far removed from actual wrestling. Thus, a *** hardcore match obviously doesn't compare to a *** standard bout, but is as entertaining in its own right nevertheless. This was a fun one for sure.
Final Rating: **½

Back to the talking heads, and Chris Jericho thinks the Undertaker is hardcore because of the way he works and how long he has been around. Not that he is trying to score political points or anything. It seems they have ran out of guys who want to talk about the subject, so they go to timekeeper Mark Yeaton who throws out the names Mick Foley, Al Snow and Steve Blackman. This is fairly redundant. A few more guys chime in as this just becomes a list of names of guys on the roster. Tazz in the next link marks out for Edge mentioning him, thrilled that someone has remembered that he was a wrestler once before he became a bad announcer.

Hardcore Match
Ivory vs. Tori

To the women, and a thong-wearing Tori attacks Ivory in a bathroom while a naked Jacqueline watches from in the shower. Ivory calls Tori a "little slut" so Tori throws tampons at her. "What are those!?" asks JR. Ivory takes to washing out Tori's mouth with soap and scores a near fall in the wet shower, before the brawl ends up in the men's locker room. Albert, Droz and Viscera get an eyeful of Tori's very exposed ass as she shoves Ivory off a table. They continue to fight/throw things at each other, and then things go from perversely amusing to slightly uncomfortable when Ivory smashes a mirror over a barefooted Tori's head and scores the win. Things get more disturbing after the "match" when Ivory grabs an iron and brands Tori in the back with it, causing her to scream in agony as hissing sound effects are pumped in from the truck. There is a point where things become just a little bit too much and go too far, and watching two half naked ladies beating the piss out of each other with weapons while their nipples and their dinner's are exposed, seems like that is probably it. What it says about me that I hypocritically had a good time watching it, I do not know.
Final Rating: **

WWF Hardcore Championship
Hardcore Holly vs. Al Snow

This comes from *St. Valentine's Day Massacre* with the belt currently vacant. Michael Cole throws out the "cup of coffee" line about Holly's previous Intercontinental and Tag Team Title reigns, which bothers me. A cup of coffee reign is brief, so I can accept that being the case with the tag belts, which he held for a couple of days. But Holly was never Intercontinental Champion, he just wasn't! The WWF have claimed this before, but in reality champion Jeff Jarrett was beaten by Holly in 1994, but the decision was overturned and the belt held up, with Jarrett winning the rematch. Holly was never recognised as the champion. If you are going to count him as a title holder, then we need to count Savio Vega too, we need to recognise Chris Jericho's 2000 WWF Championship victory over Triple H, and also count Andre the Giant and Ted DiBiase as former WWF Title holders. I know it doesn't *really* matter, but things like this where they chop and change their history and don't really pay it any respect, grates on me as a wrestling historian. The majority of this bout takes place outside in the dark, which makes it tough to see what is actually going on. The endless plunder shots are now losing their lustre having just watched plenty in the previous bouts, and the relative lack of creativity in this bout combined with the messy nature of it leaves one uninspired. The finish sees Holly wrap Snow in a mesh fence and pin him, with the idea being he is unable to get his shoulder up. Only, his shoulder is CLEARLY up, making the whole thing pretty dumb.
Final Rating: ¾*

A bunch of the guys discuss the worst injuries they have sustained, with many seeming to view them as badges of honour. There was a time when wrestling injuries made you tough, and working through them even tougher, but years later it just seems idiotic. The main feature of the piece is Hardcore Holly, who had his arm broken in half by an errant Kurt Angle moonsault during a match on *SmackDown!* and just continued anyway because he is a badass. What this has to do with a tape about hardcore matches I am not sure, because the bout

---

FURIOUS ABOUT: CRASH HOLLY

Crash is one of the most decorated wrestlers of the era holding the hardcore title 22 times, along with European title, Light Heavyweight title and the tag titles with his "cousin" Hardcore Holly. 25 in total. To put that into perspective; The Rock has held 17 titles in his entire career. Of course Crash went for quantity over quality and many of his hardcore title reigns lasted minutes and even seconds. Considering his size and lack of high-flying ability, Crash did well for himself in the WWE as an underdog. He was initially aided by teaming with established Bob Holly before striking out solo. By the end of his WWE run he found himself relegated to playing third fiddle to Matt Hardy and Shannon Moore before his release in mid 2003. Tragedy struck later in the year when he choked to death on his own vomit. He was only 32.

---

was just a standard match with a botched spot. In his book *The Hardcore Truth* Holly talks about how when they were planning the match backstage, it was his idea for Angle to hit the moonsault, as previously he always missed it. Angle was not confident about it, but Holly told him it would be fine. Famous last words. When the spot came, Holly realised that Angle had placed him too far away, and when Kurt launched himself into the move, Holly rolled towards him to protect himself but ended up taking a shin to the forearm, resulting in the following exchange:

Holly: "You broke my fucking arm! Cover me!".
(Angle did, but Holly decided to show he was tough and stick with the script, so kicked out.)
Angle: "What the fuck are you doing?!"
Holly: "Just hit me!"
Angle: "What!?"
Holly: "Fucking hit me, Kurt!"

I get that Holly is a hard guy and wanted to stick to the script, the show must go on and all of that, but it was just a throwaway match on a taped show, and he was losing anyway. Just stay down! Holly claims he figured it was just badly bruised because he had been able to continue, but from the way he was favouring the arm it was clear to everyone watching that it was broken. For his part, Angle was incredibly apologetic and did everything he could to make it up to Holly, such as turning up at the hospital, helping him make his flight the next day and sending him care packages while he was off. Commendable stuff. Vince McMahon later called Holly and praised him for working through the injury but chastised him at the same time because of the potential risks of doing so, such as if one of the broken bones had cut an artery and caused Holly to bleed to death. Like I said, he should have just stopped the match.

WWF Hardcore Championship
The Big Bossman (c) vs. Al Snow

This comes from *SummerSlam* '99, with Road Dogg coming out and earning his money by becoming the "roving Road Dogg" and following Bossman and Snow around to provide commentary. This doesn't even make the ring, and they brawl backstage, using all manner of plunder including a product placement Pepsi machine, which is empty. In a funny moment, a random guy on crutches is hobbling past and Bossman casually takes one of his crutches and belts Snow with it. Is it wrong to be amused by that? They brawl outside of the arena and into the street, and smash up some of Minneapolis on route to a bar. The drinking establishment is full of people wearing WWF merchandise, which rather gives away that this is all set-up and they are plants. Well, expect one drunk homeless guy who shouts obscenities and one delighted mark on his mobile phone, who gets in the way and is thrilled that he is on PPV. The bar brawl is good fun, though obviously it is all just hitting each other with stuff and there is no actual point or purpose to it. A technical masterpiece it ain't, but it is entertaining for sure. Road Dogg is a riot on commentary, but Bossman gets annoyed with him shadowing them and shoves him away, so Dogg belts him with a nightstick and Al pins him on a pool table. Al runs back to the arena, making sure to avoid traffic when he crosses the road, and catches Stevie Richards and the Blue Meanie seemingly trying to dognap Pepper. The poor guy from earlier is still hanging around, so Al takes his other crutch, which sends him to the floor, and he beats on the former bWo members while his music plays in the background. It is like an additional scene in a movie that runs during the end credits. This was all harmless fun and entertaining to watch.

Final Rating: **½

In a link, Tazz claims to be a tough guy and tells a story about smashing someone's face into a brick wall in a bar. Well, let me tell you another story about Tazz: once he pissed off Rob Van Dam so much that RVD came up to him backstage at an ECW show and told him calmly: "Pick the hand". Tazz, unsure what he meant, laughed it off and asked him what he meant. Van Dam responded that he wanted him to pick either his left or right hand, because he was going to smash his face in with one of them and he didn't care which. "Tough guy" Tazz backed off.

Next we go to the classic brawl between Cactus Jack and Triple H from *Royal Rumble 2000*, a bout that did more for Hunter's career than he gives credit for. Mick Foley made Triple H, there is no doubt about that. The match itself was a 30-minute war, and there is not enough tape time to feature it in full here, so we get highlights of the big bumps and stunts set to the creepy choir music that the WWF liked to use in their video packages at the time. It makes things seems intense, real and dangerous, as opposed to the wink-wink, nudge-nudge nature of modern day WWE from the Cena era, where everything is just a big joke. The match sees both guys take a pasting, with Hunter suffering a huge wooden splinter from a smashed crate going through his leg, and Cactus taking shots from Barbie and bumps into thumbtacks. Furious rates the bout at the full ***** shebang elsewhere in this book, though I don't quite go as high as that, but I agree that it is a sensational match and probably the best hardcore style outing that the WWF ever did. Following the highlights, we get another highlight package of the same bumps we have just seen, set to different music. Erm, okay then.

The riotously entertaining Crash Holly and his 24/7 title defences are covered next, and man was this ever a blast. Crash found himself in all manner of increasingly ridiculous scenarios, including fighting in a children's play area, being smashed over the head with a glass jar by Ivory while getting a massage and being attacked by referees, and he made every one of them work brilliantly. Crash was booked perfectly in this role, and it is a shame the run didn't last longer than it did. Some think it cheapened the title to have silly champions and 24/7 defences, but the hardcore division was a bit of light entertainment and an excuse to do silly things in one place at the bottom of the card rather than in the important matches. I was fine with it.

The series of ladder matches between the Hardy Boyz, Edge & Christian and the Dudleys is featured next, though again these are not really hardcore matches as such. I mean, you would never describe Shawn Michaels vs. Razor Ramon and their ladder bouts as being "hardcore", and the same applies here. Full of stunts and big bumps sure, but hardcore is a different thing.

Next, the talking heads discuss their favourite hardcore memories. Steve Lombardi and Howard Finkel both go old school, with Lombardi picking Superfly Jimmy Snuka's much hyped cage leap and Fink going for the famous Alley Fight between Sgt. Slaughter and Pat Patterson from 1981. We get more of Mick Foley's wild bumps from over the years and then the APA smashing through everyone. None of this has much in the way of structure or any threads holding it together, it is just footage.

Because Shane McMahon is such a tough guy, he had to have a Hardcore Title run to go alongside his equally unwelcomed European Title reign from the prior year. We see highlights of his match with Steve Blackman from *SummerSlam 2000*, which is a sluggish and dull affair, remembered only for the ridiculous bump that Shane takes at the end. The glory stealing McMahon sibling ascends the scaffold surrounding the set and is chased up by Blackman, and takes a few cane shots to the leg that cause him to fall backwards onto a big landing pad. What an egotist. Hey, watching people fall from great heights just over a year after the death of Owen Hart, who fell from a great height, is just swell.

And that is your lot, other than Tazz reminding everyone that "I am Tazz, and you're not". Great, thanks for that.

VERDICT

The content on offer is all for the most part entertaining, but there is just too much of it in one go. My complaint is actually that the tape is too long, and would have been better served at 45-minutes. There is just not enough variation for over an hour of stuff when the majority of the matches are very similar. Hardcore wrestling works well as an interlude and a change from everything else on a card, not as a whole standalone presentation. By the end of this I was completely desensitised to the weapon shots, big bumps and blood. It is all very samey after a while.

47

CRASH HOLLY

LITA - IT JUST FEELS RIGHT

CAT NO: WWF279
RUN TIME: 59 minutes (approx)

James Dixon: Having debuted in the WWF as the valet of aerial sensation Essa Rios, Amy 'Lita' Dumas quickly gained a cult following due to her unique grungy look and high-octane involvement in her charge's matches. It didn't hurt that she was pretty hot either. Outgrowing Rios, Lita was teamed up with the Hardy Boyz to form Team Xtreme, and she was a perfect fit, with her look and style proving to be the missing piece of the puzzle for Matt and Jeff. Lita was a trailblazer in the women's division, and while she was pretty appalling in the ring at times, her popularity, especially amongst teenage girls, was never in question. Well, that is until she became a filthy two-timing ho-bag and copped off with one of her boyfriend's (Matt Hardy) best friends (Edge). But that was all later, and when this tape was released, Lita was still over as the cool alternative chick that the girls wanted to be and the guys wanted to bang.

Stephanie McMahon, looking all gangsta in her leather hat, opens the tape by calling Lita "sexy". We get further talking head intros from JR, an uninterested Jeff Hardy, Trish and Matt Hardy. Matt refers to her as a pioneer, which she probably is. Essa Rios turns up to offer a few words! "She is something marvellous" he says in subtitled Spanish. Well, yeah, she got you over! Lita talks about her style and says she has added her own elements to standard wrestling formula. By elements does she mean the ability to make all of her moves look like she is falling uncontrollably from a height, only to recover at the last moment and bust out a flip? She is the only worker in the world whose style I would describe as "baggy". She is to wrestling moves what super loose fitting clothes are to fashion. Almost on cue, we get lots and lots of footage of her rana and moonsault, done on various people. They are her only two moves...

Next, Lita talks about the trials of the road: "we are a strange breed" she admits. Lita then claims to be living the dream and says she can't think of anything else she would rather be doing... expect being in a band, I guess

Back we go to her childhood, which is a feature of these tapes that I find incredibly dull. At least it is brief before we move on to her athletic background, which WWF loves of course, and it's revealed that she trained in muay thai kickboxing and judo. If she had come along a decade or so later, she might have ended up doing MMA and throwing down with the likes of Ronda Rousey and Miesha Tate in the UFC, rather than as a sports entertainer. But as it is, she says she got hooked on wrestling after watching, get this, SUPER ASTROS (the WWF's attempt to crack the Hispanic market by featuring Mexican wrestling stars in self-contained within the program storylines), which only actually first started airing in 1998, two years before her company debut. Her excessively subtitled book *Lita: A Less Travelled R.O.A.D - The Reality of Amy Dumas* actually contradicts that somewhat, with her claiming to have been a fan of Rey Misterio Jr. and deciding to train after seeing him work. Either way, Lita had her mind set on becoming a wrestler so in a bold move she upped and left for Mexico to seek training. She talks about how she fell in love with the culture in the country and embraced it, and that she loves new experiences. Whether that includes her time spent as a club dancer to pay for her bills, is not mentioned...

We go to her kitchen at home and see her vast mask collection, with her pointing out the likes of La Parka, Rey Misterio Jr, Psicosis and Aguila -mentioning that he became Essa Rios, which I am pretty sure the WWF didn't mention when the character debuted- as well as outing Val Venis as having worked under a hood across the border in a pre-porn star life (as Steele). I didn't realise she was such a super geek, but I kind of like her for more knowing that she is. It is interesting that all of her influences and heroes were guys that had at this point made their name in America with WCW, and the WWF having recently bought out the company are only just willing to show brief snippets of footage from the group.

After a spell in Mexico working for EMLL, next up for Dumas was a return to America. She tells the tale that she turned up at an ECW show and got talking to Tommy Dreamer, asking him for a chance to work out with some of the guys and just generally hang around. She ended up talking to Tajiri and Super Crazy, who she knew from Mexico, and worked out in the ring with Tajiri a bit, which got her on the evening's card. She had a run as Miss Congeniality, but it was hardly a memorable one, truth be told. It wasn't the ECW run that got her in the WWF but rather her training at Dory Funk Jr's Funkin' Conservatory, with the immortal Hoss having got her a spot in the company after going to bat for her. For whatever reason, the WWF decides to ignore this and skips right over it. Talk about gratitude. Lita says that for her meeting with the WWF, she wore a suit for the first time in her life. Despite going against her roots and natural instincts, she was still hired because JR saw her potential (and had obviously seen Dory's tapes) and liked her positivity.

The Lita character was introduced alongside the former Mr. Aguila and Papi Chulo, the artist now known as Essa Rios. The two fiery characters were a perfect fit for one another, and as the accompanying footage shows; they were an explosive and exciting doubles act. We see Lita's company debut alongside Essa on *Heat* where Rios defeated Gillberg to win the presumed abandoned WWF Light Heavyweight Title, a belt that Rios competed for but never won while under the hood as Aguila years previous. An amusing piece of commentary crops up here, with Kevin Kelly saying of Gillberg: "He is yesterday's news, he is so 90s". Lita was a breath of fresh air to a stagnant women's talent pool, and at times she really WAS great in her first few months. Watching the duo at the time, you could feel the swell of support for them, and for Lita in particular, as they started to get over more and more. They were explosive and used their precious TV minutes well. Lita's gimmick was mimicking Essa's moves, and it worked a treat, but the WWF couldn't help themselves and split them up after just a few months. They had bigger plans for Lita.

Enter: The Hardy Boyz. The split takes place after Essa first annoys Lita by having sexy time with the Godfather's hos, so she shoves him off the ropes during a subsequent match and causes him to lose. Then in a bout against Matt Hardy, Essa uses Lita as a human shield, and she gets bumped during the contest. Post match after he loses, a frustrated Rios powerbombs Lita, and mid-move her peachy little bottom gets exposed to the world. Before selling the considerable viciousness of the move, Lita first stops off to pull her trousers back up, rather lessening the impact somewhat. I guess this was a lesson to her about the perils of not wearing underwear, because in later years she became famous for having her thongs pulled high above her trouser line. Rios follows up the powerbomb with a beautiful moonsault, and that brings out the Hardys to save Lita. And thus, a union was formed. It was a shame for Essa, who I really enjoyed, but he is reflective about it, and says how happy he is for her subsequent success.

It turns out that Lita knew the Hardys before their WWF grouping, having trained in their OMEGA promotion and became good friends with them. We see home shot video of the Hardys, Lita, Shannon Moore and Shane Helms having a good time, as Jeff says they taught her "how to jump off buildings", which would be about right. Matt then kayfabes their storyline relationship and plays it off like it was real, describing their first onscreen kiss in far too much detail. Urgh, he is like a friggin lovesick Disney puppy. "I think of them as big brothers" says Lita. SICK.

We break from the storyline for Lita to tell an amusing story about her entrance, which she says was unplanned and she just went with the flow, because when she was told from behind the curtain: "Go! NOW!" she didn't have much time to think about it. She adds that she enjoys the walk to the ring and reading the signs that the crowd bring, because it is like instant feedback.

FURIOUS ABOUT: TOO COOL

The three year run of Too Cool was widely overshadowed by the popularity and success of other tag teams during the same era (E&C, Hardyz, Dudleyz). But make no mistake, they were extremely popular, thanks to a dancing hip-hop gimmick, and were surprisingly entertaining in the ring. Christopher & Taylor were originally paired together as Too Much, a generic heel team with homosexual tendencies. In June 1999 they established the dancing gimmick and took off. Combined with gigantic assed Samoan Rikishi, they danced their way into people's hearts. The group's success was undermined by better teams and Rikishi's sudden heel turn in 2000. Grandmasta Sexay was fired in 2001 for crossing a border with illegal drugs. Scotty moved on to teaming with Albert, which continued the gimmick to lesser success. Too Cool held the tag titles and Scotty won the Light Heavyweight title. Scotty remained in the WWE until 2007.

To *WrestleMania X-7*, the greatest *WrestleMania* ever. Lita talks us through the full week's worth of festivities that occur before the event itself and we get exclusive footage of the building the night before the show when it was empty, which is pretty cool. Lita counts the experience of being on the card as the greatest of her career, but hindsight rather ruins it thanks to this unintentional humdinger on commentary from JR: "By God, Lita's here, jerking Edge off!". Given what occurs between them in a few years time, that is a belter.

The problem with Matt's earlier kayfabing is that when Lita then marks out over being beaten up by Steve Austin on *RAW* in a vicious chair assault, it just makes her seem like a sadomasochistic mental case. She says how thrilled she was to have been trusted enough to be involved in the main event, and with someone like Austin. It didn't do a great deal for the Hardys mind you...

Back in time eight months to the feud with Stephanie McMahon-Helmsley over the WWF Women's Title, which Steph-Diddy calls "a challenge", because Lita's high flying moves are apparently hard to take. They are not really, you just lie there for the moonsault and all you have to do on the rana is stand solid and catch it, then go with the flow. If you can't wrestle, Steph, then why were you the Women's Champion in the first place, you silly cow?! "She paraded around like she was the Women's Champion" says Lita. Erm... she *was* the Women's Champion.

Extended highlights air (without music, thankfully) of the main event title match from *RAW* on August 21, 2000, with Steph accompanied to the ring by Kurt Angle and Triple H, which worries the challenger. Fortunately WWF Champion the Rock is the guest referee, giving her some protection. To her credit, Steph does at least give it the good old college try, and she had clearly worked hard to be up to a semi reasonable standard, but parading around as Women's Champion rankled with me. I guess it is sports entertainment and she is no worse than most of the Divas anyway, it's just the sheer unabashed nepotism that pisses me off. Triple H helps out Steph by tripping Lita, so the Hardys come out and belt him one. Steph hits a pretty decent looking DDT, but only gets two off it, and Rock has to keep her in line when she gets all pissy about the count. The finish to the match is spectacular, with Rock preventing Angle from interfering with the title belt, and then beating the piss out of him for trying. Triple H "nearly decapitates" (JR) Rock with a punch, then almost makes a bollocks of the planned spot that follows, where Angle accidentally clobbers him with the title belt. Rock needed to be standing so that Angle could charge him from behind, but Hunter went for the Pedigree by kicking Rock in the gut, which would have make Angle look like a complete fool flying in from behind and swinging at a bent over Rock, only to then shift and go high to hit Trips. Fortunately, Rock realises this and stands up and then ducks instantly, in a piece of perfect timing that shows what a true ring master he was. "Oh shit" says Kurt as he decks Hunter, before eating a Rock Bottom from the champ. Steph motions to nail Rock with the belt, but Rock catches her with a spinebuster and tells Lita to go up top as the crowd explodes. She hits her moonsault and covers for the win and the title, as the place goes crazy. It's women's wrestling in the Attitude Era at its absolute best and most dramatic, even if it did involved SMH.

We skip Lita losing the belt to Ivory in a four-way match on *SmackDown!* and go to the rematch at *Survivor Series 2000*. Of note is that Lita gets busted open in the match when an errant boot catches her in the face during an innocuous spot. In a shoot interview with Kayfabe Commentaries, Ivory later referred to Lita as "like wrestling Gumby" (the claymation character), because you never knew if she was going to just suddenly fall out of the ring, land awkwardly off something innocuous or cut herself open hardway from seemingly nothing, as she did here. The match doest even come close to the Steph battle on *RAW*, and barely scrapes onto the snowflake scale. After highlights of the match set to techno dance shite, which Lita lost, she calls her mom to tell her she is okay. Cute. That segues into Lita's relationship with her mom, who she claims to be closer to now she never sees her, and basically calls her a mark. We meet Lita's dog, and also see a little more of her house. She has no furniture at all! Not even a couch! Maybe she had just moved in. What happens to the dog when she is on the road?

The feud with Trish comes next, even though the matches featured took place months before the prior footage (and there it is, my old Coliseum Video continuity migraine has returned), set to more repetitive techno music and some sound bites from Michael Cole. It's the perfect marriage of horrid and horrible. Trish puts Lita over big, then we see more from *RAW is Techno* as Lita teams with Rock to take on Trish and Triple H, all of this prior to the Steph match. Before her association with Edge, Lita was previously rubbing shoulders with the top of the card because of how over she was. I can't concentrate for the mind altering music, but I do catch JR putting over H's decapitating clothesline again...

Chyna next, who comes out for her match with Lita at *Judgment Day 2001* (almost a year after the previous bout) looking like a cross between a peacock and a Vegas drag queen. "Is there any way I can get out of this?" said Lita of the bout. Chyna smashed through her, just like she did all the other women on the roster, then they have a hug and a smile immediately afterwards. Wins and losses don't matter; this is the WWF!

Next, Lita gets sexy in a program with Dean Malenko. I didn't like this at all. Malenko was just too good a technician to be reduced to stupid angles. I have to muster all my resolve to refrain from making any wildly inappropriate and tasteless comments when Chris Benoit interjects himself into the feud and puts a Crossface on Lita...

"It's hard to piss me off" says Lita, who professes to be mellow. We go to a Diva shoot on a beach, which is apparently *not* typically clichéd according to our gal, because she had never done it before. Yeah, it might not be clichéd for *you*, but the whole practice sure is. But hey, they released those cut and paste identikit Diva tapes year after year, so obviously people were buying them. Dirty people, who you would never borrow a tube sock from...

Talk moves on to her tattoo which she says was unplanned (no kidding) and that it represents her spontaneity from when she was in Amsterdam. Her stupidity more like; it's horrid. Apparently her thong look came about when she bought one and showed it to EDGE, saying of her pants that she "pulled them down for him... but not in that way!" in order to show him how it looked. Wow, this shit writes itself.

Then, yet another photo shoot, because nothing screams excitement like watching someone take pictures. We get lots and lots of talk from Lita about her fans, and I tell you what she has some very odd people who like her, some of whom are probably stalkers for sure. She gets all manner of crap sent to her from people with too much time on their hands, from poems to letters to oil paintings and pictures, even scrapbooks of her STORYLINES. My God, I would love to meet some of these people to hear their take on some of the WWF's glaring inconsistencies over the years. I can only assume that any WCW fans who attempted something similar gave up and threw themselves in front of a train out of sheer frustration and desperation.

"Lita, like Chyna, has done a lot of stuff with some of the guys". Thanks Steph, that will round us off nicely...

VERDICT

I came into this with preconceptions and expected it to be a wholly uninteresting and insufferable experience. In fact, it was quite the opposite. Lita came across exactly as she was portrayed at the time; as a cool girl you would want to hang out with, but who you would also want to do lewd things with given the chance. As well as opportunities to grab an eyeful now and again, there is also a lot of genuinely good content on here. The stuff with the masks is pretty neat, some of the footage is unique and rare and a lot of the action is quite exciting too. Lita was not a good wrestler by any means, and when she started working longer matches she was rather exposed. But with either smoke and mirrors or in the role of a corner person, she was made to look pretty great. I am a fan of Lita from this era, and this tape is a very good representation of what was one of the most fun times in her career. A must have for any fans of hers, and a pretty damn good watch for everyone else too. To my huge surprise, this comes recommended.

73

LITA

BEST OF RAW VOL. 2

CAT NO: WWF280
RUN TIME: 101 minutes (approx)

Lee Maughan: Hosted by Jonathan Coachman, sporting a WWF New York denim shirt that I can't imagine was even considered cool back in 1999. Coach brings us completely up to speed on where we left off last after *Best of RAW: Vol. 1*, noting that the Undertaker had a Ministry, Mr. McMahon had a Corporation, Steve Austin was kicking ass, and Mankind was always having fun. Given that this tape picks up from the night after *Survivor Series: Deadly Game*, I'm not sure I'd quite buy that assertion, but that's a WWF studio host for you.

1998 Survivor Series Aftermath
Steve Austin presents a legally binding contract to Mr. McMahon, guaranteeing him a shot at the Rock's newly "won" WWF Title. We know this contract to be legally binding because professional boxing referee, *Celebrity Deathmatch* claymation character and reality TV courtroom judge Mills Lane is on hand via video link to authorise it. McMahon however makes Ken Shamrock an offer he can't refuse, and Shamrock officially joins the Corporation by saving Vince from a vengeful Mankind (always having fun, remember?), allowing the Undertaker to smash Austin over the head with a shovel behind the distracted referee's back.

Following the gardening-based attack, Austin "blacks out" after a house show match at the San Jose Arena (in a ring still sporting the old red, white and blue rope motif, incidentally enough), and then, in a truly ridiculous angle, Undertaker and Paul Bearer attempt to "embalm" Austin alive, only for Kane to make the save. Austin returns fire by whacking Undertaker across the face with a shovel of his own, then he and Kane shove Bearer down a manhole into a sewer, somehow leading to McMahon announcing a Buried Alive match for *Rock Bottom: In Your House*.

This was all basically just presented as a promo package for that pay-per-view, which on the one hand managed to cover a month's worth of main event angles in one fell swoop, but on the other, just served to hype up a match that you obviously weren't going to be seeing here. Never let it be said that the WWF didn't maximise the footage they already had though - a re-cut version of this hype video actually aired directly before the Austin-Undertaker match on that very show.

No Disqualification
WWF Championship
The Rock (c) vs. Mankind
[29/12/1998 (aired on RAW is War, 04/01/1999) - Centrum, Worcester, MA]
Weirdly, the on-screen graphic places this match at August 30th, 1999, which obviously isn't the case. Sadly we skip the pre-match angle here in which Mankind, having been robbed of the WWF Title twice (at both *Survivor Series* and *Rock Bottom*) kidnaps Shane McMahon and threatens to break his arm unless he gets another shot at the Rock's title. Mr. McMahon agrees, and believe it or not, there's an actual match on this tape!

Naturally it *is* joined in progress with Rock getting two off a side Russian legsweep and another two off the Corporate Elbow, but you can't win 'em all. Mankind fires back with a swinging neckbreaker but the Big Bossman gets involved, allowing Rock to deck Mankind with the belt. A second shot misses so Mankind hits a double arm DDT on the belt and clamps on the Socko Claw, and then it all kicks off as Ken Shamrock dives in the ring and belts poor Mankind over the back with a steel chair. This is a No Disqualification match however, so Billy Gunn jumps in to kick-start his feud with Shamrock over the Intercontinental Title, and then DX engage in a mass brawl with the Corporation on the outside.

That ruckus is halted only by the sound of glass shattering that can only mean 'Stone Cold' is on his way! The reaction is absolutely *thunderous*, and he puts Rock down with a steel chair across the skull that's enough to give Mankind the pin and his first WWF Title. Austin flips Vince the bird, Vince flips out, and Mankind cuts an impassioned Rocky Balboa-esque victory speech which Vince and Shane in particular sell with incredible gusto. When wrestling is done right, there's nothing on earth quite as much fun, or quite this exciting, and while the match itself isn't much to write home about, this is one of those moments so thrilling that you can just watch it over and over again, and it never gets old. Just a truly heart-warming piece of business that the great Mick Foley deserved entirely, and a great slice of television that proves sometimes, just sometimes, nice guys do finish first.

Corporate Rumble
[11/01/1999 - Compaq Center, Houston, TX]

#1 is **Ken Shamrock** and #2 is **Billy Gunn** but Shamrock eliminates himself immediately by leaping over the top just to kick the shit out of Gunn. Man, what a mercenary. #3 is the **Big Bossman** who predictably works Gunn over before the Outlaws' music plays to herald the entrance of #4... **Test**. I smell chicanery! **X-Pac** joins the fun at #5 but Billy and Test trade some hiptoss reversals that end with Gunn getting tossed all the way out of the ring.

Test drops X-Pac with a pumphandle powerbomb before **Road Dogg** joins the fray at #6, still covered in blood thanks to a bloodbath earlier in the night from the Brood. **Kane** is #7 (after not winning the title earlier in the evening), and he puts Road Dogg out with a clothesline right across the nose. #8 is **Triple H**, who ducks a clothesline from Test, Test nailing Kane instead before getting chokeslammed out for his troubles. Kane quickly follows thanks to a double clothesline from behind from Triple H and X-Pac, and Bossman dumps X-Pac in kind leaving Triple H and the Bossman as the final two. And then the buzzer sounds...

#9 is **Mr. McMahon** who slinks in and dumps Bossman and Triple H from behind, the tears his tank top in half like the ghost of Hogan. And then the buzzer sounds again... #10 is **Chyna**. Pat Patterson and Gerald Brisco attempt to block her path so she decks them both, and then out comes Steve Austin to draw Vince's attention, allowing Chyna to hurl him over the top and out to earn the #30 spot in the actual *Royal Rumble* match. Vince it should be noted practically took his own head off like a guillotine taking that bump over the top, the mad old bastard.
Final Rating: ***

Mr. McMahon Prepares for the Rumble

Vince had designated Austin the number one spot in the *Royal Rumble* but had delegated authority over all other WWF superstars to Commissioner Shawn Michaels. When Vince himself opted to enter the Rumble, Michaels figured that made him a WWF superstar and subsequently ordered Vince to enter the match at number two. Vince tried to worm out of it by ordering the Corporate Rumble that we've just covered, but when that plan backfired, he had no alternative but to actually train to fight Austin. Cue a truly hilarious *Rocky*-style montage with Shane McMahon barking out classic lines while Vince gulps down raw eggs ("You gotta eat lightning and crap thunder!"), chases a live chicken through a snow-laden field ("Grab that chicken, make the Colonel proud!"), beats his meat ("Tenderise Austin's face!") and drops Dr. Tom Prichard with some truly rotten Stone Cold Stunners ("Number two in the *Royal Rumble*, number one in your heart!") Absolutely classic stuff.

Chyna and Mark Henry

For some reason, presumably because Vince Russo thought it was funny to pair up a chunky black man with a muscular ugmo, heel and former Nation of Domination member Mark Henry began courting DX bodyguard Chyna, taking her on a cheap date to Baltimore Jack. Mark reads poetry to Chyna as Percy Sledge's *'When a Man Loves a Woman'* plays in the background (I'm surprised that scene wasn't cut given the royalties they'd have to pay on it) then takes her dancing where a group of local douchebags hit on Chyna. When she rebuffs

FURIOUS ABOUT: MAVEN

The winner of *Tough Enough* series one, Maven is an all-round nice guy. His initial push saw him defeat Tazz on TV and eliminate the Undertaker from the 2002 Royal Rumble before facing Chris Jericho for the WWE title on RAW. He even pinned Undertaker for the hardcore title, thanks to the Rock. His push soon faltered as interest in *Tough Enough* waned and Maven's star began to fall. He spent two years in the midcard before scoring a big win over Batista in 2004. His push faltered again and Maven was turned heel, resulting in a terrible feud with IC champion Shelton Benjamin, where he lost on PPV in a matter of seconds at New Year's Revolution . Maven moved on to tagging with Simon Dean before being released by the WWE in July 2005. Despite retiring and entering rehab for drug problems Maven remains permanently upbeat

them, one calls her a bitch so Mark batters all three of them. That chivalry, as am I sure you all guessed, leads to Chyna bringing her girlfriend Sammi into the relationship for a threesome, only for Mark to find a cock and balls in his hand when he goes to give Sammi the magic fingers, causing him to vomit uncontrollably in a toilet. Har har har, transphobia, cheap laughs, giggle, guffaw, vomit.

Leading to WrestleMania XV

After Mankind beat the Rock for the WWF Title as covered earlier, the two continued to square off in a series of rematches for the belt. A brutal I Quit match at the *Royal Rumble* was followed by a silly but highly entertaining empty arena match on a special Super Bowl Sunday edition of *Halftime HeAT*. A last man standing match followed at *St. Valentine's Day Massacre*, with the final confrontation coming on *RAW*, a ladder match with Steve Austin at ringside. Sadly, this is covered by a quick series of clips rather than the full outing, but the Rock wins when Paul Wight chokeslams Mankind off the ladder, setting up both Rock vs. Austin for the title and Mankind vs. Wight at *WrestleMania XV*.

Corporate Ministry into Austin as CEO

Right then, let's see if we can make sense of this enormous pile. One week on *RAW*, the Undertaker cut an in-ring promo on Mr. McMahon, stating that "in time, your World Wrestling Federation will belong to me" and claiming to "own the key to [McMahon's] heart and soul." Later that night, Undertaker's Ministry of Darkness abducted Shane, gave him an envelope and told him to deliver it to Vince on behalf of the "Lord of Darkness."

Rather unhelpfully, none of that is explained on the tape and coverage instead picks up with Vince angrily booking Undertaker in an Inferno match against unwilling Corporation robot Kane, which Undertaker wins. During the match, Paul Bearer brought a bear to guest commentator McMahon, which the Undertaker then burnt as McMahon fell to his knees, melodramatically screaming "Noooooo!"

Following on from there, Vince began talking about the Undertaker as a character, labelling him a "creation" that Mark Calaway had actually morphed into. You know, because as per

> **FURIOUS ABOUT: CHUCK PALUMBO**
> Palumbo was one of the many graduates from WCW's Power Plant. A terrible wrestling school that flooded WCW with poor talent after all their ex-WWF wrestlers got too old to compete. Palumbo was one of their better graduates and settled into WWE life after facing a quick stint in OVW to polish his skills. Despite being one half of the tag team champions, with the superior Sean O'Haire, Palumbo found himself jobbing those titles in quick order to the Brothers of Destruction and finding himself repackaged as quasi-homosexual tag team partner of Billy Gunn. The Billy & Chuck tag team won tag gold in February 2002 and held the belts twice before Gunn got injured and the team was split up. Unfortunately for Chuck, this was his best WWE run; almost a year of being called 'gay' only to fail at that too. Chuck stayed in the WWE until 2008.

the Vince Russo directive, everything you've seen previously has been fake, but what you're watching now is actually real. He also revealed that the envelope contained photographs that invaded the privacy of his daughter, Stephanie, the first time her presence was acknowledged on WWF television. The bear was also Stephanie's, a present Vince had given her as a child.

Later, the Ministry abducted Stephanie from the McMahon family mansion and attempted to crucify her in a black wedding to the Undertaker, only for Steve Austin to make the save with a steel chair and Mr. McMahon thanking him for his help. Then, as if this heel vs. heel feud wasn't convoluted enough, Shane overthrew the distracted Vince as the leader of the Corporation, firing corporate stooges Pat Patterson and Gerald Brisco along with him, and turning Vince babyface in the process, before merging the Corporation with the Ministry.

With Shane admitting to being the mastermind behind Undertaker's abducting of Stephanie, Vince gets his ass handed to him by the entire Corporate Ministry prior to a McMahon vs. McMahon showdown on the May 3rd, 1999 edition of the *War Zone*.

Vince McMahon vs. Shane McMahon
[02/05/1999 (aired on RAW is War, 03/05/1999) - Sports Arena, San Diego, CA]
Shane destroys Vince in the aisle, Vince himself having apparently been destroyed in the locker room by Triple H and the Undertaker, and works in the Bronco Buster early. Vince's selling and movement is appalling by the way. Shane gets in Vince's face and gets cocky before Vince comes back with a clothesline and a Stone Cold Stunner for the pin in short order. I think it's fair to say the dynamic worked much better at *WrestleMania X-SEVEN*, with Vince as the heel and Shane as the babyface.

- Ridiculously, the Undertaker began talking of a "Higher Power" even greater than he, leading to many fans guessing his identity at any number of names from Mankind to Raven to Jake Roberts. All would have made solid candidates, but instead it was revealed that Vince himself was the mastermind all along in one of the biggest brain farts in *RAW* history. It was yet another one of those mystery storylines that Vince Russo was so fond of, where he began with a great idea but had no clue what the payoff was going to be until he just wrote himself into a corner and delivered an outrageous ending that defied all logic and common sense. Vince (in character) explained it as "just business" but how can anybody justify the things he did, the terror he put his daughter through, the beatings he took from those he was secretly allied with, and the lengthy feud with the Undertaker? Why go to such elaborate lengths? And who was the hoax even aimed at, Austin? I mean, what did they even accomplish? It's not like this whole charade cost him his title or anything, or even included that as part of its agenda. I mean the Big Bossman got HUNG at *WrestleMania XV*, for heaven's sake! It may have kept viewers guessing week after week back in '99, which is all that was important to Russo, but this was just a useless storyline that led to absolutely nothing other than changing then restoring the status quo of Vince as the tyrannical boss and Austin as his blue collar employee. Drek.

But it doesn't end there, as Undertaker beats Austin for the WWF Title thanks to a fast count from special referee Shane McMahon, making this one of the very rare instances of footage from *Over the Edge '99* making it onto an official WWF release. That leads to Vince's wife Linda McMahon installing Austin as CEO of the WWF for some amusing skits all compressed into about 30 seconds of music video-style recaps, much as the entirety of this Corporate Ministry nonsense has been presented.

Beer Truck Incident
We shoot schizophrenically back in time to the March 22nd, 1999 edition of *RAW* as the Rock threatens to kick Mankind's ass until suddenly, Steve Austin arrives with a beer truck. He cuts a pretty standard promo building up his match with Rock for *WrestleMania XV*, then sprays Rock and the McMahons with a giant hose full of joy juice. A classic *RAW* moment.

WrestleMania XV Aftermath with Title Belt
At *WrestleMania XV*, Steve Austin beat the Rock for the WWF Title in a **** match. Austin soon introduced his own custom made "Smoking Skull" belt design (so you can indirectly hold him responsible for John Cena's ludicrously garish blinged out spinner belt years later) so the McMahons stole it and gave it to the Rock. In a neat call-back to Austin tossing Rock's Intercontinental Title in a river (back in December '97), Rock tosses Austin in a river and chucks the belt in after him.

The next week, Rock holds a funeral for Austin, yet curiously, he's wearing the Smoking Skull belt he'd purported to have thrown in the river last week. Austin arrives in a monster truck and crushes the Rock's new Lincoln with it. He then drives the Truckasaurus 3:16 into the arena and drives over the funeral hearse for good measure before meeting Rock head-on in the aisle for a red hot brawl. Austin dumps Rock in the grave and pours beer all over him, only for Shane McMahon to blast Austin from behind with a shovel during his post-fight celebration. Hilariously nutty stuff that had the crowd going wild. Unfortunately for the Rock, Shane's special guest refereeing at *Backlash* did him no favours, so he cut a solidly babyface promo the next night on *RAW*, rid himself of the Corporation, and kicked Shane's ass for fun too.

Triple H
Having been a part of D-Generation-X, the Corporation and the Corporate Ministry, Triple H finally struck out on his own in July '99, calling out Steve Austin. Oddly enough, his big coming out party at *SummerSlam '99* actually saw special referee Jesse Ventura raise odd man out Mankind's hand at the end of a

triple threat bout for Austin's WWF Title. Hunter however would only have to wait 24 more hours before his crowning glory.

WWF Championship
Mankind (c) vs. Triple H
[23/08/1999 - Hilton Coliseum, Ames, CA]
The action picks up here with a brawl around ringside where Chyna (in the middle of a weird period where she's still seconding a heel Triple H and works accordingly, despite feuding as a babyface with Jeff Jarrett, often on the same show such as this one) slams Mankind legs-first against the steel steps. In the ring, Mankind misses a weak clotheslines and gets hit with a neckbreaker. Hunter throws Mr. Socko into the crowd and sends Mankind shoulder-first into the post, then avoids a Mankind comeback with a jumping knee. "Mankind sucks!" declares special guest commentator the Rock.

A double clothesline puts both guys on the outside where Mankind throws Triple H onto Rock's lap. Shane McMahon then hits Mankind from behind with a chair before Hunter blasts him with one of his own, then in an awesome spot, rears up for a second swing but turns at the last second and decks Rocky. Shane then knocks Earl Hebner out and Triple H lands a Pedigree with Shane making the pin to give Hunter the first of many WWF Titles. "The first of five times" as Coachman notes. Keep counting, bud. Rather pedestrian match for a World Title change, and Rock's commentary was rather obnoxious, even if he did keep telling Michael Cole to "Shut up!"
Final Rating: **

'Y2J'
During 1999, talk of the new millennium had reached a fever pitch, and the WWF began airing a clock counting down to it. Only, it wasn't due to reach zero hour at midnight on New Year's Eve and herald the next century. No, this clock was due to count down during an episode of *RAW*, coincidentally right as the Rock was in the middle of cutting an angry promo on the Big Show. The explosion that greeted the arrival of former WCW midcarder Chris Jericho was absolutely enormous, but the promos that followed saw Rock completely put Jericho in his place as just that, a midcarder.

Jericho also managed to make political enemies in the WWF during his feud with new Intercontinental champion Chyna, fresh off her victory in a "Good Housekeeping match" over Jeff Jarrett at *No Mercy*. Chyna would bafflingly win their scrap over the gold at *Survivor Series*, but as Jonathan Coachman points out, Jericho eventually became a three-time champion anyway. That statement there dates this release as being from 2001, as Jericho would actually go on to pick up the belt a further six times after that.

Rock 'N' Sock Connection
At the end of August, Mankind offered himself up as a one-time only tag team partner for the Rock in a tag team title match against defending champions the Undertaker and the Big Show. When Undertaker walked out on the match, Rock blasted Big Show in the head with a steel chair, and a double People's Elbow signalled new champions.

Injecting a healthy dose of comedy into proceedings, Mankind began using the Rock's catchphrases before hosting a special, improvised edition of *This Is Your Life* during a record-setting episode of *RAW*. Jerry Lawler's joyous reaction to Rock's debuting of the "poontang pie" line is a thing of beauty. In another trivia note, this was the sketch in which Mankind actually named the team, presenting Rock with a black sports jacket with 'Rock 'N' Sock Connection' emblazoned across the back in gold lamé. Less successful was the introduction of Mankind's latest sock puppet, Mr. Rocko.

The End of D-Generation X
Kevin Kelly narrates a piece on the demise of DX next, as the fun-loving group of rebels fell apart amidst greed and jealousy (apparently) as Chyna turned on Triple H with a low blow, Triple H turned on X-Pac at *WrestleMania XV*, the New Age Outlaws turned on each other... and then they all reformed as heels when X-Pac turned on the Rock during a match with Billy Gunn.

For reasons not covered here, Mr. McMahon insists "We're not going to have another DX night!" (it also goes unexplained what exactly a "DX night" is, but it was simply DX running the show one week), so Vince books Road Dogg against Rock (Rock wins by disqualification when DX get involved), Gunn against Steve Austin (Austin wins by disqualification when DX get involved), X-Pac against former partner Kane (Kane wins by disqualification when... well, you get the picture), and a WWF Title match with Triple H defending against Shane McMahon. Unfortunately for Vince, an errant belt shot from Vince knocks Shane out, giving Triple H the victory.

At *Survivor Series*, Mr. McMahon made himself the special guest referee for a Triple H vs. Rock vs. Austin triple threat title match, only for Austin to get run down in the parking lot by a high speed car, later revealed to be the masterplan of Triple H himself. On to *Armageddon*, and Triple H beat Vince in a bloody (not to mention bloody boring) No Holds Barred match after Stephanie turned on her father and sided with her husband.

1999 Highlights
Oddly, this selection of clips features the *No Mercy* ladder match between the Hardy Boyz and Edge & Christian, before finishing with a montage of 1999's champions, reminding everyone of the absurd fact that the WWF Title actually changed hands an astonishing twelve times over the course of just one calendar year.

VERDICT

There's two ways you can divide this tape up. The first way is that the content at the beginning of the tape covering late 1998-early 1999 is generally highly entertaining stuff, whilst mostly everything from around spring 1999 onwards is pretty rotten. The second is to say that most of the material centred around Steve Austin, Mankind and the Rock is well worth watching, whilst the content built around the Corporate Ministry and Triple H is anywhere between faintly tedious to completely dire. As for Mr. McMahon? Well, his entertainment value stretches both ways, largely depending on who he's working with/for/against, and you'll grow sick of the sight of him before long. It's a shame because although this release starts out fairly strongly, I was just begging for it to be put out of its misery as it limped over the finish line, much like the majority of the WWF's output in 1999. Mildly recommended, with a suggestion to hit the eject button sometime around April.

51

DIVAS IN HEDONISM

CAT NO: WWF281
RUN TIME: 53 minutes (approx)

James Dixon: Yes, it is another tape dedicated to the WWF's fairer sex contingent, with the usual promise of breasts that aren't delivered upon. This time we are in Jamaica. WWF Senior Photo Editor Noelle Soper gets booted off the beach because she is in shot and her breasts are too natural, presumably, before she discusses the shoot in past tense before we have even seen it. She tells us that over 20,000 pictures were shot, which is a ridiculous number. For those interested in this sort of thing, the girls choose their own clothes. Noelle talks about the hard life the Divas all have, as we see shots of the girls basking in the sun. It certainly looks tough.

Terri
We start with my favourite haggard Diva, who lets some locals paint her up while she stands there with her shirt off and her arm covering her tits. Terri says she wants to represent the WWF, which is a horrific thought. What is she a representation of? Someone with no wrestling talent who married into the business and got a spot based on a willingness to flash her ass and get implants? Terri reconnects with her roots as she rides some horses, then claims to be allergic to them. Nice try. "For some reason, everyone associates me with horses" she says. Gee, I wonder why!? This whole bio is one of the fluffiest pieces of glad-handing trite I have ever seen, and nothing she says here means anything at all.

Jacqueline
I have noticed this before, but Jacqueline talks like a female Stephen Hawking. Her interview is even less interesting than Terri's. Did you know that in her spare time she likes shopping and hanging out with friends!? What an animal, huh? Oh, and she is proud of her ass: "I have such a small round butt, like an onion". She then turns from female Hawking into every black stereotype ever, all rolled into one unintelligible package. It's like listening to Faarooq but with the addition of enormous silicone honkers. We don't get many sexy shots of Jacqueline during this, but instead footage of her in the ring. That is for the best as wrestling is definitely her better quality, because she isn't exactly a looker and her promo skills are worse than Dean Malenko's.

Tori
Tori gets all philosophical about the pace of life in Jamaica, and calls the culture "more evolved" than in America because the folk over there are kinder to each other and are not swamped in commercialism and TV culture. Kind of a strange thing to say for a woman representing an American based global corporation that makes the majority of its money from television rights and sponsorship... Tori then puts on some burlesque outfits and does some squats, with her full areola area clearly visible in some shots. Thus it is delightfully ironic when Tori talks about the things that you don't see being more exciting. Ah the good old slow motion video makes a comeback, with an awful lot of footage of Tori bending over while wearing revealing thongs. No prizes for guessing *her* position of choice. Tori goes diving in the sea for the first time, overcoming her previous fears, then revealing her antisocial side as she talks about the potential for escape underwater to get away from the real world.

Trish Stratus
"There's just so many locations to shoot at" says Trish. There sure is; the beach, the pool, further up the beach, deeper in the pool, even further up the beach. She shows a surprising childlike delight at the daily appearance and disappearance of the sun and then takes up waterskiing for the first time and says "it's a lot like skiing". Yep, she is blonde alright. "I was supposed to be a doctor" she later claims. Sure you were love, sure you were.

Debra
Here is someone I just don't understand the appeal of. She looks like someone in her fifties trying to dress herself up as a younger woman. She makes me chuckle by referring to her "Debra character", which is a laugh because her so called character is just the same hick she is in real life but with a low cut suit on. She says she is really, really sensitive and doesn't like large groups of people, which makes one immediately question her decision to get into wrestling. "I wanted to be in soaps". I see. Debra talks about then husband Steve Austin and says he is a strong personality, but she likes that because she doesn't want a man she can push around. No, apparently

TRISH STRATUS

she prefers a man who can push her around... Debra overcomes her fear of heights to dick around on a trapeze, because she would have regretted it for the rest of her life if she hadn't, apparently.

Chyna
Chyna spends a lot of time pointing out that she is a girl who likes girly things, and that people shouldn't get the wrong idea from the way she looks. She reckons that once people hear her voice they change their perception of her. They sure do; once they hear that grating nasal whine they want to leave the room. Chyna talks about the shoot and talks about the "odd looking plants" in Jamaica. You might know them as trees. She then claims to have picked bold colours for all of her outfits for the shoot that represent her personality. Then they show her in bright pink. Yes, we get it, she is a girl! Of the outfits, she says there is "something very Chyna about them, but without the black leather". So, not very Chyna at all then. She talks a bit more and at one point refers to some coffee as "Chynalicious". How did Trips put up with her for so long!?

Lita
Most of this is also featured on the Lita tape which came out two releases before this. "It's hard to piss me off" says Lita, who professes to be mellow. We see footage from the shoot on a beach, which is apparently *not* typically clichéd according to our gal, because she had never done it before. Yeah, it might not be clichéd for *you*, but the whole practice sure is. She goes over her journey into wrestling via Mexico and her current relationship with the Hardy Boyz. She considers their relationship with her to be "brotherly", which is pretty sick when you think about it. She mentions how she loves being on the road but enjoys going home to pay bills and remember what her place looks like. Remember what it looks like!? From the footage we have seen of her house on various releases, there is nothing even in it! Talk moves on to her tattoo which she says was unplanned (no kidding) and that it represents her spontaneity from when she was in Amsterdam. Her stupidity more like; it's horrid. Apparently her exposed thong look came about when she bought one and showed it to EDGE, saying of her pants that she "pulled them down for him... but not in that way!" in order to show him how it looked. Wow, this shit writes itself.

Noelle sums things up for us by pointing out how women in wrestling have never been portrayed this way in the past. Well yeah, but who the hell would have wanted to see the likes of the Fabulous Moolah, Judy Martin or - God help us - Bertha Faye like this anyway? "I have never seen such great photography from a sports entertainment company as what we are gonna have in this magazine" says Noelle. Wow, that goofy WWF-speak really sounds extra stupid when you hear it used in sentences like that.

VERDICT

The relative lack of slow-motion videos that offer nothing makes this a little better than *Divas - Postcard From The Caribbean*, and is really more a series of brief bios featuring a few gratuitous shots here and there. Some of the pieces are okay, others are screamingly dull, it depends who is featured, but they are all so brief that it doesn't really matter. Once again, who the tape appeals to outside of undersexed perverts, I don't really know. If that is you, pick this tape up and get your jollies on, but for the rest of us who like wrestling for the, you know, wrestling, it is a definite miss. Avoid.

15

INSURREXTION 2001

CAT NO: WWF282
RUN TIME: 147 minutes (approx)

Arnold Furious: Thanks to the WWF's tape sequencing, this actually took place at the start of May and therefore before *Judgment Day 2001*, so you'll have to cast your mind back nine reviews to find the actual logical place for *Insurrextion* in the tape timeline. Yet another logistical nightmare caused by the WWF's inexplicable choice of tape numbers. If only we could go back in time and do everything chronologically! *Insurrextion* first took place in 2000, as the WWF tried to eek every last pound coin from the UK public while the wrestling boom was hot. The yearly PPV event lasted three years in London before a final event in Newcastle. Falling attendances and buyrates caused the UK PPV experiment to come crashing to a halt and the WWF decided to make the UK fans pay for the American PPV's instead, therefore retaining their income stream without filling the world with pointless UK only PPV events.

We're in London, England. We start backstage where William Regal informs Kurt Angle via telephone that the whole card has changed. He's interrupted by Vince McMahon accusing him of being power crazy, but Regal points out that Linda McMahon altered the card, not him. Linda shows up to stop Vince going off on a rant and saying the changes were for the fans. It's like a mantra, regardless of content. I booked this shit-heap main event for the fans. Like Will Ferrell in *The Campaign*. For the troops! The only good thing about this McMahon-fest was Regal's facial selling in the background. Less is more. Vince closes by making fun of the Foot and Mouth Disease outbreak. His delivery is weird and off.

Hosts are Michael Cole and Paul Heyman. In my head I jokingly said to myself; at least we get a good commentary team and I'd even typed JR's name out. Then a little voice in the back of my head said "but what if it's Coleslaw". Nooo! Oddly enough I hate coleslaw too.

Grandmasta Sexay vs. Eddie Guerrero
Originally GMS was advertised as wrestling against Rhyno for the Hardcore Title, but the reshuffling of the card has that changed and Eddie gets booed more than usual for just being in the match. A pity as Eddie is on the verge of getting the boot for drug use. It probably saved his life though, for a few years, and guaranteed a sensational comeback a year later that would lead to a WWF Title win. You'd never know that here as he works a comedy opener with his character displaying a total lack of humour. On commentary Cole decides to talk about the Undertaker and thus ignore the match, occasionally returning to it in robotic fashion. GMS gets jumped while dancing, causing Eddie to mock the dancing with horrible dancing of his own. It's wonderful old school heel work and Eddie is just wasted here. They have reasonable chemistry, as Eddie did with anyone competent, and GMS has fun with bits of dancing and stealing the superkick. Hip Hop Drop misses and Eddie gets a roll up with the ropes to win. The chucklesome roll up had Eddie desperately trying to find the ropes with his feet and only barely finding them around the three count.
Final Rating: *¾

Backstage: Triple and Steph, complete with chav hairstyle (pulled back hard enough to stretch skin over scalp), besmirch England. Hunter calls it a "craphole", just in case you were wondering whether he was a heel or not.

Six Person Tag Match
Dean Malenko, Perry Saturn & Terri vs. The Hollys
Terri cuts a horrible pre-match promo blaming English shops for not having wrestling boots and trying to remove herself from the match. Not that she can wrestle anyway. If Eddie was wasted in the opener, words don't do Malenko's role service here, stuck as he is in a throwaway tag that focuses mostly on Molly Holly. Such a waste. Saturn, realising this is a rib, dresses like Hulk Hogan complete with bleached blonde Hogan-esque moustache. Hardcore Bob can't quite find his rhythm and not even Malenko can make him look good. Holly was one of those guys that everyone was champing at the bit to get pushed and yet he didn't do it for me. Truly great wrestlers tend to have good chemistry with anyone else that's even remotely good. His timing with Saturn is embarrassing. I think Saturn had a few issues but great wrestlers could cover for them. Check out his singles match with Eddie Guerrero, where Saturn was in worse shape than he is here. Crash has similar issues with Saturn where Perry doesn't really commit to the spots until they're already halfway done. The ladies catfight a

bit, which shows how completely useless Terri is, and Saturn nails Crash with the Moss Covered Family Three Handled Credenza for the pin. Oh now they put the Radicalz over! Match sucked and had barely any Malenko in it.
Final Rating: ½*

Video Control gives us footage of William Regal doing the press junket for this PPV. The fans are nice for a change. "Stop besmirching our bloody commissioner". Compared to previous tours, Regal gets hearty pops and much love from his adoring public. We return to the PPV and backstage Regal has the Queen's Cup on his desk. After all that babyface stuff Regal then heels on the fans by claiming he'll get a bigger pop than Chris Jericho. They just couldn't leave it alone, could they? Video Control moves on to the Big Show-Test match, which has been cancelled because Test is injured.

The Big Show vs. Test
Show comes out to call Test a yellow-bellied coward, which brings Test out to defend his good name. Test has injured ribs but still flew out to the UK. Presumably they were going to work a short match or some such, but he's too hurt so instead Show squashes him. Sideslam. Final Cut. Zebras come in to call it for Show and it's basically a no contest. I have no idea why they didn't just call this a match and end it with a pin. Show grabs the mic and demands competition. When nobody comes out he goes to leave, but is met by Bradshaw.
Final Rating: SQUASH

The Big Show vs. Bradshaw
The booking here is screwy as Show doesn't really utter the words "I challenge anyone in the back to wrestle me". He merely stated that nobody could take him one-on-one and Bradshaw doesn't say anything, he just comes down and attacks Show. It's a botched angle. Bradshaw gets an initial pop but then people realise it'll be a match and lose interest. Bradshaw gets beaten down so Show goes back to the injured Test, only for Test to kick a chair in his face and Bradshaw finishes with the Clothesline from Hell. A pretty dreadful match, but at least it was short.
Final Rating: ¼*

Backstage: Steve Austin calls the Undertaker stupid for asking for a handicap match against him and Triple H. Austin goes for cheap heat by saying the Undertaker's career will come to an end in a "piece of crap country" like this. Like Hunter earlier he's reminding the slow-witted fans at home who the actual heels are tonight. It's "Marvel Comics syndrome": every wrestling show is someone's first wrestling show, like every comic is someone's first comic.

Elimination Match
Edge & Christian vs. X-Factor vs. The Dudley Boyz vs. The Hardy Boyz
This was originally billed as being for the tag team titles, but Taker & Kane won them to put the kibosh on that. Apart from that it's as advertised, which sets it apart on a massively re-juggled show. The Dudleys gets a huge pop and the Hardys get a huge girly pop. Everyone has a good time in this one, clearly not taking it too seriously. Edge's over the top celebration for Christian scoring a move on Matt Hardy is almost as funny as Christian promptly breaking out a lame version of the Hardys taunt. Jeff and X-Pac decide to increase the speed and it's credit to Pac that nothing is sloppy. While no one wanted to see X-Pac in 2001, he was still a good worker. Not great like he was before the neck injury, but good. Poetry in Motion brings everyone into the ring. Albert tries to save X-Pac but misses his splash and Jeff puts X-Pac out with the Swanton. X-Factor are eliminated. Jeff gets double teamed by E&C immediately and the Unprettier dumps the younger Hardy. The Hardys Boyz are eliminated too. This sets the Duds up as the definite babyfaces and the crowd want tables. The match actually slows up as the Hardys and X-Factor had been having a blinder. Unfortunately the straight up tag that remains is half the match and a lot of it is heat on D-Von. Bubba's hot tag is pretty good as Bubba had gotten the hang of cleaning house as a babyface. WAZZZZUP headbutt scores on Edge. "They may get wood in Earl's Court" says Cole, without a hint of emotion, as the Duds bail for tables. Bubba gets GORE, GORE, GORED by Rhyno though and Edge scores the pin. Wait a minute, Rhyno? What's he even doing here? He's not on the card. Spike Dudley runs down to even the odds and hits the Dudley Dog on Edge. Rhyno takes 3D through a table and that gives us the happy ending. This started and ended really well, but the heat segment on D-Von that sent the match careering to halt in the middle was disappointing.
Final Rating: **½

Video Control takes us to a gala dinner full of rich people. The highlight of this is Stephanie McMahon getting called a whore and taking it out on Michael Cole with a vicious slap. Ringside are Chris Tarrant and Gianfranco Zola. The latter gets booed. Not many Chelski fans in tonight.

Backstage: Kurt Angle complains about Benoit stealing his gold medals.

Promo Time: Stevie Richards & Ivory
Apparently we should be ashamed of ourselves because of Page 3 girls in the Sun newspaper. Stevie suggests people should come to England to see Big Ben (I think he means the Palace of Westminster) and London Bridge (I think he means Tower Bridge). Americans; still confused by bridge names even after we flogged one to Lake Havasu. Right to Censor announce the women's battle royal is cancelled and offer this as an opportunity for the WWF ladyfolk to show a change in their ways (and because the match would suck). Jacqui, Trish and Lita all come out to be disparaged by Ivory. "A bunch of street corner slappers". The ladies take offence and rip off Ivory's clothes. She does a tremendous sell on the underwear reveal and scurries to the back. Stevie gets upset so the ladies whip his trousers off. DDT from Jacqui, and Lita adds in a moonsault. Score one for the slappers. Goofy segment inserted to break up the action, but it at least got reactions. Shame the ladies were deemed incapable of wrestling, but based on some of their matches from 2000-2001 you can see why the WWF was concerned.

2 out of 3 Falls
Chris Benoit vs. Kurt Angle
This feud rumbled on after Benoit beat Angle at *Backlash*. Benoit promptly stole Angle's gold medals in the hopes of shutting him up about IOC rules and such. This match takes the *WrestleMania* rather than *Backlash* route, and opts to be fast and furious rather than slow and methodical. I personally like the *Backlash* match, but *WrestleMania* went over better with most folk so that's what they go for here. They do some masterful mat countering at speed, which 99% of the locker room just couldn't do. It continues to boggle my mind that they booked Benoit like this and yet Malenko ended up in a bunch of silly, pointless tags. The counters continue and they do standing stuff into suplexes with as much confidence as the ground work. It is simply two incredible all-rounders in the ring going at it. Unlike some wrestlers, who treat international tours

RIGHT TO CENSOR

as holidays, they don't rest at all. Rolling Germans set up the Swandive headbutt and Kurt counts lights to end fall one.

2nd Fall: Angle starts out desperate to even the falls but then quickly transitions into the match's only rest hold; a protracted chinlock. As Angle goes for repeated pins, Cole finally says something worthwhile by pointing out how much energy you burn kicking out of a pin. Well, it'd be exhausting for normal people but both of these guys are machines. The counters continue as Benoit switches his weight to avoid the Angle Slam. It's very subtle. I like subtle. Rolling Germans leads to another Swandive headbutt, repeating the finish to fall one, but Angle rolls out of the way. The suggestion being that Benoit is now a little worn down and took longer to climb. You could argue Angle is more worn down too but hey, that's the story. Angle goes for the ankle lock, countered beautifully into the Crossface in a sensational bit of wrestling. Angle rolls out of that and, rather pleased with himself, gets caught in an inside cradle. Benoit takes it two straight falls! I remember this match being better but that's probably because it was hidden away on such a weak show that it felt like a hidden gem. Regardless, like every match in their series, this is pretty good. Benoit reveals the gold medals were down his tights the whole match. His personality remains missing.
Final Rating: ***½

Backstage: Steve Austin tries to treat Debra as his servant, which leads to Triple H and Steph doing the same thing. Debra gets a bit fed up and points out that Undertaker is a badass.

Queen's Cup
William Regal vs. Chris Jericho
Like the last UK PPV Regal gets a mixed reaction, thanks to his tireless promotion of this show, and despite that Cole puts it over as hatred. The "Queensbury Rules" match at *Backlash* was a bit disappointing, but here they go a different route. Jericho actually worked in Germany for a while and was pretty good friends with Regal's old pal Robbie Brookside, so when Regal attempts to boss with European style, Jericho understands it and is able to work around it without resorting to doing it himself. Jericho knows he needs big spots to keep the crowd on his side and yet popping off a super rana gets very little reaction. Regal dumps Jericho on his head and stops off to wave at the crowd, which gets a big pop. Cole calls it a boo because he's so blind to anything that happens outside of the WWF's own script that he just can't hear reality. He's a freakish little twat. The wrestling world is worse for him being in it, but he sure is photogenic with his stupid hair frosting and sexless delivery. Heyman has to work overtime to get anything worthwhile out of him. As the match progresses it feels as though there's no plan; Regal runs through his stuff, Jericho survives it and then switches to his stuff. I do like that Jericho uses the enzuigiri, as he was an enormous Owen Hart mark, but unless you'd read his book you wouldn't know that. Jericho could have benefitted from one of those sit down interviews detailing his past that worked so well for Mick Foley. Seeing as the WWF had rights to the ECW and WCW footage by this point, it would have been easy business. Unfortunately his babyface push had stalled. Lionsault gets knees as Cole starts to get way too excited for what's been a decent match but not a classic by any means. Jericho gets the Walls of Jericho and Regal taps out immediately. Jericho wins the Queen's Cup, which is a little trophy that nobody cares about. Regal jumps Jericho and bashes him in the head with the trophy, breaking it in the process. Jericho barely kept himself face here and the fans were so eager to cheer anything fun Regal did that the heel-face alignment was out of whack. Not that Cole noticed.
Final Rating: **¼

WWF Championship
Steve Austin (c) & Triple H vs. The Undertaker
Taker has to pin Austin to win the title, which is announced before the match and gives them an out on the finish. Because of the stipulation the match is an uneven mess with both heels allowed in there at once. At one point both of them just waddle into Taker's "soup bone" right hands and take arbitrary back bumps. Presumably the original plan, before Kane injured his elbow, was to have a tag team match here in a repeat of the awful *Backlash* main event. Like most three-way matches they work in a spot where Austin sells for ages on the floor to allow an actual one-on-one contest. Then, for no apparent reason, Austin resumes the match on the apron and we have a tag team contest. Logically, because only Austin's title is on the line and only he can lose it, there's no reason for him to ever tag in. It's another hole in this match. The only reason for him tagging in is to give Taker a beating, which he does and gets popped for it because it's a babyface move. Hunter and Taker collide allowing Austin a chair shot on the Dead Man while Steph distracts. The spot is awkward but at least it leads to a more realistic section of the match with Taker absorbing heat. It sure is boring. Meteorically so. Hunter's assertion that the match needs a lengthy sleeper spot is misplaced. I guess Taker couldn't go full out for the whole match, but the last UK PPV had a 9-minute main event, which was way better than this. This bout drags to an unwelcome 17-minutes. At least it wasn't a replication of the 27-minute yawner at *Backlash*. It occurs to me that Austin's heel turn didn't really take until after this terrible feud with Undertaker was done. Or perhaps rather the Two-Man Power Trip was disbanded following Hunter's quad injury. Hunter takes a chokeslam through the announce table, which he helpfully prepped earlier. Austin's knee braces have looked like they were about to fall off all match and that's bad news for Taker as he takes a rope ride and busts his ear into pieces. The injury would require surgery to repair it. I can only assume Austin is wearing new knee braces as they are gold and shiny, but look inadequate. Chokeslam on Austin and Hunter helpfully yells "cover him, cover him, COVER HIM" practically into the mic. Taker obliges and Hunter breaks the fall. Pedigree is countered and Heyman acknowledges the blood, which allows Cole to acknowledge it too as it wasn't planned so he'd not actually said anything about it. It is hilarious how inept he is both as a commentator and as a person. Vince McMahon strolls down and miscues a chair shot by hitting Hunter, so Taker hits the chokeslam and wins the match but not the title. Taker's ear injury is fairly horrific, in that there's lots of blood but you can't see it like you could Mick Foley's. The match is exactly what you'd expect from three overhyped main eventers in a convoluted contest. Hunter was only here so the face could go over in the main event without winning the title. Flimsy booking.
Final Rating: *½

VERDICT

There's something about 2001 that irks. The top guys stay on top and everyone else hits their head on the glass ceiling, regardless of how absolutely desperate the WWF were for new blood in the main events. *Insurrextion 2001* is the perfect demonstration. They only had three main eventers left, but unlike at *Fully Loaded 2000* where they had three main eventers and paired them up with three aspiring talents in a triple header main event, here the WWF just tossed all three into an insipid main event. I personally would have had Austin and Hunter defend the tag team titles in the main event, thus putting over the tag division as something worthwhile and letting guys like Edge & Christian, the Hardys and the Dudleys get a main event rub that they deserved. You could even switch the belts here and not affect the North American storylines (apart from the big Jericho-Benoit win that challenged the glass ceiling). Seeing as they pretty much threw the card out of the window, they could have come up with something fun! Something totally different. Instead it's Austin, Hunter and Taker. At least the midcard got some time to entertain. Angle-Benoit is naturally a top notch wrestling match and the tag team elimination match is okay, but I think the card reveals the lack of creativity in the company at the time. WCW folding left them to their own devices and wouldn't you know it; Undertaker gets another main event run during an era where his in-ring was the pits. In short, UK PPV's were mostly non-events and this is no different. Generic house show fare.

32

TRIPLE H - THAT DAMN GOOD

CAT NO: WWF283
RUN TIME: 120 minutes (approx)

Arnold Furious: Of the three of the scribes in this office, I think I'm arguably Triple H's biggest fan. In that I don't completely hate him and at one point, admittedly not for very long, he was my favourite WWF wrestler. Pretty much just for 2000 and early 2001 until he tore his quad. This is a tape that covers that particular era, so we're all good. Host is Triple H. He calls this a highlights package of some of his best matches so we can see why he is "that damn good". The first bout is from *Armageddon*. It is a terrible pile of shit and not the best match to demonstrate Hunter's ability in the ring.

No Holds Barred
Triple H vs. Vince McMahon
The stipulations are as follows: if Vince wins, Hunter's marriage to Stephanie is annulled. If Hunter wins he gets a title shot and the marriage continues. Interesting to note this match takes place after Vince had been "banned from WWF TV forever" about six months ago. He's actually had a WWF Title run since then. Only in wrestling. I remember being shocked by Steph's post match heel turn as she'd been utterly useless as a babyface, but she took to the role like a duck to water. It's just a pity Hunter and Vince decide to have a dick measuring competition first, as they go 30-minutes. Vince isn't a wrestler and doesn't have any spots. Hunter, with all due respect, has never been adept at carrying people of lesser ability. It's a recipe of disaster and the match is a humongous waste of PPV time. Seeing as Vince can't wrestle at all they fill the match with brawling. Unlike when Austin-McMahon headlined a PPV it's not filled with moments to excite. The difference with that match was, as a heel, Vince was getting his comeuppance. With this match it's just brawling for the sake of it. Yes, it is a personal feud, but Hunter as the wrestler should dominate, and he does but why, unlike the showboating Austin, does he not go for the finish quickly? He doesn't want to punish Vince, he just wants to win so he can go back to what really matters; the WWF Title. The match is dying a death so Mankind wheels out a shopping trolley full of weapons for Vince. His "use these bad boys" assertion makes me chuckle. Hunter at least inserts psychological common sense by washing his eyes out about 10 minutes after a powder shot from the chairman of the board. As if to say "I was only losing because I couldn't see". Mick's hardcore weapons make the match marginally more interesting but it still drags something fierce. It boggles the mind that the WWF won the wrestling war with PPV main events like this. It goes to show just how awful WCW was at the same time.

The set for *Armageddon* features several military vehicles. Hunter gets creative with the props and uses a machine gun to knock Vince down. Vince manages the same with a flap from a helicopter. The weird thing about all the garbage shots is the lack of selling. Various objects are bounced off Hunter's head, then off Vince's head, rinse, repeat. When that gets boring Hunter just flat out disappears. As in we head to the parking lot and he's nowhere to be seen. This is the month after the hit and run on Steve Austin and Hunter tries a similar trick on Vince, but McMahon hops over a rail to survive a badly lit, badly shot attack. A replay shows how close Vince came to serious injury. After that they resort to the same deal; bouncing heads off objects over and over again. To mix things up they add in a silly bump with both guys climbing a tower by the entranceway before Vince falls off onto a safety landing mat. Vince blades from the bump, which makes little sense. The match contains shit for the sake of it. It needs blood so Vince just bleeds. Hunter stops off to cut a promo in front of Steph before grabbing Sledgie, his trusted sledgehammer. Vince kicks him in the balls, steals the hammer and Steph leaps in the ring to demand her own vengeance. Hunter takes the hammer off her and wears Vince out with it for the pin. At least they never lost the crowd, apart from me, so it stays out of negative snowflakes, but it's a chore to sit through and I don't recommend it.
Final Rating: ½*

Back to the studio and Hunter mumbles through another segue before calling the upcoming match with Cactus Jack one of the best matches of his career. This is a fine choice for the tape as the energy levels and emotion are superb. Foley does an amazing job of covering for his lack of conditioning and a lot of that is on Hunter and how good he was at the time.

Street Fight
WWF Championship

Triple H (c) vs. Cactus Jack
Interesting they don't bill Cactus as being from Truth or Consequences, New Mexico. Plenty of "Foley is God" signs out there. To this point I felt Mick's best match in the business was his classic with Shawn Michaels at *Mind Games*, despite the lack of finish. That's about to change. The only beef I have with this match is that it should have gone on last, after the Rumble. Foley was so broken down by 2000 that it's a minor miracle he can move around with the athleticism that he does. I guess he knew he had two matches left so he could leave it all in the ring. This match is all about progression and building. They start out on the floor brawling and Cactus takes a shot with the ring bell, which was enough to put Mankind down. But Cactus Jack isn't Mankind. Not anymore. He's gained a mythical power that lifts him above that. Hunter grabs a chair so Cactus demands a shot with it and Hunter delivers. Mick goes down like a sack of spuds but he gets back up! They don't do much wrestling, they don't need to, but Jack uses swinging neckbreakers and backdrops on the floor, as if to pay homage to wrestling in an unusual setting. They insert a crowd brawl but it's merely to get to a New York style alleyway part of the entrance. This leads to Hunter taking a suplex on a pallet. Much to his horror he discovers a piece of wood stabbed him in the leg during that spot. Lots of blood from that and it's right in the calf. For all the flak we've given Hunter, he sure knew how to man up and work with pain. In order to push the envelope Cactus grabs his 2x4 wrapped in barbed wire, which gets a massive pop. As per usual for Mick, bringing a weapon into a match backfires, as Hunter nut shots him and uses the 2x4. The WWF had seen nothing this violent beforehand. Double arm DDT but, in a rare moment of weird selling, Cactus stays down far too long before pinning. Hunter rolls his shoulder while the ref is hiding the 2x4 so they can switch to a fake weapon. "Where's the bat?" screams Cactus at Earl Hebner. Jack lays out Hugo Savinovich for not giving him the bat from under the Spanish announce table. Hunter then takes a 2x4 shot right in the noggin. Hunter kicks out and the fans are already biting on the near falls. Also Hunter is bleeding like a stuck pig from the head and the leg. He's having to earn this title in blood, sweat and tears.

Like his hero Ric Flair, Hunter's blond hair is turning a shade of red as Cactus beats at his bloody head. It's a crimson mask! Cactus, remembering his last win over Hunter, goes for a piledriver on the announce table to replicate that famous MSG win from *RAW* in 1997. Hunter feels it coming and backdrops out, breaking the table before the main event. Hunter sets for the Pedigree and unfortunately does it in line with the buckles, rather telegraphing the reversal. Hunter then face bumps onto the barbed wire... for 2. Hunter has juiced so much that the fans buy everything as a near fall now. Cactus Clothesline sets up Jack to take a hip toss onto the ring steps. Cactus follows that with yet another knees-first bump into the ring steps, which makes you wonder if he was planning on even walking after this match, let alone wrestling a main event the following month. Hunter, always the cerebral assassin takes out Cactus' leg. This allows him to handcuff Jack. People get depressed at the sight of Mick Foley getting cuffed as it brings back memories of the Rock's brutalisation of him at *Royal Rumble '99*. It also ends the fans hope that Cactus can win the title. Hunter goes after the ring steps but Cactus manages to drop toehold him, in a superb piece of defensive wrestling. Hunter then wears him out with a chair, which creates a great visual as part of the chair breaks off and flies towards the crowd. As Jack starts begging Hunter to hit him properly, the Rock runs out and chair shots Hunter so the cops can unlock Cactus' cuffs. Now it's a fair fight again and Jack's first call of business is to hit that piledriver on a table. The Spanish table does not oblige and stays in one piece. Because it's not falls count anywhere Cactus has to take it back into the ring and on the way picks up a massive bag of thumbtacks. Stephanie McMahon can't take it anymore and runs out to appeal to Jack's sense of fair play. Hunter takes the opening and backdrops Cactus into the tacks. Great sell from Stephanie on that. PEDIGREE! ONE-TWO-THR... NOOO! KICKOUT! This was outstanding business as the Pedigree was death and nobody ever kicked out of it. Hunter's one-legged complaint to the ref is brilliant, but as soon as Cactus is up a second Pedigree on the thumbtacks gets the job done. A brutal ballet that had a ridiculous escalation of violence for the WWF. Hunter's selling and bleeding made the match and the match made him.
Final Rating: *****

Back to the studio and Hunter calls Chris Jericho "a constant thorn in the side of me" and implies that when Jericho got his real shot at 'the Game', he came up short, before putting him over as tough. He also puts the match over as great, which it is. He's already 2/3.

Last Man Standing
Triple H vs. Chris Jericho
The opening shine sees Jericho beat the crap out of HHH and if there's one thing Hunter did well in 2000 it was getting other people over. It almost pains me to watch Hunter in 2000 because he was such a tremendous talent and yet he deliberately stopped being it. Jericho has an out as Hunter injured his ribs with a sledgehammer prior to the PPV and HHH works that area. Like a bastard. There's a bit where Hunter rams his shoulder into Jericho's ribs in the corner relentlessly. It shows both his cardio and his aggression. He's a beast. Jericho takes such a beating on the ribs that you feel he's done, which is a huge turnaround from the opening shine. Jericho gets a series of hope spots culminating in the Lionsault, which gets knees into the injured ribs. Because Jericho can't catch his breath he can't stand. Hunter goes to finish with the Main Event Sleeper, eager to capitalise on the situation he's created. Jericho does a great job of selling how close he is to being finished with his rubber legs and his begging Hunter to kick his ass, if he can. Jericho manages a weak crotch chop and a Pedigree! As Jericho starts to stir Hunter bails for a chair, pissed off that Chris won't stay down. He even chair shots the ribs, continuing his unrelenting focus. The escalating violence was a trademark of Hunter's best matches. Hunter figures a Pedigree on a chair will do it, but Jericho goes low to save himself. Jericho comes back with a chair shot and Hunter bleeds a gusher off that. It's hideous, a massive cut with loads of juice from it. Now it's a total reversal as Hunter has the weakness and Jericho, like a shark, smells the blood. The match had previously worked on a "periods of dominance" strategy. They switch to a back-and-forth, which creates an exciting conclusion as the match is wide open. They duel with monitor shots but both survive the 10 count. Pedigree is countered into the Walls of Jericho and Hunter taps out, but that's not in the rules. Jericho just wants to cripple Hunter's legs so he can't stand. Hunter gets into the ropes then realises there's no DQ so the ref can't break it. Steph realises that means she can interfere and jumps in there, only for Jericho to slap her in the Walls of Jericho and Hunter has to save. Hunter pulls out the sledgehammer but misses and he gets catapulted into the post. Jericho gets in one of those sledgehammer punches to set up a table spot. Hunter goes low to block it and back suplexes Jericho through the announce table. Jericho's defence for losing is that his head hits the floor after the table. Hunter gets up, just, and Jericho stays down. Hunter wins.

Great match. Another classic from Hunter's 2000 run.
Final Rating: ****½

Back to the studio and Hunter, showing an increasing lack of charisma, recaps the issues with Kurt Angle at SummerSlam 2000 and how proud he was of how the match turned out.

WWF Championship
The Rock (c) vs. Kurt Angle vs. Triple H
Before we get underway, and before the Rock is even out here, Hunter and Angle brawl all over the place to get over the hatred between them regarding Steph. See, Kurt was in the Helmsleys' business and had "carnal intentions" towards Steph, which royally pissed off Hunter and practically turned him face for a while in 2000. His assault on Angle leads to a Pedigree through the Spanish announce table and the table gives way mid-move, thus dumping Kurt face first on the surface. As JR points out "his eyes are glazed over" as Kurt is just staring off into space and can't do anything. With Angle out of the game, Rock and Hunter have to improvise a match, which isn't hard for them seeing as they've worked a bunch of times since 1996 and they're both considered top guys in the company. The only real issue is throwing the whole match out of the window, thanks to Kurt's head injury, and coming up with something new on the fly. That's probably why Hunter likes it enough to feature it on this tape as winging a match is a lot harder when you need to call everything in the ring. Angle gets stretchered out, unable to do anything and there is a suggestion that it's a work as Hunter goes after the stretcher to get another lick in. I don't know what Hunter was thinking seeing as Kurt genuinely had a concussion, but my guess is he wanted it to feel like a legitimate match. To make a real injury look like a worked one, which is the opposite of what they usually go for. The idea being that they incorporate a real injury into the worked match. Hunter actually dealt with the whole situation supremely well from the point of impact and Angle's recovery as he holds Angle down when Kurt tries to get back up. Steph comes out and they improvise a goofy missed belt shot, which presumably was supposed to be an Angle spot. Hunter decides he doesn't want to do any more of those spots and sends Steph to the back, which makes sense after her miscue and also because improvisation isn't her strong point. Hunter grabs the sledgehammer as there's no DQ, not that there's ever been DQ's in a three-way as you can't DQ one guy and then carry on. He hits Rock in the ribs, not the head, and uses the spot to build rather than a false finish. It's a combination of things as Hunter needs to reinforce his heel status as the stuff with Angle was turning him face and he wants to wear Rock down and beat him his way. Hunter is looking very muscular by the way. He's carrying none of the weight around that'd plague his later career and he looks incredible. You can see his quad muscles straining as he walks around the ring and you can see why it snapped like a guitar string. Considering the lack of structure this turns out to be a decent match, which is testament to Hunter's leadership and Rock's raw ability. It's also the answer to a frequently asked wrestling question; what would happen if something went wrong in a big match? Well, they'd improvise and carry on wrestling. The show must go on!

Steph drags Kurt back out and he looks goofy but not as out of it as beforehand. Angle trips Rock to set up the Pedigree and also manages to pull Hunter off the cover. Concussed Kurt even gets a near fall off Hunter's hard work. Angle manages to get himself enough together to come up with a belly-to-belly and they try to return to the match. Rock is very careful while setting Angle up for a DDT, but Kurt's composure has returned. Hunter prevents a pin after a Rock Bottom, with excellent timing all around. Steph gets to do some more plunder improvisation by throwing the sledgehammer in, but Angle grabs it and Hunter accidentally punches Steph out. That was a much better spot. Angle nails Hunter with the sledgehammer but Rock spit-punches him out of the ring and hits the People's Elbow on Triple H to retain. They did one hell of a job to get a match together after the early injury to Angle, but it does make you wonder how great the match could have been if everything played out as it was supposed to. I remember slightly disliking this at the time, but in retrospect it's a commendable effort. If there's ever been a match to get over Hunter's ability to lead in the ring it'd be this one.
Final Rating: ***

Back in the studio Hunter gives a seriously neutral shill for his Three Stages of Hell match with Steve Austin at *No Way Out*. He calls it the highlight of the Austin rivalry and "one of the craziest matches you'll ever see".

Three Stages of Hell
Steve Austin vs. Triple H
First Fall: As Hunter puts it this is "straight up". Hunter, the cerebral assassin, goes after Austin's surgically repaired neck. When Austin comes firing back Hunter switches to the permanently injured knee instead. Showing Austin's weakness right from the off immediately casts doubt over what seemed like an obvious Austin victory. The way Hunter dissects those body parts, which are already injured, serves to make him the favourite. It also allows them to slow the pace, which is smart because it's not a short match. Hunter then hooks a figure four putting doubt in Austin's mind because it's 2 out of 3 falls. Will Austin give up to save his knee and instead come back in the last two falls? Eventually he manages to turn it over, thus reversing the pressure (what a load of bollocks that is) before waffling Hunter with his knee brace-covered leg. Hunter just about avoids the Stunner and counters into a neckbreaker, even inserting a deliberate switch in position to not confuse the fans by thinking the Stunner hit. Hunter tries for something off the top, which is somewhat out of character and drops right into the Stunner. 1-0 Austin. Which, if anything, is the only major flaw in this match. The face shouldn't really take the first fall in 2 out of 3 falls. It should always be about his fight to overcome the odds but I guess they wanted to throw some realism in there.

Second Fall: Street Fight. The street fight stipulation REALLY suits both guys as Austin loves brawling and Hunter has his best matches in a no DQ environment. Austin wears Hunter out with a chair, which gets a massive ovation. Austin gave Hunter a hellacious shoeing there. Austin pulls out a barbed wire 2x4, which Mick Foley must have left lying around, but it backfires and Austin blades off it. Hunter gets caught calling spots on camera again. Maybe it's just his deep, manly register but it's amazing how many times he gets caught, compared to everyone else. Austin bleeds a gusher so Hunter lines up a Pedigree only to get backdropped through the Spanish announce table in another hellacious spot. Lawler getting freaked as Hunter passes him in the air makes for a wonderful visual. Maybe he's just freaked out about having to follow this as his match is next. Hunter goes back to his original tactic and hits a neckbreaker on a chair. In an even better spot Hunter counters a headlock into a back suplex on the same chair and they nail it. Hunter goes after his Scott Hall-esque "finisher by the ropes" spot and gets backdropped to the floor. On the floor Hunter gets whacked in the face with a chair and that allows him an opportunity to bleed too. Austin adds in the ring steps to make sure but he needn't have... there's blood everywhere because both guys are bleeding absolute gushers. Hunter grabs his trusty sledgehammer and Austin goes for the Stunner, but Hunter pushes him off, hits him with the hammer and finishes fall two with the Pedigree. Outstanding second fall. The crowd jeer the finish but they're getting a third fall!

Third Fall: Down comes the cage to the ominous "cage lowering music". The cage leaves no space around the ring but all the weapons were left in there including the barbed wire 2x4. They both use that, which causes more blood and more vicious plunder shots. The match starts to slow down at this juncture as both men are fatigued and the crowd is burned out after the second fall too. After a few minutes of whaling on each other Hunter goes to climb out with JR pointing out you can't win by escape, only pinfall. The slower pace of the third fall puts over how tiring the match has been. Stunner is countered into the Pedigree, but Austin shoots his shoulder up at 2 ½ with the fans going nuts at the prospect of Hunter going over. Hunter adds in a chair shot and simply tosses the chair to one side. It reminds me of the match with Cactus Jack, where he got a bit dispirited at not winning with a Pedigree and felt all melancholy about the violence for a moment. Austin gets a sloppy Stunner after countering another Pedigree but this time Hunter kicks out. Very weird bump. Hunter grabs the sledgehammer and Austin the 2x4 and they hit at the same time, but it's Hunter who lands on top for the pin. The match is a brutal ballet (I know, I know, I've already used that one once) and I like it slightly more than James. It's not quite full boat because of the third fall where they tried to force spots to mean a lot. Also, as a traditionalist, I think Hunter should have gone over in the first fall but hey, these are minor quibbles and it's a very, very good match, but it's often somewhat forgotten because Austin and Rock went and had a barnburner at *WrestleMania* the next month.
Final Rating: ****¾

Back in the studio Hunter talks about tearing his quad in May and missing 8 months. He points out he wouldn't take no for an answer and "made my triumphant return". Video Control gives us footage of Hunter's return on RAW in January 2002. The respect Triple H gained from finishing the match when he tore his quad turned him into a legend while he was away. He gets a loud and sustained pop, one of the biggest of his career. "I am the Game and you can bet your ass I'm back" gets an enormous pop. Back in the studio Hunter, in his silly worked voice, points out he won the Rumble and went to WrestleMania to once again become champion.

WWF Unified World Championship
Chris Jericho (c) vs. Triple H
I think this match about sums up why Hunter's face turn failed. When he returned the fans were jazzed about it and thrilled to have him back, but two months later a large chunk of the audience has mentally checked out. That's how little they now care, having already been treated to one of the great pieces of sportz entertainment earlier in the night with Rock vs. Hogan. Unlike that match, this one is a foregone conclusion with Jericho being treated as an afterthought to the Hunter-Steph storyline. Hunter tries to bring a storyline with him, as his leg is heavily taped, and he sells it hard from the opening. At least that brings some cohesion to the action, even if the fans don't give a crap about it. The camera constantly lingers on Hooty McBoob at ringside and her enormous cleavage. Steph is completely uncoordinated and an attempt at raking Hunter's eyes results in her falling over like a chump. As if it wasn't immediately obvious what the *real* match was; Hunter drags Steph into the ring and looks for a Pedigree only for Jericho to save. Jericho is so unimportant to the booking, he might as well have been replaced by a cardboard cut-out. But hey, he's headlined *WrestleMania*! Jericho continues to work the leg while Steph gets in cheap shots. It's not a bad match, but for the main event of *WrestleMania* it's a massive underachiever. I don't remember the match at all back in 2002 as I'd been drinking rather heavily during the undercard and myself and the people I was watching with were still talking about Rock-Hogan. In fact, I think another friends of mine may have called me up during this match to discuss said contest, as it was so important. That feeling is evident on tape too as the fans start aimlessly chanting "Hogan" at one point. That about sums up *WrestleMania X-8*. Not that either guy wanted to go on last, citing that the fans wouldn't be into it. I think if they'd gone on third last, this match might have gone over a lot differently and be remembered with greater fondness. But the crowd is dead and the match doesn't do enough to get them involved. If you have to follow Hogan vs. Rock you'd better have a big match and the limb work doesn't really cut it. Maybe if it was a focus of part of the match it'd be okay but Hunter is so into selling it, the leg takes over. They do work in an announce table spot for the first half-decent pop of the match, where Hunter signals for the Pedigree but is predictably backdropped through the other table. Hunter kicks out of the Lionsault, not that Y2J had used that as a finish for his entire WWF run. They run a flubbed bulldog counter, which leads directly into a Pedigree, countered into the Walls of Jericho. Hunter passes out from the pain, which doesn't make a jot of sense considering he carried on working with a torn quad. Eventually Hunter gets into the ropes and there's no reaction at all from the crowd. Steph jumps in the ring hoping for a DQ, which would prevent Hunter winning the title, but the Tripper hits her with a crowd-pleasing Pedigree, showing from a reaction stand-point what the fans actually wanted to see. Hunter turns into a chair shot and the kick out gets popped as the match is finally getting some traction. They work in a nice counters sequence before Jericho falls to the Pedigree and Hunter takes the title off him. Honestly, you could clip this down to the final quarter of the match and lose nothing of consequence. From a storyline perspective it makes sense to finish here as Hunter won the title, but the match is decidedly mediocre.
Final Rating: **¼

VERDICT

I could have lived without Hunter's in-character links in the studio. Rather the tape would have benefitted from a little insight from 'the Game' on why he thought stuff was good and why he'd picked these matches to represent his time at the top of the industry. That said, there are several belters here. The *Royal Rumble* Street Fight is one of Hunter's best matches, the Jericho Last Man Standing Match is another. I'm pleased to see Hunter-Austin from *No Way Out 2001* on here too, as I thought I was going to miss out on that one. During the planning of the tape reviews I pointed out how great I thought it was, and luckily James came around to my way of thinking when he re-watched it. Considering this is a two hour tape, you've got three great matches on here over ****½, which is grounds for an easy thumbs up and the strongest recommendation. Even more so when you look at Triple H's "definitive" DVD collection *Thy Kingdom Come*, which features none of these top matches.

92

BEST OF RAW VOL. 3

CAT NO: WWF286
RUN TIME: 107 minutes (approx)

James Dixon: This is the third and final instalment of the rebooted "Best of RAW" series, covering late 1999 until the end of 2000. Hosted by the Coach

We begin with the Attitude Era's answer to Randy Savage and Miss Elizabeth: the relationship and proposed marriage between Stephanie McMahon and Andrew 'Test' Martin. "The power of their love would soon be tested by real life's uncertainties" says Michael Cole in the most contrived manner possible. Who talks like that? The relationship hit a few snags, not least Davey Boy Smith inadvertently hoying a metal bin in the direction of Steph's face and causing her to have that old soap opera staple; amnesia, forgetting all of her feelings for poor Test. When reminded of them, she broke with tradition and proposed, which summed up who wore the pants in that relationship. To the ceremony, which is interrupted by Triple H and his revelation that he is already married to Steph, thanks to a helping hand from Rohypnol and a less than observant attendee at the drive thru chapel. Rather than having the marriage annulled, which seems like the most logical thing to do, instead Hunter and Vince McMahon have a match at *Armageddon* to determine the future of young Stephanie. Only in wrestling. Vince agrees to the stipulations imposed by Triple H that if he wins he gets a title shot but if he loses then Steph is free, and his face furls with apoplectic rage when Hunter seals the deal with a kiss. Erm, with Steph, not Vince. Either that or he had a particularly perilous situation occurring "down south" that had already started to rear its ugly head, so to speak. It's hard to tell with him sometimes. Even though this is a tape covering happenings on *RAW*, we see the finish of the *Armageddon* match and Stephanie's subsequent heel turn on her pops, which ushers in a horrifying new era: the McMahon-Helmsley Regime. Reality aped storyline over the next few years, with the two hooking up for real and ending up married with kids. Incredibly, some fourteen years after this there was another McMahon-Helmsley era in WWE, only this time they gave themselves the scripted and forced moniker of 'The Authority'.

Back to *RAW*, and an irate Vince smashes DX's locker room door down with a sledgehammer as he tries to find Hunter. Later on in the ring, Steph explains her actions and... her justification actually make sense! She brings up the angle from a few months back where Vince was the infamous "higher power" in the Ministry of Darkness, and had Steph abducted and almost forced into a Satanic marriage to the Undertaker just so he could screw with Steve Austin. You can see how something like that would mess with a girl's head. I am actually not sure how Vince is the babyface in any of this when I think about it. Steph puts an exclamation point on things by gleefully telling her dad how much Trips turns her on. There is something not quite right about that family.

With the power mad McMahon-Helmsley era gathering momentum, Hunter targets the Rock 'n' Sock Connection, and he declares partners Rock and Mankind will compete against each other in a "pink slip on a pole match", which means the loser gets fired. It's a smart angle, and eventually resulted in the brilliant Hunter-Foley feud of the next few months. We see action from the match, which is joined in progress with Al Snow coming down and belting Rock with Head to prevent him from winning. Mankind doesn't want to win it that way, and instead of grabbing the slip he belts Al. They brawl back-and-forth some more, with Rock hitting a Rock Bottom and Mankind the Socko Claw, but neither gets the job done. They fight up by the pole where Mankind takes a bump to the outside, and Rock grabs the slip and seemingly ends Foley's career. Rock's reaction to winning is great, as he just storms off in rage because of what he has been forced to do.

Triple H continues to jibe at Foley after he has gone, which is in keeping with the WWF's unflattering tradition of ripping into guys when they leave the company. Hunter hires an imposter to mock Mankind (Dennis 'Phineas Godwinn' Knight in the only entertaining role of his career), and this results in some genuinely funny skits as "Mankind" finds himself in various embarrassing scenarios. It is the real Mankind who gets the last laugh though, as the entire roster clubs together and demands he be reinstated or they will go on strike, which leads to an 8-man tag on *RAW* featuring Triple H and his DX buddies against Rock, the Acolytes and Mankind. Hunter and Mankind end up as the last two guys standing, but WWF Champion

216

Helmsley pins Foley to prove his superiority. The real story comes after the bout, as Mankind symbolically removes his mask and beats the crap out of Hunter, and he stands bloody and proud afterwards.

A few weeks later Mick Foley has transformed into Cactus Jack, and is credited for bringing the Radicalz quartet of Chris Benoit, Eddie Guerrero, Perry Saturn and Dean Malenko into the WWF. They joke around backstage about the fact there is a crowd out there, which they are not used to, but soon afterwards Hunter reveals that it was he who gave the group contracts, and they turn on Foley and beat the crap out of him to tremendous heat. "Cactus Jack doesn't have any stroke" says Benoit in order to justify their actions.

More footage not from *RAW*, with Tazz making his debut against Kurt Angle at the *Royal Rumble* in what turned out to be the highlight of his WWF run. Back on *RAW*, Kurt protests that he is still undefeated because he was illegally choked out, and he challenges the Rock to a match later on the show. We get a decent chunk of the bout, but again not the whole thing. It's a strong back-and-forth contest, though not a patch on their excellent PPV outing at *No Way Out* the following year. Angle at one point goes to leave but is prevented from doing so by Tazz, and Rock befalls him his first pinfall defeat, in front of his hometown crowd no less.

The night after *Royal Rumble 2000*, the Big Show complains to Triple H that he was robbed in the Rumble match because Rock's feet touched the floor first. He is right, but listening to Show talk is a chore because he is really bland when it comes to delivering promos. It is one of the reasons he didn't get over to the level many thought he would, because he was surrounded by a bunch of guys who could talk up a storm. Show wants a match with Rock at *No Way Out* for a title shot, and Hunter agrees if Show can give him evidence to back up his claims. Show gives Polaroid shots, testimonies from a security guy who had a close-up view of the elimination and finally footage, getting him his match with Rock. He wins thanks to help from Shane McMahon, and Hunter beats Cactus Jack in the title match on the same show, setting up the horrific sounding Triple H vs. Big Show *WrestleMania* main event. "If Triple H vs. The Big Show is going to be the main event of *WrestleMania*, then *WrestleMania* is going to absolutely suck!" says the Rock. Oh, he is so very right. Much convoluted McMahon-heavy nonsense follows, resulting in the even worse fatal four way match also including Rock and the suddenly unretired Mick Foley, with the joyous addition of a McMahon being in every corner. They should have just had a McMahon family four way, because that was the real focus of the match. It all ended up with silliness as it always does, with Steph and Vince forming an alliance and uniting behind Hunter (rendering the past few month's storylines as nonsense), who became the first heel in history to walk away from *WrestleMania* with a successful WWF Title defence. Of course he did.

Hunter was not amused with Rock decking his wife with a Rock Bottom following *WrestleMania*, and set about tearing him apart in a cage, busting him open and leaving him lying after smashing his face in with brass knuckles. This kind of thing happens to Rock after 'Mania every year. This would result in an epic showdown at *Backlash*, but before that Triple H was forced to defend the title on *RAW* against the red hot Chris Jericho. Jericho won the match to an immense pop, but later in the night Hunter bullied pussy referee Earl Hebner into reversing the decision because he "screwed" him and counted the fall fast, before firing him and beating the snot out of him.

Anyone who saw this that was still a fan of WWE in 2013-14 probably experienced a strong sense of déjà vu, because the exact angle was repeated between the Authority and Daniel Bryan following the latter's WWE Championship win over Randy Orton at *Night of Champions*.

More Jericho next as we finally take a break from Hunter, and we bafflingly get clips from his match against Chris Benoit *prior* to the previous bout, with Kurt Angle serving as the commentator. This ended up leading to a triple threat match at *WrestleMania*, but the post match attack on both guys from Angle is missed off and the inclusion of this on the tape is rendered somewhat pointless.

Next we see the same Hardcore Title 24/7 video that has turned up on a bunch of these tape releases, showing the trials and tribulations of poor Crash Holly as he strives to retain his belt. We go to a *King of the Ring* qualifier between Crash and his cousin Hardcore, which ends in a DQ win for Elroy thanks to interference from Pat Patterson and Gerald Brisco. Brisco ends up decking Crash and beating him to win the Hardcore Title, but when celebrating backstage with Pat he gets turned on by his fellow stooge and smashed over the head with a champagne bottle and pinned.

Next up: sex! Included in the segment is the harrowing relationship between Mae Young and Mark Henry, which results in them in bed together with the insinuation being that they have just bumped uglies. We then briefly see Kurt Angle wearing a billboard promoting abstinence and a really bizarre Trish Stratus promo where she gets aroused by tables. Following that, we see Eddie Guerrero trying to gain access to the Playboy mansion so he can destroy Chyna's recently shot pictures, presumably as a service to all mankind. Eddie apologises then claims to be ill so that Chyna will wrestle her friend Rikishi in his place. Eddie turns up at ringside and 'Kishi beats him up, but Eddie maces him. Unable to see, Rikishi hits the Samoan drop on Chyna and then when he can see, he crushes her with the Banzai Drop. Eddie does nothing to save her. A little more about the relationship and the aftermath of this would have been beneficial and appreciated.

Charisma black hole and original Vince McMahon approved automaton Linda McMahon gives Kane, the Undertaker and the Rock a stern ticking off for fighting each other, then tells them to be united in order to get the WWF Title back off Triple H. This leads to a nonsense match at *King of the Ring* where Rock pins Vince to win the title in a six man tag. How horrible. The next night Vince hijacks a Rock promo to talk about how from this point on he is going to dedicate himself to Linda, and that the two are going to try for another baby because he is a "genetic jackhammer". What gruesome imagery that conjures up. Rock is equally appalled and calls Vince an "asshole" before giving him a Rock Bottom. Also that night, Shawn Michaels turned up with a major announcement: Mick Foley is the new WWF commissioner... Pleasingly that means a Foley skit with Edge & Christian, who were perfect foil for him, the one shown being where the duo are forced to defend their tag titles against the Undertaker and Kane because they disrespect Mick by making him get them sodas. The chemistry the three have is wonderful.

More from Kurt Angle next, who comes over all King Mabel following his *King of the Ring* victory, and dresses in the full regalia while taking his new position altogether far too seriously. Angle's program with the Undertaker follows, which was a bad idea. The build up is decent enough but the 7-

minute match at *Fully Loaded 2000* was crap, with Angle's momentum dealt a major blow by an unnecessary clean and decisive job. Once again this "best of *RAW*" tape shows highlights of the PPV match, meaning what this release actually appears to be is a "best of 1999-2000" tape.

While Angle's feud with the Undertaker was booked badly, his love triangle with Stephanie McMahon and Triple H was brilliant. Initially. First Angle complains about Mick Foley and gives Steph an innocent hug that Triple H sees and gets all pissy about. Angle protests his innocence and gives Michael Cole a hug to show that it meant nothing. Things take a turn for the worse for Hunter when Steph walks in on him demonstrating a dodgy looking reversal on Trish Stratus that leaves the two in a compromising position, and Steph flips her lid and trashes the locker room. The two make up but Mick Foley calls them on it all being a public facade, and then backstage Trish apologises for her role in their problems. Steph doesn't buy it and claims Hunter and Trish have eyes for each other. Steph then asks to be shown the same reversal that Hunter showed Trish, which Trips does, but then he accidentally calls her "Trish". Uh oh. Steph needs space, but things get worse when Hunter ends up getting a chair shot from the Rock and ends up in a "69" position with Trish, and Kurt Angle steps in to be the shoulder to cry on for Steph. Unfortunately the payoff doesn't come, because they have decided to split the story into two parts on this tape. How frustrating.

We see the formation of Right to Censor, which came about because of unbearable real life do-gooders the Parents Television Council, who wanted to police all television that didn't meet their so-called standards. They campaigned hard against the WWF for their supposed excessive violence, negative portrayal of women as sex objects, lurid characters and whatever other drivel they came up with in their smear campaign to try and get them off the air. The WWF's typically mature response was to mock the group on TV by forming their own storyline censorship group, which served the dual purpose of mocking the PTC but also removing some of the edgier characters from television to reduce the flak. When Steven Richards forms the group, he tells the crowd: "You do not know what's good for you, but I do" which is an obvious and fair jab at the PTC. Richards converts the Godfather, Val Venis and Bull Buchanan to his cause, and then finally Ivory who we see chastising Trish and Lita for having a bra and panties match. Good LORD the ass on Trish... Ivory claims to have "seen the light" and says "not only have you been stripped of your clothing, you have been stripped of your pride". She plays the "prissy teacher" type very well.

To William Regal, who is sitting having a tea party giving lessons in etiquette. His British accent and persona was so very stereotypical and cartoonish that it bordered on ridiculous, but he played the role so well that it was richly entertaining. He tries to teach Americans how to use a handkerchief, and offers the brilliant words of wisdom: "never wipe or smear, that is for another orifice". Jericho interrupts and promises a tablecloth magic trick, but instead just throws the contents of the table out of the ring. That doesn't lead anywhere in particular, but the focus stays on Regal as he commentates on a European Title match featuring champion Al Snow, who has perturbed Regal by confusing Greece with Grease. We don't see any of Al's match, just the comments from Regal that Al is disgracing his continent. Regal then beats Al for the title when they go head-to-head soon afterwards. His disingenuous manic smile after a vicious assault is great and almost Hannibal Lecter like.

Back to the Angle-Hunter-Steph love triangle. Hunter asks Steph to stay out of his match with Angle and she intends to, but then runs into Chris Benoit backstage and slaps him. Not wise. She decides to come out and get involved in the bout anyway because she can't follow instructions. She stops Angle using a chair but then Benoit pulls her off the apron and smacks Hunter with a chair, and Angle hits the Olympic Slam to win. Hunter storms off, furious with Steph. This leads to an assault from Benoit and Angle on Rock and Hunter, with Steph berating Angle for attacking her husband, before Benoit promptly shuts her up with a headbutt. Ace.

Steve Austin had been gone from screens for almost a year, brief appearance at *Backlash* aside, but the *RAW's* debut on TNN saw him return to TV, and the whole "who ran down Steve Austin" can of worms gets reopened again after nearly a year on the shelf. Austin does some investigating, but he is the worst sleuth in history because he doesn't even really question anyone, he just beats the shit out of people. Mick Foley cracks the case: it was Rikishi. This was one of the worst payoffs to an angle that I can remember, just illogical, nonsensical bullshit. He wasn't even at the show where it happened! If ever an angle jumped the shark, then it was this one. Backstage before a tag bout, Rock gets attacked and taken to hospital, so Austin has to work the match as a handicap bout. He gets the shit kicked out of him. It then turns out that Triple H was responsible for the whole hit and run thing and was the mastermind behind the attack. Of course he was involved, he just has to have a hand in everything.

We finish things with Mick Foley and Kurt Angle arguing about being each other's wives, and Mick forcing Angle to defend his title against bosom buddy Vince McMahon. Naturally Vince is able to ground the Olympic gold medallist during the course of this with an amateur takedown. Mick gets involved and ends up beaten up by an Edge & Christian Conchairto, but Steph comes down and prevents further assault because she has some... papers! The papers apparently say that due to "mental incompetence" Linda McMahon's CEO powers have been given to Vince. There are a whole host of jokes relating to that one. Vince immediately fires Mick and that finishes up the tape.

VERDICT

There is plenty of good stuff on here, though very little of it is actually given time to be digested before we move onto the next thing. Except Triple H and Stephanie of course... Oh there is plenty from both of those on here, and if you are not sick enough of them and can stomach it, their angles and segments are actually pretty good. The biggest bugbear with this tape is obviously the glaring lack of wrestling, with no matches shown in full and in truth very little actual wrestling shown at all. But that is *RAW* in the Attitude Era for you, and you know what to expect when coming in. Scatterbrained and occasionally suffers from the typical WWF questionable slicing and editing, but the near two hours go past pretty quickly and there is definitely nothing you would categorise as "bad" on here. Well worth your time.

73

THE HURRICANE

ACTION!

CAT NO: WWF287
RUN TIME: 87 minutes (approx)

James Dixon: Harking back to old school releases from days long forgotten, this is a compilation tape promising "action". Replacing what would have been the superior Sean Mooney as host, is the far less endearing Jonathan Coachman.

WWF Hardcore Championship
Raven (c) vs. Tazz
First up is the WWF's answer to what they perceive to be ECW; the hardcore division, taken from the New Year's Day episode of *RAW* from 2001. The two brawl around the building as is customary in these things, with one particularly unpleasant spot seeing the two battle into a women's bathroom, where Tazz flushes Raven's head in a piss-filled toilet. Charming. As ever, others want to get in on the act and the Holly trio and Steve Blackman join the fun. Raven wallops Crash with a fire extinguisher and then pins him to win the match, which doesn't make any sense at all.
Final Rating: ¼*

WWF Hardcore Championship
Rhyno (c) vs. The Big Show
Four months later Rhyno was the reigning champion, because he was another ECW guy that the WWF didn't quite understand what to do with. In many ways he was similar to Tazz, in that ECW booked him well and made him seem like a monster even though he was chunky and short, the opposite of what the WWF want. Thus, they squandered his undoubted talent and made him work these short and pointless garbage matches. Big Show can probably empathise a little, though ironically he has the opposite problem in that he is too big for the brain trust that is WWF creative to come up with how to book him. How is it hard to book a giant? Keep him strong, put him in fairly short matches, don't use him on television every week and kill the special attraction, and this is key; do not have him do half assed comedy weapons matches where he sells being hit with a bin lid like he was just shot. Because Rhyno has been with the company for, oh a couple of months at most, the WWF obviously has to job him endlessly until he learns how to work in a way that they feel is marketable. And also learns how to grow six inches. A chokeslam onto a soft aluminium bin ends it.
Final Rating: ½*

WWF Hardcore Championship
The Big Show (c) vs. Chris Jericho
A week later in Canada, Chris Jericho is forced so low down the card that he is competing for the jobbers' comedy belt. They sure were on the ball in 2001. The match is very short, or at least what we get shown here, with Jericho kicking the steps into Big Show's face (which is telegraphed horribly by the lumbering Show) and then winning the match following a Lionsault to add the Hardcore title to the tag team gold he already holds. But as he is walking up the ramp Rhyno appears through the curtain and smashes Jericho with a Gore, taking advantage of the 24/7 rules to reclaim the title. The footage of the match is too short to rate, but that Gore on the ramp was pretty sweet.

We change tact for a new form of action, according to Coach, one that promises the liberation of puppies but almost never delivers. Yes, the dumb Divas and their staple bout of the pre-PG era: the bra and panties match.

Bra And Panties Match
Trish Stratus vs. Ivory
This comes from March 2001 on *SmackDown!* and Ivory is the reigning WWF Women's Champion. She is also part of Right To Censor, and thus refuses to compete in this "degrading encounter". Trish isn't interested and jumps her, and the match is on. Is Trish ripping Ivory's clothes off against her will a form of sexual assault? Things don't last more than 30-seconds before Chyna wanders down and forces Ivory's garments off, as the build for the pair's match at *WrestleMania X-Seven* continues. Much like in that bout, Chyna is completely, overwhelmingly dominant here. Ivory scarpers with her, erm, tail between her legs, thoroughly humiliated by the experience. Again, this can't really be rated.

Bra And Panties Match
Terri vs. Trish Stratus
From May, and this is the only kind of match that Terri can actually do, because she is not a wrestler by any stretch and has zero aptitude for in-ring competition. She sure can gallop

around the ring though. Paul Heyman on commentary mocks the WWF's absurd booking and treatment of its womenfolk, claiming this is in keeping with the spirit of the Funks and the Briscos. The whole thing when looked at objectively is a somewhat perverse voyeuristic practice. "Come to the sports entertainment and see our girls pretend to fight in a really fake looking way while trying to strip each other of their clothes!". Usually the stewards need mops for those kind of shows. Questionable moral practice aside, this is what it always is; two girls rolling around and embarrassing the great traditions of the business before revealing as much skin as the network will allow. This time though, we have the added bonus of Perry Saturn wandering down and revealing himself to be wearing a bra and thong of his own. Hey, nothing sells tickets and signifies career progress like a man turning to cross dressing. I know he used to do it in WCW too, but if the WWF are going to copy their harebrained ideas then we might as well all pack up and go home. The distraction causes Perry's manger/girlfriend/whatever the hell Terri to get her skirt ripped off, costing her the match and revealing her barely covered ass. And by barely covered I mean fully exposed, with only the tiniest sliver of skin coloured thong visible at the very top or her cheeks. Other than that, there is more crack on display than at a Sunny house party.
Final Rating: DUD

Joy of joys, the next segment is the "recent evolution" of Perry Saturn! It starts with the APA repeatedly powerbombing him on his head during *RAW*, in a couple of really vicious bumps. Backstage Saturn's eyes are crossed, and all he can manage to mutter is "You're welcome". Then on *SmackDown!* things get worse for poor Perry, when Raven hits his Raven Effect DDT onto a steel chair. Backstage, Terri is concerned. Rightly so it seems, because Saturn comes out of his locker room acting all loopy. To SD again and Saturn teams with Dean Malenko against the Dudleys, but spends the majority of the match stood on the outside staring out the timekeeper. When the Duds hits "Wazzup" Perry grabs a pair of their glasses and mounts the top rope, as he wants a go of doing the move... on his own tag partner! The Dudleys are amused and let him. Saturn then grabs a mic, pushes D-Von and tells him to "Get the muffins... You're welcome". That rather dies with the crowd, and Saturn gets drilled with 3D to finish the match. These silly antics continue over the next few weeks, with Saturn and Terri going out on a double date with Dean and a random model. Saturn, who orders a bowl of mustard and a side order of crayons, gets hit on by Dean's date, and it pisses off Terri. Deciding she has had enough, Terri goes to wallop her with a tray but misses and hits Perry. Yes boys and girls, repeated blows to the head ARE funny. Chris Nowinski would hate this angle, he really would. Instead of getting Perry proper treatment, the WWF continues to book him in weapons matches, and he squares off with Test on *SmackDown!* in a hardcore match. Saturn tries to belt Test with a mop but a kick in the face, another blow to the head, wins it for Test. Afterwards, Saturn gets all concerned for the wellbeing of the mop, and thus "Moppy" is born. Clearly inspired by Tom Hank's character in *Castaway*, who makes friends with a volleyball, Saturn gives the mop a face and treats it like a person. A jealous Terri (yes, she is jealous of a mop) asks him to chose between them. He chooses Moppy. He chose... wisely. Now while I cannot condone using concussions and head injuries as a silly angle now, at the time the issues caused by repeated head trauma were not widely known. The WWE later developed a very commendable attitude towards concussions and other head injuries, working alongside Chris Nowinski to get better educated on the subject and introducing ImPACT testing to make sure guys were okay to work after suffering blows to the head. So while this Saturn stuff is all slightly unsettling viewing when you consider what concussions did to his one-time Radicalz partner Chris Benoit, the intention was merely light entertainment and it was never supposed to be taken too seriously, and when viewed from that perspective it is a lot of harmless fun.

Vince McMahon's obsession and affair with Trish Status comes next, starting when Steph talks to Vince (who is supposedly at a soup kitchen) on the phone during the Christmas Day episode of *RAW*, and hearing a woman's voice in the background. Vince claims it is just some giddy women thrilled to meet him, and throws in a McMahonism: "Quite frankly Steph, they're asking for me to come back and ladle out some more soup". Steph confronts Trish about the rumour that she was the "giddy woman" and becomes increasingly disturbingly jealous about the Vince-Trish affair. There is every chance that this may well have been the start of a proposed Vince/Steph love affair/pregnancy story that Vince had talked about doing... because he is a nutcase. Thankfully more than a few people talked him out of that one, Steph and Shane included. It all boils down to a match between Steph and Trish at *No Way Out*, which was the idea of WWF commissioner William Regal. Vince warns Regal that because the match was his idea, that he has to "do the right thing" with regards to engineering the outcome. Regal gets flustered trying to decide, and in the end drills Trish so Steph can win. Seemingly that was the wrong decision and he is forced to team with Steph against Vince and Trish on *RAW*. At one point it looks like Vince may deck Steph, but instead he turns on Trish and the three beat her up and throw dirty mop water on her to "clean this situation up". Yuck. Vince calls her a toy he got bored of, which translates to: he got to kiss her on screen and now it is someone else's turn to be part of his disturbing middle aged crisis fantasies. The next week on *RAW*, Trish begs for forgiveness, leading to an infamous and controversial angle where Vince tells her to get on her hands and knees and crawl around like a dog. "I want you to tell me in dog language just how sorry you are. Speak Trish, speak. Bark like a dog! Come on, tell me you're sorry!" What the hell were they thinking with this? Vince later made Trish strip down to her bra and panties, which is shown only in photos, and when she takes her bra off it convinces Vince that she has done enough. "You have no idea how far I would degrade myself for the right cause" she tells him. Oh that could be said of many people who have worked for Vince. After Vince kisses Trish in front of Linda on *SmackDown!*, Shane turns up on *RAW* and batters him for his indiscretions, leading to their match at *WrestleMania X-Seven*. The WCW purchase is deemed so insignificant to their rivalry that it is not even mentioned.

Street Fight
Shane McMahon vs. Vince McMahon
This is the well executed and very well booked smoke and mirrors brawl between father and son from *WrestleMania X-Seven*, which is joined in progress with Shane diving through a table from the ring. Shane being out cold allows the sedated Linda (though it is hard to tell much difference to the norm) to be wheeled out, and then Trish and Steph take centre stage. Trish slaps Vince to break up their relationship for good, so Steph slaps her in return, and that leads to a brawl. Guest referee Mick Foley breaks it up so Steph slaps him, then legs it down the aisle with Mick and Trish in pursuit. But then the footage from the bout suddenly ends, cutting out the best part (Linda's zombie rise from the wheelchair to kick Vince in the plums)! Well that is a very strange editing choice, I must say.

FURIOUS ABOUT: THE HURRICANE

"Sugar" Shane Helms came into the WWE with a reputation as a great high flier and the saviour of WCW's cruiserweight division. Naturally the WWE found out he liked comic books and turned him into a superhero. Not that it was a bad idea. He gained traction much quicker under the gimmick and rapidly became a fan favourite. Not an easy task for a WCW wrestler in enemy territory. His early WWE career involved forming a team with Lance Storm, another wrestler the WWE were keen on, and gained a sidekick called Mighty Molly, the former Molly Holly. Once the Invasion angle finished Hurricane turned face and competed, once again, in the cruiserweight division. The cruiser style caused him issues long-term and in 2007 Helms broke his neck and missed a year. He remained in the WWE until 2010. Wrestling Observer gave him the accolade of 'Best Gimmick' in 2001.

Once again, not enough of the match is shown to rate, but the full thing is an easy *** slice of sports entertainment.

On *SmackDown!* Spike Dudley annoys Crash Holly by talking to his cousin Molly, leading to a match later on. We see the last five seconds, with Spike winning, which pisses off Hardcore Holly. Spike and Hardcore then have a match, which we get a little more of. Hardcore wins but he is still ticked off with Crash, who gets hit with a 3D following the bout. The Spike-Molly relationship continues to blossom as an Attitude Era version of *Romeo & Juliet* with the addition of incest, tables and man-on-woman violence. The Hollys and the Dudleys have a match on *RAW* which ends when the Duds 3D Hardcore through a table. They spot Molly and try to powerbomb her through a table, because they are the Dudleys and that is what they do, but Spike pleads with them not to. Bubba pie faces him, so Spike lies on the table to protect Molly from the impact and sacrifice himself. On *SmackDown!* Spike tells Molly through the camera that he "really likes her", and she responds from WWF New York on *RAW* that she "really, really likes him too". During a match on *RAW* soon after that, the two end up face-to-face in the ring with everyone else down, and they do the clichéd slow movie walk towards each other before finally embracing with a kiss. Aww. The crowd mostly pops this, and the whole angle and love story has actually been really well booked, with an air of innocence (well, tables aside I guess) that you rarely see from WWF storylines. I suppose we have Steph and her team of soap opera writers to thank for this one. Hey, at least someone on the undercard actually had a storyline. Guys in the PG era would have given anything for an angle like this.

Steve Austin is the next focus, as the tape finally gets a bit of star power. A brief highlight video shows Austin turning heel at *WrestleMania X-Seven* and joining forces with Vince McMahon. To *SmackDown!* where Jim Ross interviews Austin and tells him he feels like he is losing his best friend. Austin doesn't care, knocking JR's hat off and telling him to take a swing at him. Ross declines and apologises for getting out of line, but Austin belts him from behind and beats on him. Vince comes out and makes him stop, then tells him to bust Ross open. Austin obliges. Three months later Austin is forced by Linda McMahon to defend his WWF Championship against both Chris Benoit and Chris Jericho at *King of the Ring*, and he is livid about it. He forces Vince to choose between him and Linda, then goes on a rampage attacking people. He starts a petition to get the match cancelled, but Spike Dudley rips it up when Austin insults Molly by calling him a bimbo. Austin is incredulous and cries to commissioner William Regal about it and demands a match with him. We see very brief footage of Austin beating Spike on *SmackDown!* before going back to Austin's ultimatum to Vince: him or Linda. Vince is torn and tells Austin that "I think you know which way I'm going to go" implying he will choose Linda, but Austin misunderstands and thinks Vince is going to pick him, and gives him his favourite hunting crossbow and hat as a present. Hang on, just a few months ago Vince and Linda were getting divorced and Vince was dicking around, literally, with Trish! It's sometimes impossible to keep up with the McMahon family leanings and relationships. In keeping with most everything else on this tape, just as one's appetite is whetted, we move on to something else. How frustrating.

Vince McMahon and his "challenging year" are featured next, and the Vince-Linda issue is covered, with Vince sharing his opinion that he believes divorce should be outlawed. Vince, as a "role model for America", refuses to grant Linda a divorce. For whatever reason, Debra comes out and tells Vince she doesn't believe a word of what he just said, and that he has had a negative influence on her husband Steve Austin. Vince denies all accountability, something he has become pretty good at over the years, but does say he is proud of what Austin has become. Vince then tells Debra that she is the exception to the old adage that "behind every good man there is a good woman", so Debra slaps him. Meanwhile, Trish over at WWF New York says she will fully support Linda if she wants to go through with divorcing Vince. Time travel then occurs, as we go back a month to Vince buying WCW and the famous simulcast on *RAW* and *Nitro*. We see Shane informing Vince, from *Nitro*, that he has bought WCW, which is footage that should obviously have been shown earlier when the Shane-Vince feud was covered. The schizophrenic editing continues as we skip forward three months to June and a backstage segment with Kurt Angle, Steve Austin, Vince McMahon and hanger on Debra. Kurt tells Steve that they have a lot in common and could "almost be related", then we go to the segment in the ring where Austin tells Kurt that he is no longer welcome in the Vince-Austin relationship and calls him a jackass. The two then bicker, with Angle professing that he is a hero, but Austin squabbling back that he is a jackass. Vince has had enough of the childish jaw jacking and tells them to fight, but instead they take turns hugging Vince. I love the Austin-Angle-Vince segments and relationship, I think it is one of the finest things the WWF ever did in the post Attitude Era. As I have said before; the Austin heel turn was a huge mistake for business, but the character was a riot.

Now the WWF's worst ever botch: the invasion angle. Instead of making millions of dollars for years on end and running two viable companies that toured separately, instead the WWF systematically destroyed everything about the fantasy warfare that fans had been begging for over the last decade. Not only did they not bring in the key players and big stars that would have made a difference (the likes of Goldberg, Hulk Hogan, Scott Steiner, Kevin Nash, Scott Hall, Jeff Jarrett, Ric Flair, Rey Misterio Jnr and even Eric Bischoff) but they also booked the whole thing like it was just another scripted storyline. We start out with Mike Awesome winning the Hardcore title in the hallowed halls of MSG, prompting Vince to declare that "he raped me". Booker T then shows up at WWF New York and calls out Austin, so 'Stone Cold' and Kurt Angle go to find him, only to discover he has already left and gained access to MSG, where he beats up Vince before fleeing. A decent start, but hardly the mass hostile takeover attempt the thing was screaming out for. Within a few days it became all about Vince and what a stud he is, when Torrie Wilson turned up backstage on *SmackDown!* and implied that she wanted to nail him. A jealous Austin hugs Vince, and when McMahon invites Torrie to dinner, Austin says "I'll check my schedule". "Me too" says the equally oblivious Angle. It's funny stuff, but this is supposed to be the ultimate showdown between the two biggest wrestling companies in the world, there is no place for silly comedy. Alas the courtship continues, with Vince and Torrie looking for a place to shag, but finding themselves frequently interrupted by Kurt and Austin. Torrie takes Vince to a laundry closet and strips him off, then tells him to close his eyes. When he opens them, he sees his wife Linda standing there in Torrie's place. Yes, it was a set-up all along. Vince stammers a denial while stood there in his pants, but Linda has heard enough. So now the potentially biggest angle and feud in the history of wrestling is serving as a mere backdrop for the trials and tribulations of the McMahon family.

And it gets worse too. After the WWF nearly saves the angle with the reformation of ECW on *RAW*, they then blow a year's worth of storylines in one night by having the WWF and WCW unite (which made no sense) to combat the ECW threat, only for the WCW and ECW crews to merge into one big super faction. This sort of made sense because of the sheer lack of star power on the WCW side, but it meant that the invasion was in fact not an invasion at all, but rather just a faction of WWF midcarders and a few new names alongside them. It could have been avoided if the WWF had brought in all the big stars from WCW, but they didn't want to pay the contracts. Ultimately they all, except Jarrett, ended up back with the company on fat contracts anyway, and they would have easily repaid what they were earning with the mass amount of tickets and merchandise revenue they would have generated, not to mention the buyrate spikes. Things actually get even worse before the night is out, with Shane introducing Stephanie McMahon as the new owner of ECW, instantly killing the entire thing dead on the spot. The last thing ANYONE wanted to see was the McMahon fingerprints all over this thing. Eric Bischoff should have been leading WCW, Paul Heyman ECW and Vince the WWF, with the rest of his family off television and out of the way. As soon as they were involved it was just another angle and despite the strong buyrate for the *InVasion* pay-per-view, it was just a spike because of the novelty. After that things flattened out and the whole thing was dead in the water by *Survivor Series* just four months later. I specifically avoided covering any invasion era shows in this volume because of how furious it makes me, and now I am all riled up about it. Well over a decade later, the missed opportunity and unfathomable booking still pisses me off.

For reasons I cannot begin to explain, we go back to April prior to the invasion, for the fantastic segments with Steve Austin and Kurt Angle singing to Vince McMahon backstage. I love these things, but why are they being shown now? Honestly, you can get a headache from watching this. It's impossible to follow!

Fast forward again to Vince begging Austin to become the "old Stone Cold" once again and lead the WWF into *InVasion*. He wants the needy, guitar-playing, hug-giving Austin to disappear and the ass kicking Austin to return. He begs for Austin to beat him up and give him a Stunner, but Steve walks away dejected. Austin spends an episode of *RAW* in a bar contemplating what to do, while the WWF faction gets inspired and focused thanks to stirring speeches from Bradshaw, the Undertaker and the legendary 'Classie' Freddie Blassie. Meanwhile over in the WCW/ECW locker room, Steph rouses her troops. Yeah, you can see why this failed. While the Steph stuff undoubtedly sucks, the Austin inner turmoil is fantastic and the brilliantly made music video outlining all of this causes goosebumps, especially when Austin snaps and hits the arena, taking out everyone that moves from the Alliance side. The old 'Stone Cold' had indeed returned, and on *SmackDown!* the following week Vince sings to him to welcome him back. Austin tells him his guitar is out of tune and then smashes it over Vince's head to a big pop. Then as *InVasion*, Austin nonsensically turns on the WWF and joins the Alliance, becoming the new leader of the group. They needed the injection of star power for sure, but Austin shouldn't have been that guy. Austin should have been the one leading the WWF in the fight. It wouldn't have been so bad if it made sense, but Austin spent the entirety of the *InVasion* main event beating on the Alliance, only to join them at the end. It's one of many, many plot holes. Austin's justification for turning on the WWF? Vince was hugging Kurt Angle and grooming him as the next WWF Champion. Right, great.

To counter the defection of Austin, Vince reinstates the Rock. Shane however makes a play for him, reminding Rock what Vince has done to him over the years. We don't see the payoff, instead seeing Kurt Angle beat Booker T to win the WCW Championship and thus giving the wacky scenario where the WWF Champion is with WCW and the WCW Champion in with the WWF. Oh, did I say wacky? Sorry, I meant FUCKING STUPID. To annoy me further, Coach then says we are wrapping up and thus we don't even get to find out whose side Rock joined. What an incredibly annoying tape!

VERDICT

It's all over the goddamn place. Six months of action, cut up and shuffled around, with illogical and baffling editing decisions that confuse timelines and ruin the flow of the stories shown. It's a shame too because if it was done coherently with a sense of structure, it would be a good tape. There is a lot of very entertaining footage on here, but it is strictly snippets and the impact is lost for some of the stuff with it appearing out of context. The inclusion of the invasion angle ruins things for me too, because that whole period of time really killed wrestling for me. As a tape to throw on and relive some footage rarely revisited by WWE it is worth your time, but it certainly doesn't work as a timeline piece.

48

THE UNDERTAKER - THIS IS MY YARD

CAT NO: WWF288
RUN TIME: 56 minutes (approx)

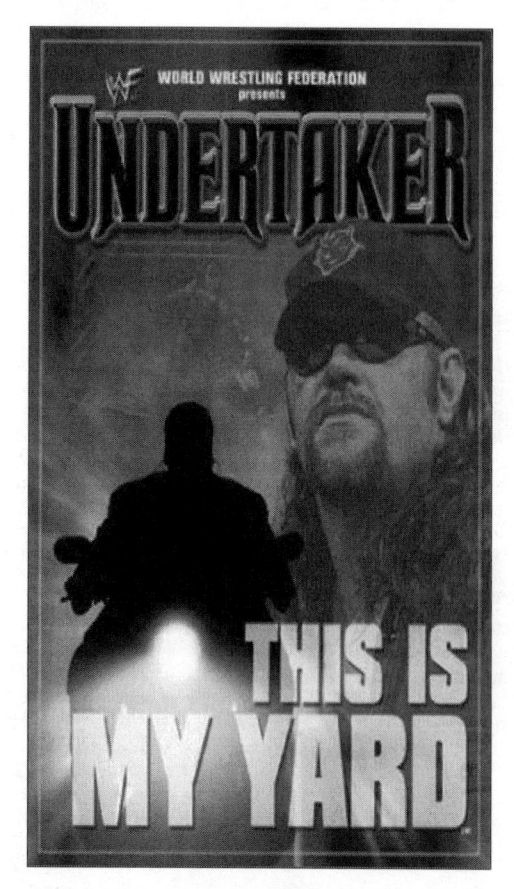

James Dixon: Despite the plethora of Undertaker tapes that have been released previous to this one, this marks the first time that he has been given the WWF bio treatment, as opposed to just a stream of bad matches one after another as is the case on his prior outings. You can understand why of course, with his supernatural gimmick not lending itself to behind the scenes footage and out of character interviews. Now as the 'American Badass', Texas redneck biker, he is fair game. He gives a rare non kayfabed sit down interview exclusive for the tape, and he is an affable and engaging subject. Even so, it is still fairly jarring to see Skyscrapers footage and hear Taker discussing his life before he was erm, dead. He recounts how an unnamed genius in WCW told him that: "No one will ever pay for a ticket to see you wrestle". I wonder how that guy feels now that the Undertaker is the most enduring personality in WWE history, one of the most famous people on the planet and one of the all-time great industry draws. Let's be frank, all those *WrestleMania* shows from the John Cena Era were sold on the back of Taker's famous winning streak at the show ahead of anything else on the card. As an example, did anyone buy *WrestleMania XXV* to see the advertised "main event" of Triple H vs. Randy Orton? Of course not, no one cared about that, they came to see the Undertaker against Shawn Michaels.

Growing frustrated with a lack of opportunity in WCW, Taker claims he attempted to get a meeting with Vince McMahon about heading over to New York, but he describes the ordeal as "like trying to get an audience with the Pope". The reality is that Taker worked alongside Hulk Hogan on fun for the family movie *Suburban Commando,* and Hogan hooked him up a meeting with his holiness. Of course, Hogan is not back in the WWF good books at this point, so the credit isn't given. Instead Taker says that the call eventually came, with the proposal leaving him taken aback. "You're going to be the Undertaker" he was told. Taker was less than convinced about the potential for the gimmick at first, describing his thoughts as "What the hell *is* this!?". Even with the doubts, Mark Calaway still played the character with a commendable conviction and was thoroughly imposing and impressive at Survivor Series '90 on his TV debut. Taker talks about the origins of the character some more, saying how Vince envisioned him in the style of a mortician from classic Western flicks, and then he stops off to put over the great mind of Jake Roberts, who he learned a lot from. Probably things like where the best strip joints were and how to drink yourself into oblivion on a night and still perform at a high level the next day...

A whole host of superstars have leaped on board to be involved in this release in an attempt to score political brownie points with the locker room leader, all offering up glowing appraisals. The sycophants include DDP, The Fink, Edge, JR, Matt Hardy, Chris Jericho and the ever-present Steve Lombardi, whose official WWE job title is seemingly "talking head". We then see the finish of the Undertaker vs. Hulk Hogan WWF Title match from *Survivor Series '91* where Taker won his first title only a year after his WWF debut. Pat Patterson though, thinks the trigger was pulled six months too late! Yes, he thinks A YEAR was too long to wait for the zombie to win the richest prize in the game.

We skip ahead SEVEN YEARS to the Inferno Match at *Unforgiven '98,* as Edge and Kane mark out about Taker's topé over the flames. Taker says it was hot and he couldn't breathe because the air was burning. He tells the story of when they came to him with the idea for the match (I bet this was Russo), and he thought "That sounds like a real good idea... Pfft.... Yeah [right]". Ever the company man, he went along with it and it turned out pretty well. The bout often gets criticised, but I enjoyed it in a perverse way. We see a few highlights, including the infamous big fake arm finish, with Jim Ross describing the bout as "challenging". That's Jim Ross speak for the shits, but it also segues into the Hell in a Cell match at *Badd Blood* some six months before the Inferno Match. We get more highlights, this time set to that creepy dramatic instrumental music that the company loved so. Jericho calls the bout the epitome of

THE APA

Taker's career, which in 2001 when this was released it probably was, but he has done so much more since then. There is no one with as many legendary moments in their career. Unfortunately we then see a few moments that are not so legendary, with idiot Lombardi discussing how he enjoyed the death and rise to Heaven of the character at *Royal Rumble '94* and Fink getting a kick out of the woeful Undertaker vs. Undertaker match at *SummerSlam '94*. He is the only one who did.

We stop of briefly for X-Pac and Matt Hardy to gush over the honour of being in the ring with Taker, before footage, inevitably, of one of his most famous matches, the insane Hell in a Cell match from *King of the Ring '98*. Taker disputes claims of it being the greatest cage match of all time, clearly realising that it is remembered for Mick Foley's ridiculous bumps ahead of the actual bout. JR claims he had the willies prior to the show and a feeling that something was going to go down, but I am inclined to not fully believe him on that one. DDP's reaction to Foley's famous first bump is simply: "Good GOD". Jim Ross throws out his dismissive argument against people who claim: "Those wrestlers know how to fall". Well allow me to retort... While the bumps certainly hurt and Foley has a helluva lot of fortitude to take them, there is no doubt that pro wrestling training, specifically training how to bump, helped to prevent him from getting seriously injured. Landing correctly in a way to break your fall does significantly reduce the risk. That's not to take anything away from Mick, or indeed any wrestler for any big bump, but the fact is they DO know how to fall. Anyway back to the tape, and Taker calls throwing Mick off the cell an out of body experience, which he says felt like it lasted a lifetime and we get replays of the bump from every angle approximately twenty times. "It was off the charts, man" he says. The other, more painful, bump through the cage is ignored. This would have been better on a Mick Foley tape really, and he should at least been here to comment at the very least, but it is interesting to hear Taker's perspective on it.

We skip approximately a year to the Ministry of Darkness, which Taker calls the last hurrah for the old character. Ha, not quite. I enjoyed the Ministry, and it may even be my favourite Undertaker era. It was way out there and probably went too far at times with the crucifixions and kidnappings, but Taker looked like a badass motherfucker, and even though it was borderline Satanic and often quite disturbing, it was a blast. "It looked so genuine because it was" says Taker, before adding that the character was "natural" for him. Yes, because he is a big ginger mosher at heart. Taker says the Ministry was good for others because the likes of E&C and the APA were given a chance and a break via the faction, which he was happy about. "Those were the good old days" he says, before also adding that it was a low point too because he allowed the character to be subservient to something/someone else, referring to the horrible Higher Power angle and formation of the Corporate Ministry. "Naturally with the McMahons involved, the issue's gonna revolve around them". Some things *never* change.

We move on to late-1999 and Taker talks about his injuries and having to nearly retire because of them, but says a bike ride cleared his head and made him realise he had to return. And return he did, in style at *Judgment Day 2000*, to an immense reaction. This was the debut of Taker's new 'American Badass' look, which signalled the end of the zombie character (for a few years) and a transition to Hell's Angel, essentially. JR puts over the new gimmick, while Taker talks about his initial apprehension with it being a new character. Personally, I detested this gimmick. It was just DOA 2000, and Taker started to suck in the ring too. Actually, he sucked way worse in the early 90s, but at least he had a zany persona to counterbalance that and it was almost expected and accepted because of the nature of the gimmick. But here, for the first time in his career, the Undertaker became boring. Taker says the American Badass character is the real him. That's a shame.

We touch upon the Angle-Taker feud, which features some typically stellar work from Angle. "I've been scared of a man who rides a bicycle" he says, and then drives around on a little scooter. Footage from their shitty 7-minute match a *Fully Loaded 2000* airs, with Taker destroying the red hot Kurt Angle cleanly with his new Last Ride finisher, nearly killing all of his momentum just as he was primed to explode. Three months later, Angle won the WWF Championship and struggled to get over fully as champion. Gee, I wonder why.

And now, a tedious piece about motorcycles! Insight of the tape: Taker loves skulls. Now, that's a revelation! Oh good, a feature on his then wife and now ex-wife Sara too. My wife thinks Sara is the spitting image of Michelle McCool, and that this is somehow surprising. Of course, it is not surprising at all because Sara is small and blonde, which is obviously his type. "I think that Sara rounds out the Undertaker's character very well" says Kane. No! She killed it. Oh jeez, now the talking heads are putting over Sara! I am not on board with this at all. To permanently shatter all illusions of Taker's aura, we see Sara beating up Taker with a cross arm breaker, and he taps out. Yes folks, his only ever tap out, and it was to a woman. Taker then discusses his tattoos and mentions the prominent Sara one on his neck. No regrets on that one then...

Back to wrestling, and resident genius Steve Lombardi calls Undertaker a "high flyer". Jesus. We return to *Badd Blood* and Kane's debut. We really are all over the place chronologically. Kane talks us through it and then the discussion moves on to him and the potential struggles he might have had portraying the role. Not because of Glenn Jacobs' ability, but because of the footsteps he had to follow. Obviously, he took to it rather well, and the Kane character is second only to the Undertaker himself in terms of company tenure. Taker puts Kane over big and says that *WrestleMania XIV* was one of his favourite matches, describing it as an "all time, all-out physical war" while Kane says: "He always brings out the best in Kane". The matches they had opposite each other would strongly suggest otherwise.

Fast forward to mid-1999 and Chris Jericho's *RAW* promo just after debuting, where he runs down Taker (and Big Show) as boring, and says people watching them clamour to change the channel. Jericho claims he probably wouldn't have said the same things now, which reading between the lines suggests he got chewed out, because he says he re-evaluated what he said from then on. Kurt Angle next, and Taker calls him "prodigy like" because of the speed he learned both as a performer and a personality. He is absolutely right. Outside of the Rock, who else comes close to the levels of progression in such a short time frame as Angle achieved? Triple H is next in line for the Undertaker seal of approval, with the no-longer-Dead Man referring to him as smart and a student of the game, declaring him his heir apparent in the WWF. Well, he certainly was the heir, but to Vince McMahon rather than the Undertaker. As much as he thinks he is in the same bracket as the likes of the Undertaker, Steve Austin, the Rock, Hulk Hogan, Shawn Michaels and other WWF legendary figures, he is not. No matter how hard he pushes himself as being in that truly elite upper echelon.

To the spring 2001 Steve Austin feud, which was set up by Austin pulling a hoax on Taker that claimed Sara was involved in a car crash. That resulted in Taker beating the piss out of Austin and then stealing his ambulance commandeering gimmick from four years earlier, revealing himself as the driver when Austin was set to go to hospital, and beating the piss out of him some more. It ended up coming to a head at *Judgment Day 2001*, in a long no holds barred match, which I peg at around ***. Taker says there will be more between them in future. There was; a hideous outing at *Backlash 2002* which flirted with negative stars and was their last match together.

Much discussion of "the yard" and Taker's stroke/respect backstage follows. Paul Heyman says that in twenty years, the locker room will remember him even more than the fans. 2021? He will be at *WrestleMania XXXVII* for sure. "I've got a lot of fights left in me" says Taker to wrap things up. No kidding: thirteen years after this release, which is longer than his tenure in the company prior to this tape, and he is still going!

VERDICT

I had a blast watching this. The Undertaker character and indeed the man behind it, have both often been shrouded in mystery. The WWE rarely lets Taker speak or appear not in character, and thus a chance to glimpse the man behind the monster is a welcomed one. Long time fans won't learn anything they didn't already know, unless you particularly want to see Taker's bike collection or watch him horseplay with his ex-wife, but the hour flies by and is entertaining and interesting throughout. Highly recommended for all Undertaker fans, and definitely worth a gander for everyone else. Good stuff.

75

THE UNDERTAKER (CIRCA, 'AMERICAN BADASS')

WWF / WWE HOME VIDEO

WWF54101
WWF54103
WWF54105
WWF54107
WWF54109
WWF54111
WWF54113
WWF54115
WWF54117
WWF54121
WWF54125
WWF54127
WWF54129
WWE59313
WWF59327
WWF59331
WWE59333

UNFORGIVEN 2001

CAT NO: WWF54101
RUN TIME: 163 minutes (approx)

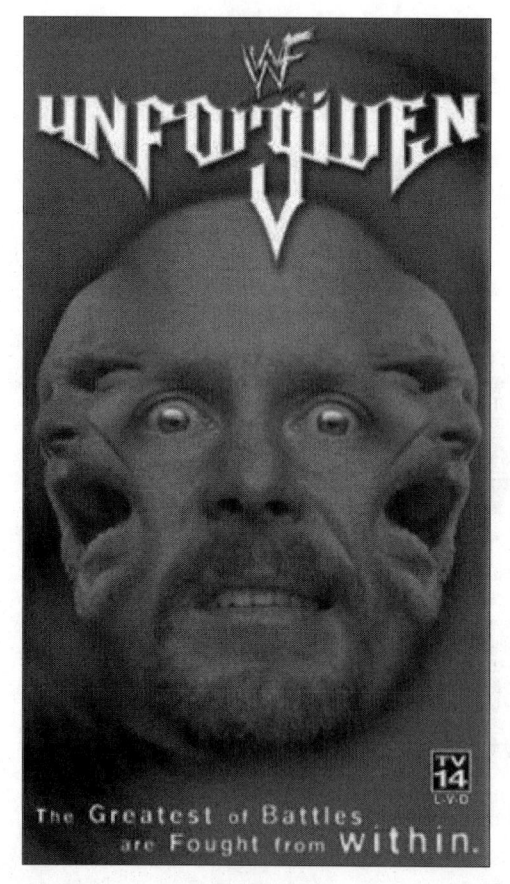

Arnold Furious: The wrestling world, nay the entire world, was thrown into chaos in September 2001. The terror attacks on New York City sent ripples out across the planet and in the USA in particular patriotism was top dog. *Unforgiven* came about just two weeks after the 9/11 attacks so the WWF had a chance to put the world right by having their own all-American Olympic hero Kurt Angle chase the WWF Title. All of a sudden it was like being back in the 80s, and what a babyface Kurt would have been in the 80s! We're in Pittsburgh, Pennsylvania. Hosts are Jim Ross and Paul Heyman. We kick off with a super patriotic rendition of *'America the Beautiful'* by Jennifer Holliday. The atmosphere is charged, but it won't stay that way.

WWF Tag Team Championship
The Dudley Boyz (c) vs. The Hardy Boyz vs. The Hurricane & Lance Storm vs. The Big Show & Spike Dudley
On the WWF's *SmackDown!* game my friend created a super heavyweight version of the Hardys called the Lardy Boyz. They had the exact same moveset, mannerisms and high flying style, and every time I see the Hardys wrestle it makes me think of Fatt and Beef Hardy. Excellent team. This is after the Duds had turned heel and joined the Alliance. I am amazed, staggered even, that Show doesn't turn heel during the Alliance angle as he tended to turn at the drop of a hat. Hurricane is supposed to be a heel but he's so goofy that the crowd pop his stuff, mainly because he rocks manly superhero poses. His partner is the contrasting Lance Storm, the super-serial heel. Lance is one of the few technical wonders that WCW had (after the Radicalz left) and really should have been pushed hard by the WWF into matches with fellow technical masters. Instead he found himself mired in obscurity, which makes me almost as sad as the WWF's treatment of Dean Malenko. Those are two guys who deserved better. Hurricane busts out the cape and Heyman makes a "whoosh" noise as he hits a crossbody. JR puts over Hurricane as having good personality and being a young star. As if to say; WCW sucks but some of their talent are okay. In other words the ones that the WWF picked up. Show gets a hot tag as JR suggests the only thing he wanted more was a cheeseburger. Oh man, it's a wave of insider comments from the commentary table this evening. Show clears everyone out and allows Spike to dive off his shoulders to the floor in a cool spot. With everyone on the floor Show decides he's going to dive only for the Dudleys to stop him. No Lucha-Show! Hurricane tries to chokeslam him, which is hilarious. Show shrugs him off and chokeslams Lance for the opening pin. Storm and Hurricane are gone. The Dudleys then lay out Show with a devastating back suplex, which shows how great they were as a team, eliminating even the biggest of threats. Matt tries for a Twist of Fate on Spike only to have it countered into a sensational neckbreaker. However that's all null and void moments later as Matt just hits the Twist of Fate to dump Spike and Show.

Dudleys vs. Hardys for the tag titles then, and that's very familiar. I was actually enjoying the other elements, but like in the heavyweight division, the WWF had a hard time letting go of something that was successful. With Edge & Christian split and gone into singles, this is the tag team division. You can tell the Duds are heels as they do the Wazzup headbutt without the Wazzup and instead of getting the tables, D-Von gets a chinlock. Way to suck all the popularity out of that spot! Seeing as the WWF had been running Hardys vs. Dudleys since January of the previous year, in various guises, the crowd is not as hot as you'd expect. This is the biggest issue with tag team wrestling. When you finally get two teams over that don't suck, the temptation is to run the match until there's nothing left to do. Here it's totally played out and the two teams sleepwalk through half the match, which is a contrast to the opening 7-8 minutes, which was really good. Matt eats a 3-D but Jeff saves the match with the Swanton, eventually. Not the best timing in the world. Bubba Bomb finishes anyway just seconds afterwards, so if Jeff was late it wouldn't have meant anything. This started out as a wildly entertaining four-team match and little bits from Hurricane and Show were fun. As soon as it dropped into the standard old Hardys vs. Dudleys match it lost that momentum.
Final Rating: **½

Backstage: Rob Van Dam tries his hand at acting (whatever you do don't watch RVD's feature film *The Wrong Side of Town*, he is terrible) by looking around for something. I can tell he's looking around for something because he stops walking

RAVEN

every other stride to do so. Acting does not come naturally to him. Stephanie shows up to wish him luck and offers her services. RVD claims to be a one man team. Where's Fonzie again? "I can't seem to find a locker room big enough to contain my superstar status" so Steph tells him to take any locker room. Rob's talent did not lie in the world of promos.

Video Control takes us to ringside and Kurt Angle's whole family is there, in his home town. Michael Cole interviews Kurt's Mom Jackie and his brother Dave. The latter can't hear anything, which makes for a stunning interview. Cole just coasts through it anyway.

Video Control again takes over as Raven feeds Moppy into a wood chipper. Raven's falsetto voice while pushing it in there is brilliant.

Raven vs. Saturn

This is one of Raven's typical psychological feuds, where the match plays second fiddle to him messing with Saturn's head. So he stole Saturn's girlfriend and when Saturn didn't care about that because he was more interested in a mop, he stole the mop too. The biggest problem Raven had in the WWF is that his best skill was getting angles over with unusual promos, yet the WWF didn't trust him to talk. Because WCW is now part of the WWF, JR references the Flock and Heyman points out that Saturn screwed up the whole Flock angle. Saturn wasn't in the best of condition in 2001 and I'm not sure why he deteriorated as rapidly as he did. Watch his ECW stuff and the man was a machine. He was good enough that he totally carried one of ECW's best ever tag teams, the Eliminators, and got signed by WCW when Kronus was left behind. But here he's sloppy and can't quite get his timing right. Raven is not the guy to carry anyone who's unpredictable. Check out his solid

match with Terry Gordy from ECW for proof that he *could* carry people, but he couldn't reign weird guys in. Saturn might even be working weird because of the angle but it sure makes for a messy match. He seems to set way early for everything and these guys should be a lot better. The match meanders toward a finish and Saturn hits the Moss Covered Family Three Handled Credenza for the win. The match has no structure at all, the fans didn't care about it and both guys would have been better suited to a different kind of match. Heyman should have booked this angle as he seemed adept at covering for their weaknesses in ECW. Here everything was left hanging on show and it wasn't pleasant.
Final Rating: *

Tangent: The strange career trajectory of Perry Saturn, where he rapidly ascended to the top of ECW, got a solid WCW push before being part of the WWF mega-group that was the Radicalz before falling off badly to the point where the WWF just let him go, is nothing compared to his strange personal life. After departing the WWF in 2002, just as other companies were opening for business and the indy scene was hotter than ever before, Saturn disappeared. Not just from wrestling either. He then saved a girl from being raped and got shot in the process. During his slow recovery he dropped off the grid. He didn't resurface until 2009, revealing he'd been homeless, before marrying his fourth wife and moving in with her and her kids. In a business where people regularly die of drug overdoses, Saturn's return to action in 2011 must have been a massive relief to those who suspected he'd joined a long list of young wrestling deaths. Saturn's disappearance was pretty unusual though, even for wrestling.

Backstage: Lillian Garcia questions Christian's motivation for destroying his friendship with Edge. Christian retorts by saying that everyone is a failure but him and if he wins the IC Title it'll have been worth it.

WWF Intercontinental Championship
Edge (c) vs. Christian
I love Christian's new singles music, which is very operatic. Edge himself has switched to Rob Zombie, which makes him feel like a bigger star. Considering these guys were not only a tag team for two years but also lifelong friends, you'd think they'd have better chemistry. You'd think they'd have a match planned out that they could work in their sleep. What they do have is a lot of brawling, which I appreciate stems from the hate and the heel turn but surely they're better at counters and wrestling. Christian tries like hell to get more heat by yelling "come on Edge, you son of a bitch", which gets no reaction at all and indeed, as they're storyline brothers, he's also calling his own mother a bitch. Maybe Edge was adopted. Who'd call their son Edge anyway? When Edge makes it about wrestling, by countering Christian's aggression with wrestling skill, the match is a lot better. Christian accidentally busts open Edge, just under his eye, and is able to switch gears to pounding the cut. Not that his aggression fits into his in-ring style. It's only when he goes after wrestling moves and Edge is able to counter out that the match is good. It doesn't help either guy that the Pittsburgh crowd just doesn't care about any of this and sits on their hands. There's nothing worse than a quiet crowd. Christian lifts the spear but Edge kicks out as there's no momentum behind it. Christian's lack of plan here hurts the match and I think he was blamed for the poor quality of the feud in general. Christian goes for the one man Conchairto but Edge sweeps the leg; he must have been a big *Karate Kid* fan. The ref stops Edge doing the Conchairto himself and Christian nut shots Edge with the other chair to win the title. He's also bleeding from the face. I'm afraid this was only sporadically good and a major disappointment. The WWF probably should have moved both guys on to other feuds but instead dragged this out for a few months.
Final Rating: **

Backstage: Coach interviews the Brothers of Destruction, the WCW Tag Team Champions. Undertaker cuts one of his biker promos. He should never be allowed to do this again. No wonder the WWF wanted him to go back to being the 'Dead Man'. "Let's roll, bro" is his out line but everything that preceded it was too quick. I know I've criticised Taker for being slow beforehand, but there's a middle ground between the two. Also using the WCW Tag Title as a bongo should be punishable by wrestler's court.

WCW Tag Team Championship
The Brothers of Destruction (c) vs. KroniK
KroniK were one of the worst hires the WWF made during the invasion angle. They were both bad in the ring, and the WWF should have remembered just how bad they both were in the WWF when they wrestled here before as Adam Bomb and Crush. Bryan Adams hasn't really changed, which is a bad thing but Bryan Clarke has gotten a lot worse. A pity really as Clarke had that WWF physique. He looked like a goddamn monster and he's able to make Kane look quite small, even though Kane is more muscular. Taker and Kane are not blameless in this match but Clarke can't take a decent bump as he not used to being thrown around by other big dudes. A shoulderbreaker off Kane looks particularly awful. If Raven-Saturn from earlier was plodding and directionless then this takes plodding and directionless to a whole other level. Taker embarrasses himself by whiffing on a punch by a good two feet. Adams reacts to it anyway but at least he didn't back bump it. The match rumbles on as Kane cleans house with a series of increasingly lacklustre big boots. Taker gets a tag and misses another punch on Adams by some distance. What's wrong with him today? Steven Richards runs in, pissed off with Taker about the destruction of Right to Censor. He gets laid out easily and Adams hits a jawbreaker, which Undertaker blows the bump on. The more you analyse this match the more obvious it is that Taker makes more mistakes than anybody else in it. KroniK set for the double chokeslam but Taker makes his own save and finishes with a chokeslam. This has a reputation for being a horrific match and it deserves it but it's not into negative stars. It's just rubbish. Steven Richards runs in post match to take a chokeslam off Kane and it's the best bump in the entire match.

The match got KroniK fired as nobody was impressed with this performance. Taker, despite his massive failings in the match, was friends with Bryan Adams from his days as Crush. Apparently he was offered a spot in OVW to get back into WWF condition (although Christ knows what they expected him to do, seeing as Crush was routinely terrible during his WWF performances in the past) while Clarke was cut loose. Luckily the Alliance had killed WCW by this point so the burial of KroniK doesn't matter at all. In the long run it probably helped the company as they didn't have to pay a terrible tag team to do a shitty job.
Final Rating: DUD

Tangent: The invasion was pretty much doomed from the off as the WWF weren't overly keen on giving WCW stars anything successful to do. What happened after that was the WWF's own stars finding it easier and easier to cement their place at the top of the card. The top WCW guys coming into the

KRONIK

invasion were Booker T and Diamond Dallas Page. Both were babyfaces when WCW closed, both turned heel to work in the WWF. Booker managed to score a black mark against his name by not protecting Steve Austin on his debut. After that they cut his legs off and took the WCW Title from him. DDP meanwhile was turned into Taker's bitch as Vince McMahon just couldn't bring himself to push a top WCW guy. After WCW's stars debuted they soon found their gold gone and their pushes nonexistent. The WCW Champion, Booker T, lost his title. The US Champion, Kanyon (given the belt), lost his title. The WCW Tag Team Champions, the Natural Born Thrillers, lost their titles. It turned WCW into a collection of jobbers who couldn't even hold onto their own titles. Only one man is to blame for this and that's Vince McMahon. His insistence at never booking anyone strong against the WWF has seen numerous strange occurrences over the years, but the WCW angle must surely rank as the worst piece of business he's ever conducted in the wrestling ring. Buying the company was shrewd but it was more for the video archive than anything else and it was the fans who were salivating at the idea of a WWF vs. WCW war. The reason it never really came about was Vince's assertion that WCW just weren't very good so they tried to rebuild the brand, but in the process kept jobbing the WCW guys out. I shouldn't really complain about how dumb the booking is though, as I happen to agree that the WCW guys weren't that good. Booker wasn't as good as the Rock. DDP wasn't as good as Steve Austin, or the Undertaker, or Triple H. KroniK weren't as good as the Dudleys. There were very few WCW talents that were worth taking and the majority were midcard guys with no history of superstardom. Guys like Lance Storm or Shane Helms were the true stars in the making and because they'd been tainted with that same WCW brush, Vince wasn't interested in pushing them either. When WCW didn't work out solo the WWF further diluted the concept by adding ECW wrestlers and indeed WWF wrestlers to give WCW a sense of threat, but in doing so changed their name to the Alliance, therefore rebranding WCW out of existence and ending most fans' interest in the angle. The only fun I got out of the whole thing was seeing some of my favourite wrestlers from elsewhere finally get a shot at the WWF. The main one was Rob Van Dam...

Backstage: Booker T is preparing for his match with The Rock but Tazz accidentally offends him by pointing out it'd be embarrassing if Booker lost despite a 2-on-1 advantage.

Elsewhere: Stephanie goes looking for Rob Van Dam wanting a birthday present: Chris Jericho being humiliated. Unfortunately for her nobody is there, apart from Jericho, who's standing behind her. "Birthday huh, how old are you going to be? 37?" When Steph points out she'll be 25, Jericho suggests that's how many men she's been with in the last week. Jericho wishes her the "breast of luck", which JR thinks is hilarious. Nothing kills a joke quicker than a commentator repeating it, pointing out why it's funny and doing a horrible fake laugh. I expect better from you, Jim.

WWF Hardcore Championship
Rob Van Dam (c) vs. Chris Jericho
Despite being part of the Alliance and supposedly a heel, RVD is over huge. As is Jericho. They start out with the mat counters wrestling sequence that Rob used to do with anyone who could keep up and Jericho can certainly do that. ECW matches often started like that so they could immediately prove to the fans they could work, just to get them off their backs for a while. Rob made a healthy living in ECW because he took that opening sequence counters thing and turned it into 15-20 minute matches with the likes of Jerry Lynn. They do that here too with various counters until Jericho kinda blows a couple of roll ups so the fans get duelling chants going. They have intricate stuff planned such as RVD going for a legsweep and Jericho jumping over it into an enzuigiri. It's clinical and RVD at his best. Smart spots, good counters and solid bumps. This being a hardcore match RVD hits a slingshot crossbody to the floor and can pin after it. Before that the match had been clinical technical stuff. RVD goes to one of his patented spots; the corkscrew legdrop off the apron to the rail, but Jericho moves. Jericho goes after Rob's shoulder, which probably isn't a good idea as RVD's matches tended to be better when he stayed away from selling and based the match around athleticism. WWF had trouble getting RVD to sell but they'd have been better off just letting him do his thing. Maybe reining him in a bit. Jericho knows how to make the match about the big spots and goes after his Walls of Jericho. RVD has powerful legs though so is able to get out and hit Rolling Thunder. Split legged moonsault gets knees and Jericho follows with a bulldog. It's been a very competitive match.

Lionsault misses and Jericho stands up to eat a spin kick, which is so stiff it cuts Jericho open hardway. Frogsplash misses so Jericho shoots the half for 2. Jericho's eye is badly swollen and cut from that spin kick. Brutal stuff. Another complaint about RVD is that he was too stiff and Kurt Angle bitched about it in particular. Basically if you don't want to get kicked in the face, you shouldn't wrestle RVD. RVD climbs up a ladder so Jericho throws a chair at his head and gets the Walls of Jericho over the top of the ladder, the same spot he worked in against Benoit back at the *Royal Rumble*. The violence in this match is the second phase, on top of the earlier technical stuff to show the guys are gifted at both. RVD goes for a topé and Jericho nails him with a chair. I've seen that done better but it's a good spot. Jericho looks in a lot of pain with his busted eye. The swelling is nasty. As if sensing that area might be sore, RVD clocks Jericho with a step through heel kick right to that bad eye. Jericho takes exception and hooks a Fujiwara armbar, deciding he's better off taking it to RVD with submissions. Jericho grabs a chair to try and wear RVD out with it, Stephanie runs down to distract, which sets up the VAN DAMINATOR! I love it when RVD works that into a match logically. Five Star Frogsplash finishes for Rob and he retains in a thriller. JR calls it a five star match, which is nice of him but it isn't. It is very good though with Rob sticking to his strengths, mixing it up well with another top talent in Jericho, and delivering a top notch PPV contest. Putting Rob in the hardcore division allowed him to do his thing without limitations but as soon as they moved into normal matches the allure went away somewhat. Keeping him hardcore allowed him to be ECW RVD and do all the spots he'd spent years perfecting. I consider this match to be one of the most underrated of the year and a low end MOTY contender.
Final Rating: ****½

Backstage: Booker T tries to figure out to do 6-time hand signs. Shane McMahon comes in to point out it doesn't matter who wins the title as long as it comes back to the Alliance.

WCW Championship
The Rock (c) vs. Booker T & Shane McMahon
This match is a booking problem as there's been no belief in WCW's top stars and Booker, being the champion, needed to avoid jobs where possible. The first WWF move with Booker? Jobbing him to The Rock. Because the WWF stars are better than WCW's stars, which is what the WWF has been saying for years and years and years, regardless of whether it was true or not. Here it is true. Rock is a better wrestler and a bigger star than Booker T but in order to keep the Alliance and the invasion strong, WCW needs to get their belt back. Seeing as the match is 2-on-1 they even have an out for the Rock as he could be double teamed. I just don't get it. Because this is WCW, Nick Patrick is the ref. Rock at least does his part, exploding into his offence like the WCW Title is important to him. He handily beats up Booker and then beats up Shane. It's entertaining but the booking is wrong. Incidentally the Pittsburgh crowd, which is one of the worst I've ever seen, continue to sit on their hands here as they've done for most of the show. Rock puts Shane in the Sharpshooter, which is sloppy but he doesn't fall over so it's better than Shane's Sharpshooter, and Booker has to save. Booker rarely looks like anything other than a chump with the Rock constantly having his way with the former five-time champ. Shane gets more joy! Even when Booker tries for a chair shot Rock still dodges it and Shane lays Rock out instead. All the hard work in the world from the Rock can't compensate for the way WCW are booked. Booker finally gets some love with a precision knee drop before the Spinneroonie and Rock rolls him up for 2. Even when

Booker is dominating, he's still a loser. The WCW guys try to double team but Rock puts them both down. At least everyone takes hearty bumps but it's the same dilemma as the WCW Tag Titles match, where the WCW guys get treated like bitches and still lose. Here Booker gets treated like a bitch and he still loses. Shane tries for a belt shot but miscues and hits Booker. Keystone Cops stuff. Nick Patrick, one of Shane's employees, lets him hit Rock anyway and that's another potential out for Rock. Not only is he outnumbered but the ref is crooked too. The heels continue to bumble their way through the match until Shane decides to do a People's Elbow. Rock nips up in the middle of it and hits the Rock Bottom. Spinebuster for Booker and Test runs in to give Rock a third out for jobbing. Bradshaw runs down to chase Test off but this is after he's stopped Rock winning and big booted him. Nick Patrick throws Rock back in so Mike Chioda runs down to complain on the behalf of zebras everywhere. He lays Patrick out so Booker lays Chioda out. Rock escapes the Book End and hits the Rock Bottom. This is yet another out as there's no ref and Rock can say he had it won but Earl Hebner runs in to count three and Booker jobs yet again, despite a 2-on-1, a crooked ref and a Test assist in his favour. So basically WCW's top star can't get the job done regardless of how much help he has. WCW is now officially dead, two months before *Survivor Series*. The match is pretty good but the sheer stupidity of the booking hurts the rating.
Final Rating: **¾

Backstage: Torrie Wilson and Tajiri persuade William Regal to let her be ringside for Tajiri's match with Rhyno. Video Control takes us to WWF New York where Stacy Keibler shows us how she shaves her legs. Is it weird that they lift Sunny's music for her? They are both stunners but Stacey Keibler is one of the best looking girls to ever work in the wrestling business.

WCW US Championship
Tajiri (c) vs. Rhyno
Tajiri beat Kanyon for the belt and I'm not sure the WWF were taking the US Title seriously. Not that WCW had done but still, you need to get the second belt over. Jobbing it, along with the WCW Title and the WCW Tag Titles to WWF wrestlers was nothing short of idiotic. Rhyno had been getting over as a face when the Alliance angle started but he jumped ship to join his former ECW buddies. Torrie is also an Alliance member, which makes her partnership with Tajiri a bit weird. She gets in the way and Rhyno threatens to kill her, which is like him. One of his ECW spots was piledriving women through tables… off the apron! Rhyno tries for the Gore on Torrie but Tajiri cuts him off with a sensational kick to the face. Brilliant spot. Tajiri's injured ribs rather prohibit any of his spots. That and the size contrast to the thick set Rhyno. The challenger escapes the Tarantula and mows Tajiri down with the GORE, GORE, GORE for the US Title. And finally an Alliance wrestler actually wins a WCW title, albeit an actual WWF guy that they turned heel.
Final Rating: *½

WWF Championship
Steve Austin (c) vs. Kurt Angle
Austin's feud with Angle is the peak of his return to form during 2001 as he deliberately went into the feud doing a ridiculous amount of cardio, just so he could hang with an Olympic gold medallist and blow him up. Angle lifts the Thesz Press in the early going, which is a cute spot. Austin hesitates to go for his gut kick to set up the Stunner because it involves waving his boot near Angle's hands. Austin takes a beating so he decides to walk out, perhaps trying a different tactic to get something out of the crowd. Angle catches him up and throws him off the ramp. It's a 6-foot drop but Austin lands on his feet and rolls to prevent injury. Austin obviously feels Angle was trying to injure him as he goes after a piledriver on the floor, something he'd recently done on TV, and the match is largely about neck injuries. Angle goes for a piledriver too only for Austin to backdrop out. Austin gets cut hardway, which takes the bizarre tally of accidental bleeding to an astonishing four on the evening. Austin goes after Angle's neck again by dropping his knee brace-protected knee. Austin gets in some superb personal work with the crowd by bailing to middle finger salute Kurt's relatives in the front row. The match has a dour middle section with Austin deliberately slowing the pace, albeit with sensible chinlocks that work the neck area. It picks up again afterwards as Angle heads into the rolling Germans. Predictably that hurts Angle's neck. Austin takes over again and Angle looks badly gassed so they keep inserting double downs, which is pretty lazy considering the talent involved. Angle hits the Stunner but it doesn't quite look right and Austin kicks out. Austin counters the Angle Slam and tries for his own, only for it to come out like a back suplex. Austin goes back to the neck, wanting a piledriver as that's the big story of the match. He nails a piledriver and the crowd's reaction of "oh, no" is one of the few they actually contribute to the evening. Kurt kicks out but he's clearly hurt now. Austin goes for the gut kick, but as he feared earlier it gets caught. Ankle lock and Austin taps out. Controversy reigns though as Austin was clearly under the ropes when he tapped and Earl Hebner just ignored it. The crowd don't care and the Angle family pile in to celebrate with the new champion, which is a moment not unlike the Hart Family after *Canadian Stampede*. Again though, I'm actually stunned at how quiet the crowd is despite the WWF basically booking their hometown guy over for the title. Compare this to say Austin in Texas at *WrestleMania* or C.M. Punk in Chicago. It's bizarre and there are times when a poor crowd can tank a show. Luckily this was a pretty good match in spite of the crowd, rather than because of it, but a hot crowd could have turned a good match into a great one.
Final Rating: ***½

VERDICT

People remember Angle's title win but for me this show was all about Rob Van Dam and the kind of awesome matches he could have with willing and talented opponents. Unfortunately the WWF switched gears and wanted to see what he could do with the likes of Angle and Austin and whether he could be a real player, which meant taking away all his spots and forcing him to do WWF Main Event Style. Their attempts to tame RVD took away a lot of his mystique and this remains the pinnacle of his WWF career (big win over John Cena aside). They spent the rest of 2001 trying to mould RVD and it wasn't really his thing. He still had decent matches, but by the time 2002 rolled around he'd settled into IC Title contention and stayed there. Somewhat of a missed opportunity if this stunning match with Jericho was anything to go by. I know I've spent the whole review whinging about the crowd, but honestly most of them were probably still in shock from 9/11, and while escapism is nice they probably had their minds on the news.

63

NO MERCY 2001

CAT NO: WWF54103
RUN TIME: 158 minutes (approx)

Arnold Furious: Coming into *No Mercy* I'd become a massive cheerleader for Rob Van Dam. I felt his clear-cut different style could allow him to be "the man" in the WWF. RVD was a distinctive talent and they don't come along too often. Ultimately the WWF decided they'd pop him into a main event to see how he coped. For a moment there, albeit a short one, it seemed as RVD would establish himself as a genuine contender and a top player in the WWF at a time when they were desperate for new top stars. Rob was positioned as the biggest star to have joined the WWF that year, and while the likes of Booker T and DDP had already been beaten by WWF talent, they'd kept RVD strong. Elsewhere The Rock had begun a program with Chris Jericho over the WCW Title, as the two had developed a misunderstanding. It was the beginning of Jericho as a heel main eventer. Sort of. *No Mercy* sees the WWF on the cusp of creating two huge main event stars, and at the time I was hugely optimistic about the future of the company. Unfortunately In the months that follow, it all goes wrong somewhere. We're in St. Louis, Missouri. Hosts are Jim Ross and Paul Heyman.

WCW Tag Team Championship
The Hardy Boyz (c) vs. Lance Storm & The Hurricane
Yet another WCW championship lies in the hands of WWF performers. Ivory is in Storm's corner here and I really don't remember her switch to the Alliance. 2001 was a confusing time for allegiances. Hurricane has Mighty Molly in his corner and that at least makes sense as she's been re-fitted as a superhero and they're both over. Heyman tries to put over the history between Hurricane and the Hardys in the Carolina's without actually using the word OMEGA. I guess they didn't want to put Matt Hardy over as an independent promoter. Storm and Hurricane have developed some decent teamwork with Hurricane doing the flashy stuff and Lance holding it together. JR isn't afraid to start reeling off St Louis wrestling history, which makes me feel all warm and nostalgic. I may have watched *Wrestling at the Chase* on tape many years after it happened, but it was good shit. The Hardys keep the pace strong even when Jeff is taking heat. They've only got 8-minutes so there's no need to take a breather. The lack of tags allows both teams to get in their team spots such as the double superkick from the challengers. Molly tries to interfere allowing Lita to run in and spear her. Ivory makes the save so Jeff slaps her about. I thought Matt was... Never mind. Jeff taps to the Maple Leaf but Lita saves him with a flying rana. Twist of Fate on Hurricane and Jeff finishes with the Swanton bomb. Team Extreme brought the big team spots, Hurricane brought the laughs and Storm held it together. The typical hot opener that you want tag teams to have on PPV. For all the upward mobility many WCW talent got in the WWF (I'm thinking Benoit, Guerrero, Jericho, Booker), Lance Storm found himself in the same boat as Dean Malenko, where his delivery was monotonous and the fans found him a bit dry. Which is a pity because Storm, as Malenko, was one of the best technicians in the business and massively underrated by the WWF.
Final Rating: ***

Backstage: Rob Van Dam arrives and is confronted by William Regal about RVD frogsplashing Steve Austin on *SmackDown!* RVD says he's not on Vince McMahon's side, he's on RVD's side. Elsewhere: Vince McMahon arrives. Michael Cole is on hand to suck up to him and drop his jacket like a dingus. "Next time you drop my jacket, I'll drop you". Oh, I wish he had.

Test vs. Kane
So, Test jumped to the Alliance. Presumably because everyone in the Alliance was too short to feud with the Brothers of Destruction. Considering it's Test vs. Kane, they set a decent pace and work hard. Test brings the kind of bumps you don't normally see from a 300lb man, including Kane pressing him out of the ring. Test absolutely waffles Kane with the ring bell but WCW senior official Nick Patrick, whose impartiality is questionable, doesn't see it and therefore can't call it a DQ. My favourite Kane spot has always been his punches. His uppercuts are probably the best in the business so I'm pleased when he belts Test with one. One of Test's best spots is his Savage Elbow, which is impressive for a big man, and he gets that in only for Kane to move. The levels of effort are commendable considering this is a total throwaway midcard match and most people would be happy with clubberin'. Kane does manage to screw up a pin as he leans across Test's stomach and doesn't even apply any pressure. It's perhaps the

worst looking lateral press I've ever seen and Jim Ross feels the need to admonish him for it. The WWF had been trying to get Test's big boot over, by having Taker job to it the previous week, but Kane kicks out after one on the floor. Test in turn survives a chokeslam, albeit with a delayed cover. Both guys continue to work hard as the match moves on, making this an unexpected success. Kane misses his flying clothesline and gets planted with a pumphandle slam but kicks out. The Savage Elbow is able to connect this time around as Kane is already down. Kane again kicks out and this match has been a real surprise hit. They try and work in an RVD-style chair spot where Kane dropkicks it into Test's face. Nick Patrick, using his usual level of impartiality, stops Kane using the chair afterwards. Test punts Kane in the balls and kicks him in the face for the win. Considering who was involved this was a wild match with great near falls and fun booking. It's really not what you'd expect a match between Kane and Test to be. Maybe the WWF employed the old Bill Watts trick and had a payout for "best match" tonight? Just to really pop the shit out of St Louis, Kane hits two chokeslams and a powerbomb on Nick Patrick. One of the best singles matches of either guys' careers and a genuine contender for "most surprisingly competent PPV match" of the decade.
Final Rating: ***

Backstage: The Coach goes to get words with Steve Austin but the champ refuses an interview. Debra translates an interview from behind closed doors as he yells stuff. It's a funny bit as Debra switches "son of a bitch" to "SOB" and "ass" to "butt". Elsewhere Stacy Keibler shows off her lingerie to Matt Hardy. He's almost caught red-handed by Lita and does a wonderful "phew" reaction shot to camera. I know the WWF is widely barracked for doing all this backstage comedy stuff, because so much of it sucks, but when you get people who are good at it, it can flesh out weak characters and make strong characters stronger. Unfortunately it also papered over people who could do their own stuff. There are pros and cons for "Creative" but the biggest con is that it makes everyone behave the same way. When you're writing creatively, the hardest part is to develop individuality, and the WWF were often rubbish at it, which is why the truly big stars tend to have their own distinct style of their own creation.

Lingerie Match
Stacy Keibler vs. Torrie Wilson
Two hot chicks who can't wrestle; it's the Divas! To be fair to Stacy and Torrie, they probably didn't ask to be wrestlers and have no background outside of being valets. Stacy can at least do a cartwheel so they work that in twice. Both ladies get a big pop for disrobing and Stacy gets a bigger one for using a whip, which shows how unimportant the heel/face structure is. Stacy has a style based on her best assets; her long legs, whereas Torrie has nothing approaching a style. In a bit of insanity, they lift the near falls sequence from Guerrero-Malenko, which is probably Dean's doing as he trained divas. Good work if you can get it. After that they run out of spots and Torrie's handspring back elbow is an embarrassment. It's also the

---

FURIOUS ABOUT: THE ROCK (1999-2002)

When Austin went down with a neck injury, there was only one obvious replacement for him and that was The Rock. Luckily for the WWF, Triple H got good around the same time. Rock was already a star in 1999. He was PWI's most popular wrestler that year and had already won three WWF titles. 2000 was a year where Hunter and Rock had to carry the company and while Triple H took up the workrate slack, Rock filled Austin's charisma void. He stepped up to the plate and delivered some of the best promos in the business. He electrified crowds like no one else. When Hunter wasn't carrying the ball in 2000, the title belt found its way around Rocky's waist. He won a fourth title at Backlash 2000 and a fifth at King of the Ring. In between he contested a remarkable Ironman match against Triple H. A match that proved both men's ability to be the companies biggest stars. Into 2001, Rock was required to headline WrestleMania and did so by winning his sixth WWF title before contesting a match of the ages against the returning Steve Austin. After losing his title, the Rock headed to Hollywood to shoot the *Scorpion King*. It was the movie that would turn the wrestler into a legitimate movie star. When he returned from set he was pitched into the Invasion angle, defeating Booker T for the WCW title and scoring the triumphant pin to keep the WWF in business. He also had a terrific feud with Chris Jericho, which elevated Y2J from 'damaged goods' to heavyweight contender. It was only Stephanie McMahon's booking that returned him to midcard mediocrity. Not content with that, Rock went out to have himself another classic WrestleMania moment in 2002 by challenging Hulk Hogan. The fans sided with Hogan but Rock coped with the pressure and delivered another classic match. In 2002 he began to reduce his schedule, as Hollywood beckoned, but he still had time for another WWE title run. On his way out he put over Brock Lesnar because Rock understands the business.

---

finish. At least both girls looked hot, which is basically what the match was for. It ends the PPV's ***+ streak but it was also over so we'll give it points for that and effort. It's not the cleanest wrestling contest in the world but they were working in lingerie so that's where the bar was set. Kudos for attempting the same near fall sequence that Chris Jericho botched a month earlier.
Final Rating: ¼*

Backstage: Kurt Angle gets interviewed but he's interrupted by Vince McMahon. Kurt responds by saying he doesn't need luck. Elsewhere: Christian complains that he was overlooked by everyone who rated Edge as the star of their tag team. Christian gets a bit of cheap heat by criticising the Cardinals and steroid era home run king Mark McGwire. Big Mac had just retired but his home run record was handily beaten by another steroid user and professional asshole Barry "Barroids" Bonds in 2001, so it was fair game for Christian to use.

Ladder Match
WWF Intercontinental Championship
Christian (c) vs. Edge
Christian has also joined the Alliance to try and give them a shot at credibility by adding as many WWF stars as possible, which they wouldn't need to do if they hadn't buried all the WCW talent with the booking. These two had an

underwhelming first match at *Unforgiven* so they've thrown the ladder gimmick in to try and get the feud over. Much like at *Unforgiven*, I'm surprised at how little they seem to have planned. You'd think these guys would have a match they'd always wanted to do for years and years and would have spots coming out of their ears. Once the ladder comes into play matters improve slightly but the spots, while quite creative, aren't much fun. Like them both standing on a ladder and Christian getting punched until he drops groin first onto it. I've not seen the spot before but it lacks the "wow" factor. Another issue is the waiting between these spots as they can't hit a fast pace in a 20-minute match and also having to sell the bumps as they're so big. The match structure is somewhere between the Shawn-Razor kind of ladder match and the TLC matches with the tables removed. For whatever reason Edge and Christian never had a great match together. This is arguably their best match and I've seen it rated up near ****. For me it rather pales in comparison to even Jericho-Benoit from the same year in terms of good ladder contests. Edge wouldn't get really good in singles until the following year and Christian seemed to hit a brick wall of career progression around 2000.

JR manages to get the slow climbing over by claiming Edge has cramp in his back as Christian works on that general area to get some psychology into the match. Both guys take monster bumps off the ladder to get the match over and because of their history, there's an excellent level of trust. You could argue if you don't trust your opponent you're not going to have anything approaching a good match regardless of personal history, something that was evident in the Bret-Shawn match at *Survivor Series*. No complex and big bumps in that match, as there was no trust. After a spot off the ladder Christian goes for the Conchairto to finish only for Edge to kick the chair into Christian's face. What follows is Edge setting up a ladder across two chairs, which seems unnecessary and Edge hits a splash on it that looks more painful than effective. At least there is consistency in the selling as Edge stays down thanks to his previous back/rib injuries. Christian climbs and Edge goes up the buckles to spear him off in the match's best spot, albeit a re-tread of TLC spots, usually involving resident fraggle Jeff Hardy. The ladder match had the gloss taken off it a bit when the TLC matches started and with this one they still used chairs. That was the nature of how the ladder match had evolved. This one struggles to live up to the legacy. Christian gets up the ladder but Edge low blows him with a chair, as a receipt for *Unforgiven*. To cap off the match Edge grabs a pair of chairs and hits the Conchairto on top of the ladders. They only needed to set up three ladders and two chairs to do it. Edge pulls down the IC Title to regain it.
Final Rating: ***¼

Video Control gives us a shill for *Survivor Series* next month, pointing out tickets are still available. That shows how the company was doing at the time! Imagine an Attitude era PPV from just a year beforehand not selling out that quickly. At WWF New York, Spike Dudley is enjoying a few drinks. Paul Heyman tries to destroy his confidence by pointing out he got dumped by Molly a month ago, but Spike's too busy hitting on rats.

WWF Tag Team Championship
The Dudley Boyz (c) vs. The Big Show & Tajiri
This is the 5th of eight WWF Tag Team Title reigns for the Dudleys. Tajiri starts, giving the Duds a big advantage, but D-Von still gets caught with a thrust kick and a standing moonsault. Show gets an early hot tag but there's almost no reaction for it. Tajiri gets into trouble again and the Dudleys run heat on him with the usual typical beats like the ref missing the hot tag. The Dudleys at least used the heat in their own way by hitting the Wazzup Headbutt with the ref distracted. Inserting trademark spots as cheating was clever stuff because it allowed them to remain interesting but still heel. When Show does get a hot tag he does the Razor Ramon and Andre the Giant posing to get a pop. Tajiri gets a blind tag and hooks the Tarantula on D-Von. Handspring back elbow allows Tajiri to avoid a potential 3D. Ref gets misted, which means he misses Show chokeslamming Bubba. Rhyno runs in – GORE, GORE, GOOOORREEEE! Tajiri still hits the Kick of Death on D-Von but the blind ref takes his time getting over to the pin. The Dudleys rapidly move into position for the 3D, which looks great, and Tajiri takes the loss. This was a patchy outing from all involved but it was mostly fun. I'm surprised, in retrospect, at how over Big Show wasn't. I guess the stint in OVW had taken the edge off him.
Final Rating: **½

Backstage: Rhyno complains about public perception of the Alliance as a joke and says he'll single-handedly change that. Within a week he'd be "suspended" and would miss a year with neck surgery. Elsewhere: Booker T congratulates Test on beating Kane and Shane McMahon claims tonight is about respect. Booker promises the Undertaker will be "one dead sucka". Heyman stops off to chill Saliva's '*Click, Click Boom*', which is the theme music of *No Mercy*.

Booker T vs. The Undertaker
Poor Booker. First he was booked to look like a chump against The Rock, eventually losing a match where he teamed with Shane against 'the Great One'. Even with Shane in the match, Booker still took the pinfall. Now he's gotten lumbered with Undertaker, who has given nothing to any WCW guys since the invasion began. He gives Booker slightly more respect than DDP, but that's the thing with the Undertaker; until you earn his respect he doesn't sell for you. Another issue is the clash of styles with Booker favouring kicks and having to switch to brawling in order to get Taker to loosen up. Ross talks about the psychology of working the left side, claiming as a right-hander Booker's left arm is probably weaker. Not that it's a wrestling convention to work the left side or anything... Unless you're Mexican. Taker at least uses the arm stuff to set up Old School. They work in a nice piece of mirroring where Booker goes after the ring bell but the ref is now WWF official Timmy White who takes it off him. Booker goes to his kicks after that but Undertaker goes through the motions of selling them, rather than actually selling them. Heyman almost sells out by saying the Spinneroonie is the most electrifying move in sports entertainment, before pointing out Shane paid him to say that. I really miss the Ross-Heyman team because it was so professional. They covered all their bases but they were both quick on their feet. So they'd get the storylines over and the nuances of wrestling while still hitting the back-and-forth banter that you need on commentary. It was a big loss when the WWF went back to using Jerry Lawler after the invasion angle ended. Booker gets a tidy pop for doing the Spinneroonie, which shows you how smart the WWF was with getting goofy stuff over. Booker hits the axe kick and Taker finally shows a bit of respect by using the rope instead of kicking out. Booker, like an idiot, then mounts the buckles for the ten count punches and gets countered right into the Last Ride. Considering Booker was supposed to be WCW's ace, as he came in as WCW champion, he can't buy a win on PPV. At least he got a decent WWF career out of this run, eventually, but this was another piece of booking that showed how useless the WWF guys figured WCW were. The case in point being that they split the

FURIOUS ABOUT: STEVE AUSTIN (1999-2002)

Before a neck injury put Austin out of the business in 2003, he had one final awesome run at the top. After missing a year of action with surgery, Austin returned with renewed vigour. He was determined to cement his legacy in 2001. First off by having a brilliant 2 out of 3 falls match with Triple H, followed a month later by an even better WrestleMania main event against the Rock. Not content with having the two best matches of the calendar year before April, Austin went on to have one of the most storied heel runs in wrestling history. Not everyone agrees with the decision to turn Austin, nor the style of his heel persona, but once the decision had been made, Austin took that ball and ran with it. His performances 2001, and a decision of his own to change his style to a harder-hitting, technically superior one, turned him into the wrestler of the year. He was absolutely outstanding in 2001. Something that probably accelerated the end of his career. Austin obviously favouring the "it's better to burn out than fade away" school of philosophy. Austin had a string of belting matches in 2001. Whether it was against Hunter, Rock, Taker, Jericho, Benoit, Angle or anyone else, he delivered the best matches of the year. Everything after 2001 is best forgotten. Austin reverted to a stereotypical and tired version of the enigmatic babyface of the Attitude era. He slowed down in the ring, changed his style again and the MOTYC's dried up. The booking began to reflect that and Austin became disillusioned. Firstly he was stuck against Scott Hall in the midcard of WrestleMania X8, possibly as punishment for turning down the Hogan match. He no-showed Raw citing exhaustion and his interest in wrestling waned. Austin then refused to job to Brock Lesnar on free TV and went home. A pity as the WWE had just started a feud between Austin and Eddy Guerrero, which would have been superb. Austin returned in 2003 for one final match, where he put the Rock over at WrestleMania XIX.

---

booking of Alliance vs. Brothers of Destruction and it's Test that goes over. A WWF guy.
Final Rating: *½

Backstage: Coach grabs Chris Jericho for an interview. He says it's time to put up or shut the hell up. Jericho adds it's time for him to go and win the big one.

WCW Championship
The Rock (c) vs. Chris Jericho
Two things of note. 1. This is the most over match on the show and it features two WWF guys wrestling each other. 2. The match is for the WCW Title and features two WWF guys wrestling each other. That sums up how well the invasion angle is going. Jericho accidentally bashed Rock with a chair to set up the feud but soon both guys' promo skills built the match up as a genuinely big one. Rock's assertion that Jericho hadn't won a big match because he wasn't good enough was sufficient motivation for Jericho, the character, to turn up and give it his all here. Behind the scenes both guys were on good terms, which shows in the ring as they're both keen to have a good match. Ross stops off to bury WCW by saying Jericho worked there for three years and never had a title match.

These guys have decent chemistry right off the bat, with counters and sequences taking place at a solid speed. Rock doesn't quite get into his armdrag bumps right but otherwise they complement each other well. The crowd gets a stirring "Rocky" chant going, which shows you who the big star is here, although Jericho gets a hearty pop for socking Rocky with a big slap and a "Y2J" chant breaks out. I'm not convinced they needed to turn Jericho heel as he was going toe-to-toe with the biggest star in the business and getting favourable reactions. Obviously Rock is the bigger star but that doesn't mean Jericho had to turn. The best part of this match is that Jericho, the smaller man, is booked on a par with a genuine megastar in The Rock. It makes me sad that Rock didn't give Booker the same treatment or that Rock wasn't around to help get guys over in the years that followed. Jericho is a different beast to many others. He's a friendly guy, a charismatic yet goofy wrestler and a master of different wrestling styles. It set him apart as he didn't work WWF Main Event Style. It shows how great both guys are that despite this being a big match with a big match atmosphere, they keep the pace moderate and don't burn themselves out. So instead of rushing through spots they keep stuff happening and there aren't many rest holds. It's interesting to note the fan reactions during the match as both guys get support. So the guy hitting the move gets popped, whether that's Rock or Jericho. Rock is a bit sloppy here and there are spots he attempts that he has no clue how to execute. A belly-to-belly is closer to a judo throw than a suplex.

As the match progresses Rock's bursts of energy allow him to boss proceedings. Jericho's WCW run turned him into a bumping machine as that was the best way for him to get over the bigger guys he wrestled (although he spent most of his WCW career in the cruiserweight division). So Rock's offence sees Jericho fly around the ring taking abuse. This match doesn't have the same athletic excellence as Jericho vs. Van Dam and yet it's possibly a better showcase as Jericho is going up against "the man". Earlier in this book I stated that Jericho, in 2000 at *Fully Loaded*, peaked as a superstar. You could argue that match is his peak, as I did, or you could argue this one is. While he beat the hell out of Triple H, he goes back-and-forth with Rock. Jericho gets a huge pop for lifting the Rock Bottom. Lionsault follows but Rock kicks out. Everyone thought it was over because of the impact of the Rock Bottom followed by Jericho's signature move. It's a great false finish and the crowd takes ages to settle down after it. Not content with one piece of trademark thievery, Jericho hits a bulldog to set up the People's Elbow but Rock moves. Rock's first move after that is a really sloppy, rushed dragon screw leg whip into a Sharpshooter. Jericho making the ropes shows how divided the audience is, and the commentators, as Heyman suggests that Jericho is a choke artist. And yet Jericho was playing his role slightly heel. Rock drags Jericho out of the ring, apparently pissed off by the Rock Bottom and People's Elbow theft, and hits a Rock Bottom through the Spanish announce table. Jericho can barely stand after that and you sense it's over, and yet Jericho elbows out of the Rock Bottom before running into the spinebuster. People's Elbow is blocked as Jericho trips Rock up and flips him into the Walls of Jericho. It's a great spot and the fans eat it up. Rock doesn't escape and Stephanie

McMahon runs down to throw a chair in. Rock takes exception and nails her with a Rock Bottom. Breakdown on the chair! Jericho has a hell of a job getting the chair out of the ring, in that he tries to shove it out three times and it keeps sticking on the apron, before pinning for the title. For those who don't remember the Breakdown, it was the same move as Jeff Jarrett's Stroke.

The match is a tough one to rate for a number of reasons. It's certainly a big breakthrough for Jericho and yet Stephanie's interference hints at something sinister and unwelcome. The crowd make the match a little better than it should be as they popped everything hard and were actively interested in both men winning. Rock wasn't exactly nailing everything clean, shall we say, and several of his moves were flubbed including the dragon screw, which looked completely wrong. That said, the match had a "big match" atmosphere, and you can't buy that. Post Match: Rock looks upset and hands the chair to Jericho, as if to say "I know you cheated". The great part of this is that both guys are still babyfaces even after the match is done. Unfortunately booking dictated one of them had to turn and it was Jericho. His turn wasn't particularly well received as people still wanted to cheer him, as was evidenced here. Tough match to rate but a good one and a low end contender for MOTY on crowd reactions alone.
Final Rating: ****¼

WWF Championship
Steve Austin (c) vs. Kurt Angle vs. Rob Van Dam
Austin and Angle had exchanged the WWF Title over the summer months, but RVD was getting so damn popular he got put into the mix too. Considering RVD only joined the company in July, he's already in the main event at an astonishing rate. In my opinion he was popular enough for the WWF to switch gears and put the belt on him here leaving everyone suspicious as to where his loyalties lie. Angle, almost the forgotten man, makes a point of starting hard and fast. He's also the only WWF guy while the other two are Alliance, so Angle gets his ass kicked 2-on-1. Rob must be loving the momentum rise to the top of wrestling and the moment where he points at himself unveils a massive RVD chant. Like at *Unforgiven* when he lost the belt, Austin goes for the Stunner gut kick and gets caught in an ankle lock. The difference here is RVD has his back to protect the belt. The crowd bite on RVD, big time, and chant his name whenever they can. Honestly, I think they should have struck while the iron was hot and just pushed him all the way here. You don't get a ton of chances to create new main event stars so you'd better take them. Rob doesn't cover himself in glory as the storyline has him selling a leg injury and he's terrible at it. "Arrrgh, ow. Arrgh. Ow. Ow" says Rob as Austin works a half crab. He sounds like a tool. Triple threat matches often have issues related to selling and RVD basically has to stay down selling his leg while Austin and Angle brawl around ringside. Because he's not good at it, he stays down for a while and then pops up and starts using the ropes, which is why he shouldn't attempt it to begin with. Angle then turns it up a notch by hitting a capture suplex on RVD and adding in a moonsault. Angle and Austin trade on Stunner attempts, showcasing how well they know each other after a run of main events. Five star frogsplash and both guys move. Stunner! Rob stops the pin, showing he's in it to win it. Split legged moonsault on Austin, and Angle showing weird selling inconsistency, pops up to save. Angle Slam and Austin saves his title. Austin and Angle go for an announce table spot before faking us out and RVD hits a tope. With all guys down, out comes Vince McMahon. RVD goes after the frogsplash but Angle runs the buckles into a superplex. Weird seeing Rob check his positioning so many times to give Angle the chance to hit the spot. Austin runs back in; Stunner but Angle falls out of the ring. Austin stalks RVD instead and Vince runs in to chair shot the champ. Vince is in the process of ordering Angle back inside; Frogsplash! Angle barely stops the count with RVD one second away from winning the WWF Title. Rob was criticised for being dangerous but Vince McMahon's chair shot (to the back of the head mind you) busted Austin open hardway. Angle hits the rolling Germans so Shane McMahon runs down to even up the McMahon involvement. Vince lays him out with a sensational diving punch. In the ring RVD is dead weight and Austin nails him with the Stunner to retain. I still think Rob Van Dam should have gone over here as it would have created a load of intrigue toward the end of the invasion angle, but I guess they felt Austin had to stay strong. Rob's critics pointed out how stiff and dangerous he was and the de-push began. Kurt's wife Karen was the most vocal detractor of RVD's style (after RVD accidentally bloodied him, Jericho and others on TV) but I guess that was to allow Kurt to save face. Criticise the boys via proxy. Rob ended up demoted into the IC Title division where he became smoother yet less interesting as a worker. Like they trained the fun out of him. My favourite RVD moments in the WWF all come at the front of his run there; the Hardy match, the great match with Jericho and his interactions at the top of the card that ended here.
Final Rating: ***½

VERDICT

This is a great show, make no mistake about it. The feeling of optimism and change is in the air and you can feel the guys respond to what they consider to be the opening up of top spots. RVD and Jericho getting their main event opportunities showed the other undercard guys that their spots weren't just there for protecting; advancement was a possibility. Of course this all changed somewhat and the spots earned by Jericho and RVD were soon handed over to Ric Flair and Hulk Hogan in 2002, which is what happens when the ratings and buyrates go down. But the fans weren't responding negatively to Jericho and Van Dam and you can tell from the crowd reactions here. The WWF should have retained their fans with smart booking and strong performances from their stars and had faith in people, instead of all the hot-shotting that took place in 2001. It was the frequently changing landscape that made Jericho and RVD able to get these chances, but they got them for a reason. The WWF knew they needed to affect positive change. When you look at the buyrates for 2001, they're not actually that bad and the panic changes the WWF made, and booking errors like the never-ending Triple H title run, actually made the buyrates worse in the years that followed. I think they expected viewership to go up, but instead of gaining WCW's fans, those Southern fans who liked a different style just stopped watching. All I really care about is the quality of the wrestling and it was good here from the hot opener through to the thrilling conclusion to the show. Jericho's title win was a gutsy booking move but it came at the expense of a poorly judged heel turn and there were still too many McMahon's involved. From top to bottom it's one of my favourite shows from 2001 though, *WrestleMania X-Seven* is obviously a lot better, but apart from that it's up there. A top five PPV for 2001.

76

TOMMY DREAMER

HARDY BOYZ - LEAP OF FAITH

CAT NO: WWF54105
RUN TIME: 58 minutes (approx)

James Dixon: Following a release covering the series of matches between the Hardy Boyz, Edge & Christian and the Dudley Boyz in 1999-2000, as well as a tape about the Hardys' manager Lita, the brothers get their own hour-long profile release. It starts with the revelations that Jeff likes coming home at least once a week to relax and that Matt likes to sew and used to make all of his own gear. A strange way to start out. Matt then calls Jeff an oddball, which is not news, and Bubba says how stunned he is that the brothers are related because they are so different and have nothing in common. We see Jeff's wacky house which is full of life-size fibreglass figurines, fake rubber plants and his embarrassingly bad self-crafted statues, which look like the handiwork of a child. "Jeff is not here with us on Earth" says Michael Hayes, a man who has met more than his fair share of off-the-wall guys over the years, as Edge brings up Jeff's frankly cringe inducing "emoetry". "The perfect description of me is "weird"" says Jeff. Oh, we know. Edge adds that he would like to go on vacation in Jeff head because he thinks it would be serene. I think it would be like being at a techno rave while on acid.

Matt says he enjoys the road, making him the first wrestler in history to do so, because they to make it fun. We then see Matt sitting in the corridor of the Gund Arena in Cleveland, venue of the famous *No Mercy* ladder match, and he puts over the nostalgic feel of the hallway, calling it hallowed ground to him and Jeff. That's all a bit too much like "emoetry" to me, but the match itself certainly was important for them. Matt takes credit for the idea of doing the ladder match, and then the brothers talk about it a little. Jeff says the one thing that kept running through his head was the directive "safe and spectacular" that they were told by Shane McMahon. And then sure enough, Matt botched the very first spot, making a cock of running the ropes at the same time as Jeff and whiplashing his neck off them. Much credit to him then for quickly pulling it together and not letting that minor mistake play on his mind, and then being able to deliver the far more dangerous and complex stuff that followed. Christian talks about the first big pop of the match (which was a ladder tug-o-war leading to a garrotting in the corner) and how the audience reaction built from there. It did; every move, every spot, every high risk bump climaxed wonderfully and all combined made this one of the most memorable and important matches of the era. Christian tells how he noticed one of the ladders was broken and that Jeff took it upon himself to fix it, which was a risky thing to do when they had to then climb it and use it for more spots, especially when they had plenty of spares. Matt discusses the worst bump he took; an innocuous looking ladder shot and bump over the top, which caught him square on the ear. I can imagine that one stung. Jeff says he remembers everything that happened in the contest, but his favourite spot was the famous and innovative seesaw spot, which is definitely great, but watched post *Armageddon 2006* conjures up images of Joey Mercury getting his face brutally smashed in by the same move (indeed it was Jeff who executed the move that night too. Yes, seven years later and the Hardys were still doing ladder matches. Not that WWE were bereft of fresh ideas or anything). Jeff says the spot was the thing that injured him the most in the bout, giving him a bruised tailbone from the landing. The two teams then describe the finish in detail and Matt rightly states that the match did a lot for all of them and points out that the Hardys have come a long way since debuting... in 1998! Yes, he conveniently forgets the four years they spent with the company as job boys, which would be fine except that in a few minutes we see them putting over such luminaries as King Kong Bundy, Crush and Waylon Mercy from 1994 onwards, contradicting what Matt just said.

To the story of how the Hardys became fans of wrestling and watched *WrestleMania IV* when growing up, and we see their home videos from when they used to wrestle each other as kids with all their cute little characters. We skip them training themselves, though Edge rather drops them in it: "They wrestled around the backyard, which we can't condone..." he says. Hypocritical of him really, what with him and Christian having done the exact same thing in their school. We get some highlights of the Hardys' early indy work, then a really bizarre shot of them and two unidentified guys in nWo shirts. The thing is, as stated Matt and Jeff started with the WWF in 1994, and were pretty much there ever since on and off. Parading around in shirts of the opposition's hottest act was a silly thing to be doing. They talk about how their father wasn't impressed with the lack of money they were making and that he wanted them to get a real job, though now they are rich and famous he likes the business, obviously. Bruce Prichard puts them over for their hard work and heart, and talks about them being with the company as semi-regulars for years before they were finally given a contract. We see the contract, which they didn't even read and just signed. Marks. "There's a lot of very cool stories of how guys got here" says Edge, before putting over the Hardys for training themselves and working hard to get to the WWF. He reckons it could be a movie. Well yeah, it is a nice story and a feel-good story at that... when this was filmed. But the way they both turned out as drug abusers, rehab frequenters and in the case of Matt, a woman beater too, makes this more sad when viewed with the benefit of hindsight.

We see the Hardys winning the tag belts in a fluke win over the APA and positively fly through their associations with Michael Hayes and Gangrel. Things get confusing as we return to the feud with Edge & Christian and the ladder match that we have already seen, and Jeff calls Mick Foley "Nothing but inspiring" for his comments (telling them that they just "made" themselves) post *No Mercy*. Foley responds, saying that the dressing room knew what the Hardys could do but everyone needs that one match to convince the fans as such, and *No Mercy* was that one match that got them over. The scatterbrain format continues as we go from that back to their childhood, as they briefly talk about their mum dying young from cancer, and their dad (who Jeff says is his hero) raising them alone and disciplining them well (though, look how they turned out...). We then get a random video interlude set to their dad strumming away on an acoustic guitar, which includes then still friends Matt and Edge playing around with the picture special effects on a handheld camera, and Jeff talking about how comfortable he is with sexual exploits, but that he believes they should be kept private. That comment probably didn't help quash any of the many rumours at the time about what his "deal" was.

At *WrestleMania 2000* they took the *No Mercy* bout and added the Dudleys to the mix, and the results were much the same. It's a tremendous bout, though not quite career defining in the same way, but still another in a long list of stunt matches featuring the teams that is definitely worth hunting out. The continued innovation of the ladder match continues with this effort, and the addition of two extra bodies makes for some great spots, such as Bubba's three stooges helicopter impression with the ladder, a sequence towards the end where all six guys climb for the belts and take wild bumps, and then the brilliant "table mountain" spot at the end with a table set up over two ladders. Watching this makes me wonder why the other two teams didn't get their own tape releases too. A lot of the stuff may have been repeated, but each duo had done plenty of other things as well to make it worthwhile. I suppose they did release the *TLC - Tables Ladders Chairs* tape that featured all three duos. We see all six guys hugging and thanking each other backstage after the match, then move to the treatment room as it turns out that Jeff knackered his heel

---

FURIOUS ABOUT: THE UNDERTAKER (1999-2002)

This is not a good era for the Undertaker. A lot of his mysteriousness disappeared, and later the WWE tried to recapture that lightning in a bottle. The gimmick switch from zombie to biker didn't sit well and not only did his interviews become tiresome but his matches became an absolute chore to sit through. When he returned to the darkness in 2004, a move some were cynical about, somehow his in-ring improved again. In this post-Attitude era, his in-ring was terrible. During the Invasion Taker gained this massive chip on his shoulder, which made him think he was better than everyone else. Whether this was just the booking or whether the booking reflected his backstage persona is anyone's guess. But the way he handled various WCW guys just wasn't professional. The destruction of Diamond Dallas Page stands out but Taker gave a few WCW guys the same short shrift in the ring. Often cutting people off before they'd had a chance to do anything. One of the worst Taker matches, ever, was the tag team match against KroniK during the Invasion. It was chronic, all right. Not content with being terrible as a babyface biker, Taker was turned heel after the Invasion angle ended and he became even worse. A generic, pointless, worthless heel character who didn't fit into the company and didn't fit into Mark Calaway's years of work as the Undertaker prior to 2001. If it wasn't for a feud with Brock Lesnar late in 2002, it would be his worst year in the business. The heel run was so diabolical that he didn't really get his mojo back, in the ring, until 2007. The Invasion era could have ended the Undertaker before "The Streak" was even a big deal. Taker's "Streak" wins in this era aren't that memorable either. A decent win over Hunter at X7 and a midcard battle with Ric Flair at X8. Undertaker has had a few stints where he wasn't good in the ring, like before 1996, but this 3 year spell really hurt because he'd been great and he wasn't anymore.

---

with a crazy Swanton off the huge ladder, which he describes as "12-foot but feels like 50". We see Francois Petit working on his leg as Jeff expresses surprise that he even hit the table because with the pain of the landing he just figured he had skimmed it at best. Talks turns to the duo's kick ass entrance music which Edge says he sings along to when they are coming to the ring, but he admits to preferring their old theme. I disagree. This is brief and doesn't offer much. It would have been nice to hear from Jim Johnston about it actually, especially as the newer piece was used as token WWF music atop highlight packages before it was given to the Hardys. A missed opportunity for some insight.

To *SummerSlam 2000*, and the first ever TLC match, a genuine ***** epic that builds properly and is far more than just spots for the sake of spots. It's yet another memorable and groundbreaking match that will be remembered long into the future. The highlights don't really do it justice, because while we see the big impressive bumps and weapon shots, none of the psychology is retained and the flow is lost. Matt Hardy's insane backwards bump over the ropes through a stack of tables doesn't lose any of its lustre though, and seeing Edge spear Lita inches away from a ladder is still disturbing of how close she came to a serious accident. Jeff's bump after being swatted off the hanging belts is nasty too, as he lands on his feet. That could have caused serious knee problems; just ask Jim Cornette.

FURIOUS ABOUT: CHRISTIAN

Like his 'brother' Edge, Christian made his name through the E&C tag team between 1999 and 2001. Through a series of high risk, dangerous matches with ladders, chairs and tables, Christian became established as a star in the WWF. In 2001 when Edge won the King of the Ring, Christian's jealousy overwhelmed him and he turned on his long-time partner. The failure of their feud to gain any traction was blamed squarely on Christian and he found himself mired in the midcard afterwards. At least Christian was able to secure an IC title reign from the Edge feud and his popularity among fans remained strong as they'd not forgotten how entertaining he'd been during the E&C team. In the early days of E&C, Christian had been the better wrestler. His fundamentals were better, his promos were better and his personality was better formed. Their heel run in 2000, where they abandoned the boring gothic lifestyle and became a couple of dorks, was enormously entertaining. They were successful in the ring too, having the PWI MOTY in 2000 and 2001 and amassing seven tag title reigns. Christian's frustration at being overlooked in the WWE eventually resulted in him becoming the first high profile wrestler to defect to TNA in 2005. He did so in order to win his first world title, the NWA belt, in early 2006. On his return to the WWE he eventually won their secondary world title in 2011, twice, but has never won the WWE title itself.

Next some footage of Jeff being a daredevil and his short attention span. We see him on dirt bikes (he has a track in his garden) and a quad, as well as more of his insane bumps. Matt says he has no fear. An epilepsy-inducing video follows, and Jeff says he has to be more careful now that he is a WWF superstar... then we see him crash his bike. He says his motocross track was getting boring so he built a volcano in his backyard to jump over... Erm... Okay then! Actually it is just a hill with a barrel on fire on top of it, and a trail of burning gasoline down the side. It's pretty cool, but to call it a volcano is a stretch. Who outside of Bam Margera does this stuff in real life?

The Hardys commentate on their cage match at *Unforgiven 2000* against Edge & Christian and modestly call it "great" (Lee called in **¾ elsewhere in this tome). Jeff went out early but still got the piss kicked out of him a bunch of times while on the outside. The psychology here was fairly good, as Jeff realised he had screwed up by leaving the cage with Matt now being outnumbered. Matt took some meaty bumps and talks about them sucking, then Jeff whacked the ref, which was a little out of character, but he was worried about his brother's wellbeing and needed to get back into the ring. He ended up making things worse, but then Matt ducked a Conchairto and fired back. Jeff brought a ladder into play and frustrated Edge because he couldn't get to him, and as he climbed the cage everyone in the building rose to their feet, and he hit a wild corkscrew moonsault off the cage. Lita followed with a sick rana off the ladder on Christian, which with her sloppy track record was a risky spot. A Conchairto on top of the cage to Edge finished him off and the Hardys dropped simultaneously to win the belts. I generally hate tag cage matches for their shitty psychology, but they coped with it quite well here.

We get a few seconds of the forgotten ladder match between the teams on *RAW* and the subsequent Los Conquistadors shenanigans because Edge & Christian weren't allowed another tag title shot. It was all good fun, albeit occasionally confusing for the fans, and ended with the Hardys donning the gear themselves and outsmarting Edge & Christian at their own game before beating them to regain the belts. Jeff claims people were surprised when they revealed themselves as the Hardy Boyz, but no... Everyone had just seen them do the Twist of Fate and the Swanton and got it right away, so that is just nonsense.

To the brilliant TLC II match at *WrestleMania X-Seven*, which Matt and Jeff again watch from home and commentate on. It's interesting to hear them discuss the spots actually, and makes me think that a release with "performer commentary" like you get on say *Red Dwarf* DVDs would have been pretty interesting. Jeff rails on Bubba for a powerbomb through Edge on a table, which saw him land head-first rather than with his back on Edge's stomach. Then Matt gets pissed about Bubba too, this time for cracking him with a ladder in the head that bust him and caused stitches, but didn't look like anything special at all on camera. "Why, Bubba? Why?" pleads Matt. When watching the stuff back Matt comes across like such a mark, which is actually endearing rather than annoying. It is nice that he was still into wrestling even after years of being involved in it. Annoyingly we don't see the end of the TLC II, but rather Matt asking Jeff if the super-ladder Swanton that he did on Spike Dudley and Rhyno is "living for the moment". Jeff doesn't really answer, looking dismissive and bored.

We round things off with other guys putting the duo over as talented and full of heart, with Christian saying they will probably fly solo down the line. They did, eventually, and Jeff ended up as WWE Champion for a while there too and one of the most over performers in the company, before leaving due to burnout, getting busted for alleged opium trafficking and going to rot in the career graveyard that is TNA. Matt on the other hand surprised everyone by being the Marty Jannetty of the two (though he doesn't hold a candle to the outrageously underrated Marty), though he was pretty entertaining as "V.1". Matt says he wants to be respected and be a locker room leader like Steve Austin, the Undertaker or Triple H and that he is "a good person", all of which is just hilarious in hindsight.

VERDICT

It's a fun hour of big bumps and stunts, with some interesting comments and insight into some of the brothers' more famous matches. A lot of what is on offer has been seen before on the *TLC - Tables Ladders Chairs* tape and some was rehashed for the *Before They Were WWF Superstars* release that came out just after this one. But for Hardy Boyz fans there is enough new stuff here to make this a worthwhile watch, and while it might not be among the best profile tapes that the company has put out, it still warrants a viewing. Recommended.

63

NAKED MIDEON

BEFORE THEY WERE WWF SUPERSTARS

CAT NO: WWF54107
RUN TIME: 68 minutes (approx)

James Dixon: This is the chance to go behind the scenes and learn the stories of how some WWF superstars got to the dance. It sounds a bit like watching paint dry to me.

Kurt Angle
Like with all of these mini bios, we start with a snapshot of Kurt's childhood, complete with comments from his brothers and mother. He was a calm kid who didn't get into trouble, so his brothers wanted to toughen him up and sadistically forced him and brother Eric to have boxing matches. His dad used to playfully beat on him too, the poor kid. Kurt says he went into his first wrestling match aged 7 full of confidence because of the tough reputation his surname carried, but he got beat. The experience made him stronger and he trained 3 ½ hours a time, which he says he didn't enjoy but at the same time looked forward to. Talk moves to the unexpected death of his father which served as his inspiration to succeed in wrestling. He went on to beat Sylvester Terkay (yes, the same one) in the NCAA finals, which was the start of his run to Olympic gold. We see some of his insane workouts and training regimes to prepare, such as his 250 hour months (about eight hours a day) where he would do wacky things like sprint up super steep hills with people on his back. As everyone knows it did pay off for Kurt and he took home the gold, which Angle says stirred feelings of relief rather than elation. At least his mother was pleased though, calling it the best feeling of her life, and brother David, wearing a WWF branded shirt, says he was concerned that his mother might die after the win. I bet he doesn't feel inadequate at all in the shadow of his brother's success. Angle rounds off a pretty dull segment by claiming that: "The Olympics is what I was meant to do, but the WWF is my calling". He says he wouldn't want things to have worked out any other way, and that the WWF has been the time of his life. Yes, yes, I'm sure it has.

Molly Holly
Nora 'Molly Holly' Greenwood grew up in an idealist feel-good movie town by the sounds of it, building tree forts in the summer and sledging in the winter. I thought people only did those things in movies? She did some sports, as seemingly all WWF stars did, with her power-lifter dad training her. He doesn't look anything like a power-lifter, he looks like an office worker! Molly was a bit of a tomboy and used to restore cars, which is pretty cool. She is like Megan Fox's character in *Transformers,* only not as stunning. Or slutty. She worked at Subway as a "sandwich artist" (which is Subway company speak, but she still refers to herself as such, making her a perfect fit for the buzzword loving WWF) and she got talking to someone from a wrestling school who encouraged her to give it a try. I wish strangers in the street would randomly direct me towards something that turns out to be my calling, just out of the goodness of their hearts. Sorry, but this whole story is just a little bit too cutesy for me to buy. We see some early footage of Molly training, and then her debut on an outdoor show in Florida in front of a dozen people in the rain. It's pretty cool that they managed to get hold of that. Molly did some indies and received a WCW tryout, which impressed Dean Malenko who invited her to train with him. Randy Savage is brought up and we even see footage of him in WCW to accompany, and Molly tells how he asked her to help train his girlfriends. She did, and ended up on Team Madness, and then on television became one of the many victims of Hulk Hogan's women beating ways. She ended up in the WWF, and was one of the best female performers they have had in my opinion. Natural, different (see: not slutty), pretty and she could work. She was one of the good ones.

Bradshaw
The future JBL talks about growing up in Sweetwater, Texas which is only famous for a Rattlesnake Roundup, which for non-American fans who don't know, picture "Whacking Day" in the Simpsons. Bradshaw says Sweetwater used to get a lot of heat for the barbaric practice from animal rights groups, but his response is: "How in the hell you can be cruel to a snake I will never know! But we weren't cruel to 'em... we just caught 'em and killed 'em" That comment is met with UPROARIOUS laughter from the people shooting this. Apparently Bradshaw

played football... everyone in the WWF played football at some point. He talks about what he did to make a name for himself, but I couldn't care less about football so this is all white noise. All I gleamed from it is that he snapped his leg and it stopped him from being in the NFL. We see old footage of him as a youth cutting a Hulk Hogan promo, which is a pretty neat and funny inclusion. Bradshaw brings up his tag partner on the indies, the late Bobby Duncam Jnr, who he lived with and rode with. Like a few others on this tape, he discusses the perils of the independent scene, the lack of money, the injuries, not being able to eat, etc. It was a different world and made guys into men and made them respect the business more and learn their craft better. When he finally got to the WWF, he was kicked out of the locker room by Tony Garea on his first day, but after a match with Savio Vega he was hired. Of course he was hired; he is tall. Bradshaw recalls working with the Undertaker on a live *RAW* not long after his debut, and he recounts looking around during Taker's entrance and turning to manager Dutch Mantel and asking "What the *hell* am I doing here!?". Dutch told him to just "be aggressive!", so he was, and Bradshaw gives Taker a lot of credit for getting him through it. We wrap up his segment with him saying how happy he is to be in the WWF and that it was worth the hardship to get there. Are you sensing a theme here yet? Everyone loves their jobs with the WWF and everything they did in their lives prior was with the ultimate goal of getting there. Rinse and repeat.

Spike Dudley
"Matthew loved being a fish" says Spike's mother as his parents tell stories about him diving for rocks when he was just two years old. Spike, who is a very good speaker in interviews like this and comes across really well, says "I've always been getting beat up, it's who I am". I kind of feel bad for the guy. He tells how all of his brothers played hockey, but he turned it down because he wanted to watch wrestling instead, because "Bob Backlund was more important to me than anything else". Crikey. Even *he* played football, and says his coach didn't buy it when he first started out because he was so tiny, but he gave him a try and he turned out to be decent enough, though not great. You ever notice in these stories that the coaches are always good guys and supportive, usually progressive thinkers too? You never hear "my coach was an asshole" do you? Unsurprisingly given his stature, Spike didn't make it as a footballer and ended up being a teacher, which he didn't really want to do. In 1993 he saw a commercial for a wrestling school and went for it, determined to live out his dream. "It was brutal" he says, because there were loads of big guys who enjoyed beating him up and throwing him around. He was like a human practice dummy. Spike's parents didn't approve of his drastic choice of career change, because they had spent a fortune on him going to college. "He probably won't need that (for) wrestling" says his mother. Spike worked under the not very creative moniker "Sensational" Matt Hyson, and on his debut he tried a flip plancha from the top, but his opponent was too far away and he sacked it. Big time. He landed squarely on his head and to be honest he is lucky to be alive. The match was actually filmed, and the WWF show the footage. The bump is horrible. Spike was proactive about getting jobs in the big leagues rather than just waiting for opportunities to come his way, and he put together a promo tape and sent it out to prospective promoters. The WWF and WCW rejected him of course, but ECW signed him up. Spike mentions an interviewer once telling him that because of his size he would need to learn crazy flips and aerials in order to make it in the business, but he disagreed because he figured that if you can work then it doesn't matter. The guy told him he would never make it if that was his attitude, and Spike says he would love to hear what he thinks now. Spike's is a nice theory, and in an ideal world that is how it would be, but for 99% of guys that just isn't the case. Size trumps talent in the big leagues, always.

Stacy Keibler
Stacy's background was beauty pageants, dancing, and being a Ravens cheerleader. None of these things are even remotely interesting. She talks about her boyfriend of seven years in school, who she went to all the school dances with where she got to wear some nice dresses... Jesus this is TEDIOUS. She complains that girls go to prom now with their bellies out. Yes, having being influenced to show skin by the likes of you! One Monday evening she was watching *Nitro* with her boyfriend (though I can't quite figure why anyone would have chosen *Nitro* back then) and saw an advert for a competition to be a Nitro Girl. She applied and ended up winning it, and boy I bet her now ex-boyfriend regrets that fateful night to this day. Stacy was briefly in the Nitro Girls, but she was hotter than them all and had the most incredible legs in wrestling, so WCW for once did something smart and put her in a more featured role as Miss Hancock. And then they asked her to work matches after 5 minutes of training, rather than just let her flourish as a non-wrestling performer. We see her wedding to David Flair on *Nitro* as Stacy talks about how much "acting" is involved in wrestling, and that it's like a soap opera. Then she says she always wanted to be in movies and be on television. Well, we knew that one already. This piece was awful.

Billy Gunn
Billy is not a confident interviewee, speaking too fast and punctuating his comments with nervous laughter, even about unpleasant subjects such as the death of his father. He puts over his folks in a big way, saying how his best friend is his mum. He sounds lonely. He then reveals that he lives with his sister and that *they* are best friends. Hang on, what about your mom!? Are you surprised to learn that Gunn played football? Good lord. He was also professional rodeo cowboy before wrestling, which we already knew of course. He says it is very similar to wrestling because you are on the road constantly. That and it is full of carnies. He talks about what a rush it is to ride a bull, and compares it to working in front of 20,000 people. He says it was getting old and too much like a job, which he was told is the sign to get out or you will end up getting hurt. It just so happens there was a wrestling show at the rodeo, and he got involved and had fun. He did some indies for a few years but claims here that he and tag partner Bart Gunn got signed "real quick". Four years is fairly quick in those days, but it was hardly rodeo rink to WWF rings overnight like he implies. Billy says the Smoking Gunns gimmick was inspired by his background, and his rodeo days helped make them feel more natural and legitimate. I can't say I particular agree. I thought the Gunns were hard work to watch and their gimmick was a cartoonish throwback to a bygone era.

William Regal
We go to visit Blackpool with an accentless William Regal, which is one of the biggest shitholes I have ever been to in my life, but Regal puts it over big as the "second most visited city in Europe". He talks about his early days wrestling at Blackpool Pleasure Beach, where carny promoters would offer drunk punters shoots with the wrestlers. The matches were far from predetermined, they were all legitimate. A loss to one of the punters meant game over for the wrestler, because it cost the promoter money. We actually see some footage from Regal's days working there, which includes the promoter inviting any "perverts and queers" to get involved, with a reward of £10 cash if they could survive. Regal takes us to some of the

dumps he has wrestled in and tells a story about kicking a heckler in the head when he tried to get in the ring, which got him popped by the rowdy crowd. We take a turn off into the rough part of town, and Regal takes us on a tour of the dossholes and fighting bars, before telling a story of walking into a pub and getting glassed the second he walked through the door. Yep, that sounds like Blackpool to me. We see footage of Regal against the woeful Giant Haystacks during the post glory days of British wrestling, which handily demonstrates exactly why the razzmatazz of American wrestling quickly overtook it in popularity. Regal gets all emotional about the shitty building he used to wrestle in, and says that while it is an honour to be part of the "biggest show in the world" with the WWF, the Blackpool venue remains the best. Uh huh.

The Hardy Boyz
This is the same footage as from the Hardy's VHS, but obviously reduced down. Matt hasn't changed at all since he was about three. They briefly talk about their mum dying young from cancer and their dad (who Jeff says is his hero) raising them alone and disciplining them well (though, look how they turned out...). Matt says they always loved wrestling, and we see their home videos from when they used to wrestle each other as kids with all their cute little characters. We skip them training themselves and see some of their early indy work, then a really bizarre shot of them and two unidentified guys in nWo shirts. The thing is, Matt and Jeff started with the WWF in 1994, and were pretty much there ever since on and off. Parading around in shirts of the opposition's hottest act was a silly thing to be doing. They talk about how their father wasn't impressed with the lack of money they were making and wanted them to get a real job, though now they are rich and famous he likes the business, obviously. Bruce Prichard puts them over for their hard work and heart, and talks about them being with the company as semi regulars for years and then finally giving them a contract. We see the contract, which they didn't even read and just signed. Marks. It is a nice story and a feel good story at that, but the way they both turned out as drug abusers, rehab frequenters and in the case of Matt, a woman beater too, makes this more sad when viewed with the benefit of hindsight.

Lita
Holy shit was Lita ugly growing up. All of this is just taken from the Lita tape *Lita - It Just Feels Right*, as we go over her experiences in Mexico and her love of the culture, though whether or not that includes her stint spent doing erotic dancing to pay for her training is not mentioned. We go to her kitchen at home and see her vast mask collection, with her pointing out the likes of La Parka, Rey Misterio Jr, Psicosis and Aguila - mentioning that he become Essa Rios, which I am pretty sure the WWF didn't mention when the character debuted- as well as outing Val Venis as having worked under a hood across the border in a pre-porn star life (as Steele). I didn't realise she was such a super geek, but I kind of like her for more knowing that she is. She then tells the tale that she turned up at an ECW show and got talking to Tommy Dreamer, asking him for a chance to work out with some of the guys and just generally hang around. She ended up talking to Tajiri and Super Crazy, who she knew from Mexico, and worked out in the ring with Tajiri a bit, which got her on the evening's card. She had a run as Miss Congeniality, but it was hardly a memorable one, truth be told. We briefly meet her dog and get a story about a job she had at a dog pound, before she tells fans who write letters to her to stay focused and make sure everything they do leads to their dreams. She was a pretty good role model actually, until she became a two-timing ho bag and the crowd majorly turned on her.

Edge & Christian
The two lifetime best buddies first met each other at school, with the majority of this piece being a tour of the building while the pair reminisce. We see some of Edge's artwork that he did when he was younger, and it is actually quite brilliant. He is a hell of an artist. Christian used to play hockey and at one point considered going pro, and in a strange coincidence he once won a trophy that was named after Edge's late uncle. Edge took the death of that uncle hard because he was like a father figure to him, and he found wrestling to fill the gap in his life, though his mother dismissed aspirations of him becoming a pro, telling him "I'm not sure wrestling will be around then". Christian on the other hand got hooked while resting up on his couch recovering from a hockey injury. Like every other kid who pays no attention to the "don't try this at home" warnings, he used to wrestle with his brothers in their living room, and then later with Edge at school, where like the Hardys they had dozens of creative characters. Edge couldn't afford wrestling training as it cost $3000, but in a bout of fortune the Toronto Sun ran an essay writing competition where the winner would receive free training, and Edge won it. He thus attended Ron Hutchinson's wrestling school, a school that would later also produce the likes of Beth Phoenix, Trish Stratus, Joe Legend and of course Christian. Christian took an altogether different route, flunking out of his final semester of college but taking his student loan to pay for the training. His dad is amused about it now, but freely admits that he wouldn't have looked back on it with such humour if he hadn't ended up making it. It makes you wonder how many alternative stories there are out there of guys and gals who have tried something similar and failed to make the grade. The pair talk about their horrific experiences wrestling in the backass ends of Canada where you could only get to the venues via boat or plane, or by driving over the frozen lakes in the winter. They tell a hellish story about the power going out in -40 weather, and nearly dying as a result. Those guys paid their dues and earned their WWF spot and their story is genuinely nice. Edge ended up as a World Champion and in the WWF Hall of Fame, and Christian had a long tenure in the company, twice actually, and held multiple titles and is generally well respected. Neither guy ever did anything to shame their careers either (other than Edge having a thing for the ladies), and their story of breaking through and living their dream together is a great one, and a good end to a drab tape.

VERDICT

Whether this tape is good or bad really rather depends on your tastes. If you are into the stories of famous guys and gals before they were known to the world, then this is the tape for you. If on the other hand like me you skip the parts in autobiographies about people's tedious childhoods, then you won't like this either. I found it unspeakably boring. Everyone played football or some other sport and then turned to wrestling when they were either too injured or too crap to do it anymore. Everyone loves the WWF and are living their dreams. Well great big whoop-de-do. The odd tiny slice of interesting footage aside, this is a pass.

26

EDGE & CHRISTIAN

SURVIVOR SERIES 2001

CAT NO: WWF54109
RUN TIME: 156 minutes (approx)

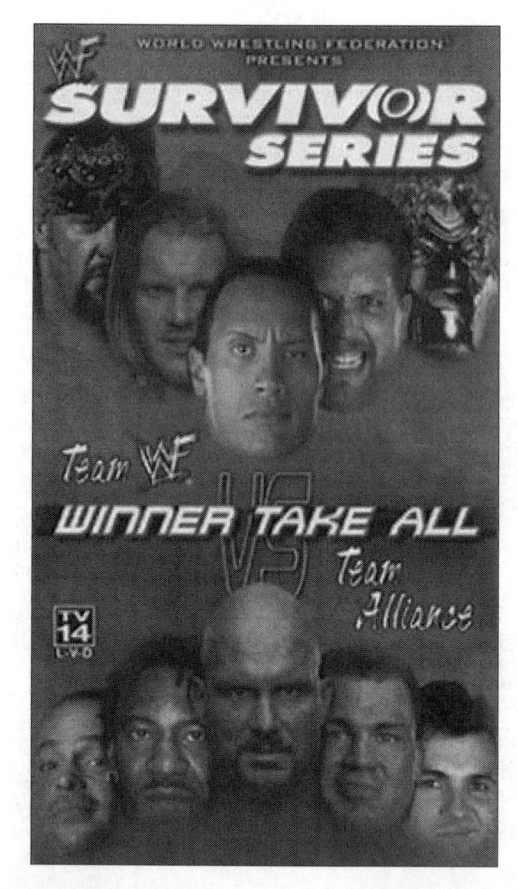

Lee Maughan: Barely four months have passed since the whopping 770,000 buys pulled by the *InVasion* pay-per-view, and already Vince McMahon has decided to draw a line under the whole WWF vs. Alliance issue. But why did it follow in the footsteps of the Jim Crockett Promotions buyout of Bill Watts' UWF group to become such an unmitigated critical and commercial failure? Well, firstly there's the fact that none of the major names associated with WCW came along for the ride, leaving Booker T and DDP to lead the charge early on. There was the introduction of Paul Heyman's ECW and said group aligning with the WCW invaders, a move which made absolutely no sense to anyone who knew the history of the Extreme organisation, and served to blow at least a year's worth of storylines in the span of about an hour.

There was the fact the entire invasion was simply a backdrop to yet another chapter in the McMahon family feud saga that was already played out, with Shane McMahon heading up WCW in place of Eric Bischoff, and the presentation of Stephanie McMahon-Helmsley as the owner of ECW, even though Paul Heyman himself was sat right there at ringside every Monday night, calling the action.

And then there was the burial of the Alliance's top talent, with Booker T losing several times over to the Rock, and DDP getting continuously battered by the Undertaker until his credibility was completely shot. There was also the installation of the WWF's top star and champion, 'Stone Cold' Steve Austin, as the leader of the Alliance group in a vain attempt to add more credibility to the outfit. Aside from the fact no WWF fan wanted to boo Austin, the whole exercise simply served to render the invasion yet another WWF vs. WWF feud, emphasised further when names like the Dudley Boyz, Rhyno, William Regal (all ECW or WCW guys in the past but since established as WWF names) and the likes of Christian and Test (WWF creations to the core) jumped ship to bolster the Alliance crew. Hardly anybody bought into it, certainly far fewer than the 770,000 who literally bought into the *InVasion* show, and McMahon felt he had no choice but to abandon the whole thing and hit the reset button on *RAW* the next night.

Before that however, there's still the small matter of mopping up the debris with this show, a card ludicrously labelled "the most important, most significant pay-per-view sports entertainment extravaganza of all times" during the show opening. Mick Foley, again working as commissioner has declared all the titles will be unified tonight, and there'll also be an immunity battle royal to guarantee at least one year of survival for whoever wins it, with either the WWF or the Alliance going out of business based on whoever wins the big 10-man main event elimination match later on this evening.

From the Greensboro Coliseum in the old WCW stomping grounds of Greensboro, North Carolina. Hosts, sadly for the last time, are Jim Ross and Paul Heyman.

WWF European Championship
Christian (c) vs. Al Snow
This was set up on *Sunday Night Heat* right before the pay-per-view went on the air so, yes, we're actually kicking off this most important supercard of all time with last-minute filler. Snow is on something of a renewed push as the head trainer for MTV's *Tough Enough* and co-host of *Sunday Night Heat*, although how important this match really is can be traced back to the November 1st edition of *SmackDown!* (taped October 30th in Cincinnati, Ohio) where Christian won the title from Bradshaw in a match that was actually cut from the broadcast due to time constraints.

Christian hits an inverted DDT that JR erroneously calls the Unprettier, then he rolls through a crossbody for two but gets blasted with a brutal Snowplow for a nearfall, getting his boot on the ropes at the count of two. On the defensive, he tricks Snow into chasing him which he turns to his advantage by crotching him on the ropes, and that's enough to set up the real Unprettier for the win in about six-and-a-half minutes of a pretty decent match.
Final Rating: **½

- In the locker room, the Alliance team begins to unravel thanks to Mr. McMahon planting the seeds of doubt regarding a claim that Steve Austin is secretly a mole and is going to turn on the

Alliance tonight and rejoin the WWF.

- Elsewhere, Mr. McMahon assuages Linda's fears about the end of the WWF by calling the elimination match tonight a "calculated risk", just like all of his business decisions. Vince sure has some gall to put himself over like that in the year the XFL lost him a reported after-tax $36.2 million. Roving reporter Michael Cole drops by to ask for some thoughts on tonight's main event with Vince replying "You seem a little dejected Michael Cole, like you might be out of a job tonight!" If only.

William Regal vs. Tajiri
This was set up by Regal landing a butterfly bomb on Tajiri's girlfriend Torrie (an Alliance member who has sort-of switched sides thanks to the relationship, thus guaranteeing her job security), and is something of a blow-off for Tajiri having spent most of the year as ex-commissioner Regal's houseboy of sorts. This match is also a replacement for Tajiri's originally scheduled WWF Light Heavyweight Title vs. WCW Cruiserweight Title unification match with X-Pac, scrapped when X-Pac picked up an injury. Oddly, the WWF would skewer from usual procedure following this show and actually scrap its own belt in favour of retaining a rebranded WWF Cruiserweight Title.

Regal catches a kick to the face early and his nose starts bleeding, which was actually a big problem for him around this period until he got surgery to correct it in 2002. They blow the Tarantula on the first attempt but Regal improvises so well that they actually get back into it without making it look at all hokey. Kudos. Then they work in a brutal looking Cactus Jack-style hangman's noose spot with the top and middle ropes as Tajiri wails and screams in pain, so supervillain Regal starts pulling him by the legs in an attempt to strangle him! Back in the ring, Tajiri escapes a butterfly bomb with a huracánrana and sets up for the Buzzsaw Kick, but Regal ducks and finishes with the butterfly bomb around three minutes in. Torrie slides in to check on Tajiri after the match so Regal gives her another butterfly bomb before pulling a classic gurn as the blood continues to gush from his nostrils. Paltry amount of time aside, this was delightfully stiff stuff.
Final Rating: **

- In the make-up room, Test gets oiled up by a seamstress before Stacy Keibler arrives to caress his buttocks. They'd pair up as an on-screen couple the following year, based on their real-life relationship.

WCW United States Championship
WWF Intercontinental Championship
Edge (c) vs. Test (c)
JR explains that the overall victor in tonight's "winner takes all" match will determine which title survives, kind of negating the entire concept of unifying the belts in the first place with the suggestion that one will actually be dissolved rather than absorbed. Given that the Intercontinental Title would be unified with Triple H's newly declared World Heavyweight crown in 2002 only to be exhumed in 2003, followed a short time later by the introduction of a new United States Championship exclusive to the *SmackDown!* brand, it's not like any of this mattered anyway.

Speaking of not mattering, Heyman brings up the names of Johnny Valentine, Ric Flair and Harley Race to sprinkle some prestige over proceedings, but curiously refrains from mentioning the likes of Jim Duggan, Konnan, Steve McMichael and the One Man Gang. Also unmentioned is the sheer volume of title changes both belts had undergone in recent times. Indeed, the Intercontinental Title had changed hands as many times over the course of the previous three years as it had over its first sixteen, with ten different wrestlers trading the belt in 2001 alone, followed closely by the U.S. Title on nine. With that much activity, it was hard to keep track and consequently, the titles quickly began to mean less and less with each passing month, week and day.

The bulk of the match is controlled by Test, cutting a slow pace with power moves and chinlocks. His big boots, pump-handle slams and full nelson slams are all fine, but there's no sense of urgency or excitement to the match at all, at least until Edge finally starts mounting his comeback with a big spear. Unfortunately, the big finish is Edge scoring a cheeky roll-up off a full nelson slam for the pin, which is about the cheapest ending you can deliver without running any interference, as Edge was dominated almost the entire way, coming out of it looking like a fluke rather than a guy who just made history. In fact, the match felt more like an audition for Test, even though foresight from most at the time suggested Edge was the horse to bet on. Hindsight proved those betters right.
Final Rating: **

- Back in the locker rooms, Stephanie McMahon-Helmsley spills her guts to Kurt Angle that she can't bare the thought of losing everything with the death of the Alliance and being forced to become a "normal person."

- Elsewhere, Lita worries openly to Jeff Hardy about a curiously absent Matt Hardy's recent behaviour. Matt soon arrives from his locker room to lay the blame on stressing out over the fact he might soon be out of a job, an explanation Lita accepts… until Trish exits the locker room shortly afterwards, building to a feud that never really happened, at least not until much later.

Steel Cage Match
WCW Tag Team Championship
WWF Tag Team Championship
The Dudley Boyz (c) vs. The Hardy Boyz (c)
Heyman, refusing to go out any other way than kicking and screaming on his last night at the booth, tries to inject a modicum of interest into this one by pointing out that these two names have never actually squared off inside a cage before. Points for trying, but this feud was pretty well played out by this point. Amazingly, they'd still be rumbling come *WrestleMania X8*.

There's some rather dumb rules in effect here (rather choreographing the finish too, I might add) as either both members of one team need to escape the cage to win, or one member of the opposing team must be pinned. They also start by actually adhering to regular tag team rules, which I've never much cared for in cage matches, though that's soon dropped in favour of an all-in brawl, negating the entire opening portion of the match. Once they actually get going they run through their usual routine before the cage finally comes into play and Heyman, referencing history like the ghost of Tony Schiavone tonight, barks "Ooooh, what a rush!" as the Dudleys hit the Dudleyville Device.

In a couple of painful looking spots, Matt first gets avalanched face-first into the cage by Bubba Ray before getting his right leg trapped in the steel bars at the top of the cage, leaving him hung upside down where Bubba rams him into the wire mesh a few times. I imagine the torque on his shinbone and calf muscles there must have been excruciating. Bubba then calls for the tables, but they're in a cage so Stacy flashes her buttocks at Nick Patrick and picks his pocket… for the key I mean, unlocking the door like a chastity belt before slowly sliding in her big, hard plank. Matt blocks a 3D attempt however, but like a total moron, opts to clamber out of the cage, leaving his brother alone with both Dudleys, the *exact same* thing that happened to DDP when Kanyon fled the cage in their match with the Undertaker and Kane at *SummerSlam* and indeed in the brothers' own cage match against Edge & Christian back at *Unforgiven 2000*.

Jeff hurls D-Von into the cage as JR breaks out one of his increasingly bizarre lines about how the steel "does not taste like chocolate." Clearly this whole invasion thing was the straw that finally pushed the guy completely off his rocker. And speaking of being completely off his rocker, Jeff actually makes it up the cage but just can't help himself, launching a Swanton off the top, crashing through the table in the ring but missing the previously prone D-Von who rolls out of the way. The pin there is academic as three seconds just isn't enough time for Matt to get back in the cage as, just as had happened at *SummerSlam 2000*, the Hardys blow the big one in their home state. That finish would be the catalyst for a Matt heel turn that didn't really go anywhere, even though Jeff was the one being selfish. Good enough for a cage match with no blood, although the tolerance for more Dudleys vs. Hardys is now wearing extremely thin.
Final Rating: ***¼

- In an absolutely ludicrous piece of scheduling, there now airs a commercial advertising all of the WWF's upcoming live shows. You know, just in case they don't go out of business tonight. Oh, and they promise Steve Austin and Rob Van Dam will both be there too.

- Over at WWF New York, Commissioner Foley accidentally manages to piss off two sets of fans, the ones in Greensboro and those watching the pay-per-view at home, by not bothering to show up to "the most important, most significant pay-per-view sports entertainment extravaganza of all times", and also his home state fans and fellow revellers by proclaiming that he'd rather be at the show after all than stuck… right here… at WWF New York! More importantly, Mick quite rightly points out that the if the commissioner has to answer to Vince McMahon anyway, then the whole concept of a commissionership is a joke, and he'll be at *RAW* tomorrow to raise the issue with Vince. Man, imagine how downbeat and dejected he would have felt if he'd been an interim assistant general manager whose jurisdiction was strictly limited to *SmackDown*!

- Back in Greensboro, Scotty 2 Hotty bumps into Test, who asks Scotty if he's in the battle royal then kicks his ass and takes his place. Poor Scotty. Last year he was part of one of the most popular acts in the company, but with Rikishi and Grandmaster Sexay both gone, he's become a complete geek.

Immunity Battle Royal
Your competitors: Lance Storm, Justin Credible, Raven, Stevie Richards, Diamond Dallas Page, Tommy Dreamer, Billy Kidman, Shawn Stasiak and Hurricane Helms for the Alliance, and Crash Holly, Funaki, Perry Saturn, Albert, Spike Dudley, the APA, Billy Gunn and Chuck Palumbo for the WWF, Palumbo having switched sides since he began teaming with Gunn. Test is also in there after punking out Scotty, but why an Alliance guy should get to replace a WWF guy is beyond me.

Some of these guys (DDP, Raven and Storm in particular) feel wasted being in this thing. Stasiak doesn't, and he gets his comedy charge in immediately and gets sidestepped and flung out by Bradshaw. Raven and Richards wind up going nose-to-nose in a really nice nod to long time ECW fans, as Test and Albert explode on the outside. Tazz quickly arrives, having missed the opening bell and with no loyalty to either side after previously quitting the Alliance. JR asks Heyman if Tazz might be "homicidal, genocidal?" Er, wrong guy, Jim. Tazz eventually gets dumped out by Gunn whilst jaw jacking with Heyman, allowing Tazz to go after Heyman who hides behind JR. That of course is all the ammunition JR needs to break out the sexism, blithering: "You old broad! You old woman! Sit down and act like a man for once in your life! You ran like a woman!" Thankfully, Heyman calls him out on it, to which JR has no comeback.

Bradshaw clotheslines Hurricane out, prompting Heyman to go on yet another history-fuelled tirade about how in the glory days, over the top rope was a disqualification in the NWA and Bradshaw should be eliminated. Albert dumps out Saturn, which is a WWF guy eliminating a WWF guy. I know that it's really every man for himself and only one guy gets immunity, but wouldn't you all team up to eliminate the opposition first and guarantee that at least one of your crew gets the immunity? Palumbo hoys out DDP from behind, perhaps finally paying off all that Insiders vs. Natural Born Thrillers stuff from WCW earlier in the year, but Storm and Credible decide to reunite the Impact Players in another nod to ECW, striking Palumbo off the list with a double superkick.

From out of nowhere, former Misfits in Action General Rection and Lieutenant Loco, the current Hugh Morrus and Chavo Guerrero, join the fray dressed in street clothes, having been fired from the Alliance. They get absolutely no reaction but manage to dump Credible, Raven and Funaki anyway. I wouldn't worry about it, Funaki would seemingly carry immunity with him all the way through to April 2010, when he was finally released by WWE after 12 years of doing almost nothing of note.

From there, the eliminations come thick and fast until just four remain: Bradshaw, Test, Storm and Gunn. Test thinks he's dumped Gunn, then dumps out Bradshaw, who's busy brawling with Storm on the apron. He turns round and sees Gunn still in the ring so they charge and Billy ducks a big boot but eats another on the rebound and that puts him out, giving Test immunity from being fired for the next year. Lucky us.
Final Rating: *

- And now, another tweaked airing of the Creed '*My Sacrifice*' video, because what this show was crying out for at this point was yet more filler material to eat up pay-per-view airtime.

Six-Pack Challenge
WWF Women's Championship
Trish Stratus vs. Ivory vs. Mighty Molly vs. Lita vs. Jacqueline vs. Jazz
The title is vacant here, with previous champion Chyna having vanished from WWF television after discovering the real-life affair between her boyfriend Paul 'Triple H' Levesque and Stephanie McMahon. Jazz is a mystery entrant into the match but she gets absolutely no reaction from the crowd who have no idea who she is, and probably didn't even know who she was while she was in ECW. She also makes the classic first night mistake of being overexcited, going overboard on a spear attempt and making a mess of a tumble through the ropes to the outside. One of the things they try to drill into you as a

wrestler is that if you ever feel like you're going too slow, you actually need to slow down, and Jazz was quite the opposite here.

With six women in there and less than five minutes to go around, there's no time for any story to develop, and not much time for anyone to do anything, although Jacqueline gets a few stiff chops in and Mighty Molly hits a nice somersault butt splash from the top. Lita and Jacqueline team up for Poetry in Motion but Jackie quickly double crosses her, which makes sense because this is first fall takes it all. Jacqueline is just on fire here, working in a pinfall reversal sequence with Ivory before Trish comes in to a big reaction, once again confirming that Divas wrestling in the WWF is all about magazine cover good looks and big plastic tits rather than wrestling ability.

Lita hits a moonsault that looks to be the finish but Trish backdrops her out to the floor, and Trish then reverses something from Ivory that leads to the Stratusfaction for the win and Trish's first title, at a time when she was still seen as a valet rather than a worker and somewhat undeserving of the accolade. That said, while she was still pretty green here (and indeed, she initially went for Stratusfaction too early and Ivory had to pull her back), she was showing vast improvements in the ring over her rookie season last year.
Final Rating: *½

- Backstage, Vince gives his team a big pep talk. I think we can all just be thankful that he isn't giving it to himself, as had been the original plan before an injury (or common sense, depending on who you believe) prevailed and saw Big Show replace Vince on the team. The idea that this whole match was going to centre around Vince and Shane is yet another clue to the shortcomings of the whole stupid angle.

Winner Takes All Elimination Match
Team WWF (The Rock, Chris Jericho, The Undertaker, Kane & The Big Show) vs. The Alliance (Steve Austin, Kurt Angle, Rob Van Dam, Booker T & Shane McMahon)
Where to start with this catastrophe? The final showdown of the one feud fans had waited years to see, and the one feud people were still prepared to believe was real to them, dammit, and the Alliance team is built around WWF stalwarts 'Stone Cold' Steve Austin, Kurt Angle and son of the boss Shane McMahon. Brilliant. Worse still, if you stop to consider the stakes as laid down by the mandate that all current champions will be retained, you'll realise that very of the Alliance guys have anything to lose. If the fact that Christian is the European champion, the Dudleys are the tag champs and Test has immunity isn't enough to tip you off to the finish, or the fact that they were all established WWF guys by the time the invasion began, then also consider that Austin is the WWF champion and RVD is the Hardcore champion, making both safe regardless of the outcome. On top of that, Shane is still Linda's son, and it was her who allowed him to bring WCW to *RAW* in the first place just to screw with Vince, so he has a fallback, and (spoiler alert) Angle is the WWF's mole, meaning he has nothing to lose either regardless of which side wins.

Perhaps worse still is that fact that if you delve just a little deeper, you may recall that Austin was fired for real by WCW in 1995, that Angle debuted for the WWF after they'd all but won the *actual* war with WCW, and that Van Dam had previously made his name working for an organisation known to detest WCW, meaning that, along with WWF lifer Shane, you've got what was presented as a WCW built around just one guy still associated with the brand in the eyes of the fans, Booker T, who has just spent the last several months being made to look second rate by genuine headline star the Rock. Gee, I wonder who'll win this?!

Earlier, I noted that the Hardy Boyz-Dudley Boyz feud felt pretty well played out by November 2001, and as if to hammer home the increasingly repetitive nature of WWF booking by this point, things kick off with another Rock-Austin showdown, two guys who have been scrapping on and off since 1997, and with two *WrestleMania* main events against each other to their credit. In the years to come, WWE would book the likes of John Cena and Randy Orton against each other almost to the point of self-parody, rustling up just about every conceivable gimmick they could to keep the feud going until they actually ran out and felt forced to present the idea of a non-gimmicked, straight wrestling match between the two at the 2014 *Royal Rumble* as a novelty.

The first elimination comes almost 13-minutes into the bout and it's the disposable Big Show (and how ludicrous it is to label a seven foot-plus, five hundred pounder as "disposable") after Angle, Booker and Van Dam all hit their finishers on him. Naturally, Shane is the one who gets to polish him off after a big elbow. What a shrewd move that was from Vince, to pick a giant who did absolutely sod all before getting his head caved in. In fact, Shane scoring the pin after all those finishers makes sense when you consider that Vince was supposed to be in that spot originally, and it harkens back to an amusing story Bret Hart wrote in his book *Hitman: My Real Life in the Cartoon World of Wrestling*, recalling a time in a strip club in 1991 when a drunken Vince was blasted with the Doomsday Device by the Legion of Doom and also took a Hart Attack from Bret and Jim Neidhart. Shane himself is sent packing a couple of minutes later after taking a string of finishers from the babyfaces, Jericho getting the honours after a Lionsault.

Kane and RVD go at it next, before Booker comes in from behind to help out Van Dam, as I suddenly realise how many different sets of past and future tag team champions there are in this match: Rock & Undertaker, Rock & Jericho, Undertaker & Big Show, Undertaker & Kane, Undertaker & Austin, Jericho & Big Show, Kane & Big Show, Kane & RVD, and Booker & RVD, with Angle and Shane the only guys to never hold the titles with anyone at all. Van Dam hits the Five Star Frog Splash and a flying kick to polish Kane off.

Undertaker destroys all four remaining Alliance members by himself (of course he does!) and gives Angle the Last Ride, but Austin sneaks in and nails him with a Stunner, putting Angle on top to eliminate him at 20:02, leaving it 4-on-2 in favour of the Alliance, with just Jericho and the Rock on the WWF side of things. God, where's Triple H when you need him? He could squash all four Alliance guys by himself *and* the WWF team for good measure! Regardless, Rock pins Booker once more for old time's sake, reducing the deficit to one.

Jericho and Van Dam go next, with Jericho landing his new finisher, the rather short-lived and mostly forgotten Breakdown, completely out of nowhere, pinning RVD to almost zero reaction. You can perhaps blame that on the fact the Breakdown hasn't had enough time to get over yet, along with the notion that, despite being part of the WWF team, Jericho is something of a heel given his ongoing feud with Rock, coupled with the overwhelmingly positive babyface reactions drawn by RVD. And for those wondering what the Breakdown actually is, it's a full nelson facebuster, similar to the Miz's Skull Crushing Finalé.

25-minutes in now, and down to 2 against 2 as a four-man brawl breaks out, Texas Tornado style, with Rocky taking a catapult into the ringpost. Jericho starts hesitating on spots, then Austin goes for a middle rope elbow but decides Jericho is too far away and doesn't bother. Rock eventually gets back in and catches a dragon screw leg whip on Angle, finishing him with the Sharpshooter at just under 32-minutes. Which brings up a good point: why did Angle just spend the best part of half an hour fighting *against* the WWF team? I can only presume he was hedging his bets in case the Alliance pitched a shutout. Bwahahaha! I know, I know. With the WWF leading, Jericho can't finish Austin off and gets caught with a roll-up for the elimination, angrily blasting Rock with the Breakdown on his way out, not because he's joining the Alliance, just because he's a jerk, and a returning Undertaker chews him out over it, which doesn't really go anywhere.

That leaves Rock and Austin as the final two. Can you say "déjà vu?" Unlike the aforementioned Cena and Orton or the Hardys and Dudleys however, Austin and the Rock are just on another plane completely so the action remain exciting rather than tiresome, and the parameters have also changed to where Austin is now the heel and Rock the babyface, so the bout at least doesn't feel like a carbon copy of what came before. Nowhere else is this role reversal more prominent than when Rock blasts Austin with the Stunner and Austin returns fire with a Rock Bottom. Of course, the conclusion to a major WWF pay-per-view match doesn't come and go without shenanigans, so Alliance official Nick Patrick knocks out Earl Hebner but fails to give Austin an easy fast count (perhaps an unintentional reference to the controversial finish to the Hollywood Hogan vs. Sting match at *Starrcade '97*), so Austin unwisely knocks him out. That gives Angle the opening to slide in and smash Austin in the chops with the WWF Title belt in a nice full-circle call back to Austin's heel turn at *InVasion*, and the Rock Bottom finishes for the WWF, confirming that no, we won't be watching *Nitro* tomorrow after all.

On a positive note, the match did pick up a lot after the more tokenistic guys vanished and it never felt anything close to its 45-minute running time, but it just didn't come anywhere close to the level of epic a winners takes all, losing promotion vanishes forever 10-man elimination tussle should, nor was it ever going to. Worse still, it just came down to Rock vs. Austin yet again when it could have been used to elevate someone like Jericho (who admittedly got a massive push the next month at *Vengeance*), Booker or Van Dam, and the final shot wasn't even of any of the wrestlers, but of Vince McMahon with his arms raised in triumph, like he'd been responsible for all of this. Which, in many unflattering ways, he was.
Final Rating: ***¾

VERDICT

And like that, it was gone. In fact, it may as well have never even happened, as the WWF completely set the rest button the following night on *RAW*, as with no outside force to defend his kingdom against, Mr. McMahon regressed to his standard heel character, along with Kurt Angle whose WWF-saving heroics somehow turned him into a villain in the eyes of the fans. Not to worry, because that alignment allowed Steve Austin to once again become the promotion's top babyface for absolutely no reason, even though the damage had already been done.

In addition to those changes at the top of the card, Paul Heyman was removed from the announce booth for real and replaced with the returning Jerry Lawler, despite his wonderful edgy chemistry with JR, intricate knowledge of wrestling psychology and status as the being the best talker to come along the pike in years; Stephanie McMahon-Helmsley was reinstated by simply apologising to daddy dearest, clearing the path for her to form a bizarre alliance with Chris Jericho in his feud with the returning Triple H; and William Regal was reinstalled to the active roster after becoming the first unwilling participant in McMahon's ludicrous "Kiss My Ass Club", completely restoring the status quo to pre-*WrestleMania X-SEVEN* levels. In time, many of the remaining Alliance losers would beg their way into regular spots on the WWF roster, after being humiliated one last time in portraying out-of-work scrubs or being show in demeaning janitorial roles at WWF New York, as was the case for Lance Storm.

Perhaps most frustratingly of all was the fact that the WWF refused to bring in any of WCW's top names like Eric, Bischoff, Scott Steiner or Bill Goldberg to add depth and genuine star power to the Alliance squad, instead preferring to pepper it with WWF contracted guys. At the time, the WWF's excuse was the cost of bringing those names in would upset locker room morale and the company's pay structure (WCW's top names weren't actually signed to contracts with WCW, but rather with parent company Time Warner owing to their giant million dollar-plus salaries.) Of course, Bischoff, Steiner and Goldberg would all debut in WWE over the next couple of years anyway, along with the New World Order contingent of Hollywood Hogan, Kevin Nash and Scott Hall. All of those guys would have paid for their over-inflated contracts several times over if the *InVasion* pay-per-view buyrate was anything to go by. Even guys like Rey Misterio, Jr. (who later became a main event star in WWE) and Ernest 'the Cat' Miller eventually made it onto McMahon's various broadcasts, long after it was too late to make a difference. And infuriatingly, Ric Flair, the man fans most associated with the WCW brand (aside perhaps from long-time WWF holdout Sting) and a personality who could have made a genuine difference to the whole thing, appeared on *RAW* just *one day* after the angle was killed stone dead.

Ladies and gentlemen, once again I give you Vincent Kennedy McMahon, Wrestling Genius.™

57

STING - LONGTIME WWF HOLDOUT

THE ROCK - JUST BRING IT!

CAT NO: WWF54111
RUN TIME: 77 minutes (approx)

James Dixon: This is the third Rock VHS release, all of which came out during the years covered by this volume.

The subtitle of the tape ("just bring it") is the first point of discussion, with Rock giving us insight on how he came up with it. He talks about a particularly gruelling schedule where he went from filming for *The Mummy Returns* in Morocco to appearing live on *RAW* a day later, and his reaction to it all was "just bring it, bring all of it". He says he liked it and it ended up becoming part of his persona, and it does indeed fit the character perfectly. We go to brief footage from the absurd main event of *King of the Ring 2000* where Rock pinned Vince McMahon to win a six man tag match and also the WWF Championship. Don't ask. Rock modestly says that selling out arenas and doing large buyrates is a collaborative effort from everyone in the WWF, and is not just down to one guy. He is right of course, because from the Attitude Era and beyond it was the company brand that sold tickets rather than any individual talent, but there is no doubt that Rock (along with Steve Austin) being on the cards made a huge difference in getting the company to that level, and either of them appearing was a difference maker.

We get some rare behind the scenes locker room footage of Rock preparing for his match and generally larking around with some of the boys. Scotty 2 Hotty wants to get his cock out but Rock is having none of that: "I've seen it already. Now I know why they call it the Worm". Rock wanders around a bit and finds an embarrassed Kurt Angle in the shower, who quickly hides his manhood and pleads with Rock to go away. "You're begging me to turn heel, aren't ya?" jokes Angle to Rocky. Next, rare house show footage from a match against Steve Austin! Not much of it is shown, but we do see Rock wearing Austin's waistcoat and prancing around, which is a spot they lifted and used again for their *WrestleMania XIX* ultimate blow-off match. Following the house show bout, the two fierce rivals put their differences aside and do some impromptu karaoke together, then Rock gives Austin a Stunner. Backstage immediately afterward Rock is unlacing his boots, and he comments that Austin is still out there entertaining the fans with his post-show antics. We see similar footage of Austin doing the same thing on his *Stone Cold Steve Austin - What?* Video release, again showing what a dedicated performer he is and how he is willing to go that extra mile to make sure the punters get their money's worth. It is something he deserves more credit for than he perhaps gets.

We go behind the scenes of *The Mummy Returns*, which is kind of bittersweet to watch because it was ultimately the first step that took Rock away from wrestling, but at the same time catapulted him into the mainstream consciousness and made him a huge star. We hear Arnold Vosloo who plays Imhotep in the franchise and he talks about first hearing of the Rock, asking in his distinctive South African accent: "What's this "rock" business?", which tickles me somewhat. The film's director Stephen Sommers puts Rock over, and they discuss a fantasy match between the Mummy and the Rock characters. If it was made in the 80s, you can guarantee Vince McMahon would have done it on PPV too.

Back to wrestling, and Rock talks about promos, saying how he feels that every one of them means stepping up to the proverbial plate. In keeping with that analogy, it is fair to say that Rock had a higher homerun ratio that nearly anyone else in the history of the business. We see some highlights from recent Rock promos, including him asking Steve Austin for a hug and verbally decimating Booker T. Rock talks about finding the balance between seriousness and adding humour, then lets us in on the fact that all of his backstage promos are done live, before adding that he likes to reference things about the city he is in that night in order to make the interviews more personal. Or get cheap pops... same difference.

That leads us to *Fully Loaded* and the excellent Rock vs. Chris Benoit main event for the WWF Title. Rock had some great matches on PPV in 2000 and this is another, probably one of the best actual wrestling matches of his career, though it is also a slugfest and a brawl too. There is a little bit of everything. The match is shown in highlight form set to dramatic music, though the structure and flow is fairly well retained, which is a change from the norm on these kind of releases. The finish sees Shane McMahon get involved and belt referee Earl Hebner with a

> **FURIOUS ABOUT: LITA**
>
> Lita has a unique history. She became enchanted with Mexican wrestling in her early 20s and, being a mark for lucha, moved to Mexico to train. On returning to US soil she continued to learn and worked on various Indy shows before being spotted by Paul Heyman and signing for ECW. She was mainly a valet for Danny Doring called Angelica. She continued to train, now with Dory Funk Jr. Dory sent her tape to the WWF and they signed her. All of this took place inside of a year. A meteoric rise! On signing for the WWF, they utilised her love of lucha and knowledge of Spanish and paired her with Essa Rios. That only lasted a few months before her flying ranas got her too over to be with him and she was put in Team Extreme with the Hardy Boyz. They gained an enormous following with Lita frequently getting involved in Hardyz matches. She eventually got into the women's division, as she was something different, and won the women's title four times. Along with Trish, she was the first woman to headline Raw, and the duo managed a ***+ match in the Observer in Trish's retirement bout.

chair, then Rock chases Shane away and seemingly beats Benoit with the Crossface. But when Earl recovers he instead calls the match for Benoit via DQ, which also happens to be a title change because of the pre match stipulations. Commissioner Foley disagrees and calls for a restart, and a bloody Rock wins it the second time around with the Rock Bottom.

We see more of the Rock's crazy schedule, with him constantly doing something when he isn't wrestling due to how in demand he is away from the ring. This time he does a photo shoot with some baseball player from the New York Mets that I have never heard of and don't particularly care about, and they debate which is better; baseball or the WWF. Well, baseball is one of the most boring sports I have ever seen so for me that is an easy one.

No Mercy 2000 saw Rock come up against Kurt Angle with his WWF Title on the line, as Kurt looked to complete an incredible rookie year by capturing the belt. He has Steph at ringside to serve as distraction and she does that pretty well, interjecting herself too and giving Kurt the title belt to use as a weapon for a near fall. Steph prevents the People's Elbow on Kurt and takes a Rock Bottom for her troubles, then Rock goes for the elbow on her, but Angle prevents it. Triple H comes down and attacks both guys, then Rikishi lumbers down and accidentally decks Rocky and costs him the match. It's a decent enough contest, but Kurt was pretty much buried as champion from the off as he needed all manner of assistance to win the belt.

Rock buries Superman for not showing any "jeopardy" and says that when he watched him as a kid he wanted to see him get punched in the mouth. It's the same argument most fans would have against John Cena a decade later. This somehow segues into Rock-Rikishi at *Survivor Series*, which was not one of the finer programs of Rock's year. The crux of the story was Rikishi ran down Steve Austin for Rock, and Rocky didn't approve. It was all fairly bollocks. The WWF tried their best to make Rikishi into a legitimate threat, including having Rikishi do a hit and run with a sledgehammer in the build up, but Rock still picks up the win to put the whole sorry affair to bed.

And then a segment about music. There is not a great deal in the way of threads holding this together, but each little snippet is at least fairly entertaining. This feature has Rock in Jim Johnston's studio "singing" for an upcoming WWF music album and a song called *'Pie'*. It's about eating pussy. It's also really horrible. Rock makes it clear that he wasn't actually TRYING to sing and that it was just a bit of fun. He gives himself 1 or 2 out of 10. Truth is he is actually not a bad singer, as his many "Rock concerts" have shown over the years. One segment on *RAW* in 2013 where he sang to and about Vicky Guerrero stands out in particular. Jim Johnston claims there will be more music projects together, but while his mouth says the words his eyes scream "NOOOOOOOOOO".

Back in the ring we skip ahead from the WWF Title loss to Rock winning the belt back at *No Way Out 2001* months later. Literally *everyone* knew Rock was winning going into this, because Rock-Austin was always a lock for *WrestleMania* the following month. This match is good though, really good, and is quite famous for Angle's potty mouth: "I will break your fucking ankle" he yells at Rock while he has him in the ankle lock. It's no surprise that the sound gets turned down for that. The Big Show gets involved, which in an unwelcome sight, but it doesn't take away from a tremendous effort from both of the guys in there. There are near falls aplenty, a hot crowd and the whole thing has an epic feel for its 16-minute duration, though it probably doesn't get the credit it deserves and is often overlooked. There were a lot of genuinely great matches in 2001 though, despite the unflattering booking going on around them all. Rock obviously gets the job done and wins the title back, and the showdown in Houston is on.

Rock talks about the "special feeling" of a Rock-Austin match, which is right. They were the two biggest stars of a generation and both were red hot at the same time, which rarely if ever happened before or since on an international stage. Their bout at *WrestleMania X-Seven* is something else, it is absolutely brilliant in every way. From the wonderful pacing to the impeccable timing and the superb series of near falls, each one of which could genuinely have been the finish. The match is a titanic clash between the two biggest stars of the Attitude Era, and in many ways is the final exclamation point on that period. We get tons of highlights from the match set to high-tempo, frenetic music. There are many cute moments that ape other bouts, such as Austin with a bloody Rock in the Sharpshooter in an homage to *WrestleMania 13*, and Rock trying to get the same fall over Austin that Bret Hart did at *Survivor Series 1996*, and then Vince gets involved and effectively ends the Attitude Era with Austin turning heel. He needed freshening up but once he turned heel, interest in the product dropped because the fans' hero had done the unthinkable. Losing a lot of other main event stars didn't help the product either of course.

The next night on *RAW,* Rock beat up Vince with a Sharpshooter until he agreed to give Rock a rematch against Austin that night, and Vince made it a cage match. Rock has the match won until Vince interferes, so Rock locks the cage door and beats the hell out of him. Austin saves Vince with a low blow and he and Vince do a number on Rock. Triple H, Austin's perennial rival of the last few months, comes down seemingly to save Rock from the pounding and begin a

> **FURIOUS ABOUT: LANCE STORM**
>
> It's a crying shame that Lance Storm isn't considered on a par with Jericho, Benoit, Angle or any of those guys. He was a tremendous talent and yet the highest star rating Meltzer has ever given him is ***3/4. For a man of his talent that seems ridiculous. Misfortune had a lot to do with it. Storm was graceful, elegant and smooth. Putting him in ECW seemed like a weird fit. It worked against ECW's more talented grapplers and he had good matches with Candido and Lynn. He also formed a very good team with Justin Credible called the Impact Players, which was as good as Aldo Montoya ever got. Storm was signed away by WCW after 3 few years but never got anywhere in that promotion at a time where they couldn't put on good matches. He did ascend to the US title level while there but just as he was taking over their upper midcard WCW went out of business and he had to join the WWF and start over. The WWF were interested and pushed him into a few decent matches (vs. Edge at SummerSlam, tagging with Hurricane) but in his four years there was vastly underrated.

babyface run opposite 'Stone Cold', but instead they put the last few months of wars behind them and align to form the Two-Man Power Trip. It was a bad time for the WWF creatively, and no one wanted to see any of this at all.

Rock getting the shit kicked out of him was of course so he could take some time off and go and film his first feature film where he had the starring role, *The Scorpion King*... Rock does well in it and comes across like a natural, but it's a boring ass movie. Really boring. Obviously his performance did impress the right people though, because it catapulted Rock into the stratosphere and set him on the way to becoming a legitimate box office attraction and a genuine movie star. In 2013 he was the highest grossing actor in the world. Impressive stuff. We get loads of footage from behind the scenes of the movie, which is nearly as dull as the film, unfortunately, apart from Kelly Hu getting all wet about the prospect of kissing Rock in the movie. Rock talks about doing his own stunts and claims: "Am I nervous to walk through fire? Nah I'm not nervous to walk through fire. The Rock walks through fire every single night in the WWF". He must be confusing his character with Kane's.

We see Rock's return a few months later in Philly where Vince and Shane McMahon both begged Rock to join their side in the WWF vs. WCW/ECW Alliance war. Rock seemingly joined the Alliance when he Rock Bottomed Vince, but then he gave one to Shane too, because why book when you can overbook? What a shame too, because Rock could have been the spike that the Alliance needed, even if it would have made no sense. I guess they could have gone with the story of Rock never having forgiven fans for the "Die Rocky Die" chants years earlier and for turning on him for going to make movies. It might have worked. But no, instead the WWF thought firmly inside the box when Rock picked the WWF. Rock claims to have been "invigorated" by the chance to work with new guys from WCW, specifically Booker T. He says he watched Booker use the Rock Bottom while he was in WCW and he thought it was "interesting". We see a brief snippet from an amazing *SmackDown!* promo where he asks Booker if he is the "WCW champion sucker?" and then a promo from *RAW* where he says "motherfucker" on the authority of Stephanie, which apparently enraged Vince. The Rock-Booker match at *SummerSlam* for the WCW Title follows, which somehow was the main event ahead of Austin-Angle. I guess it was Rock's return match, but positioning the WCW Title ahead of the WWF Title was a surprising choice from the company after they had been decimating the group on television for weeks. Of course, the reason was so Rock's victory was seen as more important, but the title situation got so ridiculous that quite quickly the WWF guys held most of the WCW belts and vice versa. Something like that should have been saved for a year or two into the angle, not done within a month. They just had no idea what they were doing with this at all.

Next we take a look at Rock ripping into Kevin Kelly on a weekly basis, including a segment where he forced poor Kev to spend an entire promo with his finger up his own nose. A few minutes of Rock working out in a gym follows, which as ever with these things is like watching paint dry. At least give us some cheesy porno music like we used to get on Coliseum tapes when the likes of Power & Glory would get features like this. After that Rock talks more about life on the road and gives us a snapshot of his day, which like everyone else on the roster includes waking up early, doing long drives and trying to find a few minutes of solitude away from pestering fans. He doesn't actually say that mind you, but it is implied.

Finally we get a glimpse at some of the great work the Rock has done for the Make-A-Wish Foundation, which is one of the finest and most genuine things that the WWF/E is associated with. At the point this tape was filmed Rock was up to 30 wishes, which is very commendable and warranted him receiving an award, but it is absolutely dwarfed by John Cena's remarkable 300+ wishes. For all of his detractors, there is no doubting that Cena's dedication to that particular cause deserves endless plaudits. Whether 30 or 300, it is a helluva job and takes a lot of mental strength to do due to the upsetting nature of the work.

VERDICT

Coming in I was expecting another generic Rock tape just featuring a bunch of matches, but it's a little bit more than that thanks to a decent portion of stuff away from the ring. It actually starts a lot better than it ends up, and more of the real backstage shenanigans and house show match stuff would have been great, and much better than seemingly endless *Scorpion King* crap. It really is a tape that goes back-and-forth between really good and fairly boring, but as with any profile tape your enjoyment will depend largely on how much you like the guy profiled. I have a lot of time for the Rock and found this to be an easy hour or so watch, though just be warned it is far more "random footage from a twelve month period" than a coherent career retrospective. Recommended.

61

THE ROCK AS THE SCORPION KING

VENGEANCE 2001

CAT NO: WWF54113
RUN TIME: 157 minutes (approx)

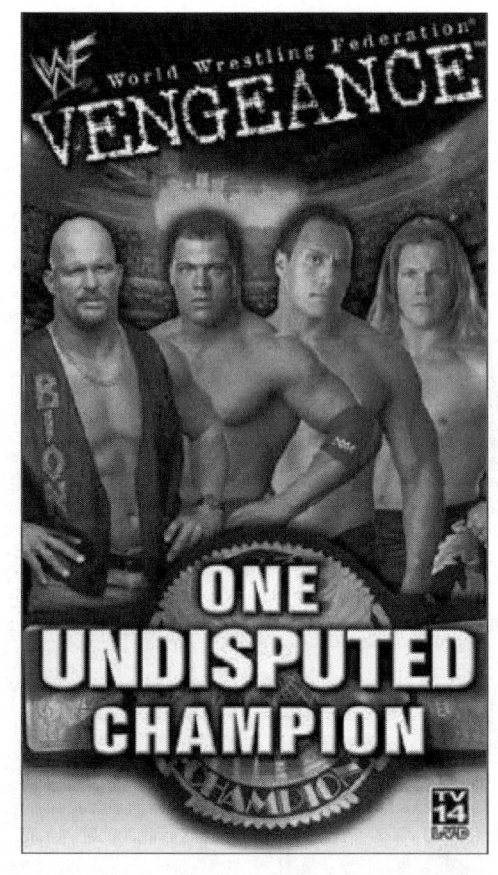

Arnold Furious: With the WCW/ECW Alliance angle firmly put to bed at *Survivor Series* the WWF found themselves in an unenviable position. Even though they flubbed the invasion angle, for reasons noted elsewhere, how do you follow it? The biggest cross-promotional angle of all time may have sucked but fans still bought the *InVasion* PPV and the *Survivor Series* PPV based on promises of inter-promotional matches and a once in a lifetime experience. With *Vengeance* falling into the usual stop-gap dead-end month of December, the WWF felt they needed to do something equally as big to pop a buyrate. Their decision was a somewhat confusing one; to unify the WWF and WCW World Titles. It made sense at the time, as the whole crossover angle was finished, but with the benefit of hindsight and the WWF's desire to expand into branding (*RAW* vs. *SmackDown!*) it made no sense at all. Ultimately they would need two titles and two different champions to give their shows distinctly different feels. Whatever the reasoning was for unifying the titles, it did nothing to pop the buyrate and indeed 2002's December PPV, headlined by Triple H and Shawn Michaels, picked up more buys. At this point most of the casual fans had gone. We were down to the hardcore fanbase that would buy just about anything with WWF in the title. The WWF learned during 2002 that they didn't really need something mega-special to sell a PPV event but in late 2001 the feeling was if they didn't go into *Vengeance* super-hot then no one would buy the show.

Tangent: The WWF got even sneakier than that with their advertising. Leading into *Vengeance*, it was clear that Triple H was approaching acceptable fitness levels and there was a suggestion he'd be available to wrestle at the PPV. Ultimately the WWF weren't going to take that risk with him and his return instead came at the *Royal Rumble*. But that didn't stop them using his picture on the *Vengeance* poster and pointing out on WWF programming that he "might" be there, which in wrestling terms means he will be. It was underhanded stuff. Some of the WWF's more devious marketing during 2001 turned fans off.

Another Tangent: Between *Survivor Series* and *Vengeance* the WWF landscape had changed quite dramatically as the WWF's victory party didn't last long. Almost as soon as the balloons and streamers were brought in, so was Ric Flair, which makes you wonder why he wasn't used during the invasion angle as there are few figures in all of wrestling that scream "WCW" more than the 'Nature Boy'. He was WCW champion eight times, plus he had another ten reigns as the NWA champion before that. Despite a brief WWF run in the early 90s he was synonymous with WCW. Anyway, the WWF brought him in as 50-50 owner with Vince McMahon, claiming Naitch had saved enough money to buy Shane and Stephanie's stock. Those who know his lack of financial stability would find that laughable. Flair's first act was to stop Vince's power-mad attempts to get the WWF Title off Steve Austin (that sounds very familiar), with Vince blaming Austin for almost tanking the WWF against the Alliance. This whole scenario turned Vince, who owned the company, and Angle, who saved the WWF against the Alliance, into heels while the champion Austin, a heel pretty much since *WrestleMania* and a guy who attempted to destroy the WWF a month ago was a babyface, and invading former WCW champion Flair was a babyface. No, it didn't make any sense to me either. I think they got the whole thing backwards. Either way the co-owners eventually agreed to book a mini-tournament rather than Flair's initial idea (Austin vs. Rock for all the marbles) and that's why this show is considered a bit of a mess.

9th December 2001. We're in San Diego, California. Video Control gives us a bit of history with Fred Blassie watching old footage of wrestling with the WWF claiming there has never been an "undisputed" World Champion. It's a pretty cool idea if it was true and there had never been an undisputed champion in the past. Lou Thesz unified all the available World Titles in the early 50s, for example. It wasn't really until 1960 when the AWA split from the NWA and then in 1963 when the WWF did the same that the waters were muddied and different World Champions existed. If they'd said; there hasn't been a unified World Champion in 50 years then I'd buy it because that would be closer to the truth although various Japanese and Mexican promotions could lay claim to World Titles and dispute this unified World Title. Although, their titles aren't really defended globally so I'm not sure they'd count. Hosts are Jim Ross and Jerry Lawler.

Promo Time: Vince McMahon.
The chairman of the board opens the show, recapping RAW for anyone that missed it, which is just a fine use of PPV time. Lawler immediately pisses me off by constantly interjecting in between pauses as if he can't deal with quiet. He's like a child. If anything his commentary has gotten worse during his time off. Vince misquotes "he who laughs last" by saying "he who laughs last, laughs loudest". It's "longest" actually. It would be nice if someone had just corrected him before his promo escaped onto PPV. Not that it had any business being on PPV as he had nothing relevant to say. Ric Flair eventually gets bored and comes out to announce the PPV is starting now.

Scotty 2 Hotty & Albert vs. Test & Christian
Vince is still in the ring when Scotty and Albert come out here and for one glorious moment they consider giving McMahon the *Night at the Roxbury* treatment (in your head '*What is Love*' by Haddaway is playing). I think Vince's reaction to Albert dancing in his face rather put them off doing it, but it would have been epic. Test & Christian are Alliance survivors whereas Scotty was left alone by Grandmasta Sexay getting fired and Albert was left alone after X-Factor collapsed. Albert switched characters to fit in and became the "Hip Hop Hippo". Scotty is a weird case study as everyone remembers him as being half of Too Cool and yet he spent longer in the WWF after GMS left than he did as part of the team. Albert does a bit of dancing and actually gets himself over. There's a bit of laughing but it's mostly pops. He even makes his moveset fun by hitting the giant swing on Christian. Test prevents the Baldo Bomb but Christian finds himself in position for the Worm, counters into a reverse DDT and Christian does it instead. Albert runs in but Test follows to add a big boot and Scotty saves. Bulldog on Test and the Worm connects. Christian runs back in for the Unprettier but Albert blocks it and hits the Baldo Bomb to win. Believe it or not this was a lot of fun and Scotty & Albert were an entertaining team. I guess either Albert's heart wasn't in it or the WWF had no belief in the team as they only lasted about four months before being broken up. They certainly slotted into the hot opener here and sometimes the WWF accidentally gets something right by sheer luck and then loses interest in pursuing it. If there's one thing to learn from the whole experience it's that dancing gimmicks get you over.
Final Rating: **

Backstage: William Regal gets quizzed about the "Power of the Punch". Regal points out he's been fighting since he was 15 years old, Edge has incurred (or "in-cured" as Regal says) his wrath and Coach is a pillock. Top promo work from Regal.

WWF Intercontinental Championship
Edge (c) vs. William Regal
Regal's unorthodox style, which is a mixture of different styles not just the classic British style, doesn't quite mesh with Edge, who's halfway between technical and flier. Regal's striking is particularly strange for the US audiences as he tends to throw knees and forearm uppercuts, which are completely different to the traditional punches and kicks. Edge does a decent job of selling them but you can sense he's not comfortable. Edge accidentally spears the ring steps and Regal goes to retrieve brass knucks, which he'd stashed behind a different post. He may have been better off just going for the pin as he gets a three count, albeit aborted by Edge getting his foot on the rope. The major issue with Regal's tough-man style clashing with Edge's flying is that when Edge clips Regal with a flying kick it looks really soft. Regal's style is far more realistic so he looks daft doing the same selling for less vicious spots. Even when he adopts American or Japanese moves, they're hard-hitting. He plants Edge with a couple of butterfly powerbombs but can't get the job done. Regal pulls out the knucks but Edge spears him to retain. The match is an interesting one as Regal gets to bully a potential big star and dominate a match but it leaves a sour taste in the mouth. As if being superior to someone in every conceivable way doesn't get you anywhere if you don't look like a movie star. Edge was in training to be a main event star and that meant working against different guys with different styles. It wasn't really until his feud with Kurt Angle after *WrestleMania X8* that people started to consider him viable in such a role. Another fine example of the better wrestler being used to put over the possible star.
Final Rating: **¼

Backstage: Ric Flair is on the phone when he gets a visit from Kurt Angle. The latter points out Flair will never be a gold medallist and won't be an undisputed World Champion. Flair hadn't quite picked up on the WWF creative team's "jokes", so this bit is supposed to be funny but it isn't. Why anyone would want to script Ric Flair interviews is beyond me. He's one of the most entertaining talkers the business has ever known. Just tell him what he's supposed to get across and let him loose.

Elsewhere: Matt Hardy points out to Lita that he's the brains and the better wrestler of the Hardys. Lita says she's the referee so she has to call the match down the middle. Matt was trying to be heel here but it didn't work. They'd get to do a better brother vs. brother feud later but this one was such a damp squib the angle not only tanked, mainly because of the reasoning behind it, but they'd be re-teamed almost immediately afterwards. Eventually Matt turned heel properly but this run made the WWF less than convinced of Matt's ability to put together a match and an angle. They knew Jeff was over and would draw but Matt was the actual talent behind it all. I'm sad to see how the whole thing panned out although Matt Hardy V.1 remains my favourite Hardy run in the company and that's still to come.

Jeff Hardy vs. Matt Hardy
Lita is the referee with Matt, Lita's boyfriend, expecting her to favour him. The angle is immediately a downer as the WWF just ran Edge vs. Christian and doing another tag team split and feud didn't sit well with the fans. Especially as they didn't really want Team Xtreme to split up, though they wanted them to continue in singles, as they'd both had singles success in 2001. Matt probably figured he could turn himself into a Shawn Michaels esque star by instigating the break up. The silence these two wrestle to is indicative of how little anyone wanted to see the split (and also that this San Diego crowd sucks). It doesn't help that the match is patchy at best. They do insert some fun spots, like Matt going for a sunset flip to the floor only for Jeff to counter into a rana, but like Edge and Christian the lack of chemistry is surprising. With Matt and Jeff it's even more surprising given their history (as brothers the trust level is even higher and they'd worked together their whole lives). Lita is a non-factor and Matt just works the match vaguely heel, leaving the fans disinterested. Matt holds on too long when Jeff gets the ropes on a half crab, but there's no flat-out cheating. Remember this came about because Matt accused Jeff of being selfish and a showboat. The match revolves around Matt working Jeff's knee and stopping him flying. Jeff's selling is usually pretty strong so he hobbles around and doesn't do trademark dives because of the injury, which is technically great but makes the match a bit dull. I like that Matt is able to counter the Twist of Fate, based on his knowledge of the move and Matt finally does something heel-ish by grabbing the ropes

on a pin attempt. Lita kicks him off and there's finally a bit of tension but it takes them ages to get there. All the leg work amounts to nothing in the end as Jeff hobbles up top and hits the Swanton. There's a crafty moment where Matt gets his leg on the rope on the pin, but Jeff sweeps it off. Who's really the heel here? Matt storms to the back completely pissed off at being robbed and rightly so. The fans are not impressed. If this angle was leading anywhere it was quickly dropped and Team Extreme were restored as if nothing had happened (albeit after they were taken off TV). The match itself is slow and psychology based, which would be fine if the team weren't renowned as daredevils. It reminds me of the Shawn Michaels vs. Marty Jannetty singles match at the 1993 *Royal Rumble* where they opted for psychology over high spots and everyone hated it. I actually like it and think it works well in retrospect (Shawn vs. Marty, not this) and gave it ***½ in the *Complete WWF Video Guide Volume #2*. Jeff vs. Matt wasn't that good because Matt Hardy isn't Shawn Michaels and Jeff Hardy isn't even Marty Jannetty, but Jeff's selling held this together.
Final Rating: **½

Tangent: For those wondering about that Jeff/Jannetty comparison, Jannetty of 1993 would smoke Jeff of 2001. It's not even close.

Backstage: Trish Stratus goes to see The Rock and put over his actions on *SmackDown!* Trish wishes him good luck so Rock lays the moves on her. Not a good segment and the third one tonight where the whole thing felt forced. And when your writing makes the Rock look bad on the mic, you know you suck. All the promos tonight have felt stilted. Even the good one from Regal.

WWF Tag Team Championship
The Dudley Boyz (c) vs. The Big Show & Kane
Show and Kane were a terrible idea for a team. Where's the vulnerability? Where's the guy who'll take bumps? It's like trying to find something to mix chocolate with and settling for chocolate. The Dudleys try to get the angle over by having them reluctant to tag in and just bumping around like mad. They also have Stacy Keibler out here but what is Stacy going to do with Kane or Show? Kane is something out of a horror movie and Show is a giant. Stacy runs in to do something or other and Show strips off her shorts and lays in a monstrous spanking right hand. So yeah, that's what Stacy is here for. The Dudleys eventually isolate Kane, which is a dreadful idea and he seems content to just take spots and lumber through all this business. The fans are actually hot for the match but I have no idea why. Basically WWF fans, you only have yourselves to blame for WWF booking. Also, I now hate San Diego (a whale's vagina), a town I'd only previously connected to *Anchorman*. Way to go jerk offs. Both challengers do a bunch of no-selling until Kane miscues on Show and that's the real reason for having this match. Even with the challengers feuding with each other the Dudleys still get swatted like flies. Bubba exposes a turnbuckle and the champs double flapjack Show onto it for the win. "It was not a pretty match" says JR. That's WWF language for a bad match. Crowd were into though. Bastards.
Final Rating: ½*

Backstage: Lita apologises to Matt for not seeing his foot on the rope. Again, this angle went nowhere. Back to ringside and JR shills Drowning Pool's '*Sinner*', which is the background noise for this PPV.

WWF Hardcore Championship

Rob Van Dam (c) vs. The Undertaker
After the invasion ended Taker turned heel, thus making a thoroughly boring Underbiker character into an even more tedious one. What it came down to was Taker suggesting he wasn't getting any respect. There are two ways at looking this match. 1. That RVD was put in with Taker because the WWF wanted to get a look at him with a big man and considered him a potential main event star. Or 2. That RVD had been stiffing guys with his kicks and they wanted Taker to show him how to work. Rob had used the Hardcore Title to allow him to work his own matches inside the WWF's environment, which was a perfect use of the belt and I'd have been quite happy for them to carry on doing that forever. Amazingly these guys mesh perfectly with Rob's unorthodox stuff keeping the Undertaker guessing and interesting. Taker can be boring and grounded all he likes as RVD has enough fun spots to keep the match ticking over, though it's nowhere near as good as RVD's matches with Jeff Hardy and Chris Jericho because he can't do all the technical countering stuff and the flying is limited. RVD does hit a dive off the cheap seats over the entranceway but Van Dam's best matches came against guys who could work his style with him. Taker uses his power sporadically and manages to javelin RVD into the Titantron head-first. RVD uses the same Tron to escape a Last Ride on the stage but that doesn't go anywhere. What follows is equally perplexing as Taker grabs a chair and ISN'T hit with a Van Daminator. Instead Rob kicks him in the guts, hits Rolling Thunder and surfs the chair into Taker's face. I appreciate variety as much as the next man but the logical spot was the Van Daminator. Taker ducks a Van Daminator attempt and chokeslams Rob off the stage through two tables for the win. As much as I hated the idea of these guys working together and the fact Taker won, the match turned out really well. They brought some interesting ideas and had a cool finish. Unfortunately RVD's career nose-dived after this and he headed into the IC Title division.
Final Rating: ***

Backstage: Ric Flair is on the phone again and gets interrupted by Chris Jericho. Y2J points out nobody thinks he can win but he's already beaten the Rock twice. Flair again stumbles through a promo whereas Jericho looks assured. Jericho had a knack of reeling off whatever nonsense creative had him saying. It's the most coherent promo of the night because it doesn't sound like jokey dialogue that some penis has written. Instead it sounds like a wrestler talking about wrestling.

Video Control gives us a Triple H video set to U2's '*Beautiful Day*' showing his recovery from quad surgery. While Hunter was a big loss during 2001 the fact so many midcard guys finally got their big break in his absence can't have been a coincidence. Given his stunning 2000 programs I was thrilled to have him back at the time, but knowing the booking that's to follow makes this a bittersweet video to watch. I don't think the song is appropriate either.

WWF Women's Championship
Trish Stratus (c) vs. Jacqueline
Trish won the title at *Survivor Series* in what was considered an upset win from someone considered as a virtual non-wrestler at the time. Of course history views her differently but there were rumblings about her skillset and whether she'd be able to match up to an actual wrestler. Trish certainly looks green here and looks weird hitting the ropes and selling. The crowd are far more interested in her looks and chant for "puppies" within seconds. Trish has an issue where she staggers backwards instead of bumping. It looks entirely natural but shows her lack

of wrestling experience. Jacqui manages a superb legsweep when Trish goes for her high kick and the bump gets an "OOOOHH" from the crowd and the spot merits a replay. Jacqui shoves her off on the Trishdog and looks to be bossing it. A very awkward double down follows and Trish finishes with a backslide. The match was a hard-hitting mess. There's an old wrestling adage that goes something like this: if you can't fake it, just beat each other up. Jacqueline figured she couldn't make Trish look good unless she actually kicked her ass so that's what she did. Trish wasn't quite sure how to react but they ended up having something resembling a match. I'm a big Trish fan but they really should have gotten her more seasoning before putting the title on her.
Final Rating: ½*

Video Control gives us footage from *SmackDown!* where The Rock made Vince McMahon kiss somebody's ass. First suggesting his own, then Jim Ross' before offering up Trish Stratus and taking it away. Eventually Vince takes a Stinkface off the returning Rikishi. Presumably Rock had forgiven him for the whole "running Austin over" thing. Jerry Lawler makes fart noises during the sequence, showing his maturity. Over at WWF New York is Rikishi, who's still wearing the gloves and shades he used when he was a heel. Back to Video Control and the fallout from *Survivor Series* where Vince went to award the title to Kurt Angle. He's stopped by Ric Flair who tries to book Austin vs. Rock and Vince switches it to two matches leading to an undisputed match, which everyone figured was just the same thing. They could easily have just made it a four-way elimination match and the winner takes all. It would have given the fans their Austin-Rock match and still allowed Chris Jericho to walk away with the title. Hindsight is 20-20, I guess, but that's what I would have done.

WWF Championship
Steve Austin (c) vs. Kurt Angle
Angle might have been red hot over the summer months but going into the year's end, he was very much the outside shot for the title. Especially as Austin's last year has been wiped away and he's back to the same guy he was before *WrestleMania X-Seven*, character-wise. JR brings the history by mentioning George Hackenschmidt and Frank Gotch before stumbling onto the last unified champion Lou Thesz by tying Austin's Thesz Press into him. He doesn't mention the unified title business though as the whole PPV was sold on the first ever unified champion being decided. They start slow and the fans aimlessly chant "what?", reminding me that 2001 was the year that Steve Austin ruined all heel promos forever. They repeat the standard spot where Austin goes after a Stunner, countered into the ankle lock but Austin instead of tapping out immediately rolls through it, as if to say he knew that hold and Angle wasn't going to catch him in it. Instead it's Austin who bosses the technical stuff by going after Angle's arm. Its only when Austin tries for a German suplex that Angle is able to get anywhere, by countering out and into the ankle lock. Austin has no counter this time and gets the into the ropes. Angle's working of the leg is not only to his benefit but also to Rock and Jericho's as both of those guys have submission finishers on

> **FURIOUS ABOUT: CHRIS JERICHO (1999-2002)**
>
> Chris Jericho's decision to quit WCW at the height of the Monday Night War was a ballsy move and he received more attention in his WWF debut than he had bouncing around dead-end feuds in WCW the previous three years. Like most of WCW's cruiserweights he'd worked hard but found himself up against the glass ceiling. The non-feud with Goldberg about summed up his WCW run. Goldberg refusing to work with him because he "didn't do comedy". Jericho's WWF run looked as if it might head the same way after a dramatic debut opposite The Rock. He found himself paired with Chris Benoit in the midcard. He enjoyed a brief run opposite Triple H, including a phantom WWF title win and an excellent Last Man Standing match at Fully Loaded 2000, before returning to the midcard to work feuds with X-Pac, Kane and Regal. The second attempt to elevate Jericho came during the Invasion where he received a title shot at Steve Austin. Again coming up short the suggestion had become that he couldn't win the big one. Which changed, albeit for a short time, when he defeated the Rock for the WCW title late in 2001. The matches between Rock and Jericho were all about mutual respect and wanting to put on the best possible match. It was a refreshing new approach to the main event scene that had been plagued by politics. I enjoyed Jericho against the Rock because it was just two guys who both wanted to be the best. The ill-advised Jericho heel turn killed all that. He changed into the whiny heel he'd been in WCW without the complete cowardice that made him entertaining. It was a big mistake. Jericho may have become the first undisputed world champion but it killed his main event run.

the legs too. Angle tries to lift Bret Hart stuff to get into Austin's head, including the ringpost figure four. Austin escapes a second ankle lock, but the fans are not buying into Angle at all. There's not much in the way of selling, which is also disappointing. Angle goes to the rolling Germans, which visibly knock Austin about as his neck was troubling him again. Perhaps feuding with Benoit and Angle and taking all those suplexes in 2001 wasn't such a good idea. Angle misses with a picturesque moonsault and they head into the hot finish. Austin manages his own shoddy version of the rolling Germans, although you can forgive him for not wanting to take too many bumps on that neck. Low blow sets up the Angle Slam and the fans are finally buying into him winning. He makes the mistake of going for the Stunner though and Austin counters into his own for the win. Austin retains the WWF Title and advances to face the winner of Rock-Jericho. At this point even JR is pointing to the setup being perfect for Austin-Rock adding that "a lot of fans" were expecting that outcome. Match wasn't up to the standard of the summer ones, where Angle was the babyface, but is still pretty good. Austin didn't look to be saving himself for later.
Final Rating: ***¼

Backstage: Trish Stratus is re-applying her makeup when Test busts in to offer a kiss. Test calls her a tease when she refuses and goes off on a rant about how he can't be fired, regardless of sexual harassment as he won an Immunity Battle Royal. Damn, that'd be pretty sweet. A year of immunity from being fired means you can do anything. Imagine the customer complaints? Oh, we're sorry, he has immunity madam so that's why he pissed in your handbag. I can't promise he won't do it again, even, because he's safe for a year.

WCW Championship
The Rock (c) vs. Chris Jericho

Jericho finally "won the big one" and captured the WCW Title back at *No Mercy* but Rock beat him on *RAW* about a month ago to reclaim the strap. It caused issues between them at *Survivor Series* and Jericho almost cost the WWF the match, simply out of hatred for Rock. I realise WCW tried to tie their title's history into the NWA one that went back to the 40s, but the WCW Title itself is only 10 years old. Rock and Jericho have superb chemistry, which led to their match at *No Mercy* being super and despite turning heel there's still a strong "Y2J" chant. The early going is in favour of Jericho, who uses the ropes to control, both by jumping off them and choking Rock on them. Jericho turning fully heel at *Survivor Series* really took the heat out of his run and this match and the crowd are different. Instead of being hyped, they're decidedly uninterested. The structure is still quite similar but I don't understand why they couldn't just be characters, as they were both hugely over, and have this match. Why does one guy have to be the heel? It worked perfectly fine as a babyface match the first time. In fact the only time the crowd is into it is when some of them start to chant for Jericho. Lionsault misses and Rock starts to fire away with punches but again the crowd is strangely dead, just waiting for their Austin-Rock match. Lionsault scores at the second attempt but Rock kicks out and Jericho pitches a fit showing how his character has fallen off in the last month. Jericho takes an amazing bump to turn the tide. He flies clear over the top, into the ring post and down to the floor, over the top of the cameraman. Even after that Jericho continues to boss and there's a suggestion they wanted Jericho to look strong for the main event but the fans just think he's staying strong because he's losing. Jericho goes after the Rock Bottom through the announce table but spends too long setting it up and Rock counters into a DDT. Earl Hebner could easily count them both out but instead opts to leave it and let us get a decisive winner. Rock stalks Jericho and in a rare piece of countering Jericho escapes into the Breakdown. Despite that move pinning Rock at *No Mercy* Jericho doesn't pin. Presumably because he just got DDT'd through a table. You never start with the head, it leaves you all woozy. Jericho goes for the People's Elbow but Rock trips Y2J up into the Sharpshooter, but Jericho counters out into his own Sharpshooter, which is actually properly applied as Jericho is from Canada and knows how to hook it. Rock fades but the fan support gets him into the ropes. Jericho goes after the Walls but gets rolled up… for 2. Rock Bottom! The delay on the cover gives away the result of that and kills the crowd again. Out comes Vince McMahon, because we can't have a big match without a run in. Rock slaps him off the apron and hits a spinebuster. Vince gets slapped again and the People's Elbow scores. Jericho goes low though and finishes with his own Rock Bottom. Jericho scores his second WCW Title but this time he needed Vince to do it. That, and the crowd, takes the shine off this a bit but the match is still very well structured.
Final Rating: ****

WWE Undisputed Championship
Steve Austin vs. Chris Jericho

Austin charges down to start the match right away only for Angle to chair shot him. Rock evens the numbers again with a Rock Bottom on Jericho before chasing Kurt off. The WWF then throws up a stupid flashing graphic for the Undisputed Title (it's awful) and the crowd chant "Triple H" because as noted he's been rumoured as a returnee on this show. The horrible stench of failure is already all over the match as the fans take a collective dump on being presented with Austin vs. Jericho. Given the benefit of hindsight the booking of Jericho-Rock was enough for Jericho to get over. He could have taken the title after this show. Austin-Rock is what people came to see and they didn't get it. Austin goes right after the Stunner to at least send the fans home slightly happy but Jericho squirms out of it. This leads into a brawl around ringside, which might be "vintage" Austin, but is counterproductive to Jericho's strengths. Onto the Spanish announce table and Austin goes for a Stunner, countered into the Walls of Jericho (like the one on Triple H after he got injured), but Austin powers out. Neither of those spots would have done more damage by being on the announce table though. A strange choice. Jericho starts working Austin's arm, which is contrary to the entire Austin-Angle match where Kurt worked the leg. Jericho slaps on the Walls of Jericho and there is a bit of a pop and an audible "tap" chant from the smarks. Austin gets the ropes and Jericho flying forearms the ref to an audible groan before the "Triple H" chants start again. Jericho lifts the Stunner, seeing as the Rock Bottom finished the Rock. Out comes Vince McMahon with less than impartial referee Nick Patrick. Ric Flair pulls Nick out and socks him one so Vince goes after Flair. Austin wakes up and bails to knock Vince on his ass as Jericho rapidly becomes secondary to his other feuds now. Austin gets the Walls of Jericho on Jericho and he taps out but there's no ref. Jericho is really getting screwed here. Booker T runs in to blindside Austin, thus showcasing a third feud that has nothing to do with Jericho. Y2J hooks a leg and becomes Undisputed World Champion. Shame he had to play second fiddle to Vince vs. Flair and Austin vs. Vince and Austin vs. Booker. Also he tapped out clean. I still don't get why they turned him full on heel as early as they did. I was pleased for Chris getting the title though, as he thoroughly deserved it, and the booking had everything to do with his failure to get over as champion. Had he been given a modicum of quality control over the booking, his reign would have worked. Instead he became a Stephanie McMahon surrogate by *WrestleMania* and never won the big one again (despite 3 "world" titles, the WWF Title eluded him from this point onward).
Final Rating: **¾

VERDICT

This should have been one of the all-time famous wrestling shows as the WWF unified their title with the WCW World Title, but Jericho's win aside it's barely remembered, and rightly so. Rock-Jericho was far better when they were both working face and people could cheer for who they wanted. What they wanted here was Austin-Rock and they didn't get it. The result is a flat crowd for the final three matches. The wrestling throughout the card is decent but *Vengeance* is a forgettable show.

54

ALBERT

REBELLION 2001

CAT NO: WWF54115
RUN TIME: 137 minutes (approx)

Arnold Furious: As I have mentioned before, I held a position in 2001 as UK PPV reporter for several websites, and my coverage generally reflected what I thought the mood was concerning the shows. Namely that they were glorified house shows with no purpose existing. However even a house show main event between Steve Austin and the Rock is nothing to be sniffed at and Chris Jericho also defends his WCW Title here against Kurt Angle. I was quite harsh on the ratings then because of my general malaise when it came to UK shows; that they meant nothing in the long run. But looking back, and having them as standalone shows, I can just kick back and watch the wrestling. After all the booking can't really get in the way as they never bothered booking anything that would interfere with the American storylines anyway.

3rd November 2001. We're in Manchester, England. Interesting to note that the dark match was Billy Gunn & Chuck Palumbo wrestling against the tandem of Lance Storm & Justin Credible, otherwise known as the Impact Players and the highlight of Aldo's career. Hosts are Jim Ross and Paul Heyman, who make a point of shilling Austin-Rock in tonight's main event.

Steel Cage Match
WWF Intercontinental Championship
Edge (c) vs. Christian
Due to belts changing hands all over the place Christian already has one strap; the European Title, which meant less than nothing by this point. Keep in mind that this show is in Europe, and yet the European Title is just hanging around as a secondary prop. Christian beat Bradshaw for that belt, which makes two title reigns I don't remember at all. He'd lose it to DDP before William Regal regained the title and then it faded into the background and got unified with the IC Title in July 2002. They could easily have jettisoned the belt here as the WWF had way too many titles with all the WCW ones knocking around. This match is pinfall or escape, which at least gives it moments of tension with near falls. Like with their ladder match at *No Mercy 2001*, these guys try to get over the toughness of the environment. In the ladder match any contact with the ladders was treated like death. Here, any contact with the cage is a near fall. It's smart work. I wish more wrestlers treated their environments that way. Let's face it, cage matches lost a lot of popularity after Hell in a Cell started up so the selling needed to reflect how harsh those metal bars were. Unfortunately I don't think the majority of the roster had the respect for cages, or ladders, that Edge and Christian had. Not only that but top rope moves are automatically intense near falls. Luckily the Manchester crowd, lively from the get-go, buy into the cage and top rope near falls and gasp at kick-outs. A great crowd can make an enormous difference. The commentators make me chuckle. "You and I would never be argumentative" – Ross. "I disagree with that" – Heyman. Honestly, the end of the invasion angle caused the biggest loss of all; Heyman from commentary. He made such a difference and got people over. The only people Lawler ever got over in the WWF were ones with big tits. Unlike the last two matches these former partners had, this one has a lot more counters. So when Christian goes after the Unprettier, it's countered out into the Edgeomatic. It's as if they'd been saving these spots for a big blow-off match that wasn't forthcoming. Or maybe they just used them on house shows. Christian actually climbs out of the cage and gets most of the way down but Edge nut shots him, ties Christian's boots together through the cage and climbs out to retain with Christian helpless. Interesting idea but the execution took ages. Thanks to some of the countering and familiarity stuff this was one of their better matches against each other, but it still dragged a little at 20-minutes. I slightly prefer the ladder match from *No Mercy,* but this is more fun.
Final Rating: ***

Backstage: Roving reporter Chavo Guerrero Jr promises hot Diva interviews, but gets interrupted by Hugh Morrus, aka Bill DeMott, who's also here to interview the Divas. They barge in and Trish is getting changed. She's topless but covered up by a towel. The suggestion of nudity on the UK PPVs was a long term tease after Jacqueline got the puppies out. It got to the point where they put these teases out on every UK PPV. Nobody likes a tease.

Scotty 2 Hotty vs. The Hurricane
This screams "house show" as there's no feud. They're just two cruiserweight guys. Hurricane was the most charismatic and

FURIOUS ABOUT: KURT ANGLE

There has never been anyone in the wrestling business who's learned as fast as Angle, who's improved as fast as Angle and who's remained as consistently excellent as Angle. When it's all said and done, he may go down in history as the best wrestler of all-time. He was already an Olympic Gold medallist and an outstanding amateur wrestler before the WWE but not every amateur can make the transition. Angle quickly developed a character for himself and a persona that would allow him to conquer the professional wrestling world. He rapidly rose through the ranks with assured promos and excellent matches. The WWF rewarded him with a shaky first WWF title run where he captured the belt with botched interference. He'd go on to retain the title through dubious means. The title run ended up a failure because of the WWF's lack of commitment to it and Angle was unseated by The Rock at No Way Out 2001, which in itself was overshadowed by Hunter and Austin in the midcard. Angle floundered into the midcard himself, battling the likes of Chris Benoit until his star had risen so much that he became the focal point of the WWF once more. This time, in 2001, it was for real and a babyface Angle defeated Steve Austin for his second WWF title. The Invasion was, by and large, booked around Austin and Angle as Kurt found himself rubbing shoulders with everyone at the top of the card. Despite this Angle only managed 2 weeks with the title in his second run and had to wait until late 2002 for his third run, during an extended feud with Brock Lesnar. When involved in midcard feuds, Angle continued to give the same levels of effort as during his main event programs, which endeared him to the fans, despite them wanting to hate him for his pomposity. A feud with Edge, where Angle lost his hair, catapulted the young Canadian up the card. Angle improved everyone around him and after three years in the business was already a lock for the Hall of Fame.

exciting from a batch of WCW cruiserweights when that division was all the company had left. The last few PPVs were just cruiserweight showcases and a bunch of crap. A pity Jamie Noble didn't come in to the WWF as hot as Helms, as he was a terrific wrestler. Hurricane and Scotty are more about posing and goofing around. Hurricane is the more creative of the two as Scotty's character was deranged. Obsessed with the Worm. No matter how hard they work there's no disguising this; it is filler, but at least they do work hard. As Hurricane reaches for his cape JR points out "this is borderline ridiculous", which is sometimes an issue with WWF wrestlers and gimmicks. You see these two and think; are they believable? Are they real? Interesting to note the proliferation of superkicks in 2001, with Shawn Michaels out for three years and showing no sign of returning. Everyone started using it as a transition. Scotty does one here and as if that's not enough, so does Hurricane. Hurricane tries to mimic Scotty, by hopping his own Worm out, then uses the ropes on a pin. Mockery followed by cheating from the "heel". Not that most of his act was about working heel. After a bit of terse countering Scotty gets a sloppy bulldog and finishes with the Worm. Like anyone with half a brain, I hate that damn move. It's not like the People's Elbow because at least that has an elbow drop at the end of it. The Worm is a chop. Who jobs to a chop? Considering what a filler match this was on paper, the actual delivery was okay. I think Hurricane should have gone over but if you're doing filler the rule is usually to send the fans home happy.
Final Rating: **

Backstage: Chavo and Bill get tips on interviewing divas from a now fully clothed Trish Stratus before walking in on Lita getting ready. These guys are total pervs. Elsewhere: DDP with his perfect teeth and perfect attitude gives a motivational speech. The motivational speaker gimmick was about as useful as his stalker gimmick. Why couldn't he just be DDP?

Diamond Dallas Page vs. The Big Show
Page's injuries were mounting up by this point and Big Show was as fat and lazy as ever. So this doesn't match up to their WCW bouts where both guys were eager to do something different. The work is sloppy, loose and unconvincing. DDP tries to put on a figure four but can't work out how to do it properly, which makes me really sad. Show goes for a lazy looking chokeslam, which is countered into the Diamond Cutter in the only decent piece of wrestling in the match. For some reason, after only a couple of minutes, Page decides to sell like Ricky Steamboat 30-minutes into a one hour match, and lies around for ages. Show inevitably kicks out and finishes with the chokeslam. I think this about sums up what the WWF thought of WCW and their wrestlers. Not that you'd blame them based on the workrate. This wouldn't have been out of place on a WCW PPV in 2000. That's not a complement.
Final Rating: ¼*

Backstage: The tedious adventures of Chavo and Bill continue as they burst in on Mighty Molly without her cape on. "Holy total strikeout" says Chavo. "We got nothing… booo". During the *No Mercy* review I made a comment about the WWF's creative team. Basically they wrote this comedy stuff the same way for everyone and either you could do it and got over as part of the machine or you sucked at it and didn't. This was not who Chavo was so he's not getting over. At all. In fact his terrible delivery is making me actively hate him and Bill DeMott. Which is a pity for Chavo who's actually talented.

Elsewhere: Shane McMahon, Kurt Angle (freshly turned), Debra and Steve Austin sit around discussing tonight's matches. I don't understand why it's shot in total darkness. Angle points out their table is round so they could be the Knights of the Round Table. He compares himself to Sir Galahad and Shane to Merlin. "If we're good knights, we need bad knights" – Angle. "I'm having a bad night right now. Merlin, can you make me disappear?" – Austin.

WCW Tag Team Championship
The Dudley Boyz (c) vs. The APA vs. The Hardy Boyz
The WWF's once electric tag team division of the previous two years finds itself relegated to the same teams competing ad nauseum. These were the same three teams on top of the division in late 1999, two years beforehand. Bubba, who's solid for a big man, takes a load of armdrags to try and get Matt over. "A lot of boos for Bradshaw" says Jim Ross. "A lot of booze in Bradshaw" responds Heyman, lightning quick. The APA get no reactions for most of the match, which shows you

how tired their gimmick has gotten. The crowd girly pop the Hardys while everyone else chants for tables. This is the problem you have when a tag team division has been established on big bumps and insane matches. You can't then go back to having the same teams just working each other in a normal match, which is where the actual lack of depth in the WWF's tag team division became apparent. Keep in mind they had the Impact Players on the pre-show. One of the WWF's most glaring faults is the "if it ain't broke, don't fix it" approach to their divisions. If nothing grows and there's no progression, there's no point. Faarooq gets double teamed by the Duds and Matt pins him with the Twist of Fate.

This is an elimination rules match, which confuses some fans who figured the Hardys just won the belts. Instead the APA head to the back and Bubba orders D-Von to get the tables! That gets a huge pop for the heel team. They don't follow through on it as Bubba decides they'll get more heat by promising wood and then not delivering on it. The Dudleys and Hardys had so many matches during 1999-2001 that they could wrestle in their sleep, and that's what the match feels like: by the numbers. Poetry in Motion on D-Von misses but Jeff lands on the ropes, just about, and D-Von falls into position for the Swanton, which also misses. Good spot though. Matt turns around into the 3D and the Dudleys retain.
Final Rating: **

Backstage: Vince McMahon mediates a sit down chat with Chris Jericho and the Rock, who'd been having issues of late. Vince points out they're both on Team WWF and they must get together to defeat the Alliance. Vince talks them into shaking hands and all is well until Jericho asks Rock to try not to lose again tonight, which provokes another brawl.

William Regal vs. Tajiri
The best part of Regal's pre-match promo is that he drops the accent completely and thanks the fans for spending their dole money on tonight's show. Regal's European style doesn't mesh well with Tajiri's puro intensity. I'm surprised how often Regal clashed with people considering how wonderful his own style was. I'm not pleased at how the old British and European styles have gone by the wayside. It was unique and beautiful to watch. I blame not only Vince McMahon, for trying to change everyone into the same worker, but also the likes of Big Daddy. Considering the styles clash they have a decent little match with Regal throwing in his strikes and holds while Tajiri uses his own strikes defensively. Both guys are so unconventional, especially for the WWF, that it's hard to find common ground. Regal's European stuff wins out over Tajiri's mixture of puro and lucha. Tajiri gets in some stiff strikes, and the Tarantula but misses a moonsault and Regal finishes with the Regal Stretch. Tajiri responds with the green mist. I'd like to have seen more of this. They were building towards something and then the match finished. It felt very abrupt. I like both guys and I enjoyed seeing a WWF match with two styles nowhere close to the norm for that company.
Final Rating: **¼

Backstage: Kurt Angle says the audience look like escapees from Strangeways prison. He moves on to Jericho calling him Y for Yellow, 2 for a turd and J for Jerk.

WCW Championship
Chris Jericho (c) vs. Kurt Angle
Yet another title is knocking around here as Angle holds the US Title. Jericho has the deck stacked against him, despite wavering with heeldom. He's wrestling against an Alliance

FURIOUS ABOUT: MIKE AWESOME

I distinctly remember my first exposure to Mike Awesome. It was ECW's Heatwave '98 against Masato Tanaka. The match is all sick chair shots, ridiculous dives and awesome powerbombs. As soon as I saw that match I knew Mike was destined for big things. The Tanaka feud continued both in Japan, for FMW, and Stateside as Awesome captured the ECW title. ECW being ECW, they couldn't hold onto him though and the former Gladiator joined WCW, which pretty much killed his career. They gave him an assortment of dumb gimmicks and his size was no longer impressive in a bigger company with lots of big men. Standing at 6' 4" and 295lbs, he didn't stand out in WCW or the WWF like he did in Japan and ECW. Awesome was signed when the WWF bought WCW but only lasted a year in McMahonland, saying "it sucked", he "hated it" and was happy to get fired. Awesome made a one match comeback at ECW's One Night Stand, putting in one final great shift against Tanaka before retiring in 2006. He seemed to have done enough to merit a contract. Tragically Mike hung himself in 2007. He was a 2-time world champion.

wrestler for the WCW Title and the referee is Nick Patrick, a guy Jericho once wrestled against in WCW and isn't known for his impartiality. These guys start out with technical stuff on the mat, which is really solid as Jericho can just about hang with Angle. Jericho then busts out the Three Amigos to no reaction. Angle responds with a cracking release German suplex. Jericho gets a nice block on the Angle Slam and goes right after the Walls of Jericho. Angle used to love working matches where the finishers were the focus. They'd get better than this, but Jericho could work that style with him. As if to emphasise that Angle goes after the ankle lock and Jericho has to counter out. Jericho rams Angle into the ring post and hits a shoulderbreaker, trying to take Angle's arm out of the match. Angle defensively goes for a sunset flip but Jericho rolls through it into an armbar, although it was a perfect position for the Walls, and Angle counters out. Very tidy wrestling from both guys and the psychology involved was good. Angle goes after the Walls of Jericho, as if to stick it to Jericho, but Chris counters out as he knows the mechanics of the move. Unfortunately the match then slows up and a typical house show spot; the sleeper with hand dropping makes an unwelcome appearance. Jericho picks the pace up again with the ankle lock but Angle, as a heel, doesn't counter and instead drags himself into the ropes. It puts Jericho over big as he could escape his hold, the Boston crab, but Angle couldn't wrestle out of the ankle lock. Angle goes after his own ankle lock but Jericho counters out of that too, to really put Y2J over big, into the Walls of Jericho. Again Angle can't find a way out and is forced into the ropes. I'm wondering if anyone was paying attention here as this match, along with the one with the Rock, made Jericho look like a legitimate main event star. And yet by *WrestleMania* he was playing second fiddle to Steph as a boring heel. Go figure. Angle goes after the Angle Slam but Jericho is able to counter out because of all the shoulder work earlier in the match, and gets a roll up to retain the belt. This

match is way better than I remember and is dripping with clever spots and work. All Jericho's little tactics come together into one big plot and it makes him look like a star for having the tactical nous to overcome not only a former WWF Champion, but also an Olympic gold medallist. There's a thought process here where it makes no sense for Angle to turn heel and immediately job to a guy who was below him on the totem pole, but in a way it makes perfect sense. Jericho was soon to become the Undisputed Champion and putting him over here showed he was ready for the responsibility. Unfortunately the booking turned kooky between now and *Vengeance* where Jericho won the title, but for a minute there Jericho was looking good. This is an underrated match. I underrated it hugely myself back in 2001.
Final Rating: ****

Backstage: Michael Cole points out that The Rock might find it hard to concentrate on tonight's match. Rock goes off on a lengthy tangent about Cole being "one of the leading journalists in the world today" before mocking him. Rock questions which way he swings. "Well.."- Cole. "IT DOESN'T MATTER HOW YOU SWING". Rock sometimes came across as a bully when he was dealing with announcers but when it comes to Michael Cole, nobody cares.

Mighty Molly & Stacy Keibler vs. Torrie Wilson & Lita
Trish Stratus is the guest referee in this sandwich/toilet break buffer match. Lita gets a substantial pop. Stacy and Torrie had a match at the last PPV, which involved a little bit of cartwheeling, which they do again here, and some actual technical wrestling, but it was all pre-planned whereas the actual wrestling in this match is terrible. Including Stacy throwing herself into Lita's arms for a scoop slam, then getting confused about the mechanics of being Irish whipped, doing a drop down and taking a poor bump off a suplex. She looks very confused and is completely out of her depth. Torrie whiffs on a gut kick so badly that JR has to call it. Torrie and Stacy's inexperience didn't show against each other because they just planned every second of the match. Here they try and incorporate themselves into Molly and Lita's actual "call-it-in-the-ring" match. It's during these exchanges where Torrie and Stacy are exposed. They are not wrestlers. Lita vs. Molly is okay and Lita finishes with a Twist of Fate (or as I've seen it dubbed, the Fist of Twat) in short order. Stacy gets pissy with Trish and gets bulldogged for her troubles. Trish had nothing much to do and most of the match was a friggin' disaster. If four men had wrestled this match it'd easily be into negative stars, but seeing as I'm feeling generous we'll call it a DUD instead. It is an embarrassment though.
Final Rating: DUD

WWF Championship
Steve Austin (c) vs. The Rock
Austin comes out first, which is a bit weird. The WWF must have gone mental during 2001 as they consider this to be a throwaway PPV match, rather than an actual US PPV main event, and the two weren't matched up again until 2003 when Austin was done and Rock was a movie star. Austin jumps Rock during his entrance but Rock comes back with a neckbreaker, aiming at Austin's surgically repaired neck, and goes right after the Rock Bottom. Austin elbows out and they head into the usual brawl around ringside. Maybe these guys have been watching Ric Flair tapes all afternoon as they lay into each other with chops throughout the entire opening segment. They head up the ramp and Austin twice gets countered, first on a suplex and then a piledriver. The suggestion being that, in a fair fight, Rock has Austin's number now. It might have taken four years but he's there and that's why Austin needed help at *WrestleMania*. He sensed it beforehand. Rock also moves on a rope ride, but Austin puts the brakes on and flips off the crowd. He turns to see Rock coming with a clothesline, ducks and hits his own. The back-and-forth is brilliant as both guys have become so familiar with the other's moves and abilities. Back in 2001 I didn't consider Rock-Austin to be essential viewing (mainly because of the midcard talent that had risen into the main events that year) but looking back it's quintessential viewing. The very essence of pro-wrestling. Especially with all the chops. It gives this match a different vibe to their other Attitude era matches. Rock fires back as they seem to be running on empty but Austin explodes with a Thesz Press and a triple rope hitting FU Elbow. Austin's proclivity for flipping people off has been taken to another level tonight. Yeah, it feels like a house show but since when is having fun a bad thing? That's evident as Rock steals the Thesz Press AND the triple rope hitting FU Elbow. They do some sleeper counters and both guys look badly winded, which isn't surprising seeing as they've worked flat out for most of the match. The hard work helps to compensate for the feeling that there's no way they'll change the title here. Earl Hebner gets clobbered and thus misses Rock hitting a spinebuster and slapping Austin in something approaching a Sharpshooter. Great sell from Hebner, who leans backwards over the apron like a dead swan. Austin replies with his own badly applied Sharpshooter. How hard is it to figure out the mechanics of that move? Rock counters into his own, and now third, badly applied Sharpshooter and Kurt Angle runs in with a chair. Chris Jericho runs down to save but Rock assumes Jericho hit him. Rock actually gets heat for laying out Jericho. Austin sneaks up behind Rock but the Stunner is countered into the Rock Bottom. Still no ref so Angle jumps back in only to get overpowered. Spinebuster for Austin and Rock goes for the People's Elbow but Angle trips him, nails Rock with the title belt and the Stunner finishes. The overbooking towards the end was a bit much. I was quite happy with the Jericho misunderstanding and that should have been enough but they just kept on going! So it loses points for the booking but the chops, counters and middle digit salutes that dominated the first half were enough to put this over as a worthy entrant in the Austin-Rock series.
Final Rating: ***¾

VERDICT

This show was a real surprise. I remember being down on it at the time but then the WWF's booking had gone a bit wonky in 2001 and it was hard to get excited about what amounted to a puffed up house show. But as far as house shows go… this is one I would have loved to have been at. There was a big main event between Austin and Rock, which delivered, and a solid secondary main event featuring Jericho and Angle. Plus a cage match between Edge and Christian. The backstage stuff was awful, as was the Divas match and Show-Page but everything that was bad, was short. Everything that was good, took up the meat of the show. This is one of the last UK only PPV's that was genuinely worth checking out, in retrospect, for a snapshot of how much fun the WWF was at the time. Even if it didn't seem that way when we were living it. Definite recommendation.

66

ROYAL RUMBLE 2002

CAT NO: WWF54117
RUN TIME: 164 minutes (approx)

Lee Maughan: Presented by Square's *Final Fantasy X*, from the Phillips Arena in Atlanta, GA. Gee, it's almost like they booked an arena in the heart of WCW country like they expected to be running some kind of interpromotional feud here, huh? Hosted by Jim Ross and Jerry Lawler.

WWF Tag Team Championship
Spike Dudley & Tazz (c) vs. The Dudley Boyz
In kayfabe terms, you do have to wonder which quack doctor allowed Spike to wrestle in a neck brace tonight. I guess we've come a long way since the days of "if you don't work, you don't get paid." The Dudleys start by immediately working over Spike (of course) but he avoids a suplex with the Dudley Dog (WWE's sanitised renaming of the Acid Drop). The referee misses a hot tag to Tazz and the Dudleys take back over with a double flapjack, but D-Von misses a diving headbutt, allowing Spike to get the tag on the second go round. Tazz runs wild with his array of suplexes and even locks Stacy Keibler in the Tazzmission until D-Von saves her. Spike tries for another Dudley Dog but gets dumped on the outside for his requisite big bump of the match, but that leaves D-Von open for the Tazzmission and he taps immediately. Hot opener, but there's only so much you can do with five minutes. This would also be the peak of the short-lived Spike & Tazz duo, as they dropped the belts to Billy and Chuck in February before Tazz retired to become the full-time colour commentator on *SmackDown!* after the brand split.
Final Rating: **½

WWF Intercontinental Championship
Edge (c) vs. William Regal
These two have been feuding for a while based on Regal's continued used of brass knuckles to win matches, and to that end, referee Nick Patrick has a rummage around the front of Regal's trunks and finds a pair attached to his winky. Regal breaks out a brutal side-release German suplex with Edge landing right on his nose, ironic given Regal's own troubles with constant nosebleeds around this time. Edge backdrops out of a butterfly bomb and into a bridging pin but Regal hangs on to the arms and rolls through into an underhook powerbomb for two. What a great spot, and they follow by colliding head-first for a double knockout after Edge lands a DDT on the ring apron.

I do appreciate the stiffness on display here, with Regal landing another German suplex but Edge popping right back and blasting him with a lariat before immediately falling down to sell the original blow. That spot was rather popularised by the likes of Kenta Kobashi in All Japan Pro Wrestling main events in the 1990s where it worked exceptionally well because those matches often used to run to the 30-minute mark and beyond. This match however doesn't even reach ten, and the crowd aren't particularly hip to the style they're working. They only really react to the big spots rather than the silence between the notes, finally coming alive for the Regal Stretch that they buy as a potential finisher, with Edge making the ropes.

Regal tries for a superplex but Edge pushes him off and blasts him with a spinning wheel kick and sets up for the spear. Regal pulls Patrick in the way however, then decks Edge with a second pair of brass knuckles for the pin and the title. Post-match, Regal denies everything, crediting his victory to the "power of the punch." There wasn't a lot wrong with the execution of the match, but I do have to concede that it wasn't massively exciting either, thanks in no small part to the crowd who weren't really au fait with the style.
Final Rating: **¾

WWF Women's Championship
Trish Stratus (c) vs. Jazz
Jacqueline is a last-minute addition as the special guest referee here, mainly to set up her being part of the Trish-Jazz feud, but possibly also because her in-ring experience will be valuable in helping call the action. Trish has her hand heavily taped thanks to an attack from Jazz, who slammed it in an equipment truck pre-match. Jazz attacks Trish as she's taking her coat off, then they immediately go into the sunset flip reversal sequence for a bunch of near falls. Jazz continues the aggression, wrapping Trish's arm around the bottom rope but she winds up in an argument with Jacqueline, who refuses to count for some reason. The distraction allows Trish to his Stratusfaction, but Jazz rolls through for a two count in a very

awkward spot. Jazz follows with a DDT but Trish blocks a charge and wins it with a regular bulldog to retain the title. Well, they tried hard, I'll give them that.
Final Rating: *

Street Fight
Ric Flair vs. Vince McMahon

Hilarious fact: Both of these guys are previous *Royal Rumble* winners, but while Flair won it from the #3 position, McMahon actually one-upped him and claimed it from #2. No wonder we've got a street fight to settle things! In reality, Flair returned to the WWF the night after *Survivor Series* and revealed himself to have bought Shane McMahon and Stephanie McMahon-Helmsley's WWF stock, making him co-owner with Vince. How Linda was supposed to fit into that with Vince and Flair owning equal stock isn't covered, but things obviously didn't sit well with Vince, leading to months of one-upmanship and interference in each other's business until Flair stumbled over a contract that described Vince as a "wrestler" as well as an owner, giving Flair jurisdiction over him that for some reason he wasn't able to override by, you know, just cancelling his wrestlers contract or something similarly logical.

Vince is just absolutely jacked to the gills here, and Lawler practically gives himself an orgasm as he verbally slavers over McMahon's physique. Interesting to note too that Flair is wrestling his first WWF match since 1993, and his last PPV appearance was nine years ago, also at *Royal Rumble* curiously enough. Oddly, McMahon more or less dominates right from the off, likely because they both realise how rotten a wrestler he is and want to avoid his lumbering ways as much as possible. Flair works in the Flair flop early, then pulls a gory blade job off a shot to the head from a steel sign. Vince drags a bloody Flair over to where Flair's kids are sat at ringside and actually steals a camera from Flair's daughter Megan to take selfies with in a terrific piece of heeldom.

Back inside, Vince locks in the figure four to rub metaphorical salt into the literal wound, but Flair escapes so Vince dashes outside and grabs a lead pipe. Flair blocks his attempts to use it with a low blow and busts Vince's head open with a monitor from the Spanish announce table, stopping off to watch a reply of it. From there, he drags Vince over to his kids and has Megan take pictures as he bites Vince's forehead like the ghost of Dracula. Back inside again, he blasts Vince in the grapefruits and clonks him over the head with the lead pipe. The figure four is academic from there, and kind of an odd choice for a finish when you've just smashed a guy's brains in.

At the time, it was tremendous fun to see Vince take such a clobbering, and fans were thrilled to see a reasonably in-shape, t-shirtless Flair dishing it out like the good old days, given what a sad little wreck he'd become in the dying days of WCW. Unfortunately, while wrestling in many ways is about the now and giving the fans in that moment in time exactly what they want, this match just doesn't hold up years removed. If you look at things from an objective viewpoint, it mostly just consisted of two middle aged blokes wandering around, smashing each other with plunder all whilst bleeding all over the place, which can be a pretty sorry sight to see when viewed in that light. Still, the live crowd were going absolutely mad for it the entire time so we'll split the difference and call it **½.
Final Rating: **½

WWE Undisputed Championship
Chris Jericho (c) vs. The Rock

Jericho of course became Undisputed Champion last month at *Vengeance* after winning a four-man tournament, beating the Rock for the World Title in the semi-finals and Steve Austin in the finals to unify the World and WWF Titles. Sadly since that time, he's been presented as less of a star than Rock, Austin and Triple H, devaluing the titles, and the angle is that nobody is taking Jericho seriously as champion, Jericho even draws attention to that by proclaiming "This is not a joke! I am not a joke!" It is a baffling way to attempt to elevate someone, and the upshot was that the fans didn't take him seriously in the role after having that point drilled home over and over again. Who could possibly have imagined such consequences?

Jericho talks trash to start and motions for Rock to "Just bring it!" (drawing an audible gasp from the crowd), so Rock kicks his ass with a Samoan drop and Jericho hightails it. 'Y2J' comes back with a suplex and channels his WCW character with the arrogant, one-foot cover before removing one of the top turnbuckle pads. That he instead slaps on the Walls of Jericho instead of trying to use the exposed steel before being cut off seems like a lapse of psychology, making it obvious it's being set up for something later. He also manages to drag the match down a touch with a chinlock, not something you see out of Jericho all too often.

Picking up the pace, Rock comes back with a superplex and a belly-to-belly, and Jericho fires back with a bulldog and the Lionsault for a near fall. Jericho argues with referee Earl Hebner over that one, and the hesitation causes him to whiff on a missile dropkick and get caught in the Sharpshooter, which the fans actually buy as a finish despite Rock winning few matches with the hold. The fact Rock beat Jericho with the move in a tag team match on the January 10th edition of *SmackDown!* might have something to do with that however. It's certainly enough to bring Jericho's chums Lance Storm and Christian out, during the period that they were hinting at doing a new Team Canada group that wound up becoming the Jericho-less Un-Americans. They distract Hebner who misses Jericho tapping out (what a loser), so Rock beats them both off... in the sense that he kicks their asses, not that's he's auditioning for a place on the team alongside Billy & Chuck.

Jericho lands a Rock Bottom for two and goes for the People's Elbow, but Rock kips up and they fight to the floor where Rock gets a Rock Bottom through the announce table. Back in the ring, another Rock Bottom is countered into the Walls of Jericho, but Rocky grabs the ropes then counters into a small package for two. Jericho ducks on a flying clothesline and Rock wipes Hebner out, giving Jericho the opportunity to blast Rock in the head with the WWF Title belt, and Nick Patrick scoots into the ring to count a near fall. Jericho is aghast at that and stops to argue with Patrick, giving Rock the opening to land a DDT on Jericho... but Patrick refuses to count. He eats a Rock Bottom for that, and Jericho suffers a spinebuster and the People's Elbow but there's still no referee. Jericho recovers as Rock tries to revive Hebner and hits a low blow before ramming Rock head-first into the exposed turnbuckle (see what I mean?) and finishes with a schoolboy and his feet on the ropes.

I could complain further about the booking of Jericho here, as it took lashings of interference before he was able to score a cheap, indecisive victory, but Rock at least did more to put him over with a good, if formulaic, match than the grumpy Steve Austin or Wrestling God and Supreme Leader of the Grand Universe Triple H did during Jericho's reign as champion. Good match once all the entirely expected nonsense kicked in.
Final Rating: ***¾

- Over at WWF New York, JR asks Shawn Michaels to predict a *Royal Rumble* winner. 'HBK' can't choose just one and goes for fellow statesmen Steve Austin and the Undertaker, which in wrestling parlance is essentially a guarantee that neither of those will win. Michaels actually has a habit of selecting multiple winners and getting the call wrong despite a clear winner going in (in this case Triple H), as he plumped for CM Punk and all three members of the Shield prior to the 2014 Rumble, which in fact went to overwhelmingly obvious candidate Batista. The moral of the story is, never let Shawn Michaels pick your lottery numbers.

Royal Rumble Match

Channelling the spirit of 'Million Dollar Man' Ted DiBiase, **Rikishi** draws #1 after last year pulling #30, whilst the returning **Goldust** is #2. This is kind of a reset for Rikishi, who turned babyface last May at the behest of then-commissioner Mick Foley after a lousy run as a heel, before a shoulder injury just a few weeks later put him on the sidelines for the entirety of the invasion angle. Goldust is also on the verge of a rather unexpected rebirth after leaving the WWF in 1999 for an underwhelming run under the Dustin Rhodes names in WCW. Goldust goes over the top but hangs on a couple of times to visually explain that you have to hit the floor to be eliminated. #3 is the **Big Bossman**, nearing the end of his usefulness to the WWF (and arguably long past it), followed at #4 by **Bradshaw**. Rikishi gives Bossman a Stinkface, and a standing superkick and clothesline leave him with the indignation of being the first guy eliminated. **Lance Storm** is #5, immediately buried by JR sarcastically dubbing him "Mr. Personality" as Vince McMahon no doubt bellows down his earpiece. Ross does at least call Storm a "great athlete" to even things up, but why would you draw attention to a guy's perceived deficiencies? Whatever happened to the old ECW philosophy of "accentuate the positive"?

Head *Tough Enough* instructor **Al Snow** joins the fun at #6, just in time to see Storm have his head all but ripped off thanks to a Clothesline from Hell by Bradshaw, and #7 is **Billy**, having lost his surname *and* all his nicknames since partnering up with Chuck. Originally a generic babyface team, they're now being pushed as heels on account of their apparently growing affection for one another. Forget the progressive, forward-thinking nineties, this is new millennium, yet for all of pro wrestling's blatant homoeroticism it's shockingly still a case of "Boo! Spit! The gays are coming!" Billy of course takes Bradshaw from behind... and eliminates him. You know, because he's a big gay wrestler. One-time ECW teammates Snow and Storm trade superkicks on the apron with Snow coming out ahead, eliminating Lance. Perhaps surprisingly early as one of the genuine contenders, the **Undertaker** is #8, and he destroys everyone, eliminating Goldust with a chokeslam, hurling out Snow, clotheslining Rikishi to the floor, and hoying out Billy. **Matt Hardy** is #9, which is rather convenient since Undertaker had a minor feud going that reunited Team Extreme after their little split in late 2001. Undertaker immediately grabs him by the throat so **Lita** slides in and kicks him square in his big, ginger plums. JR and Lawler wonder aloud how Matt might need some help and probably won't get it, telegraphing the arrival of **Jeff Hardy** at #10.

Matt gets a neckbreaker and Jeff hits the Swanton Bomb off the top, but Undertaker catches Jeff on Poetry in Motion and dumps him out, then blasts Matt with the Last Ride and wangs him out too. *Tough Enough* champion **Maven** is #11 but Lita and the Hardys jump Undertaker (to a smattering of heel heat), then in a famous spot, Maven eliminates Undertaker with a dropkick from behind. This could have served to make Maven a one-night superstar, or at the very least set up a pay-per-view grudge match between the two. Instead, Undertaker spends the next few minutes beating Maven's ass all over the arena, bloodying him up and leaving him laying in a mess of concession stand popcorn, stopping off only momentarily to confirm what a geek **Scotty 2 Hotty** (#12) has become by knocking him out for a couple of minutes solid with a single punch. European Champion **Christian** is #13 and he can't believe his luck, taking it easy and picking at Scotty's carcass until **Diamond Dallas Page** joins the fray at #14. Scotty recovers enough to get the Worm in but DDP yongs him out from behind as **Chuck** hits the ring at #15, renewing hostilities with Page for the honour of the New Blood and the Millionaire's Club.

The Godfather is #16 in a resetting of his character after the Right to Censor stable ran its course and he was surplus to requirements for the invasion angle. He's now gone "legit" with his escort agency to explain his character rebirth, but as with Rikishi, the whole thing is like trying to put the genie back in the bottle. DDP gets eliminated off-camera by Christian and **Albert** joins the battle at #17, Chuck grabs him from behind and tosses him off... err, out, with help from Christian, and they also put Godfather out with a double clotheslines after he misses the Ho Train in the corner. **Perry Saturn** is #18 in some ugly Dalmatian (or cow) print tights JR gets in a few gay jokes of his own, noting that Christian has Chuck "deep in the crotch" and suggesting that they make "strange bedfellows." Boo! Spit! The gays are strange! Lawler asks what Ross is inferring to really hammer the point home. Where's Paul Heyman when you need him? The last few minutes have felt like dead wood, which should tip you off to the fact that **Steve Austin** is #19, and he immediately throws out Christian, Chuck ("Goodnight, sweet prince!") and Saturn in short order. With nobody left, Austin drags Christian and Chuck back into the ring for a pair of Stone Cold Stunners and eliminates them again. **Val Venis** is #20, the third of five returning superstars tonight, having also been left with no direction for the invasion after the conclusion of the Right to Censor angle. Unlike the Godfather, no explanation is offered for Val's return to the porn star gimmick.

#21 is the immune **Test**, and he and Val team up and dominate Austin. What is this, War Games? Austin clotheslines Venis out after a misplaced big boot from Test, and Test in turn eats a Stunner and a clothesline to put him out too. Test was such a pussy for a guy with a year of guaranteed immunity. #22 is **Triple H** in his first appearance since tearing his left quadriceps muscle in a tag match last May, ironically where he had Austin as a partner. They run a double down in the middle as the **Hurricane** flies into the ring at #23 and goes for a double chokeslam on the former Two-Man Power Trip, who shoot each other a cursory glance, send Hurricane for a ride, and resume hostilities. **Faarooq** as #24 as the clock has gotten noticeably quicker. Remember 1997, when he was a bigger star than the other two guys currently in the ring? Austin drops him with a Stunner and Triple H puts him out. **Mr. Perfect** hits the ring at #25 to a *very* strong reaction as JR erroneously claims he made his Rumble debut in 1993, ignoring no less than three prior Rumble appearances from 1989-1991. He actually made his *final* Rumble appearance, prior to this one, in 1993.

Kurt Angle ups the star power further at #26 and sets about Triple H, revisiting their old rivalry. #27 is the **Big Show** who tries a Hurricane-style double chokeslam on Austin and Triple H, but they fight out of it again, only to eat a double clothesline.

Kane is #28 after his dominating performance last year, and he bodyslams the Big Show over the top and out in impressive fashion. Unfortunately for him, he eats a Stunner then takes an Olympic Slam over the top to put him out. #29 is **Rob Van Dam** who almost slips on his way into the ring, but blasts Angle with a Five Star Frog Splash and wipes everyone out with kicks to a thunderous reaction… except for Triple, who ends the fun by killing him stone dead with a Pedigree. Oh, don't you worry, dear RVD fan; there'll be *plenty* more of that to come. Perfect lands a suplex on Angle as **Booker T** rounds out the field at #30, and he throws Van Dam out, still down from the devastating effects of the clearly atomic Pedigree. A celebratory Spinneroonie leads to Booker walking into a Stunner that bounces him out over the top, leaving just the final four.

Final Four: Steve Austin, Triple H, Kurt Angle, and rather surprisingly, Mr. Perfect. Angle avoids a Stunner attempt and shoots Austin off, who counters the Pedigree with a catapult into an Olympic Slam from Angle. Kurt follows with rolling Germans on Austin, but Austin blocks with a low blow. Austin tries to eliminate Perfect so Angle surprisingly dumps Austin out from behind, with 'Stone Cold' blasting everyone in the ring in the head with a steel chair in retaliation. Populist theory at the time suggested the match would come down to Triple H vs. Austin so his elimination there is quite the shocker, but with Triple H being presented as a babyface, it makes more sense to leave him alone with two heels. That being said, the last time we saw Perfect and Triple H on TV together back in '96, they we in cahoots as Hunter took the Intercontinental Title from Marc Mero, so why aren't they the ones teaming up on Angle? I guess because Triple H kicked his mentor to the curb after he got what he wanted out of the deal.

Miscommunication leads to Angle clotheslining Perfect over the top but he hangs on to an enormous reaction, and comes back for a Perfectplex on Angle to an even bigger response. He follows up with a rolling neck snap on Angle but gets clotheslined out by Triple H immediately after, which is one of those things that probably sounded good on paper, but they really should have called an audible and had Angle be the one to eliminate Perfect given the overwhelming babyface response he was getting. And who wouldn't salivate at the potential of an Angle-Perfect *WrestleMania* match to pay it off? Perfect actually got a contract out of his performance here, only for the WWF to quickly realise they had no plans for him, leaving him to bounce around mostly in dark matches and on weekend television before he was released for his part in the notorious "Plane Ride from Hell" where he grappled with Brock Lesnar some 15,000 feet in the air and nearly out of the door, before finishing out his career (and sadly his life) with NWA-TNA in 2003. For one last glorious performance however, here he was absolutely *perfect*.

Triple H tokenistically teases an elimination but hangs on like Shawn Michaels in 1995, and as Angle celebrates, Hunter blasts him with a facebuster and clotheslines him out for the slightly anticlimactic and hugely predictable (but unarguably correct, at least so it seemed at the time) win at a shade under 70-minutes, sending him coursing ominously towards the main event of a *WrestleMania X8* and a showdown with Chris Jericho. Fun Rumble in all.
Final Rating: ****

VERDICT

Over the course of our two Attitude Era *Complete WWF Video Guide*s, we've seen an incredible amount of change in the WWF; The promotion turning the corner creatively in 1997, taking off dramatically in 1998, hitting the mainstream in 1999 and reaching its peak in 2000. But, just as the rot set in with WCW in '98 before its eventual decline in 2001, the same can be said of the WWF here. Of course, the consequences weren't as severe, but no clearer was the downswing evident than in 2001's invasion storyline, with the WWF continuing to push their own branded megastars ahead of anyone with the potential to supplant them. Why fix it if it ain't broke, right? Sadly, that attitude would continue throughout 2002, as the same names who were on top three and four years ago remain, so whilst the promotion masks over its own short-sightedness by pretending to push Chris Jericho as a new star in putting the Undisputed Title on him, whilst covertly (albeit transparently) presenting him as a fluke, a "joke", and a fall guy for the real heir to the throne, Triple H.

The whole thing just has a real air of late-era WCW about it, particularly to incidents in which then-booker Kevin Nash and top star Hulk Hogan worked programs with Rey Misterio, Jr. and Billy Kidman respectively to "prove" their willingness to work with talented yet smaller individuals, only to completely bury them throughout their programs. The Undertaker meanwhile was on a similar rampage, at his counterproductive worst in flattening Maven and the Hardy Boyz, hot on the heels of his destruction job last year with Diamond Dallas Page. Realistically, the only guy to break through the mould and become a genuine headline attraction was Brock Lesnar, who managed to justify all of WWE's fears about pushing new headliners before they'd "earned it" by flaking out and quitting in early 2004. Never mind the money he drew for them over the two years he spent on the main roster, quitting at the top was seen as an act of treason, and he became the go-to example for not building new stars once John Cena finally found himself permanently rooted to the top of the card. Sure, guys like Kurt Angle and Edge (and to some extent C.M. Punk and Daniel Bryan) were eventually able to squeak through, and hand-picked golden boys like Randy Orton and Batista ticked all of WWE's boxes, but the sheer volume of potential breakthrough stars who came along in that 15+ year period who WWE passed on, and in many cases, refused to even try with, was a stinging indictment of their skewered promotional policies that were growing increasingly evident here. Still, good show though!

75

NO WAY OUT 2002

CAT NO: WWF54121
RUN TIME: 157 minutes (approx)

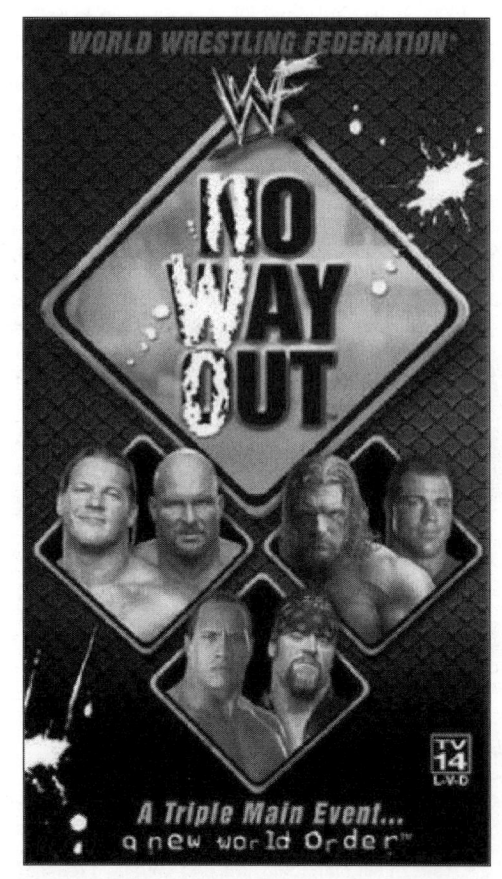

Arnold Furious: There were times during 2002 where my interest in the WWF product dropped down to a minimum. With no competition the WWF started to coast a bit and to liven things up Vince decided to re-hire Hulk Hogan, Kevin Nash and Scott Hall. These guys would have come in handy during the invasion! I had a few immediate and pressing concerns regarding them being rehired and I will address them now:

Hulk Hogan. The consummate politician, Hogan had effectively ruined WCW for his own financial betterment. He pocketed Eric Bischoff and controlled the company through his puppet owner. Vince Russo realised his hands were tied with booking Hogan and ran a shoot angle to get him off TV as he couldn't write Hogan out of the main events due to Hogan's contract clauses. Obviously Vince McMahon had significantly more control over Hogan and really only brought him back for the nostalgia element he'd bring. However in the ring Hogan's last good match was six years earlier, at the beginning of the nWo angle at *Bash at the Beach*, and he wasn't actually even in the match! For an actual honest to God good match with Hogan competing you have to go back to 1994 and his series with Ric Flair. His deterioration in the ring was clear-cut and he wouldn't be doing much quality wrestling. Also, he looked older than dirt.

Kevin Nash. He's a bullshitter and no mistake about it. Nash's basic qualities as a wrestling guy were to establish himself and then coast on that reputation. As a booker he was a disaster, putting over his buddies and generally ignoring the talent. He referred to Benoit and Malenko as "vanilla midgets". His first act in charge of WCW was to put himself and Hall over in a tag match and then put Hall over for the US Title. The Kliq never dies. Nash's last good singles match was in 1996, against Shawn Michaels. The entire time he was in WCW, he used the minimum of effort but continued raking in the cash and stayed at the top of the card.

Scott Hall. Besides behaving like a total jerk backstage, as is evidenced in many wrestler interviews and Chris Jericho's book, Hall was a liability. He was an alcoholic and when he'd been drinking he was an asshole, which is a terrible combination. I like Hall as a wrestler but his in-ring had deteriorated since switching from the WWF in 1996 and, like Nash, his last good singles match was back in 1996. The common denominator of these three then, is that they've not had a decent singles outing in the last six years, but they were name stars and people thought they were cool. That was the biggest issue of all. The once cool nWo was showing signs of aging. Hall was in the best condition of the three and he was 44 and broken down because of taking too many bumps and abusing his body outside of the ring. Nash was slightly younger but injury prone with bad knees. Hogan was pushing 50 and in horrible condition. These guys were not cool anymore, and that was the nWo's main selling point.

Tangent: It should be pointed out the last "big" WCW star that the WWF signed was DDP. What did Page do tonight? Headlined *Heat* against the Big Bossman. That should have been a warning.

17th February 2002. We're in Milwaukee, Wisconsin. Hosts are Jim Ross and Jerry Lawler.

Promo Time: New World Order
The nWo music is cool and I'm glad they didn't try to alter it and put a WWF spin on it, like they normally do. "You never say never in this business" says Jim Ross and that about sums up the wacky world of wrestling. I wouldn't have paid any of them to come back, but that's just me. Nash points out they have "heat with the boys" as the fans "WHAT?" along. Austin just destroyed heel promos with that business. Nash mewls that being labelled as "company killers" hurts their feelings. Nash claims they just want a chance. Hall gets a big pop for the "…hey, yo". He calls the nWo "marks" and as fans they want to work in the WWF. I love him saying "we might get to drink some beer with the boys" and Nash and Hogan immediately wag their finger to say no. However that's papering over his real life issues and turning it into a joke. It made me smile but he got fired a few months later for falling off the wagon. Hogan sucks up to the fans and actually gets them cheering as he says "God bless America". Ross doesn't believe a word of it. Considering what a giant in professional wrestling Hogan is, it's

274

shocking how little he actually said. I'm just relieved a 10-minute promo didn't become a 20-minute promo.

Tag Team Turmoil
#1 Contendership Match
Scotty 2 Hotty & Albert vs. Christian & Lance Storm
The winners get a title match at *WrestleMania*. Nice mix to open up with the fun-loving babyfaces against the uber-serious Canadian heels. Albert and his funky trousers make the biggest impact. He throws around the heels and hits a giant swing. He's fun. It was around this point that I really started getting into Albert as a worker. It's shocking how good he is as a babyface. It's weird because he's spent the rest of his career working heel. The match breaks down really early for the Worm but Lance interrupts it and Christian hits the Unprettier.

Christian & Lance Storm vs. The Hardy Boyz
The Hardyz had been out of action after the split and feud angle fell on its face. The fans have been burned a touch though and chant for "Lita" instead, who came out of the angle smelling like roses. The smell of failure lingers on Matt, and Jeff gets the bigger reactions in the ring. Storm slots into Edge's role with ease, inserting his spots where Edge's normally are. Including the awesome rolling Maple Leaf. Twist of Fate on Storm sets up the Swanton and the Hardys advance.

The Hardy Boyz vs. The Dudley Boyz
Anyone else getting déjà vu? There's a potential six-person inter-gender lined up as the Duds now have Stacy Keibler in their corner. Bubba switches it up and looks for a submission on Jeff with a standing figure four. I'm surprised he didn't incorporate that into his singles repertoire. They run a truncated version of their normal match, working noticeably quicker than usual. Matt almost gets the win with the yodelling legdrop and the Hardys work over Bubba with some innovative double teaming. Stacy jumps in and Lita stops her; CATFIGHT! Matt saves Lita and takes the Bubba Bomb. Lita takes revenge with the Litacanrana on Bubba. Jeff hits him with a crazy suicide senton. Matt counters D-Von's inverted DDT into a roll up and the Duds are sent packing after a frantic couple of minutes. Jeff eats 3D on the floor as a measure of revenge.

The Hardy Boyz vs. Billy & Chuck
Chuck & Suck get NO reaction whatsoever, which about sums up the problem with booking the division around them in 2002. Matt finds himself isolated and Billy takes it with the Fameasser to thunderous X-Pac heat.

Billy & Chuck vs. APA
Palumbo has ridiculous pigtails this evening in an attempt to make him more effeminate. Chuck never really got the gimmick though. He was a blank slate, personality wise. Faarooq takes heat while the fans chant "faggots". It's one of those rare occasions where I actually feel sorry for Billy Gunn. If they were desperate to put him in a tag team, why not just rehire Road Dogg! Clothesline From Hell! That'll do it. APA get the title shot at *WrestleMania*. Oddly enough it'd be against the team they beat here as Billy & Chuck won the tag belts between now and then. It ended up as a four-way with the Dudleys and Hardys both in there too, which renders this match utterly useless. It was at least good fun though. The Dudleys-Hardys bit showed how great both those teams were, but I wish both of the opening teams had gotten more of a fair shake.
Final Rating: ***

Backstage: Ric Flair gets quizzed about the nWo and claims the locker room is united against them. Undertaker strolls in to make vaguely weird threats about "keeping his eye" on Flair.

Goldust vs. Rob Van Dam
Goldust returned at the Rumble, and again he could probably have been used during the invasion, but hey if they didn't use Flair or the nWo, why bother with him? The RVD feud is basically the same as the Razor Ramon one from 1996 with the exception that RVD isn't homophobic and doesn't really get Goldust's gimmick so there's no hatred at all. Plus Van Dam has gone from mixing it up with main eventers to this dead end in two months. RVD does all the stuff in this match that irked the WWF's management. Instead of Rolling Thunder he switches to a cartwheel moonsault for no reason, other than he can. He hits a spot and then stops to pose a bit. Goldust tries to slow him up and time waste. That lasts about five seconds before RVD hits the corkscrew legdrop onto the rail. Jerry Lawler isn't interested and starts talking about movies including his favourite movie line of all time… "this one time at band camp" from *American Pie* but JR shuts that down. RVD's flexibility allows Goldust to work some interesting spots including stretching him backwards over the ring post from the top rope. Rob's side of the offence is not as good as he just gets his shit in. I guess he feels frustrated at being dumped in a match with a guy who's not always treated seriously and certainly wouldn't have been in ECW, which is an insult to Dustin as a worker. Especially as Rob no sells his uppercut. They run into a few other similar problems before RVD finishes casually with a Frogsplash. Now, RVD was blatantly above Goldust on the card and should have gone over but his attitude during the match was worrying. Despite a clash of styles I thought this came off quite well.
Final Rating: **¾

Backstage: Steve Austin runs into the nWo. They don't attack him but instead bring a peace offering of Budweiser. Austin takes the beer and casually tosses it over his shoulder. Awkward, dead segment.

WWF Tag Team Championship
Tazz & Spike Dudley (c) vs. Booker T & Test
Tazz & Spike are the underdog tag champs and the challengers are both huge. Tazz has lost all his momentum from 2000 and is no longer a badass. This was between phases of being a commentator. Spike is a more traditional giant killer and is perfect for taking heat. Spike gets beaten down, takes the axe kick and Booker even has time to hit the Spinneroonie before pinning. Tazz has to make the save as Spike was toast. The tag to Tazz is completely heatless, showing exactly how little interest the fans had in this. The inconsistent booking of Tazz hurt him. He handily outwrestles Test before Spike runs in to hit the Acid Drop. Test argues a count, which gets him caught in the Tazzmission and the champs retain via submission. It feels like I wrote very little about this match but that's because very little happened.
Final Rating: *

Backstage: The Rock gets interviewed and is unimpressed by Coach's questions. The Rock is energised, as per usual, about whupping Taker's ass all over Milwaukee.

Brass Knucks on a Pole Match
WWF Intercontinental Championship
William Regal (c) vs. Edge
If you want a clue to the quality of this match, note the "on a pole match". In general on a pole matches suck. They wisely avoid the stipulation to begin with and just work a straight up

FURIOUS ABOUT: nWo

To find the roots of the nWo you have to go back to 1984 and New Japan. It was there that Riki Choshu turned heel on Antonio Inoki and formed a group called "Ishingun". They opposed Inoki but soon fell out with the promoter and left, as a group, turning up in All Japan as New Japan invaders. The angle was red hot and almost swayed the Japanese wrestling war in favour of AJPW. Having discovered this angle, Eric Bischoff decided to do something similar in WCW. He'd hire two top tier WWF wrestlers and have them 'invade' WCW. His idea was that they'd be portrayed as being WWF wrestlers, in WCW. By the time WCW were forced to confess that neither Scott Hall nor Kevin Nash were actually under WWF contract the damage had been done and the angle was unstoppable. The whole thing went nuclear at Bash at the Beach '96 where the duo faced off against a trio of WCW main event stars, claiming they didn't need a mysterious "third man". It was at the conclusion of the event that Hulk Hogan turned up and revealed himself to be the third man. Thus turning heel for the first time since 1980. A 16 year run of pure babyface main eventdom. From there the group grew and was diluted. Some additions made sense (Ted DiBiase) as they were ex-WWF guys, some did not (The Giant). The booking went on for too long and the nWo never got their comeuppance. The WWF's attempt to re-do the nWo lasted a few months. Hulk Hogan turned face, Kevin Nash got injured and Scott Hall was fired.

match. Sadly the stipulation kicks in and they try to climb the pole. It's annoying because I know full well they can have a perfectly serviceable match and the stipulation hinders that. Also, the stipulation provides a strange situation where the knucks are legal, so what constitutes a DQ? Any other cheating? Or is it no DQ? The ref doesn't seem to know and Regal hides his other cheating. Plus this all overwhelms the IC Title, like knucks are more important! Edge inserts a big bump and then takes a butterfly powerbomb on the floor so they can establish his ribs as injured. Regal Stretch is on and again I'm not sure about the stipulations. Edge pops the old blood capsule gimmick to try and oversell those ribs with some Ken Shamrock internal bleeding. Regal attempts what would have been a sickening powerbomb to the floor but Edge clumsily counters into a rana off the apron. I say "rana" but Edge couldn't get into position and Regal just flip bumped himself. Regal somehow recovers quicker and pulls down the knucks but gets back superplexed. Edge tries to nail that coughing up blood gimmick as Regal kicks the knucks out of the ring. At the fourth attempt. This has not been a good match. Edge grabs the knucks but Regal pulls out a second pair of knucks, from his knucksack, and belts Edge in the jaw to retain. The gimmickry of the match hindered them and they had a much better straight up match than this.
Final Rating: *½

Backstage: Kurt Angle addresses confidence and says Stephanie McMahon will do an honest job as referee before pointing out he's superior to Triple H in every way.

The Undertaker vs. The Rock
This came about because Rock thought it was funny that Maven eliminated Taker from the *Royal Rumble*. Wouldn't Taker vs. Maven be the appropriate match for that storyline? Because Taker has no sense of humour, he's out to teach Rock some respect here. Good luck with that. Rock sprints down to the ring and it's a pity the whole match doesn't have the energy of his entrance. It's weird because add Kurt Angle to mix in five months time and you have a great match, but this one is a stinker. 2002 is the year where the Undertaker began to regain his mojo, mainly through a feud with Brock Lesnar, but when the year began he was in an absolute funk. This match runs for 17-minutes and they're entirely forgettable. Taker stomps away, Rock attempts a comeback, Taker cuts him off, Taker stomps away, Rock attempts a comeback, Taker cuts him off, Taker stomps away, Rock attempts a comeback… you get the picture. It's massively popular, for some reason, as both guys are still over on their Attitude personas. Taker looks in better condition than he had been for the past couple of months but the match is creatively devoid of ideas. Taker's offence hits "plodding" before too long and I again find myself mentally questioning the need for 17-minutes of this. Rock attempts a comeback, Taker cuts him off, wait, we did that already. Just before this show, Taker caused Rock a neck injury and that's never addressed here. It's never an issue and Taker works away at the ribs instead, which was also Edge's injury in the last match. The difference is that Edge actually sold his injury. Rock fires up, hits a DDT and a spinebuster to set up the People's Elbow but Taker grabs the goozle. Rock kicks him square in Death Valley to break that and you'd think it was a DQ because it was so obvious. Taker pulls a chokeslam out of his ass but decides this would be a good time to do some selling. Taker bails to mess about with his bike. "What is Undertaker doing here?" speculates Jim Ross. Indeed. Taker can't find the pipe he hid and takes ages pulling it out, thus giving Ric Flair time to run in and stop him. Taker no sells the chops and boots him. Rock ducks the pipe shot and straps Taker in the Sharpshooter. Vince McMahon runs down for the save so Rock kicks his ass. Taker goes for the Tombstone but Flair nails him with the pipe and the Rock Bottom finishes. All this really served to do was set up Flair-Taker at *WrestleMania*. I sure wish they'd found a way to do that which didn't involve a 17-minute snoozer. The last 3-4 minutes would look great as highlights. The rest of the match? Tedious.
Final Rating: *¼

Video Control takes us to WWF New York where Mr Perfect runs down New Yorkers. "Even the rats are ugly here". His promo is so incoherent they leave it at one question. JR plugs Rob Zombie's '*Feel So Numb*', which he claims is available "on 8-Track, or whatever".

#1 Contendership Match
Triple H vs. Kurt Angle
Hunter won the Rumble but thanks to shenanigans, Kurt gets to challenge him for that title shot here. Although the overwhelming story is Hunter's relationship with Steph, but seeing as he can't wrestle her, he's wrestling Angle, a surrogate. Steph is the guest referee though. Angle immediately goes for roll ups, knowing Steph will count Hunter down quickly, leading to a rarely heard WWF incantation of the "she's a crack whore" chant. Hunter is feeling suitably motivated to beat the crap out of Angle and Kurt is always good

so this works, despite Steph's shambolic officiating. She's bang in the middle of her "mega-sexy" phase, by the way, so she's wearing a very tight top and leather shorts. Angle accidentally clotheslines her out of the ring to put paid to the special referee gimmick. Hunter gets a MASSIVE pop for strolling over, taking a look at Steph unconscious on the floor and laughing. Triple H; spouse of the year! Timmy White jumps in the replace Steph while two other zebras drag her carcass out of here. Angle makes a couple of dubious decisions, regarding moveset, including a back suplex that looks almost identical to the Angle Slam. That's like Austin using the jawbreaker. Or Hunter a pancake slam. You shouldn't use a move that looks similar to your finisher. Hunter's only crime is calling spots too loudly. I was talking to James Dixon about this the other day and we concurred that he's been caught calling spots on camera more than anyone else in WWF history (with the possible exception of John Cena). "Reverse it" he yells at Kurt before an Irish whip. Gee, I wonder what'll happen here? It all gets a bit uninspired after a fiery opening and they slug it out doing a lot of Attitude main event stuff. Then Hunter steps his game up and starts with the trademarks; high knee, spinebuster, facebuster. That causes Angle to take a powder and eventually knock Timmy White out. Angle then has an opening to go low and hit the Angle Slam. This brings a recovered Steph back out here and she can't even quick count properly, with JR blaming her neck injury sustained earlier. Steph is so dumb she stands right behind Hunter when he's applying the ankle lock. Naturally Hunter kicks him off and bumps Steph again but it's a blindingly obvious spot. She didn't even move around into position, she just stood there. Not content with that they bump Timmy again. How many ref bumps are in this damn thing? Angle grabs a chair but Hunter ducks it and hits the Pedigree. Tim recovers to count 2 but Steph runs over and elbow drops him before hoofing the fighting Irishman in the Shamrocks. Hunter goes to kick her so Steph points out how great her tits are. No wait, that she's the referee! My mistake. Angle chair shots Hunter twice and the Angle Slam robs Triple H of his *WrestleMania* main event. Well, not really. They overbooked the hell out of this but gave enough effort in between to get the match over. Worryingly, this is the best match on the show.
Final Rating: ***¼

Backstage: The nWo stop off to chat with the Rock. Hulk Hogan takes a photo with Rock before disparaging him. Rock makes fun of all three guys with hilarious impressions. The Razor Ramon one is good, the Diesel one is wonderful. In about 20 seconds here Rock was more entertaining than the rest of the card.

WWF Undisputed Championship
Chris Jericho (c) vs. Steve Austin
I think some people expected Austin to go over here, especially after the booking weirdness of putting Angle over Hunter. Austin confessed an obsession with the WWF Title before this match, referring to himself as a "drug addict". It would certainly explain the booking of the last four years where Austin's personality changed dramatically but it all had one connection; the title. Jericho's title run was an uninspired couple of months but at least he's allowed to fail solo here, unlike at *WrestleMania*. Austin develops an interesting Flair tribute act where he focuses almost entirely on chops. It's not Flair-Steamboat or anything but it is a shitload of chops. It's about half the damn match. Austin then ups the ante with a superplex. Then another superplex. Then ANOTHER superplex. It's a bizarre choice of moves, not like three consecutive German suplexes, and Jericho just kicks out. Back to the chops! Normally I really dig the whole striking deal but it's certainly not clicking with the fans so that counts against it. Austin must be feeling frisky as he does the Stun Gun, turning back the years and continuing his WCW tribute. Seeing as we're doing WCW finishers, Jericho tries for the Lionsault and misses. JR starts ragging on Jericho for a poorly executed sleeper, which looks fine compared to the old Sags chinlock scale. Was Ross asked to bury Jericho's technical skill here? Austin gets a bit haphazard with clotheslines and Jericho makes a sufficient hash of the Lionsault that he re-does it. Given that nothing else has worked Jericho goes back to the chops. There's a great spot where Austin goes for the Thesz Press and Jericho uses his leverage to block it and turn Austin into the Walls of Jericho. I don't think I've ever seen the Thesz Press countered so that's a cool spot. Austin's mojo was not there in 2002 and it shows here. He seems to be taking it easy. Jericho bails for a title belt and they make a mess of a spot involving a ref bump. Jericho takes a bump on the belt for a near fall before Jericho counters the Stunner into the Breakdown onto the belt in a sensational spot but, Austin kicks out of that. Earl Hebner takes a proper bump with Jericho taking his head off on a clothesline. Austin hooks the Walls of Jericho and the champ taps out. Surprisingly no reaction from the crowd again. Stunner! This brings in the nWo to attack but Austin fends off all of them, because they suck. I'm surprised no one comes out to help Austin as the nWo was supposed to be universally hated. A lame beat down ensues and Jericho crawls across to retain. That finish leaves a sour taste in the mouth. Some of the wrestling got really good down the stretch with a couple of wonderful counters highlighting. I have big question marks over the strange format of the match, an Austin match with virtually no brawling, and the lacklustre crowd reactions. As if the design just wasn't what the crowd wanted. I did enjoy the chops and the final third, until the actual finish, but the rest of the match is a bit tiresome for a PPV main event.
Final Rating: **¾

VERDICT

The PPV is remembered as the one the New World Order first appeared on, giving us the first Hogan appearance on WWF PPV since *King of the Ring 1993*, some nine years earlier. I'm not what you would call a Hogan "fan" per se, so for me it's not a big occurrence and certainly not as memorable as Hogan vs. Rock at *WrestleMania*. The rest of the show is an insipid, uninspired mess. Almost a protest to the nWo being signed! It's like all the boys got together before the show and decided to tank the PPV. I know that's unlikely, as this isn't WCW, and Hunter-Angle is pretty good, but the second best match on the PPV is the opening tag team turmoil match, a bout that was totally meaningless. Speaking of which; the top contender stipulations here, the ones that were supposed to shape *WrestleMania*, meant next to nothing. Angle didn't get a title shot and ended up stuck with Kane, of all people, in the midcard. Hunter got his title shot back. The tag teams almost all ended up in the tag title match. RVD ended up getting the IC Title, despite his petulance against Goldust and Edge fought Booker T over a shampoo endorsement. Basically as a set up show for *WrestleMania* this was a failure. As a wrestling show it was mediocre. Not recommended.

38

WRESTLEMANIA X8

CAT NO: WWF54125
RUN TIME: 221 minutes (approx)

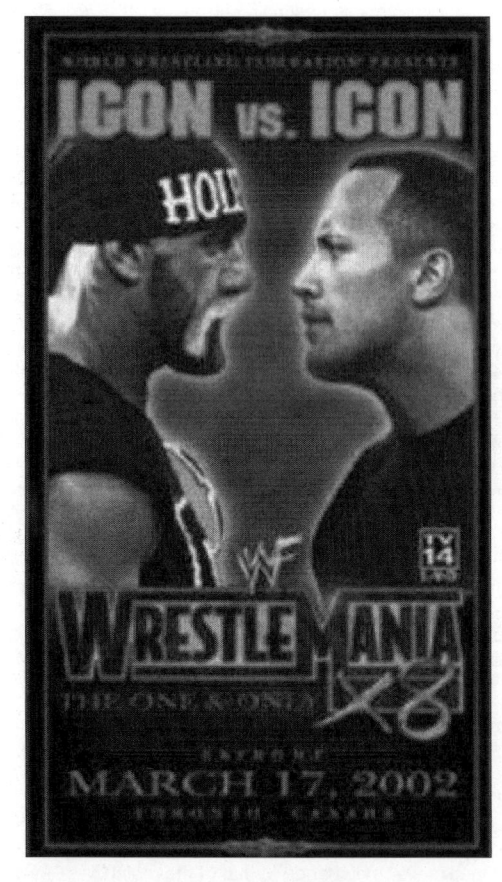

James Dixon: In many ways *WrestleMania X-Seven* was the start of a new era for the annual sports entertainment extravaganza, with the show frequently taking up residence in stadiums across North America from that point onwards. While undoubtedly already a major household name in the mainstream prior, following the legendary 2001 event, the WWF (and then WWE) began to put more and more emphasis on the show each time out, making it the genuine focal point of the year both in terms of promotion, culminating major feuds and storylines and bringing back legendary figures from the past. *WrestleMania* had become a weeklong celebration of everything WWF past, present and (sometimes) future. *WrestleMania X8* was especially notable on the nostalgia front, as it would see three former WWF Champions making their first appearances at the show in years. Not only that, but the event took place in the mammoth SkyDome in Toronto, Canada, the home of *WrestleMania VI*.

It was previously and would again become tradition for *WrestleMania* to open with a rendition of the American patriotism piece *'America The Beautiful'* (which I have always thought was a little insular on a globally broadcast show) but instead we get Saliva busting out a dirge that gets lost in the ethers of the building.

WWF Intercontinental Championship
William Regal (c) vs. Rob Van Dam

Two years running Regal has been in the *WrestleMania* opener and in the Intercontinental Championship match, which is a little strange really as his style is not exactly indicative of "hot opener". Speaking of style, this is quite the clash with Regal's European based counter wrestling and technical acumen not meshing well with RVD's high-octane, kick happy and occasionally unrefined stuff. Rob got smoother (though less interesting to watch) as his WWF run went on, but here he is still in the mode of hitting a spot and then pausing, before going into the next spot. It is fairly noticeable, especially when he is throwing his kicks, and it is almost as if he is checking that Regal is ready each time. Last year he got a lot of heat from management and some of the boys for being dangerous and busting guys open with his kicks, so perhaps he was trying to rein himself in. It doesn't work if so, because Regal ends up with a bloody lip, something that had become almost a signature of an RVD match. Regal is guilty of dallying too, taking an age to retrieve some brass knuckles from his tights, only for RVD to kick them out of his hand almost immediately. They have a few more awkward moments such as RVD going for his rolling monkey flip in the corner, but Regal either not being ready or Van Dam thinking he wasn't ready, and they just stop dead before Rob hits a makeshift dropkick then repeats the spot in the opposite corner. I am not sure if this stuff is just glaringly obvious to me as a former worker or to everyone, but either way it ruins the match for me a little. None of what they do here means a great deal, it is just exhibition stuff. Regal does at least break out the head drops to entertain, drilling RVD with a brutal Kenta Kobashi style half nelson suplex that folds Van Dam in half. It seems to knock him silly briefly too, and he stops off on the outside to recover. Regal then retrieves the knucks from earlier, but the referee spots him and takes them away, only for Regal to pull out another pair from his trunks. How did he struggle for what felt like a minute to find them earlier, when he had two sets down there!? They don't work again anyway, with Van Dam again kicking him to prevent the big knockout punch, then connecting with the Five Star Frogsplash for the very popular win and the title. Very rushed, very sloppy and completely disjointed, but the odd exciting spot carried it through.
Final Rating: *½

WWF European Championship
Diamond Dallas Page (c) vs. Christian

Here's a game: Name me one guy who came into the WWF and retained a gimmick that was already over from exploits elsewhere, who ended up more over, or their WWF run considered better. Goldberg? Raven? Taz? Scott Steiner? nWo? All of them were ruined by the WWF/E. Add Diamond Dallas Page to that list, because the WWF turned a guy who was very popular and fun to watch into a nobody midcarder. He cut his hair, changed his gear and got inferior music, all to the detriment of his popularity. After less than a year with the company he was just another guy lost in the shuffle. This match is worthless and feels very much shoehorned onto the

card, because the feud between them has only been going on for a few days. Christian is also unconvincing as a singles guy currently, probably because he still sports the same gear he wore when competing in a tag team. Would Shawn Michaels have made the step up if he carried on wearing his Rockers' gear? Yes, but not as quickly. The only thing interesting about this match is the involvement of DDP, who other than Hulk Hogan is the only person on the card who competed at *WrestleMania VI* in the same venue some twelve years prior. Well I say "competed"; he was the Cadillac driver for Rhythm & Blues. I guess by that token we can also count Edge as having been there, as the young Adam Copeland was sat in the crowd. This turns out to be DDP's only *WrestleMania* match, and he left the company shortly afterwards and pretty much retired due to injuries. At least he got to go over though, beating Christian after an uninspiring 6-minutes with a Diamond Cutter to retain his European Title. The Undertaker is not the only one with a *WrestleMania* unbeaten streak! Post match, Christian throws a tantrum in the ring after his loss, which is just stellar character booking.
Final Rating: *

Backstage, the Rock gets BOOED when he tries to do a promo with Coach. "Hogan, Hogan, Hogan" chant the crowd. They do sing-a-long with him anyway, but this initial response should have been a sign to the WWF and the guys in the match of things to come later... Rock asks Coach if he has taken his vitamins and said his prayers, and then chews him out for reneging on the latter. Rock then forces organised religion on poor Coachman, who gets on his knees, looks up to the sky and says: "What up, G?". Rock is not happy, and kicks him out of the segment. Rock then gets serious and cuts a typically decent promo on Hogan, aping him but at the same time using his own shtick, and it works well.

WWF Hardcore Championship
Maven (c) vs. Goldust
Goldust wastes little time and blindsides Maven before he makes the ring, and the *Tough Enough* winner takes two big bumps on the outside. Back in the ring Maven uses his one big move, a dropkick, to smash a golden trash can into Goldust's face. It doesn't get him far. The crowd is dead as Goldust brings a golden shovel into play, and remains so when the two knock each other out with fake looking bin lids. Nobody buys those as a serious weapon, they are just noisy. It gets the job done though, but not for either of the guys involved in the match. No, instead Spike Dudley marches down and pins Maven, thus winning the Hardcore Title. Man, does this belt ever feel past its peak. Three minutes it might have been, but this was horrid. After the match, the no longer over Crash Dudley hits the ring looking to reclaim the belt that made him so much fun to watch, but Spike does a runner.
Final Rating: DUD

And now, here are Drowning Pool to "tell the story" of the Triple H-Stephanie McMahon feud (featuring WWF Champion Chris Jericho). What that means is they play their repetitive song to no response while a hype video for the main event rolls in the background. For the PPV viewers they could have at least played the video instead of showing Drowning Pool boring everyone. Sadly the band's singer Dave Williams died just six months later from cardiomyopathy. He is not the first, and unfortunately not the last performer at a *WrestleMania* show to die from heart problems.

That segues rather unfortunately into Crash Holly, who has caught up with Spike and is brawling with him backstage. Al Snow makes a cameo, trying to run them both down with a golf cart, but he misses and crashes through a pile of very conveniently and entirely unnaturally placed boxes. Spike escapes, but then the Hurricane flies in on a rope and kicks Spike, gently, and pins him for the belt.

Kurt Angle vs. Kane
If any match sums up the mess that the company's booking was in 2002 then it is this pairing. You don't waste Kurt Angle in a match with a 7-foot lumbering monster. Angle tries to gain an advantage by using the ring bell before the match starts, but it doesn't take long before Kane comes back with his slugging shots. Angle tries, but you can't build sympathy on a monster no matter how technically gifted you are, and the crowd again fails to respond. They have not been given much in the way of quality tonight thus far. Angle goes to a front face lock but Kane powers out, so Angle ups the excitement with the triple German suplexes. Angle gets cocky and uses Kane's own clothesline from the top, so Kane ups his game with a lovely tilt-a-whirl powerslam. They continue to battle away and the effort levels are acceptable enough, but it just doesn't feel any more important than a standard television match. Kane goes for the Tombstone but Angle slips out and soon has the ankle lock on, but Kane escapes with an impressive enzuigiri. The hold has no effect on the 'Big Red Machine' who happily climbs the ropes looking for his clothesline, only to get caught with Angle's always impressive super fast climb belly-to-belly before he gets chance to hit it. Unfortunately they then make a real mess of the finish, with Angle catching a roll up in the wrong place and having to reposition himself to go to the planned finished of winning with his feet on the ropes. It made Kane look worse than if he had just kicked out of the first one and then they had organically worked into the second spot. It's not like it affects a great deal anyway, because the match was a yawner.
Final Rating: *½

Backstage, the Hurricane hides out in the Godfather's locker room and catches an eyeful of the hos. Cue the usual WWF "comedy" when a broom is misinterpreted as an erect penis.

No Disqualification Match
The Undertaker vs. Ric Flair
This was a well booked feud for the most part and did a good job in making people want to see the match, but there were some strange storyline snafus involved. One glaring example was where the WWF's board of directors, chaired by Linda McMahon, revoked Flair's status as co-owner of the company because he intended to wrestle this match. They then gave full control back to Vince McMahon, a man whose track record for the last four years was significantly worse than Flair's in terms of heinous acts, not least his recent decision to bring in the nWo to kill the company. Furthermore, why is there a board of directors anyway when Vince and Flair supposedly own a 50% stake in the company each? Nonsense. This is Flair's first *WrestleMania* in a decade, and only his second overall at this point. Last time out he was involved in a classic with Randy Savage at *WrestleMania VIII* where he lost the WWF Championship. Flair, eager to avenge the attacks by the Undertaker on his son David and best friend Arn Anderson, jumps Taker right away and brawls with him on the outside, but soon gets overpowered. For the record, this is my absolute least favourite version of the Undertaker. Here he is a short haired heel doing the rotten 'American Badass' gimmick, and stylistically he is all about clubbing blows and little else, without any of the aura, razzmatazz or presence that makes him such a unique attraction as the 'Dead Man'. Taker sits Flair on a chair on the outside of the ring and just punches away at him,

and for his second *WrestleMania* appearance in a row, Flair juices a gusher. Taker just bullies Flair, until he finally manages a few meaty chops, but they don't have much effect. I would describe some of the moves being used, but there are none. It is just lots and lots of punches from the Undertaker, though a massive superplex is very impressive. That would seemingly finish it, but Taker picks Flair up at two. All of this, and what has gone before it in the storylines, is screaming out for an heroic babyface ending in favour of the 'Nature Boy', but given the show I probably don't need to write "spoiler alert" when telling you that it doesn't happen. Flair gets a brief moment of respite when pulling Taker off the ropes when he attempts Old School, but Taker is soon back in control. Flair brings more chops, but that really is all he has. Realising this, Flair attempts to live up to his moniker of being the "dirtiest player in the game", and he grabs a lead pipe from Taker's bike and wallops him in the head with it. That busts Taker open, but almost immediately he is back in control as they brawl in the aisle. Jesus, give the guy *something*. Back in the ring, Flair uses a low blow to block a chokeslam and then puts on the figure four to a good reaction from Toronto. Taker sits up during it and Flair's facials at that are great, then Taker powers out and hits the chokeslam. Taker then decides to belt referee Charles Robinson, though it is a no DQ match so what is the point? He brings his lead pipe into the ring but Flair prevents it with chops, then as Taker comes off the ropes Arn Anderson bursts into the ring from nowhere and hits his perfect spinebuster for a near fall. The crowd bought it too. Taker doesn't appreciate the intervention and belts Arn, busting him open to give us a triple juicer. Taker puts Anderson in the dragon sleeper, but gets belted with a chair from Flair, though that doesn't get the job done either. Taker then goes for the Last Ride but they make a colossal mess of it, so Taker improvises and finishes with the Tombstone. So to sum up: Taker attacked Flair's family and friends, cost him his job, beat him to a bloody pulp for 20-minutes and then won anyway, despite the 2-on-1 odds. I wonder if any consideration was ever given to Flair winning here, prior to the Streak being a really big deal and one of the key selling points of the show. It would have made a lot more sense. Historically I am glad that didn't happen, and I sure as hell bet WWE are too, but looked at in isolation the result doesn't make a lot of sense. This match is fairly well liked by a lot of scribes, but not me. It was just a mostly lethargic brawl dominated by Undertaker, with not a lot going for it outside of the odd big spot. Decent effort from Flair, but not worth going out of your way to see by any stretch.
Final Rating: **

Backstage, Booker T talks to Frosty the Coleman about "Einstein's theory of relatives" as he puts over his intelligence. Oh, I see what they did there... Sew up my sides.

Booker T vs. Edge
This is Booker's *WrestleMania* debut, and what a program he has been given to work with! Yes folks, this is the famous match that was fought over a SHAMPOO endorsement. Whoever was on the booking team was completely clueless. Oh right, it was Stephanie McMahon. No sexism intended, but I just can't see a man ever coming up with this as a reason for two guys to work a feud. I guess at least they had a storyline though, because there came a point from around 2008 onwards where angles seemingly ceased to exist, with feuds set up by either attacks, interfering in promos purely for the sake of creating an issue between two performers or the guys just wrestling each other a bunch of times. Edge is the hometown boy here and as mentioned earlier this is quite the full circle night for him. He gets a good response when he makes his entrance, but the rest of the match is contested in front of a bored crowd. They don't get much time to do a great deal on what has been an underwhelming and overbooked show, and like the first couple of matches they just run through some of their moves without any real purpose or conviction. Booker, the heel, pops the crowd with his Spinneroonie, but Edge kicks out of a subsequent axe kick. Edge gets a near fall of his own from a spear, then tries a Spinneroonie of his own. Not so good. They do a quick hook and switch sequence to follow, then Edge hits his naff jumping DDT to finish. This didn't belong on *WrestleMania* either, and like pretty much the rest of the card, it felt like a *RAW* match.
Final Rating: *

Backstage, the Hurricane denies that he is a "hurri-perve", and then his sidekick Mighty Molly appears on the scene and decks him with a frying pan, pinning him to win the Hardcore belt. Yes, the joke is wearing a little thin now.

Steve Austin vs. Scott Hall
The man who has carried the company through to a new era of success since exploding onto the scene in 1996/97 has been reduced to working in the midcard due to an ongoing wrangling with creative, which will ultimately lead to his leaving the company in three months time. Originally Austin was set to work with Hulk Hogan in the ultimate WWF vs. WCW dream match that fans had wanted since both got red hot in their respective roles with each company, but politics made it an impossibility and unfortunately it never happened. The solution from the WWF was to put Austin in with Scott Hall, giving them Austin vs. the nWo but with someone they could sacrifice to appease him. "Thanks to Mr. McMahon, we have that man to deal with" says JR as Hall makes his entrance, and that my friends is a shoot. Head of talent relations JR wouldn't have to deal with him long mind you, because Hall was fired two months later following the infamous "Plane Ride From Hell" coming back from England following *Insurrextion*. Hall brings Kevin Nash out with him, as Austin mouths "what the fuck is that!?". Many others over the years have said the same thing when watching big Kev phone it in. Even many years later, it is still very strange indeed to hear and see the nWo music and branding at *WrestleMania*. They start quickly exchanging strikes before Austin takes over with the Thesz press and then leads the crowd in a chant of "what?" as he slams Hall's head off the buckles. Austin unloads with chops on the outside and waffles Nash for fun, but back in the ring Hall turns it around and belts Austin with a helluva chop of his own. Nash takes an age to remove a turnbuckle pad so they fight in the opposite corner for a long time, before Hall finally sends Austin back-first into the exposed steel. The match plods on from here, with Hall working over an uninterested Austin in front of a fittingly uninterested crowd. You would think they would react big to seeing the nWo wrestling on PPV in the WWF for the first time, but nobody thinks Hall has a chance here, even with Nash there. A half assed spinebuster from Austin is the extent of the hope spots, with Austin noticeably showing far less fire than usual, before hitting a desperation Stunner. "Dammit" shouts JR as Nash pulls the referee out of the ring and decks him to prevent the fall. A 2-on-1 ensues, but Austin prevents a chair shot with a Stunner on Hall and another one on Nash for good measure. Jack Doan finally arrives after an age to count the fall, but Nash drops an elbow on him and Hall goes for the Outsider's Edge right by the ropes. It's Furious' favourite spot! Austin of course reverses it and Hall takes his usual bump out of the ring, and then the referees send Nash to the back. Hey, why didn't the WCW referees just do that? Oh right, because the nWo were booked well in that company. At first. Hall hits a

Stunner of his own on Austin, but 'Stone Cold' kicks out and reverses another into one of his own. Hall stands there dazed but doesn't bump it., so Austin hits another and Hall overcompensates for not selling the first one in a big way, taking a ridiculous, overblown, but hilarious back bump from it that would make the Rock proud. That had to be Hall's way of taking the piss out of Austin because of the heat he had regarding the arrival of the entire nWo group. Similar to how Shawn Michaels oversold everything for Hulk Hogan at *SummerSlam 2005* in many respects. You know, I enjoyed aspects of this. It was a pointless match and they did almost nothing, but by the end the crowd were into it, and seeing the nWo in the WWF was a nice change from the norm. It shook up the roster, though as noted the politics behind the scenes played a large part in the group's ultimate failure.
Final Rating: *½

WWF Tag Team Championship
Billy & Chuck (c) vs. The Dudley Boyz vs. The APA vs. The Hardy Boyz
Saliva return to give a live rendition of the Dudleys' entrance theme, and they do a pretty good job of it. Bands playing guys to the ring with live versions of their themes is a great addition to *WrestleMania,* way better than the random and unwanted "bonus concerts" that the WWE often insisted on years later. This match has a very thrown together feel about it, especially after the bar has been set so high in the tag division with the ladder and TLC matches from the previous two years. The Dudleys and the Hardys were obviously in both of those, which rather shows that the WWF has little idea what to do with the teams other than pair them off against each other time after time. The bout feels fairly rushed at first, with so many teams all wanting to get their signature spots in, and with the aforementioned two teams especially this must feel like a real anticlimax, as they have gone from stealing the show to a throwaway nothing match that has little to no build. The APA are the first team sent packing, with Bradshaw succumbing to 3D immediately after turning Billy inside out with an incredibly vicious Clothesline From Hell. The bump was superb. The Hardys come in and hit their double team stuff at pace on D-Von and then Chuck, while Bubba sets up a table on the outside for use later on. The Canadian geniuses then chant "we want tables". And who said Canada is always behind the times on everything!? Jeff takes his shirt off to reveal a pasty white, skinny physique, so the Dudleys' valet Stacy Keibler gets on the apron and shakes her thonged ass at him. Jeff, being a gentleman, slaps her ass, kisses her against her will and pie faces her off the apron. It runs in the family... Bubba punishes Jeff for it, combining with Billy to hit a variation of the Doomsday Device before screaming "time to die Jeff Hardy" and chopping the piss out of him. Jeff gets impressive air off a back body drop and then D-Von comes in and runs through him with a clothesline. This has basically become a standard Dudleys-Hardys tag match now, with the champs reduced to watching from the apron. Jeff manages to botch his comeback DDT and then tags in Matt, which is poor logic from the Hardys. The last guy you want to tag is your partner, because why not just let the other guys fight it out and then pick up the pieces when everyone else is weak? D-Von gets shoved off the top through the table set up earlier, which looks great, before the Hardys finish Bubba with their top rope double team, leaving them alone with the champs. Pretty soon after that the champs manage to isolate Jeff and finish off following a belt shot to retain. And now anyone who watched has forgotten it already. Not a bad match, just nothing remotely memorable occurred and we have seen it all a million times before from all involved.
Final Rating: *½

Backstage, Hulk Hogan tells the nWo that he doesn't want any help tonight, because he wants to prove he can beat the Rock on his own. They are less than receptive.

Still backstage, Christian closes a door in the face of Molly Holly and pins her to win the Hardcore title.

Hulk Hogan vs. The Rock
This is a pretty huge match... The biggest star of the WCW boom period and one of the all-time icons in the industry colliding with his modern day pretender; box office blockbuster attraction the Rock. It is a showdown for the ages, a piece of fantasy booking coming to life and unfolding. Of course, it should have been the main event given that everyone buying the show was doing so to see this, and according to Triple H and Chris Jericho, they both realised that they would struggle to follow it. But Vince McMahon was steadfast in his belief that the WWF Championship match should always go on last at the supershow, even though they had made an exception in 1992 at *WrestleMania VIII,* and in later years the title was often shunted down to the middle of the show if a bigger attraction was occurring. Describing in any detail the moves, holds and sequences in the match is tantamount to irrelevant, because they don't really even matter. You know what they do, you have seen it all before, but never to a reaction quite like this. Heel Hogan gets cheered vociferously and loudly with every move, babyface Rock gets booed out of the building, as the crowd turns the WWF's booking and the match's structure on its head. The exchanges are at times weak (let's not forget that Hogan hasn't worked regularly for a couple of years at this point), but it near as makes no difference. He wins a lock up; the crowd explode, he hits his big boot and legdrop combo (which *doesn't* get the job done); the crowd explode, he Hulks Up, the crowd goes WILD... "brother". Hogan gets to kick out of the Rock Bottom, but another two followed by the People's Elbow gets the job done for Rock as the nWo guys job in both matches tonight. That is surely entirely down to politics, with the WWF brass looking to appease the current crop of top stars who were somewhat irked and concerned about the trio's arrival in the company. I think Hogan should have won here, especially with Rock disappearing again to make more movies. A loss wouldn't hurt Rock, but it would sure build Hogan and establish him as still being a genuine star, meaning when you do beat him it means much more. The WWF didn't pay much attention to the win/loss record though, and put the WWF Title on Hogan the next month in a feel-good but ill-advised piece of hot-shotting, as everyone, Vince included it seems, got wrapped up in Hulkamania Version 2.0.

Rating this is going to be divisive. I guess your level of enjoyment of this match depends largely on what you perceive to be important about wrestling. The great thing about the sport is that you can love it for many reasons. Some watch for realistic athletic contests and perhaps prefer the stellar work that occurs in Japan, others like high flying and high impact, some like big spots, others can only enjoy a match if the crowd reaction is good, some prefer storylines that have a definite antagonist and protagonist and a well refined set of characters, for others the spectacle and the setting is just as important as the moves. The list goes on. Me? I would take a hard-hitting athletic contest above most anything else and this match is almost the opposite of that... but I absolutely love it regardless. It is two of the biggest drawing names in the history of the business going head-to-head in a dream match that most assumed would never occur, on the biggest show of the year in front of the largest crowd, who just happen to be molten hot.

The sheer number of flash bulbs going off before they have even locked up is a phenomenal sight and sets the tone for the contest, the whole of which is about way more than the moves and the pace they cut. Instead it is a reunion between the hardcore fans and the ultimate hero from their childhood who they haven't seen for nearly a decade. The bond remains so strong, that current company hero and super over babyface the Rock, was turned on in a manner pretty much unprecedented at the time. It became cool to boo the faces and cheer the heels at *WrestleMania* years later, but here we get an outpouring of love for a long lost veteran returning "home". It is truly epic in nature and one of the all time great moments in company history. The match is one that will never be forgotten, and is up there with Andre-Hogan and Hart-Bulldog as an iconic bout that encapsulates the razzmatazz of the company at its very best. Noted ranty internet scribe Scott Keith once hilariously said about this match that if you watched it with the sound turned off then it sucked. When I watch Flair-Steamboat without the picture on it sucks too... You see how ridiculous that is? The crowd play a large part in the success of any match, and they are an integral part of this one. Who cares about workrate and execution when the sheer spectacle draws you in, and in such a thrilling manner too.
Final Rating: ****

Post match, Rock and Hogan shake hands (with Hogan doing a tremendous sell job of the People's Elbow for several minutes afterwards), which pisses off the nWo. They run down and beat on Hogan, prompting Rock to make the save. Rock then encourages Hogan to do some posing for a couple of minutes and his face turn is complete.

WWF Women's Championship
Jazz (c) vs. Lita vs. Trish Stratus
Oh, the poor girls. You can count the number of people in the building who care about this match on one hand, and the number is three: the girls in the ring. Everyone else is shattered from the previous bout and are using this buffer between the marquee attractions as the popcorn match, or the "piss break match" as some know it. They get a fairly generous 6-minutes, which is a lot for the *WrestleMania* divas bout, but they don't make the most of it. Instead, Lita puts in one of her less than Hall of Fame worthy "floppy" performances, Jazz throws some of the worst punches this side of John Cena and Trish sucks up to the crowd in Maple Leaf tights. The whole thing dies a slow, painful death before Jazz scores the unpopular victory following her finish from the top. An unstructured and horribly messy display, though it certainly achieved its goal of bringing the crowd right back down. Unfortunately they don't come up again for the rest of the show.
Final Rating: -*

Backstage, Christian takes too long kissing his Hardcore title before getting into a cab and leaving, and Maven rolls him up on the concrete to render the last four hours of title switches completely pointless.

WWF Undisputed Championship
Chris Jericho (c) vs. Triple H
The story coming into this match was all about the returning from injury Hunter and his soon to be ex-wife Stephanie McMahon-Helmsley, with Jericho merely an afterthought in the background who was dragged along for the ride because Hunter vs. Steph as the top liner at *WrestleMania* was quite obviously not possible. Although... you never know with this company. After all, they did put the Miz in the main event of the show. Because of the piss weak story in which the once cool Jericho became subservient to the shrill and emasculating Steph, combined with the burned out crowd from the epic Hogan-Rock match and a somewhat turgid card prior to that, this has no heat whatsoever. In many ways it is the polar opposite to the spectacle from earlier, in that the execution and psychology are both fine, but the crowd just isn't there. And it makes a big difference. It is almost like Jericho and Hunter are lethargic and tired too, with neither having much in the way of "get up and go". It feels like the main event from *RAW*, it is definitely not special and seriously lacks that "big fight feel" that the main event of this card should always strive to have. It's like neither has upped their game even slightly. Jericho spends the majority of the bout working away at Hunter's leg, which is sound strategy given his much publicised injury, but hardly good to watch. It's all just a necessary backdrop to the Hunter-Steph stuff anyway, with the two constantly interacting and nearly getting into a physical altercation, which eventually comes when Hunter drills her with a Pedigree. The crowd only pays the spot lip service, and barely react when Jericho belts Hunter with a chair. In fact the crowd is so quiet for it, that it stretches believability that referee Earl Hebner doesn't hear the shot. Jericho tries the Pedigree, Hunter kicks him off and then hits his own for the win and the title, in one of the flattest and most anticlimactic endings to *WrestleMania* ever. JR tries to mask the apathy with hyperbole, calling it the biggest display of intestinal fortitude (from Hunter) that he has ever seen, before rounding off the nonsense with the ludicrous claim that this is the *WrestleMania* "moment" we will remember above all the others. Wow, talk about force-feeding and turd polishing. With the crowd on board this probably hits ***, but without them it doesn't, which is simply not good enough for the main event at the "granddaddy of them all". Of course, we can all take solace in the fact that none of this even happened at all, apparently, as WWE erased the existence of its first Undisputed Title when they decided to merge their WWE and World Heavyweight titles in 2013 and put them on Randy Orton, declaring him the first ever Undisputed Champion. I don't really blame them for wanting to forget this match though; it was tedious.
Final Rating: *½

VERDICT

This show doesn't have a particularly bad reputation due to the Hogan-Rock match of the ages, but for the most part it is really, really average. The matches are uninspiring and would be more suited to free television than the biggest show of the year, and some of the booking choices are very strange and probably wrong. The company's hot streak was definitely over by 2002, and the booking became a real disaster thanks to Princess Stephanie being at the helm. Feuds over shampoo? A main event that shouldn't be main event booked around a marital split where the champion is the least relevant factor? The top star of the past five years shunted into the midcard due to creative not knowing how to book him? Multi person matches for titles with no actual issue in them between those involved? Wasting the best workers in mismatched styles clashes? We have all of that and more here, as this show takes its position as one of the most underwhelming 'Mania's in history. Other than the must-see Rock-Hogan match of course... Not recommended at all outside of that cracking piece of nostalgia-driven hero worship.

35

STEPHANIE MCMAHON-HELMSLEY

DIVAS - TROPICAL PLEASURE

CAT NO: WWF54127
RUN TIME: 60 minutes (approx)

Arnold Furious: I never really understood the point of the Diva tapes. If you wanted to ogle beautiful ladies in 2002, there was the internet. If you wanted to ogle beautiful naked ladies, there was also the internet, and Playboy did very similar presentations to these releases without the pretence of "learning more about your favourite Diva", only with added titties. The WWF were making tacky choices at the time and trying to milk every last dollar from the fans. There were fans out there who wanted to watch tapes dedicated to the ladies of professional wrestling, most of them sweaty awkward teens and sweaty awkward old men, so three of them exist from this "end of Attitude" era. Unfortunately I made the mistake of saying I would cover one of them and then James dumped this monstrosity on me.

Hosts are Dave McLain, Rich Freeda and Noelle Carr, who tell us all the girls are different and have personalities. I hate that. Everyone has personality. When you say anyone has a "great personality" you're trying to deflect from their lack of good looks. Because we're all about rating stuff I'll be rating each of the ladies on their sex appeal and how well they get their famous personalities across. A table will feature at the end, determining the most successful diva.

DIVA #1: Stacy Keibler

Stacy's unscripted interviews are a flow of consciousness and she does not shut up. It is a constant stream of verbal diarrhoea. She says nothing of interest and it feels like a drill going into the side of my head. Not a good start to the tape. She stops talking so she can frolic in the waves. Stacy is really, really, really, really hot. But she has nothing of interest to say. Based on her favourite outfits she likes showing off her ass, which, face aside, is probably her best feature so that's a good move. This is all sexy but mind-numbing so we move onto Stacy's actual history in the business. She says she was a fan (she attended WCW events) and entered a contest to join the Nitro Girls. She won but only lasted a month before creative (Vince Russo & Ed Ferrara) moved her into a storyline as Miss Hancock, then had her trained to wrestle. She slyly buries WCW by saying how great the WWF is and there being a "world of difference" between the two. Presumably because the WWF actually plans stuff in advance and doesn't change all the booking on a whim. Stacy shows us her skill: tucking her ear into itself. Discussion inevitably leads to her legs, which are 41.5 inches long. Stacy makes a remarkable statement by saying she felt she needed more training for the in-ring and suggested anyone thinking of taking a similar career trajectory should get trained at wrestling first. I'm disappointed they only skim the surface with Stacy in her 8-minute slot. There was too much talk about bikinis and the location rather than her actual career. It actually surprises me that a brief discussion left me wanting to know more, specifically about why she preferred the WWF to WCW and how she found the wrestling training. The fluffy nature of the interview was irritating, but hey, we're basically just here to see her ass in a thong so that happened.
Sexiness Rating: ****
Personality Rating: *

DIVA #2: Ivory

I don't really perceive Ivory as a diva but rather a wrestler, given her history in the business. Ivory puts Terri, Trish and Lita over as being her close friends. It seems they liquored Ivory up a bit to increase her sex appeal as we see her struggling to balance on a log. I swear her sense of balance is better than that. Ivory compares herself to Barbie; making her own money, being her own woman and driving a convertible. We see photographer Dave berate Ivory for not knowing how to pose. She's a wrestler, dumbass. Ivory gets herself over by stealing the camera and taking photos of him instead. She reiterates Stacy's story about taking bumps and says you need to try that first and see if you like it. She describes her co-workers as weirdoes but goes on to praise some of the chaps as sexy, including Chuck Palumbo and Ron Simmons ("always smells good"). She calls her ability to go and have a 10 minute match, and not get nervous about it, the most satisfying aspect of her wrestling life. Although she tempers that with fear and doubt that constantly nag at her. Ivory's 8-minutes is far more personal and less shallow than Stacy's, but with a significant reduction in sexiness as a trade-off. I've always felt Ivory comes across as a very genuine person. I'm not sure about her Barbie analogy or her listing off the wrestlers she thinks look sexy, but I'm sure she was pushed into certain directions when

talking about her career.
Sexiness Rating: **½
Personality Rating: ***¼

DIVA #3: Sharmell
Nice to see Mrs T. I always thought she was an underrated talent both in the ring and as a looker. She goes into her history with WCW, very briefly, about her spot in the Nitro Girls and wrestling. She swiftly changes course to discuss her holistic training, her yoga and her spiritual superoneness. It's all very Zen. She moves on to her dancing career and how she used to tour with James Brown (for over 3 years). She goes back to auditioning for the Nitro Girls after seeing *Nitro* on the Godfather of Soul's tour bus. Like Stacy, WCW eventually moved her into an angle and gave her the ring name Paisley. She claims to have gotten hooked on wrestling after taking her first bump and is getting trained in OVW, under the tutelage of Jim Cornette. Her character in OVW, Sister Sharmell, was a full-on ghetto girl with fake blonde hair. Her tag team, the Suicide Blondes, beat the Minnesota Stretching Crew for the OVW tag titles. The Stretching Crew was Brock Lesnar and Shelton Benjamin. Brock was making five times what everyone else was on but didn't have an ounce of passion for the business so he was paired up with Shelton, who was a natural talent and carried the team with his enthusiasm. Sharmell calls Jacqueline a role model for her. Sharmell, being a lesser known talent, gets a lot less time and her spot is 5 minutes long, most of which is her dancing. There's hardly any swimsuit stuff and a strange, but interesting, aside to her short OVW career made this a different segment. Sharmell picked up an injury around this time and dropped out of wrestling for four years, brought back by the WWE in 2005 as a valet for her real-life husband Booker T. I like Sharmell and thought she nailed all the Queen Sharmell stuff and was great in OVW, but OVW footage aside, this was very fluffy. Not as bad as listening to Stacy drone on about bikinis, but bland.
Sexiness Rating: *¾
Personality Rating: **

DIVA #4: Torrie Wilson
Seeing as Torrie is another big hitter, in terms of body type, they go right into the posing and the swimsuit talk. The switch in focus from personality to body is very noticeable after the Sharmell section. To try and get Torrie over as a real person she says she was shy in school and it wasn't until she went into sport and fitness that she became who she is. She tried to get into acting and worked as an extra on *Baywatch*. She'd been trying to get into acting in LA for 6 months when WCW signed her. She puts over wrestling as giving her a big break before saying she tried harder because of the "jerkoffs in the back saying mean things about me". In wrestling? Meanness? I refuse to believe this is true. She doesn't mention if this was the WWF locker room or the WCW one. It could have been either but from her shoot interviews, I would say it was WCW as the boys didn't like her inexperience. Like Stacy she goes on to talk about clothes, which isn't quite what this target audience wants to hear. Torrie covers a lot of ground but very little of it interests me. Torrie has an air-head personality. "I like board games and I like watching movies" is an actual line of her dialogue. It's painfully vacuous. If Torrie had any substance to her personality at the time, it's not shown here. She came across like a beauty pageant contestant.
Sexiness Rating: ****
Personality Rating: ½*

DIVA #5: Sara
Did they take everybody on this Caribbean trip? Sara is the Undertaker's wife, who worked as his valet for a while. She's a total BOBFOC. She calls herself a tomboy but then goes on to say she wanted to do more risqué stuff for the photo shoots because they had her in jeans and a t-shirt on TV. Somewhat contradictory. Sara tries to get over how dangerous she is by climbing trees and going out into the surf and boxing. She calls herself a "token brunette" despite spending most of her onscreen time as a blonde, and ignoring Lita and Ivory. The problem with Sara is she's not a wrestler, despite boasting a victory over DDP, and she's not really a looker. Depending on your preferences you could say the same thing about Sharmell, who'd barely been on TV at the time, but Sara was one of the boys' wives and the only thing that stood out about her was her rocking hot bod. She seems fairly interesting but only because she's not a wrestler so she talks about different things. I guess I'm just still resentful of the way she was booked.
Sexiness Rating: ***
Personality Rating: ½*

DIVA #6: Lita
This may seem a bit weird but I always felt Lita was out of place doing sexy stuff. She never seemed all that comfortable and as a personality she felt like a little sister. When she did wrestle in thongs and take her top off, it was in an athletic fashion. The first thing she says is she got over because she was different, which is a massive argument we have against the WWE of later eras; that everyone felt like the same person and the variety of performers just wasn't there. Lita was an individual and she wrestled a different style, a sloppy lucha style admittedly, but that's what got her over. Variety is the spice of life, McMahons. Lita seems awkward when she's posing, but when they get her to act more naturally it works. She's just not a bikini model, but she's sexy in her own way. She refers to photographers as "bullshitters" (bleeped) before saying she was better prepared for this year's photo shoot. The way she compares herself to her clothing is interesting as she says "you may not like it, but you've never seen anything like it". Lita points out her fan mail has an emotional connection to how she is. Having the benefit of hindsight, Lita was a unique in-ring performer and that's why she was so over. The cookie-cutter WWE production line that makes divas in a factory somewhere, doesn't create talent like this. Once again, it's all about variety and I'm constantly irritated by the WWE's assertions that if the fans like one thing, then they'll damn well like it over and over and over and over again. Which is strange because Lita was never cloned and copied like so many of her counterparts. I can name half a dozen Trish Stratus clones that appeared in the WWE but no one that reminds me of Lita.
Sexiness Rating: ***½
Personality Rating: ***½

DIVA #7: Jacqueline
She's one of the most experienced wrestlers the WWF had at the time. She moans about spending ages posing and how the photographers keep putting her in the water, which she's not keen on. She was also a tomboy and she played football with her brothers when she was younger. Jacqui puts JR over for hiring her in the WWF after her WCW contract expired and she debuted with Marc Mero in 1998. She was thrilled to win the WWF Women's title as she was the first African-American champion. I'm with Morgan Freeman on the race issue: it's only an issue because we keep talking about it. I don't think about Jacqueline as a black wrestler but rather a veteran wrestler. Jacqui likes to work out and she lifts a load of weights to burn her biceps. Sculpting those guns. When it comes to the sexy stuff, Jacqui tries way too hard, which is a frequent complaint from me about her. The really sexy divas were the ones that

didn't try that hard but were just effortlessly sexual (Sunny, Trish, Stacy). Jacqui always pushed it like Terri and Sable did. I don't find any of them attractive. She finishes up by saying she likes bad boys because she likes to experiment. It conjures up a few images that I won't be able to shake for a while. This whole segment left a bad taste in the mouth as it came across as forced. You can't push these things.
Sexiness Rating: *½
Personality Rating: **½

DIVA #8: Terri Runnels
I know my fellow writers, James especially, aren't keen on Terri and it stems mainly from two character traits. One that she's plastic, both in terms of her personality and her tits. Two that she's pretty much useless. As per usual she whinges about not getting enough sleep and being too cold and the sand being too coarse. No wonder Dustin divorced her. At least she has a wrestling history where she remembers the Brisco's and Dusty Rhodes, though her route into wrestling was through make-up work at TBS. In late 1990 WCW asked her to be Alexandra York and because the WWF bought the library we get footage of it. Nice to see a bit of background but it lasts a few seconds before Terri decides to go shopping on the island. Because that's boring I tend to focus on checking Terri's body out, and her fake chest area is weird looking. I get fake tits getting people over but if you're not naturally attractive it won't help. Terri's creative when it comes to getting undressed but she has very little to say. After Marlena, I thought Terri was a total waste of space and there's nothing here to suggest otherwise. Yeah, she has big tits, but they're someone else's.
Sexiness Rating: *
Personality Rating: ½*

DIVA #9: Trish Stratus
Now we're talking. I've always said that Trish was the complete package. Everything from the looks to the attitude to the promos to the wrestling. She could do everything and she was outstanding at anything she attempted. Oddly enough Trish's segment is all over the place as it focuses on the dolphin stuff they've been skirting around all tape and then sees all the girls chatting on the beach. It feels like filler. We get a quick bio where Trish talks about med school and her ambitions. Muscle Mag contacted her and then signed her up for a contract. We skip to Trish vs. Stephanie McMahon and their genuinely good match on PPV. Trish mentions how surprised people were by her wrestling but points out she's always been sporty. Trish connects with her male audience by saying she likes eating cheeseburgers. She must have an amazing metabolism. Trish's segment is surprisingly brisk and takes us up to the hour mark on the tape. Trish is clearly the company's big female star as she has every asset you'd need to be the ace of the women's division. She's good looking, she's ambitious, she's professional (no whinging at all, take heed Terri), she's athletic and she's likeable. She comes across extremely well and isn't just eye candy like Stacy or Torrie.
Sexiness Rating: ****
Personality Rating: ***½

Moving on we get some photographers doing talking head spots where they talk about this being a big Diva showcase before segueing into thanks and closing the profiles section of the tape. If you go for the DVD version you will see a showcase of the girls in-ring performances with an hour of bonus matches. Take or leave that...

As promised here is a table of how I rated the divas from most to least excellent.

1. Trish Stratus
2. Lita
3. Ivory
4. Stacy Keibler
5. Torrie Wilson
6. Sharmell
7. Jacqueline
8. Sara
9. Terri

I think that about sums up how I'd rate them too. Trish and Lita were both exceptional and the best all-rounders. Ivory is decent all round and worth more because of her in-ring. Stacy and Torrie look great but have very little in the personality stakes. Sharmell would improve later in her career and the others are also-rans. Terri comes out last by some distance but that could change based on personal preference. We just happen to think she's a bit crap.

VERDICT

The WWF wasn't quite sure how to do these Diva tapes. They knew they wanted to do something titillating but not be too tacky about it and not go over the top. They'd clearly seen Playboy do similar tapes and felt they could do the same thing without the nudity because of the girl's wrestling experience. That would give the tape substance. But because they try and mix titillation and information, the tape ends up as neither. It falls in between the two and neither excites nor informs. The only interesting aspect of the tape is clips from OVW and WCW making their way onto a WWF tape release. Something that would become commonplace. It gave Stacy, Torrie, Terri and Sharmell a richer history. Gaining those video libraries was one of the few perks of the Monday Night War coming to a conclusion. I'm sure most people bought this tape to see the WWF diva's parading around in bikinis, but Stacy and Torrie aside, that's not much of that going on. If anything teenagers potential masturbatory fantasies ran headlong into Terri going shopping or Ivory making fun of the photographers. It's boner destroying stuff. I feel bad for the kids who bought this tape, pre-internet, in the hopes of seeing more skin. Not particularly recommended.

23

IVORY

STONE COLD STEVE AUSTIN - WHAT?

CAT NO: WWF54129
RUN TIME: 63 minutes (approx)

James Dixon: Yet another Steve Austin tape then, with this one following a similar format combining a new interview with the man himself alongside footage from 2001, a period that saw him turn heel and revitalise his character, even if it was a bad move from a business perspective. We open up with Steve talking about fighting each year to earn his spot in the WrestleMania main event, which leads to footage of the epic match against The Rock at WrestleMania X-Seven. Austin says the match meant everything to him because it was in his own backyard, but also because it was so good, and he rightly names it the best bout between the two. It really is, it's absolutely brilliant in every way. From the wonderful pacing to the impeccable timing and the superb series of near falls, each one of which could genuinely have been the finish. The match is a titanic clash between the two biggest stars of the Attitude Era, and in many ways is the final exclamation point on that period. We get tons of highlights from the match set to high-tempo, frenetic music. There are so many cute moments that ape other bouts, such as Austin with a bloody Rock in the Sharpshooter in an homage to WrestleMania 13, and Rock trying to get the same fall over Austin that Bret Hart did at Survivor Series 1996, and then Vince gets involved and effectively ends the Attitude Era with Austin turning heel. He needed freshening up but once he turned heel, interest in the product dropped because the fans' hero had done the unthinkable. Losing a lot of other main event stars didn't help the company either of course.

We go to Austin's promo the next night on RAW, where he says he owes no explanation for his actions. He goes at it again with Rock, this time in a cage, laying a 2-on-1 beating on him along with Vince. Triple H, Austin's perennial rival of the last few months, comes down seemingly to save Rock from the pounding and begin a babyface run opposite Stone Cold, but instead they put the last few months of war behind them and align to form the Two-Man Power Trip. Back to the "live" interview, and Austin puts Vince over for his toughness, bringing up his nasty table bump at St. Valentine's Day Massacre and the manly chair shots and punches he has given Vince over the years. He talks about Hunter tearing his quad a few weeks later and still finishing the match, something he can empathise with on a personal level having had a similar thing happen to him. JR brings up the Austin-HHH feud and the match at No Way Out 2001, which Austin says he wasn't fully fit for, but that he thinks the build-up to the bout was WrestleMania main event quality. I think is very good, but often slightly overrated. It was certainly brutal, but 40-minutes of Hunter is just too much for me. There are plenty of shortcuts in it of course and the Three Stages of Hell gimmick certainly helped keep it mostly interesting, though I didn't really agree with Hunter going over when Austin was winning the WWF Title next month. Especially when he himself was just putting the Undertaker over at WrestleMania anyway. Speaking of WrestleMania, I have no idea why this was shown after the highlights from that show. Typical goofy editing from Video Control on this.

To SmackDown! in Oklahoma taped two days after 'Mania, and Austin participating in the long-standing cruel WWF tradition of humiliating Jim Ross in his home town. It's a brutal attack, with Austin potatoing the hell out of Ross with his big wild fists, busting him hardway before choking him out viciously with a belt. "We knew that was going to be a chance to get some heat" says Austin while stood with his victim when discussing it in the tape's interview. Austin follows the sympathy-generating attack on Ross by beating the piss out of Michael Cole. This didn't garner anything like the same response, because who cares if Michael Cole gets his ass kicked? The majority of viewers, much like me, were thrilled by it. We see more clips of Austin being a complete dickhead to people, with everyone from Tajiri to Tazz to his wife Debra getting either verbal or physical lashings from the new Stone Cold. Hmm, perhaps the less said about that last one the better. On SmackDown!, little Spike Dudley stands up to Austin when he calls girlfriend Molly unflattering names, and rips up a petition that Austin was trying to get people to sign so he could get his triple threat title match at *King of the Ring 2001* against Christ Benoit and Chris Jericho cancelled. They have a match later in the show and Austin batters him of course. The thing with Austin as a heel is that he WAS superb in the role and did a great job making himself hated with his actions, taking everything out of his character that people loved. But fans just played along, underneath they still wanted to cheer him.

To Austin's incredible match against Chris Benoit in Edmonton on *SmackDown!* (yes, important matches and angles really did used to take place on this show), which was utterly brutal. Even though Austin had just come back from serious neck surgery, he spent 2001 having the best matches on the card time after time, putting in some truly brilliant, career-defining performances against nearly everyone that he worked with. Well, expect the Undertaker. Their 2001 feud was the pits. The levels of effort from Austin as a heel when he could have conceivably and comfortably cruised by, deserves much credit. The most memorable moments of this particular contest include Austin dropping Benoit headfirst on the floor by the announce table in a cringe-inducing bump, and then Benoit hitting no less than ten German suplexes... IN A ROW! Considering the state of Austin's neck, that showed incredible confidence and faith in Benoit's ability. It's a brilliant match, one of the best ever on *SmackDown!* and clocks in at around ****½, if not higher. Without question it is worth going out of your way to see if you have never done so.

For no good reason, we then go back to the start of Austin's career and see him in action as 'Stunning' Steve Austin in WCW, with guys like Ric Flair and Arn Anderson putting him over. Anderson says WCW didn't have a clue how to market Austin because they didn't see anything in him. Geniuses. Though, let's not forget that the WWF didn't have a clue how to market him either for a good while, even after the Ringmaster was consigned to the annals of WrestleCrap and Austin had cut his "3:16" promo. Back in VHS real time to Austin, who dismisses comparisons to Mad Dog Vachon (who he is stylistically similar to) because he never saw him work, instead saying he was influenced rather by guys like Ricky Steamboat (who Austin calls his favourite opponent and says is one of the greatest ever), Jake Roberts and Ric Flair. We see the excellent *Clash of the Champions XXIII* **** match pitting the Hollywood Blondes against Arn Anderson and Ric Flair (which readers can check out in high quality blu-ray format on the WWE's *The Best of WCW Clash of the Champions* release), with Flair complimenting both Blondes for making him and Arn look good and being so easy to work with, which is something he prided himself on for years when he was reigning as NWA Champion.

Taking a moment out from wrestling, we see Steve Austin appearing in a number of segments on MADtv, including one where he played a long haired trailer park dude, which wasn't the biggest stretch for the gruff redneck. "It's like having Laurence Olivier turning up on set" says show star Michael McDonald, worryingly without a hint of sarcasm in his voice. Will Sasso does a dead-on Austin impression in another skit, while Austin plays a fitness instructor failing to get a word in because "Austin" keeps responding "What?". Oh, and Debra is there too, standing around and being wooden while smiling and nodding like she somehow belongs. Famous by association, love. In another skit, Austin sings and plays the guitar really badly, but he does know he is real bad at it, which is something at least. He tells how his dad was in a country and western band and has tried to teach him how to play the guitar, but he just has no musical talent whatsoever. That segues nicely into

FURIOUS ABOUT: PAUL HEYMAN

Let's get this out of the way from the start; I'm a Paul Heyman guy. I loved the Dangerous Alliance. I was a complete mark for ECW. I think Paul is one of the best managers, promoters, writers, commentators and promos in the business. If Paul had been blessed with the body to match the mind he has for wrestling, he would have been a multiple time world champion. As it stands he is a member of a small and exclusive club here at HoW of managers who became commentators who are absolutely outstanding at both. The club is basically Bobby Heenan, Jim Cornette and Paul Heyman. During the Alliance angle Paul got to use his skill to get over talent from the announce table. Rhyno in particular stands out. Where would he have been without the "GORE, GORE, GORE" call? But it wasn't just getting people over. Paul was outstanding at getting characters over. His explanation of Steve Austin's mentality sticks in the mind. His ability to get the personalities across worked wonders and I'm constantly confused as to why the WWE never had him back on the announce desk. He returned to managing Brock Lesnar in mid 2002.

the classic backstage skits with Austin, Vince McMahon, Kurt Angle and a guitar, which were done by necessity to keep Kurt and Austin on television when both were injured. Angle had stepped into the gap in the unholy union left by Triple H's injury, and the lowering of the serious tone and foray into immensely entertaining comedy led to some of the most rewarding segments of the era. In the first one, Austin outlines Vince's problems to him ("your kid's stabbed you in the back") and thoroughly demoralises him, but then says he is here to give him inspiration and solve his problems with music. It's chicken soup for the soul, he says. Austin then serenades Vince with the worst rendition of '*Kumbaya*' in history, all the while staring deep into his eyes with a steely, unfaltering glare. It's harrowing, and the crowd loves it. Austin then lets us in on the secret that it took two takes to get the segment right because he was laughing so much, and we actually see the blooper, which is a delight. Austin just can't control himself and then Vince bursts out laughing uncontrollably too! Vince! Next, Kurt Angle gets a chance to sing, and he asks Austin to budge up on the couch they are sitting on because he makes him nervous. Instead, Austin scoots closer like a purposely difficult child. Angle tries to start his song, but Austin loudly clears his throat to put him off with perfect comic timing. Kurt eventually sings an equally bad number, busting out '*Jimmy Crack Corn*', which causes Vince to walk off. Things get even better still when Austin starts doling out hugs, including one to a taken aback Vince in a parking lot. Austin's wide-eyed, complete psycho expression while hugging Vince is unbelievable. Maybe the best facials I have ever seen. Just thinking about it again now is tickling me to the point that I feel the need to watch it again. He basically turned into a comedy heel in the last few weeks of these skits, and the crowd can allow themselves to love him again, even if they are not really supposed to. It takes the edge off for sure, but makes him far more entertaining. During an in-ring segment on *RAW*, Austin gets pissy with

Angle getting in the way of he and Vince, saying he wants him out of the group because the team is Austin and McMahon. Vince tells them to settle their differences with a fight, but instead they both take turns hugging Vince. In another backstage skit where he gives Kurt a present (a tiny cowboy hat), Austin gets in a line that Angle says Steve used to use for real backstage a lot: "I like ya, not much, but I like ya". Kurt then reveals that most of these segments weren't planned at all, they just ran the camera and went ahead and did it. Spontaneity and letting guys be themselves can result in television gold like all of this was. It is yet another in a long list of marks against entirely scripted and overly-produced corporate sports entertainment.

We go to an impassioned Vince promo from *SmackDown!* in the midst of the WCW/ECW invasion, where Vince begs for the "old" Stone Cold to help him deal with the threat, rather than the new guitar strumming, hug giving bag of needy emotional wreckage that the character has become. Austin walks off with his tail between his legs as Vince pleads for him to Stunner him or knock him on his ass. Eventually he gets what he wished for, and Vince repays Austin in turn by singing to welcome him back. At first Austin seems to enjoy it, which is not the "old Stone Cold" at all. But then he smashes the guitar over Vince's head in a great spot, and all the rights are restored. For a couple of days at least.

Austin tells the tale of how the whole "What?" thing came about. The story goes that Austin was driving between towns and was bored out of his mind, so decided to call up Christian and bug him to whittle away the time. Christian didn't answer but Austin was undeterred, and spent the next 15-minutes having a conversation with himself on Christian's answer phone. On occasion he would ask a question, and respond "what?" as if he hadn't quite heard the answer. The thing got over with the boys and then Austin decided to try it out on television, and it exploded. Debra says Austin is always saying "what?" at home because he is half deaf and can't hear things in one ear. Austin says he likes how it took off, especially because it pissed off Kurt Angle so much, and the crowd were utterly merciless chanting it at him, to the point he could no longer do a promo. Eventually, the crowd took to chanting "You Suck! What!?" during his entrance as well, but that was a little bit after this tape came out so isn't shown on here unfortunately. One example of the crowd hijacking a segment with the chants is shown though, during Lillian Garcia singing the National Anthem no less! Austin had created a monster. A decade and a half later, audiences were *still* doing it at WWE shows up and down the country.

Back to in ring action and we see the incredible tour de force between Kurt Angle and Austin at *SummerSlam 2001*, which is a bloody, brutal and epic match, tarnished only by a disappointing finish non-finish. It's another incredible performance from Austin in 2001, as he continued to have great matches seemingly every other week. I am not sure there has ever been a run of so many ****+ matches in a single year from a guy at any other point in the WWF, and that is including guys like Shawn Michaels and Bret Hart. People rag on 2001 because of the horrible botch of the WCW invasion, which is fair comment, but they forget that the in ring work was often excellent.

Talk turns to the post 9/11 *SmackDown!* show, and Austin recounts a conversation with Vince McMahon when he was told the show was going ahead, and he questioned if it was the right thing to do. "The show must go on, we have to keep doing what we do" was the gist of Vince's response, and Austin agreed. I do too, the WWF was right to do that show and did it in a mostly classy, tasteful way... Stephanie's inappropriate comparisons of the attacks to Vince being on trial for steroid pushing aside, of course. With Austin being a heel, he didn't do a great deal on the show, but after it went off the air he stayed around to entertain the fans. We get some great never before seen footage of Austin dicking around with his brother in the crowd, and doing all manner of improv where he asks fans their name and their occupation, then proceeds to tell them how much he hates whatever that occupation might be. One woman says she is involved in Christian literature publishing, and that one breaks Austin, who has a good belly laugh at the absurdity of it all. It looks a lot of fun. We get plenty more rare footage of Austin doing the same thing at other shows, plus other stuff such as giving a live rendition of '*Kumbaya*'. He says that he does it because he wants to make sure the fans are entertained and thus more likely to return to next time the company is in town. Commendable indeed.

We discuss beer, with Kurt Angle giving a guide to how Austin does his beer drinking routine, and he expresses immense jealousy that he didn't come up with the idea first. Timekeeper Mark Yeaton gets some camera time, as he is the man responsible for throwing 'Stone Cold' the cans. He claims Austin "drinks" up on 24 beers on average per night, though as is pointed out he only ever gets around an ounce in his mouth, with the rest going everywhere. More insight into the man at home follows from Debra, with her noting that on television Austin doesn't crunch the can, but he does at home and it drives her nuts. That is probably exactly why he does it.

The final piece of non storyline footage involves Austin's feud with one of the WWF cameramen, who Austin frequently chases around the building when the live shows are off the air. Austin tortures him, grabbing his wire, making him run backwards and just generally goofing around. We get an interview from the cameraman in question and during it Austin turns up behind him. The cameraman asks if Austin is serious because he can never tell, and Austin says he is and that the only thing saving him from a whuppin' is the expensive camera. Then he slaps him heartily on the back, lets out a big belly laugh and cracks a joke. What a riotously entertaining guy to hang around with he must be.

VERDICT

The footage we get here, and indeed all over this tape, is brilliant. It does a tremendous job of not just repeating the same overused footage from the past and instead giving a different insight into the character and a glimpse behind the scenes that you rarely get to see. Considering this is one of over half a dozen Steve Austin tapes on the market, the fact it remains fresh and entertaining throughout is a testament to the man and a creditable job from WWF Home Video. Austin was involved in some of the most entertaining matches and segments of his career during the few months featured on this, and it makes for a really fantastic viewing experience. Very highly recommended.

90

AUSTIN HUGS MCMAHON

BACKLASH 2002

CAT NO: WWE59313
RUN TIME: 165 minutes (approx)

Arnold Furious: I have very mixed feelings about 2002. I am ambivalent towards it, unlike any other year in wrestling. For starters, it's the year that I fell so out of love with the WWF that I started watching both TNA and ROH. I needed an alternative to the WWF that desperately. Keep in mind, the WWF was available on TV for nothing whereas I had to buy tapes from America to see the other two promotions. That's how irritated and disenfranchised I had become. And yet the second half of 2002 saw Paul Heyman take over on *SmackDown!* and they produced a string of great matches that's pretty much unmatched by any other period in WWF history. The WWF had an insanely talented roster, including many of the best technical wrestlers on the planet and the undercard for this show features some tremendous talent, but then you get into the top matches and it's the same old story. The main event is Triple H, who had already outstayed his babyface welcome after a couple of months, and Hulk Hogan, hobbling along on a nostalgia pop. And they get 22-minutes! 2002 very much reminds me a great of WCW at the peak of its powers: a sensational undercard busting a gut, but terrible main events. 21st April 2002. We're in Kansas City, Missouri. Hosts are Jim Ross and Jerry Lawler.

Tangent: This is a strange old tape because it was filmed, as a PPV, as a WWF show but by the time it was released it had a WWE catalogue number. The time's they were a changin'.

WWF Cruiserweight Championship
Billy Kidman (c) vs. Tajiri
The WWF couldn't leave well alone and when Tajiri got hugely over as a babyface they turned him heel. To show how important the Cruiserweight Title was to the brand extension, Tajiri, the champion, was picked in the 12th round of the draft. That would be after Mark Henry, Rikishi, D-Von Dudley (a spoiler pick to stop *RAW* getting both Dudleys) and Maven. I remember us doing a brand extension draft on the website I was writing for, SmashWrestling, and we ended up with two decent rosters. The WWF didn't. Tajiri uses his educated feet to control the match but Kidman rapidly shows how much he's learned about WWF style. Tajiri's ECW moves are toned down too. The tree of woe dropkick is relatively soft. Lawler spends the whole match yacking about Torrie Wilson, who Tajiri has forced to dress as a geisha girl. Kidman charges into the Tarantula but then wrestles out so Tajiri flips back over him to get it. Kidman also finds a counter for the handspring back elbow by dropkicking Tajiri in the spine. Tajiri starts working the kicks again but goes for the powerbomb. For those who didn't watch WCW; you can't powerbomb Kidman. Billy's wonky SSP misses and Tajiri kicks him in the head… for 2. The crowd bought that finish and start chanting for Kidman. Tajiri goes for a super something but gets countered into a spinebuster off the top. That also doesn't get it done as JR starts to put over the cruiserweight moves on display. Kidman goes for an elevated powerbomb, a'la Last Ride, so Tajiri sprays him with RED MIST and drops on top for the title. Cracking match, reminiscent of WCW's brilliant cruiserweight division, with the added entertainment of seeing two solid workers from different worlds collide. That's what WCW's division was all about; bringing together wrestlers from America, Japan and Mexico. The WWF were never 100% behind the division, or the hybrid styles, but did have a spell of using them as hot openers. It totally worked here.
Final Rating: ***½

Backstage: the "brand extension divided" Faarooq and Bradshaw hug it out. The only point of them splitting the APA up was so they could try and push Bradshaw in singles, again. The only problem was that the fans loved the APA and didn't want them broken up. By the time Bradshaw got a successful run, over a year later, it was because he changed his persona.

Scott Hall vs. Bradshaw
Kevin Nash had already gotten himself injured so he's "suspended". Hall has X-Pac in his corner instead and the nWo has been reduced to a pair of jackasses. I'd have taken Hall and Waltman in 1994, but in 2002? No thanks. Faarooq strolls down to watch Bradshaw's back. They might as well have just done a tag match, although anyone who saw the nWo in WCW must surely have suspected Ron Simmons was turning heel here. Scott Hall looks in dreadful condition, which could place this match anywhere between 1998 and 2012. They'd have been better off having X-Pac work. Originally the nWo, in 2002 anyway, had Hall to take all the bumps and the heat because Hogan and Nash couldn't. Not that the WWF's version of the

nWo was any use at all. The whole "nWo 4 Life" mantra was abandoned at *WrestleMania* when Hogan left the group. It also didn't help that WCW ran the nWo angle completely into the ground. You'll notice I'm not talking about the actual match and there's a reason for that. JR compares it to a bowling shoe, if that helps. The only good spot is the Clothesline from Hell, which Bradshaw NAILS on Hall only for X-Pac to get Hall's foot on the rope. Ron Simmons kicks X-Pac's ass to entertain the crowd and Hall wins with a horrible looking roll up. I'd have been in favour of ditching the nWo and firing Hall at this point as it was apparent Hall couldn't do anything useful and being on the road was just turning him into a worse drunk. The WWF concurred and Hall was fired in May for his behaviour during a UK tour, but the nWo angle rumbled on for a couple of months before dying a death over the summer.
Final Rating: DUD

Backstage: Vince McMahon power walks into Ric Flair's locker room. Great to see Arn Anderson hovering over his shoulder. Vince thinks Flair understands the pressures of being in charge before calling his employees ungrateful. Vince points out Flair has put himself "between a rock and a hard spot". Wrong, again, Vince. Has he got a different popular phases book to the rest of the world? How hard is "a rock and a hard place" to get right? Was he doing this shit on purpose, just to annoy me? Vince suggests Flair shouldn't have placed himself in the number one contender's match as referee. Flair's rebuttal where he says Vince "never knew who he was and he never would" is killer. As if to publicly point out Vince never booked him properly when he had him in the early 90s.

WWF Women's Championship
Jazz (c) vs. Trish Stratus
Jazz was basically hired to show all the divas how to wrestle. Seeing as Trish was the WWF's chosen superstar in the women's division, and was most eager to learn, she got the biggest benefit. As Trish was trying to get taken more seriously she covered up a lot more. She has rockin' cleavage here but is covered up apart from that. Molly comes out to attack Trish before the match giving her a back injury and an out for jobbing. Jazz controls the pace and makes Trish look really solid by jumping around her and calling all the spots. They run a great spot where Jazz ducks the Chick Kick so Trish switches legs to hit it from the other side. Trish had been working on her moveset and her next spot is the Stratosphere, her handstand version of the rana off the jazz. Jazz has an awesome moveset, one nearer to a cruiserweight or a top indy performer, so she's popping off sit out powerbombs and stuff like that and Trish throws herself into the bumps. Trish goes for her bulldog but Jazz counters in mid-air into a back suplex. Trish, selling the back like a champ, gets strapped in the Boston crab and then the STF. The crowd rallies behind her but she can't get the ropes and has to tap out. For flaccid women's division standards this was a belter. Some of Jazz's stuff, like jumping onto the ropes twice, looked awkward but Trish looked dynamite in there and you can sense her star is on the rise. Even JR has to point out she's getting better in the ring. Trish was a great role model for the Divas because she went from being eye candy to being a legitimate wrestler and showed that here. From this point onward Trish looked like a talented performer. The best part of it was that the WWF were so happy with her as a looker they put her in with a host of actual wrestlers (Jazz, Molly, Victoria) so the women's division, for perhaps the only time in it's history, was over with the crowd and over with the office too. Trish, for me, defined this era in women's wrestling with her capacity to learn and her steady improvement in the ring. She became a special attraction that got the division over. She also had the two best WWF women's matches that didn't involve Japanese talent.
Final Rating: **

Backstage: Paul Heyman motivates Brock Lesnar for his debut. He's been with the WWF since the night after *WrestleMania* but they've been smart and held off on the debut.

Brock Lesnar vs. Jeff Hardy
Lesnar's attitude in OVW wasn't particularly good and he spent two years down there earning big money for standing around on the apron while Shelton Benjamin did the work. There was no doubting his potential though. Just looking at him would tell you that. Like several others within the business I wasn't overly impressed with Brock to begin with as he was a bit green. He'd improve very quickly though and benefitted from having Paul Heyman as a manager and mouthpiece. If Brock had spent his two years in OVW actually learning stuff he could have walked into the main events... Given the desperation of the WWF in 2002, he did anyway. Not exactly the best message to send to the locker room. Lesnar improved after hitting the main events and a year on from this he was a genuine talent. Here he's just a destruction machine. Jeff gets next to nothing and Lesnar manhandles him. It's interesting to see the crowd getting into Jeff for his comeback and Swanton bomb. Lesnar shrugs that off though, tackles Jeff to prevent a chair shot and hits an F-5 and three powerbombs until the ref, Teddy Long, calls for the bell as Jeff can't defend himself. The match is a virtual squash and the perfect way to get over the debuting Lesnar. The problem with having a monster is how to book him once he's already gotten over. It's "Goldberg syndrome".
Final Rating: *

Kurt Angle vs. Edge
Sometimes the WWF didn't need a reason to feud two guys. There's no title here, there's no miscommunication. They used to be tight but now it's just about who's the better man. Sometimes keeping it simple is the best way to go. Angle had been up to the top of the WWF card and, because he got cold really quickly, they bumped him down to get midcarders over until he got so over doing that, that he became a main eventer again. Angle's attitude during this apparent de-push was phenomenal and he was constantly out to steal the show. Edge is eager to prove his worth and potential so they go full out to impress. Edge takes superb bumps off Angle's suplexes. Both guys would end up with serious neck problems because of this hard-bumping style but it sure was entertaining to watch. There was certainly a crowd of WWF talent in 2002 that was wanting to have highly rated, show-stealing matches. They base this match around big suplex bumps, hard work and constant action. Kurt survives the Edgecution, which had stopped being any kind of finish for Edge as he'd switched to a spear. Edge heads up top but Angle runs the buckles to take him down. Edge escapes an ankle lock attempt but Angle goes right into the rolling Germans. Edge escapes the Angle Slam and German suplexes Angle on his head. Kurt's sell is amazing to the point where it looks real. He's practically inhaling the canvas. Interesting to note Edge using a lot of high risk dives after that, in an attempt to up his game and put Angle away. He felt he needed big moves to get the job done against a former WWF champion. Edgeomatic is countered into the Angle Slam in a smooth spot and a nice near fall. Edge's creativity mixes well with Angle's athleticism and finisher obsession. Edge counters out of an ankle lock into an inside cradle and Kurt barely kicks out in another great near fall. The crowd really bite on all this. Angle goes for a chair and does one of the all-time great "missing and hitting the ropes, then the chair hits you in

the face" spots you'll ever see. It's a convoluted spot but they make it work. The only giveaway being as Angle repositions the chair before he swings so it'll hit him seat first. When ridiculous stuff is coming off you know you're hot. Edge goes after the spear but Kurt punts him in the face and finishes with the Angle Slam in a wonderful sequence. These two clicked like nobody's business and this was like Edge's coming out party as a main event star. Albeit still buried away in the midcard. Make no mistake about it, this was a main event calibre match and easily Edge's best singles match to date.
Final Rating: ****½

Video Control takes us to WWF New York where Tazz does a roving reporter gig. It seems most of the people he interviewed were hot chicks. Strange that.

Promo Time: Chris Jericho
I find it hard to believe that Chris Jericho, WWF Undisputed Champion just last month, isn't booked in a match. You'd think he'd be in that number one contenders match. Jericho says much the same thing; he was Undisputed Champion a month ago but now he's a spectator like all the jackasses in the audience. It's a bit of an issue that the heel comes out for an interview and picks holes in the company's booking and he's right. He bitches about everyone on the card and everyone in the audience and then leaves. Well worth the PPV time.

Backstage: Ric Flair, now in ref's shirt, is visited by a moody Undertaker who says nothing at all. JR stops off to shill the *Forceable Entry* CD. Tonight's dirge is something by Creed called '*Young Grow Old*'. It's just background noise.

WWF Intercontinental Championship
Rob Van Dam (c) vs. Eddie Guerrero
Lawler tries to catch JR out by asking who was the first man to use the frogsplash in the WWF and Ross responds with "D'Lo Brown". Well, it's true, but only because we're not talking WCW or ECW or anywhere else. Anyway, this feud is over both the frogsplash and the IC Title. Eddie had spent a year out on the indies getting clean from his massive drug addiction problems and returned recently. RVD is a good opponent for him as he's super-over and works an exciting style. Eddie, being talented and tough, just beats the crap out of him. Van Dam is great at taking a beating so it works well. The crowd is surprisingly cold but you have to remember how exhausting Angle-Edge was. RVD does get pops for his trademark moves though and brings some interesting stuff like a suplex with immediate floatover that impresses JR. RVD still retains a few hardcore spots like the corkscrew legdrop onto the rail but you sense he's been told to keep his spottiness in check. If there's a guy who can keep you in check, it's Eddie. He systematically dissects RVD after blocking the Rolling Thunder with knees. It's vintage body part work as he takes apart the back area after RVD's mistake. But Eddie is so creative that he busts out a load of lucha spots like the surfboard, slingshot hilo and the Gory special to work the spine. Rob stops the frogsplash with kicks on Eddie, perched on the top rope, but Eddie NAILS him with a sunset bomb. The impact on that was SICK. Ref gets bumped allowing Eddie to hit a neckbreaker on the title belt. Frogsplash finishes. Really good match with Eddie at his resourceful best. It might have a better reputation if it didn't have to follow Kurt and Edge and the superb match they just had. Fun to see two of my favourite wrestlers from different companies hooking up though. I always loved RVD in ECW and Eddie in WCW so for me this was a dream match.
Final Rating: ***½

Video Control shows us the trailer for The Rock's movie *The Scorpion King*. JR puts it over calling it "phenomenal" (41% on RottenTomatoes says otherwise). He also puts it over as the highest grossing movie in April in movie history, which it was… for about a week until *My Big Fat Greek Wedding* wiped the floor with it. The Rock's movie cost $60M. Greek Wedding? $5M. And considering I'm an action movie junkie, I've actually seen the latter more times and it's the better film. *Scorpion King* made enough money that The Rock made it in Hollywood and went on to a successful movie career. I miss him and 2002 certainly could have used more Rocky, but he definitely prolonged his time in the spotlight by going into movies and he deserves every success he got in Hollywood.

#1 Contenders Match
The Undertaker vs. Steve Austin
And here's where the show goes completely to shit. Steve Austin's motivation in 2002 is questionable at best and his neck injury was clearly bothering him. His last great year in wrestling, 2001, saw him take bump after bump on that surgically repaired neck. The hard-hitting style took its toll and he did not look in good shape in 2002. Meanwhile Undertaker had turned heel and his already dull Underbiker character became even blander. One guy when they were on their best form could probably carry the other, but both guys unmotivated and disinterested creates a truly miserable wrestling match. Austin tries to avoid working and pops the crowd by doing push-ups, checking his invisible watch, instigating "what?" chants and flipping Taker off. It's like watching a Memphis version of Steve Austin, a fictional off-shoot of 'Stone Cold'. As for the crowd, they've now had two great matches back-to-back and Austin and Taker face an uphill struggle to get them involved. Not that they attempt anything. Austin grabs a hold and they sit in it and Taker treats it like a night off. They work in a few trademark spots like Old School and the Thesz press but it really feels like a house show. Austin occasionally makes me chuckle, like tidying up the Spanish announce table after Taker threatens a spot through it. It's strangely polite to the point where I'm not sure what he was going for but it still made me laugh. Because nothing is happening Scott Hall and X-Pac stroll out (for no apparent reason). Taker works at the leg in a manner I would describe as perfunctory. Mainly because Austin sells it when he's in a hold but then just works normally again. I'm sure the WWF criticised Rob Van Dam for doing that right before this. It's often one of the reasons people don't get pushes when they come from elsewhere; because they don't know how to sell. At least RVD was never boring. This match is tedious. You wonder why it receives a monstrous 30-minutes when Jericho wasn't even booked. The referee, Ric Flair, doesn't enter into the match either. JR criticises his lack of experience in the role, which causes him to count slowly, not count at all when there's a double down and miss exposed turnbuckles. You'd think he'd at least bring toughness, as he's a wrestler, but he gets bumped on a routine ref spot and stays down. It's embarrassing. Austin has it won with a Stunner while old man Flair lies around having a nap. Austin kicks out of a resultant chokeslam and they work some nonsense with a chair to distract from an Austin low blow, which goes nowhere. This is a terrible match between two guys who should know better. As if the match wasn't embarrassing enough Flair gets bumped AGAIN. Taker nails Austin with that chair from earlier but that's a damn false finish too. Quite how Flair missed the chair shot, given the massive noise from it, is anybody's guess. They go back to the chair again, Taker kicks the chair in Austin's face and gets the pin. For starters; that's a DQ. Secondly Austin's foot was on the rope. The booking sucked here as the attention focused on the indecisiveness of the referee. The actual

contest was boring, overly long and still managed to be convoluted. Taker manages to get in some bonus trash talking, which looks just awful. The least realistic and most out of character I've ever seen Taker work. Austin hits a Stunner to even the booking out.
Final Rating: ½*

Backstage: Coach grabs Flair, who he treats like a confused old folks home resident, to show him a replay of the finish. "Oh, shit" – Flair. We go from that to shilling a Divas swimsuit issue.

WWF Tag Team Championship
Billy & Chuck (c) vs. Al Snow & Maven
This is the sandwich match before the main event. Billy & Chuck (dubbed Chuck & Suck by internet wags) had a metrosexual gimmick at this point, with their manager/stylist Rico, who's a better worker than both of them. Chuck seems to have no idea what he's doing and his dancing is an example of that rarity in wrestling; someone who dances and doesn't get over doing it. For those who don't remember Maven, he was the winner of *Tough Enough* series one. Seeing as Snow was a trainer on that show, they're teaming up to go after the tag titles. Maven is incredibly vanilla, as he's only been a wrestler for a matter of weeks. He wrestles like a trainee. Admittedly he's a good trainee but the fans haven't taken to him as yet. The problem the *Tough Enough* kids had was once the WWF had used them up, they didn't know what to do and where to go. So when Maven got released his career just died. By 2011 he was being helped out by the WWE's Wellness Program before getting a job as a bouncer. Considering the guy was a school teacher before this, he'd have been better off staying put. The match is straightforward so Maven doesn't get lost. Snow manages to offset Rico's interference but that allows Chuck to sneak in and superkick Maven for the win. These trainee level matches are just white noise to me after seeing so many of them over the years. I get they wanted to do something with Maven, and he wasn't a bad guy, but this match was mediocrity personified.
Final Rating: ½*

WWF Undisputed Championship
Triple H (c) vs. Hulk Hogan
Like every other idiot, I was cheering on Hogan at *WrestleMania*, so I had this coming as much as anyone else. Hogan is up in his late 40s and would turn 50 the following year. He's looking orange and leathery but the fans still love him. Like at *WrestleMania* it's the fan reaction that makes the match worthwhile even if the novelty has already worn off a bit. Hunter is smart enough to know Hogan has no cardio and they have a series of test of strength spots lined up. It's like going back in time to 1985, with all the rinky-dink carnival horseshit that happened in all the worst Hulk Hogan matches from the height of Hulkamania. The thing that really bugs me about the way they approach this match is that Hunter takes superb bumps and Hogan only ever works when people bounce off him. Why don't they just do that match? Instead we get a monotonous amount of collar and elbow tie-ups. When Hunter finally takes over the beat down looks like a mugging. I keep wanting to call the police and tell them an old man is getting beaten up. Hogan's slow-motion comeback, where he can barely climb the buckles for the 10 count punches, stretches the boundaries of believability. Amazingly the match slows down further after the sluggish opening. Hunter breaks out his Pedigree in line with the ring post spot only for Hogan to counter it, really, really, really slowly. After that Hunter goes after Hogan's bad knee and the crowd dies. The problem with Hogan stems from his almost total immobility. He can't move around properly so Hunter decides to give him a reason for it. JR calls the crowd "very pro-Hogan" but unlike at *WrestleMania* they fade quickly and stay out of it. Mainly because the match is so fantastically boring and they're just waiting to see if the WWF is dumb enough to put the title on Hogan just because he got a nostalgia pop. Anyway, the match rumbles on as they run some more rinky-dink stuff like the sleeper with the triple hand drop. Triple H was always a throwback, which makes you wonder why he wanted to change the business so much in 1997. Big boot and legdrop should finish but Jericho runs down and lays out Earl Hebner, just to give everyone concerned an out. Hogan gets a chair shot but Hunter takes exception and tosses Y2J over the top thus solidifying his babyface status. Sort of. Hogan starts hulking up, or maybe he's asking a nurse for his meds. Big boot. Legdrop. Hunter moves, like Rock did at *WrestleMania*. Pedigree. Undertaker runs down to break the count, presumably because he'd rather wrestle Hogan than Hunter. Either way the match will suck. Chair shot! Taker throws Hogan over Hunter but he refuses help too and watching them fight is like seeing two old hobos scrapping over a sandwich. Hogan turns back around and drops the leg for the win and his record tying 6th WWF Title. I could have lived without the booking towards the end of the match, which merely served to set up Hogan-Taker, which was happening anyway, and Hunter-Jericho, which was also pretty much set anyway. I also could have lived without the match that preceded it. It was slow, overlong and incredibly weak. I agree that Hogan-Rock should have gone on last at *WrestleMania* because it was the match that everyone came to see, but there were only so many nostalgia pops you could get with this old act and personally, I was pissed off that the WWF went ahead and switched the belt here.
Final Rating: ¼*

VERDICT

2002 was a year where it became increasingly evident the top end of the card was going to be loaded with old timers and the same old acts recycled. The undercard was where the real effort and real wrestling was taking place. Edge-Angle and to a lesser extent RVD-Guerrero and the cruiserweights is where it was happening here. The two main events were both shockingly poor and relied heavily on a crowd reaction that never happened. There was a nostalgia pop for Hogan and another when the belt changed, but belt changes are almost always popped. People love seeing title changes. Ask Vince Russo. As far as Hulk Hogan goes, I like a lot of his work in the 80s and writing these books has allowed me access to matches with the likes of Harley Race, Randy Savage and Paul Orndorff, which was good stuff, but there came a point where Hogan's matches stopped being relevant and stopped being good and after defecting to WCW in 1994 you can count his good matches on one hand (a couple with Flair in '94, Rock at *WrestleMania* and against Vince at *WrestleMania XIX*). While he garnered a pleasing nostalgia pop on returning to the WWF and I'm glad he's in the Hall of Fame, he shouldn't have been main eventing PPVs. The one after this, against Undertaker, is even worse. That's a story for another time and hopefully someone else will be telling it.

50

FUNNIEST MOMENTS

CAT NO: WWF59327
RUN TIME: 63 minutes (approx)

James Dixon: I had the misfortune of covering the *WWF's Funniest Moments* tape from the early 90s in *The Complete WWF Video Guide Volume #2* and it scored a mammoth 1 out of 100. Now while this one probably doesn't feature the Bushwhackers or the Gobbledy Gooker, I am still fully aware of what the WWF classes as "humour", so my expectations are at an all-time low going into it.

Imitation (is the sincerest form of flattery)

- Promisingly, we start with The Rock, who *is* a funny guy. Unfortunately all he does is say a mock prayer in a squeaky voice, apparently as an imitation of Billy Gunn. Rock quickly ends any chance Billy has of getting over as a top guy by belittling him: "I just won *King of the Ring*, but everyone still thinks that I absolutely suck!" Yep, that was the problem.

- Edge and Christian bring out midget versions of the Hardy Boyz who have tiny little ladders with them, and then midget versions of the Dudley Boyz, who have little kiddie plastic tables. It looks like a funny skit, but we literally see just the entrances of the midgets and nothing else.

- Going back a bit to 1998, we see the quite brilliant DX parody of the Nation of Domination. Again, very little is shown, but we do get Hunter (as "The Crock") discussing doing a big poo, and Road Dogg with his brilliant D-Lo Brown impression, repeating everything The Crock says. Hunter alludes to Rock laying the smack down on himself, if you catch my drift, and Road Brown chimes in: "You hear that, the brother smacks himself down!" Mizark Henry gets some gentle ribbing too, with Crock asking how he manages to get this pecs to go "all the way around". I love this segment, so it's a shame we don't get the whole thing.

- Pre-*Armageddon 2000* the Rock cuts a backstage promo regarding the upcoming six-man Hell in a Cell match. He mocks each of the guys in the bout in his typically amusing fashion. Rikishi is dismissed as a "thong wearing fatty" and his digs at Triple H's promos are EXACTLY what I have been saying throughout this book. Elongated words, wacky inflection and random out of place pauses, it's all here. Rocky's imitation of Hunter is brilliant, and even better that Hunter's of him in the previous segment some two and a half years prior. After Rock does his best Undertaker impression by rolling his eyes into the back of his head, Chris Jericho hijacks the promo and mocks Rock's catchphrases for being nonsense and then does a funny send up of him. Rock is unimpressed.

- Back to 1996 with Larry Fling featuring the Huckster and the Nacho Man! I am amazed this made it onto the tape. It lasts all of 5 seconds, with the only footage shown being of Hogan's muscles creaking as he asks "whatcha gonna do when I walk out on you". Resentment lingers, it seems.

- More midget madness, this from 2001 with Rock having a promo battle with a miniature Booker T, who does a tiny Spinneroonie.

- The Stooges next, who take their shirts off and pose like Hulk Hogan.

Fun With Food

- No! No! NO! The goddamn Bushwhackers have made the tape! Very, very briefly, but they are on here, making imbecilic noises and acting like pigs. Oh I knew I should have made Lee do this. He never has to do the terrible tapes!

- The original DX back in 1997/98 had an unhealthy obsession with cocks, be it their own or things that reminded them of penises. One such segment, a DX BBQ, sees them get all excited over various large phallic shaped sausages.

- Then the Bushwhackers again. Kill me.

- Backstage at a Thanksgiving party in 2000, JR shows Debra his juicy chicken breasts, while the camera focuses in on her juicy silicone breasts.

- Back in the 90s, Mean Gene Okerlund hosts the WWF at Oktoberfest, and Jim Neidhart does some Morris Dancing. I swear I am not making it up; this really happened! Elsewhere, the Bushwhackers cut some cheese.

- Back at the Thanksgiving party from 2000, Debra asks if anyone wants any pie. Al asks her if it is a trick question, and Funaki says he likes pie, which is met with uproarious laughter from the rest of the roster. I guess you had to be there.

- The Big Bossman cooks Al Snow's pet dog Pepper and feeds it to him in a hotel room, with a giant winking doggy graphic on the screen in the arena giving the game away to everyone else. Bossman tells Al that it was "100% Pepper", and Al barfs. Bossman rubs his face in it and comments that Pepper "tastes like chicken". They would not have got away with this in the PG Era. It's ridiculous, but it's no worse than Earthquake cooking Jake Roberts' snake Damien and making "Quake Burgers". It's so silly that it becomes almost perversely entertaining.

- Never entertaining is Dennis 'Mideon' Knight, who harks back to his days as a hillbilly pig farmer by shagging a cooked Thanksgiving turkey (while singing "afternoon delights") and then having a smoke afterwards. "I know the boss don't like this" he says of his cig, which is the only even slightly funny thing about the whole horrible affair. Thought Katie Vick was the WWF's first foray into necrophilia? You were wrong! And with added bestiality too!

- What could be worse than anything involving Phineas Godwinn? Why, the Bushwhackers of course! They continue to eat like filthy animals, but at least they are not trying to wrestle; the funniest joke of all.

- Food fights occur at Mick Foley's 2000 Thanksgiving party, which ends with Debra throwing a custard pie in Mick's face. Another occurs on *SmackDown!*, a year earlier mind you, only this one is at ringside rather than backstage. It ends in a similar way though, with a pie to the face. The lucky recipient this time is Jerry Lawler, courtesy of a planted fan.

Dating

- Val Venis makes some innuendos that wouldn't be lost on a coma patient, such is their blatancy. I'm not sure what this has to do with dating mind.

- Ah here we go then, as Mark Henry recites some self-penned poetry to Chyna in order to woo her and get her to agree to go on a date with him. Elsewhere, Al Snow sets up Head Cheese tag partner Steve Blackman with a girl he met at his therapy group. Neither of these (completely separate) dates go very well. Chyna acts like an utter bitch towards Henry, telling him she wants to get things over with, while wearing an expression like she just walked in on a McMahon riding her boyfriend. Why agree to the date then, you miserable cow? Blackman on the other hand can't get his blind date to shut up, and she just talks and talks. Think the band camp girl (Allison 'Michelle' Hannigan) in *American Pie*. Mark Henry tries to get Chyna to loosen up by serenading her, but to no avail. He then busts a move on the dance floor and finally gets Chyna to get on there with him. Speaking of dancing, Al has himself a little go back at Blackman's date, with poor Steve utterly miserable about all of it. Back to the Henry-Chyna date again, and some dude is hitting on Chyna and won't take no for an answer. He calls her a bitch so she throws a blatantly fake punch at him (holding his head first and then pulling it big time), then Mark Henry steams in and smashes through everyone else.

- Fast forward in time, and 'Sexual Chocolate' has hooked up with Mae Young. They do some mentally scarring shagging under the covers, before we cut to Kurt Angle promoting abstinence while Big Show gives out free condoms. Back to Henry, whose timeline is all over the place here, and we see him get it on with a transsexual. "Oh sweet Jesus, you got a penis!" says poor Mark, before throwing up. He has been in some stunningly bad segments over the years.

Friendship

- Mankind proposes a union between him and the Rock, which is the formation of the fantastic Rock 'n' Sock Connection. Mankind steals his catchphrases and then later backstage asks him if he can do the People's Elbow. Rock refuses, and tells him to just concentrate on "doing the sock gimmick".

- More Foley next, this time from his WWF Commissioner run, and one of his ace segments with Edge & Christian. In this one, Christian is struggling to make weight for his Light Heavyweight Title match, so Foley provides him with a chicken suit to wear. It's a long story, involving Kurt Angle and gold medals. Christian makes himself sick to drop those few extra pounds, which is not a very smart message to send to impressionable fat kids, and finally makes weight. "Hey, my chicken suit!" remarks Kurt as Christian bumps into him.

- Back to the early 90s, Gorilla Monsoon and Bobby Heenan visit the zoo.

- In 1999, Mick Foley and Al Snow visit Vegas, leading to some very funny improv between the two. Foley drops a fruit machine and wins a bunch of quarters, so decides to spend them at a strip joint. The girls, used to notes from high rollers, are not impressed, and Foley takes a quarter to the eye.

- More from Gorilla and Bobby, this time on a movie set. Gorilla is devastated that Heenan has shown up and ruined his day, while Bobby gets all jumpy at the sight of a horse because he has "never seen anything move that fast".

- "Whoa! They call *you* the Big Show!?" asks Val Venis while staring at Show's cock at a urinal. Show smacks him into a cubicle for his cheek and calls him a smartass before walking off.

Marriage Problems

- From *Tuesday Night Titans*, incredibly enough. Butcher Vachon is Vince McMahon's guest, and he takes us to footage from the "most bizarre wedding" of Butcher and his wife, which it was. Held in the ring with George Steele eating the buckles, the set falling down and nutcase Dave Schultz slamming the groom, this was 80s WWF at its most wacky. Incredibly, this closed out the very first Coliseum Home Video tape ever released, so they have really been delving into the archives for this tape. Of all the tapes to finally be thorough with!

- A decade and a half later, Triple H and Stephanie McMahon are married but having problems, exacerbated significantly when Steph walks in on Hunter demonstrating a hammerlock reversal to Trish which involves her bending down in front of him. Steph is apoplectic with rage and trashes the room while screaming "I can't believe you!" over and over again. Everyone was excellent in this, and the Steph-Hunter marriage breakdown and love triangle involving Kurt Angle is something I look back on fondly. Yes, a Steph and Hunter angle and it was actually entertaining! Who would have guessed it?

FURIOUS ABOUT: DDP

It speaks volumes for DDP that he was willing to give up his guaranteed deal with Time-Warner, unlike a lot of guys, and join the WWF to support the Invasion storyline. There aren't many men who would do that. Page figured he had one last chance to get into the WWF and might as well take it. Of course he had been in the WWF as he drove the Honky Tonk Man to the ring at WrestleMania VI but he wanted to wrestle there. Page had been performing at a reasonable standard in WCW's final years and was certainly fairing better than the injured Scott Steiner and the likes of Sting, Savage, Luger and Hogan. He was fit, ready and able so the WWF absolutely buried him by having him debut as Sara Calaway's stalker and then had the Undertaker kick the crap out of him. He even jobbed to Taker's wife. Once the WWF had finished destroying him, he got a brief run as a motivational speaker, which faired equally as well before retiring from wrestling. An inauspicious end to a good career and another wrestler who'd spent their life getting to the WWF only to find it disappointing.

- From *RAW* in 1994, and joy of joys we revisit something that I described in *The RAW Files: 1994* as "maybe the worst thing on TV all year, and not just in wrestling". It involves Jerry Lawler pratting around in the crowd for ages as some skinny dude with a bad haircut (Mike) asks his incredibly embarrassed girlfriend with a Triple H nose (Andrea) to marry him. Mind you, Lawler had already ruined the surprise by introducing her as his fiancé in the first place. What an oaf. Lawler takes the girl into the ring and starts making bad jokes, before she says "yes". Thankfully the tape skips the part where Lawler calls Mike's ex-girlfriend a slut and both of them "dogs", but does keep in him insulting the poor girl by comparing her nose to that of an elephant. Ever the perv, Lawler goes to kiss Andrea despite her Proboscidean looks, but she dives out of dodge as her new fiancé looks on, livid. I am so glad I got to suffer through that again.

DX

- Yes, the juvenile delinquents get their own segment of the tape. We start with Christmas *RAW* from 1997, with Shawn Michaels and Triple H in bathrobes. We see some unpleasant mooning interspersed with footage of their network address where the ticklesome trio promised not to swear and do lurid things, while doing *exactly* those things. Unlike on some of the tapes it turns up on, it is censored here. As is some easy chick flashing her tits to DX Version 2.0. Shame. DX also take to the streets of New York to promote *SummerSlam 1998*, with Road Dogg having a starring role as he racistly asks a Japanese girl if she has seen Godzilla. She thinks he means the movie, he means the actual monster, and he is thrilled when she says that she has, and asks her how big his foot is.

Vince

- We move briskly on to Vince McMahon. The funniest things about Vince are his zany directives ("sports entertainment", "WWE Universe", etc) and the rate at which he changes his mind on a whim, but sadly instead all we get is a promo where he talks about his genetic prowess in the groinal department.

- Back in 1998, Vince gets his leg broken by the Undertaker and Kane, resulting in an extended stay in hospital, and thus we see the often replayed piece of footage that spawned the birth of Mr. Socko where Mick Foley tried to cheer Vince up by bringing him a clown and "kissing the boo-boo".

- Backstage a few weeks later, Vince tells basketball legend Shaquille O'Neill to leave because he doesn't have a backstage pass, and Shaq mouths that McMahon is an asshole.

- Next Vince turns up in a bar looking for Steve Austin, but he treats the barmaid like shit and gets threatened with a bat. This wasn't what I would describe as funny, but the next segment where Shane McMahon trains him for *Royal Rumble '99* a'la Rocky is. Vince chasing a chicken and punching the shit out of some meat is both excellent and bizarre.

- Then, Vince pisses his pants in the middle of the ring as Steve Austin holds a gun to his head, which turns out to be a toy. A gun! Didn't the WWF promise the USA Network that they would never do anything with guns again after the Pillman/Austin angle in 1996? I guess when you are hot you can do whatever the hell you want and get away with it.

- Back to the hospital and Steve Austin, disguised as a nurse, beats the piss out of Vince and clonks him with the funniest weapon shot ever; a bed pan to the head that makes a delightful "zing" noise.

- Back again to the "genetic jackhammer" promo, and Rock calls Vince an asshole before drilling him with a Rock Bottom.

Stone Cold

- Austin having just been appointed CEO of the WWF, turns up at Titan Towers and wants to implement some changes to how the receptionist answers the phone, preferring a direct approach: "Who the hell is this? What the hell do you want?". Austin later fires someone for looking stupid and then suggests a beer drinking contest. When looking through the finances he dedicates some money to Mick Foley's medical bills and then cuts Shane's salary.

- The back end of 1997 and *RAW* next, with Austin beating up a nasty Santa Claus who is cruel to a young dude who looks like a lady. It's a horrible segment.

- One of the great Steve Austin segments follows, with Austin playing the guitar for Vince McMahon. "This is inspiration man, can't you feel it!?". His rendition of *'Kumbaya'* is so shockingly bad it's immense and his wild-eyed reworking of *'We Are The Champions'* is unreal. But for me, nothing from this heel run comes close to the hug he has with Vince in a parking lot. The facials from Austin here are the best I have ever seen and it cracks me up every single time I see it.

- Deep into his heel run as leader of the WCW/ECW Alliance, Austin brings the "what?" chant into the world. Thanks for that one, Steve. It does mean he doesn't need another person as a sounding board to promo off of though, because he can now just argue with the crowd or even himself. Great character. Perhaps the greatest ever.

Oops! And Poops!!

- Amazingly, they show the set falling down at *SummerSlam '89* during a Mean Gene Okerlund interview with Rick Rude and Bobby Heenan. Sadly, Gene's best John Malkovich impression ("fuck it!") is not shown, nor is Jesse Ventura ripping into him with venomous glee afterwards.

- During his heel run, The Rock tries to cut a promo on WWF Champion Mankind, but his voice keeps cracking and he can't keep a straight face, and in the end just gives up and laughs.

- Next, Psycho Sid! He can't say the work "sceptics" and asks JR if they can go again, but is quickly informed "we're live pal". It's one of many excellent Sid moments they could have used. The man was a veritable goldmine for bloopers.

- After that, Trish beats up Steph McMahon and rubs her face in cow shit. I approve. After a brief Brother Love segment with Roddy Piper (and by brief I mean 3 seconds) and Gorilla and Bobby dressed as Love and The Genius, we go back to the subject of poo. The Rock directs Mankind to pick some up with a poop-a-scoop (also off the cuff telling some dogs to be quiet in a funny piece of improv) before we go to Head Cheese milking a cow. Blackman ends up with milk in the face, so belts the poor beast with his nunchcuks to get even.

- Sean Stasiak can't hit his lines for a pre-tape promo for Steve Austin Appreciation Night, and constantly breaks down laughing. He shows more personality screwing up than he ever was allowed to as a performer.

- Rock wanted Mankind to pick the dog shit up for a reason; so he could Rock Bottom the British Bulldog into it! " the dog poop, the dog poop, the dog poop!" bellows Michael Cole, who apparently needs his batteries recharging as he has got stuck in a loop. Well, that's the price you pay for hiring robots to do human jobs.

- Elsewhere in a different era, Bobby Heenan gets hurled through a window during a Western bar fight.

- A really classic understated moment next, as Rock cuts a promo alongside Rock 'n' Sock partner Mankind, only to have his sunglasses fall off midway through. Mick Foley thinks on his feet and picks them up, prompting a huge pop from a crowd thrilled to see two guys out there having fun and being entertaining, and Rock tells Mick: "The Rock thanks you for that". You couldn't have scripted something like this.

- Back to Steve Austin, who visits Vince McMahon's (real) office and dumps a few barrels of manure in there. Why didn't they just use a fake office instead of having to go through that clean up job?

X-tremely Funny

- The first thing shown? Isaac Yankem pulling teeth! Erm, odd choice.

- The next thing shown is Bubba Dudley putting Mae Young through a table, which again doesn't really strike me as a "funny" segment at all.

- The next one gets a little closer, with Pat Patterson attempting a low blow on Chyna during a match, and her no-selling it and looking at him with incredulity. To be fair to Pat, he can't be blamed for double checking, no-one really knew for sure with Chyna at this point. Chyna gets her revenge by slapping on a double testicular claw on both Patterson and Brisco.

- At *SummerSlam 1999*, Billy Gunn reveals a fat chick prior to his "Kiss My Ass" match with The Rock, and tells him that he will be kissing her ass rather than his when he beats him. For a heterosexual man, how is that worse'? Maybe it *is* worse for Billy... Obviously it all backfires, and Rock reverses Gunn's attempts to make him kiss her ass during the match, and Billy ends up eating it. The big chick enjoys it. "The Rock just put Billy Gunn's face in that large woman's ass" says JR, in one of his more unlikely match calls.

- On *RAW*, Mr. Yamaguchi promises "I choppy choppy your pee-pee" to Val Venis, who had been diddling his wife. Kaientai then kidnap him and Yamaguchi uses a samurai sword to commit the act. It is only later revealed, and not on this tape, that Venis got "stage fright" and his dick was saved.

- Then more Isaac Yankem, which segues nonsensically into Bret Hart against Jerry Lawler at *King of the Ring 1995*. It's a terrible match, but the finish is shown here because it involves Jerry Lawler kissing both his own and Hart's feet.

- Then, the Bushwhackers return to lower the tone further, doing a spot of lingerie shopping... for their mothers!

- You know what else is funny? People dying. Yes, the Big Show's father's funeral is next, hijacked by the Big Bossman who drives away with the casket. Did someone on the writing team have a vendetta against Bossman in 1999?

- Oh Jesus it gets worse, with the "Miss Rumble 2000" swimsuit competition from *Royal Rumble 2000* shown next. Yes, the one where Mae Young gets her large saggy puppies out for the world, and then wins the competition. A new low for the WWF and what a way to end.

VERDICT

It's one of the most bizarre tapes I have ever seen. The pace is astonishing, with a new clip every minute or less and some of them are horrific (anything involving the Bushwhackers specifically), but all are over so quickly that nothing rankles or annoys. I was very happy to see such a diverse mix of footage from various eras, with things from 1985 through 2002 featured, including some that I would never expect the WWF to champion (namely bloopers, because they hate admitting to mistakes and production gaffes). I was expecting a horror show here, but it was far from that. It was, to my immense surprise, rather entertaining. Obviously there is nothing to really get your teeth into due to the breakneck pace, but as something to put on for an hour and be amused by, it does the job wonderfully. Incredibly, this is recommended!

70

nWo - BACK IN BLACK

CAT NO: WWE59331
RUN TIME: 84 minutes (approx)

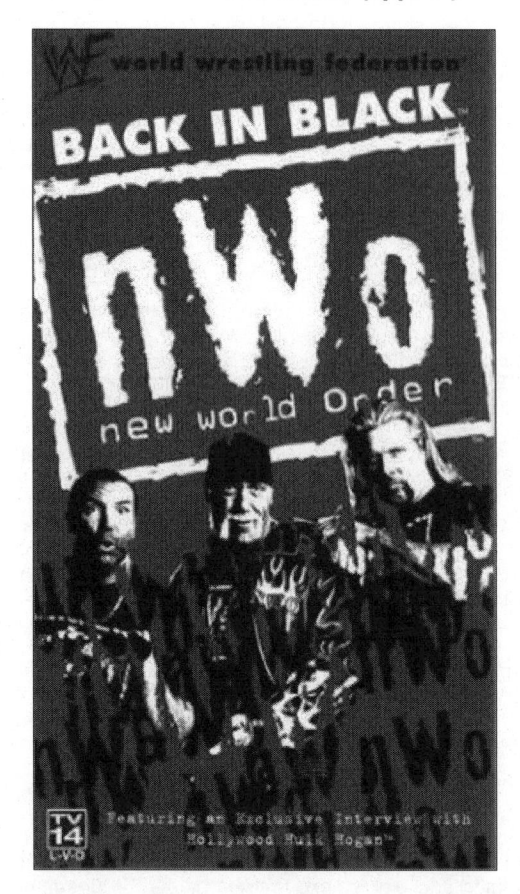

Lee Maughan: "This is the story of three men, two companies, and one organisation" notes the voiceover, setting the tone for the fact that, as you'll soon discover, this documentary isn't really about the nWo as much as it is about the three guys who started the group, and the three guys currently employed by the WWF to reprise those very roles.

"I think the nWo represented turning the corner, the attitude, the new generation of wrestlers that [were] to become the new superstars of our business" begins wide-eyed young buck of the new generation, Hulk Hogan. "It comes back to what Chief Jay Strongbow told us years ago: "In this business you can make friends, or you can make money" and I remember looking at Kev and X-Pac and going "I've got already got some friends... I'd like the money"" adds Scott Hall, in a somewhat out of context quote. Presented in this manner, it sounds like a worked reason for starting the group, but on the later *nWo: The Revolution* DVD and Blu-ray set where this specific talking head is repeated, it becomes clear that he's actually talking about his legitimate reasons for leaving the WWF. Not that there was any great cover up involved in that, but the editing choice made it sounds somewhat ambiguous. Even in 2002 the WWF couldn't help but second guess themselves when it came to opening up and shooting on these documentaries, as the looming spectre of kayfabe still seemed to blow through the essence at the Titan Tower production suite. "The nWo represented the changes that were about to become the new wrestling industry" adds Hogan, and on that one, he's not wrong.

With this being a WWF release, much is made of the company's success as a dear old Mom n' Pop's self-built independent sports entertainment outfit, only for nasty Mr. Turner and his evil corporate empire to come along and offer genuine competition through their network of cable television outlets, which you get the impression is entirely underhanded, unscrupulous and just gosh darnit poor sportsmanship, given the tone of the voiceover. I'm almost certain Vince McMahon thinks Frank Capra's *It's a Wonderful Life* was inspired by his struggles against Turner. And anyway, WCW were only *really* able to compete because they signed Hulk Hogan, the WWF's biggest star of the 80s, a wrestling icon made entirely on the platform offered by McMahon and not at all a megastar in waiting with New Japan and the AWA. Hopefully my facetious tone comes through in the black and white you see before your very eyes.

"Sometimes when you're younger, things comes easily and you don't appreciate them. The biggest difference is now the business moves a lot faster. If I was fighting King Kong Bundy or the Ultimate Warrior it would be a war that would go on for maybe a year. Now all of a sudden the wars end a lot quicker and the business seems to move with the times and changes faster" muses Hulk, who along with Randy Savage, Roddy Piper, Ted DiBiase and Jeff Jarrett were "lured to WCW with fat contracts and less demanding work schedules." The contempt with which that line was spoken is absolutely venomous. I mean, how DARE someone seek out more money for less work when they should be toiling away without any guaranteed source of income. There's only so far one of your infamous "opportunities" will stretch for an ageing wrestler with no pension security in place, Vince. And doesn't whoever made this documentary realise the war is already over? You've won! Uncle Ted's out of the 'rasslin business! As personal as the WWF-WCW war may have cut, this is the equivalent to standing on a battlefield, pumping bullets into an already decaying corpse.

In addition to the success of the 'Hulkster', the WWF was also responsible for making the careers of Scott 'Razor Ramon' Hall and Kevin 'Diesel' Nash. Few arguments there. The highlights package on both men also manages to include the entirety of Diesel's eight-second WWF Title victory over Mr. Bob Backlund at a Madison Square Garden house show in November 1994. Diesel and Razor are portrayed as "helping invigorate the business in a movement called the New Generation" along with Shawn Michaels, the Undertaker, Yokozuna and Hunter Hearst Helmsley. As noted, the war is over, there's no need for such petty politics here, even if Bret Hart was still persona non grata after Montreal. Like Hulk and the boys, Nash and Hall also succumbed to the lure of more money in WCW, and their last night in the WWF was to be at Madison Square Garden. Says

Hall: "My first match in Madison Square Garden, the arena was half full, and my last match there was sold out. I was really proud of the fact that the business improved with me and all the other guys working hard every night in all the towns."

Hall also offers coverage of the infamous 'Curtain Call' at that evening's show, although once again Hall's words are presented without any context, as they don't bother explaining the background of it to anybody not familiar with the incident in which babyfaces Ramon and Michaels shared an in-ring group hug with heels Diesel and Helmsley after a Michaels-Diesel cage match, which resulted in Helmsley being kept in the doghouse for a year and missing out on victory in the 1996 King of the Ring tournament. "Four close friends in the ring, the place was sold out, we'd made it through a successful run here and nobody [had] got hurt... we knew we were going on to WCW to see what lay waiting for us there and we felt like we had to say goodbye to the WWF fans, to the fans at Madison Square Garden. It was like 'Thank you for your support for all these years, and goodbye.' Guys (other WWF wrestlers) said we broke kayfabe and we were trying to hurt the company because we were leaving, and in fact that couldn't be further from the truth. There were no bad intentions there, it just kind of evolved, there was no plan to hurt anybody. I don't know why fans still talk about it but I find it really flattering that they do."

Despite feeling like he was selling out, Hall took Turner's guaranteed money in order to do what he thought was best for him and his family, and eight days later on Labour Day, 1996, Hall sauntered through the crowd unannounced on Monday Nitro in the middle of a Steve Doll-Mike Enos match, and cut that legendary first promo:

"Hey! You people, you know who I am, but you don't know why I'm here. Where is Billionaire Ted? Where is the 'Nacho Man'? That punk can't even get in the building. Me? I go wherever I want, whenever I want. And where, oh where is 'Scheme' Gene? 'Cause I got a scoop for you! When that Ken doll lookalike, when that weatherman wannabe comes out here later tonight, I got a challenge for him, for Billionaire Ted, for the 'Nacho Man' and for anybody else in uh… Dubya-Cee-Dubya, ha-huh-huh. Hey, you want to go to war? You want a war? You're going to get one!"

Hall admits that he didn't think it was going to be very creatively satisfying to go to WCW, and was surprised by how well the nWo got over. Hall gets another classic line at the end of the show: "Like it or not, we are taking over!" The "we" part of course referred to Kevin Nash, who debuted on the programme two weeks later, with the two "outsiders" putting out a challenge to face three of WCW's top stars in a match. At the Great American Bash, both were forced to admit that they weren't working for the WWF (an admission caused by a lawsuit from Titan Sports, Inc. which claimed Hall was still using mannerisms of his Razor Ramon character to perpetuate the impression that this was the start of an inter-promotional feud between WCW and the WWF), before a memorable angles in which Nash Jackknife powerbombed mild-mannered announcer Eric Bischoff off the stage and through a table. "WCW basically, not to knock the talent but they really didn't have anything going on, storyline wise. When I came in and when Kevin Nash came in, the rest of it just kind of fell into place. It was perceived to be a takeover… actually people thought Vince sent us to WCW to kill it." They'd think the same thing once Vince Russo showed up there in late 1999.

> **FURIOUS ABOUT: KRONIK**
>
> KroniK (Bryan Clarke and Brian Adams) were the brainchild of Vince Russo. He envisioned the possibilities of naming a team after marijuana and indeed they developed a cult following in WCW. Although their matches and angles were nothing to write home about. The team couldn't really reach the heights intended for them, thanks to WCW's bi-polar booking and their frequent changes between face and heel. Despite this, they had a cool finisher and were over enough to get hired by the WWE just after the Invasion angle started. Largely due to the name value of the team, considering the flops they'd both been in the darker days of the federation. They had two matches in the WWE. The second, and final, against Undertaker and Kane at Unforgiven 2001. The match is roundly hated by everyone and led to both men being let go. They took the gimmick to All Japan before both retiring with injuries.

Bash at the Beach in July sees the Outsiders take on a WCW team made up of Lex Luger, Randy Savage and Sting, a very well selected team given Savage's WWF past and Luger's gimmick in previous months of switching heel and face constantly, sometimes in the course of ring entrances, teaming with his babyface friend Sting despite management from the heel Jimmy Hart. As revealed years later by then-WCW booker Kevin Sullivan, Sting had actually been the backup plan for the heel turn had Hogan gotten cold feet and not gone through with it, and Sullivan had actually made Hogan sleep at his house the night before and stay away from the arena until go time to prevent anybody getting in his ear about what a bad idea the turn could be. Sullivan of course was proven right, and the reaction to Hogan's leg drop on Savage remains spine-tingling to this day. Every fan who was sick to death of the 'Hulkster' preaching his "Say your prayers and eat your vitamins" verbiage suddenly had everything they had ever hoped for - the green light to boo the hell out of him. "A career of a lifetime, right down the drain, kid" said colour commentator Dusty Rhodes during the angle. "I hope you love it. You just sold your soul to the Devil." It was a great line, but Hogan's promo was even better:

"'Mean' Gene, the first thing you gotta do is to tell these people to shut up if they want to hear what I've got to say. The first thing you've gotta realise, brother, is this right here is the future of wrestling. You can call this the New World Order of wrestling, brother. These two men right here came from a great big organisation up north and everybody was wondering about who the third man was. Well who knows more about that organisation than me, brother? Well let me tell you something! I made that organisation a monster. I made people rich up there. I made the people that ran that organisation rich up there, brother. And when it all came to pass, the name 'Hulk Hogan', the man Hulk Hogan got bigger than the whole organisation, brother! And then 'Billionaire Ted' amigo, he wanted to talk turkey with Hulk Hogan. Well Billionaire Ted promised me movies, brother. 'Billionaire Ted' promised me millions of dollars and 'Billionaire Ted' promised me world calibre matches. And as far as Billionaire Ted, Eric Bischoff and the whole WCW goes, I'm bored, brother. That's why these two guys here, the so called 'Outsiders', these are the men I want

as my friends. They're the new blood of professional wrestling, brother, and not only are we gonna take over the whole wrestling business, with Hulk Hogan and the new blood, the monsters with me, we will destroy everything in our path 'Mean' Gene.

"As far as I'm concerned, all this crap in the ring represents these fans out here because for two years, brother, for two years I held my head high. I did everything for the charities, I did everything for the kids, and the reception I got when came out here... You fans can stick it, brother, because if it wasn't for Hulk Hogan, you people wouldn't be here. If it wasn't for Hulk Hogan, Eric Bischoff would still be selling meat from a truck in Minneapolis. And if it wasn't for Hulk Hogan, all of these Johnny-Come-Latelys that you see out here wrestling wouldn't be here. I was selling the world out, brother, while they were bumming gas to put in their car to get to high school. So the way it is now, brother, with Hulk Hogan and the New World Organisation of wrestling brother, me and the new blood by my side, whatcha gonna do when the New World Organisation runs wild on you? Whatcha gonna do!? What are you gonna do!?

Back in the present day, Hogan sucks up to his current employers some more: "My favourite piece of business when I was in the WCW was bringing everything I learned from the WWF down there, and basically wiping out their whole talent pool." This is illustrated by a series of clips of beatdowns on Big Bubba Rogers, Sting, and a famous angle from the Universal Orlando outdoor *Nitro* broadcast, in which the Outsiders dismantle Arn Anderson and the American Males before Nash hurls Rey Misterio, Jr. headfirst into a truck. That leads to Hogan winning the WCW World Heavyweight Title from the Giant in a lousy main event at *Hog Wild*, where Hogan spray paints the letters "NWO" onto the belt. Going into full-on kayfabe mode, Hogan says "I knew every shortcut, I knew every way to get to a wrestler, I knew every way to get to a piece of talent in and out of the ring, and I used all my weapons to my advantage. So my favourite thing was basically stirring the pot in the WCW. That's why I'm called the "Hulk-stir."" And that line is why you're also universally referred to as Hulk Ho-pun.

An eight-man tag team match on *Nitro* pitting warring heel factions the Four Horsemen (Ric Flair, Arn Anderson, Chris Benoit and Steve McMichael) against the Dungeon of Doom ('Taskmaster' Kevin Sullivan, Big Bubba Rogers and the Faces of Fear, Meng and the Barbarian) sees the nWo destroy both sides in a red-hot beatdown before Dungeoneer the Giant arrives... and turns on his stable-mates with chokeslams on the Barbarian and Meng, a hug for new teammate Nash, and another chokeslam on Randy Savage. Sullivan later explained that his theory behind the heel vs. heel Horseman-Dungeon feud was to keep both stables occupied so the nWo could gain traction unabated, given what little sense it would have made to have just three guys run roughshod over an entire promotion, especially one already boasting two powerful groups. It worked a treat, as evidenced by the nuclear crowd heat drawn here.

Hogan waxes lyrical about how easy it was for him to be hated in the south, given his status as former WWF star. "I think the only problem I had was Nash and Hall were so cool in their image, and their "4-Life" gangsta rap and attitude that they were almost the good guys in the nWo." That "cool heel" mentality would go on to become extremely prevalent in the late 90s, not just in WCW but in the WWF as well, where natural heels Steve Austin, the Rock and D-Generation-X all became accepted as monster babyfaces. It wasn't until Edge made it to the pinnacle of WWE cards in 2006 that a new top heel allowed himself to be just that, a heel, without pandering to the fans with cutesy jokes or making the babyfaces look stupid at every turn to the short-sighted detriment of the drawing power of their programs.

Hogan laments that adding further members to the nWo watered it down and weakened it. "The nWo was so strong, you could take just a normal, everyday average wrestler, put an nWo shirt on him or put the nWo colours 4-Life on that average wrestler and he became a star overnight." Hall agrees. "A lot of fans commented that the nWo was at its strongest when there was just three, when it was Hall and Nash, and Hulk Hogan. I kinda agree too. We thought the plan was to have our own TV show, our own merchandise, everything, so that the fans would decide "Do you like WCW or do you like nWo?" instead of choosing "Do you like WCW or the WWF?""

Meanwhile, a new attitude was changing things in the WWF, as 'Stone Cold' Steve Austin and the Rock we're making a strong connection with the fans and driving the business to new levels of success. The upshot of that is Ric Flair becoming the co-owner of the WWF alongside Mr. McMahon, and an increasingly crazed McMahon bringing the nWo in to kill the promotion in retaliation. Oh, wait... You thought there were five whole years between the nWo taking over WCW and joining the WWF? Guess again, bucko. 1997-2001? Nope. Never happened. At least, not here. And what a ludicrous storyline, as Vince had just spent the best part eight months doing all he could to ensure the WWF's survival against the WCW/ECW Alliance, to then turn around and "inject it with a lethal dose of poison" in reintroducing Hogan, Hall and Nash. Perhaps even more ridiculous is the insertion of a clip at this point in which Bradshaw of all people has to explain to Flair who the nWo are. I mean, I know Flair is out of his mind, but c'mon.

So the WWF completely fails to foster any anticipation for the nWo's impending arrival at *No Way Out* 2002 by sending them out to the ring as soon as the show hits the airwaves, and the best they can muster for what should have been the monumental returns of not only Nash and Hall, but also all-time legend Hogan, was to have them cut a promo promising exactly the opposite of McMahon's proclamation that they were here to kill the WWF. "We're not here to kill the WWF, we're here to make it better. All we want to do is give the WWF fans exactly what they want!" Worse still were the backstage segments in which Austin declined a six-pack of Budweiser from the group and the Rock belittled the characters of Razor Ramon and Diesel. Why the trio had to be emasculated before they destroyed Austin at the end of his Undisputed Title match with Chris Jericho that night is something only the creative geniuses booking the WWF will know, but hey, they were the ones still in business and if they wanted to prove to a long-dead entity that the nWo was inferior to the WWF's top superstars, then that's their prerogative I guess.

An unpleasant feud between Austin and Hall followed, built around Austin torturing real-life alcoholic Hall with booze, just as the company had done during the equally disgusting Jake Roberts vs. Jerry Lawler feud of 1996 (you stay classy there, WWF), as did a dream showdown between Hogan and the Rock (the WWF's second choice incidentally, after Austin turned the Hogan match down on the grounds that Hogan had rebuffed his requests for a main event program in WCW in the mid-90s). Presented as wrestling's equivalent to a Muhammad Ali vs. Mike Tyson inter-generational showdown to determine the undisputed greatest of all-time, their initial promo in which Rock issued the challenge for a match at *WrestleMania X8* was absolutely electric. The following angle in which the nWo destroyed the Rock by caving his skull in with a hammer before smashing into the ambulance with a monster truck was, to put it frankly, complete horseshit. The nose-to-nose showdown was all the bout needed to sell itself as a legitimate contender for the biggest match in pro wrestling history, but the entirely unbelievable angle in which Rock should by rights have been crippled for life, if not have died, let alone been fit to wrestle just four weeks later, turned the whole thing into a joke, just another hokey bullshit wrestling angle.

In fact, Rock was back in the ring on *SmackDown!* less than three weeks after the assault, for a match with Hall. "Speculation running rampant the Rock's not one hundred percent" claims Michael Cole. Ordinarily I'd whinge about Cole making such dumb statements, but given that Rock works the match with taped ribs and nary a scratch on him whilst performing DDTs and kip-ups, I can't say as I blame him. Cole also claims the ambulance incident was almost "career ending" for the Rock. Given that John Cena was on the Ohio Valley Wrestling roster at this point, training for a career in the WWF, it perhaps becomes extremely clear where he picked up the idea that babyfaces weren't supposed to sell a damn thing.

At *WrestleMania X8*, the WWF's supremacy over anything and everything not directly created by them was once again underlined as Austin downed Hall in a mostly lousy match (although Hall's outrageous oversell of Austin's match-winning Stone Cold Stunner was joyously ridiculous), and Rock pinned Hogan in a technically naff but terrifically entertaining bout that saw Hogan completely undermine the Rock, going into business for himself by riding a gigantic wave of nostalgia into an initially unplanned babyface turn. Don't get me wrong, the Hogan turn was always coming, but it was Hogan's "Hulking up" and fan manipulation that accelerated the turn, freeing him of the albatross that was the nWo in the WWF. Rock and Hogan shake hands and make up after the match, letting the bygones of month-old attempted assassination be bygones, and Hulk renounces his colours the next night on *RAW*.

The following evening at the *SmackDown!* taping, Rock squares off in his first-ever meeting with Nash, winning by disqualification when Hall interferes. Afterwards, Rock eats a Jackknife through the announce table, so new best bud Hogan makes the save with legdrops on both Outsiders, only for an nWo t-shirt bedecked X-Pac to "put the band back together" and belt Hogan over the noggin with a steel chair. "And that's the real story of the nWo", or so the helpful voiceover man would have us believe.

VERDICT

They say that history is written by the winners and rarely is that more evident than here, as the always right, never wrong WWF continues to stick the knife into WCW's promotional policies whilst simultaneously brainwashing their audience with anti-WCW propaganda. They were WEAK, the viewer is lead to believe, and the only reason they had any success is because of the WWF. Meaning that even when the WWF wasn't successful and were getting their asses kicked, technically they still were because they were responsible for it. Got it?

It's a shame the WWF still had such a bug up their backside about the whole Monday Night War thing because the knock-on effect was shoddy output like this, and it was the viewers who suffered because of it. Here, the WWF had the chance to present a fascinating insight into a significant period in the wrestling industry, and with WCW coming under WWF ownership, meant that for the first time, they could present both sides of the story, complete with all the requisite archival footage. Instead, they gave a warped, potted history of the group, often lacking both depth and context, loaded up with premade highlights packages of insignificant matches and angles, particularly towards the end. That almost half the tape is dedicated to the group's two months (at that point) in the WWF in a joke; that September 1996 until February 2001 is ignored entirely is downright insulting.

The whole thing is clearly designed as a promotional tool to bring newer fans up to speed on what the WWF wanted you to believe was the history of the nWo, kayfabe intact. Problematically, by the time the release was ready to hit the market, Hollywood Hogan had already regressed into Hulk Hogan, nullifying many of his contributions, and Scott Hall had been fired. Ironically, the only one of the original trio still working for the WWF in nWo colours at the time of the tape's release was Kevin Nash, and he's nowhere to be found as a talking head. Perhaps even stranger is that, while the WWF *was* willing to admit the Big Show was once a member of the group (and he would go on to rejoin them on-screen shortly after this production was wrapped up), there's zero mention of Sean 'Syxx' Waltman's time as a member of the original 'Wolfpac' (the nickname for he, Hall and Nash), yet the tape concludes with X-Pac joining the WWF incarnation. Some background on that would have been nice, but apparently things like that require fire too much effort. Fortunately, WWE would get much less lazy as time went on, with 2012's *nWo: The Revolution* DVD and Blu-ray release offering a much more exhaustive presentation than was to be found here, although that documentary still didn't quite give fans the definitive story on the history of the influential outfit.

On a positive note, the clips on offer here *are* largely entertaining, and much like the myriad of clips found on WWF tapes revisiting the Austin vs. McMahon feud, remain just as exciting years removed as they were to watch at the time. Be warned though that if you are planning to add *nWo: Back in Black* to your collection, that it is an extremely rare tape to track down, receiving a very limited amount of time on retail shelves as one of the promotion's last releases under the "WWF" name, before a lawsuit case with the World Wildlife Fund prohibited them continuing to use those initials. By the time the WWE name was in effect, the nWo had been disbanded once and for all, and an edited re-release seemed to serve very little purpose. Furthermore, I'd also recommend the DVD version over the VHS as it comes with four extra matches, including a rarely seen Hogan, Hall & Nash vs. Rock & Austin handicap bout from *RAW*, notable as the only time Hogan and Austin squared off as opponents in a bell-to-bell match, and that if you can track down the also now out-of-print UK-only Tagged Classics release of it, you'll also get the old *Big Daddy Cool Diesel* and *Razor Ramon: Oozing Machismo* Coliseum Video releases on a bonus second disc.

40

INSURREXTION 2002

CAT NO: WWE59333
RUN TIME: 144 minutes (approx)

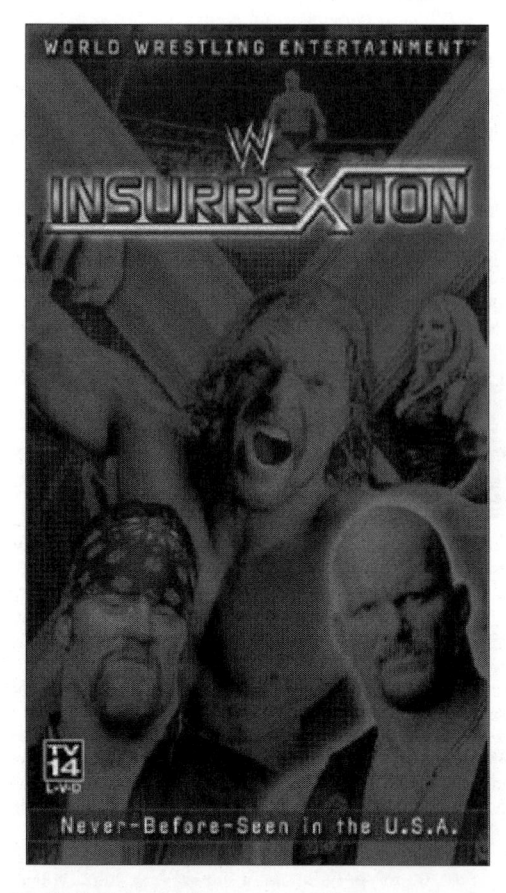

Arnold Furious: While I may have been overly harsh on some UK PPVs in the past, I have discovered a few surprisingly good bouts during the recapping process in this book, but this one isn't too good. I think a lot of the negative energy stems from this being a *RAW*-only PPV event, following the brand extension, so all the great talent over on *SmackDown!* isn't allowed to be here. Apart from one guy. We'll get to him in due course.

Tangent: The day after this show the WWF flew back to the United States and what an eventful plane journey it was. It was dubbed by industry insiders as the "Plane Ride from Hell". Several altercations took place thanks to a mixture of alcohol and boredom. Curt Hennig was fired after instigating a fight with Brock Lesnar. The big man taking exception to Curt ribbing him about his amateur career and taking Mr. Perfect down at 30,000 feet. Perhaps not the smartest thing to do post 9/11 and I'm amazed both guys didn't get slapped on the "no fly" list. Rumours soon flew around as to Scott Hall's involvement as he too found himself out of a job just days later. However Jim Ross soon confirmed Hall slept through the flight and the issues stemmed from his condition during the tour. In other words; he was too drunk to work properly. I realise I'm skating on thin ice with that implication but Hall would be the first guy to tell you he wasn't in good condition in 2002. Other incidents on the journey included Goldust drunkenly serenading his ex-wife Terri and X-Pac chopping off Michael Hayes' mullet after the former Freebird had gotten into a drunken row with Bradshaw. Ross went onto his WWE.com column the next day to describe the drunken minority as "children". There's nothing like bad PR to get the WWF cleaning house.

4th May 2002. *Star Wars* Day. We're in London, England. Hosts are JR and Jerry Lawler. This show sold out in 21 minutes. If they'd known the card, tickets would still be available.

WWF Intercontinental Championship
Eddie Guerrero (c) vs. Rob Van Dam
This is a rematch from *Backlash* where a returning Eddie recaptured the IC Title after a year out of WWF competition. To give you an idea of how over RVD is; the entire audience points to itself when he's introduced. They start out with the mat counters and the fans totally buy into this as a superb athletic contest. Rob turns up the heat and hits a split-legged moonsault for an early near fall. They're clever with how they work in their counters without getting too complicated so there's no mistakes but it's all smart stuff. A counter doesn't necessarily have to lead to yet another counter. I think Rob ended up over thinking his matches somewhat after his Jerry Lynn matches got more and more complex. Eddie keeps everything simple yet skilful. Eddie is such a masterful technician that even his straightforward matches are wonderful to watch. The fans buy into RVD's cheeky roll ups so much that they think the title might change. That should give you an idea of how big RVD was at the time. They expected him to win the title, even on a UK show that big titles never change on. Rob's suppleness comes in handy as Eddie tests how bendy his limbs are. The problem with that is Rob can't really sell a leg and I'd rather they stuck to their strengths instead of doing the body part stuff. "It's all gone Pete Tong for Latino Heat" – Lawler gets over his cockney slang. RVD makes his comeback and he's certainly learned where to insert big spots. The match flows really well and the fans continue to suspect a title switch. Eddie dodges the frogsplash and the crowd breathes out after Eddie bails for the IC Title. The ref stops him and Eddie shoves him over for the cheap DQ. Eddie chases the ref until RVD clocks him with a roundhouse, an amazing farewell dropkick and the Five Star Frogsplash. Rob wins but only on DQ. This was a tidy opening match but Van Dam was clearly being hauled into WWF style by the disciplined Guerrero.
Final Rating: ***

Backstage: Terri interviews Molly and Jazz. Both the ladies don't like Terri because she's a trashbag ho. Molly and Jazz point out they didn't do the Divas video because they didn't want to sell their bodies that way before rounding on *The Sun* newspaper. Terri exposes herself to prove a point. Presumably that she is a whoooore.

Trish Stratus & Jacqueline vs. Jazz & Molly Holly
As Jazz comes out Lawler says "you don't look at the

mantelpiece while you're stoking the fire". Who has he been talking to? The match is basically the ladies who are prepared to show the goods vs. those who feel they're above it. Jacqui gets picked off for heatless heat until a HOT tag to Trish. As Jazz takes over on her, Lawler calls her a "boiler". He's been fed a ton of English slang for tonight's show, it's just flowing out of him. It's a pleasant change from what usually flows out of him while he's commentating on women's wrestling. Unlike the psychology loaded Trish-Jazz match at *Backlash*, there's not much happening other than a straightforward 2-on-2 tag where everyone is capable. It's not a bad match and it's suitably well structured that the fans get into it. After a hot tag both babyfaces hit their finishers and the ref counts both heels down, even though only Trish was legal. There's not much to say about the match except it was smartly worked and nobody looked out of their depth. Trish was certainly coming into her own as a wrestler around this time and everyone else was capable. They nailed the formula.

Final Rating: **

Backstage: the nWo, all two of them (Big Show must be at the buffet table), banter about tonight's match. X-Pac says if he loses he'll never come back to England. "I don't know why you'd come back anyway" says Hall to nobody, after Pac leaves.

Bradshaw vs. X-Pac
I don't know why they bothered flying Hall over here. X-Pac dominates the match and busts Bradshaw open. It doesn't really make sense to me to book it that way but I think the WWF had forgotten what X-Pac's strengths were by 2002. He's just booked like a jerk here, not a talented cruiserweight. The match has wonky psychology because of that and Bradshaw's big babyface comebacks don't work at all. Eventually Scott Hall stumbles down here, looking like an absolute wreck, to hit Bradshaw with X-Pac's nunchucks. Bradshaw still kicks out. Despite all this help X-Pac can't get anything going, as if Hall actually makes him worse. Bradshaw lays Hall out but gets punched in the testicles and the X-Factor finishes. The match was passable but not a good idea.

Final Rating: *¼

Backstage: Undertaker promises to show no remorse when he beats up Triple H tonight. Like his matches in 2002, Taker's promos weren't up to much.

WWF Hardcore Championship
Steven Richards (c) vs. Booker T
Stevie won the belt on *RAW* during a match between Bubba Dudley and Jazz, which is the issue with the Hardcore Title; people tended to win the title during other people's matches, or even after them. However, one of the perks of the Hardcore Title was that it changed hands so frequently that the fans were practically guaranteed a title switch whenever it was advertised. Indeed the title has changed hands 11 times since Stevie's initial win on *RAW*. Booker tries to throw weapons into the ring but Stevie throws them all to the floor. Booker manages to sneak bits of wrestling and kicks in between the plunder, although the plunder is very soft-core. The strangest thing about this match is that Booker is way above Richards on the card and yet the match rumbles on for 10-minutes with no sense of direction. Stevie kicks Booker in the nuts, which Jack Doan sees but can't do anything about. Booker misses his sidekick into the ropes and his groin takes another beating. Stevie comes across as quite resourceful, seeing hardcore spots coming and countering them. The match actually gets better when no hardcore is involved and they break out wrestling and counters. It's probably not what was advertised but it's wrestling. Stevie somehow survives a sidekick off the top with a trashcan over his head. Steviekick! Booker kicks out but the kick looked amazing. Book End! Booker wins the Hardcore Title. Until the selling disappeared at the end of the match this was okay.

Final Rating: **

Post Match: Crash Holly runs out and rolls up Booker for the title. His sell, staring at his hand a'la Booker, is hilarious. Axe Kick! Booker wins the belt back. Justin Credible and Tommy Dreamer run in, representing ECW, looking to score title runs. This match might never end. They trade on superkicks and Booker officially retains so he hits the Spinneroonie to celebrate. Stevie dumps Booker on a table, which doesn't break so Booker kicks out and they re-do the spot. Stevie regains his title, which he'd hold for all of 48 hours before six title changes in two days on *RAW*. In between this and those six title changes the belt was renamed the *WWE* Hardcore Championship. Confused yet? Try checking out the belt's history. In less than four years there were 234 champions.

Backstage: Shawn Stasiak is all excited about Planet Stasiak and thinks their team is unstoppable. Paul Heyman tells him to sit down, shut up and just stay out of Brock's way. Heyman tells him to stay on the apron and not tag in. Stasiak doesn't get it. Lesnar makes it simple: stay out of my way, or I'll kill you.

The Hardy Boyz vs. Brock Lesnar & Shawn Stasiak
The Hardys monstrous pop should tell you how misguided attempts to split them up were. JR points out Lita broke her neck filming *Dark Angel* and she'll be out for nine months. Stasiak, like the muppet he is, starts the match. He actually does quite well but Heyman is screaming at him to tag out. Matt takes him down with the Side Effect and the Poetry in Motion would follow but Lesnar drags Stasiak across to his corner to tag. Lesnar's viciousness at assaulting Matt is psychotic. It's amazing. He's like a wild animal mauling someone who got too close to his cage. He throws Matt around like a bag of spuds. Those who read our early *RAW* recaps in the *RAW Files* will remember we used to praise the Steiners as the best "jobber killers" in the business. Lesnar would take that award if it still existed except he doesn't do it to jobbers, he does it to *everyone*. Lesnar misses in his own corner and Stasiak, against his better judgement, tags himself in. Jeff lays him out with a series of messy spots, showing how his style was falling to pieces. Twist of Fate for Stasiak and the Swanton finishes. The match was great when Brock was killing people. Otherwise it was filler. Brock destroys everyone after the match just to point out who the real star is. Both Hardys gets the F5 and Stasiak gets planted with a spinebuster and a powerbomb.

Final Rating: *

Backstage: Coach interviews William Regal, who calls himself a "truly Great Briton". He calls the English "underachieving dossers with divvy children" before calling Spike a "shytehawk".

WWF European Championship
Spike Dudley (c) vs. William Regal
Spike beat Regal by stealing his brass knucks and knocking him out. Spike looks out of his depth as Regal wrestles European circles around him. He looks screwed when Regal puts him in a cravat. Spike comes firing back with punches and dropkicks to HEAT, which shows you the UK fans didn't want Regal to lose and they were enjoying him being there. Regal avoids the Acid Drop and Spike lands funny. They call out trainers who cut Spike's boot off. Meanwhile the crowd are

happily chanting for Regal, which rather shows you how much the office misjudged Regal's popularity. Spike gets carried out but Regal throws him back in and goes after the leg. It initially gets a ton of heat until everyone realises Spike isn't hurt at all and the whole thing was a set up. Regal's beatdown on poor little Spike is greeted by hearty pops. The whole thing is perfectly set up for Regal to regain his European Title in his own country until Spike hooks an inside cradle to retain. Regal puts on the brass knucks and knocks Spike out to another massive pop and "Regal" chants follow. Shitty booking, great work from Regal. Why would you not put Regal over here? Did they just assume if Regal ran some cheap heat before the match he'd get booed? The more the WWF audiences began to dwindle the more hardcore the support was, the more partisan to great wrestlers the support got.

Final Rating: *½

Showing he learned nothing from *Backlash*, Ric Flair comes out in a referee's shirt. He's not in the ring but he is the second ref for when Nick Patrick gets inevitably knocked out.

Steve Austin vs. The Big Show

With the nWo lacking in numbers they went ahead and turned Show heel to join the flagging group, which makes the current incarnation of the nWo; Scott Hall, X-Pac and Big Show. Somehow that's not intimidating. Probably because Hall is over the hill and the other two have their own issues. The crowd amuse themselves by chanting "you fat bastard" at Big Show as Show uses his size to dominate. Austin's matches in 2002 weren't great and Show tended to sleepwalk through most of his matches too, so this match is, perhaps predictably, awful. Austin, even when he sucks, finds a way to keep the crowd amused and that's by a combination of getting people to shout "WHAT?" after every move and repetition. So he'll spend ages kicking Show in the leg so the crowd can yell "WHAT?" after each one. Technically the match is bollocks but kudos to Steve for at least getting himself over. Austin weakens Show's knee so much he can get single leg takedowns. I don't remember anyone else getting that kind of love from Show, in terms of selling, other than Lesnar. Austin decides the only way he'll get nearly 20-minutes out of Show is by working the leg and having that as a constant out. Which would be fine if Show couldn't overpower him on one leg and has no idea how to sell an injury because no one ever works him over like that. Honestly though, it makes sense and more guys should have taken that approach. After all, Andre was forced into retirement because of a combination of bad knees, which couldn't take his weight and a bad back. It seems reasonable that Show would have the same weak points. The problems in the match stem from when Show takes over and he doesn't have a similar focus. He just grinds away at holds and eats up time. He makes no attempt to win the match. By the time he grabs a bearhug, bringing up the old adage "if you use a bearhug, you suck", I'm begging for the match to end. Austin goes back to punches, because outside of the knee work, that's all he's got. Ref gets bumped. Stunner! This should be Ric Flair's moment to jump in and count but the nWo come down to stop him. Flair runs Hall and Pac to the back but there's still no ref. Austin turns around into a goozle but fights his way out. Logically that would have been the finish but why have a finish when you can have overbooking? Kevin Nash comes in from the crowd and Austin hits him with the Stunner, then Show, twice. Former nWo referee Nick Patrick crawls over and counts the pin. So basically Austin found himself 4-on-1 and still won, that's how much Big Show sucks. I have no idea why they flew Nash over just for an ineffective run in.

Final Rating: *

The Undertaker vs. Triple H

Hunter is actually a *SmackDown!* wrestler but he appears on this *RAW* tour because he has an issue with Taker, which stems from the 'Dead Man' costing HHH the belt at *Backlash*. I don't see why his issue is more important than anyone else's issue. Like, why can't Ron Simmons come and team up with Bradshaw, who's feuding with the nWo? One of the main reasons the brand extension didn't work was the WWF's own refusal to adhere to it. The reason here was probably the switch in booking that happened when Hogan won the belt. Naturally his contract didn't include overseas tours and shit like that, which is why he should never have been given the title. This match falls into one of the worst months of the Undertaker's long and illustrious career. If you'd told me in 2002 that Taker would hang around for another decade (and beyond) and constantly have one of, if not the best, match at *WrestleMania* every year I'd have called you a crazy person. JR makes me laugh when he says "Triple H jerking the Undertaker off… the top rope". The pause is noticeable. Considering how highly rated Hunter and Taker are amongst the boys, it's depressing how bad this match is. Taker's character is a disaster. Hunter's babyface character is too vanilla. So instead of a hot match, like the *WrestleMania X-Seven* one the previous year, you get two guys out of alignment and a shitty match. Taker shouldn't be begging off, even if he is a heel. The match is going badly until the top rope breaks, then it really goes into the shitter. Taker opts for the Bret Hart routine of slapping on a chinlock while they figure something out. The logical thing to do would be to change the match and go brawling around outside while someone fixes it. Instead of that they opt to do a bunch of double downs. For some reason they can't resist including pre-planned spots that involve the ropes. Mainly into the corners, which are still intact. Hunters gets whipped into the broken turnbuckle, which is really stupid and could have done serious damage. Taker counters out of the Pedigree by grabbing the arm and spinning Hunter into a chokeslam. It's the only good wrestling in the match, bar a few straightforward spots like the spinebuster. Hunter decides to no sell snake eyes and hit the high knee. Pedigree. Game over. A few counters aside this was a slack match. You'll never see Undertaker take a cleaner job in his life though, so it's got that going for it.

Final Rating: ½*

VERDICT

A glaring damnation of the brand extension as a weakened *RAW* squadron delivers one of the worst UK-only PPV events. Eddie against RVD was pretty good, but the rest is a waste of time. Like *Backlash*, the two big main event matches failed to deliver and with the guys they had on top in the first half of 2002 it was clear the WWF was desperately in need of new blood in the main events. This show does possess at least one interesting factoid about it though: it was the last ever WWF PPV. The WWF officially became the WWE the following day and the next PPV was under the WWE banner. "Get the F out!" was their slogan. After this PPV, they can "get the F out" themselves.

24

TAJIRI

WWF "800" SERIES

WWF808
WWF809
WWF810
WWF825
WWF826
WWF827
WWF843

HULK HOGAN'S ROCK 'N' WRESTLING - VOLUME 4

CAT NO: WWF808
RUN TIME: 45 minutes (approx)

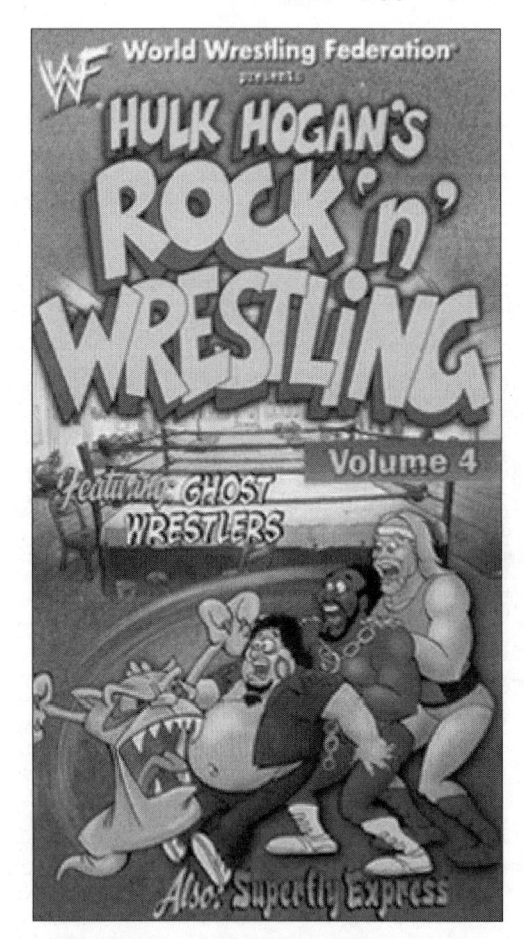

Lee Maughan: This is the fourth two-episode tape from the 1999 re-release of the 80's cartoon series.

S2, E9: Superfly Express

The gang board an overnight train to California but Superfly is awoken by Andre's snoring. Taking a late night stroll, he meets a beautiful blonde girl called Lenora. Moments later, Lenora is abducted by a couple of heavies who lead her to a mysterious cloaked woman in another cabin. The woman demands Lenora's ring but she's already left it behind in a bowl of fruit, which Captain Lou discovers and helps himself to. Screw morals, it's finders keepers here. Hulk, Lou and Wendi head down to the freezer to look for Lenora but the heavies show up and they get into a snowball fight. Because when someone's physically abducted someone, the best method of settling the score is throwing fluffy particles of frozen water at one another.

Hulk wastes an inordinate amount of time pushing a sliding block of ice against its natural incline (as opposed to, you know, just sidestepping out of the way) and Lou does a runner as the heavies give chase. Hulk, Lou and Wendi fall off the train onto a passing garbage boat but Hillbilly's skunk Naomi picks up the ring. Attempting to catch Naomi, Hillbilly and Andre fall out of the train and onto a farm where they meet Betty Jean who think they're "cute". As Michael Jackson *almost* once wailed - Betty Jean is now your lover. Cue duelling banjos.

Locked up in a River City jail, the garbage ship captain accuses Hulk, Lou and Wendi of being garbage pirates, but the sheriff recognises them as world famous wrestlers (someone eventually had to, right?) and lets them go without even asking any questions. Don't you ever again try to tell me that famous people can't use their celebrity status to bend the law in a way us normal folk can't! Betty Jean offers to fly Hillbilly and Andre back to the train on an aeroplane that looks like the Wright brothers built it, but they're too heavy to take off so Andre starts flapping his arms and they get enough purchase to fly, a bit like that infamous promo the real life 'Hulkster' gave prior to his match with Randy Savage at the October '89 Docklands Arena show. Do yourself a favour and look it up, it is *insane*. The police are also in hot pursuit with Hulk, Lou and Wendi in tow, to the point of actually jumping over a raising bridge. Never mind that Hogan promo, this *show* is insane.

Back on the train, JYD, Tito and Superfly track down Lenora but the mystery woman shows up and unlinks the axle of their carriage, sending them to almost certain doom. Luckily, Betty Jean swoops down with her rickety old plane and Superfly is able to jump on, lifting Lenora with him. Meanwhile, the cop car speeds up enough for Hulk to lean out of the window and tell the driver to stop the train. See? Insane. Reunited, the entire gang prevent the hooded lady from leaving the train and pull her hood, gasping in amazement at the reveal of... Deanna. Who?! Lenora reveals that Deanna is actually her cousin. How the hell would anybody recognise someone's cousin?! They couldn't at least have made it her evil twin?! Lenora tells Superfly that she is actually a princess of a "small country" and that if Deanna could get the ring, she'd be able to overthrow Lenora and take over the nation. What?! How on earth does that work!? That's like one of those stupid wrestling tropes where a title brings whoever holds it some unspecified "power", from refusing title defences to booking their own matches! Lenora invites Superfly to visit her country to which he agrees, though the episode's conclusion never makes it clear if she ends up mothering Tamina Snuka, or indeed, winds up being found dead in Superfly's hotel room...

S2, E11: Ghost Wrestlers

Training at Hulk's gym is interrupted by a surprise guest - Manny the Mangler, world wrestling champion of 1947 whose unannounced appearance is due to ghost sightings at his

FURIOUS ABOUT: EDGE

Adam Copeland always seemed destined for greatness. When the WWF first hired him, he had the look of a superstar. The WWF wanted to split Edge & Christian up as far back as 1999 as they believed Edge was a star in the making. The E&C tag team ended up as massive stars, hugely entertaining as both heels and faces, they dominated the tag division. The No Mercy '99 ladder match against the Hardy Boyz revolutionised tag team wrestling and made everyone in the match famous. The subsequent tag wars with the Hardyz & Dudleyz gave us a new golden age of tag teaming. During 2001, the WWF felt they had to give Edge a run in singles and turned Christian heel. Their run of matches wasn't great, which probably had the WWF a little worried but Edge's early 2002 feud with Kurt Angle proved he could compete at the highest level. While this book barely scratches the surface of Edge as a singles star, a man who'd go on to superstardom and around eight years of main event awesomeness, it does demonstrate where the potential came from. We all knew he'd make it. If Edge didn't make it, then nobody was going to. He could talk the talk and walk the walk. The TLC matches proved he was fearless and his singles work proved he could go it alone. His 2001 King of the Ring acceptance speech where he claimed he wouldn't "Billy Gunn" his KotR summed Edge up. He wasn't afraid to blur the lines between reality and booking and he wasn't afraid to make fun of people to get angles over. Because E&C were so goofy at times Edge had an uphill struggle to break out in singles but he was always odds on to do so.

---

boarding home. The crew decide to check it out but are met by Ethel, an old lady who lets Manny practice his wrestling holds on her. He attempts to give a demonstration for the guys but Ethel stabs him with a knitting needle. Whoa, very kid-friendly. Everybody takes a room for the night, but a series of ghostly goings on results one-by-one in each of the guys asking if they can sleep with Hulk. What a stud. No wonder he eventually wound up making a sex tape with Bubba the Love Sponge's wife; clearly old Terrance is just completely irresistible!

The only one who doesn't show up is Wendi, but a chilling scream leads the gang to her room where, from behind a bookcase appears a Slimer-like ghostly apparition. He's an ugly little spud, isn't he? The ghost slobbers off revealing Wendi, as Andre notices all of the elderly residents gathering outside in the graveyard. Because if you're going to build a retirement home, build it next to a graveyard so every single day you can remind the old folks they'll all be dead soon too. Curiously at this point, the intro to *Ghostbusters* by Ray Parker, Jr. plays, which must have cost a pretty penny to get the rights to, even for just those few seconds. Hell, if Parker's lawsuit over the song was anything to go by, the *Rock 'N' Wrestling* producers may have ended up having to pay Huey Lewis and the News instead, since Parker allegedly ripped his song off from Lewis' '*I Want a New Drug*'.

The crusties attempt to fight off the ghost outside but another scream leads everyone back indoors to discover the home has been completely ransacked. Down at JYD's junkyard, the gang build themselves some proton packs and head out on a ghost hunt. When there's something strange in your neighbourhood, who ya gonna call? Hulk Hogan! That leads to a series of "hilarious" mishaps in which everybody gloops everybody else, bar the ghost, and Ethel vanishes behind the bookcase. Wendi finds a secret stairway and zaps a shadowy figure behind a gravestone, revealing Lemley, the owner of the boarding house. Lemley reveals that all he was doing was following a trail of footsteps to an abandoned outhouse filled with ghoulish contraptions and Hulk decides the best course of action is get the oldies out of there.

Returning to the spookhouse under costumes, Hulk and his pals begin chasing a shrouded figure from room to room before finally glooping her. It was Ethel all along! What a swerve. Ethel says she found a letter from a Mr. Wheeler who used to live at the house who hid $100,000 under his bed with instructions that it be donated to the boarding house, but since Ethel didn't know which room he stayed in, she had to scare everyone away so she could search for it. And she would have gotten away with it too, if it wasn't for you meddlesome wrestlers! She gives a sob story about running out of money and worrying that she'd get kicked out of the house, but despite all her transgressions Lemley declares that they're still all friends. Really? After the stunt she just pulled?! Terrifying all those poor elderly folk while trying to embezzle money that didn't rightfully belong to her? Perhaps they let her off because she's got Alzheimer's or something. Manny says that Mr. Wheeler used to stay in his room so the gang check it out with Manny karate kicking his way through the floorboards to the pile of cash. He came, he saw, he kicked that floor board's ass. And just think about it - this show was made in 1986, so all those old people are probably dead by now. Spooky!

VERDICT

Two rather ridiculous plots this time, with endings almost as outrageous as the one found in 1984's, ahem, "classic" slash-em-up *Fatal Games*. *Superfly Express* is almost like a Vince Russo-penned episode where they've come up with an intriguing premise and just gone with it, only figuring out the ending once they got there. As Marge Simpson would say, "It's an ending, that's enough."

The amusingly referential *Ghost Wrestlers* is the winner this time out, although there are some curious continuity problems with the animation at one point. During the scene where all the wrestlers are helping the residents pack their belongings up to take them some place safe for the evening, Big John Studd can clearly be seen loading up the Hulkmobile despite not featuring in the episode, nor being part of Hogan's crew. A ghostly apparition perhaps? Dogs and cats living together, mass hysteria!

49

HULK HOGAN'S ROCK 'N' WRESTLING - VOLUME 5

CAT NO: WWF809
RUN TIME: 45 minutes (approx)

Lee Maughan: This is the fifth tape from the 1999 re-release of the 80's cartoon series, with this featuring three rather than the usual two episodes.

S2, E5: The Foster Wrestler

On their way to a big match at the Bombay Arena in India, Hulk and the gang are collected by a driver named Boobar and whisked off to the village of Bangpoor. Stopping off for water along the way, a baby elephant takes a shine to Andre. Arriving at the village, the group meet up with Tito's foster kid, Raji, but something seems amiss. Raji's family appear gaunt, frail and hungry despite Tito having sent them food and supplies for over a year, and their crops aren't growing. Raji explains that all they've received from Tito are letters and pictures, suggesting their shipments have been hijacked by someone. Hillbilly offers to show the locals how to farm and Captain Lou cooks up veggie burgers for everyone as Hulk's crew head out to find who's responsible for the interceptions.

At the docks, Andre, Superfly and JYD hide in wooden crates and get driven away in a large delivery truck, with Hulk, Tito and Wendi in hot pursuit. Meanwhile, the baby elephant is abducted by poachers. Back to the chase, the truck makes it all the way back to Bangpoor without stopping after driving behind a waterfall, with Boobar's car taking a shortcut over a bridge. Inspecting the truck, Hulk and Raji find Andre, Superfly and JYD all to be missing, so Hulk goes to speak with the driver. When he notices a different guy behind the wheel, the driver pulls away, unaware that Raji is still aboard, so Hulk, Boobar and all give chase yet again.

Over at a secret cave warehouse behind the waterfall, a group of captive elephants are moving boxes of contraband supplies around when the baby elephant discovers Andre and the boys, leading to the crooks capturing the trio in a large net, locking them in a box, then dumping them in the river to die. Heavy stuff! Luckily, they're picked up by a troupe of elderly elephants, whom they ride back to the cave. In the meantime, Hulkster and his team encounter trouble with a hungry tiger and a rapidly collapsing bridge, with the knock-on effect that they discover tyre tracks that lead through the waterfall and into the cave.

The boys round up the black marketeers but are forced to let them escape when Raji emerges from the back of the truck, gets his foot caught in a rope, and almost gets crushed by a working elephant. Locked in, Hogan's heroes comes face to face with the bad guys riding a horde of elephants, only for Andre, Superfly and JYD to arrive in the nick of time for an all-elephant showdown, which the babyfaces naturally win. Moments later, Boobar arrives just in time to pass out from exhaustion, having run all the way to the cave nonstop from Bangpoor. Back on the farm, Uncle Andre feeds milk to the baby elephant while cradling it in his arms, which is bizarre given that the elephant was already shown in an earlier scene to be much bigger than him. I guess that's inconsistent 80s animation for you.

S2, E2: Muscle Madness

Throughout *Rock 'n' Wrestling's* entire 26 episode run, precisely half of the episodes were actually split into two smaller stories, though this is the first time one of those micro episodes has made it onto any of these commercial tapes. This one comes from the second of season 2's episode 2.

Bumping into each other whilst out shopping for gym equipment, Hulk and Roddy both notice a poster for the upcoming Miss Muscle contest and volunteer Wendi and Moolah respectively for the big showdown. Both ladies are hesitant at first until being told the other called them a wimp. Nikolai and the Iron Sheik are sent to sabotage Wendi's training while Roddy suggests Moolah's best chance of winning is to cheat. Mr. Fuji then lies to Moolah about Piper making fun of her weight, which results in Moolah bodypressing Piper over

But wait! Fuji is such a fool that he accidentally knocks the magnet over and the weights roll onto the emcee. Moolah naturally can't lift them without any assistance but Wendi Hulks Up to finally bodyslam... er, I mean, lift the weights on her second attempt, so the judges disqualify Moolah for cheating and give Wendi first place instead. Perhaps that decision was what really triggered the infamous Madison Square Garden screwjob between Wendi and Spider Lady? Furious, Piper threatens Hogan who sticks up for Wendi by saying she could beat Moolah in any kind of sport. Piper suggests bowling and Hulk accepts, only for Wendi and Moolah to scald both guys, and they all agree to forget it.

S2, E4: Big John's Car Lot

Another micro episode, this one the first half of season 2's episode 4, which was backed with an episode called *Big Top Boobs*, which I believe was an intimate, behind-the-scenes exposé of Sable's Playboy pictorials.

Wraparound: Bobby Heenan shows Gene Okerlund how to extort money from an ATM, but gets himself arrested in the process. Okerlund of course keeps the pile of cash for himself. Hey, they don't call him "Scheme" Gene for nothing!

John Studd's father's car lot business is failing so Piper's club show up to lend a hand. With Studd Sr. out of town (why he's gallivanting off despite being on the verge of bankruptcy is never adequately explained), Piper and the boys start lying to innocent customers about the quality of the cars, having been offered a 50/50 commission on any sales. Studd the elder soon returns and can't believe the amount of money the boys have made, but all of the customers return, demanding their money back for the shoddy motors they've had pawned off on them. All except one that is, a priest who bought a convertible from the lads for just $20 but wants to return it because having cleaned it up, he's realised it's a rare convertible worth $50,000. Papa Studd scalds his son and promises to split the cash with the bible thumper.

PAUL HEYMAN

her head. "What did I tell you? She's now lifting a dumbbell!"

At the contest, Wendi posts a score of 29 out of 30 for her physique (which hardly has any muscles on it at all) before Moolah bags a clean sweep with 10 out of 10 across the board, despite the notable handicap of one of her muscles bursting. A passage of time takes us to the weightlifting portion of proceedings, with Wendi failing at 250lbs but Moolah succeeding thanks to some strategically placed magnets, and she takes the trophy.

VERDICT

The shorter episodes on offer here will perhaps make the show a little more palatable for some, although *The Foster Wrestler* did have a moderately intriguing plot (at least by *Rock 'n' Wrestling* standards). *Muscle Madness* had some decent gags but clearly not enough to carry a full length story, while *Big John's Car Lot* was rather unusual in not even featuring title star Hulk Hogan, nor any of the babyface clan.

40

HULK HOGAN'S ROCK 'N' WRESTLING - VOLUME 6

CAT NO: WWF810
RUN TIME: 45 minutes (approx)

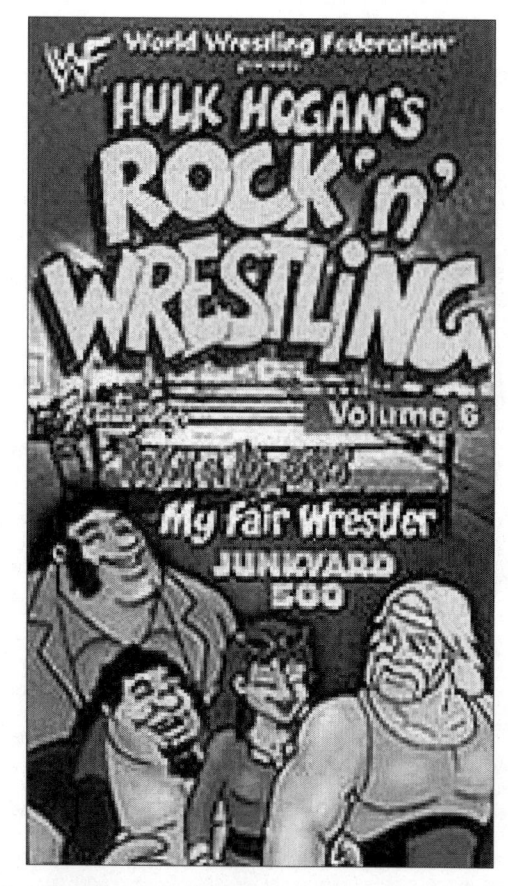

Lee Maughan: This is the sixth and final tape from the 1999 re-release of the 80's cartoon series, with this again featuring three rather than the usual two episodes.

S1, E11: Rock-n-Zombies

Bobby Heenan gives free complimentary tickets to Hulk's club and Piper's goons for the opening of his new amusement park, Rock 'N' Wrestleland. Each wrestler has his or her own themed ride, and whichever wrestler's ride gets the best attendance will also have the park named after them. Far be it from me to complain about the logical flaws in a children's cartoon, but wouldn't they all be wanting a cut of the profits, given the obviously unlicensed use of their name and likenesses?

Saboteurs extraordinaire Nikolai Volkoff and the Iron Sheik pull up a piece of the track on Captain Lou Albano's Runaway Dining Cart ride, and the train (complete with screaming children) heads wildly off course, smashing through Sheik's own theme ride (that basically looks to be a bunch of people driving cars around a dirt track). Far be it from me to complain about the logical flaws in a children's cartoon, again, but shouldn't they be arrested for attempted murder?

Roddy Piper and Big John Studd meanwhile pull the pin on Junkyard Dog's Junky Ride, but JYD's plane comes loose and flies through Piper's hot air balloon. Over at Fabulous Moolah's House of Horrors, a little child flees after hearing a monster, and he accuses Heenan of being a liar. Heenan throws the kid out of the park so Wendi gives chase as a group of zombies spill out into the park.

Catching up with the young lad, Wendi finds out that Heenan actually bought a cemetery from the boy's mother, who could no longer afford the upkeep, and built the park on it without permission. Back at the park, the zombies kidnap Wendi and take her on Hulk's Eye of the Tiger jungle boat ride, with the wrestlers giving chase on hippos. Hippos?! You know, I've gotta give it to Heenan; zombie infestation or not, he clearly spent a lot of cash on this theme park. Even so, the zombies agree with Wendi that Heenan lied to Mrs. Fulbright about leaving the site as a memorial park, so Heenan scarpers in a miniature version of Piper's Hot Rod from the auto race, with Hulk and the zombies in hot pursuit. That leads to trip around Tito Santana's Mexican Sombrero big wheel, which of course comes loose.

Catching up with the runaway wheel, Hogan demands Heenan turn the pack back into a cemetery, and the zombies all die happily ever after. Piper's still isn't happy however, as they christen the rebuilt burial ground 'Roddy Piper's Rock 'N' Rest-in-Peace Memorial Park'. "Why couldn't you have made it 'Hulk Hogan's Hulkamania Heaven'" demands Piper, "or 'Bobby Heenan's Hereafter Hotel'?"

S2, E10: My Fair Wrestler

Hulk and the crew in London for a tour of Buckingham Palace where Captain Lou cuts in line ahead of a 1920s Cockney chimney sweep and wins a prize for being the ten millionth visitor. Lou's prize is to give a speech at the House of Lords before parliament, so the gang give him a bath and paint his wacky multicoloured suit black. The chimney sweep calls Lou a Yankee and tells him to go back home, so I figure he must be a member of UKIP or the BNP. Back at the royal palace, a guard calls the chimney sweep a "dirty little street urchin" so Lou admits to stealing his prize and lays on some heavy life lessons about talking instead of fighting. Lou then reverts to form and accidentally calls the Queen a "bimbo", so he and Mickey the chimney sweep do a runner.

S1, E1: The Junkyard 500

And we end, perhaps rather appropriately given the slapdash ordering of the episodes on these tapes, with the first half of episode one from season one. Famous movie director Woody Brooks is looking for a vehicle to star in his latest monster movie, so JYD and Tito drive the Junkwagon over to the production studio. As Brooks is about to hand over $10,000 for the rights to the car, Roddy Piper and Big John Studd arrive in the Hot Rod, and a tug 'o' war breaks out with Brooks as the rope. His suggestion? A race, and the winner gets to be in the movie. Brooks sounds like a bit of a crook if you ask me.

A *Rock 'n' Wrestling* tribute to *Wacky Races* soon breaks out, with Piper jumping the gun on the start, Nikolai Volkoff and the Iron Sheik chaining the Junkmobile to the bleachers to slow it down, and Piper filling JYD's truck with smoke, blown from the oversized novelty bagpipes on the back of the Hot Rod. Further along the course, Nikolai paints over a road sign that leads JYD down a broken bridge, the Junkwagon dropping into a ravine below. Yes, attempted murder on this Saturday morning kids cartoon. The Junkmobile of course is also designed for water, and the speed of the current makes the diversion something of a shortcut for Junkyard.

Approaching the finishing line back at the studio, JYD slows down to avoid hitting a dog, giving Piper the chance to fire up his Rowdy Rocket Boosters and *fly* the Hot Rod to victory, giving Roddy the ten grand. A heel victory in the very first episode? Of course not, as a somehow previously hidden gigantic mechanical dinosaur crashes through a building and crushes the Hot Rod to pieces, as Piper angrily barks "I hate rock and roll!" Well then.

SUPERFLY JIMMY SNUKA

VERDICT

One thing that puzzles me about the release of these tapes is why they weren't themed. Obviously they decided to forgo production order when they could have released an entire season over the course of the six tapes, so why did episodes get thrown together seemingly at random? One would think the *Rock 'N' Zombies* episode here would have matched up well with *Junkenstein* and *Ghost Wrestlers*, or that *The Four Legged Pickpocket* could have tag-teamed with *Gorilla My Dreams* and *The Foster Wrestler* for an animal-themed release, but no. And where was *Rowdy Roddy Reforms*, the penultimate episode in which Piper finally turns babyface to match his real-life counterpart?

The episodes here are largely fine, no better or worse than you'd otherwise expect from this show, but they're incredibly generic and predictable. But hey, what else would you expect from an 80s cartoon aimed at the Saturday morning cereal munching pre-teen crowd? I'll call *Rock 'N' Zombies* the winner this time out, despite some obvious flaws, largely because of the mystery plotline, the zombies turning babyface, and the rare appearance of Bobby Heenan.

40

MOST MEMORABLE MATCHES 1999

CAT NO: WWF825
RUN TIME: 90 minutes (approx)

Steel Cage Match
Steve Austin vs. Vince McMahon
[St. Valentine's Day Massacre]
Arnold Furious: As I'm sure you recall, Vince won the *Royal Rumble* but gave up his title opportunity. He was just happy Austin didn't win it. As soon as he gave up the title match, WWF commissioner Shawn Michaels gave his title shot to Steve Austin; the Rumble's runner up. Vince meanwhile revealed that Austin couldn't touch him outside of a sanctioned match or he'd be fired, so he's spent the build up to this match trying to get Austin to punch him. I'd have thought punching your boss was pretty much a guaranteed firing wherever you work. I'm surprised Vince didn't just sack him when he did it the first time. Anyhow, Austin has this match to get out his frustrations. In exchange, Austin will be stripped of his title match at *WrestleMania* if he loses here. A typical February PPV main event then! One last hurdle for the company's top guy to get over before the promised land. Vince basically controls the cage by not letting Steve in until Austin pretends to blow his knee out on the floor. That suckers Vince outside for a beating. You'd think Vince would have learned from all the years of watching guys do that from ringside. I guess hatred can make you blind. Vince tries plan B; a repeat of his *Royal Rumble* sprint through the crowd. At the Rumble he made it to the concourse and Austin got jumped. Here Austin catches him and pounds him back to ringside. The more you think about this match, the more ridiculous it is. The whole thing is totally lopsided. Austin is a wrestler, Vince is not. So it's a one way ass kicking and that's all people are paying to see. They repeated this trick several times to lesser and lesser effect. To Vince's eternal credit, he takes a preposterous, insane, Mick Foley level bump off the top of the cage through the announce table. It's a huge bump for anyone but a non-wrestler and owner of a multi-million dollar corporation? Kudos, sir. It looks like it hurt. A jarring bump, certainly. That's how much he wanted to beat WCW. Howard Finkel goes to announce Austin as the winner, but Austin grabs the mic calling it "bullshit". He says the match "won't be that easy". "Is the son of a bitch still breathing?" Austin gets a massive pop for suggesting the match isn't over and he goes after McMahon as he's being carted away. Austin tipping the gurney into the cage is another terrific visual. Vince had all this coming for being such an asshole but credit where it's due, he took his beating like a man. Austin promised blood and Vince duly blades after being run into the cage. A third selfless act from the company's boss. Austin goes to leave, but the bloody Vince flips him off. That cage is rickety as hell too. I wouldn't want to climb over it once, let alone back inside again. It's the rarely ever used black bar cage. Stunner! That should finish it because now Vince is unconscious and can't flip anybody off. While Austin is busy celebrating Paul Wight, the Giant from WCW, pops up from under the ring for his debut and assaults Stone Cold. Wight pitches Austin at the cage and the rickety wall finally breaks away, leaving Austin to drop to the floor and retain his 'Mania title shot. For a moment it seemed as if the Giant was going to face Austin at 'Mania, with Mankind and Rock continuing their feud. I'll give Vince credit where it's due; his silly bumps and reckless abandon in this match made it seem more than a straightforward beatdown, which is what it was on paper. The success of this match allowed the WWF to feature Vince in a load of main event matches and *WrestleMania* bouts afterwards. Which is an unfortunate downside, but the match shouldn't be punished for it. This is probably Vince's best singles match.
Final Rating: ***

"I Quit" Match
WWF Championship
Mankind (c) vs. The Rock
[Royal Rumble 1999]
Arnold Furious: The idea behind this is that Mankind has never given up, never submitted and feels no pain so he can't lose. Putting the title on Mick Foley was one of the WWF's better booking decisions from 1999 as he felt like the people's champion. He was one of us. Meanwhile the Rock is genetically superior and a third generation star, plus he's Vince McMahon's chosen corporate champion. We get clips from *Heat* where Mankind had to wrestle Mabel in a "warm-up match". Rock never quite worked out as a heel because he was always popular and that shows when he gets a live mic shoved in his face. He makes threats and he's funny. It takes away from the serious nature of the match, which is surely not

how Foley wanted this to go down. Plus he lays into Jerry Lawler at ringside; "shut your mouth, you piece of trash". If I didn't know better I'd say Rock was trying to turn himself babyface. Rock eats the Mandible Claw, but passes out so he can't quit. They work in a crowd brawl, albeit brief, before Rock hits a superb powerslam over the rail. Rock again goes to the entertainment by singing into the mic, which would be fine if he was face but he isn't. Rock goes after a Rock Bottom through the Spanish table, but it collapses. Not the last time that kind of spot would fail. You'd think they'd re-gimmick the tables after this happened, but they didn't. Mankind looks more comfortable in the long brawling segments but Rock is fast improving. Foley's habit of main event planning was to slowly raise the bar (Hell in a Cell aside), so out comes a ladder. They use the ladder to reach the balcony and Mick takes one of his trademark bumps onto an electrical "circuit board". The lights go out as we pretend the WWF keeps all the building's electricity right by the entranceway. Shane McMahon comes out as they try and pretend this is a shoot. Considering Mick's ridiculous bumps this one was relatively safe, but it looked cool. In an attempt to escalate from there Rock puts Foley in handcuffs, which just kills the crowd as that leaves Mankind completely defenceless. This is the point where Mick puts his wellbeing in the hands of the Rock and he abuses the privilege. Mick's kids were horrified by it as Rock lay in chair shot after chair shot after chair shot. When Mick says "you'll have to kill me" here it becomes uncomfortable viewing. Especially with him bleeding from behind the mask. It takes all the enjoyment out of it and even Lawler is there saying "that's enough". When Mick feeds Rock the back, to show him no more head shots, Rock smacks him in the back of the head, which is way beyond taking liberties. He could have killed him. Mankind is unconscious, perhaps legitimately, so the WWF pump in a pre-taped "I Quit" from an earlier Foley promo. Rock regains his belt in a horrific display. I've seen this rated as high as **** but to me the meat of the match is the chair shots and they're so unsettling that I find this extremely hard to watch. Despite my reasonably high rating, I would never re-watch this if I wasn't reviewing it. Falling off the Cell is one thing as it's basically a stunt, but a chair shot is assault.

Final Rating: ***¼

Terri Invitational Tournament Final
Ladder Match
Edge & Christian vs. The Hardy Boyz
[No Mercy 1999]

The winner gets $100,000 and Terri's services. The Hardys were working as the New Brood and have Gangrel in their corner, which brings up the question of why Gangrel would want them to win as he'd have to share management duties with Terri, and was actually replaced by her. The Hardys went through a load of managers before the WWF finally teamed them up with Lita and found a winning combination. This is the first tag team ladder match and an absolute game-changer. Not only for the individuals involved, who all benefitted enormously from this exposure, but also for tag team wrestling, which leapt to importance in 2000, and the hardcore style, which gained massively in popularity in 2000 too. It's amazing looking back

---

FURIOUS ABOUT: ROB VAN DAM

When the WWF hired RVD in 2001 it made me very happy. As an ECW fan, I'd been marking out over Rob's crazy matches and insane moveset for years and was thrilled to see that happen in the WWF. And they even let him work his ECW style...for a while. His best WWF work came in the hardcore environment where he could utilise chairs and therefore get in his patented Van Daminator. His first push saw him compete against the WWF's own resident daredevil Jeff Hardy. While the Hardyz were big stars as a team, the RVD matches were Jeff's chance to prove himself in singles. Rob was already a singles star and their crazy spotfests improved several midcards in 2001. RVD then moved onwards and upwards against Chris Jericho, in what has to be the best 'RVD style' match the WWF ever saw. It was enough to force Rob into the main event scene only for his errant kicks to get him into trouble. His habit of connecting with those 'educated feet' and potatoing the likes of Jericho and Angle saw his push wane. He lost his title shot. He lost his hardcore title to Undertaker and found himself in the IC title picture. Stripped of his unique hardcore moveset RVD had to work on changing his in-ring, which he did with the help of Eddy Guerrero and became a decent WWE wrestler in the process. However if you look at the fan reactions, they never compared to when he was a renegade, working his own style. He was a lot smoother and less dangerous but he was less fun. Which is the price you pay for competency. He didn't get back into the WWE title picture until 2006 when the ECW revival allowed him to return to hardcore.

---

to see Cleveland's total lack of interest in the match to begin with. The lack of tags benefits the Hardys as they have more team moves. Timmy White gets sick of Gangrel in a hurry and sends him to the back. The early ladder spots seem quite tame compared to later ladder matches, but it works because they build to bigger things and it's organic. Christian and Jeff fighting over a ladder leads to Jeff getting jammed in the corner, allowing Christian to run up the ladder and dropkick him. As the danger increases during the match the pops get bigger. Christian does an inverted DDT off the middle of the ladder and that's a "WOW" moment for 1999. Matt goes up and Edge powerbombs him off and that gets a meaty pop too. But they're just getting going. Edge climbs and Jeff missile dropkicks him off the ladder. The spots get progressively more brutal and dangerous. At this point Christian was the biggest talent of the four, and his timing is impeccable. But it's Jeff who's the showiest and he slingshots over a ladder to hit a big legdrop. I love the planning in this match, which compared to the TLC matches is a lot better, albeit with less carnage. The spots make sense. As the match escalates they start into the trademarks off the ladders with Edge hitting the Downward Spiral on Jeff, a move he stopped doing not long after. Because they build to big spots the selling compares favourably so they can throw in the fatigue stuff, and they start climbing slower to allow spots to be set up. It's smart work. What's really important is how they got the crowd, slowly but surely, and eventually they're hanging on every spot. The see-saw spot where Christian and Matt battle over a set up ladder and Jeff dives onto the other end is inspired and gets a standing ovation. They can milk the hell out of that and just lie around afterwards as everyone gets hurt. They move up to duelling ladder spots with all four guys involved and everyone falls off apart from Jeff who grabs the cash. The finish is

THE MEAN STREET POSSE

underwhelming but the stuff that proceeded it was smartly worked, escalated nicely and got over four guys in one fell swoop. The WWF very rarely went out of their way to get four new guys over in one night, but they did here. All of them moved on to greatness and only Matt never won a World Title. Without this match to showcase their skills it could have taken them years longer to get to the top of the mountain. One of the best matches of 1999 and MOTY for most people. Follow on TLC matches would get crazier and have tremendous spots, but this was a smarter work all round.
Final Rating: ****½

Greenwich Street Fight
Test vs. Shane McMahon
[SummerSlam 1999]
James Dixon: Not content with having taken a spot on the biggest show of the year (*WrestleMania XV*), now Shane is also working the second biggest. Mind you, his match at 'Mania *was* the second best on the card and he always takes silly bumps for my amusement, so he is okay with me. The issue of contention between the two is that Test wants to date Stephanie McMahon, and protective brother Shane won't allow it. Shane's thought-to-be-injured buddies the Mean Street Posse make their way out for support, and pull up a conveniently placed sofa in the front row and drink champagne. Test being the wrestler, and a massive one at that, dominates Shane to begin with and throws him around with ease. Again, credit to Shane for his ballsy bumping and the technique on them. They go into the crowd and Test remains in control, then he press slams Shane into the Posse who go tumbling out of their couch. It's a fun visual. Because two out of the last three matches featuring weapons isn't enough, they use plunder here too, and it is largely meaningless because of the repetition. How many times can you watch the same thing, no matter how good it is, before you get bored? I guess that is the whole basis behind the less is more theory, but Vince Russo clearly takes the Frasier Crane approach to that: "Ah yes, but if less is more, just think how much more "more" will be". Frasier was proven to be mistaken, and Vince Russo is too with every shoddy, repetitive PPV that the WWF put out in 1999. The sad thing for these guys is that when viewed objectively and away from what has gone before it, this is pretty damn good. Certainly a million

times better than what you would think Shane McMahon vs. Test would be. Shane smashes a portrait of the Posse over Test's head, which shatters everywhere, but he misses a corkscrew moonsault (!) and then a leapfrog (or rana) attempt gets caught and countered with a powerbomb. Test goes for his big boot, but Shane ducks and he wipes out the ref and the Posse get involved again. But why do you need a ref bump when it is a Street Fight and thus no DQ anyway? It is just doing something for the sake of doing something, which is simply maddening. All that does is cheapen the use of ref bumps and lower their significance next time. I believe they have a place, but when they happen every show, sometimes more than once, it becomes hokey and too much. The Posse are able to take Test down and place him on the Spanish announce table for a Shane flying elbow from the ring, prompting a comical "gulp" from Steph watching backstage. If anyone else in this spot on the card was doing stunts like that they would be criticised for trying to steal the spotlight and taking away from the other talents, but hey, it's the bosses son, he is untouchable. Test kicks out of the resulting pinfall attempt and then another one after Rodney belts him with his cast, as the crowd support for Test swells. The Posse try to interfere again, but Pat Patterson and Gerry Brisco come down and fight them off, again to a big pop, then Test hits a pumphandle slam and a flying elbow to win it. Flying Elbow? Randy Savage? Steph!? Hmm... The response to Test is tremendous, and this match should have made him into a main event star, but instead his legs were cut out from under him and Triple H stepped into the role as Steph's on-screen lover, then ended up pumping her full of Helmsley for real as a result of that. If things had worked out differently, perhaps Test would have ended up as a McMahon instead of Hunter, and he may still be alive today. Curious how things work out. The most logical and emotion-drawing match on the card, though it was hurt by its placement and the close proximity to other similar matches.

Final Rating: ***

Chyna & Mr. Ass vs. X-Pac & Road Dogg
[Fully Loaded 1999]
Arnold Furious: They'd pretty much run the DX concept into the ground by this point and the reason for these two teams clashing is merchandising rights. Everyone had moved on from DX by now, as they were all acceptable singles stars and Pac was teaming with a main eventer. Road Dogg is often hugely underrated as a wrestler given his niche market of being a modern day Ricky Morton, but there were few as selfless as he was in the ring. Given that he's teaming with X-Pac you'd think

FURIOUS ABOUT: EDDIE GUERRERO

Eddie used to have a t-shirt in WCW that read "Eddie Guerrero is my favourite wrestler". That about summed him up. After Bret quit the WWF in 1997, I officially changed my 'favourite wrestler' from Bret to Eddie. He remained my favourite until his 2005 death. I persist that when Eddie was 'on' nobody could touch him. He had the technical excellence to match the likes of Benoit and Angle. He had the high flying skills of a Rey Mysterio Jr. or Rob Van Dam and he had the charisma and personality to match Hulk Hogan or Steve Austin. He was the complete package. However the era we're covering were Eddie's dark days. Addicted to painkillers, drinking heavily and out of control he was fired by the WWE in late 2001. That was after he'd spent time in rehab. Eddie may have been delivering in the ring and with his storylines, the Mama Cita stuff with Chyna was the best work she ever did in the business, but inside he was hurting. After being fired in 2001, he went into the Indies, he got himself clean and he worked his way back. His comeback and return to glory is one of the greatest stories in wrestling. His "Cheating Death" DVD is one my favourite interview pieces the WWE have ever done. When Eddie returned to the WWE in 2002, it was as a heel. Personality somewhat stripped away, they had him as a hard-nosed workhorse. To reign in spotty guys and teach them how to work. Under his tutelage both RVD and Edge improved greatly in the ring. CM Punk got a chance to work him in 2002 and, on his DVD, Punk says "I thought I was pretty good…until I wrestled Eddie Guerrero". He was one of the best.

---

it was a 50-50 as to who would take the heat, but there he is, getting his ass handed to him as per usual. He runs that Outlaw formula like Billy Gunn is waiting for the tag. The heels are both okay in the ring, but tend to rely on character rather than ability. Billy certainly has the look of a main event star. He's tall, muscular and has a full head of hair. He's Vince's dream main eventer. Hell, Vince tried to get him over as one. Pac runs on autopilot in this one; hitting his spots, albeit energetically, as if he's sleepwalking. X-Pac was still over during 1999 and quite often people forget that and just remember how hated he was after a heel turn later in 1999. Evil DX run a second heat segment after Pac gets his neck re-injured. JR has a sudden revelation that Chyna doesn't outright suck in the ring as she orchestrates everything for her team and runs heat like it's second nature. Pac gets the second hot tag of the match and this time Road Dogg gets to showcase his offensive moveset, which is mostly just juking and jiving, but it's over huge. X-Pac encourages Chyna to "suck it". Give it a few years, mate. Mr. Ass gets caught with the pumphandle slam and Road Dogg retains rights to the DX merch. I'm not sure I really cared about that, but it is a tidy little formula tag match.

Final Rating: ***

VERDICT

It's a highlights tape, so you already know what you are getting going in. In this office, 1999 is amongst our least favourite years of the WWF, and this so-called "best of" pretty much sums up why. Only one of the matches is above 4*, which is astonishing really when you look at how many matches were comfortably beyond that in 2000. That's not to say the other four bouts are not good, because they are, but they are not blow away. Not that there was much in the way of better options, mind you. If you have seen the PPVs from the year already then this is a worthless purchase, but as a quick snapshot of 1999 it is worth a look.

56

MOST MEMORABLE MATCHES 2000

CAT NO: WWF826
RUN TIME: 90 minutes (approx)

Street Fight
WWF Championship
Triple H (c) vs. Cactus Jack
[Royal Rumble 2000]
Interesting that they don't bill Cactus as being from Truth or Consequences, New Mexico as Foley was from New York (Long Island). Plenty of "Foley is God" signs out there. To this point I feel Mick's best match in the business was his classic with Shawn Michaels at *Mind Games*, despite the lack of finish. That's about to change. The only beef I have with this match is that it should have gone on last, after the Rumble. Mick jaws away before the bell, which Foley said in his book *Have a Nice Day* was actually him asking about Hunter's cologne. He does it very aggressively though. Foley was so broken down by 2000 that it's a minor miracle he can move around with the athleticism that he does. I guess he knew he had two matches left, so he could leave it all in the ring. This is reflected in his *WrestleMania* performance, when he'd been retired for a month and his body had fallen apart. This match though is all about progression and building. They start out on the floor brawling and Cactus takes a shot with the ring bell, which was enough to put Mankind down. But Cactus Jack isn't Mankind. Not anymore. He's gained a mythical power that lifts him above that. Hunter grabs a chair so Jack demands a shot with it and Hunter delivers. Cactus goes down like a sack of spuds, but he gets back up! They don't do much wrestling, they don't need to, but Cactus inserts swinging neckbreakers and backdrops on the floor, as if to pay homage to wrestling in an unusual setting. They insert a much maligned crowd brawl (in that I hate all crowd brawls) but it's merely to get to a New York style alleyway part of the entrance. This leads to Hunter taking a suplex on a pallet. Much to Hunter's horror, he discovers a piece of wood stabbed him in the leg during that spot. Not for the last time, Hunter just carries on. Lots of blood from that and it's right in the calf. That would hinder the mobility of a normal man. For all the flak we've given Hunter, he sure knew how to man-up and work with pain. In order to push the envelope Cactus grabs his 2x4 wrapped in barbed wire, which gets a massive pop. As per usual Cactus bringing a weapon in backfires, as Hunter nut shots him and uses the 2x4 on Jack. It's vicious. The WWF has seen nothing this violent beforehand. Double arm DDT, but in a rare moment of weird selling, Cactus stays down for too long before pinning. Hunter rolls his shoulder while the ref is hiding the 2x4. "Where's the bat?" screams Cactus at Earl Hebner. Mick lays out Hugo Savinovich for not giving him the bat from under the Spanish announce table. Hunter then takes a 2x4 shot right in the noggin. It's a beauty. Hunter kicks out and the fans are already biting on the near falls. Also Hunter is bleeding like a stuck pig from the head and the leg. He's having to earn this title in blood, sweat and tears.

Like his hero Ric Flair, Hunter's blond hair is turning a shade of red as Cactus beats at his bloody head. It's a crimson mask! Cactus remembers his last match with Hunter and goes for a piledriver on the announce table to replicate that famous MSG win from *RAW* in 1997. Hunter feels it coming and backdrops out, breaking the table before the main event. It's at this point that JR spots the puncture wound in Hunter's calf and sells the hell out of it. He's been working with that for 10-minutes! Hunter sets for the Pedigree and unfortunately does it in line with the buckles, rather telegraphing the reversal. Hunter then face bumps onto the barbed wire… for 2. Hunter has juiced so much that the fans buy everything as a near fall now. Cactus Clothesline sets up Cactus to take a hip toss onto the ring steps. Cactus follows that with yet another knees-first bump into the ring steps, which makes you wonder if he was planning on walking after this match, let alone wrestling a main event the following month. Hunter, always the cerebral assassin, takes out Cactus' leg. This allows him to grab handcuffs and cuff up Foley. People get depressed at the sight of Cactus getting cuffed as it brings back memories of the Rock's brutalisation of him at the Rumble in 1999. It also ends the fans' hope that Cactus can win the title. Hunter goes after the ring steps but Jack manages to drop toehold him, in a superb piece of defensive wrestling. Hunter then wears him out with a chair, which creates a great visual as part of the chair breaks off and flies towards the crowd. Sometimes props can magically help you create a better visual. Hunter is far safer with his chair shots than Rock was a year earlier. As Cactus starts begging Hunter to hit him properly, the Rock runs out and chair shots Hunter so the cops can unlock Jack's cuffs. Now it's a fair fight again and Cactus's first call of business is to hit that piledriver

320

on the table. The Spanish table does not oblige and stays in one piece. Because it's not falls count anywhere Cactus has to take it back into the ring, and on the way picks up a massive bag of thumbtacks. Stephanie McMahon can't take it anymore and runs out to appeal to Cactus's sense of fair play. Hunter takes the opening and backdrops Jack into the tacks. Great sell from Stephanie on that. PEDIGREE! ONE-TWO-THR…NOOO! KICKOUT! This was outstanding business as the Pedigree was death and nobody ever kicked out of it. Hunter's one-legged complaint to the ref is brilliant, but as soon as Cactus is up a second Pedigree on the thumbtacks gets the job done. A brutal ballet that had a ridiculous escalation of violence for the WWF. It was a massive breakthrough for hardcore wrestling to see the WWF Title defended in such a manner. I know some purists aren't keen on this, but I love Mick Foley as a talent and this was his moment to shine in a way that no one else could. The match with Shawn Michaels was a demonstration of how brilliant he could be in the WWF's PG-13 environment. This is a demonstration of what was possible when the rulebook gets thrown out of the window. Hunter's selling and bleeding made the match, and the match made him.
Final Rating: *****

WWF Intercontinental Championship
WWF European Championship
Kurt Angle (c)(c) vs. Chris Jericho vs. Chris Benoit
[WrestleMania 2000]
Angle comes in with both titles but they'll be decided in separate falls, so the first fall is for the IC Title then the second for the European Title. You'd think it'd be the other way around but such is booking in the WWF sometimes. Jericho cuts a pre-match promo, which is as daft as he is but causes crowd adoration. Three way matches are usually a bad idea as they have kooky selling and weird psychology. Luckily all three of these guys are great workers so it's less of a mess than it might have been. The selling is still odd. Benoit goes to the floor early and spends a little too long there. It's all a bit disjointed and they might have been better off having Angle wrestle Jericho first, then Benoit and vice versa. Jericho takes the first big bump off the match, off the top rope and into the announce table in the same bump Foley will later take in the main event… only Jericho lands it. I like how Lawler notices that Jericho wrestles like a heel because he's spent most of his recent career as one. It's like Ventura pointing out Hogan's flaws, only Lawler is less creative. Angle demonstrates an issue with his finisher when he hits a back suplex and it looks remarkably similar to the Olympic Slam. The match is a mess but at least everyone executes their spots clean as a whistle, seeing as they're all top guys. Angle's suplexes are a thing of beauty and his learning curve is amazingly steep. It puts the Rock's improvement from 1996 into 1997 to shame, which is saying something. They run a nice counters spot in the corner as all three guys get onto the same page. Moments like that would proliferate later, better, triple threat matches (like those from TNA featuring A.J. Styles, Christopher Daniels and Samoa Joe). Chicken-wing on Jericho and he passes out leaving Benoit to save. Benoit tosses Angle into the crowd, Jericho is still out so Benoit finishes him with the Swandive headbutt for the IC Title.

Benoit goes immediately for another pin and Angle has to sprint back in to save his European Title. Angle goes up for a moonsault, Jericho crotches him and Benoit back suplexes Jericho off, freeing up Angle for the moonsault, which misses. Good sequence. Jericho gets the Walls on Kurt but Benoit saves. Jericho just about hits his double powerbomb on Angle but Benoit interrupts the pin with the rolling Germans. As the natural fatigue selling kicks in, they're able to structure a better match. The selling is more consistent. Timmy White eats a flying forearm off Jericho but Chris turns into the Crippler Crossface and taps out. There's no ref or Benoit would have been a double champion. Benoit's attempts to revive the ref crack me up. "Ref. Ref. Ref. REF. REF. REEEEEFFFF. REEFFFFFFF!" As if he's only staying down because he's hard of hearing. Benoit misses the Swandive on Angle and Jericho hits him with a Lionsault for the European Title, thus jobbing both titles off Angle without him losing either fall. The match got better and smarter as it progressed.
Final Rating: ***¼

Last Man Standing Match
Triple H vs. Chris Jericho
[Fully Loaded 2000]
This is the peak of Jericho as a babyface in the WWF as he's shown as an equal to Triple H and this isn't long after he briefly beat Hunter (via fast count) for a phantom WWF Title run. The opening shine sees Jericho beat the crap out of HHH and if there's one thing Hunter did well in 2000 it was getting other people over. Something he's totally failed to follow up on ever since. You look at the respect he gives Foley, Rock and Jericho in 2000 and you can see how it made them. Having people go over on your big stars is how you make new ones. Jericho got over because he beat Triple H up. Triple H didn't lose any popularity and if anything he got over even more because the smart fans respected him for doing the hard work. As for the marks, he'd have them forever because he's got a cool entrance and a cool finisher. It almost pains me to watch Hunter in 2000 because he was such a tremendous talent and yet he deliberately stopped being so. Jericho has an out, like Taker did, as Hunter injured his ribs with a sledgehammer prior to the PPV and HHH works that area. Like a bastard. There's a bit where Hunter rams his shoulder into Jericho's ribs in the corner relentlessly. It shows both his cardio and his aggression. He's a beast. Jericho takes such a beating on the ribs that you feel he's done, which is a huge turnaround from the opening shine. Jericho gets a series of hope spots culminating in the Lionsault, which gets knees into the injured ribs. Because Jericho can't catch his breath he can't stand. Hunter goes to finish with the Main Event Sleeper, eager to capitalise on the situation he's created. Jericho does a great job of selling how close he is to being finished with his rubber legs and his begging Hunter to kick his ass, if he can. Jericho manages a weak crotch chop; Pedigree!

The crowd loved the crotch chop. That should do it, given that the match has been suitably brutal, but Hunter played the cerebral approach and did the work. As Jericho starts to stir Hunter bails for a chair, pissed off that Chris won't stay down. He even chair shots the ribs, continuing his unrelenting focus. The escalating violence was a trademark of Hunter's best matches. Hunter figures a Pedigree on a chair will do it but Jericho goes low to save himself. Jericho comes back with a chair shot and Hunter bleeds a gusher off that. It's hideous, a massive cut and loads of juice from it, with Hunter once again sacrificing his own wellbeing for the good of the match. Now it's a total reversal as Hunter has the weakness and Jericho, like a shark, smells the blood. But those ribs are always a weakness for Hunter to exploit too, so the match goes back-and-forth with one aspect countering the other. The match had previously worked on a "periods of dominance" strategy. This new back-and-forth creates an exciting conclusion as the match is wide open. They duel with monitor shots but both survive the 10 count. Pedigree is countered into the Walls of Jericho and Hunter taps out but that's not in the rules. Jericho just wants to

> **FURIOUS ABOUT: ALBERT**
>
> I may be the biggest Albert mark on the planet. No one I've ever met that rated as Albert as highly as I do. There's just something about his enormous head, his hairy back and his funky dance moves that make him compelling viewing. Not to mention one of the greatest Intercontinental champions of all time. His victory over Kane on June 28th 2001's episode of SmackDown is celebrated to this very day. Albert originally debuted in 1999, as a two-year pro, cornering Droz as his tattooist. Albert bounced around in tag teams after that, always under-utilised, before eventually heading off to Japan in 2005 and proving himself to be the outstanding and capable wrestler I always knew he was. As Giant Bernard he won the New Japan Cup and held the IWGP tag titles with Tomko and Karl Anderson. He returned to the WWE in 2012 as Lord Tensai.

cripple Hunter's legs so he can't stand. Hunter gets into the ropes then realises there's no DQ so the ref can't break it. Steph realises that means she can interfere and jumps in there only for Jericho to slap her in the Walls of Jericho and Hunter has to save. The timing of that is a bit weird as Hunter has to recover his legs way too quickly, but then wouldn't you to save your wife? Hunter pulls out the sledgehammer but misses and he gets catapulted into the post. Jericho gets in one of those sledgehammer punches to set up a table spot. Hunter goes low to block it and back suplexes Jericho through the announce table. Jericho's defence for losing is that his head hits the floor after the table, and Hunter gets up, just, and Jericho stays down. Great match. Another classic from Hunter's 2000 run and Jericho's defining moment as a WWF wrestler, in that he was good enough to mix it up with the main eventers but ultimately he wasn't better than them. He was so, so close. Don't even get me started on his eventual title run where he took backseat to Stephanie and Triple H having marital issues!
Final Rating: ****½

WWF Championship
The Rock (c) vs. Chris Benoit
[Fully Loaded 2000]
There's a strange stipulation here where if Rock loses on DQ the title changes hands. Which rather begs the question; why doesn't Shane McMahon just run in and hit Benoit as soon as the match starts? Having these guys work together had a twofold bonus; it helped Benoit to understand "sportz entertainment" and what he needed to do in main event matches, and also improved Rock's in-ring because as WWF champion he simply had to measure up to Benoit. Rock's explosive in-ring is complemented well by Benoit's uncanny in-ring skillset. It makes for a wonderful beginning where Benoit and Shane bounce all over the place for Rock. Benoit's ability makes it easier for the Rock to hide his shortcomings as a wrestler and it creates a very good title defence. Shane's presence is a slight distraction and he sets up a Benoit belt shot for a near fall that you feel he doesn't need. With Benoit being a technical master, he could just outwrestle Rock. Indeed he seems to counter pretty much everything into suplexes before hooking the Sharpshooter. Rock makes the ropes but Shane interferes again by lowbridging Rock to the floor. The timing was flawless on it with Shane leaping into position at the last half second. Rock responds to the leg work with his own and a figure four. Mirroring has always been a good wrestling strategy but Rock's approach is more like "an eye for eye" keeping himself creative in the process. The Rock's energy combines well with Benoit's workmanlike approach and this is a great main event because of it.

Hunter had introduced violence into the main events and blood to distinguish his stuff from Austin's arena covering brawls. Rock distinguished his main events by having them take place at frenetic pace and actually delivering in the ring, not around it. Rock has a few moments where spots appear to be on the verge of going wrong because of the complexity or the difficulty levels involved, but everything ends up working. Chalk that up to Benoit being a ring general. It makes you wonder why WCW never pushed him like this. Benoit can't talk and has very little charisma but he's a machine in the ring so he's suited to facing off with charismatic babyfaces like the Rock. Spinebuster sets up the People's Elbow but Shane distracts the ref on the pin and Benoit kicks out. As the spots continue you can see Benoit slowly coaching the Rock into the bigger spots, making sure nothing goes wrong and yet keeping the pace of the match high. It's masterful stuff and Rock really does a terrific job of keeping up. It's smart, hard work. Benoit brings a chair in but Rock steals it. Shane sneaks in and bashes the ref in the back, making the ref believe the Rock did it, which is again well-timed stuff from all involved. Rock gets the Crossface on Benoit but the ref calls for the bell. Rock thinks he's won by submission but the ref announces Benoit wins via DQ and is the new champion. Benoit celebrates with Shane and the belt and, like Jericho before him, there's a bittersweet moment where he thinks he's the champion. The WWF sure liked messing with these guys in 2000. Rock blades after the bell, courtesy of a Shane chair shot, but out comes commissioner Mick Foley to straighten everything out and he orders the match to continue. The fans who'd been pelting the ring with Styrofoam cups are able to settle down again. Benoit gets the rolling Germans to set up the Crippler Crossface but Rock survives. The timing on Rock dragging himself into the ropes wasn't right at all. It didn't feel like there was any tension behind it despite Rock bleeding all over Benoit's arm. Rock Bottom out of nowhere wins it and rather takes away all the hard work of the previous 20-minutes. However it was still a hard fought contest and one of Rock's best singles matches to this point.
Final Rating: ****¼

TLC Match
WWF Tag Team Championship
Edge & Christian (c) vs. The Hardy Boyz vs. The Dudleys
If Shawn Michaels and Razor Ramon set new standards for spectacular gimmick bouts with their ladder matches together in 1994 and 1995, then Edge, Christian, the Hardy Boyz and the Dudley Boyz raised the bar to previously unimaginable heights at the turn of the century with their incredible table, ladder and chair-based stunt festivals. Unofficially kicking off in October 1999 when doubles ladder match put Edge, Christian and the Hardys on the map at *No Mercy '99*, the Dudleys were added to the mix for a sensational triple team ladder bout that stole the show at the otherwise meek *WrestleMania 2000*. Since then, the Dudleys have introduced regular table-smashing to WWF audiences, while "chair expertise" has been crowbarred in as the speciality of Edge & Christian, giving each tandem a foreign object-based gimmick. And now, for the very first time, those elements are about to come to a head, and the results are *spectacular*...

One of the many great things about the match is how it

escalates in nuttiness, the spots getting bigger and bigger and bigger as they go. For example, they throw chairs at one another before the ladders even come into play, and when they do, nobody goes crashing through any tables for a good little while. It's perfect that way because you "Ooh!" and "Ahh!" at each spot slightly crazier than the last, but they never feel like they're regressing at any point. Christian for instance takes a full nelson bomb off a ladder which draws very audible gasps from the audience, a reaction it might not have enjoyed had the tables already been in play. Jeff then gets pushed onto a ladder balanced atop another, creating a see-saw effect that whacks Matt in the face. On the one hand that's a great spot, because unlike a lot of ladder-based spots, you just don't see it coming. On the other hand, it's the same spot that caused Joey Mercury's nose to explode in disgusting fashion at *Armageddon 2006*, so I certainly wouldn't recommend it to anyone with a ladder match in their immediate future.

The tables are then brought in with Christian eating a 3D through one, usually a sure-fire match-ender, but not here. The Dudleys then stack two tables side-by-side atop two other tables, but Edge cuts them off with a chair before they can do anything with them. That's yet another great thing about this match because so often in these types of matches you'll see someone set up a table only to crash through it seconds later in the most blatantly contrived manner possible. Sabu was notorious for it in ECW, but here it makes total sense that the Dudleys would set the tables up this way since they had success with a similar set-up just two months ago at *King of the Ring*, where they powerbombed Road Dogg from the ring through two stacked up tables, and the fact they get cut off by Edge means you completely forget the tables are set up in that manner anyway, making their eventual impact that much greater.

I also think six guys across three teams is probably the perfect number for this kind of match, because it allows for two to four guys at a time to rest and/or stay out of the way (under the pretence of selling of course) while those left standing perform their next high spot. When you have more guys in the match (such as later Money in the Bank ladder matches with ten wrestlers in there), you'd see guys drop to the floor and play dead for lengthy periods after just a couple of minutes, having taken moves that weren't particularly impactful-looking, and it hurts the credibility somewhat. You don't get that here because you also have the advantage of passing off somebody's lack of involvement as taking a respite if their partner remains active. Simply put, the tag team format of the match allows Jeff Hardy to spend a few minutes selling the pain after missing a senton off a giant ladder through a table (on the outside, mind you), but also spend a few extra moments catching his breath even after recovering as big brother Matt goes to war in the ring. I also loved that Bubba moved on that senton since he got nailed with it once before, in the aforementioned *WrestleMania 2000* match. Progressive psychology at its finest.

Remember those four tables the Dudleys parked on the outside of the ring? Bubba clambers up the giant ladder (now firmly planted in the ring), but gets pushed off sideways by Edge and Christian, sending him flying over the top, through the tables, and ending up a broken heap on the floor. Absolutely insane, and how he never blew his shoulder or elbow (or both) out doing a stunt that risky, I'll never know. And that's not even the most ridiculous bump of the match! Lita runs in and returns fire by pushing Edge and Christian sideways off the ladder, resulting in them both landing balls-first across the top rope, and then Matt begins to climb the ladder in what pretty much everyone had pegged as the big hometown hero finish. Not so. D-Von recovers just in time to tip the ladder from the opposite side, sending Matt over the top through two ringside tables BACKWARDS. He could easily have broken his neck doing that, especially if he'd come down across the ringside barrier. Just absolutely bonkers.

You'd think that would be it for the nuttiness, but Lita goes to check on Matt so Edge blasts her with a stiff spear, her head landing barely an inch away from the cold, sharp edge of an errant ladder laid across the floor. You think about how sore everyone in this match must have been for a month afterwards, but they're playing with such narrow margins that even watching it back years later you can't help but grimace at how close they all came to doing permanent damage had they just been a couple of inches either side off target. Finally, Jeff and D-Von, the last apparent survivors of this whole incredible car wreck, climb up and each grab a belt, but Edge and Christian pull the ladder out from beneath them, resulting in an impromptu game of Hang Tough. D-Von suddenly falls flat on his back, leaving Jeff alone with the belts for the second false finish as the crowd just absolutely explodes... but he can't get enough purchase to unhook the belts, so Edge and Christian SWAT him down with a ladder, then climb it to retrieve the belts.

Just absolutely incredible stuff that built and built and built to the finish with the spots getting riskier and more intense as they went along, and just when you thought they couldn't top themselves, they did over and over again. Perhaps even better than that was that not a single spot was missed, nothing felt out of place, everything was completely organic, it ebbed and flowed like any great pro wrestling battle should... Obviously there'll be some who feel a stunt show like this shouldn't compare to a technical classic, but wrestling has many forms, and as far as those stunt shows go, this one was damn well perfection.
Final Rating: *****

VERDICT

What a tape this is. Four of the five matches on offer break 4* and two of them were awarded the full boat of 5*, with only the curious inclusion of the three way causing any head scratching. I guess they just wanted to get a match from the big show on there, but there was so much better stuff around in 2000 featuring all three of those guys, that they rather missed a trick here. Still, no complaints, because this is a collection of four truly memorable matches from one of the most rewarding years for in-ring in company history. Obviously as ever with these things there is little point in owning this if you have the PPVs already, but if not then it gets the highest recommendation.

100

TAKING IT 2 XTREMES

CAT NO: WWF827
RUN TIME: 35 minutes (approx)

James Dixon: "This video is not really about tables, ladders and chairs". No, it is about ripping customers off, because it is just a re-cut and reduced version of the *TLC Tables Ladders Chairs* tape that the WWF already put out. As you can see, they didn't even change the opening voice over! This kind of thing became commonplace with Coliseum Home Video releases in the early 90s, but I thought those days were behind us now, fool that I am.

We start with the Hardys and their pretend wrestling company that they used to have in their house growing up, footage we have seen more than anything else on releases in this volume. By my count that is an astonishing four tapes that have this on them! We then cut quickly to the Dudleys talking about how they broke into the business, and the same again with Edge & Christian. It's all just the exact same stuff as in the *TLC* tape, but with large chunks cut out to make what's being said less relevant and interesting.

The main difference between this and the aforementioned release is the quality of the tape used. It is absolutely deplorable. So bad in fact, that at times the picture is almost unwatchable. One example is when highlights are shown of the Hardys on *RAW* in 1994, which looks so overexposed and grainy that it is almost like watching white noise. Don't think that it is because the tape has been watched so many times or anything like that, because this is a brand new video. If I was viewing this for anything other than review purposes, I would be livid.

It seems almost pointless going over what the contents of this offering are, because I have already gone over it in detail on the TLC tape, and I am loathe to repeat myself. It's just a far shorter, far poorer quality version of that. It harks back to some of the releases we came across in *The Complete WWF Video Guide Volume #3*, where tapes would be released with chopped up cut and paste footage from prior releases, with incredibly lazy editing from Coliseum Home Video that would result in the graphics and commentary from the original source being retained, thus confusing and confounding viewers when what appeared on screen didn't match up with the tape they thought they were watching.

One thing I will say is that this was originally a Blockbuster exclusive in the United States, and intended as a teaser of sorts I guess, but why does a 55-minute video need a 35-minute version!? It's like releasing a movie with a chunk of it cut out, filming it off TV with a cheap camera from the 80s and then giving it a completely different name and claiming it is a whole new movie entirely.

Hang about; new footage! At the end they have tacked on a few extra comments that didn't make TLC, from Jerry Lawler (wearing an XFL shirt) and Jim Ross (speaking only in his idiosyncrasies and catchphrases), as well as Bubba Dudley saying TLC at *SummerSlam 2000* can't be topped. Well, there was TLC II at *WrestleMania X-Seven* but it is down to personal taste whether you think it is better than the original.

VERDICT

A deplorable release, cashing in on the popularity of the guys involved and of the spot matches they were doing. I would have loved to have been in the room when they were discussing this tape at one of the merchandise meetings, because I can't even imagine the pitch. I guess it was: "Hey Vince, you want to make some extra money by rc cutting a release we put out a few months back and putting it on super cheap, low quality tape?" "Sure pal, let's do it". Don't even consider getting this in order to expand and complete your collection. Leave a gap, you will feel less violated if you do.

0

RIC FLAIR

HITS AND DISSES

CAT NO: WWF843
RUN TIME: 40 minutes (approx)

Arnold Furious: This is a strange tape. It was only ever sold in the USA. It barely covers anything at all, just the first four months of 2001, and it's only 40-minutes long. It's one of those tiresome tapes that needs tracking down for the book but serves no purpose in the big scheme of things. With DVD already taking over the home entertainment market, tapes like this were increasingly pointless. Who buys a 40-minute tape anyway? Well, I did obviously, but I had to. Host is the Coach.

Kurt Angle vs. Triple H
Angle comes into this segment as the champion. Triple H, Stephanie, Vince and Trish Stratus all come into play in an intertwining storyline, which exemplified Steph's best booking. The video comes across as a shill package for the PPV match but does capture what was so good about it, with Angle eventually picking Trish to corner him to offset Steph and upset Hunter. We skip ahead to the *Royal Rumble*. JIP with the ref already down and the match in its closing moments. Angle goes to use the belt but gets clocked with the Pedigree. No ref. Steve Austin runs down to kick Hunter's ass, thus building tension for their *No Way Out* match (which doesn't appear on the tape at all). Hunter gets smacked with the WWF Title belt, which causes him to blade. Stunner! Earl Hebner crawls across the ring and slowly counts three. I'm actually shocked, even though I've seen this match a couple of times, that it's not a false finish because of how slow Hebner moved.

Having Fun
Rock calls Kevin Kelly a hermaphrodite. Kaientai do their EVIL bit ("by the power of Greyskull"). Edge & Christian make fun of the Dudleys. Jericho's "I will fight Chris Benoit on a boat" bit follows. Christian and Edge do the reverse Kaientai bit where their voices are dubbed in Japanese. Rock goes off on a tangent about Hunter's mother and all the "sailors and circus midgets that have been having their way with her". Rock finishes the segment by calling Steph a whore, albeit beeped out. I'm not sure what the point of this was. Very brisk segment.

Family Business
We see clips of Trish goofing around with Vince McMahon, which leads to Vince McMahon & Trish Stratus vs. William Regal & Stephanie McMahon in a mixed tag. Regal leaves Steph high and dry against Vince. Regal brings in a bucket full of stuff he'd cleaned up off the locker room floor (hepatitis?). "Yeah, BOOOOOOOOY" says Vince as he mixes it up. Vince then turns on Trish, they beat her down and poor Trish gets mop water slapped all over her. "There's only one Daddy's Little Girl". This is what it's like inside Vince McMahon's brain. It's terrifying.

Kurt Angle vs. The Rock
Rock beat Big Show to set this up. Rock's promo work, as always, is exemplary. His hype videos feature a lot of very solid delivery and not so many catchphrases. Forward to the match and Rock kicks out of the Olympic Slam. Rock's normal approach is railroaded by Angle going to the leg. They botch the finish with Angle not kicking out of the Rock Bottom but Hebner saying he did anyway. I honestly have no idea why they do that as Rock finishes right away with the Rock Bottom. This clip didn't do the match justice at all, as it showed the worst part of it! Why would you show the botched finish?

WCW Purchase
We get the promo where Vince is simulcast on WWF *RAW* and WCW *Nitro*. Vince tells us he'll sign the contract at *WrestleMania* with Ted Turner himself bringing the papers, as Ted was begging him to buy WCW. "WCW is buried and will remain buried" says Vince. And that's a shoot! Shane McMahon appears on *Nitro*, with the *Nitro* logo next to his name, and it still gives me chills. It was a great idea but they never followed through on it. Shane announces he's bought WCW from under Vince's nose. This leads into Vince vs. Shane at *WrestleMania*, which is a superbly well booked match considering it was McMahon vs. McMahon. Zombie Linda makes me laugh too. Shane's insistence at going coast to coast, a'la RVD's Van Terminator, pops the hell out of the crowd. I wonder what they'd have done as a finish if he'd missed? Unlike Angle-Rock, this was actually a representation of the best part of the match.

Austin's Heel Turn
We get the finish from *WrestleMania X-Seven* where Austin turned heel before moving on to the next night and the

THE NEW WORLD ORDER

formation of the Two-Man Power Trip. You can almost sense the fun disappearing from the booking. Coach points out the turn made no sense as it took away what made him 'Stone Cold'. How very perceptive of him, maybe he should have been booking the show. Hardly any footage here.

Disses!
Christian gets the name of a town wrong. Angle claims he's the most requested sperm donor in Pittsburgh history. Vince takes a series of shots at Los Angeles, calling them phonies. Edge & Christian do the fat Elvis gimmick in Memphis. Angle disses Texas. "Lone Star State, my ass".

Kurt Angle vs. Shane McMahon
Angle was planning on recreating his gold medal ceremony but he's interrupted by Shane McMahon and "the WCW". Angle gets pissed off with Shane's mockery and Angle Slams him. Shane continues to make fun of Angle, so the Olympic hero challenges him to a street fight. No footage of the street fight appears, which is just bizarre, and renders this pointless.

WCW Invasion
Mike Awesome takes the Hardcore Title off Rhyno as WCW begin to sneak into WWF territory. JR treating the Hardcore Title as important makes me laugh. Vince is more irate that a WCW guy was in Madison Square Garden. Booker T calls Austin out to WWF New York so Austin and Angle go after him. The APA stand up for the WWF backstage, which is also hilarious as Haku is standing right next to Bradshaw as he does the speech. Haku, who was in WCW about two months ago. Austin shows up at WWF New York but Booker has left and arrives at MSG to lay out Vince with an axe kick. The early booking was okay but it'd soon go completely down the toilet.

We go back to Coach who signs off, promising more hits and disses soon. Or never. One or the other.

VERDICT

This bizarre relic feels like the kind of thing you'd see on Saturday morning TV. A quick recap tape for kids and people with limited attention spans to catch up on the first four months of 2001. At least it's brisk, at 40-minutes including titles, so nothing outstays its welcome. I just don't get why it exists. With the advent of DVD as a format, tapes like this were destined for the scrapheap. It would have worked better as a year in review, but that would have required patience and effort. Even the most avid collector would question the need for acquiring this tape, but if they do want it they'll have to import it from America. Or, if you're reading this in America, you can pick it up $5 or less. Not that you'd need to.

24

MISC OTHER RELEASES

867863
874463
NW001
WF298UK
WWF9998
N/A

BEHIND WWF TOUGH ENOUGH

CAT NO: 867863
RUN TIME: 30 minutes (approx)

James Dixon: Before *The Ultimate Fighter* took the world by storm and changed mainstream perception of UFC from human cockfighting to a legitimate athletic sporting pursuit, there was *Tough Enough*, a WWF and MTV combined production that aimed to create a WWF superstar of the future. Years later WWE opened up its own permanent Performance Center, which is basically just a non-televised equivalent of the show for aspiring talent that wishes to be part of the company. This taster tape promises to go behind the scenes of the first *Tough Enough* show.

There were 4000 applicants, and many of them were complete goofballs, as shown by an intro segment delightfully subtitled "The Rejects", which shows some of the videos submitted by guys and gals who didn't make it. From watching them, it is easy to see why. One nut job, 'The Custodian', a bald tattooed mini Steve Austin wannabe, beats the piss out of someone for walking on his clean, freshly mopped floor and then sings a song. Another, 'Vampyre', who looks like a fat Kevin Thorne, tries to cut a promo but keeps falling over and bringing himself to mischief on the mic. Another girl holds her nose open into the camera and says he wants to be a superstar so she can fix her face. Charming. A black guy with a stutter and a series of very noticeable ticks walks on the spot as he puts over his potential. A chick called 'Ice' clad in revealing silver lycra spanks herself and unconvincingly offers: "I'm always naughty, never nice". She then says she wants to "stupify", which is Disturbed's gimmick. Another dude beats up his mom with a full nelson...

Out of that selection of arguments in favour of abortion, the WWF/MTV managed to pick 230 people for live trials. Many of *them* are the shits too. A blonde chick with fake Kevin Dunn-esque teeth and a pretend baby bump pops Tazz, but makes Al Snow roll his eyes. Another dude smiles a lot, then punches the ring furiously before turning into either the Hulk or a dinosaur.

Finally thirteen were picked, and we go through each of them and a snippet from their promos to the panel of judges, which actually includes KEVIN DUNN! Yes, the man who hates his own face so much that he won't allow a picture of himself to be on the WWE corporate website, agreed to let himself be filmed for TV! Wow, I bet that blonde chick from earlier feels like a total douche having done that act with him there. Anyway, the luminaries and what we learn about them from this are:

- Maven Huffman: a teacher who wants to make thousands of kids happy
- Victoria Tabor: who doesn't like losing because it "sucks"
- Shadrick McGee: who is unsure if he has a girlfriend or not, even though she is right there at the tryout and thinks they are an item
- Chris Nifong: who gives an answer that only an American could about having "found himself" and that he "knows who he is" now. The panel asks him if he is an asshole, and he says he is
- Bobbie Jo Anderson: who is happy to show off her body. Gee, I wonder why she got through
- Greg Whitmoyer: who has plenty of friends and doesn't need any more
- Chris Nowinski: who wants us to ignore all of his best qualities, but then remember them again, or something
- Jason Dayberry: who is roided to hell but gets blown up delivering his promo
- Taylor Matheny: who says she is quick, snappy and witty, though doesn't appear to be any these things in her promo
- Paulina Thomas: who is tall and can't cut a promo
- Josh (Mathews) Lomberger: who wants to set the world on fire wrestling. Yeah...
- Nidia Guenard: who wants to lose her pot belly and "get it on"
- Darryl Cross: who wants to stop his mom from working

"Poor bastards", reads the caption. We get footage of Tazz throwing Rhyno around before seeing him act like a tough guy

KEVIN DUNN

prick towards everyone on the show and making some swears at them for being pussies. "I won't ever hurt you" he says, then gives a couple of reasons why he might do just that, before footage airs of him apparently "shooting" with someone. Given that the hold is a top wristlock, I'm more inclined to think that that this is just fabricated for the sake of the cameras.

Al Snow is next to get the random moves highlight treatment, and he is very much good cop to Tazz's bad cop. He is a funny guy with a good sense of humour and is much friendlier towards the contestants, more like a fun uncle who gets not angry but disappointed when they mess up. We see some more of the training, and Tazz says he has nothing to prove and then stomps the piss out of Nowinski.

Talk moves to Maven's collection of thongs, which tickles Nadia immensely. She goes through his stuff to show Josh, which is a pretty cheeky thing to do. We see more of the cast dicking around, including a prank involving shaving cream and one of the guys farting during training in the ring. It doesn't sit right with Al: "It won't clear out! I'm starting to get a headache; it's like mustard gas!" he complains in his Terry Funk sounding voice. Elsewhere in the house, there is the inevitable sexual tension that you get when you put a bunch of jacked up testosterone laden guys in there with a harem of big fake-breasted, athletic girls. Naturally, with that, comes bitchiness and denial. As well as this, there is the usual cabin fever-induced heightened levels of tension because of everyone being forced to live together for weeks on end and also being in competition with each other. Nobody likes Darryl, nobody likes

Nowinski, some other dude is weird, some chick is full of herself, etc. It's all playground bullshit.

Triple H turns up at the training centre all pissed off and snarly. He cuts a promo on everyone, in the same style that he does on television, with all the additional unnecessary punctuation and occasional shouty bits. However, what he says is actually fairly accurate and good advice. He rounds on the guys for having been given an easy path to success, and says he doesn't care that they are hurting because he is hurting every day. His biggest issue is with respect, which he says has to be earned. He leaves out the bit about pushes, which have to be politicked for...

Kurt Angle discusses pre match nerves and then says how the contestants probably know more holds than 60% of guys in the business, because it has moved away from actual wrestling. He reckons that because the business goes in cycles (though, increasingly longer cycles it must be noted) that it will come back. Yeah... when exactly? This, in the mainstream at least, did not transpire. Sure, there were some great wrestlers in WWE and there will be again, but actual wrestling itself will never be the focus. It's a dirty, dirty word. The irony of Kurt then sharing a laugh with one of the biggest detractors and murderers of good old-fashioned wrestling, Kevin Dunn, is unintentional brilliance from MTV.

Steve Austin shows what a genuine, down-to-earth, regular guy he is during his visit, as he tells stories about breaking into the business. He recounts his famous "tuna and potatoes" story from when he was breaking in, before adding that these guys have it pretty easy. He lectures that whatever they do in life, they should strive to be the best at it, be it flipping hamburgers or wrestling. Sound advice. He then touches on his ring style, saying he has cut out a lot of what he used to do because there are so many other guys doing more impressive things athletically, that nothing he does like that makes a difference anymore. Again, tremendous advice to any aspiring wrestlers. Less *is* more.

Mick Foley, whose hair is completely unacceptable, brings his latest book with him for a cheap plug, and says that even though he is a New York Times bestseller he doesn't know that many words, but it's not about the quantity, it's about the arrangement. He says the same holds true with wrestling, which echoes what Austin said, but Foley does add that a base knowledge of technical wrestling holds is important to avoid stinking up the joint when matched with certain style opponents. I agree with that to a point, though mat wrestling for the sake of it that doesn't lead anywhere and only exists to kill some time does bug me. Rick Martel and Bret Hart used to do that all the time when they worked each other. They would have a long technical sequence at the start of a match and it would go absolutely no-where at all, and then they would go to the finish. You see that shit on the indies all the time from guys who don't know how to work and just want to "do some tech" to try and make it look like they are proficient and know what they are doing.

The Hardy Boyz and Lita tell their story, which you can learn about elsewhere in this book via their respective tape offerings. Matt does the majority of the talking, with Jeff appearing to be asleep while his brother drones on. Damn those Vicodins.

We finish off with Al Snow almost breaking down with tears of pride because of the way the final five contestants have conducted themselves and how hard they have worked. But they have one final test, and that is impressing Vince McMahon and Kevin Dunn over in Titan Towers. Vince's intimidating office returns to the small screen after debuting in *Beyond the Mat*, and Dunn actually gets a few lines here. I guess the lure of MTV was too much for him to turn down, given his love of all things in the entertainment industry outside of wrestling.

"There's nothing fake about this!" says Maven to McMahon, prompting Vince's famous hearty laugh. Vince and Dunn are impressed with all of the final five (Maven, Chris (Nowinski), Josh, Nidia and Taylor), discussing how invigorating it is to see their positivity and how proud they rightly appear to be of themselves for having reached this stage. I guess this wasn't all for the cameras either, because as well as the two winners Maven and Nidia, Vince also hired Josh and Nowinski too down the line. Dunn beams about what a good group they are, with Vince offering that: "The process itself, generally, it weeds out all the assholes". They continue to shoot the shit about the contestants, and an interesting discussion takes place within this as Dunn claims: "It's a young man's business" and Vince responds in agreement: "It really is a young man's business. My dad was right when he told me that years ago". As I sit and review this, that was 13-years ago, and as of 2014 the now 68-year old Vince McMahon still presides over the empire, with many observers of the belief that he no longer understands what his audience wants and that his archaic ways of determining his stars are not in keeping with what people are clamouring for. This whole behind the scenes piece with an out of character Vince and the usually never seen on camera Kevin Dunn is absolutely fascinating, and probably worth picking up this tape for alone if you are interested in the inner workings of things.

VERDICT

I am not really sure what the purpose of this was. It seems to me like a teaser tape specifically to promote the release of the main series box set, but it rather seems like a colossal waste of time. I guess the cheap retail price was designed to work as encouragement, but surely anyone even remotely interested in the WWF would already know about the show, and wouldn't need this to remind them. And what are the chances of any non WWF fans picking this up and deciding to give it a try? Unless there is a secret underground group of people hitherto unknown to me who always buy taster/teaser tapes in the hope of discovering something new that they want to see? Somehow, I just don't see it. Anyone who does pick it up though, will probably find it an enjoyable enough waste of half an hour, but don't go in expecting a great deal of actual content, because there just isn't the time for that. As a promotional piece it does work a charm and will make you want to watch the show, but as a standalone thing it is not worth the investment.

35

MAVEN

TOUGH ENOUGH - THE FIRST SEASON BOXSET

CAT NO: 874463
RUN TIME: 450 minutes (approx)

Episode 1: Casting Special

This double episode serves as an introduction to the cast of characters and details the extensive audition process that took place. First off over 4000 tapes were sent in from hopefuls, with the range of characters varying wildly. On offer from what we see here is everything from freakish bodybuilders to jiggling fat guys, with plenty of wacky gimmicks that almost make you ashamed to associate with a sport that these people also like. The whittling down process to get the magic 230 number for live auditions was probably difficult, but not because of the quality of entrants but rather how many really sucked. Some of the people who made it are still dreadful, and it makes you wonder just how bad the ones rejected were. Actually, if you watch the companion release *Behind WWF Tough Enough* you will get to watch some of those submissions and will see for yourself.

We meet the panel of judges, which rotates throughout the course of the day but includes the likes of Tazz, who acts like a jacked up tough guy prick to everyone; Al Snow, who doesn't take anything seriously and can be frequently found rolling his eyes with disdain; Kevin Dunn, the HoW team's least favourite person in the entire company, who has broken his self imposed refusal to appear on camera because of his hard on for the MTV link up; Michael Cole, whose frosted hair should be considered a criminal offence; Jacqueline, who ranges between taking things too seriously and flirting with the contestants; Mick Foley, who is surprisingly muted and uninvolved; and John 'Big' Gaburick, who serves as the father figure to the contestants but also the man in charge onscreen.

We get endless attempts to impress from the potential contestants, whose tasks include running from side to side in the ring and touching the bottom rope, jumping over what appears to be a child's soft play toy and cutting brief promos. Notable folk who didn't make it this time around include WWF ring announcer Justin Roberts (who sent in an audition tape), Jackie Gayda (who actually won the competition the following season) and future TNA women's star ODB. There are some pretty useless people put through to this stage, some so bad that I can only guess MTV allowed them there for the purpose of getting some amusing footage of them failing. Most don't disappoint on that front, and much laughs are had when a fat guy falls down and then again when someone equally unathletic struggles to jump rope. Some of these people are so deluded about their prospects that it is frightening. "There are a lot of dreamers" says Al Snow, which is being very kind.

After what feels like days the cast is finally decided on, and an unkempt Stephanie McMahon-Helmsley turns up to deliver the news. She looks rougher than I have ever seen her, like she just got roughly sodomised while simultaneously crawling through a thorn bush. The lucky 13 are:

Maven Huffman
Victoria Tabor
Shadrick McGee
Chris Nifong
Bobbie Jo Anderson
Greg Whitmoyer
Chris Nowinski
Jason Dayberry
Taylor Matheny
Paulina Thomas
Josh (Mathews) Lomberger
Nidia Guenard
Darryl Cross

Actually Greg wasn't originally part of the series, he was added as a late replacement for a guy called Tom, who according to Big "had a change of heart", though there is an alternative story that he was only 18-years-old and his parents refused to sign the required consent forms to let him do it. If that is true, then they are some pretty selfish parents right there. Out of the qualifiers, very few have what the WWF looks for in talent and some openly admit to not even being wrestling fans. Actually, thinking about it that is exactly what the WWF likes, because that way they can mould someone from scratch to do things exactly the way they want them to, without any of that pesky wrestling training getting in the way. After giving the contestants a luxurious house in typically snowy Connecticut, Big closes the show by declaring: "These guys have no idea what they are in for"

Episode 2: Welcome to the Jungle

The first "proper" episode of the series focuses on the difficulty of the training the guys and gals have to endure, made all the more difficult by the lack of experience any of them except Chris Nowinski have. It might not make a lot of sense to people that the WWF would hire a bunch of non-wrestlers and try and train them from scratch, but that shows a lack of understanding about the purpose of the show and the message they are trying to portray. If they hired a cast full of semi-trainer wrestlers, the hardships and difficulties of the training wouldn't be evident, because the people used would be used to that and expect it. Still, that doesn't explain the trainers' attitude towards Nowinski, who has six months training with Killer Kowalski under his belt. Trainer Tori lays into Nowinski for trying to help people who are struggling by teaching them the way he was taught to do things, and she snaps at him: "We are doing things the WWF way". That's all the more amusing as Killer trained Triple H, who very much does things the "WWF way". The rest of the crew struggle to get to grips with the basics, specifically the staple first thing that everyone new to a wrestling school is shown: flat back bumps. One or two get it, but the majority suffer from the same errors and mistakes that I have seen countless times over the years as a former wrestling school trainer myself. One girl, Victoria, is particularly bad at it and constantly bangs her head on the mat, resulting in a teary conversation with Stephanie McMahon, who thickly lays on the facade of being a nice person and offers a supportive hug. She claims she was bad at bumps at first too and was scared every time she took one. That's nice and all, but the difference is that it doesn't matter if Steph sucks, because she obviously has a job for life, whereas Victoria's entire existence in the competition rather rides on being able to do things like that. You wouldn't have got forced emotional nonsense like this from real wrestling school students, and as should be obvious MTV is all about the perceived drama ahead of the genuine athletic ability.

One of the WWF's favourite places for garnering footage on some of the superstar bios in this volume is the gym, and sure enough the crew head to Titan Towers to use their workout facilities. The highlights of the piece are the rotund Big giving some pretty in shape people a workout schedule, which the incredibly ripped gym rat Jason privately mocks, and Maven smooth talking the future Mrs. Levesque while they work out side-by-side on a cross trainer. The next morning everyone is sore and whinging about how much they ache, but the training continues with that oh so strenuous task: locking up. Apparently the pain is so much that when they all head to a restaurant that evening, they "pass around the painkillers so they can keep going". With pain pills being one of the single biggest wrestler killers out there, this is fairly uncomfortable viewing. Other than that, things have all been fairly pleasant and almost Disney-like for the contestants, that is until angry munchkin Tazz arrives at the crack of dawn to give everyone the worst wakeup call ever. He rants and raves at them all, refusing to let them make their beds or shower, and in the tirade he furiously rips a Goldberg poster off the wall in one of the rooms. "I'm a prick" he tells them before forcing them to shoot wrestle in a pigpen full of shit. He comes across like a real detestable little wanker on this show, but it's pretty clear that he has been specifically cast that way so he can be "bad cop" to Al Snow and Big's father figure "good cop" roles. In the midst of all this dirty frolicking, Chyna 2.0 (Paulina, who is very tall and shares the same square jaw and nasal voice combination that defined Joanie 'Chyna' Laurer) injures her knee, which Tazz dismisses because people in wrestling are always injured and work through it. Ever the sympathetic sort, Tazz then makes the shit-caked cast run a mile and berates tub of lard Darryl for not being able to do it. The episode ends with the sorry crew grumbling and complaining like overly dramatic hypochondriacs, after what has quite frankly been a very gentle introduction to drills and conditioning training. They should have sent them all down to the Power Plant to train with Sgt. Buddy Lee Parker. Then they would know the meaning of sore.

Episode 3: Jason Crumbles

The main story of this episode is the arrival of Triple H at the Trax training centre. He is all pissed off and snarly and cuts a promo on the cast about sucking it up and working through the pain and rounds on them for having been given an easy path to success. He talks to them in the same style that he does promos on television, with all the additional unnecessary punctuation and occasional shouty bits. What he says is pretty much spot on through, and he shares some good advice as well as doing some stuff in the ring with them. The difference in snap in his bumps compared to the shoddy efforts from the upstarts is very noticeable. He also demonstrates punches very well and helps the guys with selling them. He actually comes across as way less of a dick than you would expect him to be. There are times when he acts like a bit of an asshole, but in most cases it is justified such as when he rips into Bobby Jo for not being a fan of the business and questions why she is even in the competition.

Next Hunter outlines the perils of the road and throws out a few home truths about never being home: "Your wife, she's at home, what's she doing? Don't know". Well, for most guys yeah, but not for you pal. At the time maybe this was fair comment, but looking back it's pretty hilarious. What follows though is even MORE hilarious, but for completely different reasons. It seems Triple H was clued in by Tazz that one of the contestants had a Goldberg poster on his wall, resulting in this legendary rant:

"The question I ask is; if your biggest idol in this business is a guy that's been in this business for about a year, got everything handed to him, can't have a match more than four minutes, has not wrestled probably for more than three months straight because every three months he's got a hangnail, he's got a toothache, he's got a tummy ache and he has to take time off, then I wonder where does that mentally put that person? What does that person think about the business? Is it about what we do? Is it about telling a story? Or is it just about being a big jacked up guy that stands in the ring, is fed a bunch of guys who really don't know what they're doing to mow over; he abuses that. What does it say about somebody who has no heart for what we do? No guts, no heart. You get injured, you keep going. You get hurt, you keep going. I've had to be carried to the top of the ramp to go to the ring. I've had to be helped up the stairs because I couldn't walk myself to 'em, and I've walked to that ring and I've wrestled for 45 minutes against Vince McMahon. After he fell 35 feet on my leg, [and] his big fat

ass almost busted it; I still went to the ring. I'm not bragging. I'm not that tough. I'm no tougher than anybody else in our business, but I respect our business, I love our business. I put my life on the line every day for our business and I gladly do it and I will continue to do it until I can do it no longer. Not for the fame, not for the glory of it, not so I can get laid; for no other reason but than love of the business. And I'm not saying that anybody here can't get hurt and I'm not saying you can't go to the doctor. But I question the fact that when somebody has a poster of a guy on their wall that cant suck it up enough to continue when he's on top of a business, when he's on top of a company and they ask him to go and he says "I'm sorry, I can't, I've gotta sit home for 3 months", "I can't even make it to TV", "I sorry I don't like where the storylines are going so I can't come in". I've gotta question that guy's heart. I've gotta question that guy's desire. I've gotta question the fact whether he just thinks "Hell I'm pretty jacked up, so I'm as big as these guys, I can stand in the ring with em. As long as they put me over it don't matter I'll be a big star, I'll make a lot of money, I'll be famous". You gotta ask yourself inside; where you draw the line? When do you take time off? Do you tape it up and you keep going, or do you call in sick? You guys are all on the easy track and you have to earn respect in this business. It's not given to you, you earn it. You pay your dues. And right now you guys are a mile ahead of where you should be paying dues. You guys have the greatest opportunity in the world in my opinion to be in the greatest business in the world. Do not fuck it up! Do not throw it away. Because if you do, you piss on every single person who has come before you, every single person that has paid their dues, every singles person that has busted their ass, every single old timer that's fairly crippled that can't stand up, that can't walk; you piss on them. Every single person like Darren Drozdov who's a friend of mine that sits in a wheelchair and can't feel a goddamn thing from here [motions to neck] down, you piss on them. You either want this or you don't, and if you don't want it don't waste our fucking time".

He speaks a lot of sense, and hearing his views on the business make you like the guy a little more. It would be interesting to hear his take on things since being McMahonised and turned into a corporate suit. While most guys mark out for the appearance of Hunter, the massive Jason takes his home truths badly. He gets depressed at the prospect of not seeing his girlfriend and being on the road away from her all the time. The result is that Jason calls it a day because he can't cope. I should point out that he has only been with his girlfriend for three months, so I sure hope it worked out and she was worth it. Elsewhere in the house, people rail on Darryl for being dumb and Bobby Jo was being vain and stupid. Meanwhile Nidia and Chris flirt and then have an innocent enough looking "dunking" moment in the hot tub, that MTV edits like a rape scene, complete with slow motion and dramatic music.

Episode 4: If you Can't Stand the Heat

For the first time, someone will be cut from the show this week... or at least that is the plan. But then Victoria and the vapid Bobby Jo question whether they want to be wrestlers (with Victoria making some deeply unfunny jokes about taking a load of pain pills to mask the supposed agony, including a line about overdosing), and they question if they are cut out for this. I can answer that one right now: no. They end up both talking to Big at Trax, decide to quit. No cuts this week then. What the fuck did they think they were coming here to do? And that right there is the problem with the WWF's stupid recruitment policy of hiring non wrestlers who just want to be famous. Now everyone else starts whining on the phone to their family and friends about whether they are strong enough to go through with the show. What a bunch of ungrateful dicks.

Elsewhere, Darryl smells bad so Al makes him change his pants. He rants and mutters about it as he walks away, and Al chews him out for lacking respect. No one else likes him either because he is a complete moron. Later that night, Maven and Josh are dicking around and a candle gets knocked over and sets fire to Taylor's bed. Darryl is upset that he slept through it and missed the "excitement", and decides he is being left out. Oh Jesus I wish they would all just STOP WHINING! Oh no, still more to come; this time Paulina talking about her "internal emotional struggles". I hate this psychobabble bullshit.

In an attempt to stop more girls from leaving, Stephanie McMahon turns up in her limo (with a dude carrying an umbrella to protect her precious hair from getting rained on) to take the women out for the evening. Inevitably talk turns to clothes and then boys. The "boy" in question here is of course Triple H, who Steph describes as "really funny". She then tells a story about the Undertaker making her laugh in a promo when he said Triple H "screwed his way to the top". Oh man, that one is even funnier now than it was then! Her comments on the positive atmosphere in the female locker room as compared to in the past are fairly interesting (hi, Sable) and I actually quite enjoy this rare insight into Stephanie McMahon the person with actual opinions, rather than the corporate buzzword-spouting, over-scripting, pro wrestling killer. Back with the guys in the house, Darryl has heart-to-heart conversations with the other dudes, wanting to know what everyone's problem with him is. Chris Nowinski is excellent here, dressing him down for not trying in the gym while he is simultaneously running his mouth off about how hard he *is* trying, while also telling him that people "don't like cocky assholes". Darryl to his credit takes it on the chin and vows to change. We shall see.

At Trax the next day, a miracle has occurred!: Al Snow has a match on *SmackDown!* and the cast are going with him. He warns them not to be marks, but instead they all holler, cheer and hug each other. Yeah, get it out of your system now. The footage shown accompanying this feature from "*SmackDown!*" is actually from everything but, with stuff from *RAW* and various PPVs thrown in. At least being there at a live show does seem to have the desired effect on the contestants: they now all want to be wrestlers again. Well, it's about time.

Episode 5: Dispatching Darryl

This week, the cast are having a guest over for dinner; Pat Patterson. Nowinski is tasked with buying the groceries, but he overspends by $80 and asks the rest of the house to split the cost. No one has a problem with that at all, except one man. Can you guess who? Yes, Darryl is so cheap that he pisses and moans about paying eight bucks, which results in Chris telling him he has a "personal problem" with him. Josh thinks the whole thing is like watching two chicks fighting over a hairbrush. When Pat arrives, Taylor is in there like a whippet, barraging him with questions and listening to him intently, which gets her some criticism from Paulina for being a suck up. Pat doesn't say a great deal of interest, but he does share a few stories about mooning cops and singing karaoke in his underwear. Frankly, I wouldn't have expected anything else.

Back at Trax most of the contestants still suck at even the most basic things, with Shadrick struggling to flip bump, Paulina still whining about the pain of everything and Darryl making such a mess of taking a hiptoss from Josh, that Al chews him out and threatens to make him watch from the sidelines because he is a danger to himself and everyone else. The hapless bastard is still delusional and thinks he can win the show. In the car on the ride home, he complains that Josh didn't give him "a boost" on the move. What an idiot; you take your own bump on a hiptoss. The guy is just a lazy, fat shite who wants to blame everyone else for his physical shortcomings.

At the house, Big turns up and gives everyone the "I'm not angry, I'm disappointed" line because the place is a shithole and he says it is disrespectful, but then he laughs it off and asks everyone if they want to go out. They play darts with the stipulation that the loser has to do press ups on command for the winner while saying he is their bitch. Delightfully, Darryl loses. The next day, Big gives his set of push ups to Al to use, who he does so gleefully. It's not all fun and games though, because someone will be cut in 24 hours. The pressure of that and the physical toll of the workout is too much for Shadrick, who throws up. Darryl continues to struggle, and Josh criticises him and also the WWF's big man policy, quite rightly stating that if Darryl was his size and screwing up in the same way, he would be cut, but he is kept around because he is big. There are signs of improvement in others though, with Taylor specifically looking good out of the girls. Chris Nifong calls her a "tough chick" and says that because she doesn't have kids or a boyfriend, she has the drive to win the competition. How strange then, that things ended up the other way around for her and she wound up as the one staying at home while her husband was out on the road, because in 2008 Taylor married Brian Kendrick. Yes, *the* Brian Kendrick.

It's cut time, and the judges discuss each contestant. Tazz says Shadrick has two left feet and that Paulina is clumsy, though Al counters that she is "marketable". Tazz trashes Darryl for his bitching attitude and lack of skill, and realistically there is no other option than to cut him. When he opens his locker he finds a red ribbon that signifies he is gone, and to the surprise of no one he is confused about the decision.

Episode 6: Tears Idle Tears

This is the weakest episode of the series so far, as almost nothing happens. Once again Shadrick struggles, no longer displaying the personality and confidence that got him on the show in the first place, instead comes across more like a frightened rabbit that has been dumped in an aquarium tank with a shark. He has a "definitive weakness on one side" according to Tori, which suggests that he has one side so weak that it shapes and moulds his entire being. Personally I think he has a "definite" weakness, but hey, what do I know? Some beverages at transsexual bar Lucky Chengs results in frivolity, with Greg doing a strip tease and Maven getting all glammed up and made over as a chick with a dick. He is lucky that no one higher up in the WWF ladder was paying attention, because this is the kind of thing the proponents of silly within the office would have latched on and made him do on *RAW*. Maven's mom is amused by the story when they talk on the phone, and calls him a "fag". Sure, casual homophobic slurs, why not? Back at the house the crew all watch wrestling, except for Josh. Big asks him why he won't watch and he says he doesn't like watching wrestling with other people. That he ended up as an announcer on *SmackDown!* essentially watching the show alongside a TV audience of millions and thousands in the building, is thus amusing. What he actually means is that he doesn't like watching wrestling with some of the goons on the crew, because they sit and criticise bumping technique, botched spots and whatever else they have learned that day and thus hone in on like perceived "experts". Josh finds it disrespectful and thinks that no one there has any right to criticise professionals when they have all only been involved with the business for what amounts to a cup of coffee. He is absolutely right, and I like Josh much more for having seen him on this show.

At Trax another cut is announced, and they go into armdrag drills. Most of them really, really suck at it, over rotating and coming in sideways like they are hitting a twisting body press rather than taking a smooth, crisp flip bump. The supposed pressure is getting to Shadrick, who breaks down in tears. Al takes him to one side and gives him a stern (but not unpleasant) lecture about what real pressure in the business is, and warns that if he can't handle it here then he almost certainly won't be able to in front of 20,000 people. Things get worse at the training centre when little Chris gives up and half asses his bumps, and the attempt he and Shadrick make when doing the drill with each other is appalling. Josh on the other hand is entirely aloof about everything, because he can do it all with minimal effort. He cuts a figure of someone who is bored with the same endless drills of things he can already do and do well. At decision time, Tori says that little Chris worries her and Al doesn't fancy his chances. He would be cut for sure if not for the hapless Shadrick. He has a supporter in Jacqueline, who breaks down in tears when talking about him because she can see how hard he tries. Tough, this isn't *Try Hard Enough* so he is toast.

Episode 7: A No-Win-Ski Situation

The episode begins with yet more whining about the various injuries, knocks, bumps and bruises that the cast have suffered throughout the show, which doesn't paint them in a very flattering light. I wish this series was made twenty years earlier and they were getting broke into the business by Verne Gagne, Hiro Matsuda or Stu Hart. They would know about real pain then, that is for sure. This show is all about an appearance from Kurt Angle at Trax, who gives a long, inspirational speech and then shows them some stuff in the ring. He talks about his initial misconceptions of the pro wrestling business after coming off his Olympic success, saying he was offered a multi-million dollar contract by the WWF but laughed at it and ripped it up, because he still didn't "get" it. He then became hooked on *RAW* and realised that the guys involved were real athletes, not the con artists that the amateur wrestling community had drilled into him that they were. He came back to the WWF with his tail between his legs and was given a developmental contract and told he would have to do such awful things as jobbing to Al Snow as he worked his way towards the main roster. What he does add, commendably, is that if given the choice he would take the harder second route, because it made him respect the business. That's kind of ironic when he is talking to a bunch of people who are vying for exactly that easy route into the industry.

Kurt carries on the theme of respect, talking about his time spent working in Memphis for seven months that would see him work dark matches in the WWF two days a week, train in developmental five days a week and wrestle in Memphis on the evenings. Angle then puts over the way he was trained as the best route into the business and almost buries other training schools and working the indies, which is perplexing. The biggest and best stars that the WWF/E have had have always had a solid background paying their dues and working around the circuit (The Rock aside, but he was born into the business).

Everyone from Hulk Hogan (AWA), Steve Austin (WCW), Bret Hart (Stampede), Eddie Guerrero (Various), Undertaker (WCW), Mick Foley (Various), C.M. Punk (ROH), Daniel Bryan (ROH), Randy Savage (ICW), Ted DiBiase (Mid-South) and an almost endless list of others in the pre-Performance Center days learned their craft on the road. It was and remains the best way to come into the industry and learn it properly and learn to respect it, regardless of what Angle or the WWF think.

Kurt then throws out a zinger: "If you train too hard, you wear yourself down" he says, warning the guys to not go too full-on in training because they should save their big bumping for major matches. Al's look at Kurt is utterly priceless. Kurt might has well have taken a curled steaming dump in his mouth. Angle next talks working out and says that he now trains to look good rather than for conditioning, because looks are obviously key in the WWF. Chris Nowinski raises Tazz's ire by implying that he is looking for a quick route to the top like Kurt, and he gets chewed out. Tazz says that Kurt is a unique guy and there aren't many like him, and that he paid his dues still in his own way. It's a fair point from the angry little one; none of these other fuckers have a gold medal.

Angle's jumps in the ring and takes some armdrags, which like when Triple H did some bumping a few weeks back, puts the trainees to shame. The crew then get given a treat and taken to somewhere called "Paradise Island" is the Bahamas! Pfft. This isn't wrestling training. Josh amuses everyone by playing a little wooden flute over and over again, but Nowinski is the exception and stays out of the way because he is focused and determined to succeed and has no time for silliness. Miserable and grumpy more like. Meanwhile, Paulina is STILL whining about her hurt knee. Kurt should have told how he won a gold medal with a broken neck.

Back at the house, Nowinski lets his guard down for the first time and gets inebriated, and in his drunken stupor he tries to intimidate Josh with his size. Josh doesn't back down or even flinch, and indeed tries to provoke him further. He has far more personality on this series than he was ever allowed to show on WWE television. Further issues surrounding Nowinski arise when the housemates do a draw to see which two will be allowed to have visitors. Greg is one of the lucky ones, but sells his to Nowinski because his girlfriend is scheduled to have surgery on that date. He later finds out that it has been pushed back, but the deal has already been made. Greg wants it back but Nowinski staunchly refuses to budge on the deal. In the end Greg does the right thing and lives up to his promise. Hey, a deal is a deal.

Paulina visits two doctors regarding her knee injury, and an MRI reveals that it is partially broken, partially torn and also sprained, and she is left to contemplate her future in the competition. Many have worked with much worse, and it doesn't need surgery so why is it even a question? Opportunities like this doesn't come around very often. In keeping with the lack of heart, determination and drive shown by others on this show already, she bails out. "I would love to give it a shot when I'm 100% again. I could see myself becoming a superstar, I really could". Swing and a miss.

Episode 8: Dropping Like Flies

We are told things are getting tougher now, and as far as I am concerned it is about time. Nidia and Taylor are the last two girls standing, with ALL of the others having bailed because they weren't cut out for it. Slam drills are the order of the day, and before they commence Al pre warns everyone that they are now responsible for the other person's body because they are picking them up in the air, so they have to be extra careful. Given most can barely bump an armdrag, this is a risky session. Al goes around and slams everyone to show them technique, yet despite them being safe as houses bumps somehow Josh and Nidia still manage to get injured. With the recent spate of injuries, bangs and knocks, Al senses the group are losing a little desire and he gathers them up for a talk. He tells them that injuries like this are not uncommon and no different to any other school he has taught, and that this kind of thing is just part and parcel of the industry. Despite this, Nidia still whinges about being hurt (she has what appears to be a banged shin), and she says her options are to either sit out and watch or carry on and work through the pain. She chooses the former, of course. Nidia then has the cheek to complain about Taylor getting ahead of her in the training! Later on back at the house she sobs quietly as she ices her leg, claiming to be on the verge of a breakdown. The next day it gets even more dramatic as she uses crutches to walk. Oh, come on!

At Trax, the Hardys and Lita are there to offer advice, and they have ladders in the ring with them. Maybe they will be learning career shortening ladder bumps as part of their training today... Matt does pretty much all the talking, primarily because he is the gobshite of the two but also because Jeff is permanently bored unless he is satisfying his adrenaline junkie side. Matt asks if they are all diehard wrestling fans, and Taylor pulls a face that loses her some points in my book. Lita talks about thinking the business was B.S before she got involved and that she disparaged it with the usual "it's all fake" crap that non fans love to bandy around, but adds that a bulb went off and she now, get this, understands psychology. Hmm. Josh, who is a big Hardy Boyz mark, is gutted that he has to sit out of the ring session with the trio because of his injury, and reveals in his talking head interview that he disappeared to the bathroom to cry. After the Hardys have bumped around with the class for a while and hit some of their trademark spots to amuse themselves, Matt breaks the news to them that: "When you get in the WWF, you'll never have a day where you're completely healthy" before adding that you get used to it and it's amazing how much you can do while banged up. Taylor thinks the Hardys and Lita are the most motivational and inspirational visitors yet, which I'm sure thrilled Trips.

Next to join the injury list; Greg. He does an armdrag and twists his back, reinjuring a previously herniated disc. He breaks down crying when talking to Al about it, who is out of ideas because working through injuries is one thing but having pre existing ones on top is a whole new ballgame. Al gives Greg a hug and warmly tells him "It's not over yet". The fatherly love continues as Nidia gets over with Al by (finally) working through her injury and doing extra workouts off her own bat that don't hurt her leg, which he says shows heart. It does, but she was still a baby about it earlier, and is only now working through it because Taylor is running far ahead of her and she will be out of the game if she doesn't. Nidia and Taylor end up having a match and Nidia does very well in it, leading the bout and generally showing marked improvement and displaying signs that her game as been "upped".

We end on a cliff-hanger, with Greg (who missed the latest Trax session because he was being seen by doctors) returning and giving the news that the doc doesn't hold out much hope that he will be good to go again in a few days, but he can't say for sure. "Let's not jump off the cliff yet" says Al as we go off the air. Tune in next week!

Episode 9: The Vicious Circle

Rope running starts us off this week, and everyone shows off their horrendous rope burn to show the cameras how much it hurts, though in reality rope burn actually looks far worse than it feels. Greg is still having problems and the doctor asks for his MRI scans from his previous injury in order to assess things further. He realise he is in trouble and starts to get depressed about his injury, which is out of character for him. He is one of the good guys on this show though and vows to fight on until he is specifically told he can't, because he realises just what a big opportunity this is.

In an effort to raise spirits, Al teaches them all the "circle game", which is a popular one amongst the boys. The rules are simply that you have to make a circle with your thumb and forefinger, and make someone else see it below your waist, and if they look then you punch the person in the arm. Al is a wily vet at the game and makes a bet with Maven about who can get each other the most. Nowinski eggs them both on because he wants to see the resulting forfeit (sitting on a plastic horse overlooking a busy highway while clad in lingerie) but Al is wise to his plan and drags him into the bet too. His forfeit? Walking around Yale in his Harvard boxers and nothing else, telling everyone that "Harvard sucks" and that they "chose the right college". To Nowinski, who is immensely proud of his Harvard heritage, that is tantamount to sacrilege. He ends up losing the bet after Al uses a Polaroid of himself doing a double circle and catches him out, and Nowinski has to carry out the unwanted task.

A few episodes after the draw to see who could have guests at the house, the girlfriends of Josh and Nowinski turn up. Nowinski's is a fellow Harvard alum and completely out of place in a house full of wrestlers. Josh's girlfriend on the other hand is an awful cow. Not long after arriving she decides the best thing to do in order that she support her boyfriend is to have a blazing row about him doing the show and wanting to wrestle, and generally acting like a completely unsupportive and entirely selfish bitch. "I don't care if you're "tough enough" or whatever the fuck you wanna call it" she tells him, before adding that wives of wrestlers have by far the worst life of anyone. This really does make her seem like a horrible and detestable piece of shit and is very unflatteringly edited, but stepping back you can almost see her point. Being the spouse of a wrestler or a rock star or someone partaking in any other similar vocation that involves a lot of travel and being away from home, is an awful and thankless task. But still, don't turn up on the show and go off on your guy like that when he needs to be focused and is on the cusp of something special. Her timing was shocking and in order to succeed Josh clearly needs her out of his life. Thankfully he did get rid of her and briefly married the very attractive Rue DeBona. For a couple of years at least.

Side note: Where the hell is little Chris? You know, the one who tried to "rape"/drown Nidia? He has barely had any camera time at all in the last few episodes. You could be forgiven for thinking he wasn't even on the show any more.

Back at home Greg is still struggling and he gets another call from his doc, revealing that he has in fact re-herniated the old disc and also a new one. He is broken and pretty much done, but refuses to give up. He visits the doctors again and it is revealed that he has yet another herniated disc, which amounts to half of his spine being knackered. "Can't win for losin'" he says dejectedly, and it turns out he has to go and see a back specialist and thus leave the show. See, this guy at least tried and tried to work through his pretty severe injuries, and he was forced to walk away, he had no choice. Al is emotional about it, but no one more so than Josh, who was very close with Greg and is obviously going through some emotional problems of his own thanks to his bitch of a girlfriend. He is devastated about losing his buddy. Big calls it "gut wrenching and sad" and it is. At least Greg carried on in the business and ended up fairly successful on the indy scene under the moniker Greg Matthews, working for the likes of RoH, 3PW and CZW. He was never a major star or anything, but at least he stuck at it through the injury and tried to make a name for himself. He is one of very few from this series who did.

Episode 10: Timing is Everything

We start with Chris Nifong, back from his onscreen wilderness for the first time in weeks, even though he has been around the whole time. He chats to his buddy on the phone and reveals his new nickname: CK. It stands for "career killer", because he is a klutz in the ring and keeps injuring people.

Over at Trax Mick Foley pops in for a chat looking as stylish and well kempt as ever. True to form, he has his new book with him, the great but not as good as the first one; *Foley Is Good*. He reads some exerts from it pertaining to Al Snow and Tazz, with Al doing a horrible Tazz impersonation to assist him in the process. He tells the wide-eyed students that he heard Triple H was harsh on them about the realities of the business, then almost dismisses what he said. Foley points out that while he did indeed miss some landmark family moments such as his kids' first steps and first words, that he is happily married and has been able to maintain a healthy family life. His advice on how to keep your marriage together? Avoid going out and partying every night with the boys because "nothing good can happen to you when you are out", and that the people who don't get divorced, read. A lot. Humorously he then extols the need for solid technical wrestling ability, which is true, but of all the people to say that, Foley is the one you least expect. He had a solid technical base himself of course, but he rarely if ever had cause to use it, especially as he became more notorious for his wild brawls and insane bumps.

After watching them bump around and work out in the ring a little, Foley tells the camera that the guys and gals have a lot of promise and he is impressed with them after only six weeks training, but of course he is going to say that. Amusingly, the next segment rather goes against that, with CK making another mess of things, this time when Al gives him a headlock takeover and he sets way too early because he pre-anticipated a different move rather than went with it. Al ties him up and for the first time on the show he loses his temper as he lectures him in the middle of the ring in front of everyone. Poor CK, first he is edited to look like a psychotic rapist, then he goes missing from the show for weeks, and now he can't wrestle anymore either. He is odds on favourite to be the next person cut at this stage. He knows it too.

A brief interlude shows Josh on the phone talking to his emasculating girlfriend, who cries about how much she misses him. I have no sympathy for her after the way she acted on the show. Someone I do have sympathy for is Maven, who gets word that his "mom" (actually his paternal aunt who raised him from a young age when his birth mother died) is in a serious condition in hospital relating to her battle against bone marrow cancer. Maven doesn't know what to do, but thankfully Big and Al allow him to take a few days out to be with her. Of course, instead of letting them have a private moment, the MTV cameras follow him to Washington and catch it all on film. His mom is in a bad way and Maven stays a couple of extra days with her before she convinces him to return to the show. She actually survived for another three years after this before finally succumbing to the foul disease in 2004.

In the house the mood is a sombre one, with everyone missing Maven and spirits on the verge of breaking because of the increasing difficulty of the competition. Josh breaks down on the phone to his girlfriend and says he doesn't like being in the house anymore and wants to quit and come home, but his previously unsupportive partner tells him not to because there are only three weeks left. She is probably shagging someone else...

Big is worried about morale and comes to the house to hang out and give a pep talk, because he is worried that the remaining contestants are quitters like the majority of the others who have been and gone. During this the camera zooms in on Josh's knuckles, which are bloodied from something, perhaps an altercation with an inanimate object. Big takes them all rock climbing to blow off some steam, and Josh demolishes everyone at it. He is like frigging Spiderman.

At Trax, CK tells Al and Big that he has "lost something", but he doesn't know what it is. Then how do you know you have lost it? He says he is quitting because he realises he is not good enough. He is right, but it seems stupid to walk away so close to the end. Delightfully, he then quotes Shawn Michaels directly and says he has "lost his smile", which tickles me for many reasons. I guess he doesn't get irony. The way his departure is handled compared to Greg's, is like night and day. It is incredibly understated, almost like no-one even cares.

We close out with Maven returning, and spirits in the house are immediately raised. He has a heart-to-heart with Josh and tells him that his mom isn't doing too good but he still came back, and tells him not to quit either. To put Josh's emotional problems ahead of his own pretty serious issues is a very commendable thing to do, especially when you consider that this is ultimately still a competition. He is a pretty stand-up and selfless guy all told.

Episode 11: The Rules of the Road

"I get kicked in the tits all the time" says Jacqueline as we open with the contestants botching some spots. There is a lot to get in to this episode, so we move at a breakneck pace with Al informing everyone that they are going on the road with him for a couple of days, which he is *thrilled* about as they will be at his side the whole time. Taylor's parents, who are dismissive and aloof about her choice to get involved in wrestling, are entirely unsupportive: "I think I'm gonna win" says Taylor to her mom, "I don't want you to win" says her proud parent. What a nice family. What is with the people in the contestant's personal lives on this show? Why are they all such assholes?

To the road then, and the group are introduced to the crew and help to set up the ring in order that they learn to respect everyone that works for the company and the jobs that they do. They watch the pay-per-view (*Backlash 2001*) alongside Al in the skybox, with him offering insight and opinion on what they are watching. I would be very interested to hear what he thought about the supremely tedious main event, but alas he doesn't say.

The crew head out to party, and stressed about her unpleasant parents, Taylor tries to drink her problems away and then rebuild her shattered confidence with a good shag, as she gets smashed and flirts relentlessly with Maven. Ever the gentleman, Maven spurns her advances, so she bites him hard on the arm. The next day she is rough, very rough, so a trip to Chris Nowinski's parents' house for breakfast is the last thing she wants. Nidia describes the experience as being exactly what she expected and calls Chris's upbringing "the Brady Bunch", whereas Taylor just vomits in one of the bathrooms. Classy bird. The visit actually makes her mood even worse because the environment reminds her of her own parents, and she gets all sombre about them again.

Backstage at what is assumed to be *RAW*, Nidia asks Al: "Are we gonna go backstage?" She is not the brightest. "You ARE backstage!" says a perplexed Al while rolling his eyes. And then, because it wouldn't be a WWF release without him appearing and offering his infinite wisdom, Steve Lombardi turns up and invites the cast to the pre-tape room. "I wanna see if these guys can cut a promo" he tells Al. "No, we can't" says Nidia, whose mouth often runs right ahead of her brain. She is right though, they are HORRIBLE at it, especially Taylor who just talks normally into the camera and rambles on about nothing, all the while looking like a scared deer. Hey, actually she would fit right into the Divas division... "I'm the human headlock machine" protests Josh when given the name 'The Sponge' for his promo. "You're the human headlock machine? Not in my room kid, you're the Sponge!" says Brawler. Josh cuts a pretty generic promo on Rhyno (all of these guys are thinking firmly within the box and cutting promos that you would expect non-wrestling folk to do mockingly), who then wanders into the room right afterwards and watches it back with him. They all have a good chuckle about it and the tone is somewhat genial.

It changes after Chris has done his promo though because it is appallingly trite and sycophantic, with Nowinski stuttering his way to ripping on the Undertaker and saying he will beat him because Al Snow trained him. Oh, Chris. Despite Brawler not two minutes earlier having told the room that "This is just as hard, even harder, than wrestling", Nowinski is still treated like dirt for his faux pass (and yes, it was an incredibly innocuous thing that he did "wrong", but this is the WWF and not a very pleasant place) and forced to do a punishment; ten press ups while shouting to a room full of onlookers (such luminaries as Tony Chimmel, Jonathan Coachman, Kevin Kelly, Al, the rest of the cast, etc) that "I am the Undertaker's bitch and I apologise for talking stupid". It feels like a ritualistic hazing. It could be worse I guess, at least he isn't being forced to shower with Bradshaw. Someone off camera who sounds suspiciously like Michel Cole shouts out that Chris should have to do one more for bad grammar, because it should be "stupidly". Yeah, who's Harvard now!? Nowinski to his credit recognises that he is bad at promos and realises it will be a problem for him. Maven on the other hand absolutely nails it with a very impressive promo that gets him a round of applause from everyone watching. He is starting to come into his own in this competition.

In a light-hearted moment, Josh buys a wig that looks the double of Al's ponytailed hairstyle, and he wears it to playfully mock him. Al and Josh are embroiled in a constant battle to annoy each other, and Al's reactions to Josh sending him up are priceless. "Stop it! Shut up!" he says amusedly through gritted teeth as Josh shouts at passers by that he is wrestling in the main event tonight, and then they walk side-by-side down the sidewalk, with Josh copying every mannerism. It's hilarious, and one of the most entertaining things on the entire show.

The crew are invited to catering to eat with the boys, and Tazz joins the guys and treats them... nicely! Instead of being the dick trainer like earlier in the series, now he cracks jokes and tells them stories, playfully mocking Josh in particular for being a "toothpick wrestler". The cast watch the show, which should by rights be *SmackDown!* with this being the final day of their mini tour, but it is clearly *RAW* that is shown. The footage used doesn't match up with what they claim in a couple of instances, and this is another. Al wrestles Essa Rios on the show (though on *Jakked* it should be noted, not on *RAW* itself) and the cast claim the "roof came off" when he came out. You would certainly think that from the footage shown, but it is sound-sweetened lies! Al throws in a few moves that the cast have asked him to do, and he even picks up a rare win over the no longer over Rios. Once they return home everyone is in high spirits and describe the couple of days as the best experience of their lives. And thus morale is back where it needs to be.

Episode 12: No Hill Too Tall, Nor Water Too Deep

With just a week to go, the trainers (Al, Tori and Jacqueline) along with Big go over the advantages of everyone who remains in the competition. Al is a fan of Maven's charisma, Tori says Nowinski is impressive to look at and in good shape, and while Josh isn't impressive looking at all, style wise he is. Jacqueline says Taylor reminds her of what she was like when she first started out because she is so determined, whereas Big claims Nidia is the more feminine of the two, which I disagree with actually.

At the house they wait for Big to arrive, but instead get Steve Austin! Oh and Debra comes along for the ride too, but who cares about her? He rings the doorbell but Josh dismisses it because he thinks it is a clock, and Austin gets pretty pissed off about being made to wait on the front porch. "Ain't you gonna let my wife go first!?" he curtly asks. Wrong man to piss off. Austin softens up a little once inside, but he comes across here as far more of a grumpy bastard than he does in anything else similar that I have seen him in. Years later he would head up the rebooted version of the show in 2011, which lasted for a single season (and ironically came under criticism for featuring guys who had been working for years and/or were already under WWE contract) and saw the winner Andy Leavine not even work a match for WWE afterwards.

Austin tells his story of having to live off raw potatoes and tuna while working for $20 a night in Memphis and claims: "My wife sacrificed a lot for me, and I appreciate that" before looking at Debra. Problem is they only got married in September 2000 (having first got together in 1998), so this is completely false. Obviously he was referring to his first wife, but the message to the unwitting viewer is that Debra was the one who made sacrifices for Steve. Debra shares her opinion that the women in the WWF are "candles" and it is the men who draw the money, which is true because of the way the company operates. Know-it-all Taylor disagrees of course, and says she will become more than that. How did that work out for you? Austin then warns against high risk stuff and specifically talks to Josh about making sure he keeps psychology and doesn't just do flips for the sake of them to overcompensate for his lack of size. I wish more guys on the indies would listen to that advice. "Seems to me like you all got it pretty easy" assesses Austin before he leaves. I wonder how many would have survived to this stage if all their food wasn't provided for them and they were paid a Memphis level wage each week to live on? I would wager none of them.

Note: This segment with Austin was clearly filmed prior to the last show, because Austin says he will see them Sunday (meaning the PPV) and Debra mentions that they have two weeks left to go, but at the start they said it was the last week. They can't get things past me with their creative editing!

After Josh has badgered Al incessantly to learn moonsaults, they finally get the chance to do them from the top rope onto a crash pad. Unfortunately for Josh he can't get it right, no matter how many times he tries he just keeps twisting to the side. Everyone else pretty much nails it right off, which bothers Josh significantly, because he feels flying is his forte and only realistic chance of winning. He says as much: "If I can't do the moonsault I can't win". I think it is based on more than that, but I get what he means. Later on they try the move again only this time with no protective pad, and Josh finally overcomes his fear of screwing it up and hits it right. Al is proud like a father.

Later on Big calls everyone up and tells them to pack some items for a secret trip, which turns out to be competitive trials in a quarry. Josh wins a swimming contest in a lake easily, and Big notes that everyone Josh is the most aware that they are in a competition and that because of his size he needs to try twice as hard as everyone else. Nowinski sucks at swimming and comes dead last, then bitches and complains. The next task is climbing a rock pile, and everyone does well apart from Nowinski again who takes double the time of Maven and Josh. "He handles it like a baby" says Josh as Nowinski pouts, pisses and moans. He tries to make up for it by brownnosing Big, but Josh and Maven don't care because they know the people who matter can see through it for what it is.

Back at Trax they are learning forearms to the chest when Ivory turns up and asks if she can join in, then throws herself around the ring with them all and gets stuck right in with taking bumps and throwing moves. Taylor gives a backhanded compliment about Ivory that she "isn't about looking pretty", but what she means is that she is a wrestler, and Taylor takes heart that being a wrestler and not a "candle" is a possibility after all. Ivory does say something amusing though, claiming the fans DON'T ask to see titties anymore while the girls are wrestling, which in 2001 was just not true at all.

Episodes 13 & 14: That's Not the Story / The Beginning

Live from WWF New York, hosted by Coach and Trish, this is the first part of the final! The camera pans around the final five contestants and everyone gets cheered by the fans, except for Nowinski who is roundly booed. Poor guy. Before the winners are announced though, we take a look back at the last few days of their experience, starting with a segment dubbed "The Last Supper" where the cast invite Al, Jacqueline, Tori and Big over for dinner. "You really are Captain Caucasian aren't ya? Jiminy Christmas!" says Al upon seeing Nowinski looking as sharp as a dagger in his finest bib and tucker. Everyone has a good laugh playing a Tough Enough board game that the contestants have created, which given the state of some of the WWF's merchandise over the years, I am actually surprised was never given an official release by the company. Later on at dinner, Josh once again busts out his immense Al Snow impression, adding a drawn on moustache to the wig and outfit. It is gold again, and Al is cracked by it but still protests that "I hate you" to Josh.

At Trax they work on matches, and Al goes through everyone's strengths again, surprisingly putting over Nidia's in-ring prowess, when from all the clips I have seen of her she looks like she is over-thinking everything, awkward and unnatural. Her striking is piss weak too and she still does silly things on bumps like over-rotating. Perhaps the clips shown have been unflattering to her, but to me Taylor is the far better worker.

The group get a major shock when Vince McMahon wanders into the centre unannounced, with lapdog Kevin Dunn by his side. Nowinski and Maven both sit there almost in awe and don't immediately jump up to shake his hand as he walks past them, which is not mentioned but is something I noticed right away. "I didn't know I had this level of nerves in me" says Maven. Vince and Dunn watch Nidia and Josh work a match and our Kev gushes about how they were trained from scratch in just ten weeks. In other words: "See Vince, we don't need any of these guys with experience learning their craft and doing different, wacky styles, instead we can make our own superstars from scratch and mould them exactly how we want them". Is it a huge coincidence that not long after this the company started hiring models, bodybuilders and other sports stars, none of whom had ever so much as locked up before? "The Harvard kid's got the size" says Dunn of Chris, and it is no surprise at all that he noticed that. Hey, it's the first thing the WWF looks for. Vince's assessment of Josh is amusing: "fiery little bastard".

Vince doesn't say a word to any of the contestants while at the centre and they don't utter a word to him either, with the show trying to have us believe that Vince spent the whole time there watching the matches, looking aloof and not speaking before skulking away into the night like a vampire, presumably. It is all a set up for the next part of their assessment: interviews with Vince and Kevin Dunn in Vince's famously intimidating office, making its first small screen appearance since *Beyond the Mat*. All five are nervous and conduct themselves with varying degrees of verve, though Nidia again demonstrates her slightly ignorant side by referring to Dunn and McMahon as "Kevin" and "Vince", which probably should be "Mr. Dunn" and "Mr. McMahon" to her. She probably doesn't even realise who they are... The interviews are a fascinating insight into Vince McMahon and his mindset, and he even shares some anecdotes with Maven and a few hearty laughs. Out of the five, Maven conducts himself the best and is probably the least intimidated of everyone, because he doesn't stumble over his words or run out of things to say.

Vince and Dunn are impressed with all of the final five, with Dunn over egging the pudding after each interview, throwing a side glance into the camera and then putting over the quality of the contestants in a hammy, overblown way. It is so fake and transparent that it makes you cringe. The pair discuss how invigorating it is to see everyone's positivity and how proud they rightly appear to be of themselves for having reached this stage. As Dunn beams about what a good group they are, Vince offers that: "The process itself, generally, it weeds out all the assholes". They continue to shoot the shit about the contestants, and an interesting discussion takes place within this as Dunn claims: "It's a young man's business" and Vince responds in agreement: "It really is a young man's business. My dad was right when he told me that a long time ago". As I sit and review this, that was 13-years ago, and as of 2014 the now 68-year old Vince McMahon still presides over the empire, with many observers of the belief that he no longer understands what his audience wants and that his archaic ways of determining his stars are not in keeping with what people are clamouring for. This whole behind the scenes piece with an out of character Vince and the never seen on camera Kevin Dunn is absolutely fascinating. "They are tough enough, how cool is that?" says Dunn in a clearly pre scripted line. Man, even when he isn't really doing anything wrong, that guys just annoys the hell out of me.

Back at WWF New York, Coach introduces all three of the Tough Enough coaches: Al Snow, Tazz and Jacqueline. Notable by her absence is Tori, who was unceremoniously dumped by the WWF just days before the finale. They could have at least waited until after show was finished before letting her go. She actually retired from the business following her release and went on to become a Yogini. Episode 13 ends here, though obviously this is a double episode finale special, so we continue on...

A match between cast and trainers follows, which Tori is included in. This may well even be her last match. There are some meaty bumps in this, with Tazz doling out Crossface forearms to Nowinski and Jacqueline clotheslining Taylor in the neck, but it is all in good spirits and after Josh goes over on Al, everyone hugs and cries in the ring as the reality of the journey being over sets in. The trainers get emotional saying goodbye too, with Al telling them all how proud of them he is and Tazz encouraging them to all pursue a career in the business even if they don't win.

Back to WWF New York and everyone is raving about Jacqui's vicious clothesline. "What was going through your head... other than your ass?" Al asks Taylor. She says she learned not to ever piss Jacqueline off and that she would love to wrestle her again, and Jacqui puts her over and gives her a hug. That clothesline *was* vicious mind you, especially for a training match. JBL would have looked at it and said: "Whoa, easy there girl!".

The female champion will soon be announced, and the cameras show Nidia and Taylor sat at their tables, with the ever ignorant Nidia chewing gum like a petulant child, while Taylor looks classy and attractive. We get highlight packages for both girls that show their progress and give a little background into both for anyone who hasn't been watching the whole time. Once again Nidia is shown making a horrible hash of a bunch of bumps, which suggests to me that she sucked even worse when the cameras weren't on and this was the best MTV could splice together. So, obviously, she is announced as the winner! I don't quite understand that, though I suspect her Puerto Rican heritage might have something to do with it. Cynical it may be, but that was an untapped market for the WWF at this time... Nidia bursts into tears at the announcement and is shocked, as everyone watching surely was too, but the waterworks flow even more over at Taylor's table. She is inconsolable, just devastated at having her dream snatched away when she was so close to achieving it. I tend to think she is more upset at having to go home and face her parents who will give her the "I told you so" treatment about wrestling. It's little wonder she ended up marrying a wrestler really; she was rebelling against her parents by doing the exact thing they didn't want her to do. Tazz interviews Taylor in the crowd and asks for her honest reaction. She says: "My initial reaction is that my dream is to be in the WWF and they don't want me". Wow, she really does have some severe abandonment issues.

To the men and after the highlight videos, Maven is announced as the winner. The look of disdain on Chris's face is priceless. Maven thanks everyone under the sun and dedicates the win to his mom and promises everyone he won't let them down. Al interviews Josh who says he will go home tonight and be disappointed but right now he is super happy for Maven, which is a commendable gesture indeed. "Well Tazz, I feel like I've been kicked in the face" says Chris, before promising to get the last laugh. And with that we end things, before being reminded that Tough Enough will be back for season two...

What They Did Next:

This isn't part of the tape, but I thought it would be interesting to have a look at what became of the 13 hopefuls...

Taylor worked some indies for a couple of years before "retiring" in 2003. She married Brian Kendrick in 2008 and did some work as a makeup artist for the movies *The Last Will* and *Lost Angeles* before moving into televised radio (yes, it's a thing) and working for a company called The Farmacy Venice, who specialise in organic herbal medicine and growing medical cannabis. Honest. **Nidia** was sent to OVW to tune up, a lot, before she made her full debut with the WWF. She is best remembered for her time alongside Jamie Noble, with the two being portrayed as trailer park trash, until they came into some money and began living large. With her gum chewing ways and her occasional airheaded ignorance to the world around her, the role fit her like a glove. Nidia was let go after only a couple of years with the company and she worked a few shows on the indy circuit, including for TNA, before walking away from wrestling in 2007 to become a mom and take up a culinary career with the goal of designing healthy foods for vegetarians.

Chris Nowinski is the undoubted success story of the group, but it took his wrestling career ending early through injury for that to be the case. Forced to retire because of ongoing suffering from post concussion syndrome, something previously misunderstood by major sport franchises and athletes themselves, Nowinski sought answers on the subject and researched it extensively before releasing a book about it. From there he began securing the brains of deceased sports stars for research purposes, including that of Chris Benoit, and made many significant and important discoveries in the field, then set about educating the sporting nation about the potential dangers. Far more than just a key figure in helping wrestling change its dangerous ways, Nowinski has become a pioneer throughout the sporting world. **Chris Nifong** ended up training with Crash Holly and was later asked to come and train at OVW, which he did for a year before calling it quits again. He later became a graphic designer. **Bobbie Jo** disappeared off the face of the wrestling earth after she left, having shown no passion or desire for the business whatsoever. She never did achieve her *PlayBoy* goal, but she did become a mother. **Darryl** wound up as head basketball and football coach at a school in Davenport, Iowa, but he continued to have some dumb moments on the way to that, including selling a fight with himself on eBay and once turning up in the crowd on *The Jerry Springer Show* and voicing some offensive opinions. **Paulina** worked some small indies and turned up in TNA as Disco Inferno's bodyguard during the early days of the group. She then got out of the business and became a marketing manager for pharmaceutical company Covidien. **Victoria** did stunt work until 2010 before becoming an "event specialist" providing specially tailor functions ranging from celebrity golf tournaments to corporate team building and training events for a range of clients. She also released a poorly received cash grab eBook about her experiences on the show in 2012 called *I'm Not Tough Enough*. **Josh** you should all be very familiar with, as he worked onscreen for WWE for a number of years as Josh Matthews. He filled out significantly since the *Tough Enough* days.

Maven is a disappointing one and his story is proof that the business really can poison even the nicest guys After getting pushed on the main roster and even eliminating the Undertaker from the *Royal* Rumble, Maven's push fizzled out and he was unable to shake the *Tough Enough* association and become a viable entity in his own right. He ended up released from his contract in 2005. He moved from wrestling into television and took up a job shilling things on the Home Shopping Network, as well as turning up in the final season of *The Surreal Life* and later ending up as a New York bouncer at nightclub Sutton Place. Things went sour in his personal life in 2012 when he was arrested for "doctor shopping" due to a painkiller addiction, and he checked into WWE funded rehab just over a week later. Of all the guys, he is the last one you would expect to see having such a fall from grace. **Shadrick** had a couple of matches for PCW based out of his hometown of Texas, then left the business and dropped off the radar. **Jason** became a professional muscle man and competed in various bodybuilding contests and some strongman contests. That was probably a given with how he looked. An impressive physical specimen for sure. Poor **Greg** continued to have his life ruined by injury when a bad car crash damaged his already screwed up back even further and forced him to step away from what was becoming a promising indy career that saw him work for the likes of RoH, cZw and other notably name indies. He had to call it quits for real and moved on to a job in construction.

VERDICT

Wow, what a mammoth offering this is, but it is definitely worth your time. While the business has since been exposed beyond the point of no return, at the time this show aired in 2001 there was still an air of mystique about things, and delving deep behind the scenes was fairly unheard of. Kayfabe was starting to fall by the wayside a little as evidenced by some of the tapes released in this volume, but nothing had ever pulled the curtain back quite like this. The kind of fan who craves insider knowledge will love this, because as well as breaking down the mechanics of the moves the show also gives us candid appearances from wrestlers out of character, a glimpse into the inner workings of the WWF production, more insight into the real Vince McMahon than any other program (or movie) and the coupe de gras: Kevin Dunn onscreen. Okay, maybe that last one is not so true, but the rest are, and it makes for a very watchable first series. Some of the contestants are unbearable with their whining and complaining and some moments do grate, but for the most part it is entertaining, especially with short 20-minute or so episodes. Definitely worth tracking down and watching from start to finish, though the first few shows might be a slog. Recommended.

72

WILD IN THE UK

CAT NO: NW001(UK)
RUN TIME: 60 minutes (approx)

James Dixon: Much like a few other cut price releases from around this time, the quality of the tape used for this is very shoddy, and the picture is very light and grainy as a result. Jonathan Coachman hosts this UK-exclusive tape, and breaks out the revisionist history right away by claiming *SummerSlam '92* was the first ever appearance of the WWF in the United Kingdom. What a stupid thing to say. Even discounting house shows that had been going on since the 80s, the WWF still ran UK specials such as *Battle Royal at the Albert Hall* and *UK Rampage* so it's just a patently untrue thing to claim. There is no reason behind the lies either other than misinformation, and it actually makes the company look foolish because they can't be bothered to do their own research.

WWF Tag Team Championship
Edge & Christian vs. The Hardy Boyz
[Insurrextion 2000]
These two teams are embroiled in a long-running feud, with their best work opposite each other coming in stunt filled ladder matches, which I am sure the UK audience would have loved to have seen on British shores. As it is this is just a straight-up tag match, and despite the perfectly acceptable quality of the bout, the crowd is unbelievably quiet. You might even suspect the volume of the crowd has been turned down for some reason, but it hasn't, they are just dead from a very average show. The exchanges are fine of course, but even the most basic heat generating methods don't work with the audience. It takes Matt standing on the apron and clapping continuously while Jeff is in a front face lock to get them to do anything, but even then it lasts mere seconds. It is typical London aloofness. As always with British shows, stemming back to the early 90s, there are constant air horns audible and they are unbearable. Silent, uninterested crowds and constant horns? It's like the 2010 World Cup. The match trundles on as if being contested in the AWA Team Challenge Series, while also sticking rigidly to basic and outdated tag team formula and using all the cheap tricks in the book. These guys are so much better than this, but I don't blame them. Jeff's hot tag to Matt is barely acknowledged. If I was these guys I would be taking all bumping out of the window right about now too and saving myself for an audience who appreciates it, but instead they do a tower superplex, which is an unnecessary bump on the bump card. The Hardys look to have it wrapped up but Edge uses the ring bell and gets his team disqualified, but they retain the tag belts. This would have been okay if not for the match-ruining crowd.
Final Rating: **

WWF European Championship
Shane McMahon (c) vs. X-Pac
[No Mercy 1999]
Manchester is a far more responsive audience than London, and they are solidly behind X-Pac in this confrontation. To compensate for Shane not being able to build heat because he isn't a worker, we get extracurricular from the Stooges and then Chyna. Shane dominates Pac far more than a non wrestler should, belting him with suplexes and back elbows and nearly sending him to sleep with a chinlock. He does bump impressively though, that is one thing about him that cannot be denied, and he takes a series of Pac's kicks very well. But his moveset is nonexistent, and further compensations are made for that with the bumping of referee Mike Chioda and Chyna getting involved with a belt shot. Triple H wanders out too, because every match in 1999 has to be throttled by booking. In the ring Shane tries for the Bronco Buster on Pac, but misses and gets caught with the X-Factor. Cue Chyna again, who smacks the referee and goes up top but gets crotched. She sells it too, further adding fuel to the fire in the debate over whether she used to be a bloke. At the time at least. Unfortunately for poor Pac, Triple H slides in and drills him with a Pedigree and Shane beats him. The post match beat down from the Corporate Ministry and save from Kane are left off the tape. Not bad stuff here, but it was very much a match that was "good for a non-wrestler" rather than just plain old good.
Final Rating: **¼

Queen's Cup Match
Chris Jericho vs. William Regal
[Insurrextion 2001]
The feud between these two rumbles on with Regal working as a heel in his home country, but once again the crowd are really poor. Once again, the show is in London, so it's no

coincidence. Michael Cole is especially intolerable during this with his cracking voice grating more than usual, especially when he comes out with his utterly nonsensical scripted toss. For example, the crowd cheer Regal when he waves to them and chant his name at various times, but Cole claims they are booing. Everyone watching knows otherwise, so why even pretend? It just makes him look stupid. There is really nothing going on here at all, with the minimum amount of energy exerted from both guys as they sleepwalk through their usual match and show little in the way of intensity or energy. I expect better from Regal in his home country, and better from Jericho generally. A long chinlock during the middle portion of the bout rather sums up the effort levels on display. Michael Cole sees something else to what everyone watching is viewing, getting far more excited than the situation calls for as he tends to do, before Jericho taps Regal with the Walls of Jericho. Because a trophy is involved and this is wrestling, the "cake principle" comes into play (that is, if a cake is involved in a wrestling angle or skit, someone is getting it in their face. It's like an unwritten rule and it applies for trophies too), and Regal smashes the tossy little Queen's Cup trinket into Jericho's head after the bout. Naturally, that is not shown. I found this unspeakably dull.

Final Rating: *½

WWF Championship
Kurt Angle (c) vs. Steve Austin vs. The Rock vs. Rikishi
[Rebellion 2000]
Joined slightly in progress from Sheffield, which is a far more receptive crowd than London. This had been a very middling show indeed prior to this bout, with overly long matches between guys you would rather see less than more of, and yet this only gets 9-minutes despite featuring four top guys! The WWF simply wouldn't get away with that in the United States, where a 20-minute main event is almost demanded. Midway through Angle decides he has had enough and goes to leave, which shows that his "three I's" are very much just a catchphrase, because he doesn't demonstrate any intelligence at all in doing that. It's not like he could be counted out, and he wasn't going for a breather either, he was heading to the back. Why is that a problem? Because in keeping with the horrible rules of a title defence multi man, he can lose the belt without getting beat. Dumbass. The crowd responds to the tease of Austin vs. Rock when they are left standing face-to-face in the ring, and they go nuts for them trading punches and Austin hitting a Stunner. Was there ever any doubt that these guys would be headlining *WrestleMania X-Seven*? Pinfall attempts get broken up left and right as things break down, and Austin ends up turning straight into a Rock Bottom, only for Rikishi to pull the referee out. Rock argues with Rikishi and gets caught with the Olympic Slam, but the referee is distracted and Rock kicks out when the count finally comes. Edge and Christian come out to help Angle as Rock hits the Rock Bottom on Rikishi, only for Edge to pull him out. Overkill is the name of the game as the Radicalz get involved, also to help Angle. You know what makes a champion really great? When he needs help to retain his title in every single match and he is presented as a fluke. The guy was a genuine Olympic gold medal winner; what issue would it be for him to cleanly beat someone on merit? Anyone? No, instead Rock downs Rikishi and Angle sneaks the pin on his fellow heel while Rock is dealing with the interference. Brief but fun, though I am not impressed with the finish at all.

Final Rating: **½

WWF European Championship
The British Bulldog (c) vs. Shawn Michaels
[One Night Only]
I am fairly surprised that this is on here given it is from a completely different era and this was during a time where the WWF rarely looked to the past, but nevertheless I am glad to see it because it's a phenomenal bout. We are joined in progress here though, which is a shame, just as Triple H and Chyna wander down the aisle. There is a huge difference in the audience volume here compared to the Attitude Era stuff, and a noticeable difference in the makeup of that audience too, which sounds like a lot of kids here. They chant constantly for Bulldog, but ask for Bret (Hart) when they spot Trips and Chyna because they suspect shenanigans. Curiously, there is no sign of the Hart Foundation whatsoever, which is really nonsensical booking. Necessary for the story of the match, sure, but it still doesn't add up. On the outside of the ring Bulldog goes for a running powerslam on Michaels, but he gets his leg stuck in the elevated ramp that the ring is on and seemingly injures himself. It is a clever spot, and is followed by a Sweet Chin Music from Michaels and a Pedigree from Hunter. The odds are firmly stacked against Bulldog, with Hunter, Chyna and Rude slamming the barrier into his leg and then rolling him back in the ring where Michaels removes Davey's knee brace and applies the figure four leglock. Michaels' buddies continue to cheat, and Davey becomes overwhelmed by the odds and passes out to the hold, though never gives up. As soon as the crowd realise that Michaels is the new champion and that their national idol has been defeated, there is a near riot. Garbage is hurled, people are infuriated and Michaels adds to it all by gloating. Diana Smith tries to help her husband when the assault continues, but Chyna pulls her off easily, only for the Harts to finally show up and provide backup. Where were you guys ten minutes ago? This match had far reaching consequences for Davey, who Bret says "gave up" and that the "fire in his eyes had gone" when he got beaten here. The intention of putting Michaels over was to either create a major money rematch between the two six months later when the WWF returned to the country (which would have been a great idea, though both were gone from the company by the time *Mayhem In Manchester* rolled around for different reasons) or as a way for the Kliq to disparage and get one over on the Hart family. It could have been both. I can't rate this here because it is only the finish and a thing or two more, but the full match is absolutely worth going out of your way to see.

VERDICT

This UK-exclusive tape release is in fact a very accurate encapsulation of the short-lived UK-only PPV shows, in that it features a bunch of very average matches and then one decent one, which was usually the case. I am struggling to fathom the purpose of this tape though, because is it supposed to be a teaser or a best of? Either way, there were much better options available, and I can only hypothesise that the match choice was down entirely to the runtime of the release, and bouts were chosen to fit. Of course, when the WWF turned into WWE they pretty soon stopped running UK PPV events altogether, so it's all rather redundant either way. Not terrible but not particularly worth seeing, like almost every UK event from the Attitude Era.

32

BEST OF THE WWF 2001 VIEWERS' CHOICE

CAT NO: WF298(UK)
RUN TIME: 137 minutes (approx)

James Dixon: This is a UK-exclusive release, which is a little strange because the "Best of" tapes from 1999 and 2000 were both US exclusive and didn't come out in the UK at all, but this is the opposite. The reason for that being this is just a direct to video port of a TV special that aired in the US on New Year's Eve 2001, which also got a Canadian DVD release which is super rare. The nature of the program makes it mainly just a recap of matches we have already covered, but there are a few extra things thrown in as well to keep it fresh. Michael Cole and Jerry Lawler host, supposedly "live" on New Year's Eve, with Cole looking extra idiotic tonight with his absurd frosted hair and confusingly thin bearded face. The format is a countdown of the top ten bouts of the year, and we start with this:

Ladder Match
WWF Intercontinental Championship
Chris Benoit (c) Chris Jericho
[Royal Rumble 2001]

Joined in progress, and I actually think this is slightly underrated, because it is a genuine classic to me. The brutality is off the charts, the innovation impressive and some of the bumps memorable. Jericho's octopus stretch on the ladder is unreal, even if Jerry Lawler does ruin it somewhat by commenting how Jericho can't win that way. Sadly Benoit's sickening bump from a tope through the ropes into a chair is not featured because it happened prior to the footage shown. We do see Benoit's equally crazy headbutt from the top of a ladder though, which must have been a sore one the next day. After bringing a chair into play, Jericho wins this tour de force when Benoit gets stuck outside the ring, and a new champion is crowned. Benoit was untouchable in 2001 until he got injured. With the amount of other guys on the shelf or absent for whatever reason, he may well have been given the push to the top than workrate fans had long clamoured for. As it is, it would be another three years before the company finally pulled the trigger on him. To keep things interesting, I am going to offer my own assessment of the matches featured on this tape that I haven't already covered in this volume, though please bear in mind that I am basing my rating on the full matches rather than the truncated versions that appear on here.
Lee Maughan Rating: ****½
James Dixon Rating: ****¾

Wait a minute; these are supposed to be the top ten matches. Surely they are in consecutive order rather than ranked, because there is no way there are nine better matches than Benoit-Jericho.

The Undertaker vs. Triple H
[WrestleMania X-Seven]
And this most certainly isn't better. It *is* good though, surprisingly so actually because the Undertaker had been stinking up the ring something chronic (and later in the year KroniK) since he returned as the 'American Badass'. We join this in progress again, starting from their brawl to a support stanchion in the crowd, where we see the Undertaker's impressive looking chokeslam off the structure that appears to have sent Hunter into a different underworld realm. But then Taker jumps off with an elbow and we see the nice padded structure that Trips took the bump onto, rather ruining the illusion somewhat. It's like watching a James Bond movie but with a blow-by-blow account of how the stunts were done appearing in a crawl across the screen. Back to the ring, Undertaker grabs Hunter's sledgehammer and threatens to maim him, but Hunter kicks him square in the cock. Would he have sold that when he was still a walking corpse? Do zombies even have knackers? A slugfest ensues with the referee still out bumped from ages ago, and thus he can't count when Taker hits the Tombstone. The fans boo, suspecting that Trips might well win this, especially with this show following *No Way Out* where Hunter beat Steve Austin to the surprise of everyone. Their suspicions turn to outright concern when Hunter blocks the Last Ride with a sledgehammer to the skull as the ref is reviving, but Taker kicks out. Realistically, this is probably the closest that anyone has ever come to ending The Streak. But obviously that doesn't happen, and a bloody

Undertaker manages to hit the Last Ride and score the popular victory in his hometown. This was a good fight.
Lee Maughan Rating: ***¾
James Dixon Rating: ***¼

Ric Flair, current "co-owner" of the WWF, wishes us all a happy New Year and introduces a countdown within a countdown: the top five surprise moments of the year. Is this one ranked? Too many numbers floating around...

5 - Is the merger of WCW and ECW and the announcement of Stephanie McMahon-Helmsley as the new owner of ECW. And that is the sound of the invasion angle doing a big, wet, credibility shattering fart. There was no coming back once the nasal little princess was involved. 4 - Chris Jericho becomes the first ever WWF Undisputed Champion in December 2001, which was a surprise indeed given how the WWF had booked and treated him since his debut two years prior. 3 - Drew Carey appears in the *Royal Rumble*, taking a grand total of zero bumps, doing a mammoth zero moves and not even putting anyone over as he eliminates himself. And that is how you get in the Hall of Fame before former two-time WWF Champion and all-time wrestling great Randy Savage. 2 - Undertaker turns heel and forces JR to kiss Vince McMahon's ass. Ah yes, the VKM Kiss My Ass Club, how could we forget that little gem. 1 - Ric Flair returns to the WWF... some six months after he would have been *really* useful. Flair announced he had bought Shane and Steph's stock when they sold up to buy WCW/ECW. Flair returning was great, but if anyone should have been the figurehead for the WCW invasion then it was him.

Street Fight
Kurt Angle vs. Shane McMahon
[King of the Ring 2001]
I have always been a fan of this match, even if it does see Shane once again looking to scoop the headlines away from the real workers with his wild bumps. This time he takes it upon himself to get thrown through a pane of glass, which takes some breaking but Angle doesn't give up. That is where we start things here too, though we don't see the first couple of attempts where the glass refuses to sell. I disagree with the thinking that those "botches" hurt the match and I actually think they add to it. It shows how tough the glass is and thus how tough Shane is and what a horrible bump it is to take. It adds to the gravitas, and it makes Kurt look like a heartless, focused machine, determined to achieve what he sets out to no matter what. Both guys are bloody and battered after the glass antics, but Shane shows the fire and heart of a main event babyface when he kicks out of Angle's pin attempt once he has been wheeled back to the ring. Shane has no offence to speak of so goes with a low blow and bin lid shots, then hits the Angle Slam out of desperation, but struggles to make the cover. Angle fires back with a wooden board, which he then uses to create himself a platform on the top rope that he hits an incredible Angle Slam off. The crowd goes nuts for that, and rightly so. That obviously gets the job done for Kurt. Even Shane McMahon couldn't kick out of that. Furious had issues with the match being even in places (though not in any of the footage shown here I must add) but my argument is that Angle had wrestled twice prior to this already so it makes sense that he wouldn't be on top of his game. Either way, I think this is a tremendous street fight, and easily Shane's best match.
Arnold Furious Rating: ***½
James Dixon Rating: ****

Next we see the opening of the WWF's historic post-9/11 *SmackDown!* show that took place just two days following the world changing terror attacks. Lillian Garcia does a tremendous job singing the US National Anthem in the face of adversity, and her rousing and emotional rendition sends chills down one's spine even now. The WWF's handling of the whole thing was exemplary, other than Stephanie's inappropriate comments relating to her father's steroid trial and the company's subsequent championing of themselves for being the first major production to take place after the attacks, which were a little too self-congratulatory for my liking.

WWF Tag Team Championship
Triple H & Steve Austin (c) vs. Chris Benoit & Chris Jericho
[RAW]
This is a famous match, both because of its immense quality and Triple H's torn quad. The voiceover man even informs us to look out for the injury at the end! It's a shame we are joined in progress so deep into the bout, just before Benoit's hot tag to Jericho. The crowd is absolutely electric for this, hotter than almost any modern era crowd you will see, and this was definitely a "coming out" party of sorts for the Canadian duo. Pretty soon Hunter charges into Jericho from behind and you can see his leg go and him visibly grimace. Showing what a manly mother he is, he goes ahead with the planned spot of going for a Pedigree on the announce table and getting countered into the Walls of Jericho anyway. That won him a lot of plaudits from a lot of people, as well it should have. It takes a real love of the game, pun intended, to carry on with an injury that severe. Back in the ring Austin hits a Stunner on Benoit but Jericho pulls out the ref and goes into a sensation sequence with Austin, which Hunter tries to break up with a sledgehammer. He misses and hits Austin the gut, allowing Jericho to cover for the three and the tag belts. The footage shown here doesn't quite do this full justice, though it is still amazing. Uncut, the bout is one of the greatest in *RAW* history, and incredibly Benoit and Austin had a singles bout on *SmackDown!* the following week that was almost as good.
James Dixon Rating: ****¾

Now the top five kisses, courtesy of Rikishi

5 - William Regal puckering up and becoming the first member of the VKM Kiss My Ass Club as he tries to get his job back following the WWF's victory over the Alliance at *Survivor Series*. Regal, lip balm and all, plants a kiss on Vince's pasty white backside, resulting in some wonderful facials that only Regal could do justice to. 4 - Matt Hardy and Lita's first kiss in the aisle. 3 - Rock holding Vince for Rikishi to back his ass up into his face, supposedly to end the Kiss My Ass Club. Oh, no, there are seven more years of it yet. 2 - Trish and the Rock sharing a passionate embrace backstage. 1 - Kurt Angle retrieving his gold medals from Chris Benoit's crotch and then kissing them without thinking. "That's gotta be tangy, Cole!" says Tazz. Urgh.

"It's just like being in a movie" says Cole of the WWF as he leads us into the next segment, which is just various themed clips. The first is **Singing** and features the horrible but funny (Steve Austin and Kurt Angle on the acoustic guitar serenading Vince), the good (The Rock singing *'Great Balls of Fire'* and Chris Jericho belting out "did you ever know that you're a jackass" to Steve Austin) to the just horrible (Vince repaying the favour to Austin to welcome back the "old Stone Cold" and a screechingly hideous Steph McMahon led Alliance rendition of "you are the wind beneath my *ring*"). **Romance** sees Trish in a bubble bath, Spike Dudley making out with Molly Holly in the WWF's answer to Romeo & Juliet, Terri pouring beer over her tits, a surprisingly awkward Matt Hardy and Lita backstage embrace, Tajiri getting aroused by bikinis and Trish asking Vince McMahon for a spanking. **Betrayal** sees Perry Saturn prove his faculties are in order when he picks a mop ahead of Terri, Vince trying to shag Torrie Wilson but opening his eyes to see estranged wife Linda and Matt breaking up with Lita. **Revenge** sees Linda kick Vince squarely in the McMahons at *WrestleMania*, Spike standing up for Molly to Steve Austin, Steph mopping Trish with dirty water and Linda asking for a divorce. **Toilet Humour** sees William Regal take a piss on the Big Show and then Chris Jericho take a piss in Regal's tea. "Rather tart!" he exclaims while pulling the second best facial of the year (behind Austin hugging Vince in the parking lot, of course). **Old fashioned fun** sees Kurt Angle, Steve Austin and Vince McMahon dressed in cowboy hats, the Rock picking on a midget version of Booker T and various other briefly shown frolics that get about a second of airtime each. Fun segment this actually.

Next we see highlights from the *Tough Enough* final won by Maven and Nidia, which you can read all about in the mammoth *Tough Enough Season 1 Boxset* review elsewhere in this book. Then Jerry Lawler gets all excited and makes jokes about jerking off, which can only mean one thing; Divas.

Lingerie Match
Stacy Keibler vs. Torrie Wilson
[No Mercy 2001]
This is a joke right? I'm not even going to justify this with a write-up.
Arnold Furious Rating: ¼*
James Dixon Rating: DUD

Winner Takes All
Team WWF (Chris Jericho, Kane, The Big Show, The Rock & The Undertaker) vs. The Alliance (Kurt Angle, Booker T, Rob Van Dam, Steve Austin & Shane McMahon)
So four months after it started, the invasion comes to a miserable end at *Survivor Series* with this 45-minute elimination epic. A quick glance at the teams sums up the problems with this whole thing. Only two members of the Alliance debuted in the company this year post-WCW purchase, and the rest is just long-time WWF guys. We join this at 2-on-2, with Rock and Jericho against Austin and Angle. So, four WWF guys then. Have I mentioned yet how much I detest the invasion? I think that is around the time I went from being a diehard WWF fan to becoming increasingly jaded with most things they were doing. I directly blame the invasion and the mess they made of it for that. The action between four world class performers is as good as you would think, until Angle gets eliminated via a Rock Sharpshooter and Austin gets rid of Jericho to leave him against The Rock. Jericho turns on Rock after the fact but Rock fights on and hits a Stunner on Austin, only for Nick Patrick to pull Earl Hebner out of the ring and prevent the fall. Austin hits a Rock Bottom but Rock kicks out, so Austin twats Patrick and revives WWF referee Hebner. That doesn't make much sense. It doesn't matter though, because he gets bumped again right away anyway. The finish sees Kurt Angle switch allegiance once again and belt Austin with the, erm, WWF Title belt, and Rock hits the Rock Bottom for the WWF win. It's good, but the turns are kind of silly and for me it is not a patch on the epic tag team elimination matches from *Survivor Series '87* and *'88*.
Lee Maughan Rating: ***¾
James Dixon Rating: ***¾

Trish Stratus gives us the top five slaps of 2001:

5 - Debra slapping Vince McMahon for him calling her "the exception to the rule" regarding the old adage that behind every good man is a good woman. 4 - Molly slapping Steve Austin for calling her a bimbo. 3 - Debra BELTING the Undertaker for telling her to keep her nose out of his and Austin's business. 2 - Trish slapping Vince at *WrestleMania* to officially end their illicit union. 1 - Steph slapping her own mother Linda. What a remarkably absurd family.

WWF Hardcore Championship
Jeff Hardy (c) vs. Rob Van Dam
[InVasion]
Joined in progress of course, from Rob hitting his spinning legdrop from the apron to the rail, and the crowd are firmly behind him. He wins more plaudits for taking a vicious sunset powerbomb on the outside, and this match really was the start of the hottest streak in his WWF career. Van Dam was fresh, exciting and different and fans latched onto him right away because of it. His ascent was unmatched, and three months later he was working PPV main events for the WWF Title. Of course his push stalled because of a combination of him frequently hurting guys with his wild kicks and because the WWF hates pushing guys they didn't create themselves that don't work their style. Not to worry though, they grinded him down so much that he became just another guy and then when he was a fraction as over as he was, they put the WWE Title on him. For like a week. Anyhow, this is the match that "made" Rob in the WWF and Jeff Hardy was a tremendous choice of opponent for him. Willing and able to take Rob's unique and violent moves, many of them chair based, Van Dam was able to shine thanks to Jeff's willingness to bump for him. While it has been written many times that the invasion was a complete shambles, and it was, the positive that came out of the whole ordeal was definitely RVD. As far as showcases go, this is a great one and I am a big fan of the match. In truth it is not a great deal different to what Van Dam was doing in ECW, but in the big arena environment of the WWF it just feels that bit more impressive.
Lee Maughan Rating: ****
James Dixon Rating: ****

The Rock berates a boom operator and makes him take his WCW shirt off, before making him put it back on because he is so skinny and hairy. To the top five putdowns then

5 - The Rock calls Stephanie a cheap slut. 4 - Edge tells X-Pac that 1998 called and they are sick and tired of him. 3 - Big Show impersonates DDP and has the temerity to say HE has an annoying voice. 2 - Chris Jericho mocks Steph's boob job, and she is aghast. 1 - The Rock makes Booker T look like a fool with his incredible verbal demolition job of him after returning from movie making. The putdown in question chosen here sees Rock claim T thinks two plus two equals "Thomas Jefferson sucka!" which is funnier than it sounds on paper.

WWF Championship
The Rock (c) vs. Steve Austin
[WrestleMania X-Seven]
This is number three on the list, which is absurd. It is one of the best matches I have ever seen, disappointing heel finish or not. I think it is the perfect WWF Attitude Era main event, and also the last true exclamation point on the era. It has everything, from blood to suspense to near falls to cute references to previous matches between each other and also against others. The drama is off the charts, the setting couldn't be better and it heads up the greatest WWF pay-per-view of all time. How can it be anything other than the full boat? I think Dave Meltzer of

the Wrestling Observer criminally underrated this by giving it ****½, which while a great rating is still an insult to just how fantastic this match is. Obviously it is a completely different beast to many other five star matches, but it is no less entertaining and no worse for that. I absolutely love it.
Lee Maughan Rating: ****¾
James Dixon Rating: *****

Debra next with the top five food moments of the year. Oh come on, they are pushing it a bit now.

5 - Jericho gives Stephanie an enduring classic: a custard pie to the face. 4 - Debra belts Steve Austin in the head with a tray because he insulted her cookies. No wonder he belted her. 3 - The WWF's desperate attempt to recreate the excellent Steve Austin beer bath with Kurt Angle and milk. I thought it was a transparent attempt to breathe life into something that was long gone. 2 - Steve Austin beats the piss out of Booker T in a supermarket. 1 - The Rock offers Lillian Garcia a taste of the People's strudel, and she is very, very receptive. Rock admonishes her for being unprofessional and patronisingly shushes her, because he is a bastard but an hilarious one

Jerry Lawler flat out calls Michael Cole gay, but he protests otherwise, a little too much if you ask me: "No, no, I like the pie!!!"

TLC II
WWF Tag Team Championship
The Dudley Boyz (c) vs. The Hardy Boyz vs. Edge & Christian
[WrestleMania X-Seven]
A rerun it might be, but that doesn't detract from the immense quality of this, which is the second TLC match, the third ladder match between all three teams and the fourth on PPV that the Hardys/E&C combo have been involved in opposite each other. All of their previous matches were epic and brilliant, and this offering more than lives up to the lofty standards. The fact that the three duos were able to keep things fresh in a series of similar matches, and make each one memorable for entirely different reasons, is a testament to just how good they all really were. Much like the Austin-Rock bout, this is also an exclamation point and the end of an era of sorts, with everyone going off to do other things after this. There were more TLC matches down the years of course, many of them featuring some of the guys involved in this, but as far as these three teams all being in the same ring together goes, this was it. The stunts are numerous and as they climax they raise the bar even higher from what has happened before. The spot of the match though, without question, is the incredible spear from Edge to a dangling Jeff Hardy, which is one of those "moments" that the WWF loves so much. For me it is right up there with the (overrated) Superfly Jimmy Snuka cage splash, the Mick Foley Hell in a Cell bumps and the Hulk Hogan slam on Andre the Giant. Okay, maybe it doesn't have the long term historical gravitas of those, but it is definitely one of the most spectacular. The closing sequence of the bout in general is superb too, with constant action and so much going on that there is no chance to pause for breath. The involvement of Spike Dudley, Rhyno and Lita is actually very much welcomed, as opposed to most outside interference which is a detriment. Here they all add to the match and are all involved in some fun spots. When it all breaks down, much like last year Edge & Christian are chosen as the victors, though in truth the result doesn't even matter, it's about the spectacle. On that front the match delivers in spades, and much like the *SummerSlam 2000* TLC bout, this one is five stars as far as I am concerned.
Lee Maughan Rating: ****¾
James Dixon Rating: *****

Next, a montage of Steve Austin saying "what?" and others getting pissed off about it, all set to gentle classical music. "You're being rude!" begs Vince to the audience.

Three Stages of Hell
Triple H vs. Steve Austin
[No Way Out 2001]
Inevitably I disagree with this being top dog, what with having rated four other matches higher than it. I actually cover this elsewhere in this book, and in truth I went in with low expectations, because I remembered it as overly long and drawn out like the Rock-Hunter Iron Man from *Judgment Day 2000*. I was wrong on this occasion though, because this is a bona fide classic... for the first two falls. The third has odd logic and far too much cage selling, combined with genuine fatigue. I don't blame them for being tired, because after those first two magical falls how couldn't they be, but a deciding fall should be the climax, not the comedown. Even though it was still good, it wasn't up with the superb work that preceded it and thus I don't think the match is quite as good as others think. Arn disagrees with me and rates it higher, though I am surprised by that because he is not exactly the biggest fan of WWF Main Event Style. This match is definitely that, and does it well, but the definitive example of how to work that way is Rock-Austin the following month at *WrestleMania*, not this. The version on display her starts towards the end of the first fall and then shows the rest of the bout in near enough its entirety, which does give an excellent idea of the overall quality, even if the first fall stuff that was important to the overall psychology is lost. So the match is great, unquestionably, but as we have seen there were better in 2001.
Arnold Furious Rating: ****¾
James Dixon Rating: ****½

VERDICT

Almost, but not quite perfect. Why is it not perfect? The clipping of course. Unfortunately despite the immense quality of many of the matches on display here, the fact that everything is joined halfway through is damaging. It's like watching a movie but missing the first twenty minutes, and thus you can pick up what is going on as things progress, but something key almost certainly happened that was relevant to the story in the part you didn't catch, and thus the movie viewing experience is lessened. Watching wrestling is the same, and you really cannot fully appreciate a match unless you see it from top to bottom, entrances included. Ironically the only match that gets away unscathed is the atrocious lingerie match, which gets a full airing. Colour me unsurprised by that. For UK fans without a vast tape collection or access to the WWE Network, then this is worth a look for sure, but serious collectors already have everything contained within anyway. Such is the nature of these "best of" releases I guess. Still, for sheer quality and as a standalone piece, this cannot be anything other than highly recommended.

90

CASTROL PRESENTS BEST OF SUMMERSLAM

CAT NO: WWF9998
RUN TIME: 60 minutes (approx)

Arnold Furious: This is a curious beast. It sort of appeared into existence a few years after it logically should have done. The tape covers the best match of each *SummerSlam* between 1995 and 1999. '95 is represented by the ladder rematch between Shawn and Razor, probably MOTY in the WWF. '96 is represented by the Undertaker in a truly different Boiler Room Brawl against Mankind. '97 by Mankind and Triple H in a steel cage. '98 sees another ladder match, this time the career making Rock vs. Hunter match that I've been meaning to re-watch to see if it really is as overrated as I keep claiming. Finally '99 is represented by Shane vs. Test, which is one of the all-time surprisingly good matches. '95 is a no brainer. The ladder match is head and shoulders above everything else on the card. '96 you could put in a strong argument for Shawn-Vader because it's a much better match, but it also has a very screwy finish. '97 is harder because you've got Bret-Taker, which is brilliant, but Bret was in WCW, or Owen-Austin, which would be entirely doable if Owen hadn't died and the whole Hart Family weren't up in arms about the WWF and threatening lawsuits and such. So that doesn't leave much but luckily Foley and Hunter had a solid opener. '98, despite me thinking it's overrated, the ladder match is an easy pick over X-Pac vs. Jarrett, who doesn't work here anymore, or Austin vs. Taker, which everyone is sick of seeing. '99 has a decent main event with Austin vs. Hunter vs. Mankind and it's almost a surprise they don't go with that considering the lack of Austin on the tape.

Ladder Match
WWF Intercontinental Championship
Shawn Michaels (c) vs. Razor Ramon
[SummerSlam '95]
They start extremely fast and Razor has to grab the ropes to avoid the superkick. Shawn then slips out of the Razor's Edge. 1-1. Shawn and Razor is a good match even without the ladder, but like all ladder matches it's relatively heatless until the ladder comes into play. I say "relatively", I'd argue this is one of the best ladder matches, ever, before the ladder comes into play. Shawn makes a point of throwing some bumps in to get the ladies worried for him. One bump is absolutely SICKENING. They try a suplex inside out and Shawn comes down on the rail. He must have been incredibly close to breaking his leg. They do more finisher countering, way ahead of its time, with both being dodged into a double down. They up the stakes by having Razor hit a fallaway slam off the ropes. That gives Razor time to grab the ladder but he's also remembering *WrestleMania X,* so as soon as he's close to the ring he puts the ladder down, therefore dodging the baseball slide Shawn had cued up. As soon as the ladder is in they use it to climb instead of setting spots up, which leads to Shawn taking another sick bump as his leg gets tangled in the ladder as he falls off it. With the ladder still in place Razor becomes the aggressor and stomps it. Shawn's leg is pretty much screwed so Razor piles the pressure on with continued ladder spots to the knee. It's smart work from Hall, way beyond his usual approach. The crowd buy into Shawn's injury stopping him from climbing the ladder, which is perfect. Shawn gets defensive and when Razor tries to javelin him into the ladder he slips out and shoves 'the Bad Guy' into the weapon. They both head up and Shawn back suplexes Razor off the ladder. In their first match Shawn took most of the bumps but Razor took all the early ones. It's almost a reversal of fortunes in this bout. It's at this point where the psychology changes. Up to this point both guys have been going for the win, now they start to use the ladder as a weapon. Why? Well, because you need to buy yourself time to climb that ladder and as conventional moves aren't working, the ladder comes into play in a different way. Shawn goes on the offensive by deliberately moonsaulting off the ladder and then following up with a splash off the top. The press connects, the splash does not, probably because it did at *WrestleMania X* and they wanted to play off that spot by having Razor dodge it this time, like with the baseball slide. The moonsault press was new so Razor took it. They both head up again and both spill outside where Razor pulls out the spare ladder. Shawn goes up and the Razor's Edge brings him back down. By the time he's finished messing

about we get duelling ladders and Shawn kinda botches kicking Razor off. He's too far away from the belt so he dives for it... and misses. It's amazing. It was actually supposed to be the finish, unfortunately. Razor improvises a Razor's Edge by the ropes, which is the most obvious move to get countered in the business. Nobody else went cuing up their finisher by the ropes as much as Scott Hall. Naturally he ends up on the floor and Shawn botches pulling the belt down again. He throws a hissy fit, forgetting his injured knee, and eventually manages to pull the title down to retain. I find this match almost impossible to rate because it's easily *****... if Shawn had got the belt down the first time. Or even the second time. His little temper tantrum rather takes the sheen off the finish.
Final Rating: ****¾

Boiler Room Brawl
Mankind vs. The Undertaker
[SummerSlam '96]
The backstage part of this brawl was pre-taped to give them more energy during the arena conclusion. A camera follows Taker into the boiler room, but then we cut to the other side. Taker's initial walk into the boiler room is like a horror movie. As soon as Mankind attacks it just becomes a hardcore match. Although, this being 1996, it wasn't something the WWF had been doing to this point. Like most hardcore matches the guys just bash each other with stuff. Because its pre-recorded they even insert cuts. Not by zooming into something like Alfred Hitchcock in *Rope* but by inserting "interference" while the crowd boos. Foley occasionally tries to insert his trademarks and that makes sense. Like him hitting the running knee against a roller shutter. The whole thing goes on far too long and there is no chance of it ending in the boiler room anyway, as the winner is the man who escapes, goes to the ring and claims the urn from Paul Bearer, which gives it the same quiet and weird vibe as a ladder match before the ladder becomes involved. Like the last one, in fact. They keep trying for cinematic visuals, which the cameramen aren't capable of doing because they're used to action shots. Mick climbs up a ladder, to legitimately 10-12 feet up and takes a bump off it onto a cardboard box. It looks to do nothing to break his fall. He's way above the Undertaker's head and that must have sucked to take. Mankind escapes first and tries to blockade the Undertaker in, like the Blues Brothers blocking the door when they're going to pay the taxes in Chicago at the Honourable Richard J. Daley Plaza. Taker just ploughs through the barricade, without the aid of a SWAT team or machine guns, and they brawl through the locker room area. All the boys stick their heads out, in heel/face alignment, to shout support.

When they finally hit the arena the fans are burned out from 20-minutes of staring at a video screen. It's only when they hit the ring that you realise how lame the WWF was at the time. Half the arena can't even see the Titantron, so they set up four monitors, one on each side of the ring, which are 30 inch cathode ray tube TVs. How did anyone see anything? It'd be like going to the cinema and the film being shown on a laptop. They hit the ring and Mick takes a sickening bump off the apron back-first onto concrete. A real cruncher. Taker only needs to claim the urn to win. He drops to one knee and... Paul Bearer turns his back. Mankind hooks the Mandible Claw as the fans catch onto what's happening. Paul completes his heel turn by giving the urn to Mankind, and then cracking it over Taker's head. Shocking turn, great idea for a match, not the best of execution. The match is long and poor, and the final few minutes don't really compensate for all the backstage stuff. Paul's heel turn was absolutely shocking at the time though. He'd been Taker's manager for the majority of Undertaker's WWF run.
Final Rating: **¼

Steel Cage Match
Hunter Hearst Helmsley vs. Mankind
[SummerSlam '97]
This is a result of Hunter winning the *King of the Ring* over Foley. Mankind's slow burn face turn is complete. The cage will keep the interfering Chyna out as she's been involved in almost every Hunter match since becoming his bodyguard. Hunter goes right after the door, which is perfect for his character. Their *King of the Ring* final was a real snoozer to begin with so they switch it here and have Mankind get an opening shine with Hunter trying to run away from him. The cage, as it turns out, doesn't stop Chyna as she chokes Mankind with a belt between the bars and nut-shots him as he tries to climb out. That sets Helmsley up to hit a superplex, which gets the crowd all kinds of freaked out. Hunter is a little timid in his bump but the alternative might be a broken neck. You have to be sure of your big bumps. This is a more traditional cage match than Bret-Owen from '94. Put that down to Hunter's traditionalism. Mankind doesn't slow himself up though; he just wants to use the cage as a weapon to hurt Hunter, after he was wronged by the king and his queen. Much like at KotR, the crowd go really quiet with Hunter on offence. It's a combination of Hunter's boring moveset and the crowd not feeling pain for Mankind, because he can take any pain so there's no sympathy. Both guys take some sickening bumps into the steel. My favourite is Mankind taking a backdrop over the ropes into the cage. The way he drops into the ropes looks incredibly painful. He pops right back up and Hunter must be thinking there's nothing he can do to keep Mankind down. Hunter gets tied up in the ropes, which may have been accidental and Chyna has to prevent Mankind escaping; she does by viciously slamming the cage door into his face! Ouch! She lays out the ref for good measure and throws a chair in. Chyna gets into position for a bump off the cage as Mankind slingshots Hunter into her. You can see she's very deliberate about being in position so she doesn't blow the spot, but it makes it a bit obvious. The fans buy into it anyway and it's the biggest pop of the match. As Mankind looks to climb out the crowd chant "Superfly". Chyna comes in, blowing the finish, and Hunter tells her to get out. Mankind climbs out, but wait... he takes his mask off and climbs back up to the top. If he aimed to create the same goosebumps he got from Jimmy Snuka then it's mission accomplished. ELBOW OFF THE CAGE! Massive pop. He climbs out again and now Chyna actually hits her cue to jump in and drag Hunter out. Mankind still wins by climbing quicker than Chyna can drag. The match has a couple of hugely memorable spots, especially the enduring babyface elbow drop. Chyna screwed up a few spots, but she was also involved in some of the better moments too.
Final Rating: ***¼

Ladder Match
WWF Intercontinental Championship
The Rock (c) vs. Triple H
[SummerSlam '98]
While the Rock has been champion and a potential star for some time, even feuding with Steve Austin at the end of 1997, this is Hunter and Rock's first opportunity to steal the show. The terrible DX Band play Hunter down to the ring. They could not play live, could they? Because I didn't like this match originally I've only ever seen it twice. They start out trying to get over each others' ability. The Rock looks clunky compared to his later career as the WWF's top guy. Hunter is also lacking in key areas and sets up that Pedigree by the ropes, a'la Scott

ROB VAN DAM

Hall's similarly obvious finisher reversal spot. It was like Hunter didn't trust his opponent to find a counter out and just gave them an obvious one. Lawler points out the ideal way to win a ladder match is to flat out beat your opponent into submission THEN grab the ladder and climb up unopposed. One of the major complaints about ladder matches, apart from setting up spots, is the slow climbing business. That had been largely eliminated by some excellent wrestlers partaking in ladder bouts, but it returns here. Rock is even slow picking the ladder up and carrying it to the ring. Why? Show some urgency! It's totally out of character. Because Rock takes forever to climb at his first attempt, Hunter can race up the buckles and jump off to stop him. After that single solitary spot they start selling like we're 30-minutes in! I guess that puts over the brutality of the

match but I always felt like Hunter oversold spots, compared to other people. One of Rock's worst attributes as a worker was his stomps. They looked soft as hell and almost mechanical, like his brain couldn't process the movement of his boot downward. Rock gets sensible and works over Hunter's leg, the right one (lucha style), and traps it between the ladder before nailing the ladder with a chair. It's a good spot but the crowd is surprisingly silent for it. Working the right side confuses Rock a bit too and he frequently sets for spots on the wrong side, leaving him to correct. Rock takes no spots for a couple of minutes and STILL climbs painfully slowly. Why? He took no bumps, no work on his limbs, no work on his back. He was absolutely fine. Why is he climbing slowly? Hunter, you can understand because he's got a knee injury. The ladder match is all about big spots though and if you can bring the spots, you can forgive the climbing (although the slow climb comes from the weardown of the big spots), but this match is all about psychology… apart from the climbing. Hunter does take a slingshot into the ladder on the floor, followed by a backdrop on the ladder. Again, he's taking all the big spots so I have no problem with him struggling to climb. Hunter has time to get into an altercation with Mark Henry at ringside AFTER the bump and still get into the ring before Rock can get the belt. I hope Rock lives on one floor because if he had to climb the stairs to get to bed he wouldn't get there before dawn. The best and most brutal spot of the match is Hunter dropkicking the ladder into Rock's face. Rock blades off that. Hunter brings the slow, slow, slow climb and the people actually buy it because of his injuries, but Rock knocks him off. Rock breaks out meteorically slow climbing now, taking one step at a time with both feet like he's wading through treacle. If he went any slower he'd be going backwards. They run a contrived spot where Hunter falls off the ladder and bounces back into it off the corner. It's at the wrong angle. Rock charges with a ladder and Hunter gets himself a receipt by bashing the ladder with a chair. Selling inconsistencies lead to Hunter getting slammed on the ladder and Rock hitting the People's Ladder Elbow. Hunter tries to climb but gets yanked off into the Rock Bottom. Oo er, missus. Rock actually manages to climb EVEN SLOWER than before. They have time to show a replay before he makes it to the third rung! Hunter drags him back down into a Pedigree, which is a very familiar spot. In that it just happened, the other way around. This time Hunter exerts so much energy he can't stand. Mark Henry throws cocaine in Hunter's eyes but he finds the ladder by touch. Rock climbs up QUICKLY, thus showing what nonsense the rest of the match is and Chyna runs in to low blow him. Hunter, even though he can't see, pulls the IC Title down and both guys are made as main eventers for 1999. I still persist this is overrated but I'm glad I got the chance to check it out again to make certain. The massive selling inconsistencies are what hurt the contest and Rock just didn't know how to work a long match. I will give the match credit where it's due and say that they worked hard at the intensity and making the ladder mean something, but the climbing stuff was just ridiculous. Rock might as well have screamed "THIS IS FAKE" with every rung.
Final Rating: ***½

Greenwich Street Fight
Shane McMahon vs. Test
[SummerSlam '99]
Here's a collector's item; a good match from Test! To refresh your memories this was a "Love Her or Leave Her" match where Test had to stop dating Shane's sister Stephanie if he lost. Shane was supposed to come down solo but the Mean Street Posse, complete with hilarious injuries (arm in a sling, foot in a cast, neck brace), join him at ringside. Shane has such a tremendous disregard for his own safety that it's easy to overcome his heat-stealing antics. After all, what happened to Test? Shane takes a few early spots on the floor to demonstrate his willingness to get hurt. Test goes one further and presses him onto the Posse, causing Steph to chuckle while watching on a backstage monitor. That gets the Posse all pissed off and turns it into a 4-on-1. It's a street fight though, so there's no DQ. They stay out of the ring, merely feeding Shane plunder, including a signed photo of themselves in a glass frame. Has there ever been a wrestling picture frame that wasn't shattered over someone's head? The Ultimate Warrior once even wore a baseball cap to prepare himself for such eventualities. It merits a replay, which fat idiot Pete Gas stands in the way of. Test accidentally boots the ref in the face, not that a street fight needs a ref bump because it's already no DQ. The Posse give Test another shoeing, which showcases exactly how many of them can actually work (his name rhymes with Blowy Jabs). Test gets dumped on the Spanish announce table and Shane hits an epic elbow drop through it. That merits five replays, which not even Pete Gas can ruin, and two "amazing"s from JR. Pete Gas accidentally hits Shane with plunder, because he really is that incompetent. As the nonsense continues, Pat Patterson and Jerry Brisco run down to beat up the non-wrestlers in the Posse. Test takes care of Joey Abs to even the score. Pumphandle Slam should finish but Test wants to drop the big elbow as a message. I hear Steph digs guys who drop the elbow off the top. Dig it? That gets the pin and Steph runs down, limbs completely out of control, to celebrate. Yeah, that'll last. I had forgotten how little wrestling there is in this match. It relies heavily on Shane taking silly bumps around the ring. It has half-decent structure and solid pops but it's not aged well. Recommended viewing instead: Test vs. RVD from the ECW revival in 2006. Test's best singles match, ever, I'd wager. This one was once, but it doesn't quite hold up under scrutiny.
Final Rating: ***

VERDICT

I don't want to come off like a miserable old bastard here, but some of these matches are not as good as the WWF thinks they are. For my money the Shawn-Razor ladder match is the only one that really lives up to the billing. Of course this shows how many poor matches existed on WWF PPV in the mid-late 90s if this is the best they can manage for a tape release, although you could argue this papers over Vader, Owen and Bret because they'd left the company. Politics leaves you with slender pickings! Seeing as the tape is ultra-rare you're unlikely to get the opportunity to buy it anyway unless you're a serious collector. What really irks me is an attempt to do a "best of *SummerSlam*" tape without Bret Hart. The man was a *SummerSlam* highlight reel! The Owen cage match, Davey Boy at Wembley, against the Brain Busters back in '89 and the Mr. Perfect IC Title win. All these matches are ****½ or higher! The dispute with Bret prevented the WWF from acknowledging his existence, or indeed the existence of *SummerSlam* before 1995. It's an okay tape but it's not the "best of" anything in particular really.

57

STONE COLD DEMOLITION

CAT NO: N/A
RUN TIME: 30 minutes (approx)

James Dixon: This was a special release that came with a free shirt and a mini Steve Austin figure, available from Wal-Mart. It is a strange one, because it doesn't have any catalogue number, and there seems to be no real need for it with the amount of Austin tapes already on the market. I guess with a 30-minute run time, it serves as something of a taster in the same way as the "800 Series" did with its blink-and-you-will-miss-it highlights of *WrestleMania* and *RAW* shows from 1998 and 1999.

There is no narrator, no talking heads, nothing. Just a brief video set to Austin's music before we just go right into the build up for his 'First Blood' match with Kane at *King of the Ring '98*. We see the same hype video that was used to promote the match on television, which was very good and made Kane seem intimidating like the Michael Myers type character he was originally intended to be. We go to the match, which is shown in random snippets of action set to music that sounds like a car alarm going off. Editing trickery (repeating the exciting spots from different angles) makes the match seem better than it actually was. Kane wins the bout and the title after interference from the Undertaker goes awry and Austin ends up bleeding. Putting the belt on the Big Red Machine, even if it was just for a single day, was one of the most surprising booking decisions of the year. I commend the WWF for it because no one saw it coming. The WWF Title was still very protected and people figured Austin would have a long reign, so for a gimmick character who had been around for less than a year to walk away with the gold was pretty incredible.

To *RAW* the next night and the rematch, where we curiously skip Austin's entrance but get Kane's in its entirety, before going back to the smoke and mirrors highlights. What a strange decision, especially considering how short the tape is. To put it another way; his entrance takes up approximately 10% of the entire run time! The match itself is no great shakes, though the crowd are electric when Austin hits the Stunner and regains his title belt while the Undertaker looks on. He gets too close, so the champ drills him with a Stunner too to set up a program throughout the summer between the two that dragged on forever.

Suddenly, some unbearable dance music infests the tape with its rhythmless, soulless drone, though it does rather fit with this tape, which is lacking entirely in soul. It is just chronological footage from a seemingly random point in 1998 onwards, spliced together and edited out of context. The match featured is the decent *SummerSlam '98* bout between Austin and the Undertaker, which suffers significantly from Austin knocking himself silly early on and working the rest of the match in a daze. As the match gets exciting in the home straight, the music changes to a chugging heavy metal riff, which works much better.

If *SummerSlam* had been the end of the Austin-Taker program it would have been looked back on fairly fondly, but instead the booking took over and the WWF bereft of main event talent, continued to rerun and re-jig various combinations of Steve Austin, the Undertaker and Kane. *Breakdown* saw a shitty triple threat between the three, with a terrible double pin ending in favour of the title challengers. Who was the champion? It didn't matter to Vince McMahon, as long as Steve Austin wasn't.

We skip ahead many, many months to the immense *St. Valentine's Day Massacre* opening video. The song that

---

EVIL EYE: K-KWIK

Ron Killings was in the WWF system for over year before debuting on the main roster in 2000. Green as grass and not great to watch, he had a few uneventful years with the group where the extent of his success was a handful of reigns with the largely meaningless Hardcore Title. Released in 2002, Killings went on to hone his skills and channel his undoubted charisma in garbage group XPW and then TNA, the latter of whom he spent half a decade with. Killings became a two-time NWA World Champion during his run there, before asking for and being granted his release in 2007, rejoining WWE the following year and going on to a long and at times quite successful run with the company the second time around.

accompanies it rather than the standard highlight footage is what makes this so memorable. I have researched this extensively but cannot find anything about it, so I assume it has to be a Jim Johnston piece made especially for the event. It is inspired. Instead of the usual angry metal or imposing choir, we have a 50's throwback that sounds like Marilyn Monroe, singing the lyrics:

"Crazy, you're driving me crazy / with your sweet little smile, heartbreak eyes / see right through and hypnotise me / take me, hold me close but don't break me / I'm a valentine made just for you / And I'll make mine and your dream come true / Oh baby, you're driving me crazy / Crazy, my sweet valentine / Late night when the moon is low / And the demons come out to play / I'll hide beneath my covers / Where I will chase my fears away / Oh Baby, oh my baby / Make my only dream come true / Late night and alone with you / Oh baby you're driving me crazy / Crazy, my sweet valentine / Oh crazy, my sweet valentine"

It's brilliant, the song is catchy and stays in your head and is completely different to anything else in wrestling at the time. But... it has absolutely no place at all on this tape! If it was just a video for Austin-McMahon then it wouldn't be so bad, but it's not; it covers everything on the show and is literally just grabbed from the start of the PPV and plonked in here. If it led to highlights of the cage match between the long time rivals that might be something, but instead we go straight to another music video, this the one used to hype Rock-Austin at *WrestleMania XV*. What on earth is the point of this tape!? We do at least get highlights from Rock-Austin, though randomly enough set to what would later become the entrance music of the Hardy Boyz. This tape is baffling in every respect. We actually get a good 7-minutes from that match, before going to the final segment: the same video that was used at the start of the tape as an introduction.

STUNNING STEVE AUSTIN

VERDICT

An utterly perplexing release. This tape has no soul, no heart and is of almost no worth. The majority of the stuff on here is hype videos for matches that are then chopped up, shuffled around and set to mostly horrid music. The one positive is that the footage at least gets aired chronologically, which as readers know is a rarity with most of these tapes. Well, that and the brilliant but completely unnecessary *St. Valentine's Day Massacre* video, which you should check out on the internet or the PPV itself rather than on here. I remain utterly dumbfounded by this entire effort, and must strongly recommend staying away from it because of how random and thoroughly pointless it all is.

4

COLISEUM CLASSICS

WHAT THE WORLD *WAS* WATCHING

***** MATCHES

Street Fight: Triple H vs. Cactus Jack
Royal Rumble 2000				New York, NY				01.23.00

TLC: The Dudley Boyz vs. The Hardy Boyz vs. Edge & Christian
SummerSlam 2000				Rayleigh, NC				08.27.00

TLC II: The Dudley Boyz vs. The Hardy Boyz vs. Edge & Christian
WrestleMania X-Seven			Houston, TX				04.01.01

The Rock vs. Steve Austin
WrestleMania X-Seven			Houston, TX				04.01.01

****¾ MATCHES

Hell in a Cell: Kurt Angle vs. The Rock vs. Steve Austin vs. The Undertaker vs. Triple H vs. Rikishi
Armageddon 2000				Birmingham, AL				12.10.00

Ladder Match: Chris Jericho vs. Chris Benoit
Royal Rumble 2001				New Orleans, LA			01.21.01

Three Stages of Hell: Steve Austin vs. Triple H
No Way Out 2001				Las Vegas, NV				02.25.01

Triple H & Steve Austin vs. Chris Jericho & Chris Benoit
RAW						San Jose, CA				05.21.01

****½ MATCHES

Ladder Match: The Hardy Boyz vs. Edge & Christian
No Mercy 1999					Cleveland, OH				10.17.99

Hell in a Cell: Triple H vs. Mick Foley
No Way Out 2000				Hartford, CT				02.27.00

Triple H vs. The Rock
Backlash 2000					Washington, DC			04.30.00

Last Man Standing: Triple H vs. Chris Jericho
Fully Loaded 2000				Dallas, TX				07.23.00

Kurt Angle vs. The Rock
No Way Out 2001				Las Vegas, NV				02.25.01

Steve Austin vs. Kurt Angle
SummerSlam 2001				San Jose, CA				08.19.01

Hardcore Match: Rob Van Dam vs. Chris Jericho
Unforgiven 2001				Pittsburgh, PA				09.23.01

Edge vs. Kurt Angle
Backlash 2002					Kansas City, MS			04.21.02

****¼ MATCHES

Submission Match: Chris Jericho vs. Chris Benoit

Judgment Day 2000 | Louisville, KY | 05.21.00

The Rock vs. Chris Benoit
Fully Loaded 2000 | Dallas, TX | 07.23.00

The Rock vs. Chris Jericho
No Mercy 2001 | St. Louis, MS | 10.21.01

**** MATCHES

Tables Match: The Dudley Boyz vs. The Hardy Boyz
Royal Rumble 2000 | New York, NY | 01.23.00

Ladder Match: The Dudley Boyz vs. The Hardy Boyz vs. Edge & Christian
WrestleMania 2000 | Anaheim, CA | 04.02.00

Iron Man Match: The Rock vs. Triple H
Judgment Day 2000 | Louisville, KY | 05.21.00

2/3 Falls Match: Chris Benoit vs. Kurt Angle
Judgment Day 2001 | Sacramento, CA | 05.20.01

Street Fight: Kurt Angle vs. Shane McMahon
King of the Ring 2001 | East Rutherford, NJ | 06.24.01

Hardcore Match: Jeff Hardy vs. Rob Van Dam
InVasion | Cleveland, OH | 07.22.01

Steve Austin, Kurt Angle, Chris Jericho, The Undertaker & Kane vs. Booker T, Diamond Dallas Page, Rhyno & The Dudley Boyz
InVasion | Cleveland, OH | 07.22.01

Chris Jericho vs. Kurt Angle
Rebellion 2001 | Manchester, ENG | 11.03.01

The Rock vs. Chris Jericho
Vengeance 2001 | San Diego, CA | 12.09.01

Royal Rumble Match
Royal Rumble 2002 | Atlanta, GA | 01.20.02

The Rock vs. Hulk Hogan
WrestleMania X8 | Toronto, CAN | 03.17.02

***¾ MATCHES

Chris Benoit vs. Chris Jericho
Backlash 2000 | Washington, DC | 04.30.00

Chris Benoit vs. Triple H
No Mercy 2000 | Albany, NY | 10.22.00

No DQ: The Rock vs. Kurt Angle
No Mercy 2000 | Albany, NY | 10.22.00

Royal Rumble Match
Royal Rumble 2001 | New Orleans, LA | 01.21.01

Chris Benoit vs. Chris Jericho vs. Eddie Guerrero vs. X-Pac
No Way Out 2001 | Las Vegas, NV | 02.25.01

Chris Benoit vs. Kurt Angle
WrestleMania X-Seven | Houston, TX | 04.01.01

Street Fight: Vince McMahon vs. Shane McMahon
WrestleMania X-Seven | Houston, TX | 04.01.01

The Undertaker vs. Triple H
WrestleMania X-Seven   Houston, TX   04.01.01

Submission Match: Kurt Angle vs. Chris Benoit
Backlash 2001   Rosemont, IL   04.29.01

Steve Austin vs. The Rock
Rebellion 2001   Manchester ENG   11.03.01

**The Rock, The Undertaker, Kane, Chris Jericho & The Big Show
vs. Booker T, Shane McMahon, Rob Van Dam, Kurt Angle & Steve Austin**
Survivor Series 2001   Greensboro, NC   11.18.01

Chris Jericho vs. The Rock
Royal Rumble 2002   Atlanta, GA   01.20.02

***½ MATCHES

Steel Cage Match: Triple H vs. The Rock
Rebellion 1999   Birmingham, ENG   10.02.99

No Holds Barred: Steve Austin vs. Triple H
No Mercy 1999   Cleveland, OH   10.17.99

The Hardy Boyz vs. Edge & Christian
No Way Out 2000   Hartford, CT   02.27.00

Too Cool & Rikishi vs. Chris Benoit, Eddie Guerrero & Perry Saturn
No Way Out 2000   Hartford, CT   02.27.00

Dean Malenko vs. Scotty 2 Hotty
Backlash 2000   Washington, DC   04.30.00

Eddie Guerrero vs. Chris Jericho
Insurrextion 2000   London, ENG   05.06.00

Kurt Angle, Edge & Christian vs. Rikishi & Too Cool
Judgment Day 2000   Louisville, KY   05.21.00

Perry Saturn vs. Eddie Guerrero vs. Dean Malenko
Judgment Day 2000   Louisville, KY   05.21.00

The Hardy Boyz & Lita vs. T&A & Trish Stratus
Fully Loaded 2000   Dallas, TX   07.23.00

2/3 Falls: Chris Benoit vs. Chris Jericho
SummerSlam 2000   Rayleigh, NC   08.27.00

The Rock vs. Triple H vs. Kurt Angle
SummerSlam 2000   Rayleigh, NC   08.27.00

Kurt Angle vs. Triple H
Royal Rumble 2001   New Orleans, LA   01.21.01

2/3 Falls: Chris Benoit vs. Kurt Angle
Insurrextion 2001   London, ENG   05.05.01

**Tag Team Turmoil: APA vs. Dean Malenko & Perry Saturn vs. The Dudley Boyz vs. X-Factor vs. The Hardy Boyz vs.
Chris Jericho & Chris Benoit vs. Edge & Christian**
Judgment Day 2001   Sacramento, CA   05.20.01

Edge & Christian vs. Mike Awesome & Lance Storm
InVasion   Cleveland, OH   07.22.01

Ladder Match: Jeff Hardy vs. Rob Van Dam

SummerSlam 2001 | San Jose, CA | 08.19.01

The Rock vs. Booker T
SummerSlam 2001 | San Jose, CA | 08.19.01

Steve Austin vs. Kurt Angle
Unforgiven 2001 | Pittsburgh, PA | 09.23.01

Steve Austin vs. Kurt Angle vs. Rob Van Dam
No Mercy 2001 | St. Louis, MS | 10.21.01

Billy Kidman vs. Tajiri
Backlash 2002 | Kansas City, MS | 04.21.02

Rob Van Dam vs. Eddie Guerrero
Backlash 2002 | Kansas City, MS | 04.21.02

***¼ MATCHES

Steve Austin vs. Kane vs. Mankind vs. The Undertaker
Capital Carnage | London, ENG | 12.06.98

Royal Rumble Match
Royal Rumble 2000 | New York, NY | 01.23.00

Chris Jericho vs. Kurt Angle
No Way Out 2000 | Hartford, CT | 02.27.00

Chris Jericho vs. Kurt Angle vs. Chris Benoit
WrestleMania 2000 | Anaheim, CA | 04.02.00

Eddie Guerrero vs. Essa Rios
Backlash 2000 | Washington, DC | 04.30.00

The Rock vs. Triple H vs. Shane McMahon
Insurrextion 2000 | London, ENG | 05.06.00

Tables & Dumpsters Match: The Dudley Boyz vs. X-Pac, Road Dogg & Tori
King of the Ring 2000 | Boston, MA | 06.25.00

Steel Cage Match: Chris Jericho vs. X-Pac
No Mercy 2000 | Albany, NY | 10.22.00

Edge & Christian vs. The Dudley Boyz
Royal Rumble 2001 | New Orleans, LA | 01.21.01

Chris Jericho vs. William Regal
WrestleMania X-Seven | Houston, TX | 04.01.01

Hardcore Match: Rhyno vs. Raven
Backlash 2001 | Rosemont, IL | 04.29.01

Lance Storm vs. Edge
SummerSlam 2001 | San Jose, CA | 08.19.01

Ladder Match: Edge vs. Christian
No Mercy 2001 | St. Louis, MS | 10.21.01

Steel Cage Match: The Hardy Boyz vs. The Dudley Boyz
Survivor Series 2001 | Greensboro, NC | 11.18.01

Steve Austin vs. Kurt Angle
Vengeance 2001 | San Diego, CA | 12.09.01

Kurt Angle vs. Triple H
No Way Out 2002 | Milwaukee, WI | 02.17.02

*** MATCHES

Corporate Rumble
RAW   Houston, TX   01.11.99

The Godfather, D'Lo Brown & The Headbangers vs. The Dudley Boyz & The Acolytes
Survivor Series 1999   Detroit, MI   11.14.99

Chris Jericho vs. Chyna
Survivor Series 1999   Detroit, MI   11.14.99

Chris Jericho vs. Chyna vs. Hardcore Holly
Royal Rumble 2000   New York, NY   01.23.00

Hardcore Match: Crash Holly vs. Tazz vs. Hardcore Holly vs. Jeff Hardy vs. Matt Hardy vs. Perry Saturn
Backlash 2000   Washington, DC   04.30.00

Val Venis vs. Eddie Guerrero
King of the Ring 2000   Boston, MA   06.25.00

Chris Jericho vs. Kurt Angle
King of the Ring 2000   Boston, MA   06.25.00

Hardcore Match: Shane McMahon vs. The Big Show
SummerSlam 2000   Rayleigh, NC   08.27.00

Chris Benoit vs. The Undertaker
Rebellion 2000   Sheffield, ENG   12.02.00

Kurt Angle vs. The Rock vs. Steve Austin vs. Rikishi
Rebellion 2000   Sheffield, ENG   12.02.00

Trish Stratus vs. Stephanie McMahon-Helmsley
No Way Out 2001   Las Vegas, NV   02.25.01

Hardcore Match: Raven vs. Kane vs. The Big Show
WrestleMania X-Seven   Houston, TX   04.01.01

Edge vs. Kurt Angle
King of the Ring 2001   East Rutherford, NJ   06.24.01

Steve Austin vs. Chris Benoit vs. Chris Jericho
King of the Ring 2001   East Rutherford, NJ   06.24.01

The Hardy Boyz vs. Lance Storm & The Hurricane
No Mercy 2001   St. Louis, MS   10.21.01

Test vs. Kane
No Mercy 2001   St. Louis, MS   10.21.01

Steel Cage Match: Edge vs. Christian
Rebellion 2001   Manchester ENG   11.03.01

Hardcore Match: The Undertaker vs. Rob Van Dam
Vengeance 2001   San Diego, CA   12.09.01

Tag Team Turmoil: Scotty 2 Hotty & Albert vs. Christian & Lance Storm vs. The Hardy Boyz vs. The Dudley Boyz vs. Billy & Chuck vs. The APA
No Way Out 2002   Milwaukee, WI   02.17.02

Eddie Guerrero vs. Rob Van Dam
Insurrextion 2002   London, ENG   05.04.02

HALL OF SHAME

-***** MATCHES

-**** MATCHES

Catfight: Terri vs. The Kat
WrestleMania 2000 — Anaheim, CA — 04.02.00

Evening Gown Hardcore Match: Pat Patterson vs. Gerald Brisco
King of the Ring 2000 — Boston, MA — 06.25.00

-*** MATCHES

Evening Gown Pool Match: Ivory vs. Miss Kitty vs. Jacqueline vs. BB
Armageddon 1999 — Sunrise, FL — 12.12.99

-** MATCHES

Ivory vs. The Fabulous Moolah
No Mercy 1999 — Cleveland, OH — 10.17.99

-* MATCHES

Mae Young, The Fabulous Moolah, Tori & Debra vs. Ivory, Jacqueline, Luna & Terri
Survivor Series 1999 — Detroit, MI — 11.14.99

Jerry Lawler vs. Steven Richards
No Way Out 2001 — Las Vegas, NV — 02.25.01

Jazz vs. Lita vs. Trish Stratus
WrestleMania X8 — Toronto, CAN — 03.17.02

DUD MATCHES

Kane vs. Mideon
No Mercy (UK) — Manchester, ENG — 05.16.99

Nicole Bass vs. Tori
No Mercy (UK) — Manchester, ENG — 05.16.99

The Godfather vs. Mideon
No Mercy 1999 — Cleveland, OH — 10.17.99

Mark Henry vs. Viscera
No Way Out 2000 — Hartford, CT — 02.27.00

Arm Wrestling Match: The Kat vs. Terri
Insurrextion 2000 — London, ENG — 05.06.00

No Holds Barred: Steve Austin vs. Rikishi
No Mercy 2000 — Albany, NY — 10.22.00

William Regal vs. Naked Mideon
No Mercy 2000 — Albany, NY — 10.22.00

Ivory vs. Lita
Survivor Series 2000 — Tampa, FL — 11.19.00

Bra & Panties Match: Trish Stratus vs. Terri
RAW — Minneapolis, MN — 06.04.01

The Undertaker & Kane vs. Diamond Dallas Page & Kanyon
SummerSlam 2001 — San Jose, CA — 08.19.01

The Undertaker & Kane vs. KroniK
Unforgiven 2001 — Pittsburgh, PA — 09.23.01

Lingerie Match: Stacy Keibler vs. Torrie Wilson
No Mercy 2001 — St. Louis, MS — 10.21.01

Mighty Molly & Stacy Keibler vs. Torrie Wilson & Lita
Rebellion 2001 — Manchester, ENG — 11.03.01

Hardcore Match: Goldust vs. Maven
WrestleMania X8 — Toronto, CAN — 03.17.02

Scott Hall vs. Bradshaw
Backlash 2002 — Kansas City, MS — 04.21.02

THE 41ST ANNUAL VOLUME #5 AWARDS

BEST ANNOUNCER

ARNOLD FURIOUS

1. Paul Heyman
2. Jim Ross
3. Tazz

JAMES DIXON

1. Jim Ross
2. Paul Heyman
3. Tazz

LEE MAUGHAN

1. Paul Heyman
2. Jim Ross
3. Jerry Lawler

WORST ANNOUNCER

ARNOLD FURIOUS

1. Michael Cole
2. Jerry Lawler
3. Chavo Guerrero Jr.

JAMES DIXON

1. Michael Cole
2. Scott Hudson
3. Jonathan Coachman

LEE MAUGHAN

1. Michael Cole
2. Jonathan Coachman
3. Tazz

BEST FEUD

ARNOLD FURIOUS

1. Triple H vs. Mick Foley
2. Triple H vs. Chris Jericho
3. Steve Austin vs. Kurt Angle

JAMES DIXON

1. Triple H vs. The Rock
2. Chris Benoit vs. Chris Jericho
3. Chris Benoit vs. Kurt Angle

LEE MAUGHAN

1. Edge & Christian vs. The Hardys vs. The Dudleys
2. Steve Austin vs. Kurt Angle
3. Steve Austin vs. The Rock

WORST FEUD

ARNOLD FURIOUS

1. WWF vs. The Alliance
2. The Undertaker vs. Diamond Dallas Page
3. The Big Show vs. The Big Bossman

JAMES DIXON

1. WWF vs. The Alliance
2. The Undertaker vs. Steve Austin
3. The Undertaker vs. Diamond Dallas Page

LEE MAUGHAN

1. WWF vs. The Alliance
2. The Undertaker vs. Diamond Dallas Page
3. The Big Show vs. The Big Bossman

BEST ANGLE

ARNOLD FURIOUS

1. Mankind won't challenge Triple H, but Cactus Jack will!
2. The increasing paranoia of Steve Austin
3. Stephanie McMahon's heel turn (*Armageddon '99*)

JAMES DIXON

1. The increasing paranoia of Steve Austin
2. Shane McMahon turns up on *Nitro*
3. Angle-Hunter-Steph love triangle

LEE MAUGHAN

1. The Rock challenges Hollywood Hogan
2. Mankind won't challenge Triple H, but Cactus Jack will!
3. The increasing paranoia of Steve Austin

WORST ANGLE

ARNOLD FURIOUS

1. The WWF botching the Invasion
2. DDP stalks the Undertaker's wife
3. Anything with Mae Young

JAMES DIXON

1. Stephanie McMahon - ECW Owner
2. DDP stalks the Undertaker's wife

3.   Rikishi runs down Steve Austin

LEE MAUGHAN

1.   Steve Austin turns heel
2.   The Big Bossman crashes Big Show's father's funeral
3.   DDP stalks the Undertaker's wife

BEST PROMO

ARNOLD FURIOUS

1.   The Rock
2.   Steve Austin
3.   William Regal

JAMES DIXON

1.   Steve Austin
2.   The Rock
3.   Mick Foley

LEE MAUGHAN

1.   The Rock
2.   Steve Austin
3.   Mick Foley

WORST PROMO

ARNOLD FURIOUS

1.   Linda McMahon
2.   Debra
3.   Vince McMahon

JAMES DIXON

1.   Debra
2.   Chyna
3.   The Big Show

LEE MAUGHAN

1.   Debra
2.   Linda McMahon
3.   Perry Saturn

BEST MANAGER

ARNOLD FURIOUS

1.   Paul Heyman
2.   Lita
3.   Trish Stratus

JAMES DIXON

1.   Lita
2.   Paul Heyman
3.   Trish Stratus

LEE MAUGHAN

1.   Shane McMahon
2.   Lita
3.   Trish Stratus

WORST MANAGER

ARNOLD FURIOUS

1.   Mae Young
2.   Terri
3.   Fabulous Moolah

JAMES DIXON

1.   Debra
2.   Sara
3.   Terri

LEE MAUGHAN

1.   Debra
2.   Tiger Ali Singh
3.   Sara

BEST TAG TEAM

ARNOLD FURIOUS

1.   The Hardy Boyz
2.   The Dudley Boyz
3.   Edge & Christian

JAMES DIXON

1.   The Hardy Boyz
2.   The Dudley Boyz
3.   Edge & Christian

LEE MAUGHAN

1.   Edge & Christian
2.   The Dudley Boyz
3.   The Hardy Boyz

WORST TAG TEAM

ARNOLD FURIOUS

1.   The Undertaker & Kane
2.   KroniK
3.   Lo Down

JAMES DIXON

1.   The Undertaker & Kane
2.   KroniK
3.   Right To Censor

LEE MAUGHAN

1.   The Undertaker & Kane
2.   X-Factor
3.   The Big Bossman & Bull Buchanan

GUILTY PLEASURE

ARNOLD FURIOUS

1. Hulk Hogan at *WrestleMania X8*
2. Albert
3. Steve Blackman

JAMES DIXON

1. nWo
2. Raven
3. Perry Saturn

LEE MAUGHAN

1. TLC Matches
2. The Invasion Angle
3. Steve Austin and Kurt Angle battling for Vince McMahon's affections

WORST WRESTLER

ARNOLD FURIOUS

1. BB
2. Mideon
3. Hulk Hogan

JAMES DIXON

1. The Undertaker
2. Torrie Wilson
3. Mideon

LEE MAUGHAN

1. Mideon
2. Chyna
3. The Undertaker

BEST WRESTLER

ARNOLD FURIOUS

1. Kurt Angle
2. Chris Jericho
3. The Rock

JAMES DIXON

1. Chris Benoit
2. Kurt Angle
3. Steve Austin

LEE MAUGHAN

1. Steve Austin
2. The Rock
3. Kurt Angle

WORST MATCH

ARNOLD FURIOUS

1. Terri vs. The Kat
   (WrestleMania 2000)
2. Ivory vs. Miss Kitty vs. Jacqueline vs. BB
   (Armageddon '99)
3. Ivory vs. Fabulous Moolah
   (No Mercy '99)

JAMES DIXON

1. Booker T vs. Buff Bagwell*
   (RAW)
2. Gerald Brisco vs. Pat Patterson
   (King of the Ring 2000)
3. The Undertaker & Kane vs. Kanyon & DDP
   (SummerSlam 2001)

* Not featured in book but so bad it warrants mentioning

LEE MAUGHAN

1. Gerald Brisco vs. Pat Patterson
   (King of the Ring 2000)
2. The Undertaker & Kane vs. Kanyon & DDP
   (SummerSlam 2001)
3. William Regal vs. Naked Mideon
   (No Mercy 2000)

BEST MATCH

ARNOLD FURIOUS

1. Cactus Jack vs. Triple H
   (Royal Rumble 2000)
2. Steve Austin vs. The Rock
   (WrestleMania X-Seven)
3. Chris Jericho vs. Chris Benoit
   (Royal Rumble 2001)

JAMES DIXON

1. The Rock vs. Steve Austin
   (WrestleMania X-Seven)
2. Hell in a Cell: Kurt Angle vs. Steve Austin vs. The Rock vs. The Undertaker vs. Rikishi vs. Triple H
   (Armageddon 2000)
3. Ladder Match: Chris Benoit vs. Chris Jericho
   (Royal Rumble 2001)

LEE MAUGHAN

1. TLC
   (SummerSlam 2000)
2. The Rock vs. Steve Austin
   (WrestleMania X-Seven)
3. TLC II
   (WrestleMania X-Seven)

TAPE RANK INDEX

5* TAPES

Royal Rumble 2000	100
Backlash 2000	100
WrestleMania X-Seven	100
Most Memorable Matches 2000	100

THE BEST

Judgment Day 2000	98
Royal Rumble 2001	98
Andre the Giant - Larger Than Life	95
Triple H - That Damn Good	92
Stone Cold Steve Austin - What?	90
Best of the WWF 2001 Viewers' Choice	90
No Way Out 2001	89
Fully Loaded 2000	85
SummerSlam 2000	84
Mick Foley - Hard Knocks...	84
SummerSlam 2001	81
Eve of Destruction	80
Best of RAW Vol. 1	77
No Way Out 2000	77
The Rock - Know Your Role	76
No Mercy 2001	76
The Undertaker - This is my Yard	75
Royal Rumble 2002	75
Lita - It Just Feels Right	73
Best of RAW Vol. 3	73
TLC - Tables Ladders Chairs	72
Tough Enough - The First Season Boxset	72
Chris Jericho - Break Down the Walls	70
Funniest Moments	70
Rebellion 2001	66
Invasion	65
Unforgiven 2001	63
Hardy Boyz - Leap of Faith	63
The Rock - Just Bring It!	61
It's Our Time	60

WORTH SEEING

The Rock - The People's Champ	58
Judgment Day 2001	58
King of the Ring 2001	58
Austin vs. McMahon	57
Survivor Series 2001	57
Castrol Presents Best of SummerSlam	57
Armageddon 2000	56
Most Memorable Matches 1999	56
Backlash 2001	55
No Mercy 1999	54
Vengeance 2001	54
No Mercy 2000	53
Best of RAW Vol. 2	51
S C Steve Austin - Lord of the Ring	50
Backlash 2002	50
Mick Foley - Madman Unmasked	49
Hulk Hogan Rock N Wrestling Vol 4	49
Action!	48
Hardcore	47
Rebellion 2000	44
Insurrextion 2000	42
Steve Austin - Hell Yeah	40
nWo - Back in Black	40
Hulk Hogan Rock N Wrestling Vol 5	40
Hulk Hogan Rock N Wrestling Vol 6	40

DON'T BOTHER

No Way Out 2002	38
Capital Carnage	37
WrestleMania X8	35
Behind WWF Tough Enough	35
Survivor Series 1999	34
WrestleMania 2000	34
Rebellion 1999	33
King of the Ring 2000	33
Unforgiven 2000	33
Survivor Series 2000	32
Insurrextion 2001	32
Wild in the UK	32
No Mercy (UK)	30
Before they were WWF Superstars	26
Armageddon 1999	25
Chyna Fitness	25
Kurt Angle - It's True It's True	25
Hits and Disses	24
Insurrextion 2002	24
Divas - Tropical Pleasure	23

THE WORST

Divas in Hedonism	15
Divas - Postcard From the Caribbean	10
Stone Cold Demolition	4
Come Get Some - The Women of the WWF	2
Taking it 2 Xtremes	0

SCORE GUIDE

100	5* Tape
90-99	Make sure you own this!
80-89	Highly recommended
70-79	Superb
60-69	Very good
50-59	Worth watching
40-49	Good in places
30-39	More bad than good
20-29	Worthless
10-19	Really awful
0-9	I hate wrestling.